MAKING IT
IN THE
MEDIA PROFESSIONS

MAKING IT
IN THE
MEDIA PROFESSIONS

**A Realistic Guide to Career Opportunities in
Newspapers, Magazines, Books, Television,
Radio, the Movies, and Advertising**

by Leonard Mogel

The Globe Pequot Press   Chester, Connecticut 06412

Transcript of the "Coming and Going" commercial for *ADWEEK* magazine. © 1984 The DOCSI Corporation. Printed with permission of Dick Orkin's Radio Ranch. Listings of Ten Hottest Advertising Agencies and Ten Best Newspapers are reprinted with permission from *ADWEEK* magazine.

Library of Congress Cataloging-in-Publication Data

Mogel, Leonard.
    Making it in the media professions.

    Bibliography: p.
    Includes index.
    1. Mass media—Vocational guidance—United States.
    I. Title.
    P91.6.M6   1987   001.51′023′73   87-19677
    ISBN 0-87106-770-6 (pbk.)

Cover Design: Barbara Marks
Text Design: Kevin Lynch
Manufactured in the United States of America
First Edition/First Printing

Acknowledgments

Michela Nonis researched the book brilliantly. It seemed that all I had to do was mention an area of interest, and miraculously, the next day, a huge folder appeared on my desk with reams of hard information, properly annotated. We wish her good fortune in her new chosen career.

I am indebted to my editor at Globe Pequot, Eric Newman. He provided just the right mix of goading, encouragement, tough criticism, and enthusiasm to sustain an excellent working relationship. Thanks, too, to Norma Ledbetter and Bruce Markot for their editorial contributions. I also appreciate the support of Linda Kennedy, Kate Bandos, Kevin Lynch, and the rest of the staff at Globe Pequot.

I wish to thank all the people who cooperated in the preparation of this book with data and advice. First the interviewees: Bill Pitts, Dick Low, Gene Brissie, Kay Sexton, Kathy Keeton, Jim Horton, Ruth Vitale, Midge Sanford, Sarah Pillsbury, Mark Miller, Arnold Sawislak, John Scagliotti, Ellen Hulleberg, Bridget Potter, Bruce Sidran, and Roger Bumstead. Also, thanks to the mini-interviewees: Mel Tolkin, Steven Florio, and Betsy Nolan.

Peter Pitts made an immense contribution to the chapter on television. He gave me an insight into areas of the industry I was not familiar with.

I also thank Roger Schnur for his valuable comments on the radio chapter.

I may miss a few names, but my sincere appreciation for splendid cooperation goes to The American Association of Advertising Agencies; SSC&B:Lintas; Deborah Jackson; Saatchi & Saatchi; Tony Sherwood; The Magazine Publishers Association; Ed Flynn; Jim Kaye; Women in Film; Debby Reid; the DGA; Fallon McElligott; Jack Thomas; Bozell, Jacobs, Kenyon and Eckhardt; Bob Nonis; Procter & Gamble; Bea Friedland; Book Industry Study Group; Time Inc.; Datus C. Smith; the *New York Times*; Jess Garcia; David Wachsman; Dara Tyson; Betzy Ianuzzi; Bill Brokaw; Mark Greenberg; Betsy Nolan; Carol Donner; Book-of-the-Month Club; The Association of American Publishers; New Directions; North Point Press; William Kaufmann, Inc.; John Wiley & Sons; Bridey Whalen; Lawrence Freundlich; John P. Dessauer; Joe Hanson; Steve Florio; Mediamark Research Index; Mike Levy; Standard Rate & Data Service; Elle Macpherson; American Film Institute; *Variety*; *The Hollywood Reporter*; Janet McCarthy; Michael Sloser; Neil Reiter; Diane Ekeblad; Fred Danzig; Robert Weicherding; Joel Garrick; Marcia Potash; Dr. Samir Husni; Chris Callis; Marian Smith; Charlene Soltz; Deborah Fine; *Columbia Journalism Review*; Ferdinand Teubner; Dick Orkin's Radio Ranch; Charles West; Al Bernstein; Elizabeth Martin; Terri Luke; Ramona Dunn; Ed Italo; Bob Anderson; Beth Critchley; Dow Jones Newspaper Fund; Newspaper Guild; Bettmann Archives; Newspaper Advertising Bureau; *Washington Journalism Review*; Leo Bogart; NABET; National Public Radio; National Association of Broadcasters; Arbitron, McGavren Guild Radio; Radio Advertising Bureau; Mort Miller; Television Information Office; Columbia Broadcasting System; National Broadcasting System; Capital Cities/ABC, Inc.; Cable News Network; the Fox Broadcasting Company; Corporation for Public Broadcasting; MTV; Paula Darte; Bob Bertini; Nancy Coe; Marianne Shearer.

CONTENTS

Advertising   233

INTRODUCTION

It starts with a phone call from someone I haven't spoken to in years. The conversation goes something like this:

"Hi, Len. Haven't talked to you in a long time. How've you been?" (Pause.) "I'd like to ask you a favor."

"Well, if I can help you, I certainly will."

"Have you ever met my son Richard?"

"I don't think I have."

"Richard's a terrific kid. He just graduated from _____ University with a B.A. in _____ . He's an 'A' student. Very sharp. He's not sure what he wants to do with his life, but he's very interested in music and films. He played in a band in high school and he has hundreds of records and tapes. He's a movie nut—goes at least twice a week. He thinks he might like to be a director or a producer." (Finally getting to the point.) "Do you think you could see him for a few minutes to give him some advice? I'd really appreciate it." (Without waiting for an answer.) "I'll have him call you. Oh, by the way, let's have lunch some day."

A few days later I hear from Richard himself, who's a bit nervous and seems embarrassed to be calling. Thinking that it's not worth the guilt trip to turn the young man down, I agree to a short meeting. A week later Richard arrives, neatly dressed, résumé in hand, and we begin our dialogue.

It turns out that Richard was not quite a 'A' student. He held various summer jobs while going to college, none of which leaned toward a career in film. He hadn't even read much about film, and when I suggested a graduate program in this discipline, he hesitated, saying, "I think I'd like to stay out of school for a while."

In the half hour this meeting takes, I don't want to discourage Richard by stressing the fact that the film business employs only about 200,000 people (including movie ushers) and that the odds against succeeding are enormous. I suggest a few books to read, propose that he try to get a job as a "gofer" on a music video production to gain some experience, and close the meeting with regards to his dad.

Somehow, I detect in Richard's mind fantasies of becoming a famous movie director who wears $1,000 leather jackets, drives a red Ferrari, squires beautiful actresses to screenings, and "takes" lunch with thirty-five-year-old studio heads at chic, unlisted Beverly Hills restaurants. Maybe a hundred people share this lifestyle. Richard will probably never be one of them.

Getting started in films or in any other area of mass communications is no more difficult than getting started in any other type of career. But it usually doesn't happen overnight. It takes preparation and training and then a series of low-level jobs until one either drops out, settles for a routine middle-level job—or makes it big. That's rare. The difference between a communications career and one in banking, law, or computers is that in mass communications there are far fewer jobs than in these other industries.

In my thirty-five years in communications I've had hundreds of Richards call or see me, yearning for the glamorous career they desire but are ill equipped to pursue. That's why I decided to write this book.

The book is divided into seven chapters, one for each field. Our basic approach is not to serve as a job-hunting guide but instead to orient the reader to the structure and operations of each of these seven areas of mass communications.

When we write about newspapers, for example, we'll begin with a short history of the medium, discuss the scope of the industry today, take a look at a major newspaper company and its holdings, and then talk about a small newspaper in Massachusetts.

We'll tell you about the functions of the two wire services, the Associated Press and United Press International, and then examine the operations of the nation's two largest-circulation papers, *The Wall Street Journal* and *USA Today*. We write about stringers (freelance reporters and columnists) and tell how much money they make. We also discuss Sunday supplements, the publication *ADWEEK*'s ten-best-newspaper selections, the case for journalism school, and future trends in the industry.

At the end of each chapter we include a glossary of important terms, a recommended reading list, and in-depth interviews with two industry leaders. These interviews offer an overview of the fields as well as specific tips on which areas of their specialties offer the widest opportunities.

We have not overlooked the career aspect of this book. However, we do think that before you choose radio because you want to be a deejay, or television because you want to be an MTV veejay, you'll have to learn about each job, its educational requirements, salary range, and the steps that will take you up the ladder.

We take a realistic approach to the geographical aspects of mass communications. If you want to work for the headquarters of a television network, you'll have to live in or near New York or Los Angeles. That may be fun, but it's expensive. However, you can also work at any of more than 600 network-owned and -affiliated stations throughout the United States. Wherever possible, we'll give you the salary level in a smaller city as well as in a major metropolitan area.

"Career Tips" are special pieces of information that appear in each chapter. We enlarge on these in some chapters. In Advertising, for example, we offer "Twenty Tips on Breaking into Advertising." In Magazines, we have "Six Short Tips on How to Break into Advertising Sales."

In the interest of giving our readers a typical experience, we have written a section about a hypothetical movie producer taking a project from script to release, an author pursuing bestsellerdom, a day in the life of an advertising agency, and a huge staff at CBS Sports covering Super Bowl XXI.

We emphasize the need for educational training for careers in the media professions. However, one should realize that specialized education may be the added ingredient that places one job applicant above the others. A journalism major who speaks Russian will certainly have an edge. An MBA who has taken summer publishing courses will have a decided advantage when applying for a job on the business side of a magazine or newspaper. However, there are no rules of entry into mass communications. We hope this book will help you make your choices.

There's a bonus at the end of the book. We asked a noted media specialist, Roger Bumstead, to offer some specific tips on how to get started in mass communications. Roger is a prominent New York marketing-services recruiter. Although he doesn't handle entry-level jobs, his advice is of particular importance.

We urge you to read every one of the seven chapters. Even if you are interested in only one field, you can find something of value in another chapter. Use this book as a career builder. In the advertising chapter, we write about New York's excellent School of Visual Arts, whose motto is "When the Job You Have Is Not Enough, but the Job You Want Is Out of Reach." This book will help you bridge that gap.

Now a word about sexism. Women are employed in almost equal numbers to those of men in all fields of mass communications. However, in the interest of simplification, I am omitting the unwieldy *he/she*. The word *he* in this book refers to both men and women.

My own career has been primarily in magazines. I have published books and wrote one about magazines, so I have a firm basis in these fields. At the age of fifty-nine I produced my first movie. I loved seeing my name on the screen and on billboards, so I'm doing it again. My knowledge of advertising is consequential; I've sold magazine advertising to agency people for many years. All those lunches paid off. I learned a great deal about the industry and its problems. My research into the fields of newspapers, radio, and television uncovered a rich lode of information that made these media professions seem every bit as fascinating and rewarding as the others.

Writing this book has been a wonderful education for me. Now I'd like to share it with you.

To the new people,
Susanna Trane Tolkin and Benjamin Michael Pitts.
They have expanded our family group
and filled it with joy.

My collaboration with Ann Mogel goes back thirty-eight years. It has always been a wonderful partnership. When I wrote my first book, her literary and practical contributions made the book a success. When I thought of writing this book, she encouraged me to do it although skeptical of my ability to complete it in the face of competition from my other activities.

Ann read and typed every one of the book's 160,000 words—but these. She immersed herself in its huge amount of research. She challenged, goaded, exhorted, argued, and also often praised. It is her book as well as mine. Her modesty would cause her to deny her numerous talents. I dedicate this book to her with great love.

NEWSPAPERS

Until 1987 I lived in New York City, where the only newspapers are the venerable and still vital *New York Times* and two rather sensational tabloids, the *Daily News* and the *Post*—plus some penetration from Long Island's *Newsday*. The *Village Voice*, a weekly, falls somewhere between a newspaper and a magazine. This is hardly an impressive output for the nation's number-one media market.

Now, when I was growing up in the '30s, things were different. In Brooklyn, where I lived, we had two daily newspapers, the *Brooklyn Eagle* and the *Brooklyn Times-Union*. There was even a third, the *Brooklyn Citizen*, but I'm not sure that it was a daily.

The *Eagle* performed a valuable service. When I went to Ebbets Field to see the revered Brooklyn Dodgers play baseball, I had a budget of $1.00, which comprised my savings for many weeks. A bleachers ticket cost 55¢, the subway 5¢ each way, and two hot dogs and a soda 25¢, which left me with the munificent sum of 10¢. A program purchased in the ballpark was a dime, which would have meant no peanuts. But here comes the *Eagle* to the rescue. For 2¢ I could buy the paper that had the names and numbers of all the players, plus the box score right on the front page. I had the peanuts and 3¢ left over for discretionary spending.

There were other daily papers: *World, Herald-Tribune, Telegram, Sun, Journal,* the tabloid *Mirror,* and my personal favorite, the *News.* I had a friend whose parents owned a newsstand. On Saturday nights I helped him collate sections of the *Sunday News* just to read the color comics a whole night before the other kids.

In those days New York also had four Jewish-language dailies, at least two Italian papers, and a host of other ethnic newspapers. It was the time of the Depression, but somehow the newspapers priced at 2¢ and 3¢ survived.

By the end of World War II, this profusion of papers was over. The higher cost of labor plus the penetration of television forced many of the papers out of business. This pattern was repeated in other large cities as well, resulting in mergers, consolidation, and the discontinuance of publication of many of our nation's newspapers.

Until I moved to Los Angeles in early 1987, I was an inveterate *New York Times* reader. On Sundays it cost more than $1.00 and seemed to weigh more than thirty pounds. I didn't think I could ever get along without the crossword puzzle. Now that I'm an Angeleno, I read the *Los Angeles Times,* which may be even fatter than the *New York Times*, but, like the smog, I'm getting used to it.

A Short History of the Newspaper

They say it all started in Peking, China, in the early 500s. It was called the *Tsing Pao*, a court journal produced from carved blocks. The same paper lasted until 1935. I wonder what its newspaper morgue looked like.

Roman scribes regularly sent out written newsletters to businessmen and politicians in distant cities to keep them posted on the happenings in Rome. This custom, which originated with the Romans about 1000 B.C., was continued until the 1700s, when printed papers became common.

After Johann Gutenberg's invention of printing from movable type, news pamphlets were occasionally issued in Europe, particularly in Germany. The oldest regularly published paper on record is the *Strasburg Relation* of 1609. (This is the German spelling of the border city now known as Strasbourg in France.)

The first paper published on a regular basis in England was the *Courant*, or *Weekly Newes*, of 1621. The *Oxford Gazette*, begun in 1665, was devoted to official notices of the royal court.

The first daily paper in England was the *London Daily Courant*, begun in 1702 by a woman named Elizabeth Mallett. The *London Times* began publication in 1785 as the *Daily Universal Register*.

It's interesting that many of the early newspaper names—"Courant," "Gazette," "Times," and "Register"—are still used by American newspapers today.

Newspapers in America

The first newspaper in the American colonies had the charming name of *Publick Occurrences Both Forreign and Domestick*. It seems the publisher, a Mr. Benjamin Harris, was engaging in a bit of whimsy, albeit short-lived. The paper lived and died in one issue in 1690. No one tried again until 1704, in Boston. One of the earliest was the *New England Courant*, begun in 1721 by the brothers Franklin, James and Ben.

The first newspaper outside Boston was the *American Weekly Mercury*, founded in Philadelphia in 1719, and the first in New York was the *Gazette* in 1725. The oldest continuously published daily in the United States is the *Alexandria* (Virginia) *Gazette*, first published in 1797.

By the early 1800s, there were many newspapers devoted exclusively to political subjects. Their high price of 6¢ a copy put them out of range for the masses, but the gap was narrowed in the 1830s when penny papers began publication. The first one in New York, the *Sun*, was founded in 1833. There was a *Sun* in New York up to the 1930s.

One of the greatest early journalist entrepreneurs was James Gordon Bennett, who founded the *New York Morning Herald* in 1855. It later became the *New York Herald-Tribune*, which ceased publication after World War II.

Horace Greeley, of "Go West, young man" fame, began publishing the *New York Tribune* in 1841. He was considered to be an outstanding editorial innovator and was a nationally known humanitarian as well.

What would later become great American newspapers were launched at the close of the nineteenth century. Joseph Pulitzer, an immigrant from Hungary, founded the *St. Louis Post-Dispatch*. Joseph Medill started the *Chicago Daily Tribune* in 1847. The *Atlanta Constitution* began life in the 1880s, and the *San Francisco Chronicle* was started in 1865.

The first sensational tabloid in New York was the *Daily News*, founded by Joseph Patterson in 1919. Many others followed, including the *Mirror*, known for its sensational headlines, gossip columns, and a good horse-racing section.

Consolidations of papers were significant in the first half of the twentieth century, with chains such as Hearst and Scripps-Howard being formed. Scripps-Howard had twenty-five dailies at its peak in 1929, the year of the stock market crash; by 1956 it had only nineteen papers.

The Scope of Newspapers Today

Readers who are interested in newspapers as a career will be heartened to learn that almost a half-million people are employed in the newspaper business, about five times the number employed in the magazine business, and a greater number than that employed in any other of the media.

Recent figures have put the number of daily newspapers at about 1,700 and weekly papers at about 7,800. In 1946, there were 1,763 dailies; of these papers, there were more with circulations over 250,000 than we have today. Blame it on television.

Advertising Revenues for Newspapers

Newspapers cannot possibly make money on the sole basis of their newsstand price—the cost of labor and materials far outweighs these revenues. Therefore, as with two other media in this book, television and radio, the primary revenue source is advertising (we discuss this later in the section "The Role of Advertising in Newspaper Publishing"). Further, at this writing newspapers lead all other media in overall advertising revenues with 26.8 percent of the total, compared with TV's 21.7 percent. This abundant percentage enables newspapers to make healthy profits.

Employment

Here are some employment figures of immediate interest for those seriously considering newspapers as a career. There's some good news and, inevitably, some bad. If we use 1947 as our index, the growth in newspaper employment up to the present time has not been dramatic—an increase of about 83 percent. On the female front, however, employment from 1960 rose almost 300 percent. Women now account for about 40 percent of all newspaper employees.

We will discuss journalism schools later in this chapter, but for now, let's look at where some recent journalism school graduates went to work.

	Graduates	Percent of Total
News/Editorial	4,600	21.8
Broadcasting	3,777	17.9
Advertising	4,389	20.8
Public Relations	4,325	20.5
Magazines	802	3.8
Photojournalism	295	1.4
Graphics/Design	21	.1
General Mass Communications	1,203	5.7
Other	1,688	8.0
TOTAL	21,100	100.0

Source: Dow Jones Newspaper Fund.

There are some obvious conclusions to be drawn. Given the high cost of specialized education, one might give second thought to attending journalism school—only 21.8 percent of journalism school graduates go to work on newspapers, plus another 17.9 percent in broadcasting. The reasons for this small percentage may be a lack of job opportunities, low entry-level salaries, or a disenchantment with the medium.

The figure of 20.5 percent going into public relations is interesting, as this is a much smaller field than newspapers. The 20.8 percent for advertising is understandable, because this is a high-growth area with very attractive salaries at the middle- and upper-management levels.

Daily newspapers recorded the largest salary increase of all media-related categories. The median salary for 1986 graduates hired was $14,125. Women were 66.3 percent of journalism school graduates and, in 1986, newspapers hired more women than men.

You, however, will have to make your own decision. My best advice is to visit the school of your choice and pose questions to the dean, registrar, or student journalism majors before making up your mind about journalism. You may save yourself time and money by not attending, or your initial instinct may be confirmed and you can't wait to enter this exciting profession.

Another piece of information: If you wish to enter newspaper publishing on the business side with the goal of ultimately becoming a publisher, I suggest getting your newspaper experience through internships (a list is given near the end of this chapter) or summer jobs and then pursuing an M.B.A. program to gain academic business training.

The Big and the Bigger

The five biggest daily newspapers in terms of circulation are the *Wall Street Journal*, *USA Today*, the *New York Daily News*, the *Los Angeles Times*, and the *New York Times*.

According to recent figures, the *Wall Street Journal* has a circulation of about 1.9 million; *USA Today*, 1.4 million; and the *New York Times* just under 1 million.

One might not think of the *Wall Street Journal* as a daily newspaper, but it certainly is a formidable one. *USA Today*, owned by the number one chain, Gannett (pronounced Gan-*nett*) Company, is a surprising second, as it is a national paper with news and features, launched only in the early '80s. The *New York Daily News* has the largest circulation of any tabloid in the nation. (The "tabloid" or compact-size newspaper is generally 11" × 14¾". The "metro" or full-size format is 13½" × 21¾".)

The *Los Angeles Times* is an immensely successful paper with huge advertising revenues. It is owned by the Times Mirror Company, the sixth-largest newspaper company.

The largest chain, Gannett, owns ninety daily newspapers, with a total circulation of about 5.5 million. Knight-Ridder Newspapers is second with twenty-seven dailies, followed by Newhouse Newspapers with twenty-six. Newhouse also owns the major magazine publishing company, Condé Nast. The Tribune Company, in fourth place, has eight dailies including the *Chicago Tribune.* In fifth place, Dow Jones & Company owns the *Wall Street Journal* and twenty-two other dailies.

> CAREER TIP: Give some consideration to working for one of the newspaper chains. Promotion can mean moving from advertising director at one paper to publisher of another in the same chain.

The Background of an Acquisition

The Times Mirror Company, the Los Angeles–based media conglomerate that owns the *Los Angeles Times,* fourth in circulation ranking, in mid-1986 agreed to purchase the venerable and respected *Baltimore Sun* for a sum estimated at $450 million.

The Times Mirror Company, in addition to its other media holdings—books, magazines, and so on—has four other major papers: *Newsday,* the *Hartford Courant,* the *Denver Post,* and the *Dallas Times Herald.*

The brilliant social critic H. L. Mencken was associated with the *Baltimore Sun* papers, separate morning and evening editions, from 1906 until near his death in 1956. The *Baltimore Sun* papers had a recent circulation of about 350,000.

The Times Mirror Company was a communications giant even before the acquisition. In 1985, it had an operating income of $620 million.

In May 1986, only a week before the announcement of the *Baltimore Sun* acquisition, Gannett agreed to pay about $300 million for the *Courier-Journal* and the *Louisville Times* in Kentucky. The big get bigger.

Who Does What in the Newspaper Business

The four basic divisions of a newspaper's personnel are management, business, editorial, and technical. The accompanying chart lists the various job functions for a typical newspaper with a circulation of 100,000; however, the reader should realize that of the nation's 1,700 daily newspapers, only about 10 percent have circulations over 100,000. Also, fully 7,800 of the nation's papers are weeklies, with average circulations of about 6,500. Weeklies are popular in smaller cities and in rural areas that cannot support dailies.

In this section we will describe each function and its average yearly salary. One should, of course, understand that on a larger-circulation paper the staff is larger than shown, and on a smaller-circulation daily or weekly many of these jobs are either nonexistent or doubled up.

Because there is such disparity between Newspaper Guild and non-Guild salaries and between big papers and small ones, we will quote only average annual salaries for certain job titles. These job functions and their salaries were derived from a study of 648 dailies (more than 40 percent of the nation's local daily newspaper units) made by the School of Journalism at the University of Missouri—Columbia. (We'll have more to say about the Newspaper Guild, a craft union for editorial and business employees in the newspaper industry, later in this chapter.)

Management
   Owner/Publisher/General Manager

Business
   Business Manager
   Advertising Director
   Classified Advertising Manager
   Promotion Director
   Circulation Director/Manager
   Comptroller/Director of
      Finance/Accountant

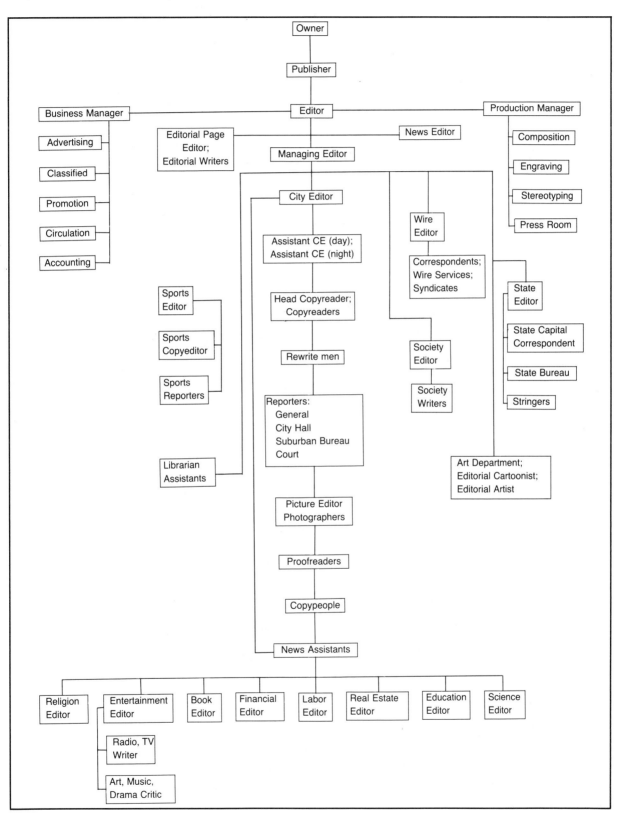

The hierarchy of a newspaper with a circulation of 10,000.

Editorial
Editor
Managing Editor
Editorial Page Editor
News Editor
City Editor
Wire Editor
Copy Editor
Specialists
Makeup Staff
Reporters
Photographers
Production Manager

Management

Owner/Publisher/General Manager: Sometimes the owner exercises day-to-day managerial control. In a chain operation, a general manager, or publisher, runs the paper and is responsible to the board of directors. This individual must have knowledge of every phase of a newspaper's editorial, business, and production functions. He is responsible for budgetary control and ultimately the bottom line. The average yearly salary for a publisher ranges from $64,000 to $68,000; for a general manager, from $52,000 to $56,000.

Business

Business Manager: The business manager is charged with the management of the vital areas of advertising sales, promotion, circulation, and accounting. Because advertising accounts for 75 percent of the average paper's revenues and circulation for 25 percent, we can readily understand the importance of this job. On a major paper, the business manager will probably have a journalism and business education. The average salary ranges from $30,000 to $34,000.

Advertising Director: The advertising director supervises the entire department, including local, classified, and national sales. In the national sales area, the advertising director works with regional sales reps and sometimes has personal contact with the newspaper's major clients and agencies. The average salary ranges from $33,000 to $37,000.

Classified Advertising Manager: The classified advertising manager runs a department that sells real estate, cars, and the like by means of want ads. The staff often includes a telephone-sales group. The average salary ranges from $24,000 to $28,000.

Promotion Director: The promotion director supports circulation and advertising sales with in-paper ads, plans radio and TV campaigns, and works with local schools and city or town on image-building. Training in public relations and journalism is a plus. The average salary ranges from $25,000 to $29,000.

Circulation Director/Manager: The circulation director supervises the sale of the newspaper through retail and subscription sources, plans campaigns, and sets goals for the field staff. The average salary ranges from $26,000 to $30,000.

Comptroller/Director of Finance/Accountant: The title depends on the size of the newspaper, but the function is basically the same regardless. This person is responsible for the general financial management of the paper, which includes budgets, periodic statements, payroll, and so on. Many are CPAs. The average salary ranges from $39,000 to $43,000.

Editorial

Editor: A look at the chart will give an indication of the scope of the editor's job. The editor is like the director of a movie, in this case calling all the editorial shots. On some papers, there is an executive editor superior in rank to the editor. In any case, it is the editor who makes the policy decisions, directs the key assignments, trains reporters, occasionally writes editorials, and hires and fires personnel—in short, he runs the editorial show.

For these demanding responsibilities, editors are paid well. Their salary range, however, varies a great deal depending on the circulation, geographic area, union versus nonunion status, and number of employees. The average salary as listed in the University of Missouri—Columbia report ranges from $34,000 to $36,000. An editors' group, APME (Associated Press Managing Editors Association), conducted its own survey in the early 1980s of 555 editors in the United States and Canada. Following are some of its findings. (Note: An inflationary factor of at least 15 percent should be added to these figures to bring them at least into the late '80s.)

- The overall average base salary of editors ranged from $37,000 to $41,000.
- The average base salary of editors working for newspapers with fewer than one hundred employees was $25,000 to $29,000. For papers with more than 500, it was $51,000 to $55,000.
- The average base salary of editors working for union newspapers was $47,000 to $51,000; for nonunion newspapers, $34,000 to $38,000.
- The average base salary of editors working for papers with circulations under 10,000 was $22,000 to $26,000; for papers with circulations of 10,000 to 50,000, $31,000 to $35,000; for

At almost any time of day or night, the newsroom will be teeming with activity. (Photograph by Suzanne Kreiter.)

papers with circulations of 50,000 to 100,000, $37,000 to $41,000; for papers with circulations of 100,000 to 250,000, $53,000 to $57,000; and for papers with circulations of 250,000 and above, it was $64,000 to $68,000. The highest individual salary in the last category was $180,000.

• The northeast had the highest average base salary, $50,000 to $52,000; the north central region had the lowest, $34,000 to $36,000.

The reader can use these figures as a guide to comparable editorial salaries for lesser job functions.

Managing Editor: The managing editor runs the entire news-gathering operation. In consultation with the editor, city editor, and wire editor, this editor decides what stories will go into the paper and directs the flow of stories, photos, heads, and so on, from the newsroom to production. The average salary range is $30,000 to $36,000.

Editorial Page Editor: Note on the chart that the function of the editorial page editor is on a par with those of the managing editor and news editor. The editorial page reflects the policy of the newspaper. On many newspapers, the staff includes two or three—occasionally more—editorial writers, usually people with considerable journalistic experience, capacity for judgment, and persuasive writing talent.

The editor looks to the editorial-page editor and editorial writers for carefully reasoned ideas and suggestions. At daily conferences, they select and assign the next day's editorials.

Editorial writers may also choose and process the letters, columns, articles, and cartoons that appear on the editorial page. In some cases, these duties are handled by a special assistant.

On a major newspaper such as the *New York Times,* the editorial page will generally run three full columns and discuss three or four issues, political or economic. Three additional columns are devoted to letters to the editor.

In the *Times,* facing the editorial page, is an op-ed page. Here, two or three regular columnists and two guest columnists write on various important issues, often political but sometimes social and economic.

Copy editors are skilled at language usage as well as publication layout. The tools of the latter and reference works are never very far away. (Photograph by Suzanne Kreiter.)

On a smaller newspaper, for example the *Berkshire Eagle*, which is profiled later in this chapter, there might be two editorial pages. Typically, two full columns are written by the editorial page staff, and three columns are letters to the editor. On the op-ed page, there are pieces by guest editors and a few by syndicated columnists such as William Safire and Ralph Nader. The editorial page content is less national in scope than that of the *Times*, but it is interesting that the basic format is similar.

The editorial page editor is responsible for these pages and approves their contents; he often writes editorials. The average salary for this job ranges from $34,000 to $38,000.

News Editor: The news editor coordinates the selection and placement of the major stories, meshing the best of the local and wire news and features into a cohesive, well-balanced, attractive product. The average salary ranges from $24,000 to $28,000.

City Editor: The city editor, aided by assistants, directs local and area news coverage. Together they schedule the shifts and assignments of the reportorial and rewrite staffs. Phone calls from "leg" reporters funnel through the city desk to the rewrite team composed of well-paid pros—usually former reporters who can write swiftly, accurately, and colorfully under the most intense of deadline pressures. The average salary for the city editor is $25,000 to $29,000.

Wire Editor: Sometimes called the telegraph editor, the wire editor sifts and evaluates foreign and national news from the Associated Press (AP) or United Press International (UPI) wire services, plus any supplementary news and features, into a cohesive, well-balanced, attractive product. The average salary is $22,000 to $26,000.

Copy Editor: The copy editor reviews and edits stories by reporters and from wire and feature services, refining or rewriting as necessary. This person often writes headlines for the stories and may also help lay out the pages. The copy editor must be highly skilled in grammar, spelling, punctuation, and writing and also have good news judgment. A copy editor's starting salary on a newspaper with a union contract is approximately $17,000 to $21,000. It may be much less on a nonunion paper.

Specialists: Depending on the size of the paper, the newsroom complement may include several subdepartments specializing in sports, business and finance, society, women's news, travel and resorts, hobbies, and the amusement and cultural spectrum of television, radio, movies, theater, art, and music.

Note, on the chart at the beginning of this section, that for a newspaper with a circulation of 100,000, the number and category of these specialists. In sports, for example, there is an editor, copy editor, and three reporters. To cover the city hall and court, there are four reporters. The state coverage has its own editor plus a resident capitol correspondent and two bureau reporters.

From time to time "stringers" are used as specialists. These are freelance writers who report news from rural and surrounding areas. They may also be used in other states and foreign countries. Stringers are usually paid by the column inch but sometimes per assignment.

As a college student or graduate, you can make extra money as a stringer by writing news or reviewing books or movies. It's good experience and can be financially rewarding. Later on in this chapter we discuss "stringing" in greater depth.

Note that on the chart there are no foreign editors or foreign correspondents. A paper of this size cannot afford this costly full-time coverage, relying instead on the wire services. If the paper is part of a chain operation, the chain will have its own foreign staff that will feed all its papers.

The specialists at the lower rung of the ladder in the chart—religion, books, and so on—may not necessarily be full-time employees of the paper, or even employees of the paper at all. They may be syndicated feature writers or provide their special services for the parent chain.

Depending on the size of the newspaper, the newsroom may include several subdepartments such as sports, business, society, and travel which may process their own copy—edit, copy edit, and so on. Generally copy (except for editorial page copy) is channeled through a "universal" copy desk that takes care of processing, editing, and copy editing the articles and features coming from every department.

Makeup Staff: The makeup staff has the job of "dummying" the pages. The "dummies" are small-scale page diagrams showing which stories and pictures belong where, on the front page and on inside pages, including the "jumps" (continuations) of stories that begin on page one.

The makeup editor has to be a wizard in making last-minute changes, trimming stories in type to fit their assigned space without loss of content or continuity, and seeing that the completed pages move along swiftly by deadline.

The makeup staff must follow through in the composing room as printers make up the pages in accordance with the dummies. On multiple-edition papers (the *New York Times*, for example), some pages may be remade several times to keep up with news developments.

Reporters: The reporters are the troops, the legpeople, the indefatigible story-hawks who badger assistant district attorneys and defense attorneys alike for the inside track on a story.

A reporter must gather information and write stories, usually under deadline pressure. He interviews people and observes events. A reporter must be able to take notes quickly and accurately, write at a typewriter or word processor, and use clear, objective language.

Certainly, under Newspaper Guild situations, experienced reporters are well paid (see the "Newspaper Guild" section later in this chapter). A degree from journalism school, however, is simply not enough to qualify even the brightest graduate as a reporter. Moreover, few training programs exist, even at large metropolitan papers.

One such program, though, has been implemented by Harte-Hanks Communications, a newspaper chain, at its Greenville, Texas, paper. There, in a ten-week program, the new reporter moves to a new assignment each week, covering such areas

Reporters often spend a good deal of their time away from the newsroom. (Photograph by Suzanne Kreiter.)

as city government, sports, schools, special interest, and so on. The trainee's week in each of these departments is spent in observation and instruction in editing copy and writing headlines, and, at week's end, in laying out pages under the editor's supervision. The reporter even spends time at the general news desk, observing and assisting the editor with rewrites, page proofs, layouts, and other chores, ultimately moving to the composing room. The final week is spent with the editor, sharpening skills in the area of special interest.

In order to give would-be reporters the experience of covering municipal politics and the courts, many journalism schools and colleges with journalism courses require students to attend town council and/or planning-board meetings and court proceedings and write stories as class assignments.

A final word on the reporter's lot. Covering city scandals and murders and interviewing the visiting celebrity may be glamorous and exciting pursuits, but starting out is not much fun—the reason being deplorable starting salaries. For talented college graduates, many of whom have bachelors' or mas-

Newspaper photographers also do much of their work on the road but often stay in close contact with the newsroom. (Photograph by Suzanne Kreiter.)

ters' degrees in journalism, salaries of $12,000 or $13,000 a year are an embarrassment. The practice exists simply because the supply exceeds the demand. Prospective journalists should be prepared to understand this reality.

Photographers: Let's accept the cliché that one picture is worth a thousand words—a picture that not only illustrates and enhances a news story but that independently tells its own story in such graphic terms that even the caption lines seem redundant.

Photojournalism has become an important specialty in the curricula of many journalism schools, yet some of our most talented news photographers have had no formal training.

The paper of 100,000 circulation typically has a picture editor and about seven photographers. This staff may seem overly large, but it's a way of ensuring that good news pictures do not "get away" for lack of an assigned photographer.

The city desk and departmental editors line up shooting schedules. The picture editor coordinates this activity. Any necessary retouching is done by staff artists to improve contrast values and crop away extraneous detail. In the University of Missouri—Columbia study, a picture editor's average salary was $23,000 to $25,000. In Newspaper Guild situations, the salary for this specialty is almost double.

Technical

Production Manager: Once the editorial people have put their day's assignments and responsibilities "to bed," and the advertising staff has done its

selling, the production manager must shepherd the paper through the composing room, the engraving and stereotype departments, the press room, and off to the trucks for delivery.

Today, as a result of technology, "cold type" has replaced the "hot" Linotype process. Cold type is a photocomposition process whereby news is processed through automatic typesetting equipment. The type is set by photographing letters rather than casting them with hot metal on a Linotype machine. Offset presses have often replaced the more expensive letterpress equipment. To remain profitable, a newspaper must keep step with these developments.

Let's take a quick run through the production stages so that we can understand the role of the production manager and his staff.

Some newspapers are fully photocomposed through automatic typesetting equipment that produces text at a rate of up to 1,100 lines per minute. This typesetting equipment is fed by the video display terminals at which most writing and editing is done.

In other systems, copy is punched into perforated tape and then fed into automatic Linotype machines, which set the type directly from the tape.

Where photocomposition systems are used, pages are pasted up, and page images are reproduced on lasermask negatives (a polystyrene plastic with a carbonlike coating). The lasermasks are then used to make planographic offset printing plates weighing only a few ounces.

In letterpress systems, the metal for the text, ads, and photos are combined into page form. A cardboardlike mat, or matrix, is pressed against the page, and the mats are then sent to the stereotype department to make a curved molten metal plate.

In offset, the planographic printing plates are wrapped around the press's cylinder and printed at high speed, up to 30,000 copies per hour of a ninety-six-page newspaper. This speed is necessary for large circulation, multi-section papers.

In letterpress, the molten metal plates are locked onto the press's cylinders. Eight or sixteen pages are printed at a normal speed of 25,000 papers an hour. Two- and four-color signatures (press sections) may be printed without loss of press time.

Most newspaper presses print from rolls of newsprint that weigh about 1,400 pounds each and are four pages wide. The press prints and folds the paper into sections in the same operation. Once off the press, the paper goes to the circulation department for its ultimate destination.

Production managers must be knowledgeable in all printing specialties. The University of Missouri—Columbia study shows production managers' average yearly salary as ranging from $32,000 to $34,000. These figures vary substantially, however, depending upon the circulation and staff of a paper.

Newspaper Jobs You May Never Have Thought of

Young journalism majors seem to concentrate on a few highly challenging jobs. They all want to be Woodwards and Bernsteins. There are other jobs, however—perhaps less glamorous but just as formidable. If you are seriously interested, start reading the classified section of *Editor & Publisher*. Here's more on those "sleeper" jobs. (Salaries for these positions vary widely and have therefore been omitted.)

Marketing Researcher: Advertising uses market research to sell more effectively. Circulation uses demographics as guides for subscription campaigns. Editors use research to learn more about readers' interests. Journalism majors with knowledge of marketing and statistics are good candidates.

Personnel Manager: Hiring, training, counseling, conducting tests, and writing manuals—these are the functions of newspaper personnel people. Journalism majors with a minor in psychology are excellent candidates for these positions.

Art Director: If art directors are on the staffs of magazines, why not on newspapers? Although not as prevalent, art directors can do much to make the paper more attractive, especially the appearance of the ads. Medium- and large-sized newspapers offer the best opportunities.

Librarian: With modern information retrieval systems, the librarian must not only be a news person but one well versed in library science. This is a small but growing field.

Labor Negotiator: Most medium- and large-sized papers have contact with unions. The job calls for a lawyer who understands the newspaper business and is also a good bargainer.

Public Relations Specialist: Informing the employees and the public about company affairs is important. The need is even greater when the paper is part of a chain and/or is publicly owned. This is a small field, but the rise to the top may be swift.

A Random Look at Journalism Salaries

Although Allen Neuharth, the chairman of Gannett (*USA Today*, etc.), earned $1.5 million in 1986, and the syndicated columnist George F. Will grossed about $1 million, lesser folk in the newspaper

Newsprint moves through the presses at about twenty-five miles per hour. (Photograph by Suzanne Kreiter.)

business earned far less. According to a recent *Washington Post* survey, here are some representative salaries from across the country:

Copy editor, *Village Voice* (New York City),
  five years' experience: $18,000
Reporter, Bucks County (Pennsylvania),
  four years' experience: $22,000
Newsman with Associated Press, based in Vermont,
  seven years' experience: $34,000
Staff photographer, Indiana newspaper,
  fourteen years' experience: $27,000
Section editor, San Francisco newspaper,
  twelve years' experience: $38,000
Editorial writer/columnist, New Jersey newspaper,
  thirteen years' experience: $44,000

These salaries are quite low compared with those on Wall Street, but the jobs are certainly more creative.

The Newspaper Guild

When we think of unions, we think of painters, Teamsters, and steel workers, but some newspaper employees also belong to a union—the Newspaper Guild. Although its membership encompasses only about 8 percent of the industry's 450,000 employees, it does represent craft people in the advertising, business, circulation, editorial, maintenance, promotion, and related departments of newspapers and allied enterprises. (It should be understood that, other than on a paper with a Guild contract, Guild membership is not compulsory.)

In 1933, in the heart of the Depression, when the average weekly salary for reporters was $29.00, Heywood Broun, the most famous columnist of his time, launched the Newspaper Guild. In its first year, the Guild signed its first contract with the *Philadelphia Record*. The reporter's minimum salary went to $35.00 a week.

In the days before the Guild, sweatshop conditions existed on newspapers. Reporters worked long, irregular hours—often seven-day weeks with no overtime—and it took the average reporter twenty years to reach the lofty salary of $38.00 a week. Even under the Guild, it wasn't until 1946 that a $100 minimum weekly salary was achieved for key editorial and advertising jobs.

Today, Newspaper Guild members are elitists by virtue of their high salaries compared with those of nonunion people. For example, in the mid-1980s the minimum weekly salaries were $885 for reporters, photographers, ad sales and circulation district managers (as high as $856 to start); $755 for computer operators; $579 for classified-ad telephone solicitors; $481 for keypunch operators; $460 for stenographers; $452 for clerks; $419 for copy carriers; $915 for magazine writers; and $613 for magazine researchers.

Translating these gross weekly salaries to annual ones shows them to be almost twice those at non-Guild papers. There are many big-city papers that do not have Newspaper Guild contracts, however, but that still pay salaries at the Guild level. This is done, of course, to attract talented people.

The Guild has contracts with most of the leading newspapers in the United States and Canada, including the *New York Times, Washington Post, Chicago Sun-Times, St. Louis Post-Dispatch, San Francisco Chronicle,* eleven Knight-Ridder papers, twelve Gannett papers, seven Scripps-Howard papers, the AP, UPI, Reuters, and twenty news and feature magazines, including *Time, Newsweek, People,* and *Fortune.*

Salaries for newspaper editorial and business work certainly do not match those for some of today's higher-paying jobs—say, for example, those of market analyst with the large New York investment banks and brokerage houses, who are paid $40,000 a year right out of college. But the Newspaper Guild has established newspaper work as a respected, creative profession—one with stability and excellent salaries as well.

What Is a Stringer?

They've been called "huckleberry" writers or country correspondents who report "backyard fence" news for papers that can't afford to employ them on a full-time basis but value their services. Yet, stringers perform a legitimate service to many newspapers by covering small communities.

Stringers are compensated in many different ways—by the word, the inch, the assignment, or by the photograph. The wire services use them on an irregular basis to complement their coverage. One of the problems in employing them is their lack of supervision and training in the use of modern technology, such as portable computers, to transmit their copy.

In some cases, a paper will have a formal compensation system with stringers and require that they submit a fixed number of pieces per week or month. Newspapers may also use stringers to write specialized articles on subjects such as gardening, home improvements, and health. Employing a local writer for these assignments may give the column a local flavor not attainable with a syndicated column. Officially, the Newspaper Guild frowns on the use of stringers, judging them competition for its full-time members.

A group called the National Writers Union, in its Boston local, published a survey showing the payment practices of area publications. A look at some of these figures may serve as a guide for would-be freelancers and stringers (see table on page 13). The survey was conducted in the mid-1980s. More than forty newspapers and magazines in the region were covered.

NEWSPAPERS

Publication	Pay Rates	Pay on Acceptance
Christian Science Monitor	$80–$200	Yes
Quincy Patriot Ledger	1,000 words: $50	No
	Arts review: $25	
	Other Reviews: $10	
Somerville Journal	Long feature: $20–$30	No
	Long news: $30–$35	
The Phoenix	Average $2 per column inch (about 5¢ per word)	No

MAGAZINES

Publication	Pay Rates	Pay on Acceptance
Atlantic Monthly	Fiction: $2,000	(Pay within one month)
	Reports: $1,500	
High Technology	Long feature: $1,600–$1,800	Long: 3 payments
	Short Feature: $1,200–$1,500	Short: Yes
	Perspectives: $300–$500	
Horticulture	Average: $750	Yes
	Low: $350	
	High: $2,100	
Inc.	Feature: $1,500–$2,500	Yes, 2–3 weeks
Yankee	Features	Yes, 2–3 weeks
	highest: $1,000	
	average: $600	
	lowest: $300	

Conclusion: Many newspapers and magazines use freelance writers or stringers, but it is difficult for these individuals to make a living at this work exclusively.

A Look at a Major Newspaper Company

A number of newspaper publishers are larger and more successful than the New York Times Company. The growth in diversification of the Times, however, from a one-product company to a communications giant in just fifteen years (1970–85) bears interest to any student of the media.

About the Newspaper

It all started in 1851 in a loft building in lower Manhattan. The first owner, Henry J. Raymond, set about publishing a paper for discerning readers. It was called the *New York Daily Times,* and it succeeded until Raymond's death toward the end of the nineteenth century.

Adolph S. Ochs, a Chattanooga newspaperman, bought the *Times* for only $75,000 in 1896. Ochs reinvested the paper's earnings in new editorial sections and staff, and, in just nine years, the paper outgrew its downtown plant and moved uptown to what was then called Longacre Square but was renamed Times Square in the newspaper's honor. One of Ochs's grandsons, Arthur Ochs Sulzberger, is the *Times*'s present publisher.

The *New York Times* is responsible for many firsts, not the least of which are the first on-the-spot wireless dispatch in history, on April 14, 1904 (it was an eyewitness account of fighting off Port Arthur during the Russo-Japanese War) and the first wire photo showing the survivors of the Navy dirigible *Macon* explosion in San Francisco in 1935.

Editorial excellence is the *Times*'s standard. Its reporters and correspondents have garnered fifty-four Pulitzer Prizes since 1918, more than any other newspaper. Its 1976 winner was Sydney H. Schanberg for his coverage of the fall of Cambodia, later made into an excellent movie, *The Killing Fields;* its 1979 winner, satirist Russell Baker for his "Observer" column.

Statistics

On a Sunday in December during the busy shopping season, a copy of the *Times* may weigh as much as ten pounds, including all its inserts. At the going rate for newsprint, that adds up to more than $2.00 per copy just for the paper. The *Sunday Times* in New York sells for only $1.25. Where does the deficit come from? Advertising—and lots of it: In 1985, there were 111,376,000 lines, leading all the nation's papers. The *Times* has an average advertising-to-editorial ratio of 65:35.

In terms of advertising pages published, in 1985 the *New York Times Magazine* became the country's leading magazine. It carried a total of 4,345 pages of advertising, ahead of *Business Week* by 130 pages.

In case you're peeved because your letter to the editor didn't make it into the paper, you'll be consoled to learn that the *Times* receives 60,000 letters to the editor each year, but because of space restrictions, fewer than 3,000 are published.

There are *Times* news bureaus in fifteen U.S. cities outside New York City and in twenty-eight foreign cities including Abidjan, Belgrade, Nairobi, and San Salvador, as well as in the major cities of the world.

Getting "all the news that's fit to print" doesn't come cheaply. Recent figures show that the paper employed 513 reporters, editors, news clerks, and photographers in New York City, seventy-three outside the city, and thirty-two in its foreign offices.

The *Times* publishes an average of 215,000 words in an average daily edition, and 834,000 words in an average Sunday edition. Each day the paper receives 1.9 million words from its own bureaus and the three major news agencies: the Associated Press, United Press International, and Reuters.

Its editorial reference library has 55,000 volumes, 500 periodicals, and twenty-five newspapers. The picture file has 3.7 million photos. The clip file ("the morgue") has 28 million clips, with 15,000 to 20,000 added each week.

The New York Times News Service provides more than 500 U.S. and foreign newspapers in more than fifty countries on six continents with a 75,000-word daily report.

It takes almost 7 million trees to print a year of the *New York Times*, but ecologists should not fear. The mills in Canada where the *Times* buys most of its newsprint engage in a natural reforestation program so that future readers will not have to read a skimpy paper.

The *Times* as a Communications Giant

The following five small papers are part of the twenty-five daily newspapers and eight weekly or semi-weekly newspapers in ten states owned by the New York Times Company: the *Dispatch* in Lexington, North Carolina; the *Daily Comet* in Thibodaux, Louisiana; *Palatka Daily News* in Palatka, Florida; the *Messenger* in Madisonville, Kentucky; and the *Harlan Daily Enterprise* in Harlan, Kentucky. The largest of these five has a circulation of only 15,000.

There are also five magazines, including *Family Circle* with a recent circulation average of about 6.5 million, *Golf Digest* with 200,000, and *Tennis* with 500,000. This division had 1985 revenues of $216.5 million and profits of $17.6 million.

As an indication of how profitable this well-managed company is, in that same year all its newspapers had revenues of $1.1 billion and operating profits of $196.99 million, or almost 18 percent of revenues—extraordinary for a company of this size.

About the Other Divisions

The New York Times Company has diversified from a single major newspaper to this nation's eighth-largest newspaper company in terms of daily circulation, with twenty-five dailies and eight weekly or semiweekly papers. The Times Company also operates a cable system in southern New Jersey and five TV stations—three in the Sunbelt, one in the Midwest, and a fifth in the Northeast. There are also the five magazines and two classical-music radio stations in New York, WQXR-AM/FM. In addition to these media properties, the company has equity positions in three Canadian paper mills and one in Maine.

At the end of 1985, there were fifty-three companies making up the parent New York Times Company. What is unusual is that twenty-eight of these companies have been acquired since 1979. The company has done it fast, and it has done it well.

How a Great Newspaper Handles a Major News Story

The day: Monday, April 14, 1986. *The time:* 7:00 P.M. EST. *The event:* Sixteen British-based, U.S. Air Force F-111 bombers attacked five Libyan facilities in the cities of Tripoli and Benghazi, in retaliation for what

President Ronald Reagan called the "reign of terror" waged by Colonel Muammar el-Qaddafi against the United States.

The raids were made particularly hazardous because the planes had to fly a circuitous route of 2,800 nautical miles—1,200 miles more than a direct route—because of a lack of cooperation from some of the United States' European allies.

That night, at 9:00 P.M. EST, in a nationally broadcast speech, the president confirmed the earlier news reports of the raid and justified them on the basis of Libyan terrorism.

At 11:00 P.M., on the network TV news, capsules of the president's speech were broadcast, and reports from correspondents in Libya were shown. The next day, of course, there was more comprehensive TV coverage of this momentous event.

Now let's shift our medium to illustrate how the event was covered in one of America's greatest newspapers, the *New York Times*.

Page one, along with four other pages in the main news section, was devoted almost entirely to the raid. By analyzing this coverage, we can now begin to understand the basic difference between how a great newspaper handles an international crisis and how it's done in the broadcast media. Television and radio are more immediate, reporting the event almost as it happens, but a newspaper can give it the depth and focus not attainable in broadcasting.

Let's analyze the *Times's* coverage and, in the process, obtain a broad perspective of the paper's news operation.

Timing and Strategy

First word of the attack came at a little after 7:00 P.M., New York time, Monday. The earliest edition that could be made was the second; it would go to press at 11:00 P.M. and hit the stands one hour later—not very much time for a major story such as this one. The first edition is off press at around 10:00 P.M. and hits the stands soon after.

The foreign editor was the commander-in-chief of this operation. The assignments were made swiftly. There would ultimately be ten *Times* correspondents covering the story: seven from Washington, one from the Hague, one from New York, and one from Tripoli, Libya, one of the major cities under attack.

There was no word count given. Basically, the directions were "Write what you've got as fast as possible."

While the foreign editor gave out the assignments, four people were involved in the editing process: the foreign editor, the executive editor, the managing editor, and the news editor. They made the

decisions about how much and what coverage was to be given to the story.

Assignments

Bernard Gwertzman covered Secretary of State George Shultz's press conference. This had been preceded by White House spokesman Larry Speakes, who made the first official announcement of the raid.

Michael Gordon reported the details of the raids as they were given to the press by Defense Secretary Caspar Weinberger and other Pentagon officials.

Neil Lewis, also reporting from Washington, covered the angle of the flight path itself and its circuitous route from England, necessitated by the rebuff of the Western European allies, who refused to allow U.S. planes to fly over their air space.

Bernard Weinraub wrote the lead article from Washington, focusing on the president's televised speech at 9:00 P.M.

Steven Roberts covered Capitol Hill, giving congressional reaction from leaders of both parties. He also wrote about the meetings the president had with some lawmakers from 4:00 P.M. to 5:00 P.M., during which time the planes had already left their bases in England. The president's national security adviser, Vice-Admiral John M. Poindexter, informed the lawmakers as late as 6:20 P.M. that the mission could still be aborted if Congress so demanded.

R. W. Apple, Jr., reported from Washington on Reagan's dispatching Vernon Walters, the chief U.S. delegate to the United Nations, to London, Paris, Bonn, and other capitals to seek their approval of the raids.

Gerald Boyd in Washington wrote of the events leading to the president's decision on the raid against Libya.

Richard Bernstein reported from the Hague on the European Community countries' decision to reduce the size of Libyan embassies in Europe and to restrict the movements of Libyan diplomats.

Robert McFadden in New York wrote about the TV networks' coverage of the event from the point of view of the live reports of their correspondents in Tripoli.

Edward Schumacher was the man on the spot in Tripoli. He had been sent there in advance because the foreign editor thought it was a good time to take a closer look at Libya, especially because of all the rhetoric during the days that led up to the event. He was there as it happened.

Schumacher received his assignment about twenty minutes after the raid. The task of recounting what happened in Tripoli was made even more difficult because foreign correspondents were not permitted to leave their hotels, so his 1,500-word piece reported only what he could see from his hotel's balcony.

Libyan radio provided official government reports of the raid. These were supplemented by statements from the People's Liaison Bureau, the equivalent of a foreign ministry. Earlier on Monday, the official Libyan press agency had threatened that Libyan "suicide missions" worldwide were ready to respond to an American attack.

Under stress, Schumacher pieced together a thorough and informative article. He had less than two hours to telephone his story to New York. All his communications subsequent to the raid were made via telephone as well. This was done to speed up the process and to allow discussions between Schumacher and his editors.

During the next few days, no additional journalists were sent to Libya because no one could get in. In fact, people were desperately trying to get out and were camping out on runways, attempting literally to "catch a plane." The airport was closed immediately after the raid.

Back in New York

The staff in New York was increased by one-third to handle the extensive coverage of this major event. These employees were mostly copy editors and a few clerks. The head copy editor assigned to the foreign desk knew what had to be done, and it was he who brought in the extra staff as needed.

The copy desk also has people who do rewrites when they are required. Most of the time, however, the correspondents send in pieces that need very little work.

No special typesetting system was used. (More about the *Times*'s system follows.) The turnaround time was kept to a minimum, as was the editing. The correspondents didn't have to write the headlines; that was done by the editors, as is customary.

Window Dressing

The front page had a small-scale map of Western Europe and North Africa, with the path of the bombers shown from their base in England to the five targets near Tripoli and Benghazi. It included the four points of air refueling that were required because of the long distance covered. All this information was provided to the *Times* by the Pentagon.

The front page also had a photo of the president speaking to the press.

The inside pages had photos of the president and his chief of staff, Donald Regan, after the congressional briefing; a fighter-bomber taking off from its base in England and bombs being transported to waiting aircraft at the base; special U.S. envoy Vernon Walters outside the Élysée Palace in Paris after talks with President François Mitterrand; the German and British foreign ministers at the Hague; a Libyan official meeting in Malta with that country's leaders; Shultz and Weinberger at their briefing for the press; and another of Poindexter and the chairman of the Joint Chiefs of Staff, Admiral William J. Crowe, Jr.

There was also a photo and line drawings of the U.S. aircraft used in the strike on Libya, together with details of their specifications and capability. This was supplied by *Jane's All the World's Aircraft* and wire reports.

The photos from the New York Times, Associated Press, and Reuters (the last two are major newsgathering organizations with correspondents worldwide) were transmitted to New York by facsimile equipment, which sends graphic matter by wire or radio.

The Next Day's Coverage

The executive editor, the foreign editor, the news editor, and the managing editor decided on the next day's coverage of the Libyan raids. Each editor made a list of what he thought should appear in the next day's *Times,* and then the "big four" made the adjustments and the final decisions.

There was a report from England from the two people sent over to cover the story from there. In the next few days, a couple of background pieces were written about the U.S. bases in England.

Typesetting, Printing, and Off to the Newsstands

The Washington and New York correspondents reporting on the Libyan event basically used portable video display terminals that delivered their material by telephone to a central computer network.

The *Times*'s typesetting is fully photocomposed. The paper converted to this system in 1978, from the slow and laborious Linotype system.

By laser-scanning of page paste-ups, page images are reproduced on polystyrene plastic negatives with a carbon-like coating and then made into

"All the News That's Fit to Print"

The New York Times

Late Edition

Weather: Partly cloudy and cool today, chance of showers; rain likely tonight. Cloudy, with continued rain tomorrow. Temperatures: today 54-58, tonight 43-47; yesterday 41-67. Details, page C14.

VOL. CXXXV . No. 46,745 Copyright © 1986 The New York Times NEW YORK, TUESDAY, APRIL 15, 1986 — 50 cents beyond 75 miles from New York City, except on Long Island — 30 CENTS

U.S. JETS HIT 'TERRORIST CENTERS' IN LIBYA; REAGAN WARNS OF NEW ATTACKS IF NEEDED; ONE PLANE MISSING IN RAIDS ON 5 TARGETS

The New York Times / Paul Hosefros

FORECAST ON TRADE GAP: Prime Minister Yasuhiro Nakasone in Washington. He predicted a decline in Japanese trade surplus with U.S. by fall. Page D1.

PARIS BARRED JETS

Weinberger Says Rebuff Added 1,200 Miles to Flight From Britain

By NEIL A. LEWIS

Special to The New York Times

WASHINGTON, April 14 — President Reagan said today that the Western European allies had assisted the United States in its military attack against Libya, but according to other high officials the action was hampered by a lack of cooperation, notably from France.

According to Secretary of State George P. Shultz and Defense Secretary Caspar W. Weinberger, the degree of cooperation ranged from Britain's allowing American air bases there to be used to France's refusal to let the American planes fly through its airspace.

"With respect to our allies, we have a variety of opinions," Mr. Shultz said in the White House briefing room. Mr. Weinberger said Prime Minister Margaret Thatcher of Britain had allowed the use of the air bases.

Route Was 1,200 Miles Longer

But Mr. Weinberger said the pilots had to use a more dangerous route to avoid flying over countries that had barred the use of their airspace. He suggested that several countries had not cooperated, but in response to a question, he singled out France.

Mr. Weinberger, in showing the flight path on a map, said that the circuitous route was 2,800 nautical miles, 1,200 miles more than a direct route.

"Obviously, if we had permission to fly a direct route, we would not have subjected the pilots to such a long flight," he said.

'That Is a Fair Description'

In response to a question whether the United States sought and was refused permission to fly over France, he responded, "I think that is a fair description."

When asked whether countries other than France had refused permission to fly over their territory, Mr. Weinberger said, "No, that would have been the direct route," an allusion to French airspace.

Mr. Weinberger said that in addition to having to fly a longer route, pilots had to take evasive actions to avoid detection.

Mr. Reagan, in his speech, praised

Continued on Page A11, Column 1

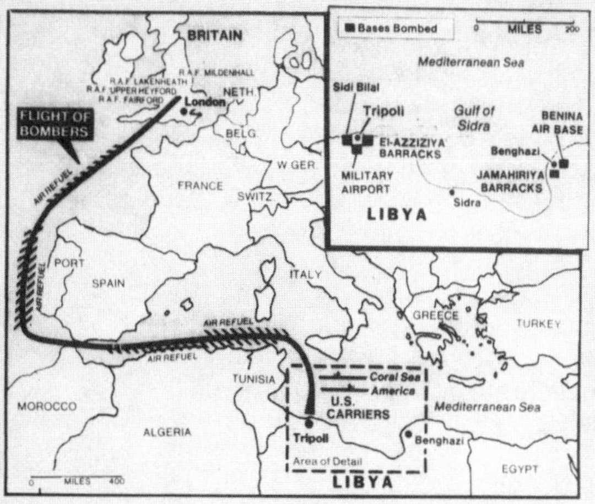

The New York Times / April 15, 1986

United States conducted air strikes against five Libyan targets near Tripoli and Benghazi. The American jets were said to have taken off from a British base and from ships in the Mediterranean.

STRIKES IN 2 AREAS

White House Lays 'Direct Responsibility' in Blast in Berlin to Qaddafi

By BERNARD WEINRAUB

Special to The New York Times

WASHINGTON, Tuesday, April 15 — The United States conducted a series of air strikes on Monday night against what the White House called "terrorist centers" and military bases in Libya.

President Reagan, in a nationally broadcast speech, said the American forces had "succeeded" in their mis-

Statements, pages A10 and A13.

sion of retaliating against Libya for what he termed the "reign of terror" waged by Col. Muammar el-Qaddafi, the Libyan leader, against the United States.

Defense Secretary Caspar W. Weinberger said later that one United States plane, an F-111 with a crew of two, "is not accounted for at this time." But he declined to say if the plane had been shot down.

Libya Says 3 Jets Downed

The Libyan radio, monitored in London, said that three United States aircraft had been shot down and that Libyans had killed their pilots and crew.

Mr. Reagan said: "Today we have done what we had to do. If necessary we shall do it again."

Congressional leaders generally expressed support for the attack on Libya, but a leading Democrat warned that the raid could lead to more violence. [Page A10.]

The French Foreign Ministry said the French Embassy in Tripoli was hit in the bombing raid, but a spokesman said no one was injured.

Foreign reporters in Tripoli, after a Government-conducted tour of a residential district today, said that the rear of the French Embassy was heavily damaged, with windows blown out, and that five or six houses in the district were also damaged. A Libyan Government spokesman said an unknown number of civilians had been killed.

5 Targets Near Cities

In his address on Monday night, Mr. Reagan said the American attack was a retaliation for what he asserted was the "direct" Libyan role in the bombing on April 5 of a West Berlin discothèque frequented by American servicemen. One American soldier and a Turkish woman died, and more than 200 people were wounded, including 50 other servicemen.

"We believe that this pre-emptive action against his terrorist installations will not only diminish Colonel Qaddafi's capacity to export terror, it will provide him with incentives and reasons to alter his criminal behavior," said a grim-faced Mr. Reagan.

An Administration official said five military targets near Libya's two major cities, Tripoli and Benghazi, were attacked.

Mr. Weinberger said American planes were forced to fly a long route to

Continued on Page A10, Column 3

Crucial Portion Of Shuttle Joint Found in Ocean

By DAVID E. SANGER

Salvage crews off the Florida coast have recovered a burned-out section of the booster rocket joint whose rupture is thought to have led to the destruction of the space shuttle Challenger, the Navy said yesterday.

The discovery provides the first tangible evidence that a failure of the joint, whose questionable design had worried rocket engineers for nearly a year before the Jan. 28 explosion, caused the disaster, which took the lives of seven astronauts.

Key 4,000-Pound Segment

After discovery of the crew cabin, which was hauled ashore last month, the search for the booster joint was the top priority for the flotilla of surface ships and submarines still combing the ocean floor off Cape Canaveral.

The wreckage, a 4,000-pound section of the aft-center segment of the rocket, was recovered early Sunday morning by the salvage vessel Stena Workhorse and an unmanned submersible working in 560 feet of water. Along one edge, where a tang fits into a groove on an adjacent rocket segment, a 2-foot-wide hole is evident, burned through the hardened steel of the rocket casing.

"It looks like someone took a giant

Continued on Page C3, Column 3

In the Skies Over Libya's Capital, Planes Roar and Bombs Resound

By EDWARD SCHUMACHER

Special to The New York Times

TRIPOLI, Libya, Tuesday, April 15 — For nearly 10 minutes, the night sky was ablaze with explosions from missiles and tracers as the American planes soared out of the distance.

Hours later, doctors said 60 to 100 wounded civilians had come to a hospital. It was not known how many people might have been killed, and the doctors did not offer an estimate.

Bombs fell on an upper-middle-class neighborhood that included the French Embassy. When reporters toured the area after daybreak, it was littered with broken glass, collapsed walls and destroyed cars.

The reporters saw one body.

The target appeared to be a communications building with a large antenna on top and several antennas behind it. The building's function was not clear, and officials would not say.

The bombs fell short of the building, and although its windows were blown out, the antennas stood intact on the roof.

The attacks began shortly before 2 A.M. (7 P.M. Monday, New York time), when the rumble of bombs could first be heard. For nearly 10 minutes afterward, the sky turned into a fireworks display of missiles and bombs.

Missiles could be seen rising into the air, but no American planes appeared to be hit.

Volleys of Antiaircraft Fire

The air strikes were met by volleys of antiaircraft fire. Smoke could be seen rising in the capital.

The reaction here was slow. The city's lights were not blacked out until 20 minutes after the attack began.

Even during the bombing, there was a strange calm on the city streets. Cars moved beneath the street lights around the harbor.

The state-run Libyan radio asserted that bombs had fallen on the barracks where Col. Muammar el-Qaddafi, the Libyan leader, maintains his headquarters, and that some members of his family were wounded in the raids. The reports could not be confirmed.

Officials said a downed American

Continued on Page A12, Column 1

PENTAGON DETAILS 2-PRONGED ATTACK

British-Based Jets Hit Tripoli, Navy Planes to Benghazi

By MICHAEL R. GORDON

Special to The New York Times

WASHINGTON, April 14 — Officials said tonight that the United States attack on five Libyan targets was a complex operation that involved separate attacks by Air Force and Navy planes and the use of aircraft for refueling, intelligence and electronic jamming.

The operation involved two strikes on separate regions of Libya, the officials said.

In one attack, Pentagon officials said, 18 United States Air Force F-111 bombers left England and attacked three targets near Tripoli. The targets were the military side of the Tripoli airport; a port section called Sidi Bilal, where Libyan commandos are trained, and the military barracks called el-Aziziya.

Planes From Carriers

In a separate attack, 15 A-6 and A-7 aircraft from the Coral Sea and the America, the two United States Navy aircraft carriers in the central Mediterranean, attacked two Libyan bases near Benghazi, Defense Secretary Caspar W. Weinberger said. They included an air base called Benina and a barracks called Jamahiriya.

Mr. Weinberger said that all the F-111's were accounted for except for

Continued on Page A11, Column 1

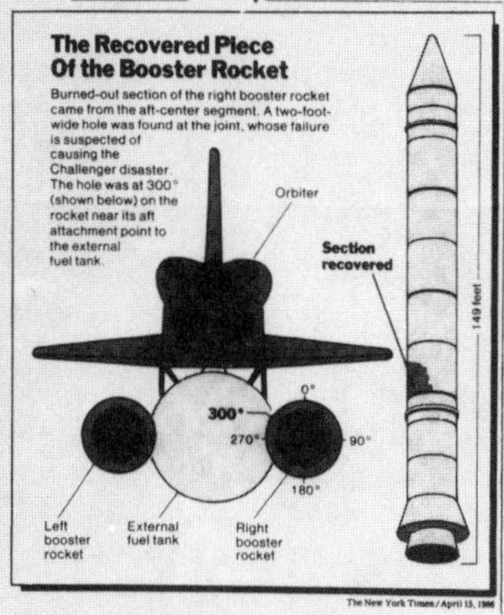

The New York Times / April 15, 1986

Plots on Global Scale Charged

By BERNARD GWERTZMAN

Special to The New York Times

WASHINGTON, April 14 — Secretary of State George P. Shultz said tonight that Libyan agents had been deployed around the world for attacks against United States embassies in as many as 30 countries.

At a news conference after the announcement of the American bombing attacks on Libya, Mr. Shultz said the raids had been necessary to deter Libya from future terrorist attacks and to retaliate for the bombing on April 5 of a West Berlin discothèque frequented by American soldiers.

He said that "we have reports and indications, quite substantial evidence, of Libyan efforts to attack — varying degrees of certainty on the evidence — up to 30 of our embassies."

Mr. Shultz said all United States embassies had been placed on special alert. Secretary of Defense Caspar W. Weinberger said United States military installations around the world were also on alert.

Administration officials said a plan by the Joint Chiefs of Staff for surgical bombing strikes against Libya was approved by President Reagan eight days ago. [Page A11.]

Larry Speakes, the White House spokesman, said tonight that Libyans were known to have been conducting surveillance and planning attacks against American diplomatic and commercial installations in Africa, Europe, the Middle East and Latin America.

He said that 10 attacks were planned in Africa alone and that in one African country, which he did not name, three Libyan agents arrived last week with the objective of bombing the United States Embassy and chancery and kidnapping the American Ambassador.

'The Primary Objective'

Discussing the American action tonight, Mr. Shultz said, "It's not a question of settling scores; it's a question of acting against terrorism, of saying to terrorists that the acts they perpetrate will cost them.

"If you raise the costs, you do something that should eventually act as a deterrent," he said. "And that is the primary objective, to defend ourselves both in the immediate sense and prospectively."

In his broadcast address tonight, Mr. Reagan said that "our evidence is direct, it is precise, it is irrefutable" that

Continued on Page A11, Column 4

HERB ENDERTON IS 50 YEARS OLD TODAY. HAPPY BIRTHDAY. CATHY, ERIC, BERT.—ADVT.

DEAR BUD, HAPPY BIRTHDAY ON YOUR 58TH. I LOVE YOU. P.K.R.—ADVTG.

The New York Times / Paul Hosefros

President Reagan speaking to journalists last night after broadcast.

INSIDE

Soviet Missile Said to Fail

United States experts said the Soviet Union had tested its largest new land-based missile, but that the test had apparently failed. Page A8.

Mets Lose Home Opener

An error by the Met third baseman, Howard Johnson, triggered a four-run burst that enabled the Cardinals to win, 6-2, in 13 innings. Page A25.

Simone de Beauvoir Dies

Simone de Beauvoir, the author and intellectual whose work helped inspire the women's movement, died in Paris at the age of 78. Page B9.

Horowitz Returns to Russia

Vladimir Horowitz, who left the Soviet Union 61 years ago, vowing never to return, arrived in Moscow to perform two piano recitals. Page C13.

Page one of the *New York Times* for April 15, 1986, the day after the attack on Libya. (Copyright © 1986 by The New York Times Company. Reprinted by permission.)

lightweight offset printing plates. The page images are transmitted electronically from the composing room at headquarters in Manhattan to the plate-making rooms at the *Times*'s printing plant in nearby Carlstadt, New Jersey.

From there, the plates are transmitted to plants in other locations: Chicago; Lakeland, Florida; Walnut Creek, California; Torrance, California; and Austin, Texas. These plants print the national edition of the *Times,* a paper with fewer pages than the New York edition.

The *Times* is printed entirely by the offset method. There are nine presses in New York and seven in Carlstadt, New Jersey. They can print up to 30,000 copies per hour of a ninety-six-page newspaper. The New York–area daily circulation is about 800,000; the national and foreign editions have a total daily circulation of approximately 310,000. On Sundays these total figures swell to more than 1.7 million copies.

The Aftermath of a Major News Event

An event such as the raids on Libya doesn't bring immediate glory to the paper and its correspondents. Costs go up, perhaps balanced by the increased number of copies sold on the newsstands. For the regular *Times* reader, however, it's what he or she has come to expect from a great newspaper.

The first day's coverage of the raids on Libya in the *Times* and the other media did not have details of the missing U.S. plane other than Defense Secretary Weinberger's statement that the F-111 "is not accounted for at this time." The reports also did not emphasize the nonmilitary targets that were hit and the subsequent civilian casualties. In the following day's coverage, however, these details were reported as quickly as they could be confirmed.

The latest time of day that a story of this magnitude could have broken to ensure coverage in the next day's paper would have been 2:30 A.M. That is when the latest (last) edition goes to press. Of course, for a story such as this one, the *Times* would have held the presses for a while in order to cover this event.

It is difficult to compare newspaper coverage of a news event with that of another medium, such as television. On the night of the Libya raids, as we mentioned earlier in this section, the president confirmed the action on TV, and later broadcasts had more details. In this case, however, TV could not match the detailed coverage of a newspaper like the *Times*. It's another story, though, when dealing with a political convention; there, the cameras are at work for five or six hours a day for four days.

One should also realize that the *New York Times* covers local news of the New York metropolitan area as well as global and national news. On Tuesday, April 15, in addition to the broad coverage of the Libya bombing, a reader could also learn of U.S. soldiers' taking part in Ku Klux Klan activities in North Carolina and of a hearing in Salt Lake City about a Mormon documents dealer charged in the bombing deaths of two Utahans. In addition, the metropolitan section contained in-depth coverage of the city's schools, courts, city hall, and crime problems. In this sense, the *New York Times* has the same news responsibilities as does the small paper, the *Berkshire Eagle,* discussed in the following section.

A Look at a Small City's Daily Newspaper

Newsweek characterized the *Berkshire Eagle* as a "rare journalistic bird," citing its commitment to cover the news fairly, its careful coverage of national, international, and regional news, and its recruitment of writing talent. The *Boston Globe* said, "The *Eagle*'s not the best newspaper of its size in Massachusetts; it's the best of its size in the country."

When Kelton B. Miller took ownership of the *Berkshire County* (Massachusetts) *Eagle* in 1891, the paper's forerunners had already been in business for 102 years. Miller changed the weekly to a daily in 1892, the same year its home town, Pittsfield, became a city. The paper and the city have thrived, and the Miller family still owns the *Berkshire Eagle.*

Today's daily *Eagle* has a circulation of 33,000, is located in a modern building in Pittsfield, employs about 200 people, and produces its product on up-to-date equipment with a capacity of printing 30,000 forty-eight-page papers per hour.

For the writers, editors, and technical staff of the *Berkshire Eagle,* working for a family-owned, small-city paper has its advantages. The Miller brothers, who run the business, are known to their employees as "Don" and "Pete." In the closeness of such an environment, it is often easier for talent to be recognized and rewarded.

Because the actual press running time of the *Eagle* is so short, the presses are available for outside customers, also. A variety of supplements are produced. For example, on Saturdays throughout the summer, the paper prints and distributes *Berkshire Week*, an attractive guide to the area's resort and cultural facilities. In February, there's a special automobile supplement; in April, a garden supplement; in May, one on outdoor living.

In a pattern that prevails in other parts of the country, the Millers own newspapers in surrounding areas: the *Torrington* (Connecticut) *Register* (circulation 12,000); the *Brattleboro* (Vermont) *Reformer* (circulation 9,000); and the *Bennington* (Vermont) *Banner* (circulation 7,000). Owning the four papers allows for group advertising programs and other economies.

The following is a brief outline of the contents of the *Berkshire Eagle* for a typical day. At the end of this chapter is an interview with Mark Miller, associate editor. In comparing this paper's operation with that of a giant paper such as the *New York Times*, the reader may be better able to form an opinion in his career choice about taking the big-paper or small-paper route.

On June 4, 1986, the *Eagle* had four sections with a total of thirty-six pages. The main news section had six pages; City and Town, twelve; Sci-Health, six; and Sports, twelve.

Page one had three national stories: one on the space shuttle system, one on the possible sale of U.S. uranium-processing plants, and one on President Reagan's appeal to Congress to finance his "Star Wars" program. All three had the byline of the New York Times News Service. (The *Eagle* is too small to have its own national correspondents. Copy that comes in via the wire services is cut, if necessary, and edited for house style and to add a local angle, if any.) The other page-one story was about a local group of middle-school students who were suspended for standing by while another student was beaten up by two other students. (The reader of a small-town newspaper such as the *Berkshire Eagle* may be more interested in reading about a local official who got caught dipping into the town's till rather than about often-depressing global events. For this information there's always the news magazines and television.)

On page one, one photo from Beirut was credited to UPI/Reuters; the other was an excellent shot of iron workers guiding steel girders into place on a local construction project. It was credited to a staff photographer. National stories and editorials filled the rest of the main news section. The average mix of advertising to editorial for the whole paper on a regular basis is 47:53. The *New York Times* runs 65 percent advertising to 35 percent editorial.

On the editorial page, there were two columns of locally written material, half on local subjects. The syndicated columns of Art Buchwald, Tom Wicker, and Mary McGrory appeared on the editorial pages. The locally written editorial conveyed mild criticism of President Reagan's approach to the SALT II treaty.

The City and Town section was comparable to similar ones in small daily newspapers across the country.

There were nine different bylines from staff reporters in this section. The writing was crisp, and the heads were good short synopses of the pieces.

Sci-Health, a once-a-week feature, was particularly well edited and occupied three of the section's six pages. More than half the feature and news stories were syndicated.

Sports coverage accounted for three pages of this section, classified ads the rest. Local sports ran half the sports coverage; national sports, covered by UPI, ran the remainder.

The Wire Services

From the earliest days, newspapers found the need for coverage outside their geographical boundaries. If a major story was breaking in Chicago or Los Angeles, a paper in New York had to have the details fast. However, it wasn't economically feasible to employ full-time correspondents in these areas. Therefore, news organizations—cooperative and private—sprung up to fill this gap by providing reporters and correspondents to bring the national and international news to local papers. The two major U.S. wire services are profiled here.

The Associated Press (AP)

In May 1848, a cooperative of six New York City newspapers, the Associated Press, was formed. The purpose: to work together to increase news coverage of the United States and the world. The first year's budget was less than $20,000.

By the 1980s, that six-paper nonprofit cooperative had grown into an organization serving more than 1,299 newspaper members and 3,890 broadcasters in the United States. Its services are printed and broadcast in 115 countries. Its present budget is in excess of $190 million.

From the outset, Washington and foreign news were staples of AP coverage. Its first Washington correspondent, Lawrence Golright, reported on such momentous events as the start of the Civil War and President Lincoln's assassination. By the early 1980s, the Washington staff numbered 128 newspeople, and the global network was staffed by ninety-three Americans and 589 foreign nationals.

In 1875, AP established the first leased wires dedicated exclusively to the transmission of news. The wires ran from New York to Washington and carried 20,000 words a day. Today, AP's telephone, cable, and satellite circuits circle the globe and carry millions of words daily at speeds up to 12,000 words a minute.

Although European agencies such as Reuters of Britain dominated international news distribution since the early part of the twentieth century, AP entered this field in 1902 at a slow pace. Interrupted by World War II, its international operations flourished in the post-war period.

The custom of illustrating stories with photos didn't really emerge until the 1920s. AP originated in 1927 what was later to become the world's largest newsphoto service. At first, photos were distributed to the member newspapers by messenger, mail, bus, or train. But on January 1, 1935, a flick of a switch dispatched a photo signal across 10,000 miles of wire to receiving machines in twenty-five American cities. By 1977, AP's leased wirephoto circuits reached every continent.

AP news wasn't available to broadcasters until 1942. Radio and television hooked up rapidly so that by 1981, AP's broadcast membership had reached 3,788. By 1977, the media devoted so much editorial space and air time to sports that AP was operating a 1,050-word-a-minute sports wire around the clock.

AP's 2,900 people all over the world use today's most innovative technology to bring to its clients—newspapers and broadcasters—the best news and picture reportage it can. These days, this pursuit often entails danger. During 1985, for example, one AP newsman was held captive in the Middle East, another was wounded and lost his daughter in a terrorist attack in the Rome airport, and an AP stringer was killed and a newsman wounded in Central America.

Restricted access, explicit or implicit censorship, pressure against correspondents, and even expulsion are some of the constraints AP staffers face in volatile areas around the world.

Job Opportunities with the Associated Press

There are many interesting opportunities available for would-be journalists at the AP. The following are some tips on how to get them:

- You may apply for AP writing, research, and technical employment at your nearest AP bureau. There, you will fill out an application, take a vocabulary and newswriting test, and be interviewed.
- Applicants for full-time regular news (reporting and editing) jobs should be college graduates with a minimum of two years' daily newspaper experience.
- A limited number of temporary openings are available for those who lack the two years of professional experience.
- Those interested in broadcasting can apply directly to Associated Press Broadcast Services, 1825 K Street, N.W., Washington, DC 20006–1253. Contact the general broadcast editor.
- You will still need the two years of professional experience for TV and radio jobs; also, experience with tape-editing equipment and other standard tools of the broadcast industry is necessary.
- To qualify as an AP photographer, you should have two to five years' experience on a daily newspaper.
- AP has a thirteen-week summer minority internship program for blacks and Hispanics who have completed their junior year of college.
- In order to work for AP overseas, you should be fluent in at least one foreign language. Once employed, you may have a choice of assignment location.

United Press International (UPI)

United Press was formed by the noted newspaper pioneer E. W. Scripps in 1907 as competition for the cartel he thought had been formed by the AP. During that first year, the UP serviced 369 newspapers. Today, it is the world's largest privately owned—as distinguished from its cooperatively owned competitor, the Associated Press—independent general news agency. It serves more than 12,000 total subscribers, including newspapers and radio and TV stations in more than one hundred countries.

In 1958, United Press merged with International News Service, becoming United Press International.

The E. W. Scripps Company owned it until 1982, when it was sold to Media News Corporation. In 1985, the financially beleaguered UPI filed for reorganization under Chapter 11 of the federal bankruptcy code. By 1986, its new owners projected the first profitable year since 1964.

UPI can claim many firsts in the news business. Here are some examples: the first news service for radio (1935); the first TTS service, enabling newspapers automatically to set and justify type from wire transmissions (1951); the first wire service radio network (1958); the first high-speed data newswire—1,200 words per minute (1974); and the first satellite data transmissions by any news agency (1981).

Through the years, UPI has attracted and trained some of America's most distinguished journalists, including Walter Cronkite, Harrison Salisbury, Eric Sevareid, and Merriman Smith.

The aspiring wire service employee should realize that both the AP with its cooperative ownership and the privately held UPI have consistently nurtured and produced quality journalism. Working for these services means creating instant history. One UPI bureau manager calls it "one of the most exciting, self-fulfilling jobs in the world."

Walter Cronkite, with UPI for eleven years before joining CBS News, thinks the edge lies with UPI. He maintained, "UPI is the best training ground for a young reporter. There is a spirit and a competitive drive to the organization that is harder and harder to find in journalism today."

Statistics

Worldwide, UPI employs 1,500 full-time people plus several thousand stringers. Of this staff, 300 are employed overseas.

Today, there are 179 UPI bureaus in the United States and fifty-two overseas.

UPI has as subscribers 729 newspapers with 37 million circulation. In broadcasting, there are 4,840 U.S. subscribers. UPI staffers produce a phenomenal 13 million words daily. The company uses 2,500 satellite dishes.

There is no formal application procedure for securing jobs as UPI staffers or stringers. For information about how to apply, write to United Press International, 220 East 42d Street, New York, NY 10017.

The UPI Stylebook

If you're going to work for a newspaper, you will have to learn not to use "weasel" words that dull the edge of a sharp phrase—for example: "underprivileged" for "poor," "sanitation" for "garbage," and "passed away" for "died." You'll also want to avoid "journalese"—such terms as "hike" instead of "increase" and "huddled" for "met."

The paper you work for may have its own stylebook. This is a handbook for writers and editors that contains rules of grammar, frequently misspelled words, misused terms, and other basic reference information for writers and editors.

One of the best stylebooks is the *UPI Stylebook*, adopted by both the UPI and the AP. Copies of this 232-page book may be ordered for $6.95 from UPI Stylebook, United Press International, 1400 Eye Street, N.W., Washington, DC 20005.

Two Giant Newspapers

USA Today: An Amazing Story

I trust this will not sound self-serving, but the first time I read *USA Today,* I found my name in an item on page one. It had been fed to the paper by my organization's press agent. This was in early 1983, and I must admit I didn't think a national newspaper had a chance to make it. I also did not take into account the muscle and determination of the Gannett Company.

When the paper first arrived on newsstands in the fall of 1982 amid much hoopla, most of my fellow New Yorkers were not too impressed. I remember reading that Gannett had also placed coin-sale boxes all over town. I had one thought: Would the rip-off rate on these boxes be 90 or 95 percent?

USA Today has made many cynics into believers. By March 1986, its circulation average for the previous six months was 1,417,077, making it the second-largest-circulation daily in the nation. In the same period, its readership (4,368,000 daily readers) had surpassed the *Wall Street Journal,* making it number one in this category.

In advertising sales, *USA Today* seems to be moving ahead. In 1985 it averaged 13.2 daily paid pages versus 8.25 pages in 1984. On a day in November 1986, there were twenty-one pages of advertising out of a total of fifty-six pages. Four-color advertising is available in all four sections.

Editorially, *USA Today* is unlike any other newspaper. Its four sections, running a maximum total of fifty-six pages, cover News, Money (business),

Sports, and Life (features, especially on entertainment). It is also expensive for a newspaper, 50¢ for fifty-six pages. Editorial color is used profusely throughout. Clearly, *USA Today* appeals to a different readership from that of, say, the *New York Times*. Its format and content seem ideally geared to a mass audience.

USA Today's technical story is remarkable. The paper is written and edited in Washington, D.C. From there it is transmitted via satellite (at a speed of three and a half minutes per black-and-white page) to thirty printing sites in the Unites States, one in Singapore (for Asia and the Pacific), and one in Switzerland (European edition). It is printed on high-speed presses (many of them used for Gannett's dailies) and rushed off to newsstands (and those coin boxes) all over the country. Eighty percent of the nation's population can read the paper on the same day of publication.

It is still too early to predict *USA Today*'s chances of financial success, although in May 1987 the publication broke even. Gannett, however, is betting a few hundred million dollars on its chances. Considering what the company has done with its other properties, my bet is that *USA Today* will make it.

The *Wall Street Journal*

It's the nation's largest (in copies published) newspaper, yet many of us don't think of it as a newspaper at all. The *Wall Street Journal* has a circulation of almost 2 million. Impeccable coverage of business news and information has made it a powerful source in financial circles all over the world. Seemingly insignificant pieces in the *Journal* have caused stocks to plummet. An incisive article about a company has resulted in the toppling of its management. Major stories that do not require immediate publication are often researched for weeks. Few "puff" pieces appear in the *Journal*.

Publishing the *Wall Street Journal* every day encompasses a network of more than 500 newspeople in thirty news offices. Let's trace a typical story from idea through delivery:

A staff reporter is "pitched" a story idea by the PR person for a small new Madison Avenue advertising agency founded by two former large-agency executives. The angle—why agency pros are eschewing the big-agency life and opening their own small shops. After lengthy interviews with the principals, the reporter proposes the story to the *Journal*'s front-page editor in a one-page memo.

When the piece is approved, the reporter spends about twenty hours talking to the new agency's founders, plus interviewing all sixteen of its employees. Then the reporter talks to the agency's clients as well as to other recent agency entrepreneurs. Weeks of interviewing and note taking have to be boiled down to between 1,500 and 2,000 words.

Informative quotes have to be developed. Statistics and facts have to be checked carefully. According to many media critics, the *Journal* is the most closely edited newspaper in the United States. The page-one editing desk gives the piece exacting scrutiny. The elapsed time between the PR person's phone call and publication—four months and one week. Of course, this story is a feature, not a hard-news piece demanding timely publication.

From the Editor's Desk to Your Home or Office: When a completed story is submitted to the editor, he writes the headline and assigns a news priority and preferred page location to the piece. After editing, the copy is transmitted electronically to two production plants—one in Massachusetts and one in Texas. At these locations, typesetters at electronic keyboards enter the stories into a central computer database.

The computer sets the type, which is then made up into pages and sent by Western Union's Westar V satellite to the printing plants. There, at a rate of 50,000 newspapers an hour, the *Journal* is printed and then distributed across the country.

Dow Jones's own carrier-delivery service delivers more than a third of all *Journal* subscriptions, and 99 percent of all subscriptions in the continental United States are delivered the day they are published. It took the reporter four months and one week to write that 1,500-word piece about the small advertising agency referred to earlier; in contrast, it took only hours to print the entire newspaper.

Dow Jones, the Company

The *Wall Street Journal* is owned by the Dow Jones company, whose recent annual revenues were just over $1 billion. The company's other activities include the Dow Jones news service, computerized financial databases, twenty-two community newspapers, book publishing, and the influential *Barron's* weekly magazine (circulation approximately 270,000).

We have highlighted the *Wall Street Journal* because of its uniqueness and its daily circulation of almost two million. Yet that alone doesn't merit our emphasis. Because this paper deals primarily with financial news and information and does so in meticulous, exacting fashion, it also enjoys an unparalleled reputation worldwide.

In the inside:

The Sunday

DACRON
Republican-Democrat

Index:

Life and Leisure	Sec. G-3	Life and Living	Sec. M-1
Living and Life	Sec. Q-5	Living Life	Sec. L-1
Leisure Living	Sec. R-1	Home and Life	Sec. P-5
Life and Home	Sec. H-7	Home Living	Sec. T-7
Living and Leisure	Sec. J-1	Home Leisure Living	Sec. W-1
Home and Leisure	Sec. Q-1	Leisure Life	Sec. V-9
Home Living and Life	Sec. Y-9	Leisure and Life	Sec. R-3
Home Leisure	Sec. K-1	Home and Home	Sec. Q-3

What happened in the Sixties? The "Now" generation back "Then."

Page R-1

Dacron's VanHusen Corp. makes twin mobility twice as affordable.

Page M-5

This week's *Newscast in Print*: "Negroes— The Problem That Won't Go Away"

Page P-2

TODAY'S WEATHER QUALITY:		OHIO
ACCEPTABLE	# DACRON Republican-Democrat	**LUCKY BUCKEYE** Daily Lottery
Data from Ohio State Weather Service O.S.W.S. DEPT. OF WEATHER	*One Of America's Newspapers*	4 6 1960 WINNING NUMBER

SECTION A   ★ ★ ★ ★   DACRON, OHIO, SUNDAY, FEB. 12, 1978   SOUTH CENTRAL OHIO COAL, GAS, ELECTRICITY, TELEPHONE & TELEGRAPH COMMUNICATIONS GROUP   TWENTY CENTS

Powder Room Prowler Strikes Anew

Photo by Rep.-Dem. Staff Photographer Prissy VanHusen

Hank's Shell Station on Dacron's West Side
. . . aftermath scene of the latest prowler attack as onlookers look on.

By LARRY MICKLE
Rep.-Dem. Staff Writer

Dacron's "Powder Room Prowler" has struck terror into the ladies room for the sixth time this year, yesterday. His latest victim, Miss Belinda Heinke, was returning from a shopping trip to the Corngate Plaza shopping center when she stopped to freshen up at a Shell station on the corner of Monroe Street and Secor Ave. It was there that the Prowler was apparently lying in wait, concealed within the Shell station's women's comfort facilities.

According to police, Miss Heinke entered a stall inside the comfort facility and had seated herself there when the Prowler dropped onto her head from a crouched position which he had been maintaining on top of the stall's partition, and forced her to be assaulted in a disgusting manner.

Henry Cobble, owner of the service station, which is known as Hank's Shell Station, was alerted to the assault by loud yelling and screams of indignation. He rushed to the women's room door but was unable to gain entrance because of Miss Heinke's having fastened a hook on the inside.

Police Called

"I don't know how this could have happened," said Mr. Cobble in a later interview. "The rest rooms are for customers only." Mr. Cobble called the police and returned to the women's room, prepared to pry the door open with a large screwdriver when, before the police were able to arrive, the "Powder Room Prowler" rushed from the powder room, struck Mr. Cobble in the face with Miss Heinke's purse, and made his escape.

Witnesses say he was wearing a bag over his head at the time.

Miss Heinke was treated at Forest Lawn Memorial Hospital for "stomach trouble" and released, and Mr. Cobble was also treated for getting slapped in the face with a purse. Police say that Miss Heinke was not able to give a very complete description of the "Powder Room Prowler" partly because she was still having a lot of stomach troubles, but that they did get some more valuable clues such as, that the Prowler was wearing unusual high-heeled shoes.

Investigation to Be Led

Assistant Police Chief Carl Leper, who has been assigned to lead a special Powder Room investigative team, said he hoped the Prowler case would be solved "as soon as we find out who did it."

Miss Heinke could not be reached, but her mother, Mrs. Gustav Heinke of 2344 Ranchwagon Rd., Dacron Dales, said the whole incident was "awful," and expressed wishes that the "Powder Room Prowler" be quickly caught before "other people's daughters get as embarrassed as mine is."

Miss Heinke, 31, who lives at home, is an ex-Dacron High School honor student who attended the University of California at Los Angeles and the Massachusetts Institute of Technology in Massachusetts and graduated with two PhD.s in chemistry and physics. She now teaches second grade.

Bring Suit in Wild Dog Pack Case

The Greater Dacron A.S.P.C.A., honored by Mayor Pilegravey last fall for capturing a pack of 30 wild dogs which were later gassed at the city dog pound, will now have a lawsuit brought against it for that action, says Dacron Estates Hunt Club Master of Foxhounds Edward Duffy. Duffy, who has been searching since last October for the Hunt Club's lost pack of 30 foxhounds, claims that the city

Cont. Sec. H, Page 5

Two Dacron Women Feared Missing in Volcanic Disaster

Japan Destroyed

CLEVELAND, Feb. 11 (Combined Sources)—Possible tragedy has marred the vacation plans of Miss Frances Bundle and her mother Olive as volcanos destroyed Japan early today.

Rep.-Dem. Archives

The Eastern Hemisphere
. . . where Japan was formerly located.

Miss Bundle and her mother departed Friday for Cleveland, where they joined other members of the East Ohio Presbyterian Women's Auxiliary Association on a one-week group tour of the Orient leaving from that city. The Presbyterian charter group was to arrive in Tokyo today, but it is not known whether they did so. The Bundles were driven to Cleveland by Miss Bundle's brother-in-law, Ed.

Miss Bundle and her mother had been looking forward to their Oriental tour for more than a year and a half, according to Rev. Elliot Dotter,

Photo by Mrs. Bundle's sister Grace

Miss Francis Bundle (left) and her mother
. . . before leaving for Cleveland on Friday.

pastor of the N. Melville Ave. Presbyterian Church. The charter excursion was available to members of the East Ohio Presbyterian women's group at a special rate of $540 per person, which included hotel accommodations and breakfast, and the Bundles had been saving diligently for some time in order to take advantage of this travel opportunity.

The Bundle family has long been prominent in Dacron church circles. Until his death in 1959, the late Mr. William Bundle, a retired assistant sales director at MacAdam, Inc., had served for years as a deacon at Melville Ave. Presbyterian. Miss Bundle

Cont. Sec. G, Page 12

AN OPEN LETTER TO THE POWDER ROOM PROWLER
From DONOVAN GROAT
Rep.-Dem. Senior Feature Writer

Dear Prowler,

Your recent attack, the sixth this year, was the most appalling attack by a powder room prowler I have ever seen color slides of. It may be senseless to appeal to your reason, you may have no more of that than the bag you wear over your head. It may be the act of an idiot with bungs in his ears to appeal to your compassion; likely you have no more of that than a fist-handed Nazi with innocent dead bodies on his hands and a million Jews on his breath . . . but all I can do is try.

I will even beg you. Yes, get off my chair and plead that you turn yourself in to the police and not into a criminal as notorious as Mac the Face or Shame-Dog Coffin.

If you are afraid of the police, you can even surrender to me. I will see you get a fair deal from them and the publishers if you choose to tell your story to both of us.

CONTINUED ON PAGE 11
OF THIS SECTION

Plan to Sell Soviet Jews

MOSCOW, Feb. 10 (OPI)—The Soviet news agency Tass has reported that Kremlin officials are debating a program to sell the U.S.S.R.'s Jewish population on the world market. The plan would reportedly be designed to reduce world criticism of the treatment of Soviet Jews and bring an estimated criticism of the treatment of Soviet Jews and bring an estimated $50,000,000 in hard currency into the Soviet economy.

"The Soviet peoples are fair and just," Tass said. "We would give discounts for quantity purchases. Maybe even arrange for lay-away plans."

CAREER TIP: Consider financial writing. It pays well and offers enormous opportunities. Jobs are available for qualified people at publications such as the *Wall Street Journal, Barron's, Forbes, Business Week, Fortune,* and so on. College training must include courses in accounting and business in addition to those in learning to write concisely and journalistically. An MBA with writing ability may become a superstar in this field.

The Role of Advertising in Newspaper Publishing

We noted earlier in this chapter that newspaper advertising expenditures consume a large share (26.8 percent) of the whole media advertising pie.

Before we discuss newspaper advertising, however, an explanation of newspaper advertising sizes is in order. A typical newspaper column is 13 picas wide. (There are 6 picas to the inch, so 13 picas equals 2⅙".) The height of a newspaper column is measured either in regular inches or in agate lines. As there are 14 agate lines to the inch, an ad 28 agate lines × 1 column would be 2" high and 1 column wide.

Now that we understand the measurements of ads, let's look at the newspaper advertising categories. There are two kinds of newspaper advertising: *local* advertising, such as the full-page advertisement for a local department store announcing a sale; and *national* advertising, such as an auto manufacturer advertising one of its cars.

Local advertising accounts for about 87 percent of all newspaper advertising. Total newspaper advertising has become big business, 20 percent higher than TV advertising. National newspaper advertising revenues are now only 13 percent of total newspaper advertising revenues. The reason for this low percentage is the competition newspapers face from TV and other media for this lucrative national advertising.

Although it often seems as though 90 or 95 percent of our Sunday papers are composed of advertising, in 1984 (the latest year for which figures are available) the average in Sunday papers was 68.8 percent and in daily newspapers 60.7 percent.

The *New York Times,* which leads all others papers in advertising-dollar volume, breaks down its linage as follows:

1983 total volume	103,987,300 lines
retail advertising	49,693,100 lines
national advertising	32,437,000 lines
classified advertising	21,857,200 lines

The *Times's* percentage of national advertising is so high because of the paper's location in the nation's number one market and its upscale demographics. Incidentally, when we talk of advertising and size, here's the *New York Times* record to date, set on Sunday, November 10, 1985—1,793,000 lines of advertising in 1,408 pages, all weighing in at ten pounds, six ounces!

The Sales Effort

We have pointed out that the bulk of a newspaper's revenues comes from advertising sales. These sales are made as they are in other media: A salesperson armed with the paper's rate card, demographics, sales advantages, and so on, visits the retailers and other establishments in his local territory; sometimes the space comes in directly from the advertiser or his advertising agency.

It is not expedient for local papers to maintain sales offices in the major cities in order to solicit national advertising. Therefore, they usually employ a sales rep firm with offices and personnel in these cities to implement the paper's sales effort. The rep companies work on a commission basis.

For example, just such a company, American Newspaper Representatives, Inc. (ANR), maintains offices in New York, Chicago, Detroit, Minneapolis, and San Francisco. It represents forty-seven hometown newspapers, including the *Shenandoah* (Iowa) *Sentinel,* the *Celina* (Ohio) *Standard,* and the *Belle Fourche* (South Dakota) *Post.*

An advertising agency in New York can see the ANR salesperson and make a buying decision for all or any part of these hometown newspapers. It is a convenience to the agency as well, as it will receive one invoice for the buy and pay for the space with one check.

A chain such as Gannett, Knight-Ridder, or Hearst will maintain its own sales offices in the six or eight largest cities. The salespeople in these offices are responsible for national advertising sales for all the papers in the chain.

A big-city paper in New York, Chicago, or Los Angeles will sell local advertisers through its own sales staff and sell national advertisers through agencies located in its home city.

Freestanding Inserts and Preprinted Tabloid Sections

Ever wonder about those pesky inserts that balloon your Sunday newspaper so that you can't get it out of your mailbox? These inserts are called either ''freestanding'' or ''preprinted'' tabloid sections— and they're big business for newspapers.

Today, inserts can be distributed in nearly every daily and Sunday newspaper in the United States. Circulation achieved is more than 59 million daily and 56 million on Sundays. More than 50 percent of all Sunday editions can distribute an insert in less than their full-run circulation, and more than 75 percent will accept a product sample attached to an insert. Many will accept an envelope, either empty or containing inserts or coupons.

The flexibility factor is important in the selling of inserts. An advertiser in a big-city newspaper may not want to reach the inner city but rather concentrate on the city's suburbs. He will then pay on a per-thousand basis for that portion of the paper's circulation used. If, for example, the advertiser wishes to insert an eight-page tabloid (10¾″ × 13″) that is preprinted into 50,000 copies, the rate would be about $42.00 per thousand times 50,000, or $2,100 plus the cost of printing the insert. In 1977, newspaper-insert advertising volume was $1.08 million; by the mid-1980s, it had reached $3.69 million.

Newspaper Advertising Bureau

The Newspaper Advertising Bureau was organized in 1913 by member newspapers to promote the efficient use of the medium for the advertising and marketing needs of individual companies. Among its services is a series of marketing research reports. Typical reports may include the following topics: how newspaper advertising affects package goods sales, estimating ad readership, time spent reading daily newspapers, cost effectiveness of newspaper versus TV advertising, redemption ratios of cents-off coupons, and advertising-to-sale ratios for selected retail stores.

CAREER TIP: When you see Robert Redford in a movie about newspapers, he's playing a hotshot reporter, not an advertising rep. Clearly, editorial work has more glamour than selling ads, yet about 19,000 men and women, as opposed to about 325,000 in editorial jobs, are fulfilling these challenging jobs at newspapers in the United States and Canada. Consider a career in newspaper advertising. It's creative, it pays well, and it offers a premium on originality, freshness, and distinction that few other occupations require or provide.

In newspaper advertising, ideas count. A salesperson can help his accounts with fresh and creative recommendations, with headlines and copy, and with layout and design.

Most advertising representatives look ahead to executive and management positions at their newspapers. More than a few aim for the very top; and more than a few make it.

For information on training programs, courses, and seminars, write to International Newspaper Advertising and Marketing Executives, The Newspaper Center, P.O. Box 17210, Dulles International Airport, Washington, DC 20041.

Two Major Newspaper Chains

Gannett

The Gannett Company, Inc., is the nation's largest newspaper group, with ninety-one dailies, including *USA Today,* and forty nondailies. Recent figures have put its total daily paid circulation at over 5.7 million, more than any other newspaper group.

In addition to its newspaper holdings, Gannett is a diversified news and information company with revenues of about $2.2 billion. The company operates TV and radio stations, and outdoor advertising, research, marketing, printing, news, and broadcast program production subsidiaries.

Talk about being aggressive: In February 1986, Gannett completed a $717 million transaction—the purchase of the Evening News Association. This involved the acquisition of five daily newspapers, including the *Detroit News*, the nation's ninth-largest newspaper, and two TV stations, including WDVM-TV, the number-one-rated station in Washington, D.C.

In 1985, Gannett acquired the *Des Moines Register*, plus two other papers in Iowa, one in Jackson, Tennessee, and one in Peekskill, New York. In addition, Gannett purchased the huge Sunday newspaper magazine *Family Weekly* from CBS and renamed it *USA Weekend*. It had a recent circulation of more than 13 million. We've already discussed the phenomenon of *USA Today* earlier in this chapter; however, an amazing fact worth repeating is that, after only a few years of publishing, the paper is the second-largest newspaper (by circulation) in the country.

What is unusual about the Gannett newspaper organization, though, is that not all of its newspapers boast huge circulations. Gannett also publishes papers such as the *Daily Argus* in Mount Vernon, New York (circulation about 9,000), the *Millville Daily* in New Jersey (circulation about 6,700), the *Coffeyville Journal* in Kansas (circulation about 7,100), and the *News Herald* in Port Clinton, Ohio (circulation about 5,800). The "littles" coexist with the "bigs" in what seems to be perfect harmony.

While other media account for about 20 percent of Gannett's revenues, newspapers are the biggest part of its business. As a growth opportunity, one should consider working for this dynamic organization.

Knight-Ridder

Before I wrote this book, I had not heard of Knight-Ridder, although I certainly was aware of a few of its well-known newspapers: the *Miami Herald*, the *Philadelphia Inquirer*, and the *Detroit Free Press*. The company must be a sleeping giant, because it is the second-largest newspaper chain in America. Recent figures show that Knight-Ridder's twenty-seven newspapers have a total average daily circulation of approximately 3.75 million and an average Sunday circulation of about 4.5 million.

As a communications company, Knight-Ridder had revenues in the mid-1980s of about $1.7 billion. Of these revenues, about 90 percent came from its newspaper business; $2 million of this was from newspaper advertising revenue, which illustrates the importance of this source.

The company got into broadcasting in 1978 with the acquisition of three TV stations. Today, it has widened its grasp to include cable TV operations, business news and information services, newsprint production, and book publishing.

Knight-Ridder's headquarters are in Miami, Florida. The company employs 22,000 people.

"Happy" Newspapers Go Straight

Back in the '60s, counter-culture publications thrived. The news is that many are still around and doing very well. There are now about one hundred such publications, of which seven have a circulation of over 100,000. New York's *Village Voice* leads the field with a paid circulation at this writing of 150,000.

As Steve Mindich, publisher of the $10 million–grossing *Boston Phoenix*, stated recently, his readers are "people who have [a '60s] political sensitivity who are now in positions of responsibility. Advertisers love this audience, because that's the group that has disposable income."

As a job source, these publications are a great place to start for popular culture–oriented people in both the editorial and advertising sales areas, although salaries may be less than on mainstream papers.

Sunday and the Supplements

Big-city papers generally have their own Sunday magazines, often more than one. However, many smaller newspapers cannot afford to have their own

Sunday magazine and, instead, insert syndicated supplementary magazines. The two leading supplements are *Parade* and *Family Weekly,* now renamed *USA Weekend.*

Parade

Parade, with a circulation of more than 30 million, claims that it is the most widely read magazine in America. It is carried by 284 Sunday newspapers and collects about $200 million annually in advertising revenues.

The first issue of *Parade,* in 1941, was a weekly sold on newsstands. During that same year, the *Nashville Tennessean* began to distribute *Parade* on Sundays. Soon, other papers followed. By the end of 1942, the supplement was carried by sixteen newspapers.

The publication went through a succession of owners until it was acquired by S. I. Newhouse & Sons, the giant newspaper and magazine (Condé Nast) company, in 1976.

Editorially, a publication like *Parade* must have a broad focus, dealing as it does with a mass audience spread across the country. Noted contributors to *Parade* have included Norman Mailer, Carl Sagan, David Halberstam, Gail Sheehy, Willie Morris, and Cleveland Amory.

Because advertising revenues pay the freight, there is a high advertising-to-editorial ratio —45:55. The only identification the local "carrying" paper gets is its name on the front page above the title *Parade.*

Parade's newspapers are among the nation's greatest: the *Washington Post, St. Louis Post-Dispatch, Boston Globe,* and *Chicago Sun-Times.* All have their own Sunday magazines in addition to carrying *Parade.*

USA Weekend

It's smaller than a tabloid newspaper and bigger than *Time* magazine (8¼" × 11"). It has 13.5 million circulation and is carried by 262 newspapers. What is it? It is *USA Weekend,* published by those enterprising Gannett people, who also bring us *USA Today.*

Actually, *USA Weekend* is an outgrowth of the Sunday supplement *Family Weekly,* which was purchased by Gannett in October 1984. In this respect, it is similar to *Parade* because it is carried by many newspapers as a supplement, in addition to their own magazine. Some papers, however, use *USA Weekend* as their only magazine.

The advertising-to-editorial ratio is 45:55, similar to *Parade*'s. The editorial content is also similar; the pieces are short and celebrity-oriented. The whole publication can be read in about twelve minutes, adding a few minutes for the vitamin and zoysia-plug ads. For the TV and videocassette generation, it's right on target.

USA Weekend seems to be an extension of its sister publication, *USA Today.* There is no sensationalism or sex in its pages; instead, there is a family mix of features on health, money management, food, books, humor, and even a column for senior citizens.

Its promotion material is very much to the point. *USA Weekend* says it is for that "generation of Americans, 70 percent of our population, who cannot remember life without television." These are the people who don't want to read heady material in their Sunday newspaper magazine section. *USA Weekend,* reaching 25 million people, has obviously decided to coexist with TV, not pull viewers away from it.

Time will tell whether Gannett's gamble on this "new" supplement will pay off. If its other operations are any indication, we can look forward to *USA Weekend* becoming the top Sunday supplement. *Parade*—look out.

The Ten Best Newspapers in the United States

Every few years the perspicacious media publication *ADWEEK* names its ten best daily newspapers, chosen by a panel of thirteen media professionals and academics. Here is the most recent list and some capsule comments from the panel.

1. The *New York Times:* This newspaper was in a class by itself—the verdict was unanimous. The *Times* won high praise for the quality of its writing, its comprehensive and authoritative foreign reporting, and the depth and detail of its business coverage.

2. The *Los Angeles Times:* This newspaper is the giant of the West in circulation and advertising. A Sunday edition in December 1984 had 674 pages. It is comprehensive, thoughtful, and very forward-thinking.

3. The *Washington Post:* The *Washington Post* won the number-three spot for its initiative, liveliness, and readability. It is held in high regard for its comprehensive coverage of politics and national affairs.

4. The *Wall Street Journal:* We have written in this chapter of this exceptional paper. One of the

panelists, Jeff Greenfield, says of the *Journal*, "They do such a good job of touching on things that you know are important but don't have the time or expertise to explore on your own."

5. The *Philadelphia Inquirer:* The panelists called it a first-rate newspaper, on a par with the *New York Times* and the *Washington Post*. It wins high praise for its award-winning investigative reporting.

6. *Newsday* (Long Island, New York): *Newsday* covers an 800,000-household market. It offers a well-illustrated paper with a strong editorial staff, an enlarged business section, and a talented Washington bureau.

7. The *Christian Science Monitor:* This newspaper won praise from the panel for being "well-written and refreshing" as well as for its serious coverage of foreign affairs—a model of explanatory journalism.

8. The *Chicago Tribune:* The *Tribune* received high marks for its clear and colorful graphics, its ability to serve several markets, and its lifestyle reporting. "A commitment to excellence in news," said one panelist.

9. The *Boston Globe:* The panelists called it the best-written newspaper in the country, eloquent and superb. It is both a writer's and an editor's paper. It is a regional paper of national importance.

10. The *Miami Herald:* "First rate" and "deeply committed to its community" were the terms used by the panel to describe this paper. It delivers prize-winning coverage of Central and South America.

CAREER TIP: If you're going to make newspaper publishing your career, consider the ten best on *ADWEEK*'s list and how energizing it could be to spend one's working life in an atmosphere of recognized quality.

Washington Journalism Review

The paid circulation is not large—only about 17,000—yet it reaches out to influence almost every important leader in broadcast and print journalism. It's a bold critic of the industry; nevertheless, it includes a hundred major media organizations in its list of advertisers.

The *Washington Journalism Review* was established in 1977 and is published monthly. What sets it apart from other media trade publications is its lack of puffery. Rather, it serves as a gadfly of the comunications business with its incisive reports on the people and issues making news.

Provocative articles in recent issues included these topics: a profile of the two NBC investigators who broke the Abscam story in 1980; a piece on the real reason ad dollars are leaving television; the competition for press coverage in Congress; the ethical decisions in journalism when doing a story would endanger a life; the specialized signals of radio news or giving listeners what they want; and puzzling problems of pictures from space.

We have been recommending a number of media trade publications in this book. Readers may not be able to afford the total investment, but we do encourage subscribing to the *Washington Journalism Review* at $24.00 a year, or at least try to find a library that subscribes. The address is 2233 Wisconsin Avenue N.W., Suite 442, Washington, DC 20007.

Columbia Journalism Review

The premiere fall 1961 issue stated its purpose and policy succinctly: "To assess the performance of journalism in all its forms, to call attention to its shortcomings and strengths, and to help define—or redefine—standards of honest, responsible service . . . to help stimulate continuing improvement in the profession and to speak out for what is right, fair, and decent."

For more than twenty-five years the *Columbia Journalism Review* has been an effective gadfly serving as a media monitor of the press, radio, and TV. It is published bimonthly under the auspices of the faculty, alumni, and friends of the Graduate School of Journalism of Columbia University.

Its recent paid circulation was 33,000. The *Review*'s influence, however, far exceeds its numbers, with an audience of the nation's opinion leaders and decision makers. Included among its subscribers are Art Buchwald, Malcolm Forbes,

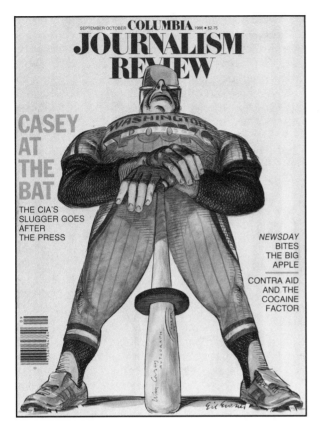

The *Columbia Journalism Review*'s editorial focus is on broadcast media as well as print. However, its greatest emphasis is on newspapers. (Reprinted from the *Columbia Journalism Review*, September/October 1986.)

Editor & Publisher, The Voice of the Fourth Estate

Editor & Publisher, more than one hundred years old, is billed as the newspaperman's guide to what's happening in the newspaper business. If you intend to make newspapers your career, you should read it every week.

In the 1880s, newspapers were just coming into their own. Future giants such as Joseph Pulitzer and E. W. Scripps were getting started. Presses and typefaces were changing. The typewriter and the telephone were revolutionizing the city room. It was in 1884 that two people founded the *Journalist* for professional journalists.

Acquisition and consolidation of four similar publications ultimately formed the *Editor & Publisher* we know today. In its one-hundred-year lifespan, the publication witnessed the increase of daily newspapers from 971 with a combined circulation of 4 million, to 1,711 with 62.5 million circulation.

The publication's guiding light for almost fifty years was James Wright Brown, who ran it from 1911 until his death in 1959 at the age of eighty-five. Brown led the good fight for verified circulation, advertising ethics, and most importantly, for freedom of the press and against government censorship.

Walter Cronkite, Bill Moyers, Mike Wallace, Garry Trudeau, and Isaac Asimov.

A recent issue contained this editorial cornucopia: Dateline Britain: How London's newspapers are dealing with the new technology; a look at the new wave of conservative newspapers on the nation's college campuses; a piece on the immensely successful suburban *Newsday* and its foray into the New York City market; plus short items on the media in Alaska, San Francisco, and northern Illinois; book reviews of works by David Stockman and Sally Quinn and of a biography of Margaret Bourke-White.

I have in this book encouraged our readers to subscribe to various publications. Here's another publication I recommend: the *Columbia Journalism Review* at $18.00 for a one-year subscription. Write to Columbia Journalism Review, 700 Journalism Building, Columbia University, New York, NY 10027.

CAREER TIP: Before you enroll in journalism school, or after you graduate from college, it might be a good idea to find a library that has back issues of *Editor & Publisher*. You could also subscribe for a year for $40.00. The address is 11 West 19th Street, New York, NY 10011. After studying this informative publication, you may either decide to go into another field, or you may be delighted to enter this noble profession.

Editor & Publisher, with an ad on the front cover. Many trade publications (*Broadcasting*, *Publishers Weekly*, etc.) carry advertising on their covers. (Reprinted with permission.)

Editor & Publisher published its first *International Year Book* in 1921. The *Year Book* is a valuable compendium of vital information to the industry. It contains a detailed listing of every daily, weekly, college and university, foreign language, black, and religious newspaper in the United States and Canada. It also lists leading foreign newspapers, news and syndicate services, comic-section groups, associations, and industry services. One can receive a quick liberal education on the newspaper business just from reading *Editor & Publisher*'s *International Year Book.*

The weekly publication has a paid circulation of 25,000, with more than four readers per copy. Its best testimonial is that it enjoys an annual renewal rate of better than 70 percent.

Editorially, the magazine is a happy blend of news stories, features, listings, and new product information. Its classified advertising section always seems to list at least a dozen newspapers for sale and a number of good employment opportunities. One recent issue offered a small central-Texas weekly for only $6,500 down.

Here are some of its important regular weekly features: Editorial Workshop—a weekly writing lesson on newspaper reporting; Advertising News Section—reports on the newest newspaper campaigns, advertising success stories, and the like; Newspeople in the News—information on people, job and title changes, and industry activities; Syndicate News—news and features on the latest in comics, columns, and other syndicated material available; plus employment opportunities and equipment lists.

The Case for Journalism School

More than 300 colleges and universities in the United States offer undergraduate journalism majors. These majors are the best preparation for a newspaper career. The courses in these disciplines account for about one-fourth of the student's total curriculum.

In achieving proficiency in these majors, the student first takes a number of core courses that serve as an introduction to the mass media. Next come the basic-skills courses such as Beginning Reporting, Beginning Editing, and Photojournalism. The advanced news–editorial courses involve training in on-the-street reporting, interviewing, and writing news stories on deadline. In addition, there are courses in graphics and media management.

Some schools are able to arrange internships for their journalism majors. Additionally, work on a college newspaper, many of which are dailies, is good experience for the budding journalist. Among the 300 colleges that offer journalism majors, there are 123 that also offer masters' programs and twenty-four that offer doctorates.

Obviously, not all journalism graduates get jobs on newspapers; yet, without majoring in journalism, it is extremely difficult to get that first newspaper job. Consider, too, that only a handful of talented journalism graduates start on papers such as the *New York Times*, the *Washington Post*, or the *Los Angeles Times* with beginning salaries of $25,000 a year.

For the rest, the first job on a daily newspaper will pay an average of only $13,000 a year. Graduates who are fortunate enough to land a place at a paper with a Newspaper Guild contract will receive higher wages. The $13,000-figure average is slightly lower than entry-level jobs in advertising and slightly higher than those in radio and TV.

The Dow Jones Newspaper Fund

The Dow Jones Newspaper Fund is a nonprofit foundation, supported by Dow Jones and Company, Inc., and other newspaper companies in cities where Newspaper Fund programs and internships are located. Each year, the Dow Jones Newspaper Fund publishes its *Journalism Career and Scholarship Guide.* The *Guide* is immensely valuable for all those interested in a career in this fascinating and exciting field.

The 1986 *Guide,* for example, contained three sections: Section I, A Newspaper Career and You; Section II, Universities That Offer Journalism Majors; and Section III, Directory of Journalism Scholarships. It is endorsed by the Association for Education in Journalism and is available free of charge by writing to Dow Jones Newspaper Fund, Inc., P.O. Box 300, Princeton, NJ 08543–0300. Another free book from the same source is the *Journalism Guide for Minorities.* It includes a list of newspaper recruiters for college students who are looking for work as reporters and editors.

Three Great Journalism Schools

For those of our readers who are seriously considering journalism as their life's work, we recommend obtaining a master's degree. Armed with undergraduate journalism and liberal arts courses and internships and work-study arrangements, the candidate becomes a top choice for a good newspaper editorial job.

There are many fine colleges and universities that offer graduate programs. We noted earlier that there are 123 that offer these programs. We have singled out three that we consider exceptional.

Columbia University

The annual enrollment in Columbia University's Graduate School of Journalism is small (roughly 180 students) and is composed of students from every part of the country, with twelve to fifteen from abroad. There is a good mix of social, economic, ethnic, and educational backgrounds. More than half of those enrolled are women, and

about 15 percent of the students are from minority groups.

Prospective students must have an undergraduate degree, not necessarily in journalism. The Graduate School of Journalism prefers students with a broad-based liberal-arts background who have writing ability. Some students are admitted right after college; others work for a year or two and then enroll. The median age is twenty-six.

The faculty of twenty-one full-time professors, each with professional journalism experience, is supplemented by seventy adjunct instructors. The program runs from September to May, full time, ending with a master of science degree in journalism.

Columbia University is, of course, one of our most prestigious educational institutions. Located in New York City, close to major newspapers and news organizations, it provides superb opportunities for journalism education, as well as being part of the cultural and financial capital of the world.

Patrick Twohy, age twenty-seven, *Pittsburg* (California) *Post Dispatch* political reporter, talks about the Columbia University Graduate School of Journalism.

I came because I didn't want to just grind out copy, I wanted to put quality in my work. . . . You become compulsive about each detail. From seven in the morning until eleven at night, I check and recheck details. . . . You're pushed to expand. You're told, "Read novels, the sports page, and every magazine printed because you'll cover everything." Last week we interviewed Daniel Ortega, the president of Nicaragua. On Monday Gerald Ford, and Wednesday Jesse Jackson. . . . I find myself talking one-to-one with people who six months ago would have awed me.

And the students are as intelligent and interesting and talented as the professors. . . . You learn about as much from them as from professors. [From a brochure of the Columbia University Graduate School of Journalism]

We think that says it best about Columbia University. For the complete course list, write to: Office of Admissions, Graduate School of Journalism, Columbia University, New York, NY 10027.

University of Missouri—Columbia

The University of Missouri at Columbia is known as one of the nation's foremost graduate schools of journalism. It is one of only twenty-four that offer a doctorate in this discipline. The graduate program takes approximately a year and a half to complete. Some areas of emphasis require additional coursework. Admission is highly selective. Upon graduation, the student receives a master of arts degree.

The program is divided into two plans. Both plans include thirty-six hours of coursework in these subjects: History of the Mass Media, Mass Media Seminar, Dynamics of Advertising or Economics of the Media, Research Methods, Advanced Reporting (at least one course), and Advanced Editing (at least one course).

Students with no journalism background are required to do a minimum of six hours of coursework in News Practicum and Editing Practicum.

Plan A, geared for those with an undergraduate degree in journalism, culminates in the writing of a master's thesis that is expected to be a contribution to journalistic knowledge. Plan B is directed toward those wishing to develop a specialized competence (science writing, for example). The choice is dependent on the students' background, career objectives, and personal priorities.

The school offers several off-campus programs for students in London, Tel Aviv, and Washington, D.C. These are designed for graduate students who wish to specialize in reporting or to do research for a thesis.

University of California/Berkeley

Not many of our readers will be able to qualify for the graduate program in journalism at Berkeley simply because the school's enrollment is only seventy-five. At the undergraduate level, however, there are courses in journalism, but no major is offered. An undergraduate major in journalism is offered at fourteen other institutions in the California State University system.

The graduate school is dedicated to training well-qualified working journalists for newspapers, magazines, and broadcast news organizations. The curriculum for this degree offers no courses in advertising, public relations, or communications research; and, other than news-related courses, it offers no courses in television or film.

Here are some typical courses in Berkeley's graduate program: Reporting the News; Editorial Writing; Political Reporting; Business Reporting; Investigative Reporting; Public Opinion, Propaganda, and the Mass Media; Introduction to Television News; Reporting for Television; and Field Study in Journalism.

Newspaper/Journalism Internships

The following is a list of newspaper/journalism internships at newspapers, universities, and specialized learning centers for undergraduates, graduates, career-starters, and career-changers. All have at least five positions in varied areas of journalism. Salaries are minimal, but opportunities for hands-on experience are priceless. If interested, write directly to the respective contact.

For a complete list of internships, the reader is directed to *16,000 On-the-Job Training Opportunities for All Types of Careers* (Writer's Digest Books).

The *Arizona Daily Star*
Box 26807
Tucson, AZ 85726

Association for Education in Journalism/New York University Summer Internship Program for Minorities
Institute of Afro-American Affairs
New York University
269 Mercer Street
New York, NY 10003

Bucks County Courier Times
8400 Route 13
Levittown, PA 19057

Buffalo News
Box 100
Buffalo, NY 14240

Center for Investigative Reporting, Inc.
4th Floor
54 Mint Street
San Francisco, CA 94103

Central Newspapers, Inc.
307 North Penn
Indianapolis, IN 46204

Chicago Sun-Times
401 North Wabash Avenue
Chicago, IL 60611

The *Courier-Journal* and the *Louisville Times*
525 West Broadway
Louisville, KY 40202

Detroit Free Press
321 West Lafayette
Detroit, MI 48231

The Dow Jones Newspaper Fund
Box 300
Princeton, NJ 08540

Institute for Journalism Education
School of Journalism
University of California—Berkeley
Berkeley, CA 94720

Los Angeles Times
Times Mirror Square
Los Angeles, CA 90053

Miami Herald Publishing Company
1 Herald Plaza
Miami, FL 33101

The News-Journal Company
831 Orange Street
Box 1111
Wilmington, DE 19899

Philadelphia Daily News
400 North Broad Street
Philadelphia, PA 19101

St. Paul Pioneer Press & Dispatch
55 East Fourth Street
St. Paul, MN 55101

Sears Congressional Internship Program for
Journalism Students
Suite 600
633 Pennsylvania Avenue N.W.
Washington DC 20004

The *Smithtown News*
Box 805
Smithtown, NY 11787

The Times Journal Company

6883 Commercial Drive
Springfield, VA 22159

The *Wall Street Journal*
22 Cortlandt Street
New York, NY 10007

The Washington Post Summer Internship
Program
1150 15th Street N.W.
Washington DC 20071

The *Washington Times*
3600 New York Avenue N.E.
Washington DC 20002

Future Trends

Circulation

Circulation growth is often a sign of health in the newspaper business. Among sixty daily newspers (each having a minimum of 200,000 circulation) charted for the half-year ended March 31, 1986, only thirty-three papers (55 percent) posted gains over the same six months of the previous period. See the table for some typical results, selected and presented randomly.

Advertising

Even allowing for inflation, newspaper advertising revenues increased dramatically in the period from 1977 to 1985. In '77, the total revenues were $10.75 billion, while in '85, they were $25.48 billion. The percentage increases were much greater than those of magazines, but TV revenues went from $7.6 billion to $20.6 billion in the comparable period. Newspapers, however, led all other media revenues in percentage gains.

Newspaper	Total Circulation	Gain or (Loss)
New York Daily News	1,275,268	(115,687)
The *New York Times*	1,035,426	22,215
Chicago Sun-Times	631,808	(27,288)
(Long Island) *Newsday*	582,388	40,315
Philadelphia Inquirer	492,374	(27,247)
St. Louis Post-Dispatch	318,587	44,803

Conclusion: Circulation is an up-and-down game, and note that three big-city papers were, in this period, "down."

Here is an interesting comparison: Thirty years earlier, in 1955, newspapers had advertising revenues of $3.07 billion, and TV had only $1.03 billion. Percentage-wise, TV has certainly caught up to newspapers.

Technology

The Linotype's inauguration in 1886 was hailed as a revolutionary event. It enabled printers to cast an entire line of type at a time rather than hand set the type character by character. Its design remained unchanged for one hundred years. In 1986, however, it was buried—the victim of new technology that enables computerized phototypesetters to set type at many times the speed of the Linotype. Soon those Linotype metal slugs will be valuable antiques.

Other technical developments in newspaper production include the perfection of photo composition, or setting type by reproducing characters photographically rather than by casting type with hot metal. Part of this photographic-composition process is the perfection of OCR, the optical-character-recognition device that scans letters on a typed page or videoscreen and then sets the material in a wide choice of typefaces.

Most major newspapers are advancing with the new technology by using VDT, video display terminals, which transmit ad or editorial copy directly into an automated system for reproduction into pages.

An obvious next step here is newspapers delivered by television. In Britain the BBC already has a system called CEEFAX, available sixteen hours a day. Press a button on your set and you get the headlines, sports scores, road conditions, and one hundred additional pages that you select. Read what you want when you want it.

Coming soon is the automated, computerized mailroom. This automation will enable the newspaper to deliver advertising speedily and economically to specific zones or to specific demographic groups. Advertising will never again be stale as a result of being prepared weeks or months in advance.

Newspapers in the Twenty-first Century

Dr. Leo Bogart is executive vice president and general manager of the Newspaper Advertising Bureau. In a report in the one-hundredth-anniversary issue of *Editor & Publisher,* he made some interesting forecasts on the role of newspapers in 2084, should there be any. Here's what we can expect:

- Newspaper organizations will be comprehensive information providers rather than publishers. They will produce a variety of products available to users through different means. These may include text and pictures (still and motion) in a video format with the option of a wall-screen or a lap-board.
- High-quality color will be universally available and printed on presses at ultra-high speed.
- No clear distinction will remain among newspaper, magazine, and book publishers, broadcasters, filmmakers, and telecommunications companies, all of which will compete directly, offering timely information in both electronic and printed form.
- Distribution systems will be competitive and comprehensive, delivering nondaily publications, advertising, product samples, and packages through professional, full-time adult carrier forces making the rounds of their assigned territories a number of times each day.
- Newspapers will include a high proportion of individually customized content. Detailed marketing and media information on individual households will be routinely available. Inkjet-printing methods will make it possible to tailor each paper to the recipient's characteristics and wishes, with optional charges for supplements to the basic package. Advertising will be highly targeted, with ad copy and art beamed to fit the profile of each reader household.
- Readers will pay a larger share of the newspaper's income than they do now, and advertisers less. This seems inevitable as newspapers provide the reader with additional values and as advertising itself becomes more competitive and more selective. By the year 2084, the classification of advertising as national or local will be meaningless, and a high proportion of product marketing will be done on an international scale.
- Newspaper content will be geared to a more sophisticated reader. A better educated, more widely traveled population will demand authoritative reporting and good writing. But they will still come to the newspaper with the same expectations that have attracted readers for some three hundred years past.

Of course, most of us will not be around to concern ourselves with these advances. Whether our news and information comes to us on a computer terminal or on newsprint, however, it will still have to be gathered and disseminated. That's where the jobs will be fifty or one hundred years from now.

Two Interviews

Mark Miller edits several small-circulation daily newspapers in New England. His editorial perspective is primarily local. For national and international news, his paper's coverage comes from the wire services. Arnold Sawislak is a veteran editor of United Press International who has covered Washington for more than thirty years. We'll see how each functions in his news-gathering activity.

Mark Miller has a bachelor's degree in political science from Middlebury College in Vermont and a master's from the Columbia University Graduate School of Journalism. He worked for United Press International and Agence France-Presse before returning to the Eagle Publishing Company in his native Pittsfield, Massachusetts, where he is associate editor of the *Berkshire Eagle*. He is also editor of Eagle Publishing's three sister dailies: the *Register Citizen* in Torrington and Winsted, Connecticut; the *Bennington* (Vermont) *Banner;* and the *Brattleboro* (Vermont) *Reformer.* In 1984, he founded the *State Line Free Press*, a free weekly newspaper based in North Canaan, Connecticut. This interview was conducted in July 1986.

How many people are there in each division of the paper: editorial, business, and technical?

There are roughly fifty full-time people on the editorial side of the *Eagle.* There are around 200 employees in total, not including the delivery people.

Is the Eagle *a member of the Newspaper Guild and/or the printing craft unions?*

No. The newsroom employees are represented by an in-house organization called the Eagle News Association. It recently negotiated a three-year contract. Our news and editorial employees have never been represented by the Newspaper Guild or any international union.

Are salaries for your employees at union level?

I'd say they are comparable. There are some larger papers that are represented by the Newspaper Guild that actually don't do quite as well by their employees as we do. We're very happy about that.

What wire services does the paper subscribe to?

UPI, which we get electronically, as we do the New York Times News Service and the *Christian Science Monitor*'s news service. [Most "wire" services are now transmitted electronically but still retain their original designation.]

What is your daily circulation?

It averages about 33,000. It is audited by the Audit Bureau of Circulation, so it is on record. We are unlike many other papers in that our circulation actually goes up in the summer rather than down because we have so many tourists and second-home people in this area, but it all averages out to roughly 33,000—and we are increasing slightly every year.

Do you have any real TV or radio competition?

Nothing serious. There are three radio stations in town, and there are TV stations in Albany and Springfield—with cable, some from Boston, Hartford, and New York City—but there isn't any local TV station.

Do the people who work in editorial double up? That is, does a reporter ever do the copy editing or proofing?

Yes, there are reporters who double as editors, maybe one or two nights a week, or when someone's on vacation.

What constitutes a big story for the Eagle? *And what is a moderately big story?*

There are "enterprise" kinds of stories that you make big by your own enterprise—by going out, getting the information, sitting down, and saying, "This is a story we really should do." And then there are stories that land in your lap. An example of that is the city council president being arrested because his family's bar had small-time gambling going on in a back room. A squad from the police department arrested him, his father, and his brother. That was a very big story. Then we had a county treasurer who was indicted and convicted of grand larceny, fraud, and all sorts of things. That was a big story, too, but that doesn't happen very often. We had a very big story on the city's water supply, which was polluted to the extent that a large number of people were getting cases of giardiasis—a disease that causes severe diarrhea and can kill people who are sick or debilitated.

One in the "enterprise" category is a six-part series we did about The Bible Speaks, a Protestant religious sect in Lenox, Massachusetts. The reporter spent about four or five months working on it. We wanted to know what kinds of enrollment techniques were being used, how they raised money, what their theology was—all sorts of questions. It was really a fascinating series.

What about the ratio between editorial and advertising?

It's roughly fifty-fifty. To be precise, it's 53 percent news and 47 percent advertising.

Can you give us a table of organization of the editorial department?

On a day-to-day basis, I am at the head of the news and editorial side of the *Eagle*. My father's title is editor and publisher, but he is going to be seventy-nine years old and is not as active as he used to be. My brother is the president of Eagle Publishing Company, and he's in charge of just about everything except the news and editorial department: advertising, distribution, business—all that sort of stuff—including printing. We have a couple of small printing businesses right here in Pittsfield.

Within the news department, the managing editor is in charge of all the news-gathering operations, and the editorial page editor is in charge of two opinion pages—editorial and op-ed. Four people work in that section. Some of the editorials go out to our other papers, which may or may not choose to use them. There is a four-person sports department and two assistant managing editors, one for soft and one for hard news. There is a city editor and a county editor. There is a copy desk that has four full-time people, three working at night and one in the daytime. There are quite a few county reporters, some of them full-time and some half-time. There are two bureaus, one in North Adams and one in Great Barrington, which are roughly twenty to twenty-five miles north and south of Pittsfield; they each have a bureau chief. Then there is a social department of two people. And that's it on the news side.

How are assignments handled?

The reporters are usually fairly self-directed. When an editor finds out about something, then it will be assigned; but for the most part, the reporters figure out their own stories. Now we are working out a system in which the county editor and the city editor are less desk-bound and are better able to get out in the community—go to meetings, receptions, and so on, so they can be more aware of what's going on and less dependent on their reporters' incentive, which by and large is excellent.

Does the paper have a particular political viewpoint, and do you back one party consistently in local elections?

No. We have a nonpartisan local government in Pittsfield. We have endorsed both Republicans and Democrats for governor in recent years. For Congress, since the '50s, we've always endorsed a Republican, Silvio Conte. He's a moderate-to-liberal Republican. Then again, we haven't endorsed a Republican for president since the 1930s. I think we're thought of as a liberal paper, but we tend to call the issues each on its own merit. We might be seen as socially liberal and fiscally conservative.

When are the day's assignments given out, and when must the stories be in for the next day's paper?

Assignments are given out every day. When they are due really depends on the story. The very early pages are the softer ones—Habitat, Kitchen, and so on. Some of the early pages are from the wire desk, stories from around the country and overseas. A reporter on a late-breaking story can have it in as late as 11:30 or midnight. Obviously, everything can't come in late, so the important thing is to have a good news flow. If there is a little fire or a little accident that happens late, you put it in the following day's paper. But if it's a terrible fire, right on North Street, with buildings burning down, you want to hold the presses and get pictures.

So how late can the paper go to press?

Press time is 12:45 A.M. That's what they aim for. Often it's 1:00 or 1:15. Occasionally, it's later than that.

(The three questions that follow were answered by Michael Miller, Mark Miller's brother.)

How many people sell space, not including classifieds?

We have seven people on the road and one telemarketer here for nonclassifieds.

How many people sell classified? How many lines per year?

We have three people on the road selling classified and six people here. We sell approximately 5.5 million lines per year.

Does the paper use a national sales rep? And what percent of total advertising is national business?

We do use a rep firm, Landon Associates. National business is about 5.8 percent of total advertising.

(Mark Miller is responding to the rest of the questions.)

Do you have internships available for college students or people interested in learning about newspapers? Are these mostly summer internships? How many do you have?

Sometimes we'll have a university like Northeastern or the University of Massachusetts, where somebody is majoring in journalism and will take a semester and come here. There are also summer internships. There is rarely more than one intern at a time. Occasionally, we have two summer interns.

Have interns worked out well in your department?

Oh, yes. Often they become reporters. We've had people from Northeastern or from Medill at Northwestern University who have later become full-time reporters.

How do you hire entry-level people? In what positions and at what salaries?

We're interested in experience, work on college papers, and recommendations. Often we try them out for a week or two. We have a lot to choose from, so we get very good people. Usually, they've had prior journalistic experience and are not coming straight out of college.

What is the salary for entry-level people?

They start at about $300 a week gross.

What relationship does the paper have to the area's colleges?

Sometimes professors will write for the op-ed page. Sometimes a Williams College expert will write about his or her field or review for the books page.

Has the Eagle *always been profitable?*

I think so. Of course, there have been years in which it didn't make much of a profit, but overall I think it's a profitable business.

Does the Eagle *employ any stringers and/or freelancers?*

There are a few, both in photography and in reporting. We have regular weekly local columnists who are not employees, and freelance reporters who write op-ed columns but not on a regular basis.

Arnold B. Sawislak joined United Press International in 1949. His first assignment was in the Madison, Wisconsin, bureau, where he covered state government and politics. In 1956, he was assigned to Washington, D.C., as UPI's first Midwestern regional reporter. Later he was transferred to the Washington bureau's general staff. He was designated a senior editor in 1972.

Sawislak planned UPI campaign and election coverage in 1974 and 1976. He prepared and supervised UPI Election Fact Sheets and wrote the *UPI Election Handbook,* a "how-to" manual for wire service campaign and election reporting and editing.

Currently, he writes a weekly "Washington Window" column of political commentary. In 1977, he was appointed Washington enterprise editor to plan, coordinate, and edit interpretive and feature news coverage of the nation's capital.

Sawislak was graduated from the University of Minnesota with a B.A. degree in journalism.

In the section of this chapter on the UPI, we noted that your organization employs several thousand stringers. Where are these people located? What kind of arrangement do they have with UPI? Is there any specific training for this function, and how does one become a stringer?

UPI employs stringers in virtually every country in the world. Stringers might work for newspapers or radio stations in their countries, or they might be spouses of American expatriates working in those countries. They might be students or teachers. UPI stringers, regardless of their vocations, will have a total commitment to accuracy, speed, and detail. They will know the fastest ways to transmit the news to the nearest UPI bureau. The transmission might be by telephone, cable, telex, or radiotelephone—even by mail.

Stringers are selected on the bases of general knowledge, accuracy, speed, news contacts, news "nose," and time availability. Reporting abilities for stringers are more important than writing expertise, but both play a large part in UPI criteria.

Some stringers receive a monthly retainer, and some are paid on a piece-work basis. The pay, modest at best, seems secondary to the UPI stringer's interest in being a "Unipresser."

What is the basic difference between AP and UPI?

Both services undertake basic news coverage at the state, regional, national, and international levels. UPI endeavors to provide more sprightly, colorful writing and more aggressive reporting to counter AP's larger staff. It also tries to provide more subscribers' special requests, whether the subscriber is a small or large newspaper or broadcaster.

UPI is a for-profit corporation that must observe strict budgetary constraints even though news generates itself at its own speed and in its own areas. UPI does not have the luxury of AP members when news coverage demands unexpected and large outlays of money.

Are regular UPI reporters paid on a par with their counterparts on a large newspaper?

In some metropolitan areas, namely New York, Washington, Chicago, and Los Angeles, top minimum-wage levels for local newspaper reporters and editors are higher than UPI levels. But in almost every middle-sized or small city, UPI salaries are as good as or better than local media salaries.

We noted that UPI staffers produce 13 million words daily. How are assignments handled for all these feature and news stories, and also, what percentage is news and what percentage features?

The spot news assignments almost always are made by the bureaus closest to the news event, although state, division or national headquarters' staffs may assist in the case of larger stories, such as natural disasters like hurricanes or earthquakes.

UPI has a lend-a-hand tradition spanning nearly a century, and UPI reporters have been known to cut short vacations to help a nearby bureau with a major breaking news story if they happen to be near the scene. One memorable occasion perhaps typifies the UPI tradition: An American editor based in Asia went to Tennessee on a long-overdue and much-needed vacation only to find that a convicted assassin had broken out of a nearby Tennessee jail. The Asian editor just put down his luggage and went out and helped cover the story. Needless to say, UPI leads the logs on that story, as it leads the logs on many stories.

Because UPI is a news wire service, spot news coverage exceeds feature output, but it would be impossible to gauge the ratio. Some days are heavy news days, and features take a back seat in number and length. Other days are light news days, and UPI can use its excellent undated feature file to provide the extras that make for diversification.

In a given year, how many new people are hired for full-time jobs at UPI? The AP requires two years of news experience for new job applicants. Is the UPI's requirement similar?

UPI trains many newspeople who have no prior experience. Helen Thomas is an example, and Walter Cronkite and Harrison Salisbury both came to United Press with very little prior experience. Specialized knowledge in a discipline—law, science, medicine—might be more help in filling a specific job slot than general news experience. In other cases, such as staffing a civil war or delicate summitry, seasoned newsmen and women would be the only staff UPI would consider.

New hires in a given year might be forty or might be zero. It would depend upon bureau expansion, news makers, staff turnover.

How is Washington covered, and how many writers, photographers, and editors are based there?

Because Washington is UPI's world headquarters and the nation's capital city, this bureau has national reporters and editors, local reporters and editors, foreign desk editors and specialized reporters, and a full complement of Spanish-speaking editors and reporters for the UPI Latin American

wire, written in Spanish. The total staff numbers well over one hundred at this writing.

Is journalism school a sine qua non for UPI employment today?

Most assuredly not. UPI's philosophy is to find experts in all fields. Sometimes it pays to hire the expert and teach him to write and report in the UPI style rather than hope that a journalism-school graduate can quickly learn the nuances of biochemistry. However, qualified J-school graduates always will receive serious consideration when UPI is hiring in any of its areas.

To what extent does UPI use satellite transmission, and what systems are used to transmit photographs?

UPI is turning more and more to satellite transmission of news and features. In addition to being much more economical than transmission by land line, satellite transmission is much faster and more reliable than old land lines, which used to cost UPI some $18 million annually.

UPI's photo transmissions presently are made by land line and received on UPI's exclusive U-II photo receivers. The U-II machine receives camera-ready photos of the highest quality available in the graphics business today. The U-II also receives color transmissions of first-rate quality.

UPI also utilizes its exclusive 16-S photo transmitter, which can send a photograph over an ordinary telephone line to a U-II receiver anywhere in the world.

The U-II also has been modified to receive top-quality photos from weather satellite stations around the world. Called GOES recorders, these U-II modifications are widely used by international airlines, the National Weather Service, the military, and by space agencies, who need fast, accurate weather photos on a twenty-four-hour-a-day basis.

Glossary of Newspaper Terms

Agate line: a term used in newspaper advertising measurement; it is one column wide, and there are fourteen agate lines to the inch.

ANPA: the American Newspaper Publishers Association, a membership group of the nation's publishers.

Banner head: the top headline on page one, often extending across the page.

Beat: a story obtained by a newspaper before its rival papers publish it; also, a reporter's assigned territory, such as police or city hall.

Byline: the name of the writer of a news or feature story or special column, usually placed between the headline and the item.

Dateline: the location and origin and date of a news story; for example, "Chicago, August 4 (UPI)."

Deadline: the time limit for stages in preparing copy to get out a certain edition of a newspaper.

Dummies: small-scale page diagrams showing which pictures, art, and copy belong where.

Edition: any issue of a newspaper; large papers issue several editions during the day or night.

Facsimile: an electronic device used to transmit photos and manuscripts from one location to another, using phone lines.

Feature: an article or story in a newspaper, about a person, situation, or trend, that is developed without regard for time constraints.

Flag: a newspaper's nameplate/logo on page one.

Folio: a line at the top or bottom of a page, with the date of the issue, page number, and title of publication.

Freestanding insert: a booklet, card, or brochure inserted into a newspaper between sections; papers often accept these inserts in a portion of their total circulation.

Jump: the continuation of an article or news item from its original page, usually bearing a "continued from page . . ." line.

Lead paragraph: the opening paragraph of a news story designed to draw a reader into the story, it traditionally answers the questions "who, what, why, when, and where?"

Masthead: box usually carried in the upper left-hand corner of the editorial page giving the title of the newspaper and a statement of its ownership and policy.

Mat or matrix: cardboardlike material impressed from type and engravings used to make stereotypes.

Morgue: the research library of a newspaper.

Op-ed: the page opposite the editorial page usually containing regular and guest columnists.

Pica: a printing measure, approximately one-sixth of an inch.

ROP: run of paper, meaning an advertiser's copy can be placed anywhere in the newspaper and does not have preferred position.

Scoop: a story obtained exclusively by a newspaper without the knowledge of its competitors.

Stringer: a freelance writer who reports news and features from rural and surrounding areas, other states, and foreign countries.

Subheads: short headings used to break up the paragraphs of a long news story.

Syndicated writers: writers of features, news, or editorial opinion for a number of newspapers.

Tabloid: a newspaper size that measures $9\frac{7}{8}'' \times 13\frac{5}{8}''$.

Thirty: typed as "--30--" and indicating "the end."

VDT: video display terminal, an electronic device whereby the reporter types a story on a keyboard; the story appears on a television screen and may be transmitted directly into a computer.

Wire services: the Associated Press (AP), United Press International (UPI), and other news-gathering services that transmit their reports to newspapers all over the country.

Recommended Reading

All-in-One Directory. New Paltz, N.Y.: Gebbie Press, Inc.

Alternative Press Directory. New York: Alternative Press Syndicate.

Ayer Dictionary of Publications. Philadelphia: Ayer Press.

Bogart, Leo. *Press and Public: Who Reads What, When, Where and Why in American Newspapers.* Hillsdale, N.J.: Lawrence Erlbaum Associates, 1981.

Cooper, Gloria, comp. *Squad Helps Dog Bite Victim—and Other Flubs from the Nation's Press.* Garden City, N.Y.: Doubleday/Dolphin, 1980.

Editor & Publisher International Year Book. New York: Editor & Publisher.

Garst, Robert E., and Theodore M. Bernstein. *Headlines and Deadlines* (3rd ed.). New York: Columbia University Press, 1961.

Grossfeld, Stan. *The Eyes of the Globe: Twenty-Five Years of Photography from The Boston Globe.* Chester, Conn.: The Globe Pequot Press, 1985.

Harrigan, Jane T. *Read All About It!: A Day in the Life of a Metropolitan Newspaper.* Chester, Conn.: The Globe Pequot Press, 1987.

Harvard Post, Editors of the. *How to Produce a Small Newspaper.* Boston: The Harvard Common Press, 1983.

Hulteng, John L. *Playing It Straight: A Practical Discussion of the Ethical Principles of the American*

Society of Newspaper Editors. Chester, Conn.: The Globe Pequot Press, 1981.

Hynds, Ernest C. *American Newspapers in the 1970s.* New York: W. B. Saunders, 1975.

Jordan, Lewis, ed. *The New York Times Manual of Style and Usage.* New York: Quadrangle/The New York Times Book Company, 1976.

Kenny, Herbert A. *Newspaper Row: Journalism in the Pre-Television Era.* Chester, Conn.: The Globe Pequot Press, 1987.

Marzolf, Marion. *Up from the Footnote: A History of Women Journalists.* New York: Hastings House, 1977.

Metz, William. *Newswriting—from Lead to ''30.''* Englewood Cliffs, N.J.: Prentice-Hall, 1977.

McKinney, John. *How to Start Your Own Community Newspaper.* Port Jefferson, N.Y.: Meadow Press, 1977.

Murray, Donald. *Writing for Your Readers: Notes on the Writer's Craft from The Boston Globe.* Chester, Conn.: The Globe Pequot Press, 1983.

Newsom, D. Earl, ed. *The Newspaper: Everything You Need to Know to Make It in the Newspaper Business.* Englewood Cliffs, N.J.: Prentice-Hall, 1981.

Notman, Larry. *Community Newspaper Management— Starting Out: A Beginner's Guide for Someone Starting Out to Manage a Community Newspaper.* Friendship, Wis.: Newspaper Services, 1981.

Prichard, Peter. *The Making of McPaper: The Inside Story of USA Today.* Kansas City, Mo.: Andrews & McMeel, 1987.

Roberts, Chalmers M. *The Washington Post: The First Hundred Years.* New York: Houghton Mifflin, 1977.

Salisbury, Harrison E. *Without Fear or Favor: An Uncompromising Look at The New York Times.* New York: Ballantine Books, 1981.

Seigel, Kalman, ed. *Talking Back to the New York Times: Letters to the Editor 1851–1971.* New York: Quadrangle/The New York Times Book Company, 1972.

Talese, Gay. *The Kingdom and the Power.* New York: Doubleday, 1978.

Udell, Jon G. *The Economics of the American Newspaper.* New York: Hastings House, 1978.

Wilken, Earl W., ed. *Glossary of the New Newspaper Technology.* New York: Editor & Publisher, 1974.

Williams, Herbert Lee. *Newspaper Organization and Management* (5th ed.). Ames, Ia.: Iowa State University Press, 1978.

In addition to the above-mentioned books, the following pamphlets will be helpful in informing the reader about careers in journalism.

A Career in Newspaper Advertising. Single copy free. Available from INAME Foundation, 11600 Sunrise Valley Drive, Reston, VA 20041.

Journalism, Your Newspaper Career and How to Prepare for it. Single copies free. Available from the National Newspaper Foundation, 1627 K Street, N.W., Suite 400, Washington, DC 20006.

Newspaper Jobs You Never Thought of . . . or Did You? Up to fifty copies free. Available from the American Newspaper Publishers Association Foundation, The Newspaper Center, Box 17407, Dulles International Airport, Washington, DC 20041.

Newspapers . . . Your Future? A brochure. Single copy free. Available from the American Newspaper Publishers Association Foundation, The Newspaper Center, Box 17407, Dulles International Airport, Washington, DC 20041.

Suburban Newspaper Careers. A brochure. Up to fifty copies free. Available from the Suburban Newspapers of America, 111 East Wacker Drive, Chicago, IL 60601.

MAGAZINES

Liberty, one of America's great magazines from 1924 to 1950, accounted for my entry into the magazine business at the tender age of ten. I was one of a legion of boys who, outfitted with white shoulder bags and a weekly supply of *Liberty* magazines (price 5¢), were told by the local sales manager (age sixteen) that we would receive a shiny pair of Union Hardware roller skates if we sold fifty copies a week for one year, door-to-door. If we sold fifty copies a week for two years, we would become the proud owners of bicycles which, incidentally, I couldn't yet ride.

This system of distribution was very successful for *Liberty;* it even had the name Boys' Sales. I never knew a kid who received the skates or a bicycle, so it must have been a profitable form of circulation.

Forty years later, in the grand tradition of all Horatio Alger heroes, I became the publisher of the revived *Liberty* magazine. My company bought the rights to the magazine and published a new version with a mix of old and new material to appeal to nostalgia buffs. We tried it for two years, but it didn't work.

Including my early experience as a *Liberty* salesman, I have been in the magazine business for more than fifty years. I still find it rewarding and challenging. Perhaps you will, too.

A Short History of Magazines

In England there have been magazines—or periodicals, as they were then called—since the seventeenth century. Those early publications were used to promote news of books and authors. By the early eighteenth century, Richard Steele and Joseph Addison were publishing the *Spectator;* and by the mid–nineteenth century, Charles Dickens was editing *Household Words.*

In France, magazines appeared in the eighteenth century and were edited by such giants of letters and philosophy as Rousseau, Diderot, and Voltaire.

Magazines were slow getting started in America, however, simply because there were not enough literate people who could afford them. Ben Franklin founded *General Magazine* in 1741, but, alas, it failed after only six issues, as did a number of others published in the next thirty years.

Many of the early magazines were literary in nature and were published by intellectual coteries in small cities such as Lexington, Kentucky. Literary greats of the time—Washington Irving, Oliver Wendell Holmes, and Ralph Waldo Emerson—contributed to these periodicals.

With the rise in our nation's population and literacy beginning in the early nineteenth century, magazines flourished. Fewer than one hundred existed in 1825; by 1850, there were six hundred. Many of America's greatest authors were involved in the launching of these publications. James Russell Lowell and Henry Adams started *North American Review* in 1815. It lasted until 1940. Henry Thoreau and Ralph Waldo Emerson's *Dial* began publication in 1840; and the historian of the American West, Bret Harte, founded *Overland Monthly* in 1868. It lasted until 1935.

Toward the latter part of the nineteenth century, new processes in printing and the rapid development of advertising encouraged the publication of still more magazines. There were 1,200 by 1870, 2,400 by 1880, and, by 1890, some 3,000. At the turn of the century, magazines became mass-market products with the introduction of the *Saturday Evening Post, Colliers, Cosmopolitan,* and *The Ladies' Home Journal.* Three of these nineteenth-century publications are in existence today, as are two others, the literary magazines *Harper's,* started in 1850, and *The Atlantic Monthly,* founded in 1857.

In the twentieth century, magazines became big business. DeWitt and Lila Wallace founded *Reader's Digest* in 1921. It became an immediate success, although it didn't carry advertising until 1955.

Henry Luce started *Time* in 1923, later to be joined by *Life* and *Fortune.* The Time, Inc., family today includes the immensely popular *People, Sports Illustrated,* and the newer *Money* magazine.

Harold Ross was the founding editor of *The New Yorker,* begun in 1925. He reigned until 1952, when his disciple William Shawn took over. Shawn officiated until 1987, when he was dethroned by the magazine's new owner, Newhouse Publications.

With the advent of television in the early 1950s, magazines, particularly the large-circulation publications, faced a new challenge for advertising revenues. Television's ad rates have escalated in recent years, however, making magazines a better buy and a viable competitor for this revenue. Later in this chapter, we discuss how magazine advertising is sold.

The Scope of Magazines Today

In a recent issue of *Writer's Digest,* an excellent magazine for writers, I learned about a new business publication with the intriguing title of *Pizza Today.* Why not? There are magazines about everything else. This one bears the subtitle "The Professional Guide to Pizza Profits," and it contains profiles on pizza entrepreneurs and unique pizza places. I wonder if there are instructional drawings on how high to toss the dough. The magazine pays 8¢ per word for articles and has its headquarters in Santa Claus, Indiana—believe it or not.

About 300 new magazines are started each year. Many will fail for a variety of reasons. Here are some of the more intriguing titles from "New Magazines," a service journalism program at the University of Mississippi, conducted by Samir Husni, Ph.D., and funded by the Meredith Corporation.

American Astrology Presents Money & Success
Archery World's Bowhunting Equipment Guide
Bathroom Journal
Beauties of Wrestling
Buns of Playguy

Catastrophe
Changes: For and About Children
    of Alcoholics
Cooking Light
Dream Guys
Forbidden Kinky Acts
Complete Guide to Single Action
    Revolvers
Honcho Overload
Inside the Mafia
Ministries Today
New Body's 10 Superfast
    Diets
Ninja Combat Training Manual
Opera Fanatic
Publish!
Rock Shots Presents Rock
    Pix
The Russian Disaster: A
    Survival Handbook for the
    Nuclear Age
Safe Sex
Taboo Letters
Three Way Lovers
VCR: The Home Video Monthly
Waldenbooks Kid's Club Magazine
Wing and Shot

If nothing else, the list does illustrate the catholicity of taste and interest evident in the magazine industry today. In the past few years, we have seen the introduction of some major publications brought out for the most part by substantial publishers. These include *American Health, PC World, W., Vanity Fair, Wood, Dial, Inside Sports,* and *TV Cable Week.* Consider the last title, a project of Time, Inc.

Time, Inc., is a giant in consumer-magazine publishing. Its flagship, *Time* magazine, had a recent weekly circulation of 4.6 million, and its *Sports Illustrated* boasts a weekly circulation of 2.8 million. Also in its stable are the monthlies *Life* and *Money,* the biweekly *Fortune,* and the weekly *People,* all highly successful publications. Time, Inc., seldom makes mistakes.

In the early '80s, however, it attempted to launch *TV Cable Week* to compete with *TV Guide.* Much research and testing went into this effort. The result was a purported loss of $47 million, an enormous price to pay for misjudging a market.

In 1985, Time, Inc., began test-marketing another picture newsweekly aptly named *Picture Week.* It was to be like *People* but on a more popular level. In late 1986, the project was killed before it ever got rolling. The result—a $30 million bath.

Yet another Time, Inc., loser, the science magazine *Discover,* was sold in May 1987 to Family Media for $26 million. At the time of the sale it had a circulation of 925,000, but it also had lost about $60 million in its seven previous years of publication.

These huge losses, plus other factors which pared Time, Inc., profits further, prompted an atypical belt-tightening program in the mid-1980s that saw the laying off of many magazine employees as part of a $75 million budget cut. Time, Inc., had always been a free-spending organization with lavish entertainment budgets and virtually no constraints in its cause of quality journalism. Even the mighty do totter.

In spite of this failure, many new magazines do succeed. Magazine revenues soared to upward of $9 billion in the mid-1980s. Magazines are a dynamic growth field employing hundreds of thousands of talented people. According to the Magazine Publishers Association, there are at least 105,000 people employed in periodical publishing.

What Is a Magazine?

Some call it a periodical; some call it a magazine. Literary and scientific journals fit into this broad category, along with newsletters. Those in the newsstand distribution business always refer to a magazine as a "title." When the advertising space salespeople meet in the reception room at J. Walter Thompson, they use the term "book," and to them there is no confusion. They'll say, "How are things at your book?" or "I hear that book is in trouble." Everyone understands. Most dictionaries define *magazine* as a publication issued periodically containing stories and articles about a specific subject or subjects. Here, we'll call it a magazine because that's what it's most often called in the industry.

The two primary divisions of magazines are *consumer* and *business* (or trade). Consumer magazines are publications of general or specialized interest either sold or given free to the public. Business magazines are those that deal with the commercial and financial aspects of particular industries or businesses.

A secondary division of the magazine spectrum, journals, should not be overlooked. Eleven publishers, located in all parts of the country, issue about a hundred scientific, technical, medical, and literary journals. Examples of some typical titles are Pergamon Press's *Solar Energy Journal,* Academic Press's

Journal of Economic Theory, the University of Chicago Press's *Journal of Women in Culture and Society,* and the well-known *JAMA,* the *Journal of the American Medical Association.* These publications—with the exception of *JAMA,* which has a circulation of about 340,000—generally have small, specialized readerships.

Consumer magazines are the largest division of magazines in terms of number of publication, circulation, and revenues. SRDS (Standard Rate & Data Service), the monthly listing service of magazines, lists approximately 1,500 consumer magazines, of which a third have audited circulation. They are audited, in other words, by the ABC (Audit Bureau of Circulation), which means that their circulation is verified twice a year. Such verification is crucial to advertisers and their agencies.

Magazines grew enormously in the post–World War II period. A recent study by Warner Publishers Services, a leading distributor of magazines, noted that there are almost 2,000 consumer magazines sold on newsstands today at 130,000 retail outlets in the United States and Canada. Approximately 500 magazines are sold on newsstands but do not choose to be listed by SRDS because they don't sell advertising.

When we add to these 2,000 magazines those that are sold only by subscription, the numerous trade or business publications, and technical and scholarly journals, we reach a total of 11,000.

Every field of interest is represented. There are more than one hundred that deal with sports; fifty-one computer magazines for consumers; thirty-five on horses, riding, and breeding; 447 trade magazines on medicine and surgery; and ninety-six on engineering and construction. There is even a magazine for people who read in the bathroom. Its title—*Bathroom Journal,* of course. The publisher claims his survey shows that about 50 million people read in the bathroom. The survey didn't show what the average time span spent there was. The bubble soap and laxative advertisers should welcome this new captive audience.

SRDS lists almost 300 farm-oriented publications, of which eighty-one have audited circulation. These include the giant *Farm Journal* (with a circulation of almost 1 million), *Successful Farming,* and *Progressive Farmer.*

Consumer magazines about business are big business. The three at the top—*Business Week, Forbes,* and *Fortune*—slug it out for circulation and advertising revenue supremacy. The list also includes such lesser lights as *Hispanic Business* and the *Oregon Business Magazine.*

As we can now begin to see, magazine publishing is a dynamic industry. In recent years, we've wit-

Omni's mix of science fact and fiction made it a winner from the outset. Its striking graphics are an important factor in its success. (Reprinted with permission.)

nessed the success of such important newcomers as *Omni, Working Woman, Inc., Avenue, American Health,* and *Personal Computing.* In the business or trade magazine area, some successes are *Information Week, Data Sources, Info World,* and *Computer Systems News.* Note that these last four are in the computer field.

Two Major Groups of Magazines

As noted, within the family of magazines, there are two major groupings: consumer and business. Within the consumer area, there are two divisions: specialized and general.

Specialized magazines, as the name connotes, deal with special, as opposed to general, interests. This seeming confusion is clarified when we examine some representative listings from SRDS's consumer book.

The following classification groupings are "specialized":

Boating and Yachting
Power and Motoryacht
Sail
Waterfront
Yachting

Computers
Byte
Lotus
PC World
Personal Computing

Dressmaking and Needlework
McCall's Needlework & Crafts
Vogue Patterns
Simplicity Sewing for Today
Woman's Day 101 Sweater & Craft Ideas

Fishing and Hunting
Ducks Unlimited
Field & Stream
Outdoor Life
Sports Afield

News Weeklies
Newsweek
People
Time
Sports Illustrated
TV Guide
U.S. News & World Report

The news weeklies are the most influential group by virtue of their frequency of publication and large circulations. It may seem odd that *People, Sports Illustrated,* and *TV Guide* are listed as news weeklies, but that is their choice of listing.

TV Guide, with a circulation of more than 16 million, has the largest circulation, followed by *Time* and the relatively new *People.* In ad revenue, *Time* leads them all with more than $169 million for a recent six-month period.

Now we come to the "general" classification:

Atlantic
American Heritage
Ebony
Harper's Magazine
Life
New Yorker
Mother Jones
Prevention
Psychology Today
Reader's Digest
Smithsonian
Town & Country

SRDS lists seventy-two magazines in this category. The mighty *Reader's Digest* has the largest circulation in the land—more than 17 million, of which all but a million is by subscription. When one considers total readership—that is, primary readers plus their pass-along audience—the *Digest* reaches 55 million people, or one in four Americans. It also has nine international editions.

Now we come to the other important category of magazines: business, or trade, as many refer to it. This grouping consists of publications dealing with industry, business, and the professions. Perhaps less glamourous than consumer magazines, for the beginner they present unlimited opportunities. For example, in the field of medical and surgical publications, there are almost 500 titles.

Professional medical people write most of the articles for these publications; however, these busy practitioners neither have enough time, nor are they usually trained writers. These magazines therefore offer rewarding and well-paying jobs for writers with some scientific background. Quality in writing, art direction, and physical presentation are of the highest order. A look at Cahners Publishing's semimonthly *Emergency Medicine,* with a circulation of about 130,000, will demonstrate the eminently high standards set by most publications in this group. *Emergency Medicine* is not sold at newsstands but may be available at your doctor's office.

Paid and Controlled Circulation

When dealing with business magazines, a discussion is necessary of paid and controlled (or free) circulation. Most consumer magazines have paid circulation; this revenue is vital to a magazine's financial health.

Many business magazines operate on a controlled circulation basis, that is, their readers get the magazine free. This policy is the publisher's decision, predicated on the premise that in his particular industry, it is more important to reach everyone than to charge a subscription rate and reach only a portion of the market.

Whether to go with paid or controlled circulation is obviously a critical decision for the business-magazine publisher. Many publishers start out with controlled circulation but are forced out of economic necessity to switch to paid. Business-magazine profits, however, come almost solely from advertising sales.

Two of the largest business- or trade-magazine publishers are McGraw-Hill and Harcourt Brace Jovanovich. The diversity of their lineup will provide the reader with a perspective of the scope of this division of magazines. Following is a broad listing of McGraw-Hill's publications:

Architectural Record
Business Week
Byte
Data Communications
Popular Computing
Aviation Week & Space Technology
Commercial Space
International Management
Professional Managerial Network
Chemical Engineering
Chemical Week
Electrical Construction & Maintenance
Electrical Wholesaling
Electrical World
Electronics
Business Week's Guide to Careers
Graduating Engineer
Engineering News-Record
The Physician & Sportsmedicine
Postgraduate Medicine
American Machinist
Metal Producing
Coal Age
Engineering & Mining Journal
Fleet Owner
Modern Plastics
Modern Plastics International
Power
Textile Products & Processes
Textile World

Chemical Engineering is a bi-weekly with a paid circulation of approximately 65,000. It has an editorial staff of twenty-five editors, including fifteen with chemical engineering degrees. *Aviation Week & Space Technology* has a paid circulation of approximately 140,000, is published weekly, and has thirty-eight full-time editors. Its publishers state that it has the biggest aerospace audience in the world.

Harcourt Brace Jovanovich, a diversified publishing company, publishes magazines as well as books. It claims to be America's largest business, professional, and farm publisher, with 146 publications in such important industries as communications, education, energy, health care, manufacturing, merchandising, paper, plastics, processing and packaging, recreation and leisure, travel and lodging, trade and consumer shows, and convention services. A random listing of its publications follows:

Pipeline & Gas Journal
Dental Management
Geriatrics
Food Management

Plastics Compounding
Candy Marketer
Flotation Sleep Industry
Meat Processing
Motorcycle Dealer News
Restaurant Show Daily

In addition to the magazines listed, Harcourt Brace Jovanovich publishes nine newsletters, including the influential *Jack Anderson's Washington Letter.*

McGraw-Hill and Harcourt Brace Jovanovich have their headquarters in New York, along with their administrative and editorial offices; their advertising sales offices are located all over the country. The addresses of these two, as well as those of other major business magazine companies, appear later in this chapter.

A written request or a visit to the personnel departments of companies such as these will shed additional light on the attractive employment opportunities they offer. (For details on such opportunities, particularly those in the editorial area, see the "Who Does What" sections of this chapter.)

One Man's Magazine-Success Story

Steve Florio's first job was as a computer operator in the research department at *Esquire* magazine. He was twenty-one, just out of college; his salary was $150 a week—not too splendid, even in 1970.

Having majored in marketing and business administration at New York University, he was attracted to magazine publishing but didn't really know where he would fit in until he went out on a sales call with an *Esquire* salesman. The guy made $35,000 a year, and to Florio, the job didn't seem too difficult.

Steve decided that his future belonged in ad sales and was fortunate in getting a promotion that enabled him to sell mail-order advertising for *Esquire.* This ad category does not have the same cachet as apparel, cigarettes, and liquor, but it offered him a chance to show management that he could sell.

In rapid-fire style, he vaulted up the ladder at *Esquire* in seven years as an advertising salesman. By the time he was twenty-eight, he was appointed advertising director. After two years at this job, he accepted the challenging offer of becoming publisher of Condé Nast's *Gentlemen's Quarterly*. He was not yet thirty-one.

A word about these two publications: During Steve Florio's tenure at *Esquire* there were three changes of ownership and concomitant redefinition of the publication's identity. Selling advertising for this magazine involved much more than being an order taker and inviting clients to chic restaurants. *GQ* had an image problem. The Madison Avenue advertising community was convinced that the book reached a predominantly gay audience and, as such, was skewed primarily to fashion advertising. Florio and his Condé Nast bosses were determined to widen their scope; in the process, they made numerous shifts of editors, ad directors, and art directors.

It worked. With its new editorial thrust, *GQ* flourished. When Steve started there, in December 1979, the circulation was about 300,000, and *GQ* was selling approximately 800 pages of advertising a year. (In magazine parlance, we add up all fractional pages of advertising, combine these with full pages sold, and come up with the total number of "ad pages" a publication sells in a given period.) By the time he left, in 1985, circulation was more than 700,000, and the number of ad pages had catapulted to 2,000.

Condé Nast, owned by the Newhouse family, publishes many successful magazines, among them *Vogue, Glamour, Mademoiselle, Self,* and *Vanity Fair.* In 1985, it purchased the venerable *New Yorker.* The company is known in the industry as a loyal employer that rewards talented people who produce results.

Florio was appointed president and publisher of the *New Yorker* in 1985 when he was only thirty-six. Here he had his biggest challenge. Many advertising savants characterized the magazine as "sleepy, stuttering, and just plain boring." Circulation was flat at about 400,000. Ad revenues were down.

In just the first year of Florio's reign, the magazine was breathing new life with larger circulation and innovative promotional advertising. It is perhaps too early for a complete verdict, but as a longtime *New Yorker* reader, I think it's moving ahead.

Steve Florio's career path can be an inspiration for those readers interested in the business side of magazine publishing. How did he do it? What about him brought success so rapidly? His detractors say that he's brash, cocky, opportunistic, and just plain lucky. His employers think that his energy, talent, drive, and aggressiveness brought him to the top. Clearly he's been in the right places at the right times. Whether or not his rise can be attributed to a

combination of these factors, the results are there for all to see.

Steve took a couple of minutes from his hectic schedule to answer these two questions:

What areas of our business do you think offer the greatest opportunity for college graduates, and do you think that an M.B.A. gives one a head start in the magazine business?

I still believe that the greatest opportunities in [magazine] publishing are found through the advertising sales departments. I believe that an M.B.A. really does give novice advertising sales executives a head start. They understand how to organize their business, and they also understand how the problems are solved.

Besides Condé Nast, what magazine companies do you recommend as good places to get started?

Besides Condé Nast, I recommend Hearst, CBS, Knapp, and Times Mirror as good places to get started.

Hold the Presses

The date: October 11, 1986. *The place:* Reykjavik, Iceland. *The event:* The epochal summit meeting between President Ronald Reagan and Soviet General Secretary Mikhail Gorbachev.

Put yourself in the place of *Time* magazine's managing editor, Jason McManus, nation editor Walter Isaacson, art director Rudolph Hoglund, and the rest of the staff. The summit meeting will be of historic importance, dealing with the elimination of nuclear testing by both superpowers for the next decade. Your obligation to your 25.6 million readers is clear: Provide them with an inside account of the meeting, in depth, in about 3,500 words and a half-dozen color pictures—and do it fast.

The problem is that *Time's* regular editorial closing time is midnight Saturday; the press date is Sunday morning. The summit meeting, however, will not conclude until Sunday afternoon, October 12. The decision is made to hold the presses for twelve hours in order to cover the complete story. On Monday morning, October 13, readers across the country picked up a copy of *Time* with the grim faces of Reagan and Gorbachev on its cover. Their farewell handshake had taken place less than a day earlier.

Let's consider the manpower and technological wizardry that enabled this operation to succeed. On the editorial side, eight reporters and five photographers were sent to Reykjavik even before the meetings were to start. Their reports to the home office in New York were filed constantly. To handle all the late reporting, a staff of writers and editors in New York were mobilized, starting their day before dawn on Sunday.

Perhaps the most difficult job was to get the photos to New York quickly. A state-of-the-art relay system was used that converted images into computer digits and then transmitted them by satellite. At *Time*'s headquarters, the data were changed back into pictures at their high-tech facility known as IMPACT (Image Processing and Color Transmission), where the magazine's stories and illustrations were assembled into pages.

Special crews were alerted at all ten U.S. printing plants to receive the late-closing pages that were beamed from IMPACT in New York. Extra delivery trucks were enlisted to rush the issue to newsstands in major cities.

Let's look at the excellent editorial coverage *Time* provided its readers, and in far less than the usual lead time for a cover story.

Preceding the story itself was a one-page introduction delineating the issues Reagan and Gorbachev would face at the Iceland summit. This piece was written in advance of the event. It was accompanied by a color photo of the two leaders, posing benignly for the cameras, taken at the start of the meeting.

The succinct headline for the cover story, "Sunk by Star Wars," set the tone. The reader could tell immediately why the summit meeting met with failure. The subhead, "An impasse over SDI zaps Gorbachev's briefcase full of proposals," gave more details.

The five-page cover story, sprinkled with five color pictures, including one of smiling Reykjavik children peering through windows, was credited to three *Time* reporters. Their writing was terse, precise, and objective.

In the "Nation" section, an essayist, Roger Rosenblatt, wrote brilliantly of Iceland's tradition of peace. He wrote also of the paradoxes in this remote land: In an underground disco, an Icelandic rock group led by a woman with her hair made up as a crow in flight sang about U.S. and Soviet journalists vying for scoops; in another part of the city, the female president of Iceland greeted Reagan at the airport.

Three other *Time* reporters covered the human-interest angle of the summit. Reagan and Gorbachev, it seems, were not the only stars of the

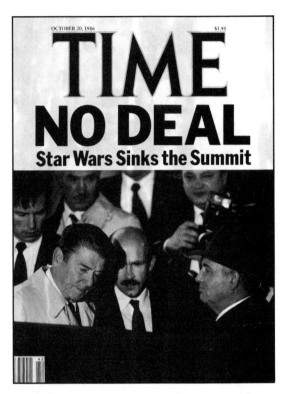

The October 20, 1986, cover of *Time*. **Rapid transmission of the photograph and split-second coordination between the editorial and production teams enabled this issue to be on the stands only a day after the event. (Reprinted with permission.)**

convocation. Miss Iceland, who is also the reigning Miss World, modeled a summit T-shirt with the faces of the two leaders. The price—$11.44.

A sidebar piece had a color picture of the chic Raisa Gorbachev and reported how she maximized the public relations advantage of her attendance and Nancy Reagan's absence at the meeting.

Also in the "Nation" section, *Time* columnist Hugh Sidey wrote a full page on his perception of Ronald Reagan's preparation, concerns, tactics, and ever-present optimism over the momentous meeting.

In a final piece, a *Time* writer compared this summit with the one between President Lyndon Johnson and Soviet leader Alexei Kosygin at Glassboro, New Jersey, in 1967. *Time* also ran an excerpt from Robert McNamara's book *Blundering into Disaster*, published in 1986, about arms control and defense. McNamara was secretary of defense during the 1967 summit.

As we see in the chapter on newspapers, a great newspaper such as the *New York Times* will provide excellent, extensive reportage on short notice for a late-breaking event like the raid on Libya in April 1986. Here we witness how brilliantly *Time*'s editorial and production staff rose to a similar challenge by reducing the time it usually takes to get comprehensive news from the writer's desk to the reader. There were many heroes in this operation.

The real-life situation just dramatized is more exciting than most. It illustrates that magazines are a glamorous, fast-paced outlet for talented people.

Who Does What on the Editorial Side of a Magazine

The people who sell advertising space for magazines eat fancy lunches almost every day with clients and agency people. They also earn more money than editors and writers, but the glamour jobs on a magazine are still editorial. Maybe it's the byline, or your name on the masthead, or just the fulfillment of a dream that started when you wrote for your college yearbook. The fact is clear—many of us do aspire to be professional editors and writers.

At the introduction to this chapter we saw that there are thousands of consumer magazines and as many business magazines. On consumer magazines, the editors do a lot of editing and little writing; this latter function is assumed by staff or freelance writers. The editors create and assign, then evaluate the material that will appear in the magazine, which is often written by others.

Included here is a chart of the editorial side of a typical magazine, but no two magazines are alike. At some large magazines, there are additional functions such as design director, assistant managing editors, executive editors, and, on a large weekly, as many as fifteen editorial assistants and forty contributing editors. The sizes of editorial staffs vary greatly. A small journal may consist of only one or two people who perform the multitudinous functions of editing a magazine. Often these dedicated individuals handle the additional chores of production and art direction. By contrast, the editorial team of a weekly news magazine may consist of between 300 and 400 people. On a monthly such as *House Beautiful*, the editorial staff consists of about forty-five employees, not including those in the art department.

First, we'll chart each job assignment, and then we'll review the editorial process for a monthly magazine.

Editor-in-Chief (or Editor; the title varies): The editor-in-chief controls the editorial content of a magazine and, in turn, usually delegates the administrative responsibilities to the managing editor. There, the chain extends to department or senior editors, to staff and freelance writers, and, ultimately, to copy editors, editorial production, and art direction.

Editors-in-chief can earn $100,000 a year or more. Readers of this book are primarily concerned with entry-level or junior positions on an editorial staff, so let us emphasize the function and salary of those jobs.

Managing Editor and Assistants: A weekly magazine such as *New York* will have one managing editor and two assistants. These individuals are responsible for giving out assignments to freelance writers and in-house staff, attending story conferences, consulting on story treatments, and supervising departmental editors. In a magazine's editorial pecking order, they are just below the editor-in-chief and above senior editors and contributing editors. Most have come up from the ranks of editorial assistant to assistant editor to associate editor. Almost all are college-trained. Many are writers themselves, but, if not, they are skillful evaluators of good writing. Their salary range depends on the size and frequency of the magazine and runs from $30,000 to $65,000 a year.

Senior Editor: The job description of senior editor varies from overall managerial function to department editor. For example, on one weekly magazine the senior editor may write and edit two pages on marketing and advertising. The importance of this material warrants the important title. Another senior editor on the same magazine may be in charge of all copy flow, a major responsibility on a weekly magazine. The salary range is from $35,000 to $55,000 a year.

Contributing Editor: On some monthly magazines, contributing editors are listed on the masthead and attend editorial meetings but actually write for the magazine only four or five times a year. They are paid a minimum annual fee, which increases proportionally to the number of pieces they write.

Often magazines use "name" writers as contributing editors, even though these people seldom write for the publication on a regular basis. On some magazines a contributing editor is a specialist—food, travel, reviews. Since the function varies so much, it is inappropriate to give an average salary.

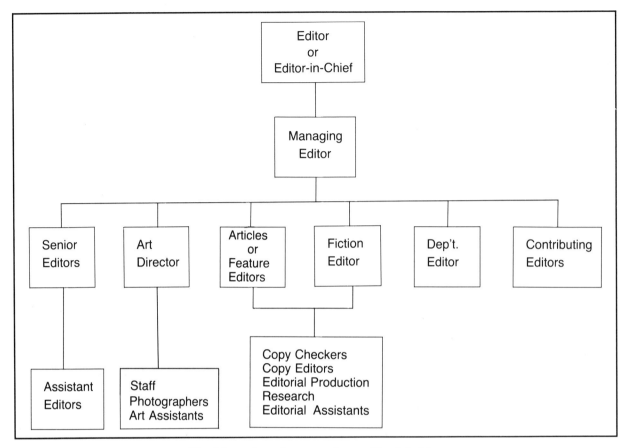

The hierarchy of a magazine: editorial side.

Copy Editor: On a small magazine, a sole copy editor reads manuscripts and does the proofreading after copy has been set. On a larger magazine, or one with weekly frequency, the copy-editing function is handled by a number of people headed by a copy chief. Meticulousness is the name of this craft. The salary range is from $22,000 to $32,000.

Assistant Copy Editor: This person reports to the copy editor and is responsible for reading and processing all manuscripts and copy for style, accuracy, facts, grammar, and editorial content. These salaries vary according to the size of a publication and the person's experience, but salaries range between $17,500 and $27,000 a year. You seldom start out your career with employment in this job; rather you progress through promotions from copy reading, proofreading, research, and editorial-assistant jobs.

Proofreader and Researcher: These individuals perform all the duties referred to in the previous paragraph. Although these job titles are somewhat down the ladder on the editorial side of a magazine, they can be stepping stones to more important situations on your own or other publications. Sala-

ries vary between $12,500 to $22,500 a year. English and journalism majors will have a decided advantage over others in applying for these jobs. Candidates are expected to have absolutely perfect spelling and grammar skills and a near-obsessive attention to detail. Attendance at a summer writing or publishing program plus an internship (see "Magazine Publishing Internships") will clearly help the job seeker in pursuing employment in this capacity. Often one progresses to this level from a job as an editorial assistant.

Editorial Assistant: The editorial assistant is the private in the editorial regiment whose work runs the gamut from "gofer" to writer contact and arranging for payment to art and photography people, plus manifold other duties. Salaries, unfortunately, are commensurate with the status of this job classification; they range from $7,500 to a high of $14,000 a year at some large magazines. As in book publishing, the competition for jobs is fierce because at any one time there are many more applicants than there are availabilities.

One doesn't start out on a magazine as an editorial assistant and then in a few years become a full-fledged editor. Before all this can happen, one must begin the process by getting a good liberal arts education at college, sprinkled with writing courses. Then, a good first step is a job as an editorial assistant at a magazine. This is where one really learns to understand the editorial function.

Contact with staff and freelance writers also furthers one's educational perspective. At some magazines, editorial assistants are invited to editorial meetings, even if it's just to take notes or serve coffee. In these meetings, the assistant can learn how ideas are presented and developed. On a magazine using art and illustration, the novice can learn how clever art direction can dress up a story.

Magazines often have special cover meetings. Here, one can learn the elements of creating good ''selling'' covers; also, it is helpful to observe the interaction of the editorial and art people.

In time, the editorial assistant will understand that the editor must create a unique personality for his magazine and that the editor must understand the magazine's audience and write for it, not for himself or his friends. It is not necessary for an editor to be a fine writer. Writing ability may be helpful, but it is far more important that the editor be an organized, critical thinker, one who can *evaluate* good writing and generate ideas and excitement into the editorial package.

As in other fields, the ambitious, talented individual in a magazine will ultimately be discovered by management and rewarded with promotions leading to top editorial positions. It takes hard work, patience, and time.

From Editorial Meeting to Presstime

The difference between a weekly or monthly magazine is basically in the size of the editorial staff. However, whatever its frequency, or whether it's a consumer or business magazine, all magazines start out each issue with an editorial meeting. There may be preliminary meetings between a few top-echelon editors, but in most cases the general editorial meeting will include most of the staff.

The format for a general editorial meeting varies. It may include a critique of the most recent issue. It may also include progress reports on future issues; the editorial team works on many issues at the same time. Future issues may be assigned to senior editors, who then will report to the managing editor and editor (or editor-in-chief) on their activity.

Magazines often work out special themes for issues. For example, *Sports Illustrated* will have cover emphasis and a lead article on a major event such as the U.S. Open Tennis Tournament or the Super Bowl (see chapter on television). Elaborate planning must be undertaken to ensure coverage of the event by staff writers and freelancers.

For the purpose of this section, we'll highlight four weeks in the editorial life of a monthly magazine.

To simplify our narrative approach, let's start on the first of the month, when we have a general editorial meeting attended by the editor-in-chief, the managing editor, senior editors, the art director, articles and department editor, the fiction editor, a few contributing editors, assistant and associate editors, and two editorial assistants to take notes. The meeting is held in a big conference room, of course.

Because two or three issues are in the works at one time, the editor-in-chief will ask the managing editor for a progress report. The group will discuss articles and fiction to be assigned for issues four and five months hence. Stories that are completed and scheduled for a specific issue will also be discussed.

Cover treatments for future issues are presented to the group in layout form by the art director. Much heated debate and give-and-take ensues. The final color proof for the current monthly issue is submitted. Most agree that it's terrific—all except the editor-in-chief. He thinks that the cover lines should be in a different typeface. The art director (who, corporately, is subordinate to the editor) disagrees. The editor wins out.

A week later, there is a smaller meeting with only the managing editor, one senior editor, the art director, two assistant editors, and, this time, only one editorial assistant. The managing editor brings a list of approved text and art layouts for the forthcoming monthly issue. There are still a few holes. The senior editor and assistants will plug them with pieces from their inventory and cartoons.

On this magazine, the managing editor directs the day-to-day flow of copy—from the writers, through copy editing, typesetting, layout, and on to press. The editorial and art staffs work on a fixed budget, which is administered by the managing editor. Meanwhile, the assistant editors have been receiving pieces from staff writers and freelancers and guiding them through their final stages in issues beyond the current one.

By the third week, the current issue is in its final stage; that is, the color separations have been made, and the type has been set and mechanically placed for the entire issue. In this color-separation process, color transparencies and art are prepared for the press by undergoing a scanning process that separates them into four basic colors. The editor-in-chief initials these pages after a final check for content, thereby approving their shipment to the printer for film proofs.

In the final week, the editor-in-chief and managing editor approve the final proofs, and that issue goes to press. After a brief respite, it's on to the next month's issue.

The Freelance and In-house Writers

It is often more economical for a magazine to rely on freelancers than to employ a large number of in-house specialists. For example, a magazine like *Texas Monthly* will call upon as many as a dozen local freelancers in a given issue, or a specialized magazine like *Fine Woodworking* will enlist a number of craftsmen/writers to share their expertise in words and pictures in each issue. *Time* and *Newsweek* rely on hundreds of home-office and regional-bureau writers to meet their demanding press schedules, in addition to "stringers" or freelance local writers (see "What Is a Stringer?" in the chapter on newspapers).

The would-be freelancer should be aware of the competition existing to get published. A magazine such as *Cosmopolitan* receives fifty unsolicited submissions every business day. Six editorial assistants share the reading of the annual volume of submissions—approximately 12,500.

Cosmopolitan has a 3 million circulation, which is why writers want to be there—broad exposure. The magazine runs only about twenty-five articles and features per issue—slim odds for the neophyte, especially as many of the pieces are by regulars and are initiated by their editorial staff.

Even if you are published in *Cosmopolitan*, you're not going to get rich. A major 4,500-word article brings only about $1,500, and you'll have to sweat over it for weeks. For an excellent report on how freelancers work with magazine editors, read an article in the August 1986 *Writer's Digest*, "How Publishing Really Works."

Freelancers are generally paid on a per-word basis—perhaps 20¢, 30¢, or 40¢. Usually the magazine pays the same word rate to all its freelance writers. Sometimes a publication will offer a particularly valuable freelance writer a minimum yearly guarantee plus contributing-editor status. The reader should note that there are various ways writers are paid by magazines. "On acceptance" means payment when a magazine receives the piece and agrees to run it. "On publication," a less favorable method for the writer, means payment when the issue of the magazine carrying the actual piece goes on sale.

Omni pays $1,500 to $2,000 on acceptance for 2,500 to 5,000 words on science, space travel, and real and projected development of many kinds.

A freelancer must work on assignments only because many magazines have a policy of not publishing unsolicited manuscripts, generally for fear of legal consequences. Also, editors have their personal favorites who get most of the assignments. This doesn't necessarily imply that there is a "buddy" system, but rather that editors are most comfortable with writers they know. Many successful freelancers are represented by agents, thus widening their scope of assignments.

Getting started in magazine writing is difficult. One approach is for a neophyte writer (who may be otherwise employed) to send article or fiction *ideas* to a particular editor (in this case, the articles or fiction editor listed on the masthead) at a magazine. If the editor is responsive, a follow-up interview may be requested.

Another approach to breaking in is for the young writer to take a job on a trade, or business magazine. Here the writing may not be that creative, often a rewrite of a press release; yet, the job pays fairly well, and the writer learns style, economy of words, and writing on a deadline.

Included here are some representative prices paid to freelance writers by selected magazines.

- *Outdoor Photographer* pays $300 to $600 for 1,500-to-4,000-word articles on techniques of outdoor photography.
- *Practical Homeowner* (formerly Rodale's *New Shelter*) pays $400 to $800 for 2,000 to 3,000 words.
- *Prime Time* pays $50 to $900 for 500 to 3,000 words on active retirement or travel for people over fifty.

For additional, up-to-date information on rates, study "The Markets" section in *Writer's Digest*.

Becoming a Writer or Editor

For those interested in becoming writers and/or editors, working for a high school newspaper is fun and often a good learning experience. A stint on a college paper or literary magazine is more serious training. A liberal arts background at college, with elective writing courses, will certainly increase one's intellectual development and hone the skills needed to enter the writing or editorial profession. Participation in a publisher's internship program or attendance at a summer publishing seminar such as those at NYU and Radcliffe/Harvard will certainly

Writer's Digest **is justifiably "the world's leading magazine for writers." One reader used its advice to sell a novel to a publisher for $350,000. It's worth reading** *WD* **for that possibility alone. (Reprinted with permission.)**

impress interviewers. (See sections on publishing internships, college book publishing programs, and writers' conferences in the books chapter.)

The would-be writer should make a small investment—$17 for a one-year subscription to twelve issues of *Writer's Digest.* This magazine, which bills itself as "the world's leading magazine for writers," is a fount of information. It has carried such provocative pieces as "The Basics of Successful Fiction," "Choosing Your Storyteller," "Ray Bradbury's Nostalgia for the Future," "Writing Poetry for Children," and "Ten Ways to Get to Know Your Market Better Than Its Editor Does." There are also regular departments and columns on language, poetry, tips on new markets (writing outlets), and selling movie and TV scripts and nonfiction.

The *Writer's Digest* people also publish a yearbook, *Writer's Market,* which contains the names of 4,000 buyers of freelance writing—book publishers as well as magazines—their pay rates and editorial requirements, as well as tips from authors and publishers on selling one's writing. They also have a

Writer's Digest Book Club and a Writer's Digest School. The emphasis in *Writer's Digest* is on the freelance writer; however, those seeking full-time writing jobs can benefit from it as well. The address is F&W Publishing Corporation, 1507 Dana Avenue, Cincinnati, OH 45207–1005.

Summer Writing Programs

The oldest summer writing program is the Radcliffe/Harvard publishing program, conducted every July. Stanford University in California sponsors an intensive twelve-day combined book and magazine seminar, as does Sarah Lawrence College in Bronxville, New York, and Rice University in Houston, Texas. New York University's School of Continuing Education runs a summer magazine program, which I originated; it also conducts continuing education courses in the spring and fall semesters on editing and other phases of magazine publishing. Columbia University's Graduate School of Journalism offers a Magazine Career Institute each June. It is a comprehensive program with excellent guest lecturers and a workshop.

Most of these programs are multifaceted, offering a variety of lectures and workshops about writing, editing, and other functions of magazine publishing. In addition, there are dozens of summer writing conferences and seminars where the craft of writing and editing is nurtured in a totally dedicated environment. Here is a partial listing (for a complete list, write to *Writer's Digest*):

La Jolla Summer Writers' Conference
University of California/LaJolla
La Jolla, CA 92037

Santa Barbara Writers' Conference
c/o Barnaby Conrad
Box 304
Carpinteria, CA 93013

National Writers' Club Workshop
1450 South Havana Street, Suite 620
Aurora, CO 80012

Wesleyan-Suffield Writer-Reader
  Conference
Box D, Graduate Summer School
Wesleyan University
Middletown, CT 06457

Christian Writers' Institute Conference and
  Workshop
c/o Helen Kidd, CWI
Gundersen Drive and Schmale Road
Wheaton, IL 60187

Maine Writers' Conference
c/o Joan D. Viles
59 Beverly Drive
Brunswick, ME 04011

Cornell University Summer Session
105 Day Hall
Ithaca, NY 14853

International Congress of Crime Writers
Mystery Writers of America
105 East 19th Street (3D)
New York, NY 10003

Miami University Creative Writing
  Workshop
c/o Milton White
Creative Writing Workshop
Upham Hall
Miami University
Oxford, OH 45056

Philadelphia Writers' Conference
c/o Emma S. Wood
Box 834
Philadelphia, PA 19105

University of Texas at El Paso Summer Writ-
  ers' Conference
c/o Les Standiford
University of Texas at El Paso
Department of English
El Paso, TX 79968

Duke University Writers' Conference
The Bishop's House
Duke University
Durham, NC 27708

Louisiana Writers' Conference
Centenary College Campus
P.O. Box 4633
Shreveport, LA 71134–0633

Highlights for Children
Second Annual Writers' Workshop
803 Church Street
Honesdale, PA 18431

Reader's Digest/Utah State University
Magazine Article Writers' Workshop
c/o Dick Harris
Utah State University
UMC 01
Logan, UT 84322

Bread Loaf Writers' Conference
Middlebury College
Middlebury, VT 05753

Rhinelander School of Arts
c/o Robert E. Gard
University of Wisconsin Extension
720 Lowell Hall
Madison, WI 53706

Magazine journalism courses and programs are
offered by a number of accredited graduate schools
of journalism. Some, like the Medill School at
Northwestern and the University of Kansas, produce
laboratory magazines to give their students practical
experience. Often, these students are evaluated by
professionals from within the industry. The National
Journalism Educators' Organization (University of
Kansas School of Journalism, Stauffer-Flint Hall,
Lawrence, KS 66045) can provide information on
these specialized graduate magazine programs.
Other schools offer special courses in magazine
instruction, sometimes known as "emphases." They
include the following:

Ball State University, Muncie, IN 47306
Bowling Green University, Bowling Green, OH
  43403
California State University, Fullerton, CA 92634
Drake University, Des Moines, IA 50311
University of Georgia, Athens, GA 30602
University of Kansas, Lawrence, KS 66045
Kansas State University, Manhattan, KS 66506
University of Minnesota, Minneapolis, MN 55455
University of North Carolina, Chapel Hill, NC 27514
University of Oregon, Eugene, OR 97403
Temple University, Philadelphia, PA 19122

Beginning writers and editors will find the following listing of organizations and publications
beneficial to understanding their chosen craft:

● Poets and Writer, Inc. (201 West 54th Street,
  New York, NY 10019) is an organization that
  maintains a listing of 5,600 poets and fiction
  writers; it publishes the *Directory of American
  Poets and Fiction Writers* and a thirty-two-page
  newsletter, *CODA* (five times a year), with information on workshops, jobs, and so on.

- The R. R. Bowker Company (1180 Avenue of the Americas, New York, NY 10036) issues a free catalogue of books on book and magazine design.
- The Literature Program of the National Endowment for the Arts, Washington DC 20506, gives grants to writers and to literary magazines.
- *Folio:* magazine (6 River Bend, P.O. Box 49, Stamford, CT 06907–0949), published monthly, is the trade publication for magazine publishers. It is essential reading for magazine professionals and those planning to enter the field. In 1985, the magazine published a superb book, *Magazine Editing—Its Art and Practice* ($49.95). In it, twenty-two top editors and publishers give a concentrated course in editorial philosophy, practice, management, and problem solving. It is primarily geared to people in the field, but newcomers will gain much from the experience of these industry giants.

Finally, a thought on becoming an editor of a magazine: Magazine greats like *Good Housekeeping*'s John Mack Carter, *Cosmopolitan*'s Helen Gurley Brown, or the *New Yorker*'s eminent Harold Ross didn't take a pledge in eighth grade vowing to become editors. Somehow it happened—by chance and circumstance, and much zeal.

As stated earlier, an editor does not have to be a great writer. What matters most is the ability to evaluate writing. This skill comes from reading fine (and not-so-fine) writing, learning to recognize style and quality, and, most of all, creativity.

At an editorial meeting, the truly creative people come up with the ideas that make a magazine great. One is probably born with this talent, yet the careful study of excellent magazines will foster this talent.

Becoming an editor still means climbing the ladder. That means starting as a lowly editorial assistant and perhaps taking orders for coffee at the editorial meetings, but spending a year or two at this job will prepare you for more important editorial assignments. If it's your dream to be an editor, prepare for it.

Art and Layout

When you visit a magazine's offices, you can always tell the art people by the way they dress. If they're male, they wear jeans or chinos, plaid shirts with solid-color knit ties (when they wear ties at all), corduroy sports jackets, and L. L. Bean bucks. The females wear jeans, plaid shirts (no ties), and L. L. Bean work shoes.

Despite their laid-back appearance, art people work at a frenetic pace. Consider their responsibility on the magazine that makes heavy use of illustrations, photography, color, and complex layouts. The art director and assistant often attend editorial meetings at which the subject of a particular piece is discussed and the editors express their thoughts on the visual approach they favor.

Although these meetings take place months in advance of a particular issue's deadline, circumstances always seem to work against the art department, requiring overtime, work on weekends, and/or work taken home. This lateness can be caused by a variety of factors—late copy, late illustrations or photography, changed minds about content. Before we discuss the functions of an art staff, let us reflect on the purpose of art direction for a magazine.

Covers attract readers to a magazine, whether the readers are newsstand browsers or longtime subscribers. The newsstand, particularly, can be a jungle of hundreds of titles vying for the prospective buyer's favor. Because all newsstand magazines are sold on consignment, a brilliantly conceived cover treatment can result in a swing of as much as 50,000 copies. Or consider *Sports Illustrated*'s annual swimsuit cover, which, as we will see shortly, enabled that issue to outsell by many times this figure those issues with covers devoted to sports heroes.

Even on a business magazine an appealing cover can be the draw that attracts the busy executive who receives dozens of magazines and can read only a few.

Trade magazines offer a unique challenge to the designer, a challenge that demands constant invention. He must overcome limited budgets and resources, along with a narrow, specialized subject matter. These magazines individually cover a diverse range of interests, but they share the common need to communicate.

An all-type layout with a provocative headline can lead the reader into an article as well as a splashy layout for a piece with little substance.

All the phases of a magazine layout are important: the typeface of the head and text, the quality of the photography and illustration, the use of white space, and, finally, the skillful positioning of all these elements in the space allotted. On the other hand, layout need not be merely a meretricious ploy: it can be an attractive means of inviting the reader into the piece.

Covers, as we noted previously, are the sales force that must deliver buyers. There is a tedious sameness to most covers. The hard-sell cover blurbs sometimes cancel themselves out to a point where one becomes oblivious to the lines of type and their accompanying illustrations.

An apparent contradiction is the success of *Cosmopolitan*. Every cover for the last twenty years has had a photograph of the same type of slinky model with exactly the same amount of cleavage showing, never a centimeter more or less—but this formula works for them. The magazine is immensely successful; however, *Cosmo* is the exception. In order to "sell," covers must be varied, unique, and visually exciting.

The Society of Publication Designers publishes the award winners of their competition in a handsome volume, which can be found at some libraries or ordered directly from the Society at 25 West 43rd Street, Suite 711, New York, NY 10036. The price is $39.95.

The Training of an Art Director, Illustrator, or Photographer

Many people show artistic talent at an early age. Often this is encouraged by parents and teachers in elementary and high school, and by the time they apply to college, a weighty decision must be made about the serious pursuit of art training.

For some, the path leads to fine art; others choose graphic design. For this training, there are fortunately many fine colleges. Included here is a list of a few schools and colleges that offer these programs:

Art Center College of Design
Box 7197
Pasadena, CA 91109–7197

Cooper Union for the Advancement
of Science and Art
41 Cooper Square
New York, NY 10003

Moore College of Art
20th and Race Streets
Philadelphia, PA 19103

Parsons School of Design
66 West 12th Street
New York, NY 10011

Philadelphia College of the Arts
320 South Broad Street
Philadelphia, PA 19102

Pratt Institute
295 Lafayette Street
New York, NY 10012

Pratt Institute has trained countless magazine and advertising agency art directors. It has a four-year B.F.A. (Bachelor of Fine Arts) curriculum, and students can major in graphic design, illustration, and art direction.

The official accrediting organization for art schools is NASA, the National Association of Schools of Art, 11250 Roger Baron Drive, Reston, VA 22090. Send $5.00 for a complete listing of their member schools. For an extensive list of accredited schools, see Milton K. Berlye's book *How to Sell Your Artwork* (Prentice-Hall, 1978).

Getting Started

The aspiring art director or illustrator can ill expect to make waves in the magazine art world. First, consider carefully which phase of art you wish to specialize in. Then, it is essential to prepare a portfolio of your *own* work, even if this work was done in school and not commercially.

Illustration is used in book and magazine publishing, at advertising agencies, and in the corporate world to a lesser extent. Unfortunately, the supply of talent in this field far exceeds the demand. At the typical monthly magazine, about five or six illustrations are purchased for each issue, yet almost a hundred portfolios, some from very talented illustrators, are offered to the art directors each month.

Many magazines do not even use illustration. For those artists determined to make it as illustrators in book or magazine publishing, or in advertising, we suggest a visit to New York City's prestigious Society of Illustrators (128 East 63rd Street, New York, NY 10021). The visitor can obtain pamphlets on illustration and have the opportunity to see the society members' work in the building's gallery.

We should understand the function of an art director. This individual creates the look of an entire magazine—its layout, choice of illustrations, and typeface. Thus art direction is a viable career choice in magazines, because virtually all of the 11,000 consumer and business magazines have an art director. Some staffs have a dozen or more people.

A good way to get started is to learn how to do "mechanicals," that is, the accurate placement of type proofs, illustrations, and photography for a layout before it goes to the printer. The work is exacting and may be tedious, but it is a beginning, even though one is executing someone else's design. The next step can often be a shot at doing simple layouts, and from there . . . who can tell?

Here is the general range of salaries in magazine art:

Paste-up: Paste-up people prepare mechanicals,

56

and skilled freelancers in New York generally make $30,000 annually. Beginners on full-time jobs are paid about $10,400 to $11,700. Outside New York, freelancers make one-third less; those on salary, from 15 to 20 percent less. (Salaries for the following professions also pertain to New York City. Those working elsewhere will earn less.)

Illustrators: Most illustrators work freelance and earn as little as $100 for a black-and-white drawing and up to $1,000 or more for a cover illustration; the general range is $500 to $600 for an inside color piece. If it takes three weeks to finish one of these works and it sells for only $500, that's not too profitable.

Photographers: Here, too, the prices are all over the place but are usually less than the fees for illustration. The top newsweeklies employ a number of staff photographers at starting salaries of $22,500 to $25,000 but have arrangements with a larger number of freelancers.

Art Directors: Assistant art directors on the top 200 consumer magazines earn from $20,000 to a high of about $30,000 a year. On other magazines, that figure is reduced 10 or 15 percent. Senior art directors earn from a low of $22,000 to a high of $50,000 a year on magazines with large art staffs. (For information regarding production managers, who work closely with art directors, see below.)

Who Does What on the Business Side of a Magazine

There are people who write, edit, art direct, copy edit, and proofread a magazine; then there are the others. These are the people who are responsible for the "business" of a publication. The business aspects include circulation, advertising sales, production, promotion and advertising, and finance. The publisher directs these activities and is often the titular head of the magazine.

To obtain an understanding of the "business side," take a look at the accompanying chart outlining this structure on a consumer magazine. Following are descriptions of the job assignments on the chart and their areas of responsibility.

Publisher: The publisher is usually the "business boss," but in some cases he is also responsible for the editorial product. Generally he is in charge of

the key areas of advertising sales, newsstand circulation, subscriptions, production, promotion, and finance. On most magazines, the publisher is also charged with budgeting financial projections and preparing profit-and-loss statements for the board of directors or the top management of the magazine. In short, the publisher controls all business aspects of the magazine. Salaries range from $30,000 to $100,000.

Advertising Director: Although we devote a whole section of this chapter to the advertising-sales process (see "Advertising Sales," p. 58), suffice it to say that the advertising director is the head honcho of this department with the considerable task of providing advertising revenues for the publication. Salaries range from $35,000 to $100,000.

Circulation Director: The circulation director is responsible for the development of newsstand sales and subscriptions. Again, the importance of the circulation division merits a separate section in this chapter (see "Circulation"). Salaries range from $30,000 to $75,000.

Production Manager: Negotiating printing contracts, ordering typography and color separations, day-to-day contacts with printers, interaction with editorial and art departments—these are some of the major duties of the production manager and staff. Salaries range from $25,000 to $55,000.

Promotion Director: As distinguished from the sales promotion manager, who works more closely with advertising sales, the promotion director and staff are charged with the duty of promoting the magazine and its image. In this respect, the job also involves public relations, which is sometimes handled in-house but more often by outside counsel. Salaries range from $25,000 to $45,000.

Business Manager: This is the individual who reports directly to the publisher on all areas of financial management, including cash flow and budget projections, profit-and-loss and monthly operating statements, preparing annual reports, and so on. Often, the business manager is an accountant or has an M.B.A.; he frequently is a corporate officer as well. Business school graduates with special interest in publishing would be wise to consider business management of a magazine. Many publishers have risen from the ranks of business managers. Salaries range from $30,000 to $65,000.

Research Director: Working under the advertising director, this individual is responsible for a magazine's research as it applies to ad sales. The research director has close liaison with the outside research specialists. A statistics and computer background is necessary for this function.

Single-Copy Sales Manager: This is the person who works with the magazine's national distributor

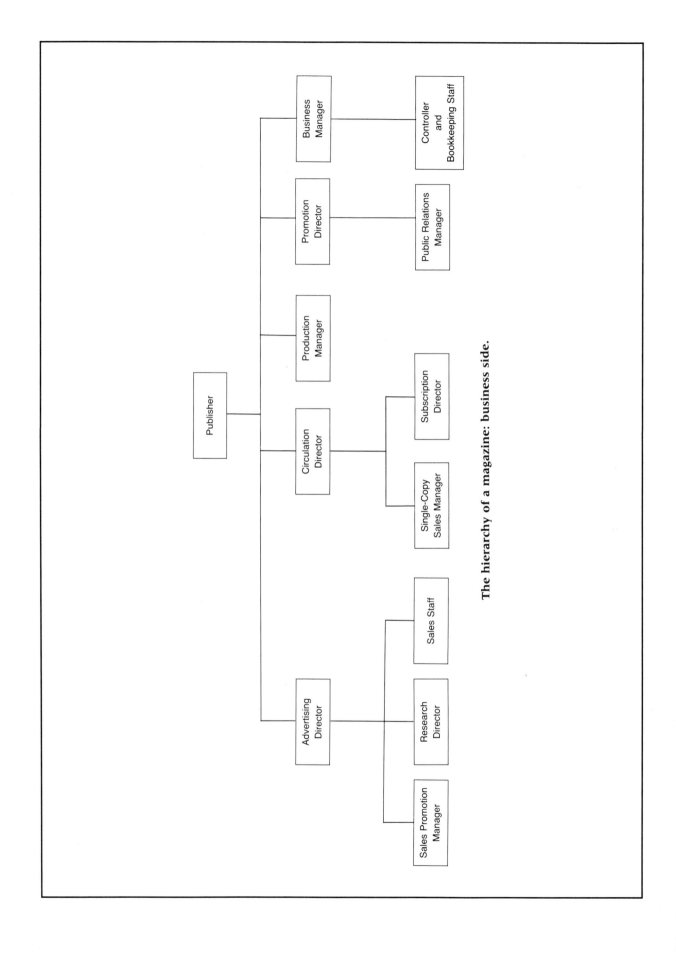

The hierarchy of a magazine: business side.

in achieving strong newsstand sales. It's a job that entails much travel to conventions and local wholesalers. Most single-copy sales managers start out working for a national distributor. The next step up may be assistant circulation director.

Subscription Director: Directly under the circulation director in rank, this individual is in charge of implementing all the subscription programs of the department. The job requires a total understanding of direct mail. (See later section in this chapter for outline of the entire circulation process.)

Advertising Sales

To someone on the editorial side of a magazine, a typical day in the life of a New York advertising salesperson looks like this:

He comes into the office at about 9:00 A.M., and after reading the morning paper over coffee, he makes the first phone call of the day, confirming his lunch date. Lunch is preeminent in the mind of a space salesperson, so there are more phone calls setting up lunch appointments for later in the week. Then he's off by foot for an 11:00 A.M. agency meeting eight blocks away ($2.20 taxi fare on the expense account). The media director to be seen is tied up in a client conference and has to cancel, but this doesn't perturb our friend the space salesperson, who passes a half-hour or so chatting with fellow space buddies in the reception room.

Then our salesperson is off to lunch at La Côte Basque with the product manager of one of his accounts. He greets the maitre d', a captain, two waiters, and at least three diners, thus establishing his familiarity in these plush digs and, he hopes, winning points with his client.

Two hours, two drinks, and $106 later, he's back at work and puts his head into the advertising director's office to announce, "I think we're on _____ 's schedule [the lunch date] for eight four-color pages." He makes a half-dozen phone calls setting up more future lunch appointments; by then, it's 4:50 P.M. and time to walk the few blocks to Grand Central to catch the 5:04 to Westport, where he'll have a couple of drinks at the station café before his wife picks him up.

All this for only $87,000 a year.

No doubt there are a few advertising-space salespeople who function this way. I don't know any. The life and times of people in ad sales are at best difficult. Yet the job pays well, and many who succeed at it go on to publishers' jobs; however, unlike editorial jobs where only the top people's performances are evaluated on a critical standard,

salespeople's results are tabulated on a calculator. If they miss their quota too often, they are replaced.

Advertising sales on magazines are big business. They jumped from about $3 million in 1980 to about $5 billion in the mid-'80s, as compared with newspapers' total advertising sales of about $3.5 billion in the mid-'80s. Consumer magazines draw about twice the volume of business, or trade, magazines.

The following is the recent ranking of the ten top consumer magazines in advertising revenues. The number-one publication, *Time* (a weekly), sells about $350 million worth of advertising space a year, and the tenth, *Reader's Digest* (a monthly), sells about $120 million worth a year. These rankings are in descending order: *Time, TV Guide, People, Sports Illustrated, Newsweek, Business Week, Good Housekeeping, Family Circle, Better Homes & Gardens,* and *Reader's Digest.*

One should keep in mind that magazines seldom make money on circulation, thus placing the profit potential of a publication almost solely on advertising-sales revenue.

For an understanding of the advertising sales function, let us assume that a consumer magazine has a circulation of 100,000 and is in the "home service" or "shelter" classification. It competes for ad dollars with seventy-five other regional and national publications, one of which, *Better Homes & Gardens,* has a circulation of 8 million and a total audience (including pass-along readers) of 32 million.

The hypothetical magazine's editorial thrust is the country lifestyle, thus making it a prime prospect for advertisers of building and renovation items, furnishings, antiques and collectibles, gardening items, wood-burning stoves, food, and so on. These advertisers and their advertising agencies are located all over the country.

To service these prospects, the magazine will employ its own sales staff plus sales representative organizations in areas where it is not economically feasible to have its own staff. The sales reps work on commission. The in-house staff is under the direction of ad managers, and over them is an ad director.

Our hypothetical home-service magazine with a circulation of 100,000 has its headquarters in Chicago, with sales offices in New York and Los Angeles. A rep firm is engaged in Atlanta to cover the Southeast and, in particular, the North Carolina furniture-manufacturing market. Because this is not a large-circulation magazine and advertising revenues are only about $1 million a year, the six-person in-house staff travels a great deal to cover about forty prospects each. Unlike our mythical

Six Short Tips: Getting into Advertising Sales

1. If you're still in school, get a job selling advertising space for your college newspaper. Getting turned down by the local record-store owner will be good training for getting turned down by more important people later on.

2. Consider where you would like to work. The big three advertising sales markets are New York, Chicago, and Los Angeles, in that order, but there are advertising agencies all over the country and, therefore, opportunities for a salesperson who is willing to relocate.

3. If you're a woman, note that space-selling opportunities for you have increased enormously in recent years. Nowadays women can (and indeed do) become advertising directors at major magazines. Consider sales-training courses designed specifically for women (such as those at David King's Careers for Women, 80 Fifth Avenue, New York, NY 10011).

4. Get a job selling classified advertising for your local Yellow Pages directory. It offers an excellent entry-level base, and these jobs are easier to get than selling jobs on a magazine.

5. Take any space-sales job at a consumer *or* business magazine even if it's at the low end of the totem pole. A successful record on one magazine will either lead to a promotion there or opportunities with increased salary and responsibilities at another magazine.

6. Get a job as an associate media planner at an advertising agency, an entry-level job where you'll be involved in developing the media plan. This work entails evaluating the various media. If you're good, you'll no doubt be promoted in short order to media planner. Then you'll be taken out to lunch every day by advertising-space salespeople. You can learn about their jobs and even get leads about job opportunities

friend who lunches daily at La Côte Basque, these people really hustle. They try to visit four or even five prospects a day and must see both the agency and client to develop an effective sales story. At an agency, they may be required to see eight or ten different people, all having responsibility for the same account.

Advertisers can easily come up with dozens of reasons why they don't want to buy space in this particular small-circulation home-service magazine—it doesn't have enough circulation; its competitors cover the market more effectively; its audience is too old or too young; its income level is too high or too low; or, they just don't like the magazine. All this sales resistance must be overcome creatively, with the further difficulty of having to sell advertising, an intangible commodity. Few advertisers can tell if advertising really works for them, perhaps only those who are in direct-response (i.e., coupon) advertising.

It is then small wonder that advertising people are well paid and that many are encouraged to entertain their prospects at fine restaurants. Advertising directors earn from $60,000 to $100,000 at major magazines. Salespeople earn starting salaries of $13,000 to $15,000 and usually work on a salary-plus-bonus or commission arrangement. Senior ad salespeople make between $45,000 and $65,000 yearly at both consumer and business magazines and are usually rewarded with numerous perks.

The ad salesperson is the foot soldier who is on the line all the time, but without a support staff, he cannot function effectively. From an informational and career standpoint, it's important to understand the other functions of this department.

Advertising Sales Promotion

On any magazine that carries a substantial amount of advertising, there is a sales promotion manager and staff. These creative people are charged with generating printed sales aids and programs used to solicit advertising. Their functions vary. These are some of the activities they perform on a day-to-day basis:

- Alerting advertisers to particular special issues of the magazine by use of printed material such as brochures.
- Arranging retail store promotions tying in advertisers, stores, and the magazine.
- Attending key industry conventions; arranging hospitality suites, and so on.
- Preparing special mailings to agencies and advertisers regarding research.
- Developing the media kit used by salespeople as "leave-behinds" on their sales call.
- Going on key sales calls with salespeople.

- Coordinating the magazine's public relations activity as it relates to advertising.

Salaries for a sales promotion manager range from $25,000 to $45,000.

Research

Today's sophisticated advertisers and marketers demand accuracy in their media buying. Once the decision is made by an advertiser and its agency to buy a schedule of advertising in magazines, the question then becomes: Which ones? Magazines spend a great deal of money defining the character of their audience—its demographics and psychographics. This is necessary ammunition for the advertising sales troops.

Some of this information is developed in house by a magazine's own research department, but more often it is provided by outside syndicated research companies. For example, advertising is bought on the basis of "total audience" rather than "total circulation." A research company in its field study must, therefore, determine how many pass-along readers a magazine has (pass-along readers are a secondary audience, that is, readers who do not actually purchase the publication). For example, the *National Lampoon,* which had a mid-1980s circulation of 290,000, actually had a pass-along factor of 8.41, which means that its "total audience" was 2,728,900.

If the reader is intrigued at this point about the subject of pass-along readership, here is a brief elaboration. Research companies such as Simmons and MRI (Mediamark Research Index) conduct a field study twice a year. Magazines pay for this statistical information. Once a magazine agrees to participate, it is committed to the results, which are then submitted to the advertising agencies that subscribe to the study.

The two studies measure magazine-reading time, along with other demographic information. The interviewers who work for the research companies visit homes and, by showing covers of recent issues of magazines and asking questions about the issues' contents, determine who the pass-along readers are.

The primary reader (who actually bought or subscribed to the magazine) and the pass-along readers are then given questionnaires measuring various data: education, income, and product usage. The results are then published for the benefit of both the agencies and the magazines. Most of the latter gather this data and evaluate it in house.

Advertising research is very challenging. For those with an understanding of computer practices

and a feeling for numbers, it can be a most rewarding career, one that pays well and offers the satisfaction of making sales by the skillful use of data. Salaries start at about $20,000. The salaries of research directors vary from $30,000 to $60,000.

Circulation

In 1960, the average price of a newsstand magazine was 39¢. A quarter-century later, that price had risen over five times to $2.05. Similarly, in 1960, the average yearly subscription price of a consumer magazine was $4.58, and that went up in the same period to $22.37. Even with these high prices, most publishers lose money on circulation. If this is the case, one may rightfully ask, why do publishers do it? We'll tell you how and why.

Advertisers want circulation and don't particularly care how a magazine gets it. Magazines, therefore, are forced to constantly increase their circulation to show vitality and to meet the advertisers' demands. Then, if the magazine sells enough advertising, it will counteract its unprofitable circulation and show a healthy bottom line.

Let's analyze the two basic sources of magazine circulation.

Single Copy: The Newsstand Jungle: Very few people in the business use the term "single copy." Most call it "newsstand," even though magazines are sold at many locations that are not newsstands. The actual process works like this: A magazine's printer ships all the copies designated for newsstands to approximately 550 wholesalers across the country: the wholesalers in turn route the copies to the 130,000 dealers in the United States and Canada; the dealers can be convenience stores, supermarkets, drug stores, and, yes, the corner newsstand.

All copies of the magazine are sold on consignment, which means that the dealer can return any unsold copies for full credit to the wholesaler, where they end up in the shredder. All this seems quite orderly and businesslike, except when one realizes that the average "newsstand" sells only 45 percent of the copies that are allocated for this purpose. Therein lies the unprofitability factor.

Why, you may ask, in today's computer society, can't publications regulate the number of copies they put out so that they can realize 80 or 90 percent sales? Unfortunately, the vagaries of distribution do not allow for greater efficiency. Yes, an occasional successful magazine like *Cosmopolitan*—which, incidentally, sells extremely well on college campuses—will sell more than 80 percent of its distribution, but most don't. The following magazines (*National Enquirer, Star,* and *Globe* are magazines by SRDS standards) have large newsstand sales, from a high of about 8.5 million for *TV Guide* (half its total circulation) to 3 million for *Penthouse* and 1.6 million for *Playboy.* They are listed in descending order of sales: *TV Guide, National Enquirer, Star, Penthouse, Globe, People,* and *Playboy.*

Newsstand percentage sales are privileged information; therefore, we cannot determine accurately the sales percentages for these magazines. We can estimate, however, that their sales average only 50 to 60 percent of the copies distributed.

Subscriptions: Many magazines that don't have much newsstand appeal because they are not entertainment oriented are forced to achieve their overall circulation objective by going the subscription route. *Reader's Digest* has 16.5 million subscribers, *TV Guide* has about 8.5 million, and *Sports Illustrated* has approximately 2.7 million. Again, in descending order, these are the top seven: *Reader's Digest, National Geographic, TV Guide, Better Homes & Gardens, Time, Newsweek,* and *Sports Illustrated.*

How do these publications reach these heights? The largest source for all magazines is "ordered by mail" and/or by "direct request." This accounts for fully 72.6 percent of all subscriptions. Who of us has seen a week go by without finding some hard-sell magazine subscription solicitation in his mailbox? In January, which is the most expedient month for these mailings, we can often count a few dozen of these pieces crammed into the box.

All this activity, plus the development of the other sources of subscription solicitation, requires a high degree of sophistication on the part of the specialists responsible for its preparation.

A fuller understanding of the circulation function is necessary to grasp its importance in the publishing process. There are a number of interesting and remunerative job classifications available in circulation. Many pay on commission:

- *College subscription representatives* solicit subscriptions on behalf of one or a number of magazines. It's a good way to get started.
- *Newsstand field salespeople* work directly for magazines or their national distributors covering a fixed sales territory. They visit supermarkets, convenience stores, and the like, setting up displays and promoting sales. This is often a good entry-level job with some long-range promotion possibilities.
- *Direct-mail copywriters* write those persuasive mail solicitations. This requires a very specialized type of writing, requiring great skill. Free-

lance writers can earn $2,000 to $4,000 for writing just *one* direct-mail letter.
- *A major magazine's own circulation managers and assistants* employ many talented people who, on a day-to-day basis, plan and execute the strategy, tactics, and systems necessary to implement an effective circulation program.

[For a more extensive look at circulation, see Leonard Mogel, *The Magazine: Everything You Need to Know to Make It in the Magazine Business* (Prentice-Hall, 1979).]

Consumer and business magazines require circulation departments. The jobs here are less glamourous than those in editorial and pay less than those in advertising sales, but they are a good steppingstone within a publishing organization to the top jobs. Many publishers got their start in circulation.

Production

We saw earlier in this chapter how *Time*'s editorial people handled the Iceland summit meeting. Not to be overlooked is the achievement of their production people, whose minute attention to detail accomplished their difficult objective.

The production staff was responsible for the electronically produced typesetting and the reproduction of the photographs. They supervised the operations of the ten printing plants and the ultimate shipping of the completed copies to the nation's newsstand delivery points and post offices.

There are constantly new technological advances in magazine production. Today, with sophisticated laser scanners, we are able to process color transparencies and artwork in minutes. Recent developments in phototypesetting utilize OCR (optical character recognition), sometimes called "the incredible reading machine." The operator types the manuscript on a special typewriter with a few symbols or commands. The typed paper is fed into the OCR, which "reads" the page and then sets the required type in any of *500* different typefaces—all this at 1,105 characters a minute and without sacrificing quality. If you've ever seen a Linotype in an old newspaper plant, you'll better appreciate this development. Herr Gutenberg, who invented movable type around 1440, would be proud. In magazine printing plants, we now see giant presses that can print up to 400,000 thirty-two-page color sections in a three-shift day.

Shepherding a magazine, big or small, through all these phases is the formidable job of production people. Experience in the graphic arts techniques are the requisites for a job in production, but there are always opportunities for trainees. Production salaries, which range from $25,000 to $45,000, are on a level with those of other business-side staffers, with the exception of those rogues in advertising sales. Another difference between these two job classifications not to be overlooked is that, while ad salespeople do the taking to lunch, production people are the ones who are taken to lunch at the same fine restaurants by their suppliers.

Production is a rewarding career with stability, even if it's lacking in glamour.

Sales Promotion: The Story of a Success

The cover of the February 10, 1986, issue of *Sports Illustrated* was graced with the alluring charms of scantily clad model Elle Macpherson. No swimming star was she—Elle was there to promote the twenty-third annual *Sports Illustrated* swimsuit issue.

This momentous occasion spurred *SI*'s advertising people to sell a record 137 ad pages. In 1985, the swimsuit issue sold 795,000 copies on the newsstands. In 1986, that figure went to more than 800,000, almost *eight* times their average newsstand sale.

On the eve of the release of this issue, *SI* threw a bash at its headquarters for a select few hundred of its advertisers and agency people. And guess who was there to greet them—of course, Elle Macpherson, who turned on her biggest smile as she autographed large-size posters of the cover.

In addition to being served the usual party food and drinks, the guests were shown a short film featuring Elle and her sister models—also scantily clad—as they were shooting the cover and the twelve inside swimsuit pages in the sun-soaked island of Bora Bora in the South Seas. After being given a copy of the magazine for their very own, the guests returned home with the memories of an evening well spent. The next day, New York newspapers, radio, and TV gave *SI*'s swimsuit issue nearly the same coverage as they gave the controversial election in the Philippines and the ousting of Haiti's "Baby Doc" Duvalier.

Consider first the financial benefits of this issue to Time, Inc.'s *Sports Illustrated*. In an average week it sells 100,000 to 150,000 copies on the newsstands. This time it sold about *two million* copies, for more than $2 million in additional newsstand sales revenue. The issue sold $14 million in advertising revenues, a huge increase over the regular issues' revenues, plus great image-building and good will with readers and advertisers.

Sports Illustrated's competitors *Inside Sports* and *Sport* both publish swimsuit issues in attempts to rival *SI*. It's hard to match the appeal of this one. (Reprinted with permission: Brian Lanker for *Sports Illustrated*, © Time Inc.; Elle Macpherson/ Ford Models.)

Sports Illustrated's swimsuit promotion is a textbook example of fine sales promotion and public-relations technique. Many talented people working diligently for many months combined efforts to make it happen. A discussion of their specific activities will offer us a clearer understanding of the functions of sales promotion and public relations:

- The art director of the magazine and his staff of photographers, stylists, and fashion coordinators worked for many months choosing the locations, interviewing the models, and making the arrangements for the shooting itself.
- The advertising salespeople and their sales promotion team prepared literature and presentations that were used by the sales staff to encourage new and existing advertisers to participate in this special issue.

- The circulation department had the job of alerting its magazine wholesalers and thousands of dealers across the country that this was the big issue of the year, with a distribution of eight or ten times the regular number of copies. The retailers were asked to display the magazine prominently in order to obtain even higher sales (such requests are made and granted continually in this industry). Circulation advertising was also used on the local level to implement this promotion.
- The sales promotion department made the arrangements for the party. These included arranging for the food and drink, printing the posters, and planning the guest list.
- Finally, the public relations people had the major responsibility of getting the message out to the trade and general press.

As we can see, it was a team effort involving many talented people. Sales promotion jobs are available on other magazines, too, although decidedly few have swimsuit issues.

Public Relations

A business, or trade, magazine is integrally involved with its industry's trade shows and conventions. There the magazine must put its best foot forward. This can include conducting parties in hospitality suites, printing daily convention newspapers, distributing literature and samples, or scheduling a speech by the magazine's editor to the convention participants.

Magazine public relations on a day-to-day basis takes many forms. It can be as simple as sending a press release to an advertising trade publication announcing a special issue of the magazine or an increase in rates or circulation, or as demanding as arranging an editor's coast-to-coast trip, which could include newspaper and radio interviews and appearances on talk shows.

Writing ability is a good prerequisite for a job in the dynamic fields of sales promotion and public relations. Creativity is always a plus.

To help the beginner explore sales promotion and publicity, we offer a few suggestions:

- An organization of importance is the New York Publicity Club. Address: 404 Park Avenue South, New York, NY 10016.
- The national association for PR people is PRSA (Public Relations Society of America). Address: 845 Third Avenue, New York, NY 10022.
- The trade magazine for PR is called *Publicist*, put out by PRSA, New York Publicity Club, and a

private firm called PR Aids. Address: same as for PRSA.
- *Media Memos* is a quarterly newsletter for marketing and media executives about promotion. A typical recent issue had two excellent promotion ideas used by the *American Journal of Surgery* and *Builder* magazine. For information on this newsletter, write to Julie A. Laitin Enterprises, Inc., 170 West End Avenue, New York, NY 10023.

The Ten Hottest Magazines

The superb marketing/advertising publication *AD-WEEK* loves doing "The Ten Best." Once a year, it selects the ten hottest magazines on the basis of increase in actual and percentage dollar volume. Here are their most recent choices in descending order: *American Health, Parade, New Woman, Modern Maturity, Country Living, Gourmet, Rolling Stone, Car and Driver, Home,* and *Motor Trend*

CAREER TIP: Why not go with the winners? If you think you have the talent the top ten magazines can use, give them a try. Or seek out the magazines just under them in the same classifications, such as *Road & Track, Smithsonian, Working Mother,* and *Ebony*.

American Health reached the top in only its fourth year of publication. *Parade* is a large-circulation Sunday supplement with ad revenues of almost $200 million. *New Woman* is owned by publishing baron Rupert Murdoch, who is giving it the support to go to the top. *Modern Maturity* is for the older set; it made the "Ten Hottest" list in three of the previous four years. *Country Living*'s circulation went from 750,000 to 1.5 million in only three years.

Gourmet has been around for a long time. Once Condé Nast acquired it, circulation and advertising zoomed. Shedding its hippy, alternative-culture image, *Rolling Stone* went straight, and it paid off. Ad revenues were at about $30 million by the mid-1980s. *Car and Driver*'s success mirrors the growth of the auto industry as does the number ten book, *Motor Trend. Home* is owned by Knapp Communications, the *Architectural Digest* people.

Although some of the editorial content concerns service reminders and developments in automotive research from Germany, other recent articles were on general subjects such as understanding the information on a wine label or where to stay while visiting Washington, D.C.

In keeping with the company's sophisticated marketing techniques, the magazine is well produced and edited and is even used by college journalism departments as a teaching tool. Many libraries keep copies on microfilm for future reference to older-model cars.

Opportunities for Women

Women are making a tremendous impact on the magazine business, both in the number of publications serving their interests and in the job market at the executive level. Standard Rate & Data Service (SRDS), in a recent edition of its directory, lists thirty-six publications for women. Indicative of the rapidly growing trend of women in the workplace are magazines like *Working Mother* and *Working Woman.*

Perhaps more significant is the rise of women on the editorial side of magazines as well as the business side. Twenty-five years ago only a handful of editors and hardly any space salespeople were women. Today, tokenism barely exists at most magazines. The question now asked is, "Can she do the job?"

Pat Carbine publishes *Ms.,* Marianne Howatson publishes *Travel & Leisure,* and Kathy Keeton is the president of *Omni,* while Helen Gurley Brown edits *Cosmopolitan.* Pat Miller is the editor/publisher of *New Woman,* and Paige Rense is the editor of *Architectural Digest.* But what is of greater importance to women coming into the magazine field is that just below these leaders are dozens of associate publishers, advertising directors, and managing editors ready for their move to the top.

Company-Sponsored Magazines

Here's a new trend—magazines like *Volkswagen's World,* published by the automobile manufacturer for its 200,000-plus owners in the United States. It is issued four times a year.

Metropolitan, Regional, and State Magazines: Good Local Opportunities

If in the past you wanted to stay near home and write, you got a job on a local newspaper. That still may be an approach, but newspapers are not the growth area they used to be. Today many large cities have only one or two newspapers.

Metropolitan magazines, however, have had an exceptional uptrend in the last twenty-five years. Also, they are no longer chamber-of-commerce handouts. Most are provocative and hard-hitting publications with independent editorial policies and extensive coverage of local politics, sports, and entertainment.

Texas Monthly, for example, was launched in 1972 by Michael Levy. It has been successful almost from the outset, with sparkling graphics and crisp writing throughout. No puff pieces here. In the issue shown, there are four articles of provocative interest: one on the current oil revolution and what it means to Texas; another called "Confessions of an Aging Pothead," a funny piece on a man who makes bad, cheap movies in Texas; and an insightful article by the magazine's former editor on his Vietnam experiences.

The articles of local interest are so well presented that one might find himself attracted to Texas even though it is a place he has never thought of visiting. The formula has paid off for advertising as well. There are ads for Neiman-Marcus and other local stores, along with national ads for whiskeys, cars, and tourism. *Texas Monthly* is big—usually more than 200 pages (of which about 45 percent is advertising), and it matches the state in vitality. The

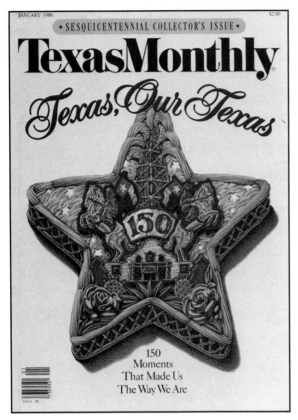

JANUARY 1986
★ SESQUICENTENNIAL COLLECTOR'S ISSUE ★
$2.00

TexasMonthly

Texas, Our Texas

150

150
Moments
That Made Us
The Way We Are

The cover of *Texas Monthly*'s sesquicentennial issue, January 1986. One of the best metropolitan magazines in the country, *Texas Monthly* has won many awards for editorial excellence. (Reprinted with permission from *Texas Monthly* magazine.)

magazine is, by the way, available in a limited number of libraries and newsstands outside Texas.

The *SRDS Consumer Magazine Directory* lists 130 publications in the metropolitan category. All have a monthly circulation of more than 100,000. The following are some representative titles: *Alaska, Chicago, Los Angeles, New Jersey Monthly, Ohio, Philadelphia, Texas Monthly,* and *Washingtonian.*

All are audited by the Audit Bureau of Circulation (ABC). Advertisers and agencies accept these audits totally and rely on them for media evaluation and planning.

Within this group, there is a trend for further specialization—metropolitan magazines about subjects like real estate, gardening, and business. Consider, for example, *Colorado Homes and Lifestyles, California Business, Indianapolis Business Journal,* and *Phoenix Home and Garden.* In New York, the people who publish the very important *Advertising Age* now put out *Crain's New York Business;* and the owners of *Philadelphia* magazine launched *Manhattan, Inc.* This lively metropolitan magazine about New York's

business and its leaders came out in 1984. By the end of its first year, it had 50,000 monthly circulation and was well on its way to success.

For additional information on metropolitan magazines, write to the City and Regional Magazine Association, 801 Second Avenue, New York, NY 10022.

Fitness and Health Magazines

The '80s saw a dramatic increase in America's commitment to physical fitness, diet, and health awareness. Concomitant with this interest is the introduction of many new magazines on these subjects—with more to follow.

First published in 1981, *American Health* had a circulation of about 800,000 by the time it was five years old. Decathlon star Bruce Jenner lends his name and affiliation to *Bruce Jenner's Better Health and Living.* Rodale Press's *Prevention* magazine has been around since 1950; it has a circulation of almost 3 million. Condé Nast's *Self,* launched in 1978, carries about $20 million in advertising linage (total amount of advertising, determined by the page) and has a circulation of about 1 million. I first published *Weight Watchers* magazine in 1968; its recent circulation is 900,000.

Getting Hired in the Magazine Industry

When it comes to looking for a job or changing jobs in magazine publishing, the question invariably asked is: "Should I work for a large publisher or a small one?" The answer is complex and really depends on a number of considerations. Here are a few:
Geography: The three largest consumer magazine companies are in New York. Many publishers with head offices in other locations maintain large advertising sales offices in New York. *Playboy* is still in Chicago, and *Architectural Digest* is in California; nevertheless, if you really want to make it in this

business, you'll have to face up to living in or near the Big Apple and paying the numbing rents.

The Case for Bigness: Often we read in the publishing trades about a Time, Inc., executive moving from one of its publications to another with a promotion. This happens at CBS and Condé Nast and other giants as well, and, of course, jobs within their corporate spheres are posted for their own employees before being offered to outsiders. The news about someone with talent and dedication to his job travels fast and soon reaches the chambers of top management. The rest follows.

The Case for Smallness: In a small publishing company, or even in a one-magazine situation, there is a distinct opportunity to learn many jobs by virtue of being exposed to them. Also, a number of such companies are located outside of New York, Chicago, and Los Angeles, making them attractive to those preferring to work in smaller cities. Companies within this category include those that publish *TV Guide, National Geographic, U.S. News & World Report,* the *Saturday Evening Post, Smithsonian,* a dozen automotive magazines, and of course a host of metropolitan and regional entries.

Another question we hear is: "What is the best approach to take in getting a magazine publishing job?" We will not repeat here what has been written in dozens of fine career books about résumés or the countless tips offered the job applicant.

Magazine companies, like those in other fields, have human resources and personnel departments. For the entry-level person, there probably is no way to bypass this traditional route. If one is attempting to improve a job situation by moving from one company to another, however, it is a good idea to write directly to the department head of that magazine. The letter might still end up in the wastebasket, but it's worth a try.

Further, any personal contact should be exploited whether that person is at the top or not. A college friend who works as an associate media planner at an ad agency may be a good source for ideas and leads about magazine space sales.

For those readers who desire to make the big move to the big publisher, here are the big four in consumer magazines and some of their publications:

Diamondis Communications, Inc.
1515 Broadway
New York, NY 10036

Car & Driver
Cycling
Field and Stream
Flying

Mechanix Illustrated
Popular Photography
Road and Track
Skiing
Stereo Review
Woman's Day

Condé Nast Publications, Inc.
350 Madison Avenue
New York, NY 10017

Bride's
Gentlemen's Quarterly
Glamour
House & Garden
New Yorker
Mademoiselle
Self
Vanity Fair
Vogue

Time, Inc
Time & Life Building
1271 Avenue of the Americas
New York, NY 10020

Discover
Fortune
Life
Money
People
Sports Illustrated
Time

Hearst Corporation
224 West 57th Street
New York, NY 10019

Cosmopolitan
Good Housekeeping
Harper's Bazaar
House Beautiful
Popular Mechanics
Sports Afield
Town & Country

There are also a number of multimagazine companies in the business, or trade, field. They include the following:

Cahners Publishing Company
221 Columbus Avenue
Boston, MA 02116

Harcourt Brace Jovanovich Publications
757 Third Avenue
New York, NY 10017

McGraw-Hill, Inc.
1221 Avenue of the Americas
New York, NY 10020

Penton/IPC
1111 Chester Avenue
Cleveland, OH 44114

Although there are not many employment agencies specializing in magazine publishing job opportunities, these two merit consideration if you're coming to New York for your search:

Howard Sloan Associates, Inc.
545 Fifth Avenue
New York, NY 10017

Jerry Fields Associates
515 Madison Avenue
New York, NY 10017

Folio:, The Magazine for Magazine People

Folio:, the most important trade publication for magazine publishers, was started in 1972. As we've said previously about a number of other trade publications, *Folio:* is an education in the magazine business. Its astute publisher, Joe Hanson, published *Folio:* on a controlled (free) circulation basis until 1977. (During those first five years, it was more important for him to reach all the influential business and consumer magazine publishers than it was to have a paid circulation and serve only a limited number. The revenue came from advertising sales.) *Folio:* was also a bi-monthly until 1977, when it became a monthly and began charging a subscription fee. It now has a circulation of 10,000 at a subscription rate of $58.00 per year.

Realizing that ad revenues from his magazine were not, by themselves, sufficient to support his operation, in 1975 Hanson launched the first Face to Face Publishing Conference. To attend its workshop seminars, publishing professionals paid the fees necessary for *Folio:*'s early survival. The annual fall conference in New York now has 200-plus seminars, and there are additional *Folio:* conferences in Atlanta in September, in Los Angeles in February, and in Chicago in April. Professional magazine people from all over the country come to the workshops to listen to industry leaders.

Here is a sampling of subjects discussed at the conference seminars: launching a magazine on a low budget, how to succeed in newsletters, analyz-

Folio: is the magazine industry's bible. In this excellent cover, the reader is drawn into the issue with five significant pieces. The lead article on writing is a standout. (Reprinted with permission.)

ing your magazine's covers, basics of selling magazine advertising, magazine writing workshop, the craft of interviewing, basics of printing, creative magazine design, and basics of magazine circulation.

In addition to *Folio:*, the company publishes several useful reference books. One is *The Folio: 400*, an annual ranking of magazine publishers by revenues and dozens of other categories. Another is *The Folio: Ad Guide*, published each June; covering consumer and business magazines, it is a detailed analysis of advertising on a category-by-category and classification-by-classification basis. It is a valuable reference tool for the magazine industry.

Folio: and its subsidiary publications are geared to the professional; however, the beginner and magazine publishing aspirant can gain much from subscribing. For information, write to *Folio:* 6 River Bend, P.O. Box 4949, Stamford, CT 06907–0949.

The Future of Magazines

If you're going to give your all to making it in magazines, you'll want to know what the future looks like.

The trend to bigness continues. A recent article in *Folio:* reported on two major acquisitions in the magazine business. The ubiquitous press and film (20th Century–Fox) baron Rupert Murdoch paid $350 million for Ziff-Davis's business magazines. He thus acquired twelve titles, including *Aviation Daily, Hotel & Travel Index, Weekly of Business Aviation,* and *World Travel Directory.* This acquisition boomed Murdoch into a top position in business magazines and added to his already profitable consumer publications, *New York* and *New Woman.*

CBS Publishing, which already owned ten magazines, including *Road and Track* and *Field and Stream,* got even bigger by plunking down the huge sum of $362.5 million for twelve Ziff-Davis consumer magazines, including *Car & Driver, Modern Bride, Popular Photography,* and *Stereo Review.* In late summer 1987, the parent company of CBS spun off its magazine division to a group of its top executives.

For the new entrant into the magazine business, Murdoch Magazines and CBS may be good places to go for jobs. A top-notch ad salesperson on one CBS magazine may not make ad director on his own book but may be moved to another in that company's stable.

The Ad Squeeze

When the economy shows weakness, one of the first casualties is advertising. When advertising budgets are cut, so goes magazine revenues. In addition, liquor and tobacco, two pillars of magazine ad revenue, have suffered reduced sales in recent years, causing much less spending in these important classifications. For the future, with fewer people smoking and with drinking patterns changing, the magazine industry will have to look to other categories to replace these revenues.

Business magazines, as well, are facing a crunch because of the dramatic reduction in computer-related advertising. For magazines such as *Fortune* and *Business Week,* the drops are as significant as 15 to 20 percent from 1985 to 1986. These and other consumer and trade magazines will have to hustle to replace this business with advertising from other categories.

In the early '80s there were eight mass market science magazines, all flourishing. Then came the inevitable shakeout. The big reason—ad revenue losses. By the middle of the decade there were only three left: *Discover* (merged with *Science 86*); *Omni;* and *Scientific American,* which was founded in 1845 and sold in 1986 to a West German publisher. Will they all last? We think so. What would a future be like without science magazines?

Magazines for Trendies, Yuppies, and Other Upscalers

At this point, we've all had it with magazine and newspaper pieces about Baby Boomers growing up, moving to newly gentrified big-city neighborhoods, and living lavish lifestyles.

Magazines appealing to this ever-increasing group are, however, cashing in. Here are a few examples, all with a circulation of more than 400,000: *American Health, Esquire, Food & Wine, Gentlemen's Quarterly, House & Garden, Success!, Vanity Fair,* and *Working Woman.*

Magazines on Computer Screens

It was inevitable. As a promotional device, *Playboy* now offers a free preview of the magazine to Macintosh computer owners. In addition to text, they even receive black-and-white computer-generated photos of the Playmate of the Month. It is hoped that this upscale audience will then rush down to the newsstand for the real thing.

Summing Up

Wall Street regards magazines as a growth industry. Witness the astronomical prices paid for some properties. *The New Yorker,* for example, is reported to earn about $5 million a year, yet Condé Nast paid $165 million for this property. Then, too, advertising revenues in the 1980s were more than eight times the revenues in the 1950s. And since 1954, magazine per-issue circulation has grown 91 percent, while in that same period the adult population has increased only 61 percent.

Anyone considering magazines as his life's work, however, should look at the negative factors as well. CBS Publishing paid $362.5 million for the Ziff-Davis properties; then it sued Ziff-Davis, claiming that it had overpaid on the basis of the magazines' real worth. *The New Yorker* is a prestige, culturally oriented magazine; clearly, though, part of the reason for its high acquisition price (far above the usual purchase multiple) is what Condé Nast regards as its potential, not its present real value.

As for the more than 300 new magazines started each year, most will fail for various reasons: lack of capital, no real market for the publication, or insufficient experience on the part of the principals. Thus, how many start is insignificant. What's important is how many cross the finish line.

Furthermore, inflationary factors account for a major portion of that eight-times increase in advertising revenues. Just as telling, in the mid-1980s we saw a scaling down of ad spending, particularly for liquor and cigarettes.

Finally, one should consider that magazines are a relatively small industry, centered in New York and a few other major cities. Employment, therefore, is limited, certainly as compared with a nonmedia industry like finance.

For myself, however, magazines have been a fascinating career for thirty-five years. It is a glamourous, exciting field, one that beckons bright, motivated people.

Magazine Publishing Internships

The following is a partial list of magazine internships available to undergraduates and recent graduates. It is also a good idea to contact the metropolitan magazine in the nearest city for possible opportunities. A more complete list of internships appears in *16,000 on-the-Job Training Opportunities for All Types of Careers*, available from Writer's Digest Books. Address: 9933 Alliance Road, Cincinnati, OH 45242.

American Society of Magazine Editors
575 Lexington Avenue
New York, NY 10022
Approximately fifty paid positions are available each summer in this ten-week internship in magazine editorial work.

Boston Magazine
1050 Park Square Building
Boston, MA 02116

Eight unsalaried editorial positions and one art position are available. Duration: about four and a half months. The program is offered three times a year during spring and summer semesters. College credit is available.

Columbia Journalism Review
Internship Program
700 Journalism Building
Columbia University
New York, NY 10027
A number of nonsalaried part- and full-time positions are available. The sessions generally run from January to May, June to August, and September to December. College credit may be arranged.

Dell Publishing Co., Inc.
1 Dag Hammarskjöld Plaza
New York, NY 10017
Four to six salaried positions are available in accounting/finance, marketing, operations/services, advertising/promotion/publicity, and editorial.

East/West Network, Inc.
5900 Wilshire Boulevard
Los Angeles, CA 90036
Three to four nonsalaried positions are available in the editorial and art departments. College credit is required.

Los Angeles Magazine
1888 Century Park East
Los Angeles, CA 90067
Five nonsalaried positions are available each semester and during the summer. College credit may be arranged.

McCall's Magazine
230 Park Avenue
New York, NY 10169
Four salaried editorial positions are available; open to college graduates.

Magazine Publishers Association M.B.A. Intern Program
575 Lexington Avenue
New York, NY 10022
Fifteen to twenty salaried positions are available; open to a limited number of M.B.A. students between their first and second year of graduate business school.

Newsweek
444 Madison Avenue
New York, NY 10022
Six salaried summer internship positions are available.

Philadelphia Magazine
1500 Walnut Street
Philadelphia, PA 19102

Four to six nonsalaried editorial positions are available. Duration: two to four months. College credit is available.

13-30 Corporation, Internships
505 Market Street
Knoxville, TN 37902

Between two and five interns are selected for salaried positions available during each of the four sessions offered.

Writer's Digest
9933 Alliance Road
Cincinnati, OH 45242

A number of salaried positions are available.

Yankee Publishing, Inc.
Dublin, NH 03444

The program provides forty to fifty salaried positions on a number of magazines concerned with preservation and conservation. Duration: average of twelve weeks. The program is offered every summer and during the school year as part of work-study programs. Send requests for applications to the National Trust for Historic Preservation, 45 School Street, Boston, MA 02108.

Two Interviews

Our two interviewees have long and distinguished careers in magazine publishing. Kathy Keeton is the founder of *Omni* magazine. Jim Horton's *Working Woman* was dubbed one of America's "hottest" magazines in 1982 and '83 by *ADWEEK*. What they have to say should be of special interest to readers considering magazine publishing as their profession.

Kathy Keeton is the author of *Woman of Tomorrow* (St. Martin's/Marek), published in 1986. In it she says, "My dream for tomorrow's woman is not that she compete for greater recognition in a man's world, but that she influence their common future with her own intellect, values, and perceptions."

As a young woman, Keeton studied dance at London's prestigious Sadlers Wells Ballet School. She used her years of classical dance training to launch a more lucrative career in modern dance, playing theaters, supper clubs, and in films, includ-

ing an appearance in *The Spy Who Came in from the Cold.*

Later, her interest in the world of business and commerce led to magazine publishing in the United States, where she ultimately became the president of *Omni,* a science magazine with a circulation of 800,000 and a total readership of almost 5 million.

Although your success has been widely publicized—in 1984 you were named the Periodical and Book Association of America's Publisher of the Year—how did the daughter of a South African farmer go from selling magazine ad space to becoming president of Omni *magazine and one of the most highly paid women executives in the world?*

Simple—hard work and an unrelenting passion to learn. Science, technology, and the "high frontier" of space have been a part of my psyche ever since I was growing up on my family's farm in South Africa. In those early years, I read as much of Edgar Rice Burroughs, H. G. Wells, Isaac Asimov, and Arthur C. Clarke as I could get my hands on, and I dreamed constantly of becoming a scientist. My family discouraged science because science was not for girls, so I was steered into ballet instead. It was years later that I was able to begin to channel that love of scientific discovery into *Omni* magazine.

We'll ask it right out: Are there still any major obstacles for women in magazine publishing today?

I don't believe that there are any major obstacles for women anywhere in America. Doors are open for women everywhere today to do pretty much anything they want to do; however, I have strong feelings about where women should begin to apply themselves if they really want to excel. Women need to carve out careers in scientific and technical fields. It's not enough for women to want to be lawyers, executives, and politicians. The future is shaped by those who generate new knowledge, create new products, and find new options for solving the problems of humanity—hunger, overpopulation, energy, and other resource shortages, and even the dangers caused by unwise use of technology today.

When I began doing research for my book *Woman of Tomorrow,* I was disheartened to learn that only 13 percent of all the scientists and engineers in the United States are women. Evidence everywhere suggests that large numbers of us sidestep math and science, ignoring the job boom in technical fields and sending sons, not daughters, to computer camps.

And yet, science and technology are the greatest forces for change in the world today. Women can do better in these fields, on average, than anywhere else. Women will never share power with men—nor should they—until they overcome their fear of science and master technology.

Space selling is one of the glamour jobs in magazines—fancy lunches, big salaries, and so on. Is there any special training and preparation you might suggest for someone seeking entrance in this field?

Persistence, persistence, persistence. In advertising sales, as in any other sales, "no" is never an acceptable response. Sales requires that you be more creative, take greater risks, and push harder than any of your competition. Learn as much about your clients—their hobbies, likes, and dislikes—and use that knowledge at every opportunity. You will get the sale.

Omni *is a success story of recent publishing history. In 1980, it was awarded the coveted title of Magazine of the Year by the American Society of Journalists and Authors. What special marketing techniques did you use in putting over this unique concept?*

By adhering strenuously to a commitment to put the needs of the readers first. If you expect your readers to return to the newsstands month after month for a copy of your magazine, then they must always be uppermost in your mind—not the advertisers, not the printers, not your competition, but your readers.

Omni readers understand that tomorrow will be different from today, and they turn to *Omni* to catch the clearest, most prophetic visions, so we hire the brightest, most knowledgeable editors and illustrators available. Our readers understand that before scientific discovery and technological development become reality, someone first has to dream—fantastic dreams that no one else has the courage to dream—so each issue contains world-class science fiction.

Publishing a magazine dedicated solely to its readers is not the least costly approach by any means. However, we know our readers don't want and won't buy a second-class product—and why should they?

I remember having an appointment with you some years back at 8:30 in the morning and was surprised to see a whole office full of people busily at work at that early hour. How do you manage to instill this old-fashioned work ethic in your staff working on such a trendy magazine?

I hire the best staff possible and leave them alone, provided they meet assigned objectives. In addition, I have always managed my time by adherence to a rule to make quick decisions on small matters and encourage my staff to employ the same technique. I

have also learned to rely more and more on the computer to manage my time for everything from routine scheduling to important research. My staff widely uses the computer as well.

Most successful publishers have development teams exploring new magazine ideas. Without divulging any privileged information, what areas of publishing do you think still represent growth possibilities?

Electronic publishing. Recently, *Omni* magazine went on-line on the CompuServe Network, and early indications suggest wide use and strong growth potential. With ever-increasing ownership and use of personal computers, electronic publishing is clearly one area likely to expand in percentages vastly larger than those of traditional print publishing.

James B. Horton began his career as an advertising salesman for the *Wall Street Journal* and moved on to *American Home,* where he rose to assistant to the president of the Curtis magazine division.

After leaving Curtis, he became the first director of print media relations for Young & Rubicam. In 1968, he became publisher of *Atlas* and then the vice-president of CRM, Inc., creators of *Psychology Today* and *Intellectual Digest.* Horton then went on to become general manager of the National Observer for Dow Jones and Co. He next became group vice-president of Playboy Enterprises, Inc., where he launched *Food and Wine* magazine for that company. Afterwards (1978), he took over a bankrupt woman's monthly, *Working Woman,* and built it into a highly profitable $20 million-per-year business.

Horton earned his B.A. from Columbia University and an M.B.A. from New York University. He is an adjunct assistant professor of publishing for New York University, where he lectures on the opportunities and pitfalls of magazine management.

You were an ad agency person for many years before getting into magazines. From the standpoint of career opportunity, what do you perceive as the difference between the two media?

I think it's a question of different strokes for different folks. Personally, I have always found publishing a good deal more rewarding than advertising. I suppose that's because I believe that the movement of information and knowledge in our society is the critical problem and opportunity of our times.

I'm sure there are a lot of valuable, useful products out there, but personally I find it hard to get my gut into spending my life persuading customers to switch brands of soap powder, cigarettes or dog food. That's not to say, however, that advertising doesn't offer some exciting and challenging jobs.

Is magazine publishing getting its share of bright young people today, or are they being sidetracked into the more lucrative fields of Wall Street and the law?

Magazine publishing is a small industry. By and large, young people are not aware of the opportunities, particularly on the business side, and it is true that at the entry level, Wall Street and the law offer better immediate rewards.

Are there any departments of a magazine, such as ad sales, circulation, promotion, or editorial, where, in your opinion, the demand for talent exceeds the supply?

Supply really exceeds demand in the editorial area, which helps to explain why entry-level salaries are so low. Every spring a swarm of graduates from New England colleges come paddling their canoes down the Hudson with stars in their eyes and English diplomas in their hands. I hope they all have rich daddies. Otherwise they won't survive the high costs and pitiful salaries of New York.

Many young people are beginning to realize the potential in advertising sales. In publishing, advertising is the fast track to big bucks. Unfortunately, it's an area where every employer wants experience, but few are willing to provide it.

As circulation revenues become more important, wide-ranging opportunities are opening up in both the subscription and newsstand areas: promotion, purchasing, analysis, marketing, distribution, subscriber service, and field sales. Production is also becoming increasingly important. Manufacturing now accounts for 50 percent of the cost structure of many magazines.

In general, it's good to remember that compensation is equal to the square of the distance from the source of the revenue. In publishing, that means entry-level jobs in advertising pay most and those in editorial pay least.

This is a question that comes up in other areas as well as in magazines, but it is of prime importance to the recent college graduate about to enter the magazine industry. Is it better to go to work for a small one-magazine company or for a large organization such as CBS, Hearst, or McGraw-Hill?

It depends on how you see your career. If you are a generalist, you will learn more about publishing in a small company. If you want in-depth knowledge about a particular area, big companies are better. Small companies for breadth, big companies for depth.

Personally, I've always found small companies more fun. It's also easier to move from a small company to a big one than vice-versa. That's because big companies spoil their employees with an expensive lifestyle and a large support system. In a small company, you are often your own support system, and you have to watch the expenditures closely.

Most consumer and business magazines have their headquarters in New York. What advice can you give someone who loves the magazine publishing business but would hesitate moving to New York because of the extremely high cost of living?

Unquestionably, there are opportunities outside New York, particularly with the growing number of local and regional magazines, but New York is still the nexus of the business. If you won't go to New York, you are isolating yourself from 80 percent of the business and 80 percent of the opportunity. Besides, it's the most stimulating, exciting city in the world, particularly for young people. True, you have to have a taste for McDonald's, small, shabby apartments, lots of roommates, and the subway, but that can be fun too—at least for a while.

There are people reading this book who are willing to defy the 10-to-1 odds against succeeding with the publication of a new magazine. Are there areas, if any, where there is opportunity for new magazines?

Opportunity abounds. The information need and the marketing needs of our society are constantly shifting, and there is always a way to do it better. The demise or decline of the big, old, general magazines has been accompanied by a rash of new, sprightly specialized publications. Some don't make it, but on balance, Standard Rate & Data Service adds about sixty new magazine listings every year.

Many of us in consumer magazines think that our field is more glamourous and exciting than business magazines. Is there validity to this premise?

In terms of job opportunities, business magazines may be better than consumer magazines. There are a lot more of them, and because they are less well known, there is likely to be less competition for jobs. The excitement of the job itself is probably about the same. It is true that big consumer magazines deal with big dollars, although that's not necessarily reflected in salaries. If you are moved by the glamour of Madison Avenue, then a consumer magazine is the place to be, but, realistically, the only difference is where the decimal point falls.

Career books generally conclude that an applicant must go through the personnel or human resources department in applying for a job, even though other approaches can be tried. Do you have any ideas about how someone applying for a magazine publishing position can circumvent this traditional procedure?

Use your contacts. Almost everybody knows somebody who knows somebody who knows somebody. If you can't make a contact, drop a note to the top person in the department where you want to work. It's the department head who usually makes the hiring decision—that is, the editor, or the advertising director. In your note, include a résumé and a statement of your objective. Always end by saying that you will call for an appointment; never ask a prospect to call you—he won't.

Do your homework. Before you make the contact, be sure that you have read the magazine and have some understanding of what it's all about. To get an appointment, it's much more effective to ask for help than it is to ask for a job. Even if the employer has no openings, ask if you can see him to get help and advice. Most people are flattered and find it hard to say no.

I've found that I'm a sucker for someone who comes in and tells me how terrific and important my magazine is. If a candidate tells me that he's bright, intelligent, and perceptive, I tend to think he's somewhat egomaniacal. If he tells me how terrific my magazine is, I find myself thinking how bright, intelligent, and perceptive he is. It helps if you really do believe the product is terrific, because you might wind up having to work on it.

Glossary of Magazine Terms

ABC: the Audit Bureau of Circulation: audits circulation of magazines for the use of advertisers and agencies.

Advertising director: the individual at a company with responsibility for its advertising; the executive at a magazine who directs and coordinates all advertising sales.

Advertising-to-editorial ratio: the ratio or percentage in a magazine of advertising space to editorial content.

Advertising linage: the number of advertising pages carried by a publication in a given period.

Agency commission: the amount (usually 15 percent) of commission paid by the media to the advertising agency for its services.

American Association of Advertising Agencies (AAAA): an organization representing American advertising agencies whose members conform to a code of rules and procedures.

Bind-in card: a card inserted into a publication to sell subscriptions, or other services, of its advertisers.

Bleed: the extension of illustrations, photos, or copy to the edge of a page.

Book: an industry term for a magazine or publication.

Business magazine: often called "trade" magazine; a category of nonconsumer publications that serve the interest of a particular industry or profession.

CPM: cost per thousand, a figure arrived at by dividing the audience or circulation of a publication by its cost per page. It is used by agencies and advertisers to determine the relative cost of various media.

Circulation guarantee: the minimum total circulation of a magazine offered to its advertisers.

Consumer magazines: the class of publications sold or given free to consumers as distinguished from "business" magazines, which relate to a reader's business or professional interest.

Controlled circulation: refers to publications that are sent free to specific individuals.

Cover lines: sometimes called sell lines; used to emphasize an issue's contents on its cover.

Demographic characteristics: the economic and social characteristics of a group of individuals or households; refers to the age, income, education, and economic levels of the audience of a magazine.

Dummy: the prototype of a new publication done in the form of artist's roughs or as printed pages.

General magazine: a consumer publication with broad editorial appeal not directed to a particular or specialized audience.

House organ: the in-house publication of a business organization or union, often used to improve employee relations.

Insert: a preprinted advertisement supplied by an advertiser to a publication and bound into its pages.

Kill fee: the fee paid to a freelance writer by a magazine when the assigned article or story is not used.

MPA: the Magazine Publishers Association, the official organization of consumer and business publications.

MRI: Mediamark Research Index, one of the two large research organizations measuring the product usage, demographics, and so on, of a publication's audience.

Media kit: a kit used by magazines in advertising sales. It contains a rate card, survey results, sample magazines, demographics, and publicity about the magazine.

Pass-along readers: the secondary magazine audience, composed of readers who are not the primary buyers of the magazine.

Rate card: a detailed document listing a magazine's ad rates, frequency, closing dates, and production data.

Regional edition: a portion of a magazine's overall circulation distributed in a specific geographical area and containing advertising (and at times some editorial copy as well) aimed at that area's readers alone.

Rep: a publication's advertising sales representatives who are not full-time members of its staff.

Simmons: a major research organization that measures product usage, demographics, and the like, of a magazine's audience.

Single-copy sales: the functional term for newsstand sales of magazines.

Specialized magazines: the classification of magazines geared to the special interests of a group of readers.

Title: term used primarily in distribution to refer to a magazine.

Total audience: the combined total of a publication's paid circulation plus its pass-along readership.

Trade magazine: the popular name for business magazines, designating nonconsumer publications that serve the interests of a professional group or industry.

Recommended Reading

Anderson, Elliot, and Mary Kinsi. *The Little Magazine in America.* Yonkers, N.Y.: Pushcart Press, 1978.

Barnhart, Helene Schellenberg. *How to Write & Sell the 8 Easiest Article Types.* Cincinnati, Ohio: Writer's Digest Books.

Berlye, Milton. *How to Sell Your Artwork.* Englewood Cliffs, N.J.: Prentice-Hall, 1978.

Business Publication Rates and Data. Wilmette, Ill.: Standard Rate & Data Service. Issued monthly.

Byron, Christopher M. *The Fanciest Dive: What Happened When the Media Empire of Time/Life Leaped without Looking into the Age of High-Tech.* New York: Plume/New American Library, 1987.

Claxton, Ronald H. *The Student Guide to Mass Media Internships.* Boulder, Colo.: University of Colorado, School of Journalism, 1983.

Click, J. W., and Russell N. Baird. *Magazine Editing and Production.* Wm. C. Brown Co., 1979.

Cool, Lisa Collier. *How to Sell Every Magazine Article You Write.* Cincinnati, Ohio: Writer's Digest Books.

Delton, Judy. *The 29 Most Common Writing Mistakes and How to Avoid Them.* Cincinnati, Ohio: Writer's Digest Books, 1985.

Donahue, Bud. *The Language of Layout.* Englewood Cliffs, N.J.: Prentice-Hall, 1978.

Ellenthal, Ira. *Selling Smart: How the Magazine Pros Sell Advertising.* New Canaan, Conn.: Folio: Magazine Publishing Corp., 1982.

Ferguson, Rowena. *Editing the Small Magazine.* New York: Columbia University Press, 1976.

Folio: The Magazine for Magazine Management. New Canaan, Conn.: Folio: Magazine Publishing Corp. Special issues: *The Folio: 400, The Folio: Ad Guide* (annual), *Editorial Index* (annual).

Forsyth, David P. *The Business Press in America 1750–1865.* Philadelphia: Chilton Books, 1964.

Handbook of Magazine Publishing. New Canaan, Conn.: Folio: Magazine Publishing Corp., 1978.

Hubbard, J. T. W. *Magazine Editing: How to Acquire the Skills You Need to Win a Job and Succeed in the Magazine Business.* Englewood Cliffs, N.J.: Prentice-Hall, 1982.

Kelley, Jerome E. *Magazine Writing Today.* Cincinnati, Ohio: Writer's Digest Books, 1978.

Kevles, Barbara. *Basic Magazine Writing.* Cincinnati, Ohio: Writer's Digest Books, 1986.

Korda, Michael. *Success!* New York: Simon & Schuster, 1977.

Latimer, H. D. *Advertising Production Planning and Copy Preparation for Offset Printing.* Chicago, Crain Books, 1975.

Lieberman, Seymour. *How and Why People Buy Magazines.* Port Washington, N.Y.: Publishers Clearing House (sponsor), 1977.

Mainstream Access, Inc. *The Publishing Job Finder.* Englewood Cliffs, N.J.: Prentice-Hall, 1981.

Mann, Jim. *Magazine Editing: Its Art and Practice.* New Canaan, Conn: Folio: Magazine Publishing Corp., 1985.

Melcher, Daniel, and Nancy Larrick, *Printing and Promotion Handbook.* New York: McGraw-Hill, 1966.

Mogel, Leonard. *The Magazine: Everything You Need to Know to Make It in the Magazine Business.* Englewood Cliffs, N.J.: Prentice-Hall, 1979.

Mott, Frank Luther. *History of American Magazines* 5

vols. Cambridge, Mass.: Harvard University Press, 1966–68.

Newsletter on Newsletters. Rhinebeck, N.Y.: The Newsletter Clearinghouse. Published monthly.

Quick, John. *Artists and Illustrators Encyclopedia.* New York: McGraw-Hill, 1969.

Rogers, Geoffrey. *Editing for Print.* Cincinnati, Ohio: Writer's Digest Books, 1985.

Romano, Frank J. *Don't Call It Cold Type!* Salem, N.H.: G.A.M.A. Communications, 1977.

Scherman, William H. *How to Get the Right Job in Publishing.* Chicago: Contemporary Books, Inc., 1983.

Spencer, Herbert. *The Visible Word.* New York: Hastings House, 1968.

Spikol, Art. *Magazine Writing: The Inside Angle.* Cincinnati, Ohio: Writer's Digest Books, 1979.

Stevenson, George. *Graphic Arts Encyclopedia.* New York: McGraw-Hill, 1968.

Strunk, William, Jr. *Elements of Style.* New York: Macmillan, 1959.

Teeters, Peggy. *How to Get Started in Writing.* Cincinnati, Ohio: Writer's Digest Books, 1986.

White, Jan V. *Designing for Magazines.* New York: R. R. Bowker Co., 1982.

Writer's Digest Books. *16,000 on-the-Job Training Opportunities for All Types of Careers.* Cincinnati, Ohio: Writer's Digest Books, 1984.

BOOKS

My first experience in producing a book came right after World War II. I was working as a printing salesman, a job for which I had no particular experience but to which I gravitated after leaving the service.

Each day I left my office in the morning, armed with my samples and much enthusiasm, got on the subway to midtown Manhattan, and began canvassing office buildings. I started on the top floor and worked my way to the lobby. Most often, I didn't get past the office receptionist. The answer was usually "We already have a printer."

On one of these frustrating trips, I went to a seedy building consisting of many small offices with a half-dozen names listed on each door. I came upon an establishment with the offbeat name "National Association of Gag Writers" painted in black on the wire-glass door.

Now, I must add that on the days I had a successful solicitation, it usually brought an inquiry for an estimate on 1,000 letterheads and envelopes, priced at a total of $20.00. On this fortunate occasion at the National Association of Gag Writers, the amiable director asked if I printed books. "Of course," was my quick response. "How many do you want?" I was elated when he said that he wanted 500 copies of a ninety-six-page book, to be spiral bound.

I could see myself leaving the chintzy world of letterheads, envelopes, and business cards and stepping up in class to the rarefied atmosphere of book production. When I brought the inquiry back to my employer for an estimate, his immediate reaction was to demand brusquely that the customer pay for the work on a C.O.D. basis.

Fortunately, the customer accepted the estimate and agreed to pay C.O.D., and I received the assignment to produce *The Mathematics of Comedy Writing*. I don't think the book had wide appeal; its basic premise was that there are only a limited number of jokes, and all one had to do was interpose a situation into an existing mathematical formula in order to write effective comedy.

My employer and I had on-the-job training in producing the slim volume. I learned about such arcane matters as book typesetting, printing multiple-page signatures, and spiral bookbinding. When the book was completed, it seemed incredibly handsome, at least to me. I was ready to print encyclopedias.

A Short History of Books

Although one may be inclined to exclude much of the schlock that passes for "literary production," a quick definition of a book might be "a printed composition forming a volume."

The first "books" were the clay tablets of Babylonia and Assyria, and the first printed books may be said to be the Egyptian writing on papyrus rolls of about the twenty-fifth century B.C. This cursive writing was even simpler than hieroglyphics

By the twelfth century (A.D.) paper mills were already set up in Europe. In the fifteenth century, with the invention of movable type by Johann Gutenberg, the demand for paper and the printing of books proliferated.

During the Renaissance, it is said, tens of thousands of books were printed, predominantly of a religious nature. Of course, Gutenberg's first work—the first book printed from movable type—was a Latin Bible, published around 1456.

Books came to America in the early seventeenth century with the Pilgrims. By the eighteenth century, there were great improvements on the early works of Gutenberg's era, particularly in the areas of paper, type, and presswork. France and England were the leaders, but Germany and Italy were not far behind.

Clearly, one of the most dramatic factors in book production was the invention of the Linotype machine by another German, Ottmar Mergenthaler, in 1884 (by which year he was a naturalized American; his machine was perfected in Baltimore). If you have ever been in an old print shop and seen the printer hand setting type character by character, you will realize how innovative the Linotype was, with an operator at a keyboard rapidly setting "lines" of type. Now, in the computer era, this method of typesetting seems as primitive to us as the clay tablets were to Gutenberg.

Bookselling in America

The first authentic reference to the trade of bookselling in America was in 1638, according to the early records of Harvard University.

In 1802, there was a "literary fair" held in New York with twenty-four booksellers participating. In the same year, the New York Association of Booksellers was formed to publish and sell textbooks. Its first book: *Cicero* in Latin and English.

Most of the books sold in America during the nineteenth century other than textbooks were imported books of English literature—Scott, Byron, and Wordsworth were favorites. After the Civil War, prices of books came down, and many publishers and booksellers became established, principally in Boston, New York, and Philadelphia.

The American Booksellers Association, the ABA, was organized in New York in 1900. This group is still the major force in the book business, sponsoring the annual ABA convention each May in a different city.

The first book club was established in 1926 with 4,500 subscribers. By 1928 there were 85,000 subscribers. Today, book clubs account for 10 percent of the multibillion-dollar gross annual sale of all books.

Paperbacks first appeared in America in the late nineteenth century but didn't become popular until the late 1930s. In my high school days during that period, paperbacks cost 10¢. The big growth in popularity of mass market paperbacks occurred during World War II, when the industry discovered that soldiers were able to carry them around in their back pockets. Because the books were so cheap, the GIs could read them, then dispose of them or pass them along to their buddies. These days they cost $3.95 and up and are a major factor in book publishing.

By the mid-1980s, the gross sale of books exceeded $9.8 billion annually. Textbooks still account for the major share of this market, although a glance at a drugstore paperback rack would seem to indicate the works of pop authors such as Judith Krantz, Irving Wallace, and Louis L'Amour dominate book publishing.

Many social commentators have tolled the death knell for books as a cultural force, and perhaps a case can be made for this position; nevertheless, despite all the developments in audio and video, book publishing is still a major factor in our society—and a vital and challenging industry. You'll learn all about it in this chapter.

The Scope of Book Publishing Today

A recent study by the Book Industry Study Group, a not-for-profit corporation that provides research for the industry, prepared a consumer research study on reading and book purchasing. The results are significant to our understanding of the book market.

America is a nation of readers; 94 percent of all adults over sixteen read books, magazines, and newspapers. And of this large group of 169 million people, 50 percent read books.

Nearly 90 percent of all adults and young people read as a leisure activity, with about 62 percent of the juveniles, 50 percent of the adults, and 34 percent of the senior citizens in the sample population reading books. Book readership begins to decline sharply after the age of fifty, especially among those with low levels of education.

Among adults and seniors participating in the study, television was the leisure activity engaged in most frequently, followed by listening to the radio and spending time with the family. Leisure reading came in fifth.

In the juvenile group, 90 percent gave TV watching as an activity they enjoy, along with playing sports and going to the movies. Reading books was a surprising fourth choice. In terms of *favorite* activities, juveniles ranked reading books third.

Who Is a Book Reader?

Book readers can be classified as "light" (one to three books in the previous six months), "moderate" (four to twenty-five books), or "heavy" (twenty-six or more books). The number of heavy book readers nearly doubled in the five years prior to the consumer research study. Book readers as a whole spend 15 hours per week reading compared with the 17 hours per week the average American spends watching television.

A Gallup survey reveals that only one in four adults reads books regularly and possesses a library card. The average American doesn't spend as much time reading books for pleasure as the average European does; however, 55 percent of all Americans read some books, and only 6 percent read no books at all.

The average book reader read twenty-five books for leisure or work over the six-month period before the study. The subject matter of the book was the most important criterion for selection, followed by recommendations of friends, author's reputation, and synopses or reviews.

Book Publishing and You

Now that we've told you a bit about the history of books and about who reads books, let's get to the point. Is there a future in book publishing for you,

The publishing industry offers something for every reader's tastes. (Photograph courtesy Waldenbooks.)

or should you forget about your love of literature, get an M.B.A., and go into mergers and acquisitions at Merrill Lynch and make $300,000 a year by the time you're thirty? Before you commit to either choice, let us tell you more about book publishing as a business.

In the United States, there are slightly more than 2,000 book publishers, and they publish about 55,000 paperbound and hardcover books a year. This relatively small industry employs only about 60,000 people. The gross sales of all books total just under $10 billion a year. Magazines do almost 50 percent more business, and newspapers do three times as much. The largest share of this $10 billion is textbooks, with about 30 percent of the total.

According to the Book Industry Study Group, New York–based publishers account for almost 45 percent of the industry's output and about half of its employees, yet starting out in the big city on an editorial assistant's average salary of $12,000 to $13,500 is rough, especially with the enormous cost of New York rentals. For this reason, perhaps, only about half of the eighty-five graduates of each summer's Radcliffe Publishing Procedures course were still in publishing five years later. They just couldn't afford to wait until they made it to the top.

In defense of small salaries, may we add that book publishing is a low-profit business, with small salaries a necessity. Why low profits, one may ask? The answers are not simple.

Although the price of books escalates each year—paperbacks averaging just under $4.00 and hardbound books $16.00 to $20.00—manufacturing costs have risen in the same proportion. Another factor is duplication. Just look at the popular-fiction racks in your local bookstore or in the cookbook and self-help sections.

Significant, too, are the high acquisition costs paid by paperback publishers for the rights to popular works by proven authors. It was certainly a major gamble when the paperback publisher Bantam paid $3.2 million at auction for the rights to Judith Krantz's bestseller *Princess Daisy*.

Consider as well the good fortune of Douglas Adams, the English humorist known for his two blockbuster novels, *The Hitchhiker's Guide to the Galaxy* and *The Restaurant at the End of the Universe*. When his contract was up at Crown Publishers in 1985, his next two comic novels (still in proposal form) were auctioned to Simon & Schuster for $2.275 million.

Clearly, a major negative factor in mass market paperback sales is the system of consignment. With certain exceptions, dealers can return unsold books for credit, so that a sale to a bookstore by a publisher is not really a sale unless the store actually sells the books. This practice is similar to newsstand sales for magazines (see the chapter on magazines).

So let's say that a publisher produces 7,000 copies of a hardbound book to retail at $19.95. If he sold all 7,000, he would make a small profit, but what would happen if he sold 4,000 copies (the average)? He would then "eat" the 3,000 books and sell them to wholesalers as "remainders" for 20¢ to 40¢ each, and the buyer would be able to pick them up at a bookstore's bargain counter for $1.00 or $1.98. Want to reconsider that M.B.A.?

The Glamorous Side of Book Publishing

Some time ago I was at a cocktail party and met a man I knew slightly who had been the president of a major book publishing house.

He had left that company for undisclosed reasons and was "at liberty." I asked him about his plans for the future. He said, "I don't know where I'll go, but it will have to involve the written word." His

response seemed pretentious at the time, but on reflection I understand it.

Although I have written just one book before this one, I have published dozens of books, gone to a hundred autograph parties, and attended many book fairs. If I seem jaded, I'm not. I can only say that the sheer excitement of the book business is matched by few experiences in mass media.

The American Booksellers Association: Let's discuss, for example, the American Booksellers Association—or the ABA, as it is usually referred to—and its annual convocation of the book industry, held in May. There, hundreds of book publishers set up booths and displays offering tens of thousands of new books (and some older ones as well) to thousands of booksellers from all over the world.

The ABA runs for four days. Many of the displays, especially those of the larger publishers, are elaborately festooned with posters and decorations. Many booths have audio-visual displays. Authors abound—for signings, interviews, or just to shake hands with the book buyers of a department store chain.

Evenings at the ABA can be quiet dinners or boisterous cocktail parties in hospitality suites. Sales are made and sales are talked about, but many are not consummated. The big publishers are there as a presence; the smaller ones are there for survival. It's all one big literary carnival—and it's great fun.

The Frankfurt Book Fair: Each year in October, in a dull, mercantile German city, hundreds of the world's leading publishers convene in a group of huge buildings called *halles* to sell books and rights. The event is the Frankfurt Book Fair; the overall effect, mind-boggling.

A first-timer is impelled to walk the aisles just to absorb the color of the place. Here's a large booth with about a dozen polite, smiling mainland Chinese quietly offering their wares. At the Israeli booths, armed guards patrol the area—conveying a grimness that does not seem to affect the participants, who are engaged in animated conversations with their fellow publishers from other countries.

The Frankfurt Book Fair's primary importance is in the sale of subsidiary rights. For example, an Italian publisher brings to Frankfurt a dummy of a beautiful art book he plans to publish. He shows this prototype to a few dozen foreign publishers, and if he is successful, sells co-editions to five or six of these publishers in their respective languages. By printing all these editions at the same time, he is reducing the cost for the foreign publishers while guaranteeing a profit for himself.

The Frankfurt Book Fair is so immense in its scope that there is no room for the host German

The "miles of aisles" at a typical ABA convention, an event held each Memorial Day weekend. (Photograph copyright 1986 Lawrence Migdale.)

publishers in the main *halle*. They peddle their wares in an adjacent building.

The pace at the fair is so frenetic that one rarely has the time to sit down and eat lunch. The custom—and not a very appetizing one—is to wolf down two large frankfurters (that's where they got the name), a roll, and a stein of German beer in eight minutes while standing at one of the fair's numerous counters—all this, including indigestion, in the name of culture.

The Wide Range of Book Publishing Activity

The *Literary Market Place* directory—or *LMP*, as it is called—published annually by the R. R. Bowker Company, breaks down book publishers by fields of activity. There are twenty-six categories, ranging from "Association Presses" to "University Presses," with "Fine Editions," "Microcomputer Software," and "Scholarly Books" also included.

The largest categories are "General Trade Books Hardcover" and "Paperback Books Trade." The word *trade* refers to books for the general public sold through bookstores. Each of these two categories lists about 650 publishers: Some are small, publishing fewer than a dozen titles each year; others are large companies, often owned by conglomerates.

Book publishing is truly diversified. In the *LMP* listings there are about seventy-five publishers of dictionaries and encyclopedias, twenty-two that do maps and atlases, 225 that do juvenile and young adult books, and 340 that publish college textbooks.

There are also publishers that specialize in books on religion, nature, art, humor, travel, politics, science, computers, crafts, and so on. If you have a strong special interest, consult *LMP* when you go job hunting. Book publishing's diversity may help you get the right job.

The Germans Are Coming: West Germany's Bertelsmann A. G. is a giant in book publishing, music and video, magazines, printing, and television broadcasting. Its management skills have enabled it to acquire thirty book-publishing houses worldwide, build sales to a $5 billion range, and operate profitably.

Bertelsmann's growth in this country started in

81

CBS College Publishing
383 Madison Ave, New York, NY 10017
SAN: 200-2108
Tel: 212-872-2000
Pres: Lisa Bayard
VP & Ed-in-Chief: Robert P Rainier
VP, Sales: John W Wood
VP, Mktg: Barbara Kimball
The Dryden Press: See separate listing.
1984: 199 titles

TransMedica Inc
One Madison Ave, New York, NY 10010
SAN: 241-466X
Tel: 212-686-8520
Pres: George Rohr
VP & Ed-in-Chief: Ann M Holmes
Dir, Planning & Admin: Cathy A Goodfriend
Medical education products, including
  medical symposia, monograph series,
  newsletters, videocassettes, films, other AV
  products.
Holt, Rinehart & Winston General Book: See
  separate listing.

CBS Software
One Fawcett Place, Greenwich, CT 06836
Tel: 203-622-2500 Telex: 96-5959
Pres: Edmund Auer
VP, Mktg Serv: Arthur Barnett
VP, Oper: Robert Lovler
Cont: Frank Serpe

**CCHS: California College for Health
  Sciences**
1810 State St, San Diego, CA 92101
SAN: 692-2643
Tel: 619-232-3784; 800-221-7374
Pubn Coord: Kimberly Hogan
1985: 3 titles. In print: 14 titles
Founded 1979
ISBN Prefix(es): 0-933195

Celestial Arts
Subs of Ten Speed Press
Box 7327, Berkeley, CA 94707
SAN: 159-8333
Tel: 415-524-1801; 800-841-BOOK
Warehouse: 1303 Ninth St, Berkeley, CA
  94710
Pres: Philip Wood
Edit Fir: Philip Wood
Mktg Dir, Adv & Direct Mail Mgr: David
  Hinds
Prodn Mgr: Mary Ann Anderson
Cloth & quality paperback originals; popular
  psychology, self-help & healing, how-to,
  cookbooks, sports; general trade nonfiction.
1985: 14 titles. In print: 85 titles
Founded 1966
ISBN Prefix(es): 0-912310; 0-89084; 0-89742
Adv Agency: Orbit Graphic Arts
Foreign Reps: Airlift (England, Europe);
  Beaverbooks (Canada); Specialist
  Publications (Australia); Tamarin
  Publications Pty Ltd (South Africa)

Center for Applied Linguistics
1118 22 St NW, Washington, DC 20037
Tel: 202-429-9292 Telex: 89-2773
Pubns Coord: Martha K Clark
Dist by Harcourt Brace Jovanovich
Linguistics, including language in education
  & bilingual education series, Indochinese
  phrasebooks, teacher-training materials &
  other scholarly works in linguistics.
1985: 5 titles. In print: 117 titles
Founded 1959
ISBN Prefix(es): 0-87281
Imprints: CAL/HBJ

Center for Migration Studies of New York
209 Flagg Place, Staten Island, NY 10304
Tel: 718-351-8800
Exec Dir: Lydio F Tomasi

Dir, Pubns: Maggie Sullivan
Mktg Dir: Mona Hesterhagen
Art Dir: Lucretia Miele
Foreign Off: CSER, Via Dandola, 58, 00153
  Rome, Italy
Journals & monographs on migration,
  refugees & ethnic group relations.
1985: 9 titles. In print: 65 titles
Founded 1964
ISBN Prefix(es): 0-913256
Adv Agency: Flagg Associates
Foreign Reps: CADEMS (Argentina); CCMS
  (Australia); Centro de Estudos Migratorios
  (Brazil); CIEM (France); CSER (Italy)

**Center for Thanatology Research &
  Education Inc**
391 Atlantic Ave, Brooklyn, NY 11217
SAN: 210-7414
Tel: 718-858-3026
Pres, Ed-in-Chief & ISBN Contact: Roberta
  Halporn
Prodn Mgr & Art Dir: Linda Avitable
Dist for Foundation for Thanatology; Health
  Sciences Publishing Corp
Thanatology books, audiovisuals & journals.
1985: 4 titles. In print: 20 titles
Founded 1976
ISBN Prefix(es): 0-930194
Imprints: Thanatology Service Series

Center for Urban Policy
Loyola University of Chicago, WaterTower
  Campus
820 N Michigan Ave, Chicago, IL 60611
SAN: 264-1836
Tel: 312-670-3112
Pubns Mgr: Janice Stockwell
Urban related monographs.
1985: 3 titles. In print: 18 titles
Founded 1979
ISBN Prefix(es): 0-911531

Center for Urban Policy Research
Rutgers University
Bldg 4051-Kilmer, New Brunswick, NJ
  08903
SAN: 206-6297
Tel: 201-932-3133
Dir: George Sternlieb
Libn: Edward Duensing
Dir, Publicity: Mary Picarella
Textbooks; scientific, technical & social
  sciences.
1985: 18 titles. In print: 55 titles
Founded 1969
ISBN Prefix(es): 0-88285

Century House Publishing
American Life Foundation
Watkins Glen, NY 14891
SAN: 217-0930
Tel: 607-535-4004, 733-9238
Acting Pres, Ed & Rts & Perms: G L
  Freeman
Adv Mgr & Publicity Dir: R Sunderlin
Educ Dir: Ruth S Freeman
Coord: L M Goodman
Antiques & Americana.
1985: 3 titles
Founded 1942
ISBN Prefix(es): 0-87282
Imprints: ABC (Antiques Book Club); Prang-
  Mark

Chadwyck-Healey Inc
1021 Prince St, Alexandria, VA 22314
Tel: 203-683-4890
Pres: Charles Chadwyck-Healey
VP, Mktg: Bertie Bonnell, 2511 Pontiac
  Trail, Ann Arbor, MI 48105. Tel: 313-662-
  2662
VP, Edit: W Mark Hamilton

Man Ed: Sandra Shaffer Tinkham
Foreign Off: 20 Newmarket Rd, Cambridge
  CB5 8DT, England
Dist for Avero Publications Ltd
Scholarly books, reference works & academic
  microform publications.
1985: 29 titles. In print: 81 titles
Founded 1974
ISBN Prefix(es): 0-85964

Chain Store Guide
Subs of Lebhar-Friedman Inc
425 Park Ave, New York, NY 10022
Tel: 212-371-9400
Assoc Dir, Res: Michael Lambe
Databases; directories & reference books;
  business.
1985: 15 titles
Founded 1933
ISBN Prefix(es): 0-86730

Irena Chalmers Cookbooks Inc
23 E 92 St, New York, NY 10128
SAN: 217-3425
Tel: 212-348-3240; 800-334-8128
Warehouse: Rte 2, Canaan Church Rd,
  Denton, NC 27239
Publisher: Irena Chalmers
Man Ed: Jean Atcheson
Dist by Kampmann & Co
Cookbooks.
1984: 14 titles. In print: 51 titles
Founded 1981
ISBN Prefix(es): 0-941034
Imprints: Books by Cooks; Great American
  Cooking Schools
Foreign Reps: Danica Imports Ltd (Canada)
Foreign Rts: International Book Marketing
  (Europe)

Chandler & Sharp Publishers Inc
11A Commercial Blvd, Novato, CA 94947
SAN: 205-6127
Tel: 415-883-2353
Chmn of the Bd, Pres & Rts & Perms:
  Jonathan Sharp
Trade & college books.
1984: 7 titles. In print: 35 titles
Founded 1972
ISBN Prefix(es): 0-88316
Foreign Rts: Inter License Ltd

Chanticleer Press Inc
424 Madison Ave, New York, NY 10017
SAN: 201-5749
Tel: 212-486-3900 Telex: 23-4692
Cable: CHANTPRESS NEW YORK
Pres: Paul Steiner
VP & Gen Mgr: Gudrun Buettner
Design Cons: Massimo Vignelli
Illustrated international editions on natural
  history, art & science.
1985: 50 titles. In print: 100 titles
Founded 1941
ISBN Prefix(es): 0-918810
Foreign Reps: Agenzia Letteraria
  Internazionale (Italy); La Nouvelle Agence
  (France)

Charter Oak Press
Box 7783, Lancaster, PA 17604
SAN: 692-4581
Tel: 717-898-7711
Shipping: 68 W Elizabeth, Landisville, PA
  17538
Original hardcover & paperback trade books
  for professional audiences via direct mail;
  business, engineering, how-to, outdoor
  recreation, psychology.
1985: 6 titles
Founded 1985
ISBN Prefix(es): 0-87521

28

A typical page from a recent *Literary Market Place*. Note that CBS College
Publishing published 199 titles, while Irena Chalmers Cookbooks did 14,
and the Center for Applied Linguistics only 5. (Reprinted with permission. Published by R. R. Bowker, Division of Reed Publishing USA, © 1986
by Reed Publishing USA, a division of Reed Holdings, Inc. All rights
reserved.)

1980, when it acquired the mass market paperback publisher Bantam Books. Having made a success with Bantam, Bertelsmann paid $300 million, in September 1986, to acquire 75 percent of RCA's record business (it already owned the other 25 percent).

A brief sojourn into the American magazine business in the early 1980s with *Geo*, a slick science magazine, failed. In late 1986, Bertelsmann acquired the publishing interests of Doubleday & Company. This encompassed book publishing and book clubs, including the Literary Guild.

The German company no doubt expects to infuse an already dynamic American market with its own aggressive management style. It evaluates this market as one with stability and a continuing capacity for growth. We hope this assessment is correct.

Magazine Publishers as Book Publishers

From almost the very beginning of the *National Lampoon*'s success as a magazine, we realized that book publishing would be a natural outgrowth. We put out a line of mass market paperbacks with various publishers; one noteworthy title, *The Job of Sex*, a parody of the well-known book *The Joy of Sex*, sold almost a million copies.

Later we both edited and distributed our own books on a regular basis. The obvious benefit to this kind of publishing is that we knew our market and, in fact, could reach it through our own magazine as well as traditional sources.

Other magazine publishers have ventured into book publishing with equal success. *Sail* magazine picked up an attractive how-to book in England, *This Is Sailing*. Distributed to bookstores through W. W. Norton and sold via the magazine, the book sold more than 100,000 copies.

Country Journal, an upscale magazine for transplanted urbans, launched the Country Journal Bookshelf, a random listing of books on subjects of interest to their readers. The Bookshelf is offered through the magazine as well as by direct mail. Although most of its books come from other publishers, the magazine is exploring publishing its own titles.

Of course, book publishing as an ancillary activity of magazine publishers may be profitable because ad space in one's own magazine is free; however, when the publisher ventures into bookstore distri-

bution and direct mail, the risk increases. It's a profit center, albeit a cautious one.

Big-Time Publishing

Conglomerates have concentrated their efforts in the past on the more profitable areas of mass communications—TV, radio, and the movies. In 1984, however, Gulf & Western acquired Prentice-Hall for $710 million. The move made Gulf & Western the world's largest book publisher, as it already owned Esquire, Inc., Ginn & Company, and Simon & Schuster. These acquisitions are significant because, in the past, book publishing has not been considered a growth business.

Time, Inc., the nation's largest magazine publisher (see the chapter on magazines), increased its position in the book business in late 1986 by acquiring Scott, Foresman & Company for $520 million.

Scott, Foresman is a major elementary and high school textbook publisher, perhaps known best for its ''Dick and Jane'' readers. Time, Inc., already owned the venerable trade book publisher Little, Brown & Company at the time of the acquisition.

In seeming contrast to such major purchases is the recent action of CBS Inc., which in late 1986 began divesting itself of its book publishing operations. For $500 million they sold Holt, Rinehart, and Winston, one of the top elementary and high school publishers; W. B. Saunders, a large medical publisher; and CBS's overseas textbook operation. The buyer was the giant Harcourt Brace Jovanovich company, a major factor in books and periodicals.

Aussie acquisition ace Rupert Murdoch, whose empire already includes newspapers, magazines, television stations, and a movie studio, made his bid for eminence in the books field in 1987 by purchasing the number-three book publisher, Harper & Row, for $300 million.

Time, Inc., gets bigger; CBS wants out. Considering the prices paid for publishing companies, one can certainly conclude that book publishing is on the rise.

We have presented a number of facts about the book industry. If you love reading books and are looking for a challenging career, we recommend book publishing. It may not be as remunerative as Wall Street, but it surely is more intellectually stimulating.

How Book Publishing Is Structured

An understanding of book publishing as a business must entail knowledge of the interaction of suppliers and related companies and individuals. We will break down these activities accordingly.

The book publisher is at the center of the accompanying chart. Every position radiates from there, ultimately extending to the users of books at the bottom. We'll start from the top and work our way clockwise around the circle.

Authors

Without the author, none of the other spokes in the publishing wheel can function. Name or celebrity authors command staggering advances from their publishers. One house, Bantam Books, formerly in mass market paperbacks, entered the hardbound ranks with a bang in the '80s. By early '86, it had enjoyed rousing success—ten of the sixty-five available spots on The *New York Times* bestseller lists.

One *Iacocca* can support the total activity of a medium-sized publisher, but Bantam's roster includes Chuck Yeager, Shirley MacLaine, Hugh Hefner, and Beverly Sills—none of them literary types but nonetheless appealing to mass audiences. Bantam also publishes the perenially bestselling Louis L'Amour, who has written ninety-five books and is working on a three-volume autobiography.

Erich Segal of *Love Story* fame is typical of those name authors who command huge fees. His novel for Bantam, *The Class*, about five Harvard alumni, fetched a $1 million advance. An *advance* is monies paid by a publisher to an author prior to publication, to be subsequently earned back from sales of the author's book. If sales don't reach this amount, the publisher suffers the loss. The author receives additional monies—a predetermined royalty on each copy sold—when sales exceed the advance.

G. P. Putnam's Sons is another publisher adept at creating bestsellers. This involves clever promotion, marketing, and effective use of public relations. When Putnam published eighty-six-year-old Helen Hooven Santmyer's first novel, . . . *And Ladies of the Club*, the human-interest factor as much as its content propelled it to high bestsellerdom.

In a period where hardcover bestsellers may sell as many as a million copies, plus 300,000 to 400,000 copies more from book club sales, the search for bestsellers is lined with gold and pursued with frenzied activity at trade book publishing houses.

But this is a world of celebrity publishing. It's the *People* magazine of books for an audience that's celebrity-mad; an audience craving for more facts, gossip, and intimate details of their heroes and heroines.

Book publishers move almost as fast as their magazine counterparts. Within weeks of the *Challenger* explosion, Random House had a Concord, New Hampshire, reporter signed up for a biography of Christa McAuliffe, the teacher/astronaut. The book came out ten months after the disaster.

The record for rapid publishing, however, goes to Bantam. Its book *Miracle on Ice*, which told of the miraculous victory of the U.S. Olympic hockey team over the Soviet team in the 1980 Olympics, came out only 46½ *hours* after the championship game. Four years later, Bantam actually cut a few hours off that time with its book on 1984 Olympic gold-medal king Carl Lewis.

In the real world, authors are university instructors desperately writing learned treatises, hoping they will be "published" before they "perish." Or they are first-time novelists submitting manuscripts to dozens of publishers, hoping they will beat the enormous odds on getting published. Authors are also "how-to" writers who are published but must grind out manuscripts at the rate of one a year in order to make a living. For the great majority, being an author is a frustrating craft.

Let's trace the path of a manuscript from author to publisher. We will use, for this example, a well-crafted historical novel by an already published author.

First, the author in question will do an outline of the novel and submit it to his agent for subsequent submission to a few dozen publishers of hardbound books. (Most authors, of course, don't even have an agent.) Because this author is established, he doesn't need to submit a sample chapter—which may be the case for an unknown.

More about agents later, but for now let's assume that the agent finds a willing publisher for the novel. A contract is drawn, and the author receives an advance of $15,000. This may seem to be a tidy sum if one has a full-time job and moonlights at writing, but if the writer is to labor over this work for three or four years, the advance seems insignificant.

The advance is paid in stages—usually a third on signing, a third at a certain stage during the writing process, and a third upon completion of the manuscript. The author will also share in subsidiary

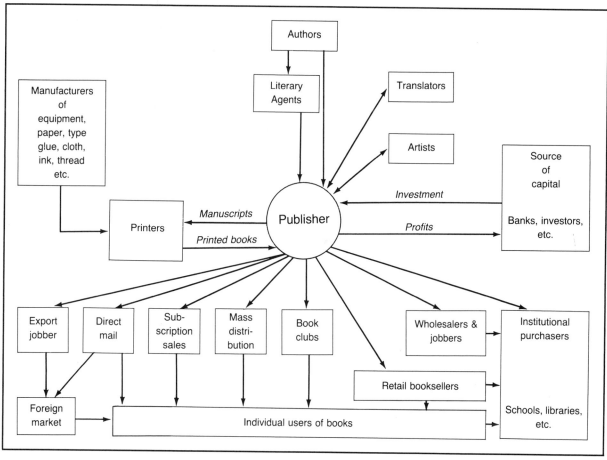

The book publishing network. (After a chart used in *A Guide to Book Publishing* with permission from the author, Datus C. Smith, Jr.)

rights—paperback, book club sales, magazine excerpts, foreign editions, movies, and so on. The contract that the agent negotiates with the publisher will specify the author's share of these rights.

Authors' royalty advances vary greatly. Bantam paid a reported $1 million for the autobiography of Geraldine Ferraro. Kiss-and-tell Reaganite David Stockman is supposed to have received a $2 million–plus advance for his memoirs. Some authors don't receive any advance at all, even for scholarly works; others receive just a thousand or two.

Once a work is published, the author may be asked to do signings in bookstores or, in some cases, go on publicity tours. For most authors of fiction and nonfiction trade books, there's only an autograph cocktail party (white wine or cheap champagne, cheese, and crackers).

If the average trade hardbound book sells 6,000 or 7,000 copies, the author will seldom receive more money than the advance. So, for our hapless author of the historical novel, his "profit" may end up being some good critical acclaim and a brief

moment of glory; then it's off to the workshop for another three years and another novel.

Literary Agents

Literary Market Place lists more than 300 literary agencies. Some are one-person operations; others are large departments of theatrical agencies. The giant William Morris Agency in New York and Los Angeles lists eight agents in its literary department. Sterling Lord, a respected veteran literary agent, represents such literary luminaries as Art Buchwald, Howard Fast, Jimmy Breslin, and Seymour Hersh, as well as a few young and unknown clients.

Most literary agents do not accept unsolicited manuscripts. Some require a nominal reading fee. A typical listing is the following:

The Betsy Nolan Literary Agency. Humor, how-to, fiction, and nonfiction. No unsol. mss.,

The agent negotiates all terms of the contract while consulting with her client. Once the contract stage is completed, the agent assumes a rather inactive role unless a paperback or movie sale is in the offing.

A study of *LMP*'s literary agents' listings will show their area of specialization—specialties such as crime fiction, young adult fiction, science fiction, romance, and so on. One should carefully examine these listings before selecting an agent. Of course, agents are most selective in choosing clients. The selection process is clearly a two-way street.

Authors seldom seem pleased with their agents. Before one makes a selection, it is judicious to discuss the situation with other professional writers, preferably from the same stable. One should be wary of agents who will take on any author just by virtue of paying a fee.

For an insight into the role of a literary agent, we talked to Betsy Nolan, a woman who has been active in this field for many years. Her comments:

After majoring in college in drama, philosophy, and English, I began work in the book business as a press agent. The years of rejection there made the pain of rejection as a literary agent a piece of cake.

My public relations background makes me look at a literary property in terms of how to sell it to the media. Since the whole thing is sales, sales, sales, this training proved very valuable.

As an agent, I have to sell the manuscript to the editor first. The editor then has to sell it to an editorial board, which has to sell it to the sales department, which has to sell it to the wholesalers and chains, which have to sell it to the bookstores.

The bookstores have to sell it to the retail customers, who, hopefully, have been sold by seeing an ad or an interview set up by the marketing department of the publisher, which also has to have been sold on spending its budget for the book.

A new agent can expect to starve unless a James Clavell walks in and says, "I need you." Barring this, even when an agent does sell something to a publisher, there is a wait to get paid. There is some money on signing, some money on completion, some money on publication, and then forever between royalty payments. Often, though, the only money an agent sees is the commission on the advance.

The agent needs a lot of clients and, hopefully, some larger ones to make ends meet. Overhead needs to be kept to a minimum. I

Although trade books represent only a small part of the publishing industry's output, it's generally regarded as the most exciting. Celebrity book signings are only part of the reason; here, Tina Turner turns on the charm in a Barnes & Noble outlet. (Reprinted with permission from Barnes & Noble.)

query first; submit outline, sample chapters, and author background; no reading fee.

The listing is self-explanatory. Nolan lists her specialties. She will not accept unsolicited manuscripts but asks that the authors inquire first; then, if approved, the authors must submit the required elements. Nolan does not charge for reading manuscripts.

After following this procedure, if the agent takes on the property, she will sign an agreement with the author establishing a commission rate, usually 10 percent (some receive 15 or 20 percent). The agent, by virtue of her experience, has established contacts among publishers. She may submit the property to one publisher at a time or as a multiple submission. Closing a sale may require repeated telephone contact, lunches, cocktails, and so on, until the agent is able to convince the publisher's editor of the merit of the work. Now the agent will earn her fee.

support my literary agency by doing public relations.

We agents sustain ourselves by thinking of Morton Janklow. This famous agent is reported to earn over $1 million a year from his literary clients—among them, Sidney Sheldon, Judith Krantz, Jackie Collins, Shirley Conran, Danielle Steel, and William Safire. Clearly, 99 percent of all literary agents are not in his league.

Many East Coast agents now charge 15 percent instead of the 10 percent that exists in the entertainment business. When an agent negotiates a movie deal, the prices are usually high, and the commissions may vary.

There is an excellent annual reference book called *Literary Agents of North America 19-- Marketplace,* available from Author Aid Associates, 340 East 52nd Street, New York, NY 10022; the price is $19.50 plus $2.00 for shipping. The publication profiles 665 agencies, including dramatic agents. A special introductory essay explains the dos and don'ts of dealing with agents.

In the current literary climate, because many publishers will consider only agency-submitted material, the choice of an appropriate agent is extremely important for the would-be author.

Translators

A gastroenterologist preparing a medical textbook on a particular phase of her specialty may require translation of articles in medical journals from a number of countries. This author might consult the American Medical Writers Association for specialist writers in the languages required. She might then work with professional writers who understand medicine and are fluent in one or a number of foreign languages.

Or, an author of an English-language version of a book might be asked to write two or three foreign-language editions. He might then seek out a translator/writer who shares his sensibilities for the work and whose writing ability matches his own. This is often a difficult search.

Some of the translators listed in *LMP* write in many languages. One must recognize the expertise and proficiency it takes to translate *and* to write professionally and in a specialized field.

Columbia University has an agency that offers translating services in thirty foreign languages including such uncommon ones as Korean, Hindi, Serbo-Croatian, and Urdu.

Translators perform a unique function in book publishing. Their special talents make it possible for works of many important foreign authors to gain acceptance in the English language. The reverse of this situation is also significant. One need only visit the Frankfurt Book Fair to see the number of English-language books translated into other languages.

Artists

Throughout this book, we will encounter the role of artists in mass communications. The magazine illustrator, the production designer and art director of a film, the visual artist in television—all are basically artists whose talents give aesthetic character to their medium.

A friend of mine, Carol Donner, is a well-known medical illustrator. Her detailed, graphically incisive color illustrations are used in various medical journals and textbooks. Carol also recently wrote and illustrated a children's novel called *The Magic Anatomy Book.* Nothing to it, right? Wrong. Her training included four years of observation in surgical and clinical procedures at hospitals and medical schools, and integral to her work is a profound understanding of the human body and its functions.

Most books are not illustrated; therefore, the artist's role may be that of illustrating only the dust jacket or cover. This is nonetheless an important assignment, as the appeal of a jacket on a bookshelf increases the book's sale. (Some books merely have black-and-white line illustrations inside, but they, too, can play a vital role in a book's presentation.)

In addition, an artist can be a book designer. A designer may select the typeface for the body text and headings, design the jacket, and/or assign the illustrations for the jacket and the inside of the book. The book designer may also be involved in the selection of paper to be used as well as the fabric for the cover.

The reader interested in commercial art is urged to read the Society of Illustrators' wonderful annual awards book. In it, there are awards given for excellence in magazines, advertising, institutional publications, and books. The works of the winners in the book category truly exemplify the significance of art in books. If you can't find this volume locally, write to the society at 128 East 63rd Street, New York, NY 10021.

Illustrators, of course, are not married to one specific medium. Often magazine illustrators work on books and advertising. The competition, however, is fierce. Only the very talented win out in this field.

An illustration that appears in color in Carol Donner's beautiful publication for children, *The Magic Anatomy Book*. **It is particularly significant in showing how a highly technical subject can be made palatable to children. (Carol Donner,** *The Magic Anatomy Book.* **Copyright © 1986 W. H. Freeman and Company. Used by permission.)**

Source of Capital

A book publishing enterprise may take many forms. It can be a large, publicly held corporation such as Harcourt Brace Jovanovich. It can be a small, privately held company, or it can be a limited partnership with investments from a number of investors.

For publishers, there is a slow payback. Authors' advances, manufacturing costs, and staff overhead must be paid before money comes back to the publisher from sales. Also, except for a runaway bestseller, a book publisher's profit comes from subsidiary sales—for example, paperback rights, book club rights, foreign rights, and so on. Thus, the publisher must wait for these revenues. In the interim, he may require bank financing to run his operation.

When a publisher enjoys a consistent period of profitable operations, he may be in a position to finance his operation without loans, saving the costs of debt service. He may also choose to use his excess capital in acquiring other publishing and media enterprises.

Sales

In this section we will discuss individually the various outlets through which the publisher gets books to its ultimate users.

Institutional Purchasers: This outlet includes schools, colleges, and libraries. Textbooks are published by many different publishers that compete forcefully for this profitable business. A sale to a school of a textbook is a true sale, unlike the consignment system of trade books referred to earlier in this chapter. Typically, in a school, each department makes its own decision on the textbooks it chooses to adopt. This is done after a review of all the available texts in a particular discipline.

Publishers employ skilled salespeople, once called "college travelers," who meet with professors and department heads in an effort to influence their decisions. In colleges, supplemental texts are also adopted for use. Books are usually sold at the college bookstore, which is often owned by the college.

The adoption of a book doesn't mean that it cannot be replaced at a later date. Often a book

88

written by a university professor will be adopted at his own school. Publishers, however, will not produce a textbook unless its potential sales extend beyond the limits of one or two institutions.

In the "el hi" field (elementary and high school textbooks), public schools buy the textbooks outright from the publisher because these schools pay for their students' books.

Libraries may buy from publishers directly or through wholesalers or catalogue operations, which simplifies the purchasing procedure. A library's discount from the publisher is less than that of a bookstore (see the section "Retail Booksellers"). Libraries generally buy hardbound editions, which are more lucrative to a publisher.

Wholesalers and Jobbers: These operations are vital to a publisher's distribution procedure. Some are huge businesses within themselves, servicing the entire country. They function, in a sense, as clearinghouses by ordering fairly large quantities of each book on a publisher's spring and fall list. A small bookstore can then place orders from the jobber for one or two each of many different books from as many different publishing houses and have them all shipped the same day if they're in stock. For the bookstore, this method is much simpler than placing orders with each individual publisher. The bookstore pays the same price to the wholesaler that it would to the publisher. The middleman, or jobber, receives a special discount from the publisher, enabling him to support this extensive warehousing and sales operation.

Two of the largest wholesalers in this field are the Ingram Book Company in Tennessee and the Baker & Taylor Company, a division of the conglomerate W. R. Grace & Co., in New Jersey. Baker & Taylor also has regional sales offices in Georgia, Illinois, and Nevada and issues annual guides to elementary and secondary school libraries. Wholesalers and jobbers provide all types of books, from trade and technical volumes to school texts.

A large publisher will, of course, have its own national sales manager and sales staff covering all the major, if not smaller, territories, the latter coverage being economically unfeasible. The smaller publisher may have its own sales manager but rely totally on sales reps to achieve its sales objectives. These reps work on commission and often for more than one publisher.

Let's look at a listing in *LMP* for a typical rep firm, Wilcher Associates, headquartered in Berkeley, California. This firm covers thirteen western states and El Paso, Texas. It represents fifteen publishers in this territory including major houses such as Rizzoli and Farrar, Straus & Giroux, plus four university presses.

These rep firms work on commission. They will cover all the retailers in their territory and function similarly to a publisher's own sales staff. They will often attend the publishers' seasonal conferences to gain perspective on the publishers' upcoming lists of new titles.

CAREER TIP: Book sales, whether for a publisher directly or for a rep firm, can be a worthwhile career for the individual who enjoys selling and does not mind traveling. Salaries are similar to those in other such sales situations. Jobs are not too difficult to find. Success in this field may lead to sales manager positions at a publisher's headquarters. Refer to the "Who Does What in Book Publishing" section for additional information.

Retail Booksellers: There are approximately 9,000 bookstores in the United States. Many are small single-proprietor establishments with small volume and small profits. In contrast to these shops are the two giant bookstore chains, B. Dalton (now owned by Barnes & Noble) and Waldenbooks. (See the section on these two book retailers later in this chapter.)

The booksellers' average discount from the publisher is 42 percent. This figure would seem to allow for a reasonably profitable operation. This factor, however, is mitigated by the nature of the business. Books sometimes sit on the shelf for a long time before they are sold. Also, because many new titles come out each month, it is difficult to maintain a proper inventory with a limited cash flow.

Book Clubs: There are 142 adult book clubs and sixteen juvenile clubs listed in the most recent *LMP*. Within the adult listing, one publishing company, Macmillan, has seventeen separate clubs. At estimated publishers' net book sales, book clubs accounted for about 5 percent of the total for all books.

The range of book clubs is truly eclectic. Here are some examples: Astronomy Book Club, Aviators Guild, Books for Accountants, Catholic Book Club, Dance Book Club, Farm Journal Family Bookshelf, Nostalgia Book Club, and Photography Book Club.

Book clubs are marketed to the public and special groups directly by mail. Usually the publisher makes a book's plates available to the club, which prints its own edition. Club members receive the books at a discount. The publisher receives approximately 10 percent of the club's price for each book printed. The author also receives a lower royalty on these sales. The prestige of being a club selection can significantly help a book's sales in bookstores.

As implied a moment ago, most book clubs are owned by book publishers. Doubleday, for instance, owns the Literary Guild and many other clubs. (Time, Inc., though not in book publishing, has owned the Book-of-the-Month Club since 1977.) In general, however, there seems to be no question regarding the objectivity of clubs in their book-selection process. Such selections are made on the basis of quality and commercial viability, not on whether they come from the club's parent publisher.

A look at the Book-of-the-Month Club, known in the trade as BOMC, will give us an understanding of the entire book club phenomenon. Launched in 1926, the club grew enormously in the post–World War II years. Recently, its membership topped the 2 million mark.

The average member is thirty-seven years old and college-educated; 52 percent are women and 48 percent men. Membership geographically falls into the same pattern as the population of the United States.

Each year BOMC sends out 9 million shipments containing 15 million books. Unlike its chief competitor, the Literary Guild, which mass-produces its books in standardized formats, BOMC reproduces the publisher's edition in the same size and format, using the same platemaking film that the publisher used.

An example of BOMC's clout in the book publishing business is its choice in 1984 of the novel . . . And Ladies of the Club by eighty-six-year-old Helen Hooven Santmyer as a main selection. As a result, the 1,176-page first novel zoomed onto the national bestseller charts. The club's choice in this case was no doubt based on the instincts of its editors and the unique quality of the book itself.

Book-of-the-Month Club News, the members' magazine from which selections are made, lists dozens of books of diverse interest about art, business, computers, history, and humor, as well as classic and current novels. In addition to the main selection, the News offers members a choice of about twenty new books and about one hundred backlist titles.

Of the 300 new titles offered to club members in the course of a year, many are by lesser-known or first-time authors. Pearl Buck was an unknown writer in 1931 when The Good Earth became a BOMC selection.

Quality Paperback Book Club, better known as QPB, was created by BOMC in 1974 to appeal to college-educated people who grew up reading paperbacks, who do not like to join book clubs or buy a certain number of books a year, and who display idiosyncratic tastes in their reading.

In just over ten years' time, QPB had a half-million members. Since its first main selection, The Nude by Kenneth Clark, QPB has distributed more than 15 million books by more than 1,300 authors. Included in its esoteric mix are such authors as Milan Kundera, John Barth, Russell Baker, Garry Trudeau, and Tom Wolfe.

Mass Distribution: In trade books there are adult and juvenile hardbound editions and adult and juvenile paperbound editions. The phrase "trade paperback" generally refers to a book that is the same size as a hardbound but need not necessarily be so. It may be in a smaller size and still be called "trade."

The distinction the industry makes is to establish a category called "mass market paperback." These are low-cost, small-size paperbacks that are usually reprints of fiction and nonfiction trade books. They are sold in the "mass markets"—drugstores, supermarkets, airline terminals, and conventional bookstores.

The vagaries of this phase of the business go beyond eccentricity. Consider this scenario:

A paperback publisher bids $1 million at auction for the rights to a bestselling hardbound novel. In this procedure the book will be submitted to several mass market paperback publishers at the same time, who will then make a successive round of bids with the contract being given to the highest bidder. The publisher then decides to make a first printing of 2 million copies. These are distributed to about 450 magazine and book wholesalers, as well as to bookstores. The publisher spends another large sum on promotion.

All books are on consignment. The wholesalers then ship the books to hundreds of outlets (drugstores and so on) within their geographical territory. Bear in mind that there are hundreds of new titles published each month. The racks in most outlets can handle only fifteen or twenty titles, usually bestsellers. Can you guess what happens to titles that don't sell fast? You guessed correctly. They go back to the wholesaler for credit.

Formerly, the practice agreed to by all participants was for the wholesalers then to strip the covers of these books and ship them back to the publishers for verification of the number unsold. This system is now obsolete. The wholesaler merely sends the publisher an affidavit stating the number of books sold. Does this leave room for error, chicanery, or a little of both? It surely does.

The point of this little scenario is to illustrate the

precariousness of mass market book publishing. Bantam, Pocket Books, New American Library, and a few others have succeeded at it for a long time, but many others have drowned in its murky waters.

Subscription Sales and Direct Mail: All of us have seen ads in magazines and received direct-mail solicitations for series such as Time-Life Books and Reader's Digest Condensed Books. These "continuity" series and others in this category are big business in book publishing. They account for almost $300 million in their publishers' net sales.

Time-Life Books is the largest direct-mail book publisher, shipping 19 million volumes worldwide. Time-Life Books market-tests about twenty series ideas per year but publishes only a small fraction of the total. (Its music division is also very successful, shipping more than 800,000 record albums and tape cassettes a year.)

Since their existence depends on mass sales, subscription and direct-mail books are produced and edited well. Moreover, their subject matter is structured so that the books will enjoy wide consumer appeal.

CAREER TIP: In addition to editors, writers, and artists, subscription marketing requires skilled direct-mail copywriters, media specialists, list buyers, and the like. Advertising agencies that specialize in direct mail work closely with their publisher clients in developing these campaigns. Most of these agencies are located in New York.

Export Jobbers and Foreign Market: The Frankfurt Book Fair brings the world's book publishers together for the purpose of selling one another's books and the subsidiary rights to these books. Typically, a publisher will attend the book fair but also engage an export jobber to maintain foreign sales on a continuing basis.

The export jobber has offices in key parts of the world, with a sales staff traveling from these points to all the important book-buying countries. The jobber will be familiar with international trade customs and duties. Jobbers work for American publishers on a commission basis.

At Frankfurt, however, the American publisher displays his wares with the objective of selling rights to his books to a foreign publisher who may not be interested in the English-language edition but may want to reprint the books in his own language. One year, when I attended the book fair, *Roots* was the big bestseller in the United States. I understand that rights were sold for this book in fifteen or twenty languages, with substantial fees paid for the rights in the larger countries.

Each year at Bologna, Italy, there is a children's book fair where rights are exchanged on a similar basis to that of the Frankfurt fair. In a major American publishing house, there will be an individual or staff responsible for the sale of children's book subsidiary rights; these people generally attend the Bologna fair.

Printers and Other Book Suppliers: Few, if any, publishers own their own printing plants. Printing is a very competitive business, affording even a small publisher the opportunity to shop for the best prices. Large publishers can call their own shots as to price, delivery, and the like. In addition, there are printers in other countries that are favorable sources for American book publishers. Japan is a leading supplier of art books for the world markets.

Publishers seldom purchase the individual elements needed for a book's manufacture, with the possible exception of paper. Large printers have their own binding facilities and are usually equipped with typesetting equipment. Other, smaller shops exist solely for the purpose of providing publishers and other customers with typesetting services.

We have now completed the full cycle illustrated on the chart, with all the supporting services of a book publisher's activities. Next, we will concern ourselves with who does what within the publisher's own organization.

Who Does What in Book Publishing

The Association of American Publishers, Inc., has prepared the following table of organization as a guide to the structure of a book publishing company. Of course, not every company employs all the positions shown, and large publishers have a staff reporting to each executive. Also, different titles mean different things in different houses. We will delineate the task for each function. Some jobs on the list will not have a description, but we will note the salary ranges for each.

Editorial

Editor-in-Chief/Editorial
   Director/Publisher
Senior Editor/Project Editor
Managing Editor
Asssociate Editor
Copy Editor
Assistant Editor
Editorial Assistant

Production

Production Director/Production Man-
   ager/Vice President Production
Production Supervisor
Cost Estimator/Production Estimator
Art Director/Design Director
Artist/Designer
Production Assistant

Marketing

Marketing Director/Vice President
   Marketing
Market Research Manager
Sales Manager
Direct-Mail Manager/Promotion
   Manager
Sales Representative
Advertising Manager
Promotion Manager
Publicity Director
Subsidiary Rights Manager
Copywriter
Marketing Assistant

Editorial

Editor-in-Chief/Editorial Director/Publisher:
Alternative titles are used for the same function. This person plans the editorial program, determines staff needs of the program, and hires and trains the senior editorial and supervisory staff. He also assigns responsibilities for implementing the editorial program, sets or approves program budgets and schedules, monitors and evaluates progress of the editorial program, and maintains liaison with the company's administrative marketing and production departments. Along with the senior and managing editors, the editor-in-chief must have knowledge of market dynamics and be able to spot market trends. The salary ranges from $39,000 to $62,000.

Senior Editor/Project Editor: The senior editor obtains management approval to acquire, contract for, and publish a manuscript (usually done in committee). He contracts with the author for a manuscript and, after obtaining an acceptable manuscript, maintains a positive author relationship. He provides editorial feedback to the author when work is in process and often obtains it from outside reviewers when work is complete. The senior editor also maintains the schedule and budget for the publishing project, supports the marketing effort, and publishes reprints and revisions. The salary ranges from $29,000 to $41,000.

Managing Editor: The managing editor coordinates the progress of all editorial functions in fulfillment of an overall publishing plan and works with marketing and production managers on planning. This person hires and trains staff for editing services, establishes guidelines and oversees procedures for hiring freelance editing assistance, assists in preparation of the editorial director's budget and publication schedule, and develops procedures for controlling flow from the manuscript to the finished product. The salary ranges from $22,500 to $27,500.

Associate Editor: The associate editor works with the senior or project editor and editor-in-chief in planning for new projects and revision of present books. He makes recommendations for authors and consultants, sets deadlines for completion of materials and projects, and is responsible for the acquisition and orientation of consultant staff to the project, including the copy-editing staff. In addition, he rewrites and clarifies manuscripts with authors and consultants. The associate editor may function as project editor as well as undertake ad hoc assignments for the managing editor/editor-in-chief. The salary ranges from $17,000 to $21,000.

Copy Editor: The copy editor handles assigned manuscripts by copy editing for style consistency, spelling, grammar, and punctuation; he also confers with editors on manuscript matters dealing with inconsistencies in style and information, and assists supervisors by checking glossaries and bibliographies. The copy editor proofreads galley proofs and checks pages against galley proofs. He meets copy-editing deadlines by working closely with supervisors and assigning overflow of work to freelance copy editors. The salary range is from $15,000 to $19,000. (The entire copy-editing and proofreading functions are often "farmed out" by publishers to freelancers, who can make from $7.00 per hour for proofreading to $10.00 per hour for copy editing to $15.00 per hour for developmental editing.)

Assistant Editor: The assistant editor works with the associate editor, project editor, and authors on deadlines for submissions of material, assists the project editor on consultant acquisition, and submits regular project reports to the project editor. The assistant editor must be able to function as project editor if necessary. He is also responsible for implementing field-test designs, whereby manuscripts, particularly nonfiction and textbooks, are read by academics and focus groups for their comments before publication. The salary ranges from $13,000 to $16,000.

Editorial Assistant: This is an entry-level position. The editorial assistant assists editors with acquisition of freelancers, works with copy editors and proofreaders on projects, and is responsible for day-to-day contact and correspondence with authors, freelancers, and the like. This person also assists in monitoring production and schedules. In addition, he is responsible for requisition of payments, advances, expenses, and so on, and application for all copyrights and correspondence with the copyright office. The salary ranges from $12,000 to $14,000.

Editorial positions (not described) and their salary ranges:

Executive Editor, College Division:
$34,000 to $48,000
Executive Editor, El hi Division:
$46,000 to $62,000
Acquiring Editor, College Division:
$25,000 to $31,000
Developmental Editor, College Division:
$20,000 to $25,000
Senior Editor, Juvenile Division:
$26,000 to $30,000
Assistant Editor, Juvenile Division:
$14,000 to $16,000

Qualifications for General Editorial Positions

A college education is a must. A passion for reading and for the touch, smell, and feel of books is a prerequisite. The would-be book publishing professional must also have a thorough understanding of grammar and current English usage. Proficiency in typing and/or word processing is also helpful. A special knowlege of a particular field or discipline such as science fiction, history and politics, and fiction in trade publishing, or perhaps of math or science in textbook publishing, may accelerate promotion. Sometimes textbook editors are former schoolteachers. Often, journalism majors go into book publishing, creating a more competitive field.

The opportunity to work with books is most appealing, yet, on the downside, the salary ranges

in book publishing are low. The fringe benefits, however, of autograph parties, day-to-day contact with creative, interesting co-workers, contact with well-known authors and celebrities (although this is the exception rather than the rule), and just being involved with the wonderful craft of books may make the financial sacrifice worthwhile.

Production

Production Director / Production Manager/ Vice President Production: The production director determines specifications and production processes for the publishing unit and establishes overall production department plans and roles. This individual hires and trains production supervisors, art directors, and estimators; he coordinates and schedules elements of the editorial and production process and supervises traffic for projects assigned. In addition to procuring raw materials, he assures quality, schedule, and budget adherence. The production director maintains relations with suppliers, purchases production-related goods and services, and oversees suppliers' fulfillment of quality, cost, and schedule obligations. The salary ranges from $34,000 to $53,000.

Production Supervisor: The production supervisor analyzes and consults with editors on specifications for paper, cloth, binding, typography, and reproduction processes. He secures estimates based on project specifications and selects vendors. The salary ranges from $23,000 to $37,000.

Cost Estimator/Production Estimator: The cost estimator provides cost estimates to production management by obtaining actual current costs from vendors of all production services and materials. He also maintains contacts and understanding of traditional and new graphic arts processes and costs. The salary ranges from $16,000 to $20,000.

Art Director/Design Director: The art director establishes overall artistic guidelines, themes, and quality control standards. His responsibilities include the hiring and training of staff, recruitment of freelance resources, assignment of work on projects, and supervision of the creative staff output. He sets and approves budgets and schedules and approves costs and bills for design and art. The art director maintains quality and artistic merit based on understanding of the market, competition, usage requirements, and the like. The salary ranges from $27,000 to $36,000.

Artist/Designer: The artist understands editorial, marketing, and production requirements and provides a design theme and artwork that meet these requirements. He works with media sources and keeps to a schedule that meets the financial and deadline requirements of the project. The salary ranges from $17,500 to $25,000.

Production Assistant: This is an entry-level position. The production assistant secures estimates and submits them to the production manager for evaluation and analysis. He coordinates movement of the manuscript to the compositor by assisting in the development of the schedule, by trafficking of the galley proofs and page proofs, and by following up against the schedule. The salary ranges from $10,000 to $12,000.

General Qualifications for Production and Art Positions

Production people are in charge of the physical design and manufacture of books. A thorough background in typography, printing processes, paper manufacturing, art and graphic design, and mathematics is necessary for these job functions. Although there are many fine art schools (see the chapter on magazines), there are few specializing in printing processes.

Salaries in this field are not high and are generally less than at advertising agencies. Often the work pace is feverish, as, for example, when a spring or fall list is closing. There is great satisfaction, however, when the finished product is completed and meets the industry's high standards.

Marketing

The book is the ultimate editorial product, and it is this product that the marketing people must sell to bookstores, supermarkets, drugstores, schools, colleges—and finally to the reader/consumer. Here are the people who make this happen.

Marketing Director/Vice President Marketing: The marketing director develops marketing objectives, policies, and strategies, as well as marketing plans by product and market. He identifies marketing capability for present and future products, spots trends, and integrates market research and product development information. He hires and trains field and staff organization in order to develop efficient and effective organization structure. The marketing director maintains good communications with the marketing and editorial departments and evaluates the effectiveness of editorial and marketing strategies. He participates in forecasting and budgets and is responsible for meeting sales and expense budgets. He also controls or affects inventory levels. The salary ranges from $38,000 to $64,000.

Market Research Manager: The market research manager identifies the needs for research on those products and markets that justify the investment, determines detailed information to be obtained in each research project, and selects methods of research and information needed for a particular market. He implements the research plan, evaluates the responses, and reports on the findings. The market research manager works with the editorial staff, using market research and data. The salary ranges from $20,000 to $27,500.

Sales Manager: The sales manager plans sales forecasting. He recruits, trains, and motivates sales representatives, conducts sales meetings, and assigns territories. He is responsible for developing budgets and for monitoring turnover, new product introductions, sales activity, and field reports. He also supervises the creation of book jackets and makes recommendations on the development of promotional materials. The sales manager makes personal contacts with major dealer chains. The salary ranges from $30,000 to $45,000.

Direct-Mail Manager/Promotion Manager: The direct-mail manager analyzes markets for books and selects appropriate lists to reach those markets. He supervises or prepares copy for brochures and sales letters and directs and supervises all graphics for direct-mail pieces. He also directs accurate record-keeping of all sales resulting from direct-mail efforts. The salary ranges from $17,000 to $33,000.

Sales Representative: Sales representatives are first cousins to the "college travelers" referred to earlier. In addition to identifying key prospects for major publications, the sales representative makes advance appointments, attends sales and training meetings, and visits buyers. The salary range starts at $12,500 for beginners and goes up, depending on experience, territory, and sales record.

Advertising Manager: The advertising manager researches markets and available media, prepares and submits the advertising budget, and recruits and trains copywriters, artists, and traffic managers. He establishes a relationship with an advertising agency or in-house advertising department; he organizes advertising schedules, books to be advertised, medium and space to be used, deadlines, and cost. The advertising manager enters joint advertising ventures with dealers and monitors actual ad placement, responses, and performance of alternative media, and follow-up sales. The salary ranges from $24,000 to $38,000.

Promotion Manager: The promotion manager schedules advertising, direct mail, exhibits, and

The Dell Dateline

A BI-WEEKLY LOOK AT PUBLICITY NEWS OF CURRENT AND FUTURE DELL BOOKS

BESTSELLERS

October 6, 1986

AFTER THE REUNION by Rona Jaffe: #10 New York Times; #8 Publisher's Weekly; #9 Baker & Taylor; #55 B. Dalton; #69 Waldenbooks; #7 Washington Post; #8 Doubleday ; #26 Ingram.

THE BRIDGE ACROSS FOREVER by Richard Bach: #13 Doubleday.

GALAPAGOS by Kurt Vonnegut, Jr.: #20 B. Dalton; #18 Waldenbooks; #5 Doubleday ; #12 Ingram.

SAVAGE GRACE by Natalie Robins and Stephen Aronson: #14 Doubleday.

AMERICAN HERITAGE DICTIONARY: #43 Ingram.

TRADE PAPERBACK BESTSELLERS

COLD SASSY TREE by Olive Ann Burns: #60 Waldenbooks; #15 Ingram.

NICE GUYS SLEEP ALONE by Bruce Feirstein: #11 Doubleday; #79 Waldenbooks

JUVENILE BESTSELLERS

TALES OF A FOURTH GRADE NOTHING by Judy Blume: #10 Waldenbooks; #16 B. Dalton.

RAMONA FOREVER by Beverly Cleary: #50 B. Dalton; #35 Waldenbooks.

(The above information was compiled from currently available bestseller lists, including: New York Times 10/5; Publisher's Weekly 10/3; Baker & Taylor 9/20; B. Dalton 9/21; Walden Books 9/20; Washington Post 9/28; Doubleday 9/20; Ingram 9/22. If you have any questions regarding "Bestsellers" or "Forecasting Frontrunners," please contact Matthew Coyne at 212-605-3467.)

A typical press release sent out by a book publisher to newspapers, magazines, and booksellers promoting its bestsellers. (Reprinted with permission from Dell Publishing.)

other promotional activities. He recruits and trains staff and assigns work to staff and outside agencies. He interacts with sales and editorial departments. The promotion manager reviews industry reports and written and visual material. He consults on catalogues and sales tools. His responsibilities include preparing copy for all book jackets/covers, supervising publicity, and maintaining contact with the advertising agency and media. The salary ranges from $20,000 to $23,000.

Publicity Director: The publicity director compiles lists of appropriate sources of book reviews for each title published and places review copies with all appropriate sources. He prepares publicity re-

leases and stories on authors and their books and distributes them to appropriate newspapers, magazines, TV programs, columnists, and so on. He plans authors' parties and organizes authors' tours around the country. He also maintains clippings files of reviews and other press coverage given to books and authors. The salary ranges from $21,000 to $36,000.

Subsidiary Rights Manager: The subsidiary rights manager keeps close communication with the editorial department. He determines the scope of potential prospects for specific types of products, maintains up-to-date files on all potential sources, and follows up to ensure receipt of material sent.

His responsibilities include monitoring and negotiating contracts. He consults regularly with the marketing manager concerning subsidiary goals and follows up each sale of subsidiary rights. The salary range begins at $21,000 and goes up, depending on the size of the publishing house and the degree of responsibility.

Copywriter: The copywriter develops schedules for copy development. He obtains information about books from the editorial and marketing departments. The copywriter writes basic cover and other copy and develops variations. The salary ranges from $13,000 to $20,000.

Marketing Assistant: This is an entry-level position. The marketing assistant maintains sales records, distributes review copies of books, and assists in the preparation of catalogues and in the writing of specialized promotion pieces. The salary ranges from $12,000 to $16,000.

Marketing positions (not described) and their salary ranges:

Regional Sales Manager:
    $21,000 to $35,000
International Sales Manager:
    $27,000 to $41,000

Book Club positions (not described) and their salary ranges:

General Manager: $51,000 to $81,000
Editor: $25,000 to $30,000

General Qualifications for Marketing Positions

As with magazines, the best editorial product in book publishing will also fall on its face if it is not distributed and marketed efficiently. The marketing people are the shock troops; they do battle with wholesalers, retailers, distributors, and college professors, their basic objective being the selling of books. Often it's not fun, but it can be financially rewarding and a source of great pride in accomplishment when a line sells well.

One needs a marketing personality to sell used cars, aluminum siding, or books—aggressive, outgoing, persuasive, and even charming. A book is a different kind of product. A book salesperson, visiting the head of the psychology department at a university, needs a keen understanding of his book as well as its subject in order to persuade the professor to adopt the text for his classes.

Similarly, the regional sales manager for a large publisher, calling on B. Dalton in its Minneapolis headquarters, must be conversant with the themes of his entire seasonal line, which may number a hundred books. Add intelligence and a love of reading to the other qualifications, and you have a book marketer.

The Making of a Bestseller

Now that we have discussed the structure of the book publishing establishment and book publishing jobs, let's trace the path of a mythical book from the author's conception to its appearance on the shelf of a bookstore.

The Idea Stage

Let's imagine that our would-be author is an associate professor of humanities at a midwestern university. He has already published his doctoral thesis and numerous articles in professional journals, but he is intent on writing a novel about post–World War II Germany, a period and place of special interest to him. He has never published fiction.

Realizing that most fiction is placed with publishers through literary agents, the professor begins a solicitation of thirty agents, sending them each a ten-page outline of the novel, his bio (brief autobiographical sketch), and reprints of some of his articles.

After months with no success, an agent from New York, whom the professor had met briefly at a professional conference, expresses interest in the book. The agent suggests a meeting in New York (at the professor's expense), where the project could be discussed more fully. During lunch at the Algonquin Hotel, a well-known authors' hangout, the agent confirms to the professor that she thinks she can sell the book but will need to see certain changes in the outline that will make the book more salable to a publisher. The professor agrees to the revisions and promises to send the new outline in a few weeks.

About a month after the agent's receipt of the revised outline, the professor receives a call from her with the good news that a major trade book publisher is very interested in the book but wants to see a completed first chapter before making a commitment. The professor is reluctant to comply without a contract but agrees when the agent says that it is common practice.

Because the professor had done a rough draft of the whole book a year prior to these discussions, it takes him only a few months to complete the chapter. The publisher reads the chapter, is impressed with its quality, and agrees to publish the book on the next year's fall list, which will give the professor about fourteen months to write the book.

(A few words about lists and seasons: Most publishers have two principal seasons, spring and fall, when they issue catalogues showing their "list." The list includes the publisher's entire list of books in print—the backlist—as well as its forthcoming titles for that season—the frontlist. The frontlist, of course, receives greater emphasis.)

Within the publishing house, before a decision can be made on a submission such as this one, the project must be approved by the top echelon in the editorial group. Any strong negative arguments—such as poor sales by similar novels—can kill the book proposal. In this case, however, the enthusiasm for the plot and the professor's excellent writing style influence the positive decision.

The agent handles the deal itself with the publishing house's editor-in-chief, and, after much negotiation, they agree to an advance of $8,000—a respectable figure for a first-time novelist. The professor had idealized an advance of $15,000, but this was not to be.

(One must understand the precariousness of publishing a work of fiction. In a given year, American publishing houses put out more than 4,500 new fiction titles to a booksellers' market that can't absorb that many works. Further, much of what sells is commercial fiction of the Judith Krantz, Irving Wallace, and Sidney Sheldon variety. Literary fiction, such as the professor's book, appeals to a much smaller market.)

After the agent and the publishing house's editor-in-chief have agreed on all points and a contract has been signed, the professor is invited to New York to meet with the publisher's staff on procedures, coordination, scheduling, and similar details.

The Author Meets the Publisher

At his visit to the publishing house, which lasts two days, the professor meets many of the publisher's people and is particularly impressed with the executive editor. Although she seems cool and detached, she does convey the feeling that the book can be a success if the style, tone, and pace of the first chapter carry through the whole book. She will be the author's primary contact throughout the writing stage.

The relationship is key to the writing process, with the editor assuming many roles. At various times, she may goad, cajole, question, and praise. Often the simple comment "What do you really mean?" or "You can do better than that" may be all that's needed to shore up a shaky section. The editor's firm hand-holding is particularly significant when working with a first-time novelist.

In our mythical situation, the professor goes home and settles down to the meticulous and rigorous task of writing a book. As with most authors, there are infertile periods and many distractions, but with stamina and self-discipline, the professor perseveres, and fifteen months after his meetings in New York, he completes the manuscript.

Only then does the laborious regimen of final developmental and copy editing begin at the publishing house. After another read for content, the manuscript is checked and rechecked for style, usage, grammar, and punctuation. When this process is completed, the manuscript is ready for typesetting, the first stage in the manufacturing process.

From Galley Proof to the Bound Book

Type is set by a computerized phototypesetting system. It has the advantage over hot-type systems by virtue of its economy and speed. When the type for the novel is set, the galley proofs (representing the text of the book set in long sheets without regard to page breaks) are read by the proofreader against the edited manuscript and, of course, by the author. A few "author's alterations" are made. These are changes that do not appear in the typed manuscript.

When all concerned are pleased with the final set of corrections, the production department orders fifty sets of galley proofs for distribution to a wide group of people. The delivery of the galleys sets in motion a number of activities.

The art director/designer reads the galleys and, in consultation with the marketing director and editor-in-chief, arrives at satisfactory designs and illustrations for the cover and dust jacket.

The marketing director, in consultation with the editor-in-chief, makes the decision to print 10,000 copies of the hardbound edition of the book, a slightly higher figure than the average for most hardbound books. Both have read the galleys and are keenly excited about the book. By this time the marketing staff, also enthusiastic, has come up with a catchy title to bolster sales.

When the first books come off the press and are delivered to the publisher, all agree that it is indeed a quality novel, perhaps one destined for great success. The editor-in-chief and the executive editor send special congratulatory notes to the author. At this point, everyone loves everyone else.

Bestselleritis

By the time the book is presented to the sales force at the fall sales conference, "bestseller" is being whispered about. The marketing director alerts his publicity and promotion staff to arrange an author's publicity tour. He has met the professor only briefly but is convinced that his personality will lend itself to a successful tour.

First novels are not easily promoted unless there is a strong gimmick—such as the eighty-six-year-old Grandma Moses–like novelist referred to earlier in this chapter—available to attract the attention of talk show hosts.

When the professor visited the offices of the publisher, the promotion manager took him to lunch. In the course of their conversation, the promotion manager learned that the professor had been in military government stationed in Germany, right after World War II. Also, the book was somewhat autobiographical, as are many first novels. In the book, the central character is an American military governor who becomes involved with a German woman who is half-Jewish but was able to survive the Holocaust by hiding her true identity.

The emotional aspect of this plot and the author's involvement are deemed to be sufficient ammunition for a media blitz. It is agreed that a six-city tour will be arranged, with radio, TV, and newspaper interviews. The logistics require a great deal of planning.

The professor finds the traveling and interviews taxing, especially when bookstore signings are added to the PR program. They do, however, pay off. One appearance on the "Today" show can mean more for the sale of a book than many full-page newspaper ads.

While this promotion activity is being planned, other staffers are moving in many directions. The subsidiary rights people have submitted the galleys to the major book clubs. Although the two largest clubs, Book-of-the-Month Club and Literary Guild, do not buy it, a smaller scholarly club elects to make the book its principal monthly selection.

(An author and his publisher do not derive a great deal of revenue from a book club sale, usually 10 percent of the club's price on selections and 5 percent on free offers. Book club selection, however, does convey a great deal of prestige and is a definite plus in promoting bookstore sales. The clubs will often print their editions at the same time as the bookstore version. On major titles, the larger clubs offer guarantees as high as $500,000 or more.)

The subsidiary rights manager of the publishing company makes solicitations early on to the major movie studios for possible movie rights. This individual will have developed contacts at the acquisition or production level of the movie companies. This contact ensures that the book is read by someone in authority so that it receives proper consideration. There can be large sums of money involved in such a sale. Usually, the sale is made as an option of the property for a certain amount, with additional monies when the film is made. Many options are picked up without the pictures ever being produced.

The movie rights solicitation may be made individually or by multiple submissions to all the studios. Also, the sub rights manager must decide whether it is feasible to make the solicitation from the galley proofs or to wait instead for the book to be on sale. If the book becomes a bestseller, then obviously it can command more money as a movie property.

Agents for established name authors make every effort in their negotiations with book publishers to retain movie rights for the author. This may not be possible for a first-time novelist. In the case of our professor's novel, movie solicitations are made, but no rights are sold. In the studios' opinion, the subject matter of the book does not seem to have the popular appeal necessary for today's movie audiences.

Another area sought after by sub rights people is first serial rights in magazines. A number of large-circulation publications will run 20,000- to 30,000-word excerpts of a novel simultaneously with its publication date. This serves as excellent promotion for the book, and the revenue from this source can be remunerative. Here, too, name authors are able to retain these rights.

Foreign sales rights are pursued early on in the process of a book's publication. Much of the contact is between the sub rights department and foreign sales agents. Larger publishers maintain ongoing relationships with certain publishers in foreign countries that receive first refusal on their properties.

A major publisher in Germany does buy the rights for the professor's novel for a $4,000 advance and a 6,000-copy first hardbound printing. Of course, the story takes place in Germany, and this explains the

THE NEW YORK TIMES BOOK REVIEW

Best Sellers

Fiction

This Week		Last Week	Weeks On List
1	**IT,** by Stephen King. (Viking, $22.95.) Childhood horrors haunt six men and a woman who grew up in a small Maine town.	1	8
2	**RED STORM RISING,** by Tom Clancy. (Putnam, $19.95.) Without using nuclear weapons, the West staves off the Russians in World War III.	2	14
3	**HOLLYWOOD HUSBANDS,** by Jackie Collins. (Simon & Schuster, $18.95.) A top New York model encounters three of Los Angeles's most dynamic men.	3	3
4	**THE PRINCE OF TIDES,** by Pat Conroy. (Houghton Mifflin, $19.95.) Complex family relationships in South Carolina's low country and New York City.	4	5
5	**WANDERLUST,** by Danielle Steel. (Delacorte, $17.95.) A rich orphan comes of age while she travels the world.	5	16
6	**THE GOLDEN CUP,** by Belva Plain. (Delacorte, $17.95.) Continuing the saga of a turn-of-the-century New York family begun in "Evergreen."	9	4
7	**FOUNDATION AND EARTH,** by Isaac Asimov. (Doubleday, $16.95.) The hero of the "Foundation" series searches for the lost planet Earth.	10	3
8	**A TASTE FOR DEATH,** by P. D. James. (Knopf, $18.95.) Inspector Adam Dalgliesh investigates a brutal double murder.		1
9	**THROUGH A GLASS DARKLY,** by Karleen Koen. (Random House, $19.95.) Romance, family conflict, power and greed mark a young woman's life in 18th-century England and France.	6	9
10	**FORTUNE OF FEAR,** by L. Ron Hubbard. (Bridge Publications, $18.95.) Countess Krak of Voltar arrives from outer space to save Earth from an invasion.	12	2
11	**ROGER'S VERSION,** by John Updike. (Knopf, $17.95.) A fiftyish professor wrestles with God, sex, science, technology, mathematics and computers.	7	7
12	**FLIGHT OF THE INTRUDER,** by Stephen Coonts. (Naval Institute, $15.95.) Navy aviators at war over Vietnam.		1
13	**THE BEET QUEEN,** by Louise Erdrich. (Holt, $16.95.) Forty years in a small North Dakota town near an Indian reservation.	8	6
14	**PERFUME,** by Patrick Süskind. (Knopf, $16.95.) An olfactory vampire kills people to steal their scents.		1
15	**THE WILD BLUE,** by Walter J. Boyne and Steven L. Thompson. (Crown, $19.95.) Six members of the Air Force at work, at play and in love.		2

Nonfiction

This Week		Last Week	Weeks On List
1	**HIS WAY,** by Kitty Kelley. (Bantam, $21.95.) From Hoboken to superstardom: an unauthorized biography of Frank Sinatra.	1	4
2	**FATHERHOOD,** by Bill Cosby. (Dolphin/Doubleday, $14.95.) Anecdotes and ruminations from the television star and father of five.	2	26
3	**THE RECKONING,** by David Halberstam. (Morrow, $19.95.) The crisis in the American automobile industry and Japan's role in it.	5	4
4	**THE STORY OF ENGLISH,** by Robert McCrum, William Cran and Robert MacNeil. (Sifton/Viking, $24.95.) Companion volume to the PBS series about the world's most widely used language.	3	4
5	**MCMAHON!** by Jim McMahon with Bob Verdi. (Warner, $16.95.) The autobiography of the quarterback for the Chicago Bears.	4	6
6 *	**ONE MORE TIME,** by Carol Burnett. (Random House, $18.95.) From impoverished childhood to television star: the comedian's autobiography.		1
7	**YOU'RE ONLY OLD ONCE!** by Dr. Seuss. (Random House, $9.95.) A checkup at the Golden Years Clinic in pictures and rhyme.	7	34
8	**DREAMGIRL,** by Mary Wilson with Patricia Romanowski and Ahrgus Juilliard. (St. Martin's, $16.95.) A former member of the Supremes tells of her time with the group.		1
9	**SNAKE,** by Ken Stabler and Berry Stainback. (Doubleday, $15.95.) The experiences of the retired Oakland Raiders quarterback.	10	6
10	**NECESSARY LOSSES,** by Judith Viorst. (Simon & Schuster, $17.95.) Life is a series of losses, the author argues, and we must confront them to grow.	11	28
11	**ONE KNEE EQUALS TWO FEET,** by John Madden with Dave Anderson. (Villard, $16.95.) Observations on football by the television commentator and former Oakland Raiders coach.	8	6
12	**DANCING ON MY GRAVE,** by Gelsey Kirkland with Greg Lawrence. (Doubleday, $17.95.) The ballerina recalls her checkered career.		1
13	**MAYFLOWER MADAM,** by Sydney Biddle Barrows with William Novak. (Arbor House, $17.95.) A member of one of America's oldest families tells of the world's oldest profession.	6	7
14	**I, TINA,** by Tina Turner with Kurt Loder. (Morrow, $16.95.) The autobiography of a Tennessee sharecropper's daughter who became a rock-and-roll star.	9	5
15 *	**MY DADDY WAS A PISTOL AND I'M A SON OF A GUN,** by Lewis Grizzard. (Villard, $14.95.) Memories of growing up Southern with a very Southern father.	12	3

And Bear in Mind

(Editors' choices of other recent books of particular interest)

PARADISE, by Donald Barthelme. (Putnam, $16.95.) Three models move in with Simon, an architect on sabbatical from his job and his wife; a very funny and often brilliant novel.

THE LEAGUE: The Rise and Decline of the NFL, by David Harris. (Bantam, $21.95.) Mr. Harris chooses to ignore the heroics of football players and focus on the shenanigans of team owners. The gamble pays off, thanks to his diligent reporting.

THE HARVEST OF SORROW: Soviet Collectivization and the Terror-Famine, by Robert Conquest. (Oxford University, $19.95.) Chronicling one of the great modern tragedies: Stalin's deliberate starvation of millions of peasants, most of them Ukrainians.

A SUMMONS TO MEMPHIS, by Peter Taylor. (Knopf, $15.95.) The consequences of a family betrayal that happened 40 years ago are the matter of this novel of manners that incorporates tragedy without the slightest huff or puff of pretension or magniloquence.

THE ENCHANTER, by Vladimir Nabokov. (Putnam, $16.95.) Written in Russian in 1939, this is the Ur-"Lolita," an unpleasant short novel about a child molester and a nerdy girl; it prefigures the mature masterpiece only in plot and humor.

A MISSING PLANE, by Susan Sheehan. (Putnam, $18.95.) From scattered bones, an anthropologist identifies 22 men lost in a 1944 Army airplane crash; then the author's reconstructive journalism recovers their lives from the memories of family and friends.

TO SKIN A CAT, by Thomas McGuane. (Seymour Lawrence/Dutton, $16.95.) The Wild West lives in the hearts of Mr. McGuane's restless, skeptical modern Americans, and at moments of stress in these stories it is apt to burst out in crazy violence that seems just right — esthetically, at least.

Advice, How-to and Miscellaneous

This Week		Last Week	Weeks On List
1	**MEN WHO HATE WOMEN & THE WOMEN WHO LOVE THEM,** by Susan Forward and Joan Torres. (Bantam, $16.95.) How to cope with overbearing men.	1	7
2	**THE ROTATION DIET,** By Martin Katahn. (Norton, $15.95.) A regimen based on the Vanderbilt University Weight Management Program.	2	24
3	**FIT FOR LIFE,** by Harvey Diamond and Marilyn Diamond. (Warner, $17.50.) A diet for weight loss and physical fitness.	3	63
4	**BE HAPPY YOU ARE LOVED,** by Robert H. Schuller. (Nelson, $15.95.) Inspiration from a California clergyman.	4	2
5	**THE FRUGAL GOURMET COOKS WITH WINE,** by Jeff Smith. (Morrow, $16.95.) Recipes to be prepared at moderate cost.		1

The listings above are based on computer-processed sales figures from 2,000 bookstores in every region of the United States, statistically adjusted to represent sales in all bookstores. In Advice and How-to, five titles are listed because, beyond that point, sales in this category are not generally large enough to make a longer list statistically reliable.

*An asterisk before a book's title indicates that its sales, weighted to reflect the bookselling industry nationally, are barely distinguishable from those of the book above.

The list of hardbound bestsellers from the *New York Times Book Review*. Note that Stephen King is in fourth place on the paperback list but first in hardbound. Danielle Steel and Tom Clancy are also in top positions on both lists. The Sinatra book made the top of the list in the first few weeks of its publication. (Copyright © 1986 by The New York Times Company. Reprinted by permission.)

November 2, 1986   THE NEW YORK TIMES BOOK REVIEW

Paperback Best Sellers

Fiction

1 **SECRETS,** by Danielle Steel. (Dell, $4.95.) Behind the scenes of a television production.

2 **THE SECRETS OF HARRY BRIGHT,** by Joseph Wambaugh. (Bantam, $4.50.) A detective's quest for a killer and the meaning of his own son's death.

3 **CONTACT,** by Carl Sagan. (Pocket, $4.95.) The commotion that follows the reception of a signal from intelligent life beyond Earth.

4 **THE BACHMAN BOOKS,** by Stephen King. (Signet/NAL, $5.95.) Four horror novels previously published as the work of Richard Bachman.

5 **THE HUNT FOR RED OCTOBER,** by Tom Clancy. (Berkley, $4.50.) A submarine driver brings Soviet nuclear secrets to the United States.

6 **THE VAMPIRE LESTAT,** by Anne Rice. (Ballantine, $4.50.) Eerie carryings-on in a tale ranging from ancient Egypt to the 20th century.

7 **THE RED FOX,** by Anthony Hyde. (Ballantine, $4.50.) A thriller in which a journalist journeys to Russia, seeking the father of a woman he loves.

8 **THE ACCIDENTAL TOURIST,** by Anne Tyler. (Berkley, $4.50.) Family and friends impose order of a kind on the errant life of a travel writer.

9 **TALES OF THE WOLF,** by Lawrence Sanders. (Avon, $3.95.) Thirteen adventures of Wolf Lannihan, sleuth and womanizer.

10 **LAKE WOBEGON DAYS,** by Garrison Keillor. (Penguin, $4.95.) Yarns about life in a small Minnesota town.

11 **GALAPAGOS,** by Kurt Vonnegut. (Dell, $4.50.) Passengers on a Pacific cruise are mankind's sole survivors.

12 **HANDS OF A STRANGER,** by Robert Daley. (Signet/NAL, $4.50.) A New York policeman torn between lust and love, vengeance and ambition.

13 **TO SEE YOUR FACE AGAIN,** by Eugenia Price. (Berkley, $4.50.) Romance and adventure in antebellum Savannah and the Georgia countryside.

14 **THE CAT WHO WALKS THROUGH WALLS,** by Robert A. Heinlein. (Berkley, $3.95.) A comic look at a future in which mankind tries to control fate.

15 **DRAGONLANCE LEGENDS: Volume Three, Test of the Twins,** by Margaret Weis and Tracy Hickman. (TSR, $3.95.) A battle between brothers.

Nonfiction

General

1 **THE ROAD LESS TRAVELED,** by M. Scott Peck. (Touchstone/S&S, $9.95.) Psychological and spiritual inspiration by a psychiatrist.

2 **WEST WITH THE NIGHT,** by Beryl Markham. (North Point, $12.50.) A woman's experiences flying in East Africa and across the Atlantic in the 1930's.

3 **DANCING IN THE LIGHT,** by Shirley MacLaine. (Bantam, $4.50.) The entertainer wins an Oscar, survives a stormy romance and has new visions.

4 **YEAGER,** by Chuck Yeager and Leo Janos. (Bantam, $4.95.) The ex-test pilot's autobiography.

5 **HOUSE,** by Tracy Kidder. (Avon, $4.50.) Building a Greek Revival house in Massachusetts.

6 **IACOCCA: An Autobiography,** by Lee Iacocca with William Novak. (Bantam, $4.95.) How the son of immigrants rose to top jobs at Ford and Chrysler.

Advice, How-to and Miscellaneous

1 **WOMEN WHO LOVE TOO MUCH,** by Robin Norwood. (Pocket, $4.50.) How to avoid or end addictive, unhealthy relationships with men.

2 **BLOOM COUNTY BABYLON,** by Berke Breathed. (Little, Brown, $12.95.) Five years of comic strips.

3 **THE FAR SIDE GALLERY 2,** by Gary Larson. (Andrews, McMeel & Parker, $9.95.) A collection of syndicated "Far Side" cartoons.

4 **DIANETICS,** by L. Ron Hubbard. (Bridge Publications, $4.95.) Revised edition of a handbook by the founder of Scientology.

5 **ADULT CHILDREN OF ALCOHOLICS,** by Janet Geringer Woititz. (Health Communications, $6.95.) Advice about a family problem.

6 **IT CAME FROM THE FAR SIDE,** by Gary Larson. (Andrews, McMeel & Parker, $5.95.) More "Far Side" cartoons.

7 **THE OLD FARMER'S ALMANAC,** by Robert B. Thomas. (Yankee Publishing, $2.25.) Lore and data.

8 * **RAND MCNALLY ROAD ATLAS: United States, Canada, Mexico.** (Rand McNally, $5.95.) For 1986.

9 **CRACKING THE SYSTEM,** by Adam Robinson and John Katzman. (Villard, $9.95.) A guide to the Scholastic Aptitude Test.

The listings above are based on computer-processed sales figures from 2,000 bookstores and from representative wholesalers with more than 40,000 retail outlets, including newsstands, variety stores, supermarkets and bookstores. These figures are statistically adjusted to represent sales in all such outlets across the United States. The number of titles within the two subdivisions of nonfiction can change from week to week, reflecting changes in book buying.

*An asterisk before a book's title indicates that its sales, weighted to reflect the book-selling industry nationally, are barely distinguishable from those of the book above.

interest. Publishers in other countries that are solicited take a wait-and-see attitude by passing on the rights until the book has a U.S. sales history.

The foreign rights people are not too disappointed because the book will be on sale for a few months by the time the Frankfurt Book Fair has begun in October. Then, if the book is successful in the States, there will be dozens of opportunities for foreign rights sales.

Another method for stimulating sales is the use of complimentary quotations from famous people on the back of the jacket. The publicity and promotion people generate these blurbs by sending the galley proofs to authors and celebrities who are affiliated with the publisher. Any positive comments by "name" authors and famous people are used on the book and also in advertising.

For a work of literary fiction, reviews are extremely important. For less-literary novels, less so. Getting the author on the "Today" show can, as already mentioned, generate the necessary word-of-mouth that makes a book a bestseller.

For serious fiction and nonfiction, a good review in the *New York Times Book Review* can sell out a first hardbound printing. Book buyers are a sophisticated lot who look to many sources before making a major commitment to a book. Reviews in the authoritative trade publication *Publishers Weekly* are significant, as are those in the prestigious Kirkus Reviews service.

Good reviews do not guarantee a book's success, but bad reviews can surely kill its chances. A book review is unlike a movie review, by which the critics have little effect on the box office, at least for most youth-oriented films.

The Aftermath

Let's reprise the sequence of events in the making of a bestseller for the professor's novel about post-war Germany.

The critics' consensus is mostly positive. Stores that didn't order the book initially now place orders for small quantities. Because of the somber aspect of the subject matter, it is difficult for the publicity people to schedule major TV talk shows.

The author goes on a publicity tour immediately after the book's publication. In some cities, he does one interview on TV, two on radio, and one for the major newspaper; yet, when he does a book signing in a large bookstore, there are few customers, causing embarrassment to the publisher's local salesperson and the store manager and frustration on the part of the author, who wishes he was back at the university.

As the author browses in other bookstores, he doesn't see his book displayed or on the racks. He is beginning to understand the realities of being an author. Physically and emotionally exhausted from the six-city tour, he complains to the marketing director, who responds, "We're doing the best we can."

The professor becomes bitter and harangues the marketing director about the lack of advertising support. The director answers placidly, "We don't have a budget for it."

So that's the story of a bestseller that doesn't happen. The book is well written. The publisher doesn't get behind it all the way, but, in fairness, this novel is not the torrid intimate memoirs of a former government official; it is a fine work of literary fiction that is difficult to propel to the top.

In the end, the publishing house makes back its expenses on the book. Other than his advance, however, the professor receives no income. He returns to the tranquility of academia somewhat disillusioned. What he must realize is that of the thousands of books published every year, only a tiny few make the bestseller lists. In other words, only a minuscule number of authors get rich from their craft.

Small Presses

There are 1,800 small presses throughout the world, most of them in the United States. They're called "small" because their average individual output of original works per year is only about twenty-five or thirty titles each. Generally, they publish authors whose works are often spurned by larger publishers, basically because they lack mass appeal. Yet it is fortunate that these small presses exist. For, although they do have the same profit strictures, they do not have to answer to the boards of conglomerates.

Small presses, known also as independent presses, publish a broad range of subjects—poetry, fiction, art, scholarly books on music, architecture, and science—usually deemed too risky for larger publishers. Authors' advances from a small house may be only a few hundred dollars each, but these authors know that their books will be published with affection and understanding.

The audience for books from small presses has widened. Where, in the immediate post–World War

II period, the audience for experimental or avant-garde literature was perhaps 25,000, today it is many times this figure. Contemporary literature is being taught at many colleges, and these paperback works are assigned by professors for class use or outside reading.

The giants of modern literature—Dylan Thomas, Tennessee Williams, Jean-Paul Sartre, Federico Garcia Lorca, and others—are now standard fare in literature courses. Professors prefer to assign a group of paperbacks rather than works from anthologies. There is no longer an impassable barrier between an appeal to the intellect and mass culture.

Although many small presses do not choose to go public about it, they do accept unsolicited manuscripts. This does not mean, however, that a poorly written work will have a better chance of being published by a small press. On the contrary, the standards of small presses are higher than those of the large houses. Nevertheless, knowing that their works will at least be considered provides encouragement to many authors.

New Directions

When the controversial poet and critic Ezra Pound told a young Harvard dropout, James Laughlin, that he must do something useful in his life, the young man heeded Pound's advice and formed the small publishing house New Directions in 1936.

More than a half-century later, one looks at the career of Laughlin and New Directions with much admiration. In his first twenty years, Laughlin lost $250,000, turning a profit only in the late '50s. As an heir to the Jones and Laughlin steel fortune, Laughlin could maintain his philosophy of literature as art, not business, enabling him to explore the avant-garde and the experimental—and explore it he did. New Directions pioneered the works of Gertrude Stein, Henry Miller, and William Saroyan, as well as the works of poets Delmore Schwartz, e. e. cummings, Dylan Thomas, and Marianne Moore.

In the '50s, New Directions broke new ground publishing the San Francisco avant-gardists Kenneth Rexroth, Gregory Corso, and Lawrence Ferlinghetti. It reprinted the notable writers Henry James, E. M. Forster, and Evelyn Waugh when others would not.

Perhaps its greatest contribution through the years has been in bringing foreign authors to American readers in translation. Consider just a few: Rimbaud, Baudelaire, Kafka, Cocteau, Neruda, Lorca, Pasternak, Borges, and Mishima.

New Directions' entire staff is equivalent in size to the subsidiary rights department of a large publisher. Eight people bring out about twenty-five original books a year, some of them paperback editions of its hardcover books. The average print run of one of its books is 1,000 in cloth and 3,000 in paper. The publishing house receives approximately fifty submissions per week.

Each year since 1936, New Directions has published its annual edition. This distinguished literary journal includes poetry and short stories by new and established writers, but, as with many quality literary journals, the press run is small, about 3,000 copies.

I was surprised to learn that occasionally a New Directions book takes off. Hermann Hesse's *Siddhartha,* a favorite of the hippie generation, sold as many as a quarter of a million copies a year in the late '60s. Lawrence Ferlinghetti's *Coney Island of the Mind* enjoyed a million-copy sale.

The Case for the Small Press

In an article in *Publishers Weekly,* author Todd Walton, who wrote three novels for major New York publishing houses—one made into the movie *Inside Moves*—eschewed the big-time approach in favor of a small San Francisco publisher, Mercury House. Here are a few of the numerous advantages Walton gives for going the small-press route:

Each book purchased is a significant investment. The author is treated with respect. The creation itself is the highest priority. The small-press editor displays a high degree of optimism, a trait not shared by his major-publisher counterparts. The author feels the total experience of participating in an effort that is harmonious, optimistic, creative, and inspiring.

Two in California

Small presses are located everywhere but usually not in big cities. One such operation is North Point Press, founded in 1978 in Berkeley, California. With a staff of only ten, North Point publishes quality works produced elegantly. North Point's *Son of the Morning Star,* an account of General George Custer and the Battle of Little Bighorn by Evan Connell, remained on the bestseller list for six months and sold more than 150,000 copies in hardcover.

In Los Altos, California, still another small publisher has been making waves, primarily because of its affinity to unusual projects. One of William Kaufmann, Inc.'s recent books deals with "AI," artificial intelligence or compuhter-induced thought processes.

Kaufmann published a $120 three-volume set about artificial intelligence. A science-fiction book club ordered more than 10,000 sets. The publisher's range, however, is eclectic, running from the environmentally oriented *New Book of California Tomorrow* to a first novel by fifty-nine-year-old Martin Gardner, *The Flight of Peter Fromm.*

A Very Unusual Publisher

I first became aware of Da Capo Press in 1982 when I had the grandiose plan of producing a big Broadway musical based on the life of America's first renowned composer/pianist, Louis Moreau Gottschalk. Gottschalk lived from 1829 to 1869; in that short span he composed a body of wonderful works performed on three continents and, incidentally, had love affairs with dozens of adoring female admirers. His memoirs, *Notes of a Pianist*, published posthumously in 1881, were reprinted in 1979 by Da Capo, a small arts press in New York.

Notes of a Pianist was immensely valuable to me. Although it is now a memento of my unfulfilled producing dream, it also introduced me to Da Capo, an extraordinary publishing operation whose catalogue reads like a candy store of the senses in music, dance, and the arts.

Da Capo was founded in 1964 as an outgrowth of a publisher of scientific journals, Plenum Publishing. It originally issued hardcover reprints of books on classical music but is now much more diversified.

In 1976, musicologist Bea Friedland joined Da Capo as executive editor. Under her editorship, Da Capo's scope widened to include books on dance, jazz, architecture, and the graphic arts. At the same time, the company ventured into the expanding world of trade paperbacks, publishing about thirty titles a year. Most are reprints of other publishers' hardcover editions; others are quality paperback editions of out-of-print classics. This category now accounts for more than half of Da Capo's volume.

One can appreciate the diversity of Da Capo's mix by reviewing the following list of some of its recent titles in both hardcover and paperback:

- *The Magic of Opera* by J. Merrill Knapp
- *Schubert: A Musical Portrait* by Alfred Einstein
- *Mingus: A Critical Biography* by Brian Priestley
- *In the Nature of Materials: The Buildings of Frank Lloyd Wright 1887–1941* by Henry Russell Hitchcock
- *The Sounds of Two Hands Clapping* by Kenneth Tynan

- *Serge Diaghilev—His Life, His Work, His Legend* by Serge Lifar
- *The 900 Days: The Siege of Leningrad* by Harrison E. Salisbury
- *On Movies* by Dwight Macdonald
- *Turner: Paintings, Watercolours, Prints and Drawings* by Luke Herrmann
- *The Art and History of Books* by Norma Levarie

Da Capo's gift to book publishing is an impressive selection of works that otherwise might be lost to the discriminating reader. It's the kind of publishing we rarely see today, and we are fortunate that it exists.

CAREER TIP: Readers who are capable of writing quality literary fiction and poetry should consider submitting their work to a small press. The chances of being published are slim, as are the advances if one is accepted; yet the reward of being published by a high-quality small press is to be accepted in the inner circle of literature.

Would-be authors would be well advised to check publishers' listings in the *LMP* as well so that they don't send a highly specific type of proposal to a house that doesn't publish that type of material.

Working for a small press can also be worthwhile and rewarding. At such a press, you won't be pigeonholed into one department with no sense of what's happening on the next floor, as might be the case when working for a large publisher. Because most have small staffs, you have the opportunity of assuming two, three, or more job functions. The salary may be less, but what better way to learn the craft of book publishing?

An excellent bimonthly magazine about small presses is *Small Press: The Magazine for Independent/In-house/Desktop Publishing*, put out by Meckler Publishing, 11 Ferry Lane West, Westport, CT

06880. It contains news and features of interest to smaller independent book and magazine publishers, writers, and others who follow publishing trends. A year's subscription costs $23.95; write to the magazine at Dept. VV, P.O. Box 3000, Denville, NJ 07834.

University Presses

There are approximately eighty-five university presses in the United States. They account for about $85 million in publishers' net book sales, just a bit more than 1 percent of the sales of all books; yet their quality far exceeds their tiny output.

These presses published only 5,300 books in 1985 but won 25 percent of the annual top book prizes. Typically, their production is directed toward the publication of scholarly works of nonfiction. Although there is obviously favorable consideration given to a university's own faculty, most of these presses maintain high standards and objectivity in their selection process.

Many books emanating from university presses are geared to academics in specific disciplines at other universities; however, there are some titles with appeal to students and the general public, and occasionally even fiction appears on their lists.

Because print quantities of these books are small, the advances received by their authors are small as well. Of course, in the "publish or perish" atmosphere of academia, authors do not write these books for financial considerations.

A look at some sample listings of university presses from the *LMP* will give our readers an understanding of their diversity. Note particularly the variety of both the number of titles and the subject matter.

University of Chicago Press: 1985 output: 262 titles. In print: 3,000 titles. Scholarly, nonfiction, advanced texts and monographs, clothbound and paperback, microfiche, scholarly and professional journals.

University of Nevada Press: 1985 output: 12 titles. In print: 55 titles. Scholarly books dealing with Nevada, the West, and the Basque people.

Harvard University Press: 1985 output: 130 titles. In print: 2,750 titles. General scholarly, medical, and scientific books.

University of Illinois Press: 1985 output: 60 titles. In print: 810 titles. General and scholarly nonfiction, especially in American studies, communications, film studies, folklore and black studies, poetry, and short fiction.

University Press of Kansas: 1985 output: 19 titles. In print: 168 titles. General scholarly nonfiction: U.S. history, government and political science, literary criticism, philosophy, and regional.

Let's analyze the University Press of Kansas: Of eleven new publications in its spring and summer 1986 catalogue, only one author was a member of the University of Kansas faculty, although most of the other authors were academics at other universities. Many of the books in the catalogue are regional in nature—for example, *Prohibition in Kansas, a History; The WPA Guide to 1930s Missouri; Exodusters—Black Migration to Kansas after Reconstruction;* and *Farming the Dust Bowl—a First-hand Account from Kansas.*

A Look at Scientific and Technical Publishing: John Wiley & Sons

LMP lists approximately 500 publishers in the scientific and technical categories. We will here zero in on one of the largest and most prestigious, John Wiley & Sons.

In 1807, Charles Wiley opened a small printing plant in downtown New York near city hall. From printing, the tiny company branched out to become a bookstore and publishing operation. Its early output included law books, reprints of contemporary European works, language texts, journals, and a new genre—the American novel.

By 1915, Wiley became recognized for publishing the best in scientific literature. In the years before World War II, the company widened its sphere to include business and professional books. In the service during World War II, I can remember studying two Wiley books, *Principles of Radio* and *Elements of Electricity,* both having sold in the hundreds of thousands.

In the 1950s, worldwide interest in science escalated with Russia's launching of *Sputnik,* and Wiley became an international scientific publisher with the publication of such prominent nuclear scientists as Edward Teller, Harold Urey, Hans Bethe, and MIT's *Cybernetics* author, Norbert Weiner.

By the 1970s, there were subsidiaries and joint

ventures in England, Australia, Canada, Singapore, Mexico, India, and Brazil. The company, run by W. Bradford Wiley, the great-great-great-grandson of John Wiley, had become a major force in world-wide technical and scientific publishing.

John Wiley & Sons Today

Since 1963, ten Wiley authors have received the Nobel Prize for achievements in various fields of medicine and science. Here are some landmark books published by Wiley, which will give you an indication of the range of this unusual company:

- *Physics* by David Halliday and Robert Resnick. This highly popular book uses easy, almost colloquial, language and cartoons ("Peanuts" is a favorite) to explain technical concepts.
- *General Virology* by S. E. Luria (Nobelist).
- *The Rorschach: A Comprehensive System* by John E. Exner, Jr. This work sets forth the first cohesive system for scoring and interpreting the Rorschach projective psychological test.
- *Basic Inorganic Chemistry* by Geoffrey Wilkinson (Nobelist).
- *Cybernetics* by Norbert Weiner. This ground-breaking work led to the development of artificial intelligence.

John Wiley & Sons publishes more than 1,000 books and related information products each year and maintains a backlist of more than 10,000 titles in more than 400 disciplines. It has a roster of approximately 11,000 distinguished authors and 1,300 employees worldwide. Incidentally, Wiley's headquarters are still in New York. The company has net sales of about $200 million.

Summing Up

Being involved in the publishing of fiction and nonfiction bestsellers by celebrity authors has its own brand of excitement, especially when you read in the next day's newspaper about the famous person whose hand you shook the night before at a cocktail party. More important, being involved in a business that disseminates information and knowledge to people who need and use it makes for a most rewarding career. Why not explore scientific, technical, and educational publishing?

Elementary, High School, and College Textbooks

Textbooks are big business. By the late '80s they accounted for almost $2 billion in publishers' net book sales. El hi books (elementary and high school texts) comprise 60 percent of this total. Commenting on its recent purchase of Scott, Foresman, a textbook publisher, a Time, Inc., executive said, "Educational publishing is the largest and, without question, the most profitable segment of publishing. The profit margins are 20 percent or more and are considerably more attractive than [those in] other parts of book publishing."

Many book publishers vie for this large and lucrative market. There are about one hundred elementary, 130 high school, and 329 college textbook publishers listed in the *LMP*. These publishers overlap in that many produce both elementary and high school texts, and some publish in all three fields.

Textbook publishing is a lot less glamorous than trade book publishing—no celebrity authors and no cocktail parties, either. These publishers function in a very structured fashion, with long-range planning in the book's preparation and a difficult selling process.

The selling process has become more complex than in the past for a variety of reasons. Formerly, the decision on a public school textbook's adoption was made at the state level. Obviously, if a book continued to be adopted year after year, it did not allow competitive publishers to get into the act. Today, that situation has changed radically. Decisions on adoptions are made at many levels: the state and city, school districts, individual schools, departments within a school, community school boards, and even by individual teachers.

When I went to school, all textbooks were hardbound. Today, paperbound books account for more than 40 percent of all el hi textbooks and about 16 percent of all college textbooks. In addition, the use of audio-visual and other nonprinted materials makes this phase of book publishing much more diversified.

My own experience with a supplementary textbook is rather positive. When I wrote *The Magazine: Everything You Need to Know to Make It in the Magazine Business* for Prentice-Hall, the marketing people considered it a good bet for adoption in

A page from the catalogue of Silver Burdett & Ginn shows some of the products available from the educational side of the publishing industry. (From *Silver Burdett & Ginn Catalog K–8,* © 1987 Silver Burdett & Ginn. Used with permission.)

colleges with journalism programs on magazines. The field staff was given advance copies of the book, promotional material, and a list of the professors teaching these courses.

Reports came back to Prentice-Hall's marketing staff, my editor, and me about the reaction to the book. As a result of the sales calls, *The Magazine* was adopted by many journalism schools. The staff was then able to use these successful sales in its selling efforts to other schools.

The job of selling to school boards, districts, and schools is indeed a specialized one. It requires knowledge of the educational needs of the prospect, as well as a total understanding of the line of books.

These sales jobs generally pay more than similar ones at trade bookhouses. Lists of textbook publishers may be found in that reliable source, the *LMP*.

Ginn: An Elementary Textbook Company

Let's look at a typical large company in the textbook field, Ginn & Company. Ginn is a division of the publishing giant Simon & Schuster, which in turn is owned by the conglomerate Gulf & Western. Ginn specializes in elementary textbooks and, in some years, publishes more than 300 titles. Currently, it has more than 4,000 titles in print.

The textbook company Silver Burdett was also acquired by Simon & Schuster in 1985 and merged into the operations of Ginn. On its own, Silver Burdett has almost 5,000 books in print. The trend to consolidation certainly seems evident in the textbook field.

Another Simon & Schuster subsidiary, Globe

Book Company, publishes about 350 titles a year, specializing in the development of materials for secondary school youngsters with reading problems and in creating skills within the discipline being taught while continuing to develop and supplement reading skills.

> CAREER TIP: Textbooks are written by academics. Although these people are specialists in their fields, many are not skilled writers and do not have the expertise necessary to write textbooks. This creates opportunities for staff writers and copy editors at textbook publishers. When writing and editing talent is coupled with expertise in specific fields such as science, history, computers, and so on, it becomes a very marketable commodity.

Ginn has been in publishing since 1867. Its range includes school systems across the United States and in more than one hundred foreign countries. Ginn's catalogue reveals the depth of this company in elementary school textbooks and educational materials.

El hi textbooks have grown in their diversity and scope to meet the educational challenge of the computer age. While there are still major problems in educating many segments of our population, the majority of sociologists and educators believe that the root cause of these problems lies in economics and its concomitant social conditions, not in the tools of education.

College Textbooks

As mentioned earlier, more than 300 publishers vie for the college textbook market. One such company is Allyn & Bacon, another of the Simon & Schuster family of publishers. Its output of 140 titles a year covers twenty-five disciplines from anthropology to theater, with computer science, educational psychology, and political science included in the mix.

As with el hi publishing, the college textbook field is a challenging area, both from the editorial and marketing aspects. An advantage, too, for job seekers is the diversified location across the country of college textbook publishers.

Publishers Weekly

In early 1987, the R. R. Bowker Company sold *Publishers Weekly* to another prominent business magazine publisher, Cahners Publishing (for more information about Cahners, see the magazine chapter). *Publishers Weekly* has been in existence for more than one hundred years and is a vital spokesman for the book publishing industry.

Anyone wanting to learn about book publishing should invest in a one-year subscription, which costs $84.00. In *PW,* as it's known in the trade, the reader will find editorials, features, reviews, lists, articles—everything that's current in the book business.

Even the ads are interesting, and, incidentally, the magazine has a good want ads section in the back. Write to the magazine at 205 East 42nd Street, New York, NY 10017.

R. R. Bowker: The Information Company

R. R. Bowker is the most important information source for the publishing and library trades. In addition to its numerous directories, it publishes the magazines *Library Journal* for professional librarians and *School Library Journal* for libraries serving children and young adults.

Referred to often in this chapter is the resourceful annual directory *Literary Market Place.* In it one can find listings and profiles of all major book publishers, book clubs, associations, suppliers to the book business, and more. A key feature is *LMP*'s "Names and Numbers" section, where one can find quick contact information on 25,000 key people in the industry. *LMP*'s present edition has 900 pages. For those dealing with the foreign market, Bowker also publishes *International Literary Market Place* (*ILMP*).

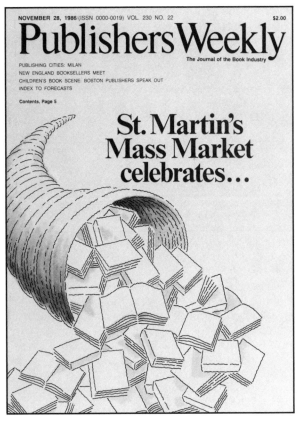

NOVEMBER 28, 1986 (ISSN 0000-0019) VOL. 230 NO. 22 $2.00

PublishersWeekly
The Journal of the Book Industry

PUBLISHING CITIES: MILAN
NEW ENGLAND BOOKSELLERS MEET
CHILDREN'S BOOK SCENE: BOSTON PUBLISHERS SPEAK OUT
INDEX TO FORECASTS

Contents, Page 5

St. Martin's
Mass Market
celebrates...

Publishers Weekly **is the bible of the industry. (Reprinted with permission of The Mesa Group.)**

Did you ever wonder where to find information on some obscure book that you're not sure is still in print? The six-volume set *Books in Print* solves that problem by providing the current price, edition, publisher, binding, and author information on more than 695,000 books. About 70,000 new titles are added each year. In addition, the set contains contact information for more than 17,500 publishers and distributors. Publishers make constant reference to *Books in Print*, often just to check the competition's output. Large bookstores may have a set of *Books in Print* for reference purposes.

Bowker's Database provides an online service for libraries and bookstores enabling these clients to access information such as that in *Books in Print* with microcomputer speed and convenience. In addition, the information company's services extend beyond the book publishing industry. Here are some other representative titles from its roster of books and directories: *The Software Encyclopedia, Audio Video Market Place, American Men and Women of Science, Directory of American Research and Technology, American Art Directory,* and *Who's Who in American Politics.*

One would do well to locate a library with access to Bowker's line. This source of information can be extremely helpful in research and writing projects, or maybe just in looking for a job.

Two Giants in Book Retailing

Waldenbooks

The Waldenbooks story takes the "humble beginnings" prize. Larry W. Hoyt opened a small book rental library in a department store in Bridgeport, Connecticut, on March 4, 1933, the day that President Franklin D. Roosevelt was inaugurated and closed the banks. In that Depression-ridden year, the 3¢-a-day charge per book was more than many could afford, but Hoyt's modest venture prospered.

Additional rental libraries followed, primarily in department stores. By 1948, there were 250, but the "paperback explosion," with books selling for 25¢ each, killed the rental business. To counter this effect, Hoyt stocked both paperbacks and hardcovers on his shelves in the department stores.

In 1962, in Pittsburgh's Northway Mall, he opened his first company-owned, independent retail store. He called it The Walden Book Store (after Thoreau's *Walden Pond.*)

Acquired by the department store chain Carter Hawley Hale, Waldenbooks expanded rapidly and, by 1981, was the first and only bookseller to operate in all fifty states.

In 1984, Waldenbooks was bought by K mart Corporation, the second-largest retailer in the world. The following year, the book chain opened its first Waldenbooks and More, a 10,000-square-foot super-store. The same year, it acquired the famous Globe Bookstore in Washington, D.C. In the fall of 1986, Waldenbooks opened its 1,000th bookstore.

The stores today may be considered educational centers, stocked as they are with magazines, audio cassettes, videocassettes, games, and computer software in addition to books. Speaking of books, Waldenbooks stocks its stores with more than 55 million of them. This comes to more than 7,000 miles of books. The chain employs 8,500 people.

An interesting innovation is Waldenbooks' in-store book clubs, with more than a million members nationwide. The clubs' specialized interests are science fiction/fantasy, romance, mystery, and children's birthdays.

Who said that bookstores aren't profitable?

B. Dalton

B. Dalton is another huge book retailer. Owned until 1986 by the Dayton Hudson Corporation, the nation's fifth-largest general merchandise retailer, it was acquired in that year by the aggressive New York–based Barnes and Noble chain for about $300 million. B. Dalton will maintain its own identity, including its buying function, but will be doing many projects jointly with the Barnes & Noble management. The company has its headquarters in Minneapolis, and its 780 bookstores are spread across the contiguous forty-eight states, the District of Columbia, and Puerto Rico. As of this writing, the company has more than 7,700 employees.

A typical B. Dalton store stocks 18,000 hardcover and paperback titles. The chain's largest store, on New York's Fifth Avenue, carries more than 33,000 titles.

CAREER TIP: Getting a job selling books at a Waldenbooks or B. Dalton outlet should be relatively easy, especially if you are willing to work odd hours. The experience you get at the point of sale can be beneficial in gaining a perspective of the entire book-marketing process. This can ultimately lead to store management or book sales for a publisher or rep.

The chain maintains a point-of-sale-based computer operation that enables it to have a full-line, in-depth selection of current popular titles and to spot trends immediately.

In tune with our developing technology, B. Dalton stores feature more than 1,200 software titles, 2,000 computer books, and accessories. At this writing, more than thirty-five stores carry this material.

The chain began selling audio and video products in the fall of 1984, featuring a full selection of nonmusic audio tapes, including fiction, self-improvement, how-to children's musicals, as well as blank tapes. However, it dropped video in 1987 because of excessive theft and shrinkage.

It is interesting to note that with the rapid rise of chain bookstores there are few independents left outside the major cities—the reason: low profit margins and slow-moving inventories plus, of course, the competitive edge of these two giant chains. Virtually every shopping mall contains one or the other—some contain both.

Future Trends in Book Publishing

Instant Books

Book publishers may take years to prepare an elaborate art book for publication, but they can also move fast when they have to. Just two days after the royal wedding of Prince Andrew and Sarah Ferguson in July 1986, Crown Publishers shipped 25,000 copies of *Invitation to a Royal Wedding* to U.S. bookstores. The book, a 120-page full-color, hardcover picture book, included photos of their courtship and wedding. Now that's swift publishing.

Vanity Publishing

When the wife of a wealthy big-city plastic surgeon wants to publish a book of her breathless prose, she may have difficulty finding an agent and, even if she does, may find it impossible to get her work published. The vanity press comes to the rescue.

The practice probably dates back a few hundred years. If one wants a literary work published, why not pay for it? It's called "subsidized publishing" or, pejoratively, "vanity publishing."

There really is nothing shameful about it. Although there are some disreputable vanity publishers, as long as no glorious promises are made to the author, the practice is perfectly legal and ethical; but *caveat emptor.*

Books on Cassettes

You can now hear every word of *Clan of the Cave Bear* on six audio cassettes or the unabridged version of *The Godfather* on five. Or how about William F. Buckley, Jr., articulating in his best Yale-speak his book *Right Reason*?

Books on cassettes may be a trend or just a fad—certainly at this writing not anything to excite the nation's videocassette publishers and distributors—yet the huge Waldenbooks chain, in a recent year, doubled its sales of these "books" over those sales of the previous year. Still, few such book tapes have sold more than 35,000 units. Somehow, we can't picture too many Sony® Walkman users trekking off to school or work listening to *War and Peace*.

The Big Business of Baby Books

Despite television's lure, today's parents are buying more books for younger children than ever before. Classics remain perennial bestsellers; but social changes have influenced the market in many ways. Br'er Rabbit has emerged as an Afro-American folk figure.

Approximately 4,000 children's books are published annually, with juvenile paperbacks growing faster than any other area of book publishing in terms of titles and revenue.

Academics and psychologists firmly believe that the earlier children are exposed to books, the better readers and, consequently, the more aware citizens they become.

Forget Dick and Jane. Today, children's books are more sophisticated, including stories about minority children, human sexuality, unemployment, child abuse, and senility.

Bookstores: The Emerging Market for Video

Unlike audio cassettes, the retail market for home video is expanding dramatically. In late 1986, *Publishers Weekly* hosted an industry seminar on the subject. The first in a series of industry meetings sponsored by the magazine focused on marketing videocassettes through major retail book chains and independent bookstores.

Proprietary Publishing

When a major Hollywood film studio buys movie houses (for example, MCA/Universal's purchase of 50 percent of Cineplex/Odeon's theaters), the other studios are concerned lest there be unfair competition in the distribution of their products. Is it so with the book business? If a book retailing giant publishes its own books, aren't they then guaranteed the best display space and, thus, the best sales?

Barnes & Noble, the New York–based book retailer, has always had proprietary products in its mail-order catalogues, but seldom in its stores. Proprietary publishing by book retailers does not in fact seem to be a major issue in book selling and does not concern the big publishers. In the final analysis, good display of books in stores does help to sell them, but books have to find their own market.

Improved Technology

As in the production of newspapers and magazines, book production has benefitted from advances in technology, too. Photocomposition has speeded up the typesetting process and made it less expensive. For printing large-run, mass-market paperbacks, web offset presses that print at high speeds, feeding rolls into the press that come out as folded sections, have kept prices of these books as well at a controllable level.

Big Books—Small Publishers

In the section on small presses, we wrote about the small independent publishers that publish ten or fifteen titles a year without expectation of selling more than a few thousand of each. Now there's a new twist—small publishers that are looking for big books.

What chance, one might ask, does a small publisher have of even seeing a big book before the giants grab it with their six-figure advances? Miracles do happen.

In 1986, Freundlich Books published *Murrow: His Life and Times*, a biography of the famous TV journalist, by A. M. Sperber. To be sure, Lawrence Freundlich is no publishing tyro. He already had twenty years of experience in the book business and had his own imprint at Simon & Schuster, thus establishing his credentials and broadening his range of contact. (Important editors are sometimes given their own imprints by a publisher. This imprint appears on the title page, cover, and book jacket. The imprint editor usually has a proprietary interest in the book or series with his imprint.)

Bookstores today offer much more than just books to their patrons. (Photograph courtesy Waldenbooks.)

The Murrow book was brought to Freundlich by a major agent, Theron Raines. It's hard to tell why. In any case, the book became a Book-of-the-Month Club featured alternate and, in a short time, had eight printings in hardcover for a total of 60,000 books.

Freundlich distributes through Kampmann, a former Simon & Schuster marketing executive who distributes for about forty small publishers. In the tradition of American free enterprise, book style, Freundlich has an opportunity to make it big, even if only on a single book.

Since the distribution process is costly and unwieldy, many small presses choose to have their books distributed by large publishers. Under this arrangement, the large publisher may provide warehousing services as well as sales help. That is, the small presses' books are listed in the large publishers' catalogue and sold by their field sales force. The large publishers do this for a reasonable profit; the small presses get major sales coverage and are willing to trade this portion of their profits for such services.

The World of Desktop Publishing

Now, every would-be writer can do his own publishing. All he needs is a desktop computer to set type, a rented laser printer to produce one copy of each page at about 30¢ a page, and a conventional printer to run off hundreds or thousands of copies on an offset press. Doing it this way can save thousands of dollars over traditional typesetting. Of course, he still needs to write the book and figure out ways to sell it.

The systems in use today enable computer owners to change typefaces and layouts at the touch of a key. If one requires a wide variety of typefaces, there are establishments now springing up all over the country that provide do-it-yourself phototypesetting services that rival professional sources.

The field is burgeoning. In 1986, there were six

books published via desktop publishing, and a national magazine called *Publish!* emerged to deal with the news and happenings of this high-tech development. *Small Press,* referred to earlier, also deals with this form of publishing.

Spiritual Resurgence and the Rise of Religious Books

The Gallup research people tell us that young American adults, particularly new parents, are returning to the religious fold. Church and synagogue attendance is up, as is, accordingly, the publishing of books keyed to religious interests.

There have always been publishers of religious books, but now mainstream publishers are competing for this market. For instance, Harper & Row's religious book division, which has tripled in size in the last seven years, carries such provocative titles as *Man in White* by Johnny Cash and the controversial Reverend Daniel Berrigan's *The Mission: A Film Journal.*

The large publisher Macmillan has created a new emphasis for these books, and the Gibson greeting-card people of Connecticut sold three million volumes in three years of *Apples of Gold* by Jo Petty, a book of religious essays. New smaller publishers have joined the "fold" as well, and, as a result, this aspect of book publishing is providing an expanding choice of books to readers with a religious orientation.

Trends in the Sale of Books

In this chapter we have already written of the book retailing giants, Waldenbooks and B. Dalton. Their success mirrors the success of the entire industry. Consider these statistics:

- Domestic expenditures on books rose 10.3 percent annually from 1979 to 1983. Their projected annual increase from 1983 to 1988 is 13 percent.
- The number of book titles rose from 38,053 in 1972 to 53,380 in 1983.
- The number of bookstores went from 11,786 in 1973 to 19,580 in 1984, primarily as a result of the growth of the large chains, and gives every sign of increasing proportionately.
- According to the Bureau of the Census, the number of book publishers in the United States went from 1,250 in 1972 to 2,128 in 1982.

In 1983, the Book Industry Study Group conducted a survey of readers and nonreaders. Unfor-

tunately, there is a large group of aliterate Americans, adults who can read a book but don't choose to; the figure is about 44 percent. Further, the study found that in the under-twenty-one age group, book reading declined in the previous ten years from 75 percent to 62 percent.

Although women read more than men, there are many senior aliterates. The Bureau of the Census states that more than 11 percent of the U.S. population is sixty-five or older. In this age group, only 29 percent are book readers, compared with 50 percent of the whole population.

What College Students Read

Although a recent study by the National Association of College Stores showed that only 45 percent of college students said that they read one to five books a year outside of their course work, books on career-related subjects were their primary interest. The survey said that 68 percent reported collecting books on this specialty. By the way, 78 percent said that they enjoyed browsing in bookstores even though they had no purchase in mind.

Just Plain Statistics

The Book Industry Study Group, led by the noted book statistician and scholar John P. Dessauer, issued *Book Industry Trends 1984,* which is a compilation of book industry statistics, including actual figures through 1983 and projected figures through 1988. Here are some of the findings:

- Per-capita consumer expenditures will go from $35.44 in 1984 to only $56.41 in 1988, not a huge increase when inflation is considered.
- The number of book units acquired by colleges, universities, and public libraries will remain the same from 1979 to 1988.
- The total number of book units sold in 1984 was 1.295 billion. In 1988, that figure is projected at 1.799 billion, not an insignificant increase.

Conclusion

Although it seems that every American is glued to his TV set watching a rented videocassette, that is not the reality. Many of us are jogging, doing aerobics, listening to music, going to the movies—and, yes, reading books. To me, the most encouraging development discussed in this chapter is the dramatic increase in bookstore openings by such progressive chains as Waldenbooks and B. Dalton. This increase is translated into more books sold; and if they're sold, they're usually read.

As a career, book publishing is a rewarding choice. Working with words, expanding human intelligence, and increasing literacy are all admirable pursuits. It may even be worth making less money.

Where to Find the Book Publishers

Unlike advertising agencies, of which the majority are located in either Chicago or New York, book publishers are spread out all over the country. For an extensive listing we again recommend the *LMP* (*Literary Market Place*), the Directory of American Book Publishing, R. R. Bowker Company, 205 East 42nd Street, New York, NY 10017. This standard reference tool may be found at almost all major libraries. The listings are valuable in that they delineate the publisher's total activity.

Writers' Conferences, Workshops, and Summer College Programs

One cannot expect to attend a four-week writing workshop and emerge as a skilled writer. Becoming a writer is a long process involving infinite hours of reading as well as studying and analyzing the technique of professionals. Such workshops will, however, along with creative-writing courses at the college level, nurture one's talent. Then it's a case of writing, writing, and more writing.

Most colleges offer excellent writing programs. Attendance at a good writer's conference or workshop is additionally helpful, however, because of the opportunity to meet successful authors. At times, a mentor relationship may be established. Just being immersed in this environment may spark creativity.

Following is a list of a few of these special programs. *Writer's Digest* magazine is a source for a more complete listing.

Annual Black Writers' Conference
Black Writers' Workshop Committee
Box 43576
Los Angeles, CA 90043
Telephone: (415) 523–6179

Aspen Writers' Conference
Box 3185
Aspen, CO 81612
Telephone: (303) 925–7189

Bennington Writing Workshops
Bennington College
Bennington, VT 05201
Telephone: (802) 442–5401

Bread Loaf Writers' Conference
Middlebury College
Middlebury, VT 05753
Telephone: (802) 388–3711, ext. 5286

Chautauqua Writers' Workshop
Chautauqua Summer School
Box 1098
Chautauqua, NY 14722
Telephone: (716) 357–4411

Childrens' Book Writing and Illustration Workshops
460 East 79th Street
New York, NY 10021
Telephone: (212) 744–3822

Harvard Summer Writing Program
Dept. 222
20 Garden Street
Cambridge, MA 02138
Telephone: (617) 495–2921

Hofstra University Writers' Conference
Hofstra University
Weller Hall
Hempstead, NY 11550
Telephone: (516) 560–5016

NYU Summer Writers' Conference
NYU School of Continuing Education
332 Shimkin Hall, Washington Square
New York, NY 10003
Telephone: (800) 852–5000, ext. 74

Romance Writers of America National Conference
Romance Writers of America
5206 FM 1960 W, Suite 207
Houston, TX 77069
Telephone: (713) 440–6885

UCLA Extension
University of California, Los Angeles Extension
Box 24901
Los Angeles, CA 90024
Telephone: (213) 825–9415

Women's Writing Conferences and Retreats
International Women's Writing Guild
Box 810, Gracie Station
New York, NY 10028
Telephone: (212) 737–7536

The *Folio*: Show in New York

Each year in October, *Folio:* magazine, the magazine industry's excellent monthly magazine, conducts seminars for professionals on more than fifty aspects of book and magazine publishing. The individual sessions are led by top industry professionals and run for an average of two and a half hours. The fee for an individual seminar is about $100. If you are employed in the industry, however, many employers will pay for the cost of your attendance. I have been a lecturer at *Folio:*'s magazine seminars, and I highly recommend both the book and magazine sessions as an ideal place to meet the experts and broaden your outlook on these professions. For more information, write to *Folio:*, River Bend, P.O. Box 4949, Stamford, CT 06907–0949.

College Book Publishing Programs

Many colleges offer book publishing seminars, workshops, and programs. Most are listed in *Peterson's Guide to Book Publishing Courses*. (See "Recommended Reading" at the end of this chapter.) Here are a few well-known programs and some typical courses.

Education in Publishing Program, City University Graduate Center, 33 West 42nd Street, New York, NY 10036. Courses include The Profession of Literary Agent: A Workshop, Selling Subsidiary Rights, Marketing and Sales for the Non-Specialist, and Copyediting and Proofreading Workshop.

Diploma Program in Book Publishing, New York University, 2 University Place, New York, NY 10003. Courses include Editorial Processes and Procedures,

Elements of Production, and Organization and Management in Publishing.

Publishing Procedures Course, Radcliffe/Harvard, 10 Garden Street, Cambridge, MA 02138. This course is an intensive six-week summer program for recent college graduates who are seriously considering a career in book publishing.

Summer Course in Publishing, Stanford University, Bowman Alumni House, Stanford, CA 94305. This intensive course covers editing, copywriting, design, advertising and publicity, marketing management, and finance.

Book Publishing Internships

A few internships are available in book publishing, and serving an internship is obviously an invaluable way to see the publishing world up close, gain some useful experience, and possibly make some contacts. Here is a sample of these offerings. For a more complete listing of media internships, see *The Student Guide to Mass Media Internships* by Ronald H. Claxton, University of Colorado School of Journalism, Boulder, Colorado.

Dell Publishing Company, Inc.
1 Dag Hammarskjold Plaza
New York, NY 10017
Four to six salaried positions are available in accounting, marketing, operations, publicity, and editorial. The internships last for three months, during the summer; open to currently enrolled students who have completed two or three years of college.

William Morrow & Co., Inc., Publishers
105 Madison Avenue
New York, NY 10016
One to three part- and full-time positions are available in contracts, children's books, marketing, and sales. Internships are offered from June to August, September to December, and January–February. Open to qualified adults, including high school students.

W. B. Saunders
West Washington Square
Philadelphia, PA 19106

A number of positions are available in editorial, marketing, and advertising. Duration: ten weeks during the summer; open to college juniors and seniors.

Yankee Publishing, Inc.
Dublin, NH 03444

A resident intern program is available from time to time to learn the publishing business. Yankee Publishing, Inc. also offers a program of forty to fifty salaried positions in preservation and conservation of New England's built and natural environment, under the auspices of the National Trust for Historic Preservation; open to college students only.

Two Interviews

Our guest interviewees come from the editing and retail end of the book business. Gene Brissie, while still a young man, has already had an important career as a book editor. Kay Sexton is a legendary lady in this field. Starting as the manager of the first B. Dalton store in Minneapolis, she went on to become vice president of merchandising communications at this major chain.

Eugene (Gene) Brissie is a born-and-bred New Yorker. He attended The Lawrenceville School and was graduated from Princeton University. Brissie started his career in books in the subsidiary rights department of Farrar, Straus & Giroux, eventually becoming director of foreign rights.

After four years, he left for the Pocket Books division of Simon & Schuster, where he started the subsidiary rights department. A few years later, he became editor-in-chief of Cornerstone Library as well as vice president and ultimately was named associate publisher of Fireside Books, Simon & Schuster's largest trade paperback imprint.

In 1984, he joined The Putnam Publishing Group, where he was named vice president and associate publisher of Perigee Books. Brissie has since become publisher of Perigee.

You have been an editor for at least the ten years that I have known you. Can you trace your career path, including your major at college and first job, that trained you for the position you now hold?

Although I am a publisher of trade paperbacks, I did indeed spend many years as an editor. I majored in English and American Literature at Princeton and worked for a couple of summers at Harcourt, Brace. My first job out of college was a brief stint as a copy editor for a very small publisher. My first real job was in the subsidiary rights department at Farrar, Straus & Giroux, where I finally became director of foreign rights after several years' experience as an assistant in the department. Then I went to Pocket Books to start their subsidiary rights department. I eventually became an editor at Pocket for their brand new—at the time—trade paperback imprint, Wallaby Books, and ultimately became editor-in-chief of that imprint. At one time or another in my years at Simon & Schuster, I was either editor-in-chief or associate publisher of three different imprints. My training was definitely on the spot—it strikes me that anything you do in this business is good training to be an editor or, ultimately, a publisher. Selling foreign and domestic rights made me a much better editor than I would otherwise have been. One of the things you do all day long is sell, sell, sell—to an editorial board, to an author, to publicists, to salesmen, and so on.

I think it helps to be willing to take the next step. I suppose I tried to do things that were in addition to those comprising my job. As a subsidiary rights assistant, I was willing—or tried to be—to help someone in the department send out books or manuscripts or make follow-up calls, which eventually led to making the deals themselves. Once you take all those other steps, it's a very short time before you close a deal. Once you close a couple of deals, you're quickly relied upon to do more.

It also helped to have bosses who expected and encouraged me to keep doing more; I've always been lucky to have that. The same was true in making the transition to editor. When I was selling rights, I also tried to bring in a couple of books. Once I brought in a couple, it was easy to bring in more. At some point, I had a boss who said, "Why don't you become an editor?" It goes back to my point that any job you do in the industry helps you to become a better editor, if that's what you want to be. The jump to editor-in-chief or publisher takes place with time and experience. At some point you realize—and your boss realizes, you hope—that you know how to handle lots of different books and lots of different authors.

As an editor of a division within a large publishing company, do you operate autonomously from your parent publisher, or if you do interact with them—what form does this take?

I don't operate completely autonomously, although there is a certain amount of freedom. I answer to the president, I buy books via an editorial board she chairs, and I am constantly getting advice from our sales manager—if he can't sell what I buy, there's no point to the exercise.

As publisher, how much of your time is spent on acquisitions and how much on editing?

As publisher, I do spend a lot of time acquiring books and a good deal less time editing, perhaps 15 percent of my time. Much of that gets done by the editors who work for me.

Do the literary agents present their best book ideas to a number of editors simultaneously, or do they single out editors with whom they have close personal and business relationships?

There are agents who submit only multiply, and there are agents who submit only selectively; and there are some who do a little of both, depending on the project.

If the answer to the last part of the previous question is yes, how does an editor cultivate the top agents?

See them; take them to lunch; respond appropriately in a timely fashion to their submissions—and for heaven's sake, return their phone calls.

When working with celebrity authors, is it almost always necessary to hire a ghost writer to work with these authors?

Not always, although much of the time.

How are these ghosts compensated, and do they receive a share of the author's royalty?

A ghost, in my experience, gets a piece of the advance, although not necessarily any of the royalties. Some ghosts, however, are worth half the advance and royalties, the maximum that could be expected.

How much time does an editor like you spend on actual editing?

Not all that much on actual editing anymore. There are still *some* books I edit. Perhaps 15 percent of my time.

How many books do you have in process at any one time?

We publish about seventy-five to eighty Perigees a year right now. At any given time I'm working on perhaps ten to fifteen books in one stage or another.

Are there any areas of book publishing that do not seem to be getting their share of bright young talent?

I don't think so. There are so many bright people coming into the business and looking for any opportunity to get into it that I don't think any areas are being ignored. Sometimes, aspiring editors make the mistake of thinking that the only way to become an editor is to become an editorial assistant first. As I mentioned previously, in my experience, everything you do in the business—production, subsidiary rights, publicity, sales—helps make you a better editor.

Is book publishing, once past the entry level, as poorly paid as has been suggested, and does the compensation structure equal the other areas of mass communication once one reaches the middle-executive level and beyond?

There is no question that the pay at entry level is low. Compensation gets much better at the middle levels and above. It's certainly competitive with advertising and magazines; I don't know about TV and radio.

You run a trade paperback division. What special kinds of books lend themselves to this format? What growth has there been in trade paperbacks in the last ten years?

Almost anything could be a trade paperback, although I think that certain categories and types of books lend themselves to the format easily: humor, how-to, hard information, self-help, puzzles and game books, and so on. Of course, the phenomenal growth in trade paperbacks came during the 1970s—I've read figures suggesting fiftyfold growth from 1970 to 1982. During the '80s, that's leveled off a bit; that kind of growth can't be sustained.

What college training would you recommend for those seeking to make book publishing their life's work?

Mostly, read everything you can get your hands on, whatever the subject. Make books a part of your life and reading second nature. That's more important than majoring in English or liberal arts or business. The people who do best in this business are the people who read and love books.

Is there really any opportunity to be published for the writer without an agent? What would you suggest?

Oh, yes. I publish a number of writers without agents. That said, an agent is definitely the path of choice for a previously unpublished writer. A lot of agents will evaluate over-the-transom manuscripts or proposals. They also scour magazines for interesting new writers, so doing pieces for periodicals is sometimes a good way to get an agent or book deal.

Kathryn (Kay) F. Sexton was graduated from the University of Minnesota and immediately began a career in books as an assistant librarian for the Arlington Hills Public Library. After a number of years in retailing, in 1967 she began her affiliation with the B. Dalton Company as store manager. Today she serves as vice president and director of merchandise communications and publications.

In addition, Sexton currently serves as vice president of the board for The Minnesota Center for the Book Arts. The mission and purpose is to establish a working museum to preserve handcrafts such as paper making, typesetting, printing, binding, illustration, and all the other arts that go into producing a handcrafted book. She also serves on the board of Graywolf Press.

You have spent a major portion of your career with B. Dalton. What special opportunities are available to one who would spend his or her entire career with such a large organization?

Yes, there are opportunities in chain book operations today. B. Dalton is diversifying and exploring new business development all the time. We view the '80s as a time of challenge, change, and opportunity.

Would you recommend field sales for a book publisher or retail book sales management as a career for bright college-trained people?

I would recommend both field sales and retail book sales management. It depends on the individual's area of interest as to which he or she selects. In either case, the individual has to prove himself. Knowledge, energy, and commitment play a large role.

If books are no longer sold on consignment, how does a large retailing chain such as B. Dalton handle the buying function when such a huge number of books are published each month

Our buyers buy by category. Our merchandise distributors distribute the books by store, category, and regional differences. Return privileges are still a part of the industry, but there may be changes in the future.

What major trends have you seen in book reading and buying during the last ten to fifteen years?

The major changes in the last ten years include many trends: the paperback explosion; the growth of discounting; the development of new strategies such as software, video, and audio; the testing of new strategies—for example, the ideas of a giant supermarket "entertainment center" and store within a store such as Dalton's test of a "children's store within a store"; the emergence of specialized bookstores such as children's, mystery, science fiction, and the occult; the reemergence of leased departments; and the growth of specialized book clubs.

Do publicity and authors' tours have a greater effect on a book's sale than reviews?

The success of publicity and authors' tours depends on the magnetism of the author and the nature of the book. Having the book and author written up in a section of the news magazines other than the book section can be effective. Bookaholics will always find the book section. We want to capture the casual reader.

Are there significant opportunities for college graduates in book publishing if they do not choose to locate in New York?

Yes. New York is good, but there are opportunities in other cities. Chain booksellers, regional publishers, specialty publishers—Sunset, Ortho, Better Homes & Gardens are examples—and small, quality publishers—Graywolf in St. Paul is an example—museum shops, and university publishers all offer opportunity.

Would you recommend summer sales positions in bookstores for college people desirous of entering book publishing when they graduate?

I definitely recommend part-time work and full-time summer work in book publishing and bookstores. The experience can be invaluable.

Of the many classes of book publishing, which ones do you think offer the greatest opportunities?

A well rounded, diversified publishing house or bookseller chain offers good opportunity. Examples are Bantam Books and Simon & Schuster for publishing, and B. Dalton and Walden for bookselling.

Glossary of Book Terms

ABA: the American Booksellers Association; within the trade, the abbreviation often refers to the association's annual convention.

Adoption: the selection and approval of a book for school or college use.

Advance: the sum paid to an author by a publisher prior to a book's publication, to be subsequently earned back from sales of the author's book.

Auction: bidding for a hardcover book's paperback-sales rights by various publishers.

Backlist: list of books published in a previous season and still available for sale.

Cold type: an advanced system of typesetting, usually done by computer; a labor-saving process over prior hot-type systems.

Colophon: the publisher's standard, imprint, or logo used on a book's spine or title page.

Copy editing: the review of a manuscript before typesetting for grammar, spelling, punctuation, and style.

El hi: a designation for textbooks for use in elementary and high schools (kindergarten through twelfth grade).

First serial rights: the sale of a portion of a book to a magazine or periodical before a book's publication.

Galleys: long paper proofs (or photocopies) of a book's text pulled prior to platemaking and printing.

Literary agent: an author's representative in relationships with a publisher; generally works on commission.

LMP: *Literary Market Place,* an annual directory of the book industry.

Mass market paperbacks: a paperbound book in a small format sold to bookstores and mass outlets such as drugstores, department stores, and the like.

Remainders: Publisher's unsold copies of books sold to bookstores at large discounts and, in turn, to consumers at reduced prices.

PW: *Publishers Weekly,* the important weekly publication of the book industry.

Subsidiary rights: a source of additional revenue for a publisher, whereby the rights to a book, for other than its original publication, are sold for book club distribution, paperback reprint, magazine serialization, translation into foreign editions, and motion picture adaptation.

Trade book: a book planned and marketed for the consumer to be sold in bookstores.

Trade paperback: a softbound book sold in bookstores, often larger than a mass market paperback.

Recommended Reading

Applebaum, Judith, and Nancy Evans. *How to Get Happily Published.* New York: Harper & Row, 1978.

Bailey, Herbert S., Jr. *The Art and Science of Book Publishing.* New York: Harper & Row, 1970.

Berg, A. Scott. *Max Perkins: Editor of Genius.* New York: E. P. Dutton/Thomas Congdon Books, 1978.

Bingley, Clive. *The Business of Book Publishing.* New York: Pergamon Press, 1972.

Boswell, John. *The Awful Truth About Publishing: Why They Always Reject Your Manuscript . . . And What You Can Do About It.* New York: Warner Books, 1986.

Bruno, Michael H., ed. *Pocket Pal* (12th ed.). New York: International Paper Co., 1979.

Cassill, R. V. *Writing Fiction* (2nd ed.). Englewood Cliffs, N.J.: Prentice-Hall, 1975.

Chesman, Andrea and Polly Joan. *Guide to Women's Publishing.* Paradise, Calif.: Dustbooks, 1978.

Chicago Manual of Style, The (13th ed., rev.). Chicago: University of Chicago Press, 1982.

Davis, Kenneth, and Joann Davis. *The Paperback Book in America.* Boston: Houghton Mifflin, 1982.

Dessauer, John P. *Book Publishing: What It Is, What It Does* (rev. ed.). New York: R. R. Bowker Co., 1981.

Ehrlich, Arnold W., ed. *The Business of Publishing: A PW Anthology.* New York: R. R. Bowker Co., 1976.

Fulton, Len, and Ellen Ferber, eds. *International Directory of Little Magazines and Small Presses.* Paradise, Calif.: Dustbooks. Published annually.

Getting Into Book Publishing (2nd ed.). New York: R. R. Bowker Co., 1979. (Pamphlet: Single copy free.)

Grannis, Chandler B., ed. *What Happens in Book Publishing. Revised ed..* New York: Columbia University Press, 1967.

Gross, Gerald, ed. *Editors on Editing: An Inside View of What Editors Really Do* (updated ed.). New York: Harper & Row, 1985.

Guide to Book Publishing Courses: Academic and Professional Programs. Prepared in cooperation with AAP. Princeton, N.J.: Peterson's Guides, 1979.

Gunther, Max. *Writing and Selling a Nonfiction Book.* Boston: The Writer, 1973.

Hasselstrom, L. M. *The Book Book: A Publishing Handbook for Beginners and Others.* Hermosa, S. Dak.: Lame Johnny Press, 1979.

Hawes, Gene R. *To Advance Knowledge.* New York: American University Press Services, Inc., 1967.

Jovanovich, William. *Now, Barabbas.* New York: Harper & Row, 1964.

Levarie, Norma. *The Art and History of Books.* New York: Da Capo Press, 1982.

Morgan, Roberta. *How to Break into Publishing.* New York: Harper & Row, 1980.

One Book—Five Ways: The Publishing Procedures of Five University Presses. Association of American University Presses, ed. New York: W. Kaufmann, 1978.

Plotnik, Arthur. *The Elements of Editing.* New York: Macmillan, 1982.

Publishing Positions: 30 Job Descriptions in Editing, Production, Marketing, Customer Service and Administration. New York: Publications Department, Association of American Publishers, 1977.

Rogers, Geoffrey. *Editing for Print.* Cincinnati, Ohio: Writer's Digest Books, 1985.

Shaffer, Susan E., ed. *Guide to Book Publishing Courses.* Princeton, N.J.: Peterson's Guides, 1979.

Shatzkin, Leonard. *In Cold Type: The Promise and Performance of Book Publishing in America.* Boston: Houghton Mifflin, 1982.

Targ, William. *Indecent Pleasures.* New York: Macmillan, 1975.

Tebbel, John. *A History of Book Publishing in the United States.* Vol. 1, *The Creation of an Industry, 1630–1865;* Vol. 2, *The Expansion of an Industry, 1865–1919.* New York: R. R. Bowker Co., 1972–74.

———. *Opportunities in Publishing Careers.* Skokie, Ill.: National Textbook Co., 1975.

Uhlan, Edward. *What Every Writer Should Know About Publishing His Own Book* (21st ed.). New York: Exposition Press, 1976.

Yankelovich, Skelly and White, Inc. *The 1978 Consumer Research Study on Reading and Book Purchasing.* New York: Book Industry Study Group, Inc., 1978.

TELEVISION

I will never forget May 20, 1949. I parked my low-slung 1948 Hudson in front of the fashionable apartment building, rode the elevator to the sixth floor, and rang the doorbell. As the door opened, my nervous anticipation was relieved when I was greeted by my date for the evening. She was at least as pretty as the picture given to me by our matchmaker, although she appeared a bit younger than twenty. You see, it was one of those fixed-up blind dates that were then popular.

After I was introduced to her parents and exchanged a few pleasantries, her father opened the rosewood cabinet doors of the wall unit, pressed a button, and miraculously this "thing" moved up and out. There, seemingly bigger than life, was this wonderful 20″ DuMont TV set showing the Friday-night wrestling matches. Six months later, the twenty-year-old became my wife, and with her came viewing privileges on the monster TV set.

In the early '50s, television for us was a magical form of free entertainment. Thursday, "crime night," we watched such stimulating fare as Jack Webb's "Dragnet," "Crime Syndicate?," and "Racket Squad." For comedy, there was the irrepressible Milton Berle, "The Honeymooners" with Gleason's memorable character Ralph Kramden, and on Saturday nights, the brilliant "Your Show of Shows" with Sid Caesar, Carl Reiner, Howard Morris, and Imogene Coca.

True, television has its share of critics, especially those with intellectual pretensions. Books have been written about how to kick the TV habit. Former FCC member Newton Minow's categorization of TV as a "vast wasteland" didn't help TV's tarnished image.

Clearly, most of us would like to see television develop its potential as an educational force and reduce its commitment to lowest-common-denominator programming. Yet as long as there are commercial considerations, this is the way it's going to be.

The immediacy of television cannot be equalled by any other form of mass media. When Jack Ruby shot Lee Harvey Oswald, John F. Kennedy's alleged assassin, you saw it live on TV. When a war or major disaster breaks any place in the world, within minutes you see it on TV. You could actually see the 1986 *Challenger* disaster live on CNN. And when it comes to events like political conventions, the Super Bowl, the Olympic Games, or the Oscars, television's coverage is unmatched.

A Brief History of Television

The first patent for a complete television system was given to a German inventor, Paul Nipkow, in 1884. In the early part of the twentieth century, inventions by an English physicist, J. A. Fleming, and an American, Lee DeForest, were giant steps in modern TV research.

Other dramatic developments followed, the foremost being V. K. Zworkin's iconoscope camera tube, which was patented in 1923. Although RCA was the leader in TV research in the '30s, the Germans were first with a broadcasting service in 1935. Regular TV broadcasting began in the United States in 1941, but because of wartime restrictions governing the manufacture of receivers, most other countries did not begin their services until the 1950s.

The first practical demonstration of color was in 1928, but widespread purchase of color receivers did not begin in the United States until 1964. More recent developments in TV systems and instrumentation include cable and satellite transmission. Large-size direct-screen TV and stereo-sound TV are also available today; these latter two technologies, however, are still being perfected and remain in comparatively limited use.

The growth in the use of TV receivers reached geometric proportions beginning in 1949, when there were 1 million receivers in the United States and fewer than five million in the world. By the early 1970s, however, there were 275 million sets in use worldwide, including 93 million in the United States and 28 million in the Soviet Union. Today, 250,000 sets are manufactured daily, and there are more than 657 million of them in use worldwide.

year's number-one show, cost $380,000. That's the most expensive spot for a regularly scheduled TV show and exceeds the previous year's record by $110,000. As we'll see later in this chapter, however, special events such as the Super Bowl rate even higher commercial prices. Two other NBC Thursday-night shows, "Family Ties" and "Night Court," drew $300,000 and $260,000, respectively, for their 30-second commercials. In the early days of television, *stations* could be bought for that much money.

As you can see, television is big, big business. In March 1985, the powerful and very profitable Capital Cities Communications acquired the American Broadcasting Company for the whopping sum of $3.5 *billion.* In the same year, a major syndicator and cable company, Viacom, purchased 66.6 percent of MTV Networks (including Nickelodeon) and 50 percent of Showtime/The Movie Channel from Warner Communications for $500 million cash plus warrants (financial instruments issued by a corporation giving the holder the right to purchase the capital stock of that corporation at a stated price at a future date). Viacom had previously purchased 33.3 percent of MTV from the public for $181 million, thus making MTV worth more than $550 million.

In 1985, Rupert Murdoch, of newspaper, magazine, and now 20th Century–Fox fame, bought seven TV stations from Metromedia Broadcasting for $2 billion. In this game of television monopoly, Murdoch sold WCVB-TV in Boston to the Hearst Corporation for $450 million. With his new stations, Murdoch formed Fox Television (see later section on the Fox Broadcasting Company), a major attempt to become the fourth network. In 1986, Ted Turner made a serious try to take over CBS but failed. Cox Communications, a cable operator, acquired WFTV in Orlando, Florida, for $185 million.

The lesson to be learned from all of this is "Don't throw away that old TV station you have in the attic." It may be worth millions.

The Scope of Television and Cable

For the 1986–87 season, a 30-second commercial spot on NBC's "The Cosby Show," the previous

What the Ratings Are All About

If you're General Mills or General Foods and spend billions of dollars on TV commercials, you must know the number of households and what types of people are in those households being reached by each program. Such information helps advertisers predict performance and, later, tells them what they received for their money. It guides advertising agencies in the buying of TV schedules and then helps to evaluate the efficiency of their buys. It serves as both a programming and sales tool for the networks, stations, and program suppliers. The major sources for this information are the Nielsen TV-audience estimates and the Arbitron Rating Company's market rankings.

A. C. Nielsen, Sr., founded the A. C. Nielsen Company in 1923. He started radio-broadcast research in 1936 with a device called an "audimeter," which provided a mechanical link between the turning dial on a radio receiver and a moving roll of paper in such a way that a permanent record of dial position (i.e., station tuned to) was produced.

Technology advanced, and in 1950 the Nielsen Television Index began, providing network-audience estimates.

In those days, 3.8 million households, or 9 percent of U.S. homes, had TV sets. Today, more than 85 million households, or 99 percent of all U.S. homes, have one or more sets.

In 1980, Nielsen issued its first cable report and was able to respond to cable, pay cable, subscription TV, and superstations by means of a monitoring device placed in selected homes on a statistical basis. (A superstation is one whose programming is carried by satellite to cable households outside its local market.) In responding to VCRs, Nielsen can tell whether a set is on playback or recording and what it is recording.

The Arbitron Ratings Company, a leading research company, defines each TV market on the basis of its Area of Dominant Influence. A geographic designation, ADI provides advertisers with a relative standing of each market area's number of measurable viewers.

For example, New York (the greater New York City metropolitan area) is the nation's leading ADI by virtue of its roughly 6.5 million TV households (homes with at least one TV set) out of the nation's total of 80 million. We therefore refer to New York as the "number-one market." In contrast, San Diego is the twenty-fifth market, with about 780,000 TV households; Spokane is the seventy-fifth market, with about 320,000; Las Vegas is ninety-ninth, with about 215,000; and Panama City, Florida, the 175th market, has about 65,000 TV households.

These market rankings are significant to advertisers, who will pay more to reach the larger markets.

Research and Ratings Today

Movie producers reading critics' unfavorable reviews of their pictures often dismiss the criticism by asking, "What does he know about movies?" Television producers and networks that receive low ratings often say, "You know that those ratings are inaccurate."

With TV households viewing an average of more than 52 hours of TV a week and with advertisers spending billions of dollars in the medium, research on this vast audience is vital. Two advertising agencies, Young and Rubicam and J. Walter Thompson, each spend more than a billion dollars per year in television. Consider, too, the cost of this advertising. In 1965, the average cost per 30-second commercial for nighttime television was $19,700. By the mid-80s, it had reached $94,700. Total television advertising volume in 1985 was more than $20 *billion.*

So now, let's find out how ratings really work. First of all, television audience research, such as that provided by A. C. Nielsen, measures the size of the audience for various TV shows, as well as the age, education, and so on, of that audience. These are quantitative, not qualitative measurements.

Nielsen doesn't take a program with bad ratings off the air; the decision is made by the network or the station, because the advertisers are also reading the ratings and generally don't want to sponsor shows with small audiences.

Occasionally, an advertiser of high-quality merchandise is willing to pay a higher cost per thousand viewers to reach upscale prospects. Clearly, the program that gets the highest rating—or votes in a sense—is not necessarily the best. It is simply what most people want to watch.

The Nielsen rating you may see in the newspaper is a *statistical estimate of the number of homes tuned to a program.* For example, a rating of 20 for a network TV program means that 20 percent of U.S. TV households are estimated to be tuned in to that program. Eighty million U.S. households now have TV sets, so a rating of 20 means that 16 million TV households tuned in. One rating point thus equals 800,000 households.

Ratings are statistical estimates because of the margin of error. They are based not on a count of all TV households but on a count within a *statistical sample of TV households selected from all TV households.* The findings within the sample are then "projected" to national totals.

How Does Sampling Work?

Nielsen samples only 2,000 homes, but the TV industry regards this sample as adequate in size to

SEASON AVERAGE RANKING

WEEK 1 (SEP 21, 1986) THRU WEEK 11 (NOV 30, 1986)
ALL REGULAR PROGRAMS IN PERIOD

NIELSEN NATIONAL INDEX

RANK	PROGRAM	WEEKS	NET	DAY	TIME	DUR	AVG RTG	AVG SHARE
1	BILL COSBY SHOW	10	NBC	THU	8:00	30	34.3	52
2	FAMILY TIES	9	NBC	THU	8:30	30	32.3	48
3	CHEERS	9	NBC	THU	9:00	30	27.8	42
4	MURDER, SHE WROTE	9	CBS	SUN	8:33	60	26.1	38
5	GOLDEN GIRLS	8	NBC	SAT	9:00	30	25.9	43
6	NIGHT COURT	8	NBC	THU	9:30	30	24.6	38
7	60 MINUTES	11	CBS	SUN	7:59	60	23.4	36
8	MOONLIGHTING	8	ABC	TUE	9:00	60	23.1	35
9	GROWING PAINS	6	ABC	TUE	8:30	30	22.4	33
10	DALLAS	10	CBS	FRI	9:00	60	22.3	36
11	WHO'S THE BOSS?	8	ABC	TUE	8:00	30	22.2	34
12	AMEN	8	NBC	SAT	9:30	30	20.4	35
13	NEWHART	8	CBS	MON	9:00	30	20.0	29
14	227	7	NBC	SAT	8:30	30	19.3	33
15	NBC MONDAY NIGHT MOVIES	9	NBC	MON	9:00	120	19.0	30

A. C. Nielsen's ranking of the regular network programs from September 21 through November 30, 1986. The top fifteen may also be considered successful if they appeal to a special target audience that advertisers want to reach. (Reprinted with permission, Nielsen Media Research.)

provide a reliable estimate of national TV viewing habits and trends.

Nielsen puts a small electronic device called a "people meter" into each sample household, where it is interconnected with up to four TV sets and VCRs. The device stores information, at 1-minute intervals, showing whether each set is on or off and, if on, to which channel it is tuned. The information is then transmitted from the device, and a full day's viewing information is automatically retrieved by Nielsen's central office computer in 5 seconds. In effect, the channel selection knob on each set in each sample household is "wired in" to Nielsen's computers so that they can determine exactly how those knobs are switched around, minute-by-minute over a 24-hour period.

The meter device determines whether the set is on, but how does it determine "who" is watching? There are about 2,000 households randomly selected, using scientific sampling procedures. Each permanent member of the selected household is given his or her own number, which is punched into the "people meter" each time the viewer turns on the set. In this way, Nielsen is able to determine what programs are watched and the demographic information on age, sex, and so on of family members. Your chance of

being in the sample is one in 60,000. You can't volunteer to be in the sample; you must be selected by scientific sampling procedures.

Because there are more than 200 local TV markets (209, according to Nielsen; Arbitron ranks 260), which would require a total of about 100,000 sample households, it would not be feasible to meter all those households, so only the very large markets such as New York City, Los Angeles, Chicago, San Francisco, and Philadelphia are metered. In other markets a diary system is used.

Nielsen then collects and tabulates all this information for distribution to TV stations, ad agencies, production companies, and the like. It is important to remember that these procedures are unbiased and that their sample is, in effect, a scale model of all TV households watching a particular network show.

Some explanatory notes based on ratings as of this writing:

- "The Cosby Show" is the highest-rated show on television, with a 34.9 rating (about 28 million TV homes) and a whopping 52 share (a "share" refers to that percentage of homes with TV sets *on* and tuned to a specific program). Note that

"Family Ties," another hit show, profits from Cosby's success because it follows immediately on the same network and thus benefits from Cosby's "lead-in."

- "60 Minutes" has always had high ratings. Often it competes with football and other sports, but here it holds its own with a 26.0 rating and a 40 share.

- The networks have been leaning toward MOWs (Movies of the Week) rather than paying high prices for recent feature films. The MOWs run about $3 million in cost and are often rerun or syndicated. In this particular week, there are six MOWs, including three on Sunday night.

- On Sunday night at 9:00 P.M., the three networks' share is 77. That leaves only 23 percent of the viewing audience watching the independent stations and cable at that time.

Career Opportunities in TV Ratings and Research

In TV research, there are only two major companies—A. C. Nielsen and Arbitron. Though both employ computer and research specialists, however, the field is limited.

The networks employ research personnel on both coasts to evaluate the Nielsen and Arbitron data. These evaluations are then passed along to the programming and sales departments.

The programming department, seeing a sudden sag in a series' ratings, then consults with the production company about possible changes. (In the chapter on advertising, we will see how an advertising agency's media department uses this research in its buying of commercials on television.)

College students and graduates with talent in mathematics, statistics, and computer science might consider employment in this demanding field. Salaries in a company such as A. C. Nielsen for the entry-level job of research analyst begin at about $15,000 a year and progress to about $20,000 in three or four years with normal promotions. Unlike areas such as TV production, there is good job stability in this field.

Now let's see how big-time sports are handled by a network.

Super Bowl XX

On January 26, 1986, in the 70,000-seat New Orleans Superdome, the mighty Chicago Bears, sparked by their flamboyant quarterback Jim Mc-Mahon and the media darling, 305-pound William "Refrigerator" Perry, clawed the New England Patriots 46 to 10.

There was a viewing audience of 120 million people watching NBC-TV over a network of 207 television stations and the Armed Forces Network, with additional feeds to stations in thirty foreign countries, including Japan, Saudi Arabia, the Philippines, and Nicaragua.

NBC had a production and technical crew of 135 people and $11 million worth of electronic gear, including twenty-one cameras, a telestrator (video chalkboard device), and four miles of audio cable.

NBC's sales staff sold fifty-two commercials at $550,000 per 30-second spot.

The national ratings were 48.3, that is, 42 million homes tuned in to every minute of NBC's Super Bowl coverage.

Veteran commentator Dick Enberg, along with former players Merlin Olsen and Bob Griese, performed valiant service in trying to make a dull game exciting for this vast audience.

Super Bowl XXI

Change the locale. This time it's Sunday, January 25, 1987, and the place is the Pasadena Rose Bowl. The participants: the mighty New York Giants, with their 14–2 season record, and the Denver Broncos. The result: a decisive (39–20) win for the Giants in a lackluster game unrelentingly hyped for two weeks by the media.

This time CBS-TV won the broadcast rights, and 130 million viewers watched the game, which was broadcast by that super-talented pair, Pat Summerall and John Madden, ex-coach and TV-commercials personality.

Commercials were priced at $600,000 per 30-second spot. Because this high ticket was too rich for many advertisers, 15-second spots were sold for the first time.

In addition to the pre-game commentators and the broadcast team, there were dozens of production executives and more than one hundred technicians involved in this extravaganza. CBS used fourteen cameras.

The contract with the National Football League for broadcast rights was completed *three* years in advance of the event. Management, including lawyers and negotiators, had to make its deals with the Rose Bowl, the individual TV and radio stations, and the foreign stations receiving the feed.

The broadcast media gained additional mileage from Super Bowl XXI with shows other than the game itself. There was a two-hour pre-game show on CBS with video diaries about two of the players; a learned treatise from Charles Osgood, a CBS senior commentator, on which state has a stronger claim to the Giants, New York or New Jersey; a

125

"Beat the Greek" call-in segment, during which viewers agreed or disagreed with Jimmy the Greek's prognostication; and a CBS reporter in Italy covering the live telecast there at 1:00 A.M.

The well-known commentator Frank Gifford announced the telecast to be fed to England. Broadcast a day earlier was NFL Films' "Road to the Super Bowl." On Saturday night before the game, CBS offered "Super Bowl Blitz," which included interviews about football with celebrities. From Zsa Zsa Gabor: "I only know that two gorgeous teams beat the hell out of each other and that American men are insane."

All this, plus three blimps in the sky at game time. Slice, a new blimp (the largest ever), carried the CBS camera in the sky.

The sales-development group assisted the sales department by preparing ratings information and demography. Then the salespeople went out to sell all those 30-second commercials at $600,000 per. They started working on the event a year in advance. This was no simple effort, either, since demand among advertisers for commercial time on sports telecasts has slackened.

The ratings for the game itself were 47.8, with an average share of 68 in the nation's thirteen largest markets. That is, 68 percent of the TV homes with their sets on during this period were tuned to the Super Bowl telecast.

The responsibility of CBS Sports' promotion and publicity departments was to get viewers. The hundreds of thousands of words of pre-game hype in the media didn't hurt a bit in promoting the TV coverage. Although much of their planning was done earlier, the promotion people couldn't start their feverish push until two or three weeks before the event, since the teams participating were not determined until then.

For all of us viewing the Super Bowl, comfortably ensconced at home with our beer and pretzels, it was a game. For the people at CBS Sports, it was how they make their living: glamorous, exciting, demanding, and remunerative.

Who Does What in Television

With the growth of television in the past forty years, its performers have become stars. For many of us,

they are the subject of fascination and envy, yet we must realize that for every on-air performer, there are hundreds of workers and technicians with less glamorous jobs whose earnings may be a fraction of those of these celebrated on-air performers and behind-the-scenes top executives.

This section may help you decide whether there is a place for you in the TV industry. By understanding the functions of each department and job, you can better comprehend the entire TV broadcasting process.

The Variability of Salary Ranges

Whenever it is available, we will include the approximate contemporary salary range for stated jobs on network affiliates and independent stations. (See sections on networks and independents later in this chapter for a description of network affiliates, independents, and O&O stations, those owned and operated by one of the major networks.)

For the technical jobs listed in this section for which there is union representation, salaries are proportionately higher. Moreover, salary ranges for all jobs at major TV stations in New York, Chicago, or Los Angeles can be as much as 40 to 50 percent greater than those listed. This situation also prevails on the fifteen O&Os.

In terms of market ranking, the general rule is the higher the ranking, the higher the salary range. The salary averages appearing on the following pages apply to a station in the fiftieth market. Stations ranked higher, however, will offer salaries from 20 to 25 percent greater than those listed here; stations in lower-ranked markets, from 25 to 35 percent smaller.

General Manager (The Boss): The general manager is most often a corporate officer who reports directly to the station's owner and board of directors. The average annual salary for this position is $69,000. Reporting to the general manager are the six major departments listed here with their key job functions. Certain production, news, and engineering jobs are represented by unions.

Programming
    Program Director
    Director of Promotion/Publicity

Production
    Production Manager
    Executive Producer
    Producer
    Associate Producer

Director
Cinematographer
Floor Manager
Lighting Director (sometimes considered part
of Engineering)
Unit Manager

Sales
General Sales Manager
Assistant Sales Manager
Traffic/Continuity Supervisor
Sales Coordinator

News
News Director
Anchors, Correspondents, and Reporters
Sportscaster
Weather Reporter

Business
Business Manager

Engineering
Chief Engineer
Engineering Supervisor
Technical Director
Maintenance Engineer
Transmitter Engineer
Audio Engineer
Video Engineer
Master Control Engineer
Videotape Engineer
Engineering Assistant or Technician

Programming

Program Director: The program director is the decision maker and overseer of the program department. With the general manager and sales manager, he determines and directs the station's policies. The program director plans the most effective programming schedule for the station. On a daily basis, he must consider the competition, the best shows for each time slot, and who should produce these shows; he is also responsible for budget and allocations of equipment and manpower.

The program director must be aware of the station's compliance with Federal Communications Commission (FCC) rules and regulations relating to programming. (More about the FCC later in this chapter.)

Most program directors get their experience from jobs described on the following pages. Some are former directors and performers. They must have thorough understanding of sales and production. A college degree is a requirement for this job, with specialization in communications, radio/TV, or marketing a plus factor. The average annual salary at a typical mid-market station is $38,000.

Director of Promotion/Publicity: This individual is a public relations professional whose responsibility is to promote the station's image, programs, and activities. Some of the many duties of this job are the conception and execution of written and taped presentations, securing advertising in other media, and, with the sales department, developing ways to keep current advertisers and attract new ones.

At smaller stations, the director of promotion also handles community relations, which include PSAs (public-service announcements) and public-affairs programming. This job function is important, since FCC regulations require stations to provide a fixed percentage of their air time for such programming. At public TV stations (more on this subject later), the promotion director assists in fund-raising activities. The salary ranges: from $15,000 in small-market stations to more than $35,000 in large. An undergraduate degree in public relations, advertising, or communications is essential.

Production

In order to better understand the importance of this department to a TV station, we will first give an example of how people operate in a typical production situation. Following the example is a description of the various jobs the department contains.

The general manager, news director, and program manager of a TV station in a major metropolitan center meet and decide to do a five-part series on the dumping of toxic waste in the area as a segment of the regular late-night news. Each segment will run about 3½ minutes on camera.

One of the station's veteran reporters is assigned to the series, which will take him almost a month to research and film. A producer and associate producer, director, cameraman, and a writer will also join the team. The reporter will do some writing and will share the coordination, scheduling, and creative functions of the project with the producer.

The key to doing this assignment well is legwork. Interviews with as many of the "dumping" companies as possible are obligatory. Many companies will not want their representatives to go on camera. Local officials will be more cooperative, but they will want to avoid responsibility for the dumping. The good investigative reporter knows how to get around the smoke screen. He will try to entice the interviewee into performing a valuable public service by telling his story to a large TV audience.

The producer will be careful to review legal guidelines with the station's legal department because this kind of reportage often has libel considerations. Quoting cancer statistics, for example, would have to include a disclaimer stating the uncertainty of whether the cancers were a direct result of the toxic dumping.

Much more footage than can be used will be shot. The videotape editing process (see description in "Engineering" section) is crucial in establishing this series as unique in this kind of coverage, as similar reports have been done by other stations in this market.

Although the original plan is to do a five-part, 3½-minute series, running from Monday to Friday, when the editing is completed, management decides to run it as a half-hour special to be shown after the station's regular 10:00 P.M. news show. To guarantee a large audience, the station will run promos for the special each night for a week or two on its nightly news shows. A particularly provocative piece of tape from the show, plus some good voice-overs by the reporter, will be used for the promo.

When the special is complete, it wins no Emmys and its crew gets no raises, but the show is significant because it offers the crew an infrequent opportunity for creativity, since most programming is supplied by other sources. There is also a volume of favorable viewer mail, which prompts top management to voice its pleasure at the show's editorial content and production values.

Now for the descriptions of the jobs:

Production Manager: On a daily basis, this individual handles the myriad details that go into producing the station's entire range of programs. The number of individually produced programs varies according to the status of the station. All O&Os, network affiliates, and independent stations, however, produce news, talk, and interview shows. The independents will produce little else in the way of original material, though, relying instead on reruns and outside programming. Thus, the production manager's role at an independent station is more limited than it is at an O&O or affiliate station and consequently commands a smaller salary.

The production manager is responsible for programs, conception, design, development, and scheduling. He often supervises producers, directors, art directors, camera operators, floor managers, and so on. Most production managers have had substantial experience in lesser positions. Salaries average $30,000. A college degree with a major in radio, TV, communications, theater, or journalism is preferred.

Executive Producer: The executive producer conceives and develops ideas for all types of programming. On smaller stations, this function can be as diverse as originating a Sunday-night weekend sports wrap-up show, an election-eve show, or a midday celebrity interview. Specific duties include determining format, framing budget, arranging financing, and overseeing promotion. This executive usually works with independent production companies at major market, big-city stations often in charge of developing shows. He must follow each project from inception to completion, for he is ultimately responsible for the success or failure of the program. In major markets, the salary ranges from $40,000 to $60,000. Some executive producers earn six-figure salaries.

Producer: The producer plans and oversees a single show or a series of shows. His job duties include the selection of material and performers, and the planning of sets, lights, props, and camera angles. A producer for news programs selects tape to accompany the news, scripts, and music. He is also responsible for a show's budget.

The producer chooses directors (not, however, newscasters or reporters) and handles contracts with performers, technicians, musicians, and so on. The educational requirements are similar to those of a production manager. Competition for this job is very heavy. The salary ranges from $20,000 to $35,000. Independent-production-company and network producers can make more than $60,000 a year.

Associate Producer: The associate producer serves as assistant to the producer, performing similar tasks. If employed by a production company producing a situation comedy or dramatic series (a story or concept that continues for a number of weeks), the associate producer is a major source of creative planning. Story lines and concepts, design, and production of special segments may become the associate producer's responsibility. Salary range is $15,000 to $32,000. Competition for this responsible position is heavy. Educational and training background similar to a producer's is recommended.

Director: The director reports to the producer. In addition to coordinating the fine details of a production, the director actually gives instructions to all of those involved in the show—performers, production staff, and technical crew, including camera operators. Most network stations and production companies employ directors on staff. Some specialize in news and special events, others in sports. The salary range is from $25,000 to $35,000. A select few earn much more. A college degree is recommended, with courses in radio, TV, and communications. Many have undergraduate degrees in film and graduate degrees from film school. A director, like nearly all of the professionals described here, needs a combination of creativity, technical knowledge, organizational skills, and the ability to motivate.

Assistant Director: The assistant director performs many of the duties of the director but for 20 to 25 percent less salary. A director depends on an assistant director to help execute all responsibilities. Educational requirements are the same as those for the director.

Cinematographer: The cinematographer is sometimes called the camera operator. Those who operate the portable electronic news gathering (ENG) cameras are called ENG operators. Use of videotape instead of film has simplified the job enormously, as this equipment plays back immediately without chemical processing and also can use simple portable lighting or available lighting in most situations.

ENG operators work alongside news reporters to record interviews and events on tape. Often they rush back to the studio and serve as tape editors. In cooperation with a producer or reporter, the ENG operator assembles the finished product. The job requires the ability to work well with other people as well as technical knowledge.

Camera operators run the video camera during the rehearsals and the broadcast of a studio-based TV program. They use a studio TV camera mounted on tripods or dollies. Typically, in the studio, a camera operator takes direction from the director through an intercom system attached to a headset.

The steppingstone to the job of cinematographer or camera operator is that of assistant camera operator, which is an entry-level position. Aspiring camera operators need a high-school diploma and some training in photography (still or motion) and/or audio-visual equipment. College training in television, film, or communications, however, will place the job seeker in a preferred spot. Some stations consider camera and ENG operators members of the production team. Consequently, they may move on into studio floor managing, producing, or directing. At other stations, the camera or ENG operator is part of the engineering department. In that case, an operator may decide to aim for the job of audio-visual engineer or technical director. The salary ranges from $15,000 to $25,000.

Floor Manager: The on-site extension of the director to the cast is the floor manager, who ensures that everything coordinates with the director's instructions. He reads scripts and cues performers during rehearsal and shooting. He also works with the art director and set designer and is in charge of props and costumes. The salary ranges

from $12,000 to $21,000 for experienced individuals.

Lighting Director: The lighting director is in charge of designing and executing lighting for all TV production in the studio or on location. This job requires technical know-how but is not as creative as a similar job on a feature film. The lighting director must overcome the technical limitations of television by using spots, floods, filters, and the like. He oversees a small crew of technicians who install and position lighting elements. The lighting director reports to either the engineering supervisor or the production manager. The salary ranges from $15,000 to $20,000. It is higher at those stations in which the job is part of the engineering department and is represented by a union.

Unit Manager: The unit manager is responsible for all pre-production scheduling and for setup, maintenance, and operation of equipment. He also organizes the stage and light crews and camera operators—all the production staff during pre-production and rehearsal. In addition to scouting locations and scheduling transportation, food, and lodging for location shoots, he is in charge of the shooting facilities and sets and technical crew. The title of unit manager sometimes describes the person in charge of the daily operation, organization, and budgeting of a series. The salary ranges from $16,000 to $28,000.

Sales

General Sales Manager: The general sales manager is in charge of producing all advertising revenue for a station or network. He analyzes the limited inventory of airtime available for commercials and works with the program director and the station's general manager in matching the programs to specific advertisers. Supervising the sales staff, developing sales plans and goals, previewing programs, and helping to set the station's advertising standards and policies are other major responsibilities.

The position requires long experience in TV sales and a thorough knowledge of the competitive market. An undergraduate degree in marketing, advertising, or business administration is essential. The general sales manager usually comes up from the station sales ranks and is highly compensated. The average annual salary is $63,000.

Assistant Sales Manager: This person helps the general sales manager with all aspects of sales and is responsible for local and national advertising sales. He supervises the sales staff on a daily basis, makes sales calls, analyzes ratings statistics, and monitors available airtime. The assistant sales manager may work with the station's national rep firm to solicit national advertising. Extensive sales experience in TV is required. The average salary is $45,000.

Traffic/Continuity Supervisor: This is an entry-level position with a lot of responsibility. The traffic/continuity supervisor schedules every second of airtime and informs the sales department of all commercial time available during and between shows, when it is sold, and how it is scheduled. This individual reports to the general sales manager, the program director, or both. He also spends time writing for announcers who give the station breaks and announcements promoting the station.

A high school graduate—particularly one who has experience or course work in broadcasting, advertising, and copy writing—would have a competitive edge. Generally speaking, a college graduate would be overqualified for this job. Yet, as a "foot in the door" opportunity, it should be considered. The average salary is $14,000.

Sales Coordinator: Found primarily at larger stations, this employee monitors the activities of the sales staff, writes orders, maintains a schedule of available airtime, and serves as a general assistant/secretary to the sales staff. The sales coordinator also works with the production staff to schedule production of commercials for the sales clients. The job requires a high school diploma; a secretarial or business school background and the ability to work with word processors and computers make the candidate that much more attractive to potential employers. The next step up is typically advertising sales jobs. The average salary $15,000.

News

News Director: The news director heads up the news department and is the final authority for the choice of all news, interviews, documentaries, and special news feature programs. He also supervises anywhere from five to forty or more reporters, anchorpersons, sportscasters, weather reporters, news writers, freelance performers, film and video-camera operators, researchers, assistants, and secretaries. In addition, he oversees the news budget and monitors the work of the reporting staff.

The news director must have news judgment—the assessment of the importance of a particular news story and the appropriate degree of coverage. Promotion to this coveted job comes after years of experience as an on-air reporter, news writer, and producer-director. If a news director runs a top-rated news show, he is highly recruited by other stations. This job has a high turnover rate. For all

this, the salary ranges from about $38,000 in one of the seventy-five smallest markets to $54,000 in one of the twenty-five largest markets. Assistant news directors need college training in mass communications, journalism, or TV. They come up from the ranks of news writers and earn about 15 percent less than their bosses.

CAREER TIP: If you think you have a sales personality, try to get a job as a junior salesperson at a TV station in a city of about 100,000 population. There you will sell to local retailers and establishments. The salary probably will not run higher than $15,000 a year plus some commission basis. If such a job is too difficult to obtain, try to gain your experience in a similar position at the local newspaper; then consider a shift to TV in the same city. Even if you're a college graduate, gain your first TV experience as a traffic/continuity supervisor or sales coordinator. Numerous opportunities are available for the right person who is alert, bright, detail-oriented, and who can operate a computer and/or word processing equipment. Then, after working at these entry-level jobs for a while, you will be in a better position to make your move into sales or programming.

Anchors, Correspondents, and Reporters: When we think of television news, we think of those glamourous people without regional accents who are paid staggering amounts of money to read the evening news. A handful of superstar anchorpersons are paid million-dollar-plus salaries, but then so are superstar actors, athletes, and rock stars. Dan Rather of CBS is said to make $2.5 million a year. NBC's Tom Brokaw is purported to make $1.5 million, and ABC's Peter Jennings, a paltry $1 million, as does Bryant Gumbel of the "Today" show and ABC's Barbara Walters.

Bear in mind, however, that these people are network stars with vast viewing audiences. Also, the swing of just one rating point (800,000 TV homes) from one network to another can mean as much as $70 million in annual revenues to the successful network. If the NBC "Today" show has a Nielsen rating of 4.5 (4.5 × 800,000 or 3.6 million homes) and its competitor on ABC, "Good Morning America," has a 3.5 rating (or 2.8 million homes), NBC can charge more for its commercial time.

Even top network correspondents are well paid. Diane Sawyer of "60 Minutes" makes close to $1 million. CBS White House correspondent Lesley Stahl, who also anchors "Face the Nation," makes a reported $300,000. A half-dozen others make from $200,000 to $350,000. The 200 other network correspondents average $100,000.

For excellent background reading on the subject of anchors, see Barbara Matusow's *The Evening Stars.*

The anchors and correspondents we've been talking about are in the big, big leagues. If you're an anchorperson in Quincy, Illinois, the country's 153rd market, you'll make only $25,000 a year. In one of the top twenty-five markets, such as San Diego, you will probably average $110,000—not bad.

All our highly paid anchors and correspondents did not, of course, start at the top—nor do they merely read the news. Today, they must be seasoned newspeople who can interview, coordinate live reports from a number of sources while on camera, and write and develop news stories.

For those interested in TV news, a background in local investigative reporting is a good starting-off point (see "Investigative Broadcasting at the Local Level" later in this chapter). ABC's Peter Jennings, anchor and senior editor of ABC's "World News Tonight," for example, began his career in 1959 as a reporter for CFJR-Radio in Ontario, Canada. David Brinkley, a forty-year veteran of broadcast news with NBC and ABC, attended the University of North Carolina and Vanderbilt University and got his start after World War II service by working for United Press International. In contrast, ABC's Barbara Walters, one of the most highly acclaimed journalists and interviewers on television, was a writer for CBS News, and before that she was the youngest producer with NBC-TV's New York station. Most anchors, though, started as reporters.

On-air TV reporters need all the attributes of a news anchor, but certain skills will be used more often. Reporters must gather news from a variety of sources, determine with the news director or assignment director the scope and length of the story, and write and deliver the story on the air. At larger stations, the reporter may be a specialist in covering politics, consumer news, crime, health, or business. Although it is not official written policy, news

Stalking the wild story, weekend anchor Betsey Bruce and cameraman Mike Favazza are shown here on assignment for St. Louis's KMOV-TV, a CBS affiliate under Viacom ownership. (Photograph courtesy Viacom International, Inc.)

anchors and on-air reporters must be physically attractive. Viewers seem to favor good-looking people. In a noted court case, Kansas City anchor Christine Craft sued her former station, claiming that she was discriminated against and fired because she wasn't pretty enough to suit her employers. She lost the case. Craft subsequently became the news director of KRBK-TV in Sacramento, California, one of 110 women in the country to hold that title as of this writing.

To give you an idea of how large the news staff is at a network, Roone Arledge, president of ABC News, in the early '80s, increased the size of his staff from 600 people to 1,200. In 1986, when Capital Cities Communications merged with ABC, it quickly cut seventy-five jobs, firing producers, writers, and other employees. Before the cut, ABC News' annual budget was about $250 million.

Other assignments in the news department include weather anchor/meteorologist, $40,000 average salary; weekend anchor, $26,000; general-assignment reporter, $24,000; sports director, $35,000; and sports reporter, $30,000. Sports anchors make more money than reporters. They earn salaries in the $40,000-to-$50,000 range. Again, these averages pertain to jobs in the fiftieth market. As we also indicated earlier in this chapter, however, salaries will be higher in larger markets and lower in smaller markets (salaries for comparable positions in the lowest fourth of all markets will, for example, average $15,000).

> CAREER TIP: Getting an on-camera reporting job is difficult in any market. The lure of fame and large salaries draws many candidates to the medium. It is best to concentrate instead on the less glamorous but more realistic jobs in television. They are described in the following pages.

Sportscaster: At larger stations, sportscasters report to the sports director. At smaller stations, sports may be a one-person department. In any case, by the very nature of the subject, many compete for a limited number of jobs. Sportscasters report the outcome of local games and contests and review, select, and report on the films and videotapes of sporting events and news of national interest.

Some sportscasters provide play-by-play descriptions of live events, interview sports figures, and create features and documentaries aired before and after major sporting events. Most have undergraduate degrees in journalism or mass communications. The salary ranges from about $21,000 to $40,000. Network sportscasters can be paid salaries well over six figures.

Doing the color coverage on sportscasts is a job that attracts former jocks. They're favored by stations and networks, especially if they are articulate and physically appealing, but mostly because (it is hoped) they will bring their established following with them as viewers.

Weather Reporter: You probably don't need a college degree to get a job at a small station, where all you'll do is read the National Weather Service's statistics. At larger stations, however, the weather reporter is usually a trained meteorologist, familiar with the latest weather-prediction technology and equipped with visual devices. Because few stations employ more than one or two weather reporters, prospects for employment in this field are limited. About thirty colleges around the country offer a bachelor-of-science degree in meteorology or, its more formal name, atmospheric sciences. The salary ranges from $18,000 to $35,000. Veteran meteorol-

ogists, particularly those in the larger markets, can earn substantially more.

Business

Business Manager: The business manager handles all financial transactions, develops business plans and goals, and supervises the activities of a business department that generally includes accountants, bookkeepers, billing clerks, and so on. Courses at the college level in business administration and accounting are prerequisites for this position. The average salary is $32,000 a year.

Engineering

Union requirements for jobs in engineering are discussed in the interview with Bruce Sidran near the end of this section.

Chief Engineer: The chief engineer is sometimes called the director of engineering. He must possess experience in all the technical aspects of broadcasting, as well as a thorough understanding of the principles of electronics. The chief engineer must be able to design technical systems that meet the station's needs. An understanding of communications law is essential. An FCC license is also desirable, along with some form of technical certification. While some chief engineers began as engineering technicians straight out of high school or technical school, most have electrical-engineering, physics, or science degrees and technical training from a technical center or college. The average salary is $37,000.

Engineering Supervisor: At smaller stations, the assistant chief engineer also performs the work of the engineering supervisor. At larger stations, this individual directs the work of audio, video, maintenance, master-control, transmitter, and videotape engineers. He ensures maintenance of all equipment and sees that sound and picture meet FCC regulations. He must be alert to equipment malfunction and failure.

Most supervisors have had a minimum of two years' experience as one of the engineers previously listed. Most also received technical school training. Some have degrees in engineering or physics, and most have an FCC license and technical certification. The next step upward is the job of chief engineer. The average salary is $30,000.

Technical Director: The technical director oversees the technical quality of a program and operates the production switcher, which controls the choice of camera images and special effects being fed into the videotape recorders and over the air. In planning a production, the technical director analyzes the requirements of production and works with the director to meet those requirements. During rehearsal and performance, the technical director sits with the director in the control room and runs the switcher, turning the director's camera and videotape choices into reality.

Most technical directors are promoted to this job after two or more years of experience as engineers. The next step upward is the job of engineering supervisor. The salary ranges from $15,000 to $30,000.

Maintenance Engineer: Maintenance engineers are much in demand. This individual performs maintenance work on cameras, switchers, audio consoles, video monitors, microphones, videotape recorders, and other equipment. He works in an engineering shop. A high school diploma is required, plus training in electronics at a vocational or technical school, and a minimum of one year of TV-maintenance experience. An FCC license and technical certification are desirable. The salary ranges from $16,000 to $28,000.

Transmitter Engineer: The transmitter engineer maintains the TV transmitter and antenna system in compliance with FCC regulations. His daily duties include testing the performance of the transmitter to ensure uninterrupted broadcasting, conducting tests, and keeping operations records for the chief engineer. He also routinely inspects the transmitter tower and building. This job requires the same training as that for a maintenance engineer. The salary ranges from $15,000 to $26,000.

Audio Engineer: The audio engineer is in charge of the electronic controls that comprise the station's audio and video equipment. His duties include placing microphones, producing special sound effects, and monitoring sound levels. During the editing process, he may add music or other sound elements to tape. The audio engineer has final responsibility for the technical quality of the program's sound. The salary ranges from $15,000 to $25,000.

Video Engineer: The video engineer sets up and aligns the cameras, controls brightness and color levels, monitors transmission quality, and creates special visual effects. At some stations, an audio/video engineer handles both functions. The salary for a video engineer ranges from $15,000 to $25,000.

Master Control Engineer: The master control engineer coordinates the video and audio portions of programming that comes from the studio, the networks, pre-recorded segments, satellites, ENG crews, and other sources; he then delivers the signals via the master control switcher and processing equipment to the transmitter. In addition, he cues and rolls the film and videotape to ensure smooth transitions from program to commercial to station break; he maintains the station log, and ensures that the output meets FCC technical requirements.

Training and background requirements are similar to those of audio/video engineers. This individual must be calm, alert, and capable of making quick decisions. He must also understand the workings of a wide variety of audio and video equipment. There is a good market for this job. The salary ranges from $15,000 to $22,000.

Videotape Engineer: The videotape engineer sets up and operates a wide variety of videotape machines that record, play back, and edit programs, although the actual editing of videotape is done by camera or ENG operators. The engineer evaluates videotapes, including satellite feeds received by the station, duplicates the taped material, and assembles tape segments for broadcast. He also monitors the audio and visual quality of videotape recordings and works with the master control engineer and other audio/video engineers.

Television photography and editing have been dramatically improved with the use of videotape instead of film. Film consumed time for developing and processing before it was available for transmission. Today, with videotape technology, film is becoming obsolete. Videotape's greatest asset is its ability to be played back immediately without processing.

Many college theater departments videotape their productions for analysis and study. Students thus gain valuable experience handling video cameras. Experience with a home-video camera can also help in mastering techniques needed in preparation for a video job.

Videotape engineers generally spend time as engineering assistants or technicians before promotion to this position. An FCC license and other technical certification are desirable. The salary ranges from $15,000 to $28,000.

Engineering Assistant or Technician: This is the entry-level job on the engineering ladder. Engineering technicians handle the setup, operation, maintenance, and construction of technical equipment and facilities. The job entails working on every piece of equipment the station owns. The opportunity to advance is limited only by the technician's own capabilities. Requirements are a high school diploma and some vocational training. An interest in electronics and broadcast-equipment operation is, of course, a plus. To enhance chances for employment, a candidate should have an FCC license

Seven Tips on Getting a Job in Television

1. For most jobs in television, college or vocational training is preferred. If you're aiming for the highest level of broadcast management, pursue a graduate degree.

2. If you want to major in broadcasting at college or pursue a two-year program at a junior college, there are more than 300 schools that offer substantial course work in radio and television. For information write to: President, Broadcast Education Association, National Association of Broadcasters, 1771 N Street, N.W., Washington, DC 20036.

3. If you want a job operating television equipment, don't waste your time as an assistant in the news department. In many stations, because of union regulations or station rules, you may be prohibited from operating the broadcast equipment.

4. The best way to get in the door after graduation is to apply for a paid or unpaid internship. Getting an internship will not only help you make contacts, it will also help you find out which department of the station you're interested in.

5. In many departments of a TV station, "vacation relief" help is hired during the summer months. If you have some experience, one of these jobs may provide you with the entry that will lead to a full-time job.

6. In order to find out the call letters and locations of TV stations, you should look through one of the industry directories. Your public library or publishers of these directories can provide you with one of the following: *Broadcasting Yearbook*, 1735 DeSales Street, N.W., Washington, DC 20036 and *Television Factbook*, Television Digest, Inc., 1836 Jefferson Place, N.W., Washington, DC 20036.

7. The National Association of Broadcasters maintains an employment clearinghouse to help increase the number of minorities and women employed in the broadcasting industry. The clearinghouse disseminates information on minorities and women in broadcasting and encourages their involvement in the industry. For information, contact: Director of Employment, Clearinghouse, National Association of Broadcasters, Minority and Special Services Department, 1771 N Street, N.W., Washington, DC 20036.

and be preparing for technical certification. The salary range begins at $12,000.

The FCC no longer conducts examinations for broadcast engineers, and a license is needed only for transmitter operations and maintenance. Technical certification now replaces the license examination and is conducted by groups such as the Society of Broadcast Engineers. (For more information, write to the Society at Box 50344, Indianapolis, IN 46250.) Tests are tailored for various areas of broadcast engineering. As one gains experience, additional certification tests are taken to demonstrate expertise in a variety of broadcast-engineering jobs. Certification demonstrates to a potential employer that the applicant is willing to work hard for the job and is interested in improving performance.

The Union and Television

A desk assistant on a news desk is an entry-level job. If you're fortunate enough to get a job at a station with a NABET (National Association of Broadcast Employees and Technicians) contract, you'll earn $360 a week plus benefits. Of course, first you have to get the job.

NABET is the major union in television. It has contracts with ABC and NBC, including their O&Os and affiliates. It also has contracts with a number of CBS affiliates but not with that network itself. NABET has contracts with many independent stations as well.

This union represents a variety of jobs, including engineers, cameramen, graphic artists, news producers and writers, technical directors, and on-air talent. Although salaries vary according to size of market, the range for these employees after three years of experience runs from $35,000 to $65,000 yearly, plus overtime and travel time where applicable.

NABET does not have an internship program of its own, unfortunately, but it does participate in station programs. Once an intern is hired on a full-time basis at a union station, he automatically becomes a union member and profits from its high-wage scale and benefits.

A Day in the Life of a Network Newsroom

Wouldn't most of us like to make a huge salary just to face the camera and read the news five days a week? The answer is an emphatic *yes*. But broadcast journalism is much more than reading the news. It's a serious, complex business with the whole world as its focus. Network-TV news reaches 96 percent of U.S. households weekly. Because the evening news is the most prominent news format on TV, we will chronicle a typical day in the newsroom of ABC News. This will provide an understanding of how a news team functions and will delineate the various job responsibilities.

The television news team is divided into two groups: the first, reporters and correspondents, who cover the news worldwide; and the second, editors and producers, who select, edit, and present the news in an interesting and informative framework.

Early in the morning the day's activities start as correspondents, producers, and camera crew receive their daily assignments. Assignment decisions are based on information received from ABC domestic and international news bureaus, ABC affiliated stations all over the country, stories from the "futures" file (which anticipates stories that may break months later), and information received from the wire services—Associated Press, United Press International, and Reuters.

The senior producers have already made a final check on the assignments the previous night in preparation for the "troop movement," or positioning of staff members.

9:00 A.M.: The senior news staff arrives. In preparation, the senior news staff has carefully read the morning newspapers and is familiar with the overnight news. They hold a "reading in" review of overnight dispatches and cables and receive the daily "situationer," which tells them where the events are happening and how they are being covered. This situationer is continually updated all day.

10:00 A.M.: A conference call is held, including all ABC News representatives in the United States and overseas. At this time, the executive producer makes special recommendations, relying on information from the field.

10:30 A.M.: The senior producers and editors hold a meeting to line up stories and choose a "lead" story. The lead may be a group of related events involving a particularly hot area of the world, such as the Middle East. The stories are then "blocked" into segments divided by commercials. At all times, the editors try to make the stories flow continuously from one to another by grouping like stories together.

10:30 A.M. to noon: By noon, the field producers have evaluated their stories, and all bureaus have reported in. Also, new information from the wire services and newly arrived videotapes are reviewed.

Noon to 2:00 P.M.: The organization of the first draft and the selection and length of stories are discussed; visuals and graphics are determined; videotapes are edited, and any technical problems regarding satellite time and late-arriving material, and the like, are solved.

2:00 P.M. to 3:00 P.M.: The lineup must be revised due to late-breaking news. If new "news" is light, it may serve as a "show ender." Typically, at this time, two or three complete changes in the lineup may be needed.

3:00 P.M. to 6:00 P.M.: Tapes of stories arrive and are reviewed. All have been edited but need cutting for time because every second counts. The hardest part of editing is balancing the visuals with the narrative in order to ensure continuity.

The anchor, especially if he serves as managing editor, is integrally involved in the selection and rotation of stories, as well as their presentation. Now the anchor's copy is prepared, his hair is styled, and makeup is applied. The anchors and writers prepare the introductions and narrations for the shorter pieces. These narrations are called "voice-overs" or "tells."

6:30 P.M.: "World News Tonight" is on the air, the first feed broadcast direct from the control room in New York City. A second feed at 7:00 P.M. is prepared so that affiliates can have flexibility in airing local news. This second transmission is used to cover later time zones and also to update stories from the first feed.

So there it is: 22 minutes of news that represents more than 24 hours of planning, writing, filming, and editing, just so that you can sit back comfortably in your living room and effortlessly absorb the most important events of the day.

All About Sitcoms and Cop Shows

You have probably watched a new show on television and then thought to yourself, "Gee, I can come up with a better concept than that." Possibly you can, but don't plan on getting it made into next fall's hot new series and becoming rich and famous. Here's why.

First, let's rule out the 99 percent of individuals who send the networks unsolicited manuscripts. Chances are that these will be returned promptly with a polite note. The networks cannot afford the risk of future lawsuits, and returning manuscripts unread is their protection.

Sending outlines and manuscripts to TV production companies like Warner, Paramount, and Lorimar will result in the same response. At Paramount, for example, I'm told that they receive 500 scripts *every day* for existing shows, as well as dozens of ideas for new shows.

For every idea that comes into a major network or production company, hundreds of similar, if not identical, ones have preceded it. Skilled submission people can categorize an outline or script almost within seconds of taking it out of the envelope.

At ABC, all material submitted for acceptance in programming goes first to the broadcast standards and practices department. There, a staff of three or four people read the submissions, write brief synopses of the properties' thrust, and then index them under subheadings (women, mystery, blood and gore, terror, or sitcom). From there, each goes to the appropriate programming department for disposition.

Readers at NBC and CBS merely open submission envelopes to see if they're unsolicited. If so, they send them right back.

Readers at the networks and production companies are a harried lot. There's always a big backlog of material, and when the backlog is reduced, there's always more. Junior readers are glorified clerks who spend most of their time going through books and files to check titles. Senior readers do the same thing but also spend more time reading and synopsizing.

At a network, the highest level reader/researcher is paid about $25,000 a year, those at lower levels a good bit less. Personnel people at the networks favor English majors who read and write fast for these jobs. If one has the right contacts at a network,

there is freelance reading work. The pay—about $20.00 to $30.00 for a thirty-five-page script. For a full novel, the fee would be $45.00 to $50.00.

The soundest approach for a writer with an outline for a series, or a script for an existing series, is to get a reliable agent, one who is known to the networks and production companies. That, too, is not easy, because agents are reluctant to take on nonprofessional writers. So, let's say that your cousin's friend is a receptionist at the powerful William Morris agency in New York City. You buy her a drink one night after work and tell her about this great idea you have for a sitcom about two New York cops. One is a bigoted Irish male and is 6'2". His partner in the radio car is a 5'2" black woman. They fall in love, and she brings him home to meet her parents, both high school principals.

After two drinks, the receptionist agrees to show the outline to her friend, an assistant agent who is moving ahead rapidly. After much cajoling, the assistant agent agrees to send the outline to the three networks. Within a few weeks, the outline comes back to the agent with two polite rejection notes and another one saying that they've received the same idea six times with only the woman's height changed.

The agent now sends the outline to various production companies: Warner Bros. Television, MTM Enterprises, Paramount Television, and 20th Century–Fox Television. The results are all the same—rejection.

A 750-to-1 Shot

What do those long-shot odds above indicate? For every ten ideas the network actually hears—that is, ideas submitted by producers and agents they know—they will order one script. A writer will then be given $20,000 or $30,000 to put the idea into script form. The network's average is that for every five scripts it commissions, one is picked for a pilot.

However, the network will not give just any writer or producer the $350,000 or $400,000 to make a 30-minute pilot. The writer or producer will have to work with one of the dozen or so established production companies, or it's no go.

One reason is that pilots and series are often made on a deficit-financing basis. The production company will spend more money than the network allocates to make sure they produce a quality product. Their hope is to recoup this deficit when the series goes into syndication. However, a show must run for two years or more to become an attractive prospect for syndication. (More about syndication later.)

136

But let's continue the odds game. One of five scripts the network orders is made into a pilot, and then one of every three pilots becomes a series. Only two of every ten series that start out in a season will make it to the second season. Thus, the ratio of ideas made into series is 150 to one, and the chances of an idea going into a second season is 750 to one.

Then there's another problem, even with hit shows. Universal Television produces "Miami Vice." The network pays Universal $950,000 for each hour-long episode, but Universal's cost is about $1.25 million. Universal is a rich and powerful studio but is reluctant to "eat" $300,000 every week in the hope of getting it back in syndication, if the show goes into syndication at all, especially when the independent stations now prefer half-hour sitcoms and game shows to hour-long dramas.

If I have dissuaded all the readers of this book from turning their skills to writing for television, that is not my intent. There are still many people enjoying fine careers in this field. Just be aware of the obstacles. If you think you've got great ideas for a TV series, forget about the long-shot odds and go get 'em. Remember, too, that television sitcoms and dramatic series are a major industry, one that employs writers, directors, camera operators, actors, producers, lighting and sound specialists, and editors as well.

For those readers still interested in TV comedy, we have some words of advice from Mel Tolkin. Mel started in television in the early '50s as a senior writer on the classic "Your Show of Shows" and "Caesar's Hour," where his co-writers were Mel Brooks, Neil Simon, Woody Allen, and Larry Gelbart.

More recently, he has written for Bob Hope, and he was story editor on "All in the Family" for five years. Mel has been awarded one Emmy, and he has received seven Emmy nominations for his work on various shows.

Mel Tolkin's Comments on Today's Best Sitcoms

(Excerpt from an interview that appeared in *Emmy Magazine*.)

"Family Ties" is beautiful. The people are beautiful, they're loving, they're permissive, they're ideal. Nobody really raises his voice. No such family exists, but it's marvelous to have that family in front of you. It's what we used to call "white on white," or a bit WASPish,

compared to "The Cosby Show," which has a certain amount of emotionality permitted.

And then there's another form of humor on television, which at its worst is sheer stupidity and at its best is brilliant. I'm talking about farce. There have been a few attempts at farce that have been so ugly and so stupid that mercifully they have died. But there have been two great successes. I'm talking about two shows that some people may not agree with me on, "The Jeffersons" and "Three's Company."

Mention "Three's Company," and some people will say, "Oh, it's just sex." But they did a miracle of writing on that show. For seven years, they kept that ball up in the air. A man is trying to make it with somebody. And it's all done in innocence. And it's pure French farce, with doors opening and closing. If you didn't like it, you didn't have to watch it, but if you wanted to see farce and little misunderstandings rising and rising, those were fine examples.

"The Jeffersons" used farce, too, that was pure Molière. The Sherman Hemsley character is right out of Molière: the bourgeois gentleman trying to rise in a world which he has just stepped into. I think that group, Sherman and the others, should do Molière. I don't know anybody who could do that better. They are great *farceurs*. They take everything lightly. You can see why that show went on and on. Think of "The Jeffersons" and "Three's Company" as pure fun. They have their sermons occasionally, too. But there is a place for comedy that is fun just for the sake of fun; nice people getting into binds.

Some of Mel Tolkin's General Thoughts on Comedy

In a way, comedy is prophetic. What it says to the audience is that if you keep misbehaving, with your petty jealousies, your foolish pride, your little cruelties, *this* is how you will end up. That is what comedy says.

To be a comedy writer you have to be an outsider. The insider takes life for granted. The outsider sees the foolishness or cruelty in it.

On Writing a Pilot for Television

Mel Tolkin also offered the following thoughts on writing a pilot. After listing the difficulties of selling a pilot, he goes on to say:

Suppose, in spite of the odds stacked against you, you still want to write a pilot. And suppose you have written this pilot. Suppose it is in the proper form, the correct number of pages, all of it neatly typed. And suppose, further, you consider your brain child marvelous, that it will bring a fresh note to tired old TV and may start a rash of imitations.

Don't put in an order for a Rolls Royce or convertible, of course, or call your lover to start packing for a weekend in Paris. Not yet. First, reread your masterpiece and ask yourself these very crucial questions:

Is your cast of characters a family unit?

By family unit I mean some cohesive, closed group, like the Huxtables of "The Cosby Show," or the staff in some hospital (plenty of examples there), or the staff in some office ("WKRP"). Or even the inmates of a prisoners' camp ("Hogan's Heroes," which ran for ages).

Note that in the above examples of "family," all the members are locked in, either because of love, or because they're too young to go out in the world, or because they risk losing a weekly pay check if they cut out. Or they're locked in because they're locked in—with locks and guards.

Unable to leave, they *must* solve their problems, fight their battle, then and there.

Do your characters have the potential to grow?

A teenage girl is an excellent example of growth. Little Jenny can marry, have a baby—two events that add millions of viewers. The potential of growth in the characters adds to the show's longevity.

Has the show some originality—but not too much?

Examine the current crop of "family" family shows. (Mom, Dad, kids, dog, etc.) They all look alike, but on examination you will see there is always some element that makes each show different. Even "Alf," the family show with one of the members from outer space—not that original. Or have you forgotten that movie *E.T.?* A talking car representing Mama was a bit much.

Is there some built-in conflict within the cast of characters?

Some basic difference of opinion is absolutely necessary. Examples: Sam the stud versus Diane the romantic in "Cheers." Archie the reactionary versus Mike Stivic the liberal. Any two people in a family who always agree aren't worth a scene.

Conflict—the life blood of comedy and drama.

Does each member in the family (as defined above) have story possibilities?

The need for such possibilities is obvious.

Have you considered the budget?

Can the permanent cast keep stories going without having to hire expensive guest stars? Or going on location?

Do *not* suggest for the pilot, "Michael Jackson's limousine breaks down in front of the Gordons' home, and he comes to love them—they're so decent, so simple, especially the dog."

Do *not* open with location shots of a festival in Kyoto, where Jim and Mary meet romantically. If that is your first line, the producers won't bother reading the second.

Are your characters funny?

Consider the cast of "The Golden Girls." One is dumb, one is a Southern belle type with rather loose morals, one is a cynic, one is old enough not to care what the others think of her cutting remarks. The jokes fly!

Now, if your answer to all the above has been *yes*, you must still refrain from shopping or phoning your lover, because you have some things to do first.

Get an agent who thinks you have something salable. Getting a reputable agent to represent you who will work hard for you is very difficult unless you've already sold a pilot, which is impossible without an agent. (Suggestion: Collaborate with a writer who has a track record. Plenty of fame and glory and money for two.)

Suppose you get an agent. Have him set up a meeting with some established producer, or a network. Pitch your story.

Suppose they like your idea. After sweating through many a rewrite, wait for the network to give the project a go-ahead.

The pilot is made. The network looks at the dozens of other pilots, makes its choice. Yours is one of the lucky ones, say.

It is on the air, scheduled between "The Cosby Show" and "Family Ties," two biggies.

Now buy the car, with cash, and call your travel agent.

By then, you may be too old to get an

automobile license. And your lover has gone to Paris with a writer with *two* pilots.

But when you get to that point, you will know that all that sweat and the waiting has been worthwhile.

So—good luck, and many renewals! You now have a track record.

By the way, I have this idea for a pilot . . .

The Fine Art of Programming

A discussion of programming must be preceded by a definition of "dayparts." A daypart is a particular segment of the broadcasting day. The day is broken down into these dayparts:

- Early Morning: 6:00 A.M. to 9:00 A.M.
- Morning: 9:00 A.M. to Noon
- Afternoon: Noon to 4:00 P.M.
- Early Fringe: 4:00 P.M. to 6:00 P.M.
- Early Evening: 6:00 P.M. to 7:30 P.M.
- Access Time: 7:00 or 7:30 to 8:00 P.M.
- Prime Time: 8:00 P.M. to 11:00 P.M.
- Late Fringe: 11:00 P.M. to 11:30 P.M.
- Late Night: 11:30 P.M. to 6:00 A.M.

Television viewing increases throughout the day, reaching a peak between 8:00 and 10:00 P.M., then declining as people retire for the night. The following is a brief analysis of the programming strategy for each daypart:

Early Morning: This daypart is traditionally dominated by talk and news shows. NBC's "Today" is the leader at this writing with about a 21 share (percentage of TV sets tuned in to TV in this time slot), ahead of CBS's and ABC's competition. The independents generally counterprogram these three shows with children's programming.

Morning: The networks run a mixed bag, including syndicated sitcoms and exercise and game shows. In this daypart, audience composition is twice as many women as men and twice as many children as teens.

Afternoon: This is the time for the soaps, those daily sagas never to be missed (more about soaps later in this chapter). Women comprise 70 to 75 percent of this afternoon audience. The three networks produce about a dozen soaps during this period. Although it takes considerable time to achieve audience involvement with a soap, once a viewer is hooked, she's trapped forever.

Stations not carrying soaps in this daypart usually go with movies, syndicated series (usually old network reruns), and game shows.

Early Fringe: This is a tough daypart to schedule. The teens are home from school, often pressuring for MTV if it's a one-set household. In late 1986, NBC encouraged its affiliates to reschedule the highly rated "Phil Donahue Show" to this daypart in an attempt to dominate the time slot. From 5:00 P.M. to 6:00 P.M., the network affiliates usually run local news or news/feature shows. Stations without news experiment with this time slot, often running popular old sitcoms to increase the ratings.

Early Evening: At this time, the networks trot out their big news guns—the Rather, Brokaw, Jennings bunch—along with their highly paid correspondents, for 30 minutes of national and international coverage.

As noted, the affiliates either precede or follow the network news with locally produced news, or they sandwich the network news between two local news programs. The independents generally do not carry news in this daypart; instead, they carry syndicated series and game shows.

Access Time: Here, the networks and affiliates program game shows. One often sees the highly successful "Entertainment Tonight" in this time slot. The independents run game shows or syndicated sitcoms like "M*A*S*H" or "Happy Days."

Prime Time: During this time, the stations hope to get the highest ratings, and commercials sell at the highest rate. This is the "big time." The networks support this programming with extensive promotion, both on-air and in print.

The independents know that they can't compete with shows like "The Cosby Show," "Family Ties," and "Golden Girls"; they rely mostly on old movies to sustain their share of rating points.

The accompanying Weekly Ratings Scorecard, which appears in the weekly *Variety*, is helpful in understanding how prime-time television functions. These ratings are for the sixth week of the fall 1986 TV season.

Note that NBC is in first place with an average rating of 19.7. Ratings are based on the 80 million U.S. households (98 percent of the total) that have TV sets. Thus, an average rating of 19.4 means that 15.5 million households are watching NBC on an average that week.

"The Cosby Show," with a gigantic 34.9 rating, was the top-rated show of that week and the previous season. That's almost 28 million TV homes.

Monday (27)	A:8.7	C:17.4	N:37.3		
				Rating	Share
8:00	MacGyver (ABC)			10.3	15
	Kate & Allie (CBS)			18.0	26
	World Series — Game 7 Pregame (NBC) (S)			23.7	37
8:11	World Series — Game 7 (NBC) (S)			38.9	55
8:30	My Sister Sam (CBS)			16.0	22
9:00	NFL Monday Night Football (ABC)			8.8	14
	Newhart (CBS)			20.0	28
9:30	Designing Women (CBS)			18.3	26
10:00	Cagney & Lacey (CBS)			15.9	24

Tuesday (28)	A:20.6	C:13.2	N:12.7		
8:00	Who's The Boss? (ABC)			22.0	34
	The Wizard (CBS)			10.9	17
	Matlock (NBC)			17.6	27
8:30	Growing Pains (ABC)			22.5	34
9:00	Moonlighting (ABC)			23.9	37
	Movie: Manhunt For Claude Dallas (CBS)			14.4	24
	Crime Story (NBC)			11.6	18
10:00	Jack & Mike (ABC)			15.5	27
	1986 (NBC)			8.9	16

Wednesday (29)	A:15.6	C:13.2	N:14.8		
8:00	Perfect Strangers (ABC)			14.7	24
	Better Days (CBS)			8.5	14
	Highway To Heaven (NBC)			16.8	27
8:30	Head Of The Class (ABC)			15.9	25
	Together We Stand (CBS)			9.2	15
9:00	Dynasty (ABC)			17.0	27
	Magnum, P.I. (CBS)			16.2	25
	Gimme A Break (NBC)			14.5	23
9:30	You Again? (NBC)			13.2	21
10:00	Hotel (ABC)			14.5	26
	The Equalizer (CBS)			14.4	26
	St. Elsewhere (NBC)			13.6	24

Thursday (30)	A:11.3	C:13.3	N:25.6		
				Rating	Share
8:00	Our World			6.0	9
	Simon & Simon (CBS)			13.1	19
	The Cosby Show (NBC)			34.9	52
8:30	Family Ties (NBC)			33.2	49
9:00	The Colbys (ABC)			10.0	15
	Knots Landing (CBS)			15.4	23
	Cheers (NBC)			27.2	41
9:30	Night Court (NBC)			25.6	39
10:00	20/20 (ABC)			17.9	31
	Kay O'Brien (CBS)			11.5	20
	Hill Street Blues (NBC)			16.3	28

Friday (31)	A:9.8	C:16.8	N:14.7		
8:00	Webster (ABC)			11.8	21
	Scarecrow & Mrs. King (CBS)			14.3	25
	The A-Team (ABC)			12.2	21
8:30	Mr. Belvedere (ABC)			11.9	20
9:00	Sledge Hammer! (ABC)			8.7	14
	Dallas (CBS)			20.5	33
	Miami Vice (NBC)			16.4	27
9:30	Sidekicks (ABC)			8.2	13
10:00	Starman (ABC)			9.2	16
	Falcon Crest (CBS)			15.6	28
	L.A. Law (NBC)			15.6	28

Saturday (1)	A:7.5	C:11.8	N:18.0		
8:00	Life With Lucy (ABC)			8.0	14
	Downtown (CBS)			11.8	21
	The Facts Of Life (NBC)			15.8	28
8:30	Ellen Burstyn Show (ABC)			6.3	11
	227 (NBC)			18.0	31
9:00	Heart Of The City (ABC)			5.3	9
	Movie: Vengeance: The Story Of Tony Cimo (CBS)			11.8	21
	The Golden Girls (NBC)			25.0	43
9:30	Amen (NBC)			19.6	34
10:00	Spenser: For Hire (ABC)			10.1	19
	Hunter (NBC)			14.7	27

Sunday (2)	A:14.3	C:22.4	N:14.7		
7:00	Disney Movie: Ask Max (ABC) (S)			11.8	18
	60 Minutes (CBS)			26.0	40
	NFL Football Runover (NBC) (S)			15.6	26
7:10	Our House (NBC)			13.3	20
8:00	Movie: Never Say Never Again (ABC) (S)			15.3	23
	Murder, She Wrote (CBS)			27.7	40
8:10	Easy Street (NBC)			13.1	19
8:40	Valerie (NBC)			14.5	21
9:00	Movie: Something In Common (CBS)			18.2	29
9:10	Rage Of Angels: The Story Continues — Pt. 1 (NBC) (S)			15.9	25
10:55	Reagan Political (CBS) (S)			12.3	23
10:56	Republican Political (ABC) (S)			10.6	19
	(S) - Special		(R) - Repeat		

Prime-time ratings for the three networks for a week in November 1986. NBC had the highest weekly average share, 19.4. (Reprinted with permission.)

The show's share was 52. Notice, too, that NBC's "Family Ties," which follows "The Cosby Show," has a rating and share almost as high.

ABC's "Monday Night Football," which at this point had been on TV for sixteen years, has been dropping in its ratings, although its low figure during the week shown is attributable to tough competition from the World Series.

Notice on the chart the programming at 10:00 P.M. of so-called "adult" shows—"St. Elsewhere," "Hill Street Blues," and "L.A. Law." Saturday night has always been a difficult daypart because traditionally many people go out then. Yet, a show such as "The Golden Girls" was able to capture a 43-percent share during the week in question.

It is significant too, that in the 8:00 P.M. time slot on Thursday, NBC and CBS together held 72 percent of those tuned in to TV. That leaves only 29 percent for ABC, the independents, and cable TV.

As we have seen earlier in this chapter, the networks are constantly developing new series to attract and hold viewers. The fatality rate is high for these new series. Over a thirteen-year period, ending in 1983, the average number of new programs canceled was 66 percent. The continual series development program of the networks means, of course, employment possibilities for writers, actors, and technicians.

Note that some of the listings for movies are for those especially made for TV. These productions have been on the increase with ever-improving production values, although their budgets seldom exceed $3 million. Networks prefer these movies because they sometimes serve as pilots for series. Another reason is that videocassettes of feature films are distributed as early as three months after their theatrical release, and the networks don't want to pay huge sums for pictures that have been so widely distributed.

Often the plot for a made-for-TV movie deals with current psychological or sociological issues. In one week in April 1986, the three networks aired *five* made-for-TV movies. Here are the subjects covered:

- CBS: "Nobody's Child." A drama of a woman's triumph over mental illness after years of being institutionalized.
- NBC: "Beverly Hills Madam." The title says it all.
- NBC: "The Annihilator." A journalist uncovers a plot to make people into robotlike killers.
- ABC: "My Two Loves." A 2-hour drama about a young widow involved in two relationships—one heterosexual, one lesbian.

- CBS: "A Case of Deadly Force." A true drama of a three-year probe into the police-shooting death of a black man.

The ratings for some of these made-for-TV movies even surpass those for feature films shown on television. Of the top ten movies shown on TV in the early '80s, for example, five were made-for-TV movies. By the mid-'80s, not surprisingly, made-for-TV movies were aired on television more often than theatrical releases.

Note on this prime-time schedule that "The Cosby Show," which attracts a whole family audience, is scheduled for 8:00 P.M., and that "Hill Street Blues," with an older audience appeal, is programmed for 10:00 P.M.

Late Fringe: Traditionally, this time slot is reserved for late news, sports, and weather, usually carried at 11:00 P.M. by the networks' O&Os and affiliates. Independents that carry their news at 10:00 or 10:30 P.M. usually run syndicated series during this late fringe period. Successful old shows like "Taxi," "Barney Miller," and "Hawaii Five-O" predominate this programming while earning huge sums for the series' original owners but seldom for the actors and writers.

Late Night: The undefeated king of this daypart is NBC's "The Tonight Show" with Johnny Carson, followed by "Late Night with David Letterman." The other networks and the independents try to compete with news shows and a grab bag of other formats.

By 1:00 A.M., when most of us are asleep, the insomniacs are watching old movies. The ratings are low, so national advertisers stay away. The pitchmen for a potpourri of products come out of the woodwork to ply their wares on a not-too-alert audience.

Program selection is a sophisticated craft. Research is widely used. Programmers scan such data as Nielsen's *Multi-Network Area Report*, which covers the seventy most populous areas in the country—those cities with at least three commercial TV stations. This sample represents about two thirds of the total number of TV homes.

The largest expenditure at the network programming level is made on series development—evaluating and assigning scripts, producing pilots, and testing. Working in network programming is clearly the big time. Successful programmers go right to the top of the networks' pecking order—with salaries to match.

But even at the local station, there is a need for programming talent. Jobs are not readily available, but persistence is the key.

Those Three Mighty Networks

In 1961, the outspoken head of the Federal Communications Commission, Newton N. Minow, pronounced television "a vast wasteland," alluding, of course, to the poor quality of its output. He also said, at the time, "When television is good, nothing . . . is better. But when television is bad, nothing is worse."

Because the three networks are responsible for most of TV's original programming, the various network heads have, in the twenty-five years since Minow's statement, seen fit to apologize for his biting criticism. Invariably, however, these apologies include basically the same rationale as that applied by movie moguls for years: "We give them what they want." At the bottom line is the bottom line. The networks are big business, and they must make money for their stockholders. If they don't deliver, their chiefs will be axed. We've seen much of this lately.

Some see the networks' current state as one of turmoil. Although they still have about three-quarters of the prime-time audience, they face dogged competition from the independents, from the new fourth network (Fox), from cable, and from the powerful lure of VCRs. The challenge offers unprecedented opportunities for the nets.

Until 1985, FCC regulations permitted each of the three major networks to own a maximum of seven stations, only five of which could be VHF. Before continuing, let's define VHF and UHF. VHF (very-high frequency) encompasses channels 1 through 13 in the United States and Canada and relates to the electronic-spectrum band from 30 to 300 megahertz. UHF (ultra-high frequency), the TV band in the electronic spectrum from 470 to 890 megahertz, encompasses channels 14 through 83.

Most early TV sets were not equipped to receive UHF, but, by the mid-1980s, close to 90 percent of all TV sets had this capability. In theory, the UHF band can handle the broadcasts of up to 3,000 stations in the United States, far beyond the 650 that can be accommodated by VHF. Because of VHF's head start and lower channel numbers, however, it has always dominated, even though in recent years many independents have chosen UHF because of availability. Consequently, by the late 1970s there were only 350 UHF stations, of which 195 were commercial.

The three networks, CBS, NBC, and ABC, are "affiliated" with another 600 stations (approximately). These privately owned affiliates are contractually obligated to carry a large share of the network's programs in exchange for money the network pays to them for carrying its commercials. This compensation amounts to about 8 percent of the affiliates' revenues. We will elaborate later on the role of "independent" stations—those with no network affiliation.

According to FCC statistics, these three networks employed about 17,000 people in the mid-'80s, or nearly 22 percent of all employees in commercial television. The rest work for network affiliates and independents.

Now let's take an individual look at each network.

CBS, the Columbia Broadcasting System

CBS, Inc., the parent company, has headquarters in New York City. It is a diversified business including records, radio, magazine and book publishing, and home video and films; it employs more than 30,000 people.

In the television network division, CBS owns five stations in the important markets of New York City, Chicago, St. Louis, Los Angeles, and Philadelphia. In addition, there are 200 affiliated stations not owned by CBS. Although the affiliates are obligated contractually to fill a large share of their programming day with network supplied programming, they retain a degree of independence.

Recent figures show CBS with annual broadcasting (TV and radio) revenues of $2.78 billion. Clearly, VCR use for viewing of purchased and rental feature films has cut into the growth of TV networks. To meet this challenge, CBS has moved aggressively into the home-video business by entering into a partnership with 20th Century–Fox (owned, as is the rival Fox Broadcasting Company, by Rupert Murdoch) called CBS/Fox, the current leader in its field.

The CBS network has three separate programming and production units. CBS Entertainment is responsible for the acquisition, development, production, and promotion of all entertainment programs for the network. CBS Sports, a major force in broadcasting sports events, has broadcast NFL football for thirty years. It also produces college basketball and the NBA world championship series, the Masters golf tournament, and the U.S. Open tennis championship. CBS News provides more than one-third of the CBS Television Network schedule. Its

"Evening News with Dan Rather" has ratings equal to those of NBC's Tom Brokaw's "Nightly News." CBS News has also produced the award-winning "60 Minutes" continually since 1967.

ABC, the American Broadcasting Company

In 1985, in a friendly (nonhostile) consolidation, ABC merged with Capital Cities to form Capital Cities/ABC, Inc. Before the merger, ABC had broadcasting revenues of $2.847 billion, with an operating income of $340.8 million. It owns TV stations in New York City, Chicago, Los Angeles, San Francisco, and Detroit. It also has 213 primary affiliates and twenty-eight secondary affiliates. A primary affiliate will agree to carry a certain amount of the network's programming, for which it will be compensated by the network. A secondary affiliate is generally the network's second choice within a given market to carry certain programming.

The merged company owns stations in the five largest market areas of the country. These stations combined reach 21 million homes with TV sets, or about one quarter of the nation's total TV homes. As is CBS, Capital Cities/ABC is a diversified company with divisions in magazine and newspaper publishing, radio, and cable television.

ABC's network division comprises six divisions of its own: ABC Entertainment, ABC News and Sports, ABC News, ABC Sports, ABC Television Network, and ABC Communications. ABC News and Sports is headed by the dynamic broadcast executive Roone Arledge, who, as group president, oversees both ABC News and ABC Sports. Arledge originated many sports shows, including the very successful "Monday Night Football," which has been running since 1970.

"Wide World of Sports," another ABC show, celebrated its twenty-fifth anniversary in 1985. In 1984, ABC broadcast the summer and winter Olympics.

NBC, the National Broadcasting Company

In 1986, the giant RCA company agreed to merge with the super-giant General Electric. At the time of the merger, RCA had sales of $8.97 billion and earnings of $369 million (1985 fiscal year). RCA owns NBC.

NBC was the number-one network at the time of the merger and first in prime-time programming. The network is a television pioneer. In 1939, RCA chairman David Sarnoff stood before the cameras at RCA's pavilion at the New York World's Fair. It was the first time that a news event was covered by television. The TV set of that era had a 9″ screen.

The network's news division, NBC News, produces more than 3,000 hours of TV and radio programming.

In technology, NBC has always been a leader. In 1985, it adopted the Kuband satellite to distribute its TV programming, which eliminated the network's dependence on land-based communication lines. This system results in a better-quality picture, improves traffic control, and reduces cost to the network.

The CNN Phenomenon

Ted Turner may be having over-extension problems, but the twenty-four-hour Cable News Network (CNN) is not one of his trouble spots. Since its inception in 1980, it has grown into a profitable organization with 38.5 million subscribers and an average household audience of 600,000.

CNN employs about 1,500 people, more than the news departments of the three major networks. However, its annual budget, of about $100 million, is far less than that of the three networks. The network, based in Atlanta, has eighteen news bureaus around the country.

It is much easier to get a job with CNN right out of college than it is to get one with the networks. In fact, CNN is eager to attract recent college graduates, but at less money than is paid by the networks. You may never earn Tom Brokaw's or Dan Rather's superstar salaries, but it's a good way to get started in the broadcast news business.

Trends

In 1971, the networks lost cigarette advertising because of government regulations regarding the tobacco industry; gains from other advertising sources, however, mitigated this heavy loss. Not until 1985 did the networks again suffer overall ad declines; this time, though, the declines persisted into 1986. If future losses are prolonged in this manner, TV faces some disturbing long-term trends.

The three networks' share of the prime-time audience slipped from 91 percent in the 1977–78 season to 73 percent in 1984–85. Austerity mea-

sures, including layoffs, seemed to be the rule at the networks in the mid-1980s.

> CAREER TIP: Don't overlook the opportunity to work for one of the networks or their affiliates even though they may seem to be having difficulties. Working for CBS, ABC, or NBC is the big time. Success with one of their stations can mean advancement in other parts of these networks' activities.

The Fox Broadcasting Company: The Making of a Network

In recent years, a number of attempts were made to form a fourth network. None have succeeded, but in 1986 along came Rupert Murdoch; with a huge bankroll and much determination, he prepared to outdo the Big Three at their own game. First, Murdoch bought 20th Century–Fox for its status as a movie major and a source for programming for his new network.

In 1985, Murdoch plunked down $2 billion for Metromedia's seven TV stations, which included the profitable WNEW in New York, now renamed WNYW. The next step was to line up independent stations unaffiliated with the other three networks. The hook: a generous package that combined cash and extra advertising time beyond the usual amount allotted affiliate stations by the networks. There were ninety-nine affiliated stations in the Fox network, FBC, by the end of 1986.

The start of progamming for the new Fox network was in April 1987, when it introduced several new half-hour sitcoms, among other entries. To catch viewers who were watching other shows, each sitcom was run at three different time slots during the same evening on premiere night.

The new network, however, needed more than attractive business terms and sitcoms; it needed a big show in prime time or late night. "The Late Show," initially starring Joan Rivers, was Fox's big gamble, running against Johnny Carson in the key late-night spot. Although FBC lined up one hundred

CNN's "A" control, election night 1986. Seated, from left, are the graphics operator, executive producer, director, switcher, and sound man (standing). Two women with phones are coordinating remotes, and above them, at right, votes are being tallied. The anchors can be seen in the center background. (Courtesy CNN.)

stations in major markets that agreed to carry the talk show, Rivers was canceled seven months after the show's start.

Fox's programming whiz is Garth Ancier, who got his start at the age of fourteen as a PBS intern. His mix includes feature films, sitcoms, and action adventure series. FBC's management forecasts an ambitious average prime-time rating of 8.0 or 7 million homes, about half of what a typical minute of network prime time gets during the regular season.

Ancier's career should be an inspiration to our readers. Right out of college, he got a job as an assistant to a top programming executive at NBC. At age twenty-three, he became vice-president of comedy programming, helping to develop the top NBC sitcom "The Cosby Show." Fox, Inc.'s chairman, Barry Diller, says that he hired Ancier (at twenty-eight) because "he's young, bright, energetic, and he's never been a senior programmer before."

Those Independent Independents

In the Boise, Idaho, market area, there are 152,400 TV households, which makes Boise the 134th market nationally. Yet, the area has six television stations: three are network affiliates, one is a public TV station, and the other two are small independents.

New York, the nation's largest market area, has seventeen broadcast (noncable) channels. Of the six largest stations, three are independents. One of these, WNYW (formerly WNEW), now a part of Rupert Murdoch's broadcasting group, is one of the most profitable stations in the country. Murdoch purchased it for about half a *billion* dollars in 1986.

What do independents like the two in Boise and

144

WNYW have in common? First, they are among the 290 that are not owned or affiliated with the three major networks, although about one hundred independents are now affiliated with the Fox network. The independents share 21 percent of the nation's TV audience. Their ad billings in 1985 were $2.5 billion—25 percent of total TV national and local sales. And most significant of all, their profit margins were more than 25 percent.

Why, one may ask, are the independents so profitable? The answer may be found in their programming. Where network affiliates primarily run network programming, the independents carry much less expensive syndicated shows. True, network prime time commands higher advertising rates for commercials, but there was also a large audience for WNYW's 1986 airing of the 1961 movie *West Side Story,* even though it ran against NBC's "The Cosby Show."

Let's look at a recent schedule for WNYW:

Early Morning: Syndicated kiddie shows such as "New Zoo Revue," "Fat Albert," and the "Woody/ Bugs Hour."
Morning: Syndicated shows such as "Leave It to Beaver," "I Love Lucy," and "All in the Family."
Afternoon: From noon until 1:30 P.M., the station runs its locally produced news and talk show. For the rest of this daypart, it's "Woody Woodpecker," "Jayce and the Wheeled Warriors," and "She-ra."
Early Fringe: More syndication—"He-Man," "Thundercats," and "The Brady Bunch."
Early Evening: More of the same—"Diff'rent Strokes," "Too Close for Comfort," and "Three's Company."
Access Time: "M*A*S*H."
Prime Time: Old movies. At 10:00 P.M., the station runs its very popular "Ten O'Clock News," which is locally produced. One of the show's claims to fame is its intro, "It's 10:00 P.M. Do you know where your children are?" videotaped by various celebrities and personalities.
Late Fringe and Late Night: Reruns of shows like "Taxi" and "Dynasty," as well as "Comedy Tonight" and other syndicated shows until 3:00 A.M.

WNYW is an immensely successful station in the nation's number-one market. Its formula of syndicated reruns and its highly rated "Ten O'Clock News," now followed by "The Late Show," has enabled it to sell out most of its commercial time—an uncommon feat for *any* TV station.

We can certainly conclude that going to work for a local independent TV station can be a positive

move. Although there's not much production work, there are opportunities in programming and sales.

Investigative Broadcasting at the Local Level

Want to be a network news reporter and expose a major purchasing scandal at the Pentagon? Well, maybe you should get your training as an investigative reporter at a local TV station covering influence peddling at city hall.

Granted, when it gets down to local stations, there seems to be a disinclination to rock the game-show/sitcom boat. Among other considerations is the high cost of setting up the investigative teams. Some stations, however, say that investigative news broadcasting is good business, in some cases improving their standing one or two positions within their market, and they are producing provocative broadcast journalism on a regular basis.

In an article in the November/December 1985 *Columbia Journalism Review,* Nancy Madlin tells of a number of such efforts. At KPRC-TV in Houston, there's an I-team (investigative team) that includes two former print reporters, backed up by a full-time researcher and cameraman. A two-person team at KTUL-TV in Tulsa, Oklahoma, has been doing it for two years. They uncovered a major fraud by a charitable foundation.

For those pursuing a career in TV news, making the I-team can be rewarding work. After all, Morley Safer and Mike Wallace had to start somewhere.

Syndication: Mining for Gold

On Thursday-night prime time in March 1986, NBC carried four series: "The Cosby Show," "Family Ties," "Cheers," and "Hill Street Blues." When these shows go into syndication, they will earn their production companies a fortune. "The Cosby Show," one of the most popular series of recent years, will earn its syndicator, Viacom International, Inc., a *half billion dollars*. By mid-1987 it had been sold to more than fifty-six stations for syndication.

Here's how it works. A network commissions a TV production company such as Lorimar, Warners, or Paramount to develop a script for a sitcom. If the network likes the script, it then commissions a pilot program from the production company for a fixed fee. The pilot is aired, and if it has good ratings, the network then orders a series of thirteen or fewer shows at a fixed "license" fee per show. The license gives the network the right to show each episode of the show twice, once in first run and once as a repeat. The network is also granted the right to order from the production company between twenty-four and twenty-six new episodes per season.

If the show has been in prime time for at least three or four years (the barometer of success, since it has to have high ratings to last that long), the production company then sells the show for syndication to local stations and foreign TV.

The package may also be sold to superstations such as WWOR in New Jersey, thus boosting profits even higher. (As noted earlier, a superstation is one whose programming is carried by satellite to cable households outside its local market.)

The network, however, can make money only from the sale of advertising time on its shows, which often doesn't cover the license fees it pays the production company. The problem is magnified when the show's ratings are low and the network cannot charge enough for the advertising. Thus, we can understand the network's demand for a stake in the lucrative syndication market.

The production company's complaint, on the other hand, is that the network's license fee often does not cover the production costs of a show. The producers must then make up the difference, which can run as much as $200,000 per show.

For example, Universal Television owns and produces the hit series "Miami Vice," which runs on NBC. The cost of one episode of this hour-long show is estimated to be $1.25 million, but NBC pays Universal somewhat less for licensing its use. Why, you may ask, doesn't Universal produce the show for less money and break even on the transaction (a common occurrence in earlier years, when production costs were comparatively low)? Well, simply because NBC will not permit lesser production values.

As just mentioned, shows can be syndicated only after they've been successful on the networks for three or four years, because in syndication they will be shown five times a week. To add to the problem, stations that buy syndicated shows are now favoring

half-hour programs in preference to 1-hour programs, but the networks continue to commission many 1-hour shows.

Also, there is the chance of overkill. When "Dallas" went into syndication in the mid-'80s while still a continuing series, the syndicated episodes suffered. (Also contributing to lower ratings for serials such as "Dallas" is that, in syndication, their suspense element is largely gone. For the same reason, CBS sometimes does not rerun "Dallas" episodes in the summer.) Still, this lucrative after-market of eventual syndication is in the mind of every production company when it launches a new sitcom.

What Is a Show's Afterlife?

After "Miami Vice" finishes its run on NBC, it will surely be a favorite on independent stations. In selling these licenses, Universal has no production costs, so at this stage it seems to be all profit.

Yet syndication has other cost factors. The syndicator must sell the independents station-by-station, which entails expensive sales costs, except of course in an arrangement such as that of the new Fox network, in which the independents have a firm arrangement to carry the programming. Also, in order to avoid the cost of making many prints of a show, one print is sometimes routed from station to station—a tedious procedure. Duplicate prints are made when a show is sold to as many as a hundred independent stations.

A New Twist

Production companies such as Lorimar Television have come up with a new, perhaps (for them) better, idea: first-run syndication. Here, game shows, animation, and family and children's programming are produced and syndicated to networks and independents right from the start. It could be a new trend.

The Game Show Mania

When Merv Griffin sold his two game-show creations, "Wheel of Fortune" and "Jeopardy," to Coca-Cola for $250 million, industry pundits were not surprised. "Wheel of Fortune," TV's number-one game show, has 43 million viewers tuning in *every day*, and "Jeopardy" is not far behind.

So powerful is the appeal of game shows to the early evening daypart that ABC bumped Peter Jennings's newscast from its traditional 7:00 P.M. slot on its New York station and replaced it with "Jeopardy." The result? In its new period, "Jeopardy" beat Dan Rather and Tom Brokaw on the CBS and NBC stations.

What's significant about the success of these game shows is their syndication advantage. These shows are not reruns but the first-run syndications just mentioned. They're produced to run daily on independent television stations and some affiliates. These stations prefer them to the more costly network reruns that don't have the same audience appeal.

"Wheel of Fortune" now airs on about 200 television stations. Since its prizes are donated by manufacturers as promotional considerations, the show's annual production costs run a mere $7 million. Its gross revenues—$120 million. That's truly mining for gold.

Don't waste too much time thinking of game-show ideas. There are probably not too many new ones. You may have more luck in trying to become a contestant. There's a school in Los Angeles called (what else) the Game Show Company that will teach you how.

Feature Films

The order of rotation of a feature film after its theatrical run is videocassete, cable TV, network TV, and, finally, syndication, five years after its first release.

Made-for-TV movies and mini-series are later licensed for local independent TV stations just as are sitcoms, dramatic series, and game shows.

Foreign TV is also a market for all this programming. In some cases, the shows are made available to these markets immediately after their U.S. debut.

Barter and Other Games

The simplest form of syndication is the straight sale of programs to stations for cash. At other times, the program is sold directly to a large advertiser, which then purchases time on stations in markets it desires and becomes the show's sole sponsor.

In a barter situation, an advertiser or agency buys a program from a production company and gives it to a station free of charge with two or three built-in commercials in lieu of payment from the station. The station then sells the remaining spots. Or, the station receives the program free of charge in exchange for commercial time, which the advertiser can place on other shows on that station.

The Coming Crisis in Syndication

We know that syndication is big business. In one recent year, advertisers placed $2.5 billion in advertising on syndicated shows. Now the reader can begin to understand why TV stations are sold for so much money.

With the sale of ABC to Capital Cities, the sale of NBC to General Electric, and the reign of Laurence Tisch at CBS, the battleground is set for the war on syndication profits. With advertising revenues down in the mid-1980s, this profit center becomes increasingly important.

Clearly, the networks want more control and revenues from syndication reruns (which they originally helped to finance) to balance their losses from pilots and new sitcoms that don't work. The production companies as well are demanding these revenues to counter their deficit on the amount the networks pay per show against their actual cost. The fight goes on. Let the viewer beware.

As a career opportunity, syndication is very exciting. Primarily, it is a sales business. There are syndication jobs at networks, ad agencies, production companies, movie studios, and organizations that do nothing but syndicate sales of other people's products.

The Soaps

What do Warren Beatty, Ellen Burstyn, Dyan Cannon, Robert De Niro, Peter Falk, Dustin Hoffman, Kevin Kline, Bette Midler, Christopher Reeve, Tom Selleck, and John Travolta have in common? Yes, we gave you the hint. They are among the famous graduates of daytime drama—otherwise known as the soaps.

Twenty million Americans watch the soaps every day, 50 million watch at least once a week, and 25 percent of this audience are men. More statistics: Soaps sold $1.8 billion in advertising in 1985, and they are purported to account for one third of ABC's profits.

The reason for this high profit margin is the relatively low cost of producing soaps. A 60-minute drama costs between $125,000 and $150,000. Prime-time series cost five or six times that amount.

Origins

Radio soaps date back to the mid-'20s. Our first TV station, DuMont's WABD in New York, experimented with soap operas in 1946. Incidentally, they're called "soap operas" because the early radio dramas were sponsored primarily by soap advertisers. The "opera" comes from their melodramatic, larger-than-life plots and highly charged emotions.

NBC and CBS got into the soap act in the early '50s. These early shows were basically adaptations of radio soap operas. ABC joined the other networks with the blockbuster "General Hospital." In early '86, "General Hospital" was a top-rated soap, along with "All My Children" and "The Young and the Restless." NBC's "Search for Tomorrow" was thirty-five years old in 1986.

With women joining the work force in rapid numbers, the boon for soap producers and viewers alike has been the advent of the VCR. Now, working soap fans merely tape their favorite daytime serials and then watch them at night.

Soap viewers are known for their passionate devotion to the medium, but new shows do not have an easy time building a loyal audience. Also, syndicated game shows have given soaps a run for it in the daytime market.

Although the three networks are constantly battling it out for the daytime market, for the fourth quarter of 1985, among women viewers, ABC held a 50 percent advantage over CBS and 90 percent over NBC.

The Plot Thickens

Soaps have been tackling the subjects of drugs, abortion, rape, and illegitimacy for years. These days, in an attempt to attract younger viewers, soap opera producers are introducing bolder themes such as homosexuality, incest, herpes, and AIDS.

Producing the Soaps

It takes about ten days and more than a million dollars to produce one episode of the prime-time soap "Dynasty." The producers of "All My Children" do the entire 1-hour show in a day, on a budget of a little more than $100,000.

Two hundred people are involved in the production of "All My Children," many working 12-hour days. Taping goes on every weekday, including holidays. It has not had a hiatus or rerun for sixteen years. The following is a brief recap of a day in the life of "All My Children."

"All My Children" first aired on January 5, 1970. It currently has a cast of thirty-two contract players, twelve noncontract players who appear regularly

on the show, plus a number of extras who vary from show to show.

The work starts at 7:00 A.M. when the director gives the actors a run-through of the day's show, going through the script and showing them exactly how they will have to move on the set. The actors don't know their lines yet; they will start learning them later on in the day.

This first rehearsal (conducted off the set) concerns just physical movement. The run-through ends at 10:00 or 10:30 A.M.; then, the whole cast plus directors go down to the set. There are generally about nine or ten sets in place for each show, every day. In "All My Children," they can include Erica's room, the hospital room, a jail cell, a car, and so forth. The actors go through the movements they have previously rehearsed with the director while he directs the three cameras through the shots they will have to take during the taping. Having three cameras tape the episode at the same time saves a lot of time because all the different shots will be done at once: close-ups, long shots, long views, and so on, and will later be edited on the tape when needed.

At 12:15 P.M. everybody breaks for lunch until 1:15, when dress rehearsal starts. The actors must be completely dressed and made up by 1:15, and most of them devote the lunch hour to this process. Those with smaller parts may have time to do it during the first rehearsal. The dress rehearsal, however, is really for everybody except the actors. During the dress rehearsal, the producer and the director sit in the control room and review how the show will look through the camera. They shout out any immediate changes they want to the actors and crew on the set.

At 3:30 P.M. there is a break, and a light fruit snack is served for the actors. The director and the producer sit down with the actors, exchange notes, and go over the show once again, pointing out changes they want made as they go along.

Taping usually starts anywhere from 4:00 to 5:00 P.M. It usually lasts 2 hours, unless the script features scenes with a lot of extras, or some great event like a wedding. In that case, it can run 1 or 2 hours more. Generally, however, the 2 hours of taping that was done two or three days in advance, ends up being the 1-hour show the audience will be watching in the next few days. Most shows are shot in studios, not on location, although much more on-location work is done these days than was done in the pre-1980s period.

Opportunities in Soaps

Soaps mean jobs for many actors, writers, and technical people. Because the networks are involved, all jobs are controlled by the various theatrical unions. Writers usually receive the Writers Guild minimum of $1,500 per week, but this work is limited to a select group of dialogue specialists.

Although there are some highly paid actors, most work for scale, and the regimen is very demanding. The AFTRA (American Federation of Television and Radio Artists) union scale is $476 a day. Actors in movies do about a script page of dialogue a day. On prime-time serials, they do three pages a day, but on the soaps, the requirement is twenty-five to forty pages a day.

Most of the soaps are shot in New York City, ostensibly because of the abundance of stage actors. If the reader is able to break into the TV and film industry through soaps, it's a good beginning—and the work is steady.

Selling Airtime for Fun and Profit

Television networks and television stations (as well as cable networks and systems) make their money selling airtime, those pesky commercials that viewers with remote controls have been known to zap, just like mosquitoes on the back porch.

Whether it's the local furniture company buying a 30-second commercial for $150 on a small local TV station, or a beer company buying a 30-second spot for $550,000 on the Super Bowl telecast, it's still airtime—and it has to be sold.

Because we devote considerable space in the advertising chapter to the purchase and production of TV commercials, this phase of television will not be covered in depth here. However, we will give here a brief outline of the selling process.

There are three basic kinds of airtime that a station or network's sales force sells: network TV, spot TV, and local TV.

- Network TV airtime is the commercial time that exists within and between programs that air on TV stations that are affiliated with one of the three broadcast networks. An example would be General Foods' buying a 30-second spot on "The Cosby Show," which would then appear on all 200 NBC affiliates.
- Spot sales are those made on behalf of an advertiser that, because of product distribution

or new product testing, elects not to advertise in every market but only in "spot" markets, selecting only those markets in which the advertiser wishes to advertise.

- Local TV airtime, sometimes called "local availabilities" or simply "local avails," is bought by local concerns to appear on the local TV station.

As we have seen in the section on ratings, network and spot airtime is sold by the networks and stations on the basis of ratings such as those developed by Nielsen and Arbitron. The networks' and stations' research staff coordinate this information, which is then used by their sales staffs to sell the airtime to advertisers and their agencies.

In the programming section, we talked about "dayparts." The cost of airtime is determined by the daypart in which the commercial is to appear. Obviously, a commercial will cost more on a prime-time program than it will late at night, because there is a much larger viewing audience.

CAREER TIP: If you have a persuasive, outgoing personality, by all means consider a career in selling airtime. It can be frustrating, but the rewards are great. A successful career in TV sales can lead to the top of the heap at a network.

Don't overlook the research and promotion aspect of sales. Perhaps less remunerative than sales, it is no less challenging. A computer background helps in research; writing courses are good preparation for promotion jobs.

As do their counterparts on a magazine, the advertising salespeople at a network TV station or rep firm entertain their clients at expensive restaurants, but that doesn't make sales. The salesperson must sell the advertiser or agency on the basis of the following criteria:

- Television is more effective than other media.
- Television reaches more people than other media.
- Television is cost efficient.

- Television advertising has a subliminal effect.
- Television advertising can be pinpointed to a specific buying group or target audience.

The networks have their own sales staffs whose employees sell advertisers network TV airtime. There are separate departments at the networks in charge of selling spot sales. In addition, stations call on "rep" firms to sell time for them.

A large rep company will have offices in many major cities, with a headquarters staff in New York or Chicago. The rep company represents many stations across the country; thus, a rep salesman will make sales calls to an agency on behalf of a number of stations. The rep companies generally work with the stations on a commission basis.

The FCC (Federal Communications Commission)

The FCC is an independent federal agency created in 1934 with powers of regulation over television, cable, and radio. Its five commissioners and the chairperson are appointed by the president of the United States. Each president appoints his own chairman for a term of five years. At this writing, the FCC has a staff of 2,000.

Through the years, the activities of the FCC have varied, depending on the dynamism of its chairperson and commissioners. In the early '70s, Newton Minow, as chairperson appointed by President John Kennedy, was a particularly vocal critic of television and its programming content. This criticism centered on TV violence and its emphasis on lowest-common-denominator entertainment.

Mirroring President Ronald Reagan's attitudes on free enterprise, his appointed chairperson in the early '80s, Mark Fowler, moved aggressively toward a policy of less governmental regulation of television and radio.

One can better understand the function of the FCC by examining some of its activities.

Broadcast Regulation

This activity concerns the allocations of frequency bands, applications for new stations, and the regulation of existing stations, which includes the licensing of transmitter operators and the transfer of a station's license from one party to another.

It is the FCC, for example, that determines the number of stations one owner or business entity may own and the maximum term of a station's license (five years), which, upon application, may be renewed.

Programming

The commission periodically reviews station performance, usually in connection with the license renewal application to determine whether the license has lived up to its obligations of serving the public interest.

During political campaigns, the FCC prescribes that all legally qualified candidates for any public office be afforded equal opportunities to state their views. This practice is commonly known as the "equal time provision."

Advertising

The FCC does not regulate individual commercials, but it does consider whether over-commercialization contrary to the public interest may be involved. In the early 1970s, the commission was instrumental in banning cigarette advertising on TV and radio.
Career Opportunities: Considerably less glamorous than working for the networks or in TV production, a job with the FCC can nonetheless be fulfilling. It may be especially attractive to those who would like to work in Washington, D.C. The FCC, for example, employs about 250 lawyers. Other than the commissioners and certain noncareer employees, employment in the FCC is nonpartisan.

The Public Broadcasting Sector

Dozier, Alabama; Bethel, Alaska; Pago Pago, American Samoa; Cotati, California; and Broomfield, Colorado, have one thing in common—they all have member stations of PBS, the Public Broadcasting Service. There are 313 noncommercial stations in this network. During an average week, viewers in

47 million homes watch public television at some point during the seven-day period.

PBS, alone among the world's public TV systems, is entirely independent of political and governmental control or interference. It is owned and controlled by its member TV stations, which, in turn, are accountable to their local communities.

Origins

The nation's first public TV station pre-dates the creation of PBS. KUHT in Houston, Texas, got its start in 1953. One of its productions, "Children's Corner," had a weekly budget of $150, which included salaries and props. We can just guess at the producer's fee.

By 1962, there were seventy-five such stations, most operated by educational institutions. The distribution system used in those days was indeed primitive. When offered for nationwide use, a program had to be "bicycled," that is, a few copies would be sent to key stations, which would air the program and then send it on to other stations.

The Public Broadcasting Act, signed by President Lyndon Johnson in November 1967, initiated governmental support for public broadcasting. At the same time, the Corporation for Public Broadcasting (CPB) was founded, basically to act as a buffer between stations and federal agencies in order to protect programming from government influence.

Consultation among CPB, the Ford Foundation (a strong and longtime supporter of educational television), and the existing public stations' representatives recommended that a "Public Broadcasting Service" be formed. PBS signed its charter on November 3, 1969.

PBS started with 128 member stations and a budget of $7 million. In the first year, its audience was treated to a diet of such productions as "The French Chef," "Washington Week in Review," and "The Nader Report."

Through the 1970s, PBS innovated such provocative programming as "The MacNeil/Lehrer News Hour," "Bill Moyers' Journal," "Nova," "Masterpiece Theatre," "Live from the Met," and the children's program "Sesame Street." By the mid-1980s, 90 million people were watching public television each week.

WNET/Thirteen

A view of public television requires a look at WNET/Thirteen in New York, until mid-1986 the supplier of more than 35 percent of all prime-time

programming aired by the more than 300 public TV stations in the United States. Major cost-reduction measures at the station forced a deemphasis in its programming role.

WNET/Thirteen then reached a prime-time audience of more than three million households in the metropolitan New York area. In the same year, four first-run series produced by WNET/Thirteen won major awards and critical acclaim. These were "Heritage: Civilization and the Jews," "The Brain," "A Walk Through the 20th Century with Bill Moyers," and "The Constitution: That Delicate Balance."

A Quantum Jump in Technology

In 1978, PBS took a giant leap in becoming the first American TV system to distribute its programs nationwide via satellite. In 1984, PBS purchased four transponders from Western Union, giving the system the capacity to provide public TV stations four streams of programming simultaneously. (A transponder is a device on a satellite that receives, amplifies, and retransmits audio and video signals.)

For hearing-impaired Americans, PBS spearheaded the development of closed captioning, whereby subtitles appear on the home screen by means of special decoding devices hooked into sets.

Programming

In the final analysis, what distinguishes public TV from commercial TV is not simply its lack of commercials but rather the innovative excellence of its programming.

Viewers of public TV have learned that educational TV can be subtle, varied, and spirited. Series such as "American Playhouse," "Wonderworks," "The Brain," and "Heritage: Civilization and the Jews" are indicative of this quality programming.

As of this writing, the three all-time, most-watched PBS TV programs were National Geographic Specials:

Title	Date	Cumulative Audience*
"The Sharks"	1/82	17.4%
"Land of the Tiger"	1/85	16.5%
"The Incredible Machine"	10/75	16.0%

*Percentage of U.S. TV homes viewing at least six consecutive minutes of a program.

In an experiment in September 1985, WNET/Thirteen positioned its alternative to commercial evening news, "The MacNeil/Lehrer News Hour" (co-produced with WETA/TV in Washington), on prime time locally from 7:30 until 8:30 P.M. It attracted more viewers than ever.

Grants and Contributions

In 1984–85, WNET/Thirteen's revenues were $100 million. These revenues were derived 60 percent from grants for designated projects, 25 percent from contributions, 10 percent from government grants, and 6 percent from miscellaneous sources. (The federal government spends less per capita on public television than just about any other developed nation in the world—in 1984–85 only 54¢ per person.) Because so much money must come from grants, WNET/Thirteen and other public TV stations pursue these funds aggressively. In 1985, for example, WNET/Thirteen received $1 million from the National Endowment for the Arts. To receive this large sum, however, the station first had to raise the even larger amount of $3 million in matching contributions from other donors. It did.

Public Television as a Career

Readers interested in a rewarding career should consider public television. Few other fields offer this combination of education and entertainment.

As we've pointed out earlier in this section, there are public TV stations everywhere. One can always get one's feet wet by becoming a volunteer fundraiser at a local PBS station. There are internships available at many of these stations; some are listed at the end of this chapter.

With the exception of sales, the table of organization of a public TV station is similar to that of a commercial station. In smaller cities, public TV jobs pay less than those of its commercial counterpart. In larger cities such as New York and Los Angeles, salaries are about equal.

Breaking into public TV is no less difficult than breaking into commercial television, unless you have exceptional skills and training. The job spectrum is about the same, the major difference being that fundraising replaces ad sales. While there is even more financial pressure to meet budgets in public TV, however, there is an esprit that may be lacking in commercial TV. Perhaps it is based on the lack of constraints from advertisers. A good route to follow is to get experience on a PBS production, even if it means being a "gofer." From there, who knows, maybe you can become another Bill Moyers or Alistair Cooke.

Hooked on Cable

Cable has had enormous growth in the past twenty years. By the mid-1980s, there were 6,600 operating cable systems serving 18,500 communities with a total of 40 million households. Yet major cities such as Chicago, Boston, Washington, D.C., and half of New York City had no cable. Pay cable (HBO, and so forth) was subscribed to by almost 60 percent of cable TV households.

A Short History of Cable

Cable TV got its start in the late 1940s as CATV (community antenna television). Its purpose was to provide better reception for areas that were underserved or unserved by standard broadcast stations.

After it was discovered that CATV could offer consumers better reception and that microwave relay stations could be used to import TV signals from distant TV stations, CATV systems began sprouting up in areas already served by local broadcast stations.

Advancements in the 1970s increased the capacity of CATV systems to more than one hundred channels; however, major CATV companies found that laying coaxial cable in cities was far more expensive than they had anticipated, and there wasn't an overwhelming demand for their services.

Then, in 1975, along came Time Inc.'s HBO (Home Box Office), which leased a transponder on RCA's Satcom 1 to distribute its "pay-TV" service. Soon others followed HBO's lead, distributing programming of their own, via satellite. This new programming increased the demand for cable dramatically, and, by the early 1980s, most cities were wired or about to be wired.

Now we refer to two types of cable networks: basic and pay. Pay-cable networks are those such as HBO, where the subscriber pays a monthly HBO-access charge in addition to a basic monthly cable charge. The pay-cable networks share part of their fees from subscribers with the cable system.

The growth of pay-cable networks continued unabated until the mid-'80s. By the end of 1985, HBO had 24 percent coverage of cable households; its main competitor, Showtime, had 10 percent coverage.

HBO, whose principal programming is movies released about a year earlier, became king of the hill in Hollywood. It was buying rights to so many movies that it seemed to control the film industry. HBO's appeal to middle-age, middle-class America was enormous, because traditionally that group doesn't go out to the movies. Why pay $5.00 for a movie when for $10.00 a month you can see twenty or thirty movies?

But as with all good things, a threat lurked around the corner in the form of a new medium—home video. By the mid-1980s, there were 20,000 video stores renting videocassettes of movies, barely *three months* after their theatrical release, for only $2.00 or $3.00.

Cable viewers, however, are not to be denied access to their favorite films. An innovative two-way cable system, recently tested, will give viewers access to about sixty first-run movies at the same time that video rental stores acquire them. Viewers using the system will merely have to punch in a personal code on their sets to select the movie showing at that time. (See the chapter on movies for a discussion of the home-video revolution.)

Suddenly, by the end of 1985, HBO's spirited growth hit its peak at 14.5 million subscribers. Cinemax and Showtime/The Movie Channel topped out as well. These premium channels soon realized that the immense popularity of home video had reduced the demand for cable viewing. On the "if you can't lick 'em, join 'em" theory, HBO wisely made its move into home video by forming Thorn EMI/HBO Video, joining forces with a large established video company.

A movie producer now making a deal for cable rights with HBO can also expand that deal to include that premium channel's home-video rights. The channel wins both ways. HBO and Showtime have reduced costs, too, mostly by producing their own comedy and drama series.

Yet another problem plaguing the cable industry in the '80s was the appearance of those unsightly futuristic backyard dishes, now euphemistically called "home satellite dishes." For an investment of a few thousand dollars, homeowners could bypass cable services. Pay TV countered by scrambling its signal so that dish owners couldn't receive cable's programming. At least one service, HBO, has made peace with the dish people and offers nonsubscribers descramblers for $12.95 a month.

One should not be quick to toll the death knell for pay TV. In 1985, consumers spent $9.2 billion on cable programming, more than they spent on going to the movies or renting home-video programs.

A Look at Cable TV's Networks

First, a word about how cable systems function with cable networks. We, the TV public, can subscribe to cable TV in all areas that are wired. We simply pay a fixed monthly amount for the service, then pay additonal fees for the premium (pay) channels: HBO, Showtime, and so on.

A cable network, in turn, charges the local cable systems a fixed amount per month, per subscriber, for the privilege of carrying that network's programming. For example, ESPN, a cable network, charges the cable system in Columbus, Ohio, 13¢ a month for each of its subscribers. Cable-system operators have the option of carrying particular networks, depending upon the terms offered by those networks.

The cable networks depend upon advertising revenues and their fees from local cable systems to pay for their programming. The local cable systems depend upon the monthly fees from their subscribers to pay the cable networks and, of course, their operating expenses.

On cable there are twelve advertising-supported networks. They range from CNN, Ted Turner's all-news network seen by 33 million subscribers, to Black Entertainment TV, which reaches only 10 million subscribers.

Among the pay-TV networks, HBO, Time, Inc.,'s Home Box Office, remains the largest and most profitable pay-TV service, with approximately 14.5 million subscribers in all fifty states.

CAREER TIP: HBO offers some paid internships, the number depending on the need of a particular season. There is a twelve-week internship for undergraduate students and a twelve-week internship for graduate students. Interested readers should write to HBO's Department of Human Resources, 1100 Avenue of the Americas, New York, NY 10036.

In the early '80s it seemed that every publication in the country carried a story on the enormous growth potential of cable TV. But, alas, there have been major failures as well. Here are just a few:

- In September 1982, CBS Cable, a cultural service run by CBS, Inc., shut down after $30 million in losses.

- In September 1983, *TV-Cable Week,* a TV-listing magazine of Time, Inc., ceased publication after losing $47 million.
- In October 1983, the Satellite News Channel, the 24-hour headline service co-owned by ABC and Westinghouse, was shut down after little more than a year's operation and an estimated loss of more than $40 million.
- In January 1987, the Qube Network, a nightly satellite feed of interactive programming, was suspended by Warner Amex because it was too costly and of too little interest to viewers. This was the network that was to revolutionize TV. Subscribers in test cities such as Columbus, Ohio, had a unit on their sets with various buttons and keys. In one experimental football game, the audience was asked to select a play for the quarterback while he was in a huddle. The audience's choice fed through the computer in seconds and was relayed to the quarterback in time to call it as his next play.
- Cinemax, owned by HBO, was started in 1980, and by 1985 had 3.3 million subscribers. Its programming is designed to appeal to the eighteen- to thirty-four-year-old audience. Subscribers can watch a broad selection of movies, comedy shows, pop concerts, and mini-series.
- Showtime/The Movie Channel is now owned by the diversified communications and entertainment company Viacom International. In 1985, this company also purchased MTV Networks, Inc. Showtime closed 1985 with 5.4 million subscribers; The Movie Channel stood at 3.1 million. The two channels are attempting to ensure their supply of feature films by making exclusive arrangements with major studios—Paramount and MGM.

Opportunities in Cable

One can probably get a job for a cable company installing new systems. It may pay well, but it surely is not very glamorous.

Cable, like broadcasting, needs bright, fresh talent—for wiring, programming, production, technical crew, directing; in short, a myriad of assignments. One need look no further than the end of this chapter for inspiration. The interview with HBO's Bridget Potter says it best.

MTV, VH-1, and Nickelodeon

When Martha Quinn was twenty-six years old, she had already been a veejay (video jockey) on MTV for five years. Her perky personality has made her rock-star famous to an audience of tens of millions of teenagers watching hours of music videos on their favorite station—MTV.

MTV is a pop-culture phenomenon of our times. From a standing start in 1981 when only a few hip music people had ever heard of music video, it became a giant success in only four years, reaching a vast audience and revolutionizing the music business along the way.

Before MTV came along, the record business was in a state of lethargy. Now, for 24 hours a day, audiences can "see" music. When they like what they see, they go out to buy records. In turn, record companies are encouraged to pick up the hefty production tabs of the videos.

In late 1985, the media giant Viacom bought total ownership of MTV Networks, Inc., for a whopping $550 million. Although MTV was not profitable in its first three years, in fiscal 1984 it earned $17 million after taxes. In 1985, it generated the highest advertising revenue of any cable-originated basic cable network, including those with substantially more subscribers.

Diversification: On the theory, no doubt, that the tastes of the twelve- to thirty-four-year-old audience are ephemeral, in 1985 MTV launched VH-1 for the "old folks" aged twenty-five to fifty-four. Instead of watching videos by Van Halen, Wham!, and John Cougar Mellencamp, the sedate set could now watch the music of Billy Joel, Diana Ross, and Kenny Rogers.

MTV Networks' other network, Nickelodeon, is considered a leader in quality programming for children. Although targeted for the two- to 15-year-old audience, its program mix seems to have maximum appeal to the younger segment of that group.

MTV's wizardry lies in its programming and promotion. In addition to music videos, viewers are offered interviews with rock personalities, music news, guest veejays, and even live concert presentations. Its 17-hour coverage of the LIVE-AID concert in July 1985 was momentous.

But by fall 1986, MTV's ratings had dropped dramatically. The sameness of the videos had worn away their novelty. MTV is meeting the challenge with veejay changes plus a number of programming changes. Only time will tell whether MTV is just a passing fad or, with these changes, can withstand the temporary drop in ratings.

Readers can learn from the launching of MTV that anything is possible in the mass communications business. MTV's founder, Bob Pittman, was only twenty-six years old when he conceived the idea of showing videos 24 hours a day on a channel designed solely for that purpose. At the time of the

Viacom acquisition, in 1985, Pittman was thirty-one years old. He functioned as chief operating officer of MTV Networks and was paid the whopping sum of $450,000 a year for his efforts. By the beginning of 1987, he was off to conquer a new horizon, this time his own record label at MCA.

Broadcasting and *Television/Radio Age*

The two leading publications in the broadcast industry are *Broadcasting* and *Television/Radio Age*.

Broadcasting

Broadcasting, a weekly magazine, was established in 1931, back in the early days of radio. Its circulation is approximately 35,000. With pass-along readership, the total audience is 138,000. *Broadcasting's* readers are advertisers, agencies, engineers, sales reps, TV and radio general managers, network executives, and students and teachers in communications.

Broadcasting publishes special reports throughout the year. Here are some recent examples: ''Annual Report on Baseball,'' ''Top 100 Companies in Electronic Communications,'' ''Satellite Special Report,'' ''Annual Report on Local TV and Cable Journalism,'' and ''Special Report on the World of TV Programming.''

Those aspiring to careers in broadcasting would find a year's subscription ($65.00) to *Broadcasting* a worthwhile investment. The address: Broadcasting Publications, 1735 DeSales Street, N.W., Washington, DC 20036. Its editorial coverage embraces advertising programming, broadcast and cable journalism, technology, and systems operation and management.

Broadcasting also publishes the *Broadcasting/Cablecasting Yearbook,* a compendium of the year's activity in these fields.

Television/Radio Age

A biweekly magazine calling itself the world's leading broadcast journal and published since 1953,

Television/Radio Age offers comprehensive coverage of the industry.

Some regular features include the following:

- *Programming and Production:* An account of activity in radio and TV programming, new programs offered by syndicators, and trends in programming on the local and network level.
- *Commercials:* A feature devoted to the latest developments in commercial production.
- *Spot Report:* A recap of commercial placements by advertisers in radio and TV.
- *Special Studies:* Several times a year *Television/Radio Age* focuses on an event or an aspect of importance to the business, such as the farm broadcast market, the black radio market, sports on radio and TV, news and public affairs, Hispanic radio, and children's programming.

A subscription to *Television/Radio Age* is $50.00 per year. Although the publication is oriented to executives in the industry, students can gain much from its definitive coverage of these media. The magazine's address: 1270 Avenue of the Americas, New York, NY 10020.

Important Addresses

New York

American Federation of Television and Radio Artists (AFTRA)
1350 Avenue of the Americas
New York, NY 10019

Screen Actors Guild (SAG)
1700 Broadway
New York, NY 10019

Writers Guild of America, East
555 West 57th Street
New York, NY 10019

Directors Guild of America, East
110 West 57th Street
New York, NY 10019

ABC Television
1330 Avenue of the Americas
New York, NY 10019

CBS Television
51 West 52nd Street
New York, NY 10019

NBC Television
30 Rockefeller Plaza
New York, NY 10020

California

American Federation of Television and Radio Artists
   (AFTRA)
1717 North Highland Avenue
Hollywood, CA 90028

Screen Actors Guild (SAG)
7750 Sunset Boulevard
Hollywood, CA 90046

Writers Guild of America, West
8955 Beverly Boulevard
Los Angeles, CA 90048

Directors Guild of America, West
7950 Sunset Boulevard
Los Angeles, CA 90046

ABC Television Center
4151 Prospect Avenue
Los Angeles, CA 90027

CBS Television City
7800 Beverly Boulevard
Los Angeles, CA 90036

NBC Television
3000 West Alameda Avenue
Burbank, CA 91523

Universities Offering Degree Programs in Television

In the chapter on movies we discuss three great film schools, those at New York University, the University of California at Los Angeles (UCLA), and the University of Southern California (USC). All three schools also offer major programs in television. Here are a few of their course offerings.

New York University: NYU offers a B.F.A. in television. Students have opportunities for internship at some of New York's TV and radio stations.

The School of Continuing Education offers a half-dozen TV courses evenings and Saturdays. Here are some degree course titles:

- Broadcasting, CATV and New Technology
- Broadcast and CATV Programming
- Station Management
- Beginning TV: Production-Direction
- History of Broadcasting I and II

University of California at Los Angeles: UCLA offers B.A., M.A., M.F.A., and Ph.D. programs in film and television, as well as television internship for credit. UCLA Extension offers a nondegree program. Following are some degree course titles:

- Motion Picture/Television Writing
- Beginning Television and Video Production
- Introduction to Film and Television Study
- Remote Television Broadcasting
- Direction for Television
- Independent Production of Feature Films and/or Television Programming

University of Southern California: USC offers a B.A. and an M.A. in journalism with an emphasis in radio-television. Here are some degree course titles:

- Basic Principles of Broadcast Production
- Broadcast Newswriting
- Radio/TV Programming
- Radio/TV Advertising
- Introduction to Telecommunications

For a complete list of schools offering two-year, four-year, and graduate programs in broadcasting, scholarships, and so forth, we recommend the book *Broadcast Programs in American Colleges and Universities.* To get a copy, write to the National Association of Broadcasters, 1771 N Street, NW, Washington, DC 20036.

The following is a partial list of colleges and universities offering degree programs in radio and/or television (for a more comprehensive list, see *The American Film Institute Guide to College Courses in Film and Television* in the "Recommended Reading" section at the end of this chapter):

University of Alabama
University, AL 35486

University of Arizona
Tucson, AZ 85721

University of California at Los Angeles
Los Angeles, CA 90024

University of Southern California
Los Angeles, CA 90007

Stanford University
Stanford, CA 94305

University of Colorado
Boulder, CO 80302

University of Denver
Denver, CO 80210

Colorado State University
Fort Collins, CO 80521

University of Delaware
Newark, DE 19711

American University
Washington, DC 20016

Florida State University
Tallahassee, FL 32306

University of Georgia
Athens, GA 30601

University of Illinois
Urbana, IL 61801

Indiana University
Bloomington, IN 47401

Purdue University
Lafayette, IN 47907

Ball State University
Muncie, IN 47306

Indiana State University
Terre Haute, IN 47809

University of Iowa
Iowa City, IA 52240

University of Kansas
Lawrence, KS 66044

University of Maryland
College Park, MD 20742

University of Massachusetts
Amherst, MA 01002

Boston University
Commonwealth Avenue
Boston, MA 02215

Emerson College
Boston, MA 02116

University of Southern Mississippi
Hattiesburg, MS 39401

University of Michigan
Ann Arbor, MI 48104

Wayne State University
Detroit, MI 48202

Michigan State University
East Lansing, MI 48823

University of Mississippi
University, MI 38677

University of Missouri
Columbia, MO 65201

Brooklyn College of the City University of New
    York
Bedford Avenue and Avenue H
Brooklyn, NY 11210

Hofstra University
Hempstead, NY 11550

Cornell University
Ithaca, NY 14850

Hunter College of the City University of New York
695 Park Avenue
New York, NY 10021

New York University
New York, NY 10003

Syracuse University
Syracuse, NY 13210

University of North Carolina
Chapel Hill, NC 27514

Ohio University
Athens, OH 45701

Ohio State University
Columbus, OH 43210

Miami University
Oxford, OH 45056

Temple University
Philadelphia, PA 19122

Carnegie-Mellon University
Pittsburgh, PA 15213

University of Texas
Austin, TX 78712

Southern Methodist University
Dallas, TX 75222

Brigham Young University
Provo, UT 84601

University of Utah
Salt Lake City, UT 84112

Marquette University
Milwaukee, WI 53233

Internships

Writer's Digest Books, located in Cincinnati, Ohio, publishes annually *19— Internships,* which contains 34,000 on-the-job training opportunities for all types of careers. Included are about sixty TV internships. Here are some highlights from a recent edition:

International Radio & Television Society, Inc.
420 Lexington Avenue
New York, NY 10170
Contact Stephen B. Labrinski, Executive Director. This is a membership organization for people in broadcasting and broadcast-related fields. Ten salaried internships are available each summer for an eight-week period.

The MacNeil/Lehrer Newshour
WNET
356 W. 58th Street
New York, NY 10019
and
WETA
Box 2626
Washington, DC 20013
There are eight paid new/research positions each semester in New York and four paid positions in Washington.

New Jersey Public TV
1573 Parkside Avenue CN-777
Trenton, NJ 08625
Nonsalaried full and part-time positions are available in various phases of broadcasting.

WCVB-TV
5 TV Place
Needham, MA 02129
Twenty-six paid positions are available; also several programs for minority students.

WCAU-TV
City Line Avenue and Monument Road
Philadelphia, PA 19131

WNET/Thirteen
356 West 58th Street
New York, NY 10019
Fifty nonsalaried positions are available each semester.

Two Interviews

Our television interviewees come from two distinctly different areas of television. Bruce Sidran gives us a perspective on the engineering function, while Bridget Potter discusses the programming aspect of pay cable.

Bruce Sidran came to work at ABC in July 1978 as a junior engineer. His first assignment was the expansion of the main technical facilities in central switching, the very heart of the TV network in New York. In January 1979, he was promoted to full engineer. He assisted with the captioning of the Sugar Bowl in 1980, the 1980 presidential inauguration, and several presidential press conferences and speeches. From September 1981 to June 1985, Sidran was the project manager responsible for providing ABC's owned and operated TV station in San Francisco. Since June 1985, he has held the position of manager of engineering for the ABC owned and operated TV stations. Sidran received his bachelor's degree in electrical engineering from the City College of New York in June 1975. While working for ABC, he attended the Polytechnic Institute of New York and was awarded a master's degree in computer systems in January 1981.

What is the general responsibility of your job?
I manage a group of engineers who design facilties for ABC's owned-and-operated stations and ABC's news bureaus.

What types of projects are you involved with?
Right now we're designing a facility for the news bureau in London. ABC bought the building, and we're renovating four floors and remodeling the facility. It will cost more than £6.5 million, roughly $9 million.

What type of training do you need for your job?
I have a bachelor's degree in electrical engineering and a master's degree in computer systems, but what I know about television, I basically learned on the job. When I was going to college, there were very few college-level courses in television engineering, so my background is generally in electrical engineering. And you learn specifics on the job as you go. Most people who work for me have been trained in electrical engineering.

Is it essential to have a background in electrical engineering, or can you pick that up on the job, too?

It's possible to pick it up on the job, but I'd say it's more difficult that way. Operations and engineering is a technical field that requires someone with technical acumen. However, there are people in my department who are self-taught. One of the most talented people who works for me has a background in general studies—no engineering courses at all. He's basically taught himself everything. My boss, who's the general manager of engineering, never went to college. He is completely self-taught and one of the brightest engineers I know, so it's definitely possible to work in the field without formal training.

Do you need an FCC license?

No. The FCC has relaxed its requirements considerably. . . . The only person required to have a license is the actual operator of the station's transmitter—and that's usually just the chief engineer.

What engineering jobs are available at a typical television station?

There is really no such thing as a typical station, so I'll describe a large one and a small one. A large one—say, an owned-and-operated station, or one in any of the top fifty markets—would be run almost like a network facility. It would have anywhere from 300 to 700 employees, of which half would be technical. It would employ people who are mostly operators to run various equipment on a day-to-day basis—transmission operators, camera people, people to do the switching from on-air shows.

Are those union positions?

It depends on the station. At the larger stations, yes, but at smaller stations, usually not. Each station, except for the ones owned by the networks, is really a separate entity unto itself. It really depends on the particular facility.

If somebody wanted an engineering job at a unionized facility, how would he get into the union?

There are two major broadcast unions: One is called NABET, the National Association of Broadcast Employees and Technicians; the other is IBEW, which is the International Bureau of Electrical Workers. It has a subsection that deals with broadcast television. Getting into either of those unions is not a problem. The problem is getting a job. Once you get a job, you have thirty days to join the union. And there's no problem getting into the union once you have a job.

Sort of a Catch-22?

Right.

What about jobs at smaller stations?

Most stations, even very small ones, have ENG—electronic news gathering—teams, who go out into the field and gather footage for the local news using mini-cams. And those are usually NABET and IBEW positions. Then there is a group of jobs for quasi-technical people: stage managers, floor managers, people who interface with the on-air talent. They require some technical expertise but not at the same level as the actual operators. At most of the ABC stations, these people belong to the DGA, Directors Guild of America, or IATSE, International Alliance of Theatrical Stage Employees and Moving Picture Machine Operators of the United States and Canada, known in the industry as IA. This union has incorporated television, film, and video over the past few years.

What about the engineers who do need an FCC license? What do they do, and why do they need a license?

One person at a station has to have the station license. The one person with the FCC license is supposed to oversee the operations of the station to be sure that all FCC regulations are being adhered to. Basically, the license allows you to transmit. The FCC gives you a piece of paper called a license, which says you can have this spectrum of space—this frequency—to broadcast on. You're very limited as to the geographical area and about the power you can transmit. There are a lot of other requirements to fulfill in order to comply with an FCC license.

And that's the responsibility of the person who holds the license?

Yes. Typically, it's the chief engineer. At some stations, it might be the owner of the station if he has a technical background. It could also be the general manager of the station, but it's usually the chief engineer. In days gone by, up until 1980, anybody who had anything to do with the transmitter was required to have a first-class FCC license. That's not the case anymore. You just need one licensee for the station, and that person can designate other people to operate under his authority. The licensee has the responsibility to adhere to all of the FCC's rules and regulations. But his staff actually handles the day-to-day work.

What are the direct responsibilities of the person holding the FCC license?

If, say, the station has interference problems with other stations in the area, the FCC will come to the person at the station who has the license to settle the problem.

What are some of the entry-level positions in operations and engineering?

A very typical entry-level position is a videotape operator. Somebody familiar with various formats of videotape and who can work videotape machines, play back, and record.

And where would that lead to in, say, two years?

He or she could become a videotape editor, and that's a well-paying, respected job. Another entry-level position is that of a chyron operator—that's electronic character generation for the words that appear on the screen.

Whom do you contact about getting these jobs?

At a smaller station, the chief engineer. At a larger station, the manager or director of operations, or the director of engineering.

How have the advancements in technology affected jobs in this area of broadcasting?

Most of the jobs in engineering have not been changed by technological innovations. The tasks are the same; only the knowledge that it takes to operate some equipment has been altered. A standard format of videotape is standard for all modes of transmission, whether by microwave, satellite, fiber optics, or telephone lines.

What role does engineering play in the transmission of a sporting event or a news event?

ABC has a division with mobile field units. These are large trucks, actually tractor-trailers 45 to 50 feet long, that have the same equipment found in a typical television studio—except it's mobile, on wheels. In the case of ABC, the truck is owned by the broadcast operations and engineering division and is, essentially, rented out to a customer—in this case, the customer would be ABC Sports. The sports department would decide that it needs one, two, three, or perhaps four trucks to do the job. The producer will decide how many cameras are needed, as well as what other items, such as tape machines, editing facilities, and communication setups, that he needs. And then it's up to us, to engineering, to provide those facilities and to actually run them during the event.

The same sort of thing goes for news events, although they tend to be more impromptu, so typically there would be one or two mini-cam crews assigned. A mini-cam crew gathers the information and either records it on videotape or transmits it back to the studio for live transmission.

So, is operations and engineering really a service division?

Yes. And most networks and most stations work the same way. Operations is a service group, aiding the production people, as well as serving as "in-house" consultants on an ad hoc basis for specific projects—like the Super Bowl.

How does a news story happening in France find its way onto the ABC Evening News that same night?

We maintain news bureaus in various areas around the world; Paris is one of them. If a major event happens in France, an assignment editor in that office sends a mini-cam team, or a stringer team, to cover the story. An assignment editor finds out about stories via the wire services, press releases, and so forth. Also, all the news bureaus communicate with one another. Sports use stringers a lot more than news, because sporting events need more people, while a news event can usually be covered by a staff mini-cam crew.

How does the footage get from Paris to New York?

There are a couple of different ways. One scenario is to edit the videotape locally—if facilities exist nearby—and transmit it in any number of ways directly to ABC News in the United States. But usually ABC gathers all the stories from Western Europe for any one day in London. And then all the stories, fully edited and with voice-overs, are transmitted as a package directly to New York, which is where ABC's "World News Tonight" with Peter Jennings is done. London time is five hours ahead of New York, so there is an advantage in doing that. ABC can gather stories all day and then transmit them later in the afternoon.

Is it prestigious to work in the operational aspects of a news department?

Yes. News and sports are equally prestigious. News is a very exciting place to work because of the immediacy of the events. The length of assignments is short—one to three days—so someone in this area is going to see a wide variety of tasks. Different places, different people, and there's a lot of travel involved; it's an exciting place to work. When I worked for CBS News, we would, on a day-to-day basis, never know whether we'd be sent to Boston or the Bahamas. Sometimes I'd have 15 minutes to get ready if it was a fast-breaking story. Usually we got a day or two's notice. We were on call 24 hours a day. When Son of Sam was terrorizing New York [in the 1970s], I got a call at 2:00 A.M. to go down to the courthouse; I was working audio on a mini-cam crew at the time. David Berkowitz had been caught, and he was going to give a statement to the press. I ended up literally camping out at the courthouse for two and a half days waiting for something to happen. That's what it's like—long periods of intense boredom punctuated by short bursts of intense activity. It's an interesting place to work. You need to be the type of person who can handle sitting outside someone's front door for three days in case he decides to come out and make a statement. And the next day you could be on a plane for God-knows-where.

Is there an element of danger?

One of the big drawbacks about working on a news crew is that there is danger present at various times. Often you're assigned to cover trouble spots, and by virtue of their being "hot," you're exposing yourself to a dangerous situation. Many of the people who have worked on news crews have at some point covered riots, or scenes of hostage takings, or war zones. There are crews that are assigned to transmit pictures from Beirut. They're shot at, beat up. Several news people have been killed; there is an element of danger involved. For some people, that adds excitement to the job.

What words of advice can you offer someone who finds operations and engineering a possible career?

It is extremely interesting and rewarding work. It is typically very well paying, and because it is interesting, rewarding, and well-paying, it's historically difficult to get jobs. Someone just starting out has a much better opportunity at a small station, away from the major markets. It is extremely difficult to get work in New York with no experience. Los Angeles, Chicago—the same story. But for someone who is really dedicated to the field, I would suggest going to a small-market station or a nonunionized facility, or starting out at a production company and gaining experience in production and engineering; then one could approach a larger station or a network. Three to five years of experience is reasonable dues with which to approach a bigger operation.

In summing up, I can only say that there isn't an area of television that's more exciting or gratifying than operations and engineering.

Bridget Potter was named senior vice-president of original programming for Home Box Office, Inc., in October 1983. She is responsible for overseeing all aspects of HBO's music, comedy, drama, documentary, series, and family programming, including all original programming for Cinemax. Potter joined HBO in April 1982, after two years at Lorimar Productions, Inc., in New York, where she was a

vice-president of production. From 1976 to 1980, she was associated with ABC-TV, becoming vice-president in charge of prime-time program development. From 1974 to 1976, Potter served as producer for Palomar Pictures International, producing and developing movies and mini-series. Previously, she was an associate producer for "The Dick Cavett Show" and also worked on the "Armstrong Circle Theatre," "The Diary of Anne Frank," and "The Crucible." Born in England, Potter came to the United States in 1960.

Your title is senior vice-president of original programming for HBO and Cinemax. To our readers this is a very glamorous and creative position. Could you tell us exactly what you do for HBO?

I am in charge of 25 percent of the programming on HBO and Cinemax, excluding sports. What I mean is that in conjunction with the management of the company, I decide what kind of programming there should be and then go about making it happen. In addition, I control the amount of money that is spent on strategy in terms of how it's put on and promotion.

Was there anything in your earlier job situations or in your college career that prepared you for this job?

I didn't go to college. I have absolutely no academic qualifications whatsoever. And I'm not a big believer in the M.B.A. school of thinking as far as a career in the entertainment business is concerned. I really don't think there is anything you can train for. I didn't know this when I started working, but I certainly believe it now. If I have any regret, it's that I never went to law school, where they train you to think in a special way. But I also think that is something you can train yourself to do on the job even though it's harder, because you don't have the discipline forced on you by somebody else. But to answer your question more specifically, this job has stretched me a good deal; everything I've done in my career has prepared me for it. I've learned the business of making TV shows by being on the production end, and I've also learned the business of programming TV shows from working in broadcast television. So I seem well equipped for this job.

For our readers about to graduate from college, what is the best way to get into TV or cable? You mentioned that there is nothing that can really train you for the job. What then?

It depends on your goals. If you're interested in making TV shows, then there is no reason to get an M.B.A. You do need business training if you're interested in the business part. Until this job, I have always been interested in the creative aspect. This job has trained me a little more in management. But if you're interested in the creative aspects of television, or the movies, or making shows, then the only way to learn is to go make shows. One starts by doing whatever one has to do in order to get a job working on a show—or working somewhere in and around the business. Entry-level jobs are hard to get, especially without some sort of connection. If one can find that connection and exploit it, that's the best thing to do. And one can't be bashful about taking a really low-level job. That's one of the problems I see with people coming out of M.B.A. programs. They're overeducated into expectations that are not realistic in the entertainment community. You really have to start at the bottom, running out for coffee. That's how I started—running out for coffee and answering telephones.

When I started, it was easy for women to get in because they would hire only women for those jobs. Men were not comfortable with having male secretaries. It's quite different now; there are a lot more men in these positions, and I think it's easier now for men to get into the bottom level of the business than it was twenty years ago. It's always been relatively easy for a woman to get the entry-level job. The hard thing has been for her to get the second job, but I hope that it's different now.

Would you suggest that a person still in college try to find something like a summer internship in the junior or senior year in order to get some experience?

Most of those internships are corporate, which has nothing to do with making TV shows. What a person should do in the summer if he or she is interested in making TV shows is to find a job working on a show, or helping out some way, or working in summer stock, or doing something that has to do with making a show. The business end really doesn't have anything to do with the creative end.

Is there much movement between jobs? Do people change jobs frequently?

Yes. In the entertainment business, people change jobs a lot, and that's the way you get ahead. One gets to a certain level, and then one finds something better somewhere else. I think that this has its drawbacks, because if network heads shift every two years and it takes two years to implement a point of view, it means that there is no time for a consistent philosophy to develop. But this is the way one moves ahead, and it is the way it's always been in the entertainment business. There are very few people I know who haven't done this. I used to change jobs every two or three years. I've been at HBO now for three and a half years, but my job has

changed, which has been a help. One has to keep moving. This is not an industry in which stability is rewarded.

How does HBO handle hiring for entry-level and higher-level jobs? And also, what do you look for in a candidate?

We hire mainly through the human resources department. For a long time, HBO was a major recruiter at colleges. I don't know whether that's still the case. [It's not.—L.M.] When I have an entry-level job to fill, I look for the brightest, most aggressive, most ambitious person I can find, wherever I find that person. I also look for some work experience or life experience that leads me to believe that person will go on to grow and develop on the job. I meet new people every day.

Are there any specific areas of cable or TV that you could suggest to our readers that would have the greatest opportunities in the next several years?

It's hard to know. The videocassette business is the newest of these new technologies and seems to be interesting. I think that people interested in the business end would be wise to look there because there will be a certain amount of growth in the future. In the cable world, there will be more cable systems built. The intelligent thing would be to find out where new systems are being constructed or will be in the future. Those will be areas of expansion.

Would these necessarily be in the major cities?

Yes. Chicago, Boston, and Washington, D.C., have no cable. These are areas that will grow. And Queens, New York City, has no cable, although the franchise has just been granted. There are big urban areas where there is no cable and where it will come in the next few years.

We would like this book to be of help to readers who don't necessarily want to live in New York or Los Angeles.

Well, if you don't want to live in New York or Los Angeles, you can still be in the TV business. Even small cities have TV stations, and there are plenty of local opportunities. It isn't an enormous business, but there are jobs out there.

You probably work in a male environment. Are there any special problems you face or have faced because of being a woman? You mentioned earlier that it is, or at least was, more difficult for a woman to advance from that entry-level position to a higher-level job. Do you think that is still the case?

The entertainment industry is probably better than most about women. I have never felt in any way that I had any difficulty or that I was discriminated against or passed over for a job because I was a woman. I may have my head in the sand, but I have never had those feelings. I think I have been extremely lucky, and I also think I had, because of my age, a different set of expectations than most women have today. When I started working in the business, there was no support for women; it was in between feminist movements. I knew I was entering a man's world, and I knew it was going to be hard. So I might belong to that generation of women which has reaped the benefits of the women's movement without ever having to actually sign up. I also think it's a question of one's personal attitude toward one's work. I have never heard a man say, "A woman couldn't do this job." I know that I was paid less, but it didn't matter to me. I had a sort of Pollyanna attitude. I didn't think it was wrong; I thought I was being given a great opportunity. I think it's useful to be a woman in a male environment, because there are ways that one can use one's difference to an advantage rather than a disadvantage.

Do you advise other women to adopt this attitude?

I don't know. My attitude isn't a contemporary one. I'm forty-three years old, and I've been working since I was eighteen. I didn't go through a college education that told me there was equal opportunity out there. I didn't expect it. So this probably isn't an accurate image of how the world really is, but it's my opinion.

How does HBO handle submissions?

We try not to take any submissions from people who aren't represented by agents. Ideas are cheap; it's getting them executed that's expensive and difficult. Everybody has an idea; the problem is getting those ideas made. If something doesn't come in under bona fide auspices, it's very hard for us to spend time looking at it.

The next question is of particular interest to me. As you're involved in comedy, what do you see as a trend in that specialty? What is today's humor?

Well, the obvious trend at the moment is a sort of conceptual, performance humor. Comics like Bob Goldthwait and Howie Mandel are wild. It's not in the tradition of verbal comedy, or character comedy like Woody Allen. Many of the new people coming up now seem to be almost out of control. They use a lot of props and strange things. It's a very weird kind of humor—a blend of low comedy from vaudeville and the nihilistic '80s attitude toward the world. It isn't a literary tradition; it isn't a tradition of jokes, or of satire or parody. It's something else

that seems to be emerging and interests me a great deal. We do quite a bit in this area. On the whole, the trend seems to be performance artists rather than comics.

Last big question: What do you see as the long-range and short-range future of cable?

Well, I'm primarily interested in pay, rather than basic, cable, although without basic cable there wouldn't be any pay. I think that long term we're going to have to provide audiences with entertainment that no one else is providing. That's our original program strategy. Give people out-of-home entertainment *in* their homes: movies, specials, concerts, and all that sort of stuff. Long term, what I think we basically have to do is establish new program forms that we will deliver and that will be perceived by our audience to be worth paying for. Short term, I just hope I make it through the day.

Glossary of Television Terms

Anchor: in news broadcasting, the principal face on camera. In a sense, the central core from which remotes to reporters and correspondents are directed.

Affiliates: the stations affiliated with a network in an arrangement where they agree to carry the network's programming in exchange for money the network pays to it for carrying its commercials.

Barter: the trading of a TV show to a station by an advertiser or agency in return for commercials.

CPB: the Corporation for Public Broadcasting; a private, tax-exempt corporation that supports the activity of public radio and TV stations.

Crawl: lettering that moves vertically or horizontally across the television screen and provides information (as performer credits and news bulletins).

Cume: cumulative audience—the percentage of U.S. TV homes viewing at least six consecutive minutes of a program.

Daypart: a particular segment of a broadcasting day.

ENG: portable electronic news gathering cameras used to transmit videotape from the field to the station.

Equal time provision: a ruling of the FCC granting equal TV time to all legally qualified candidates for public office.

FCC: the Federal Communications Commission; an independent federal agency created in 1934, with powers of regulation over TV, cable, and radio.

O&O: a station that is owned and operated by a TV or radio network.

PBS: the Public Broadcasting Service; an independent affiliation of the nation's public TV stations.

Rating: a statistical measurement of the percentage of TV households tuned in to a particular show of the total U.S. TV households.

Share: that percentage of the TV viewing audience watching a specific program at a particular time.

Spot Sales: a commercial buy by an advertiser in specific markets only, rather than in the whole network.

Superstation: a station whose programming is carried by satellite to cable households outside its local market.

Syndication: the after-market for a TV show or movie.

Telestrator: a video chalkboard device used in sports broadcasting to outline plays or sequences.

Transponder: a device on a satellite that receives, amplifies, and retransmits audio and video signals.

UHF (Ultra-High Frequency): the TV band in the electronic spectrum from 470 to 890 megahertz, encompassing channels 14 through 83 in the United States and Canada.

VHF (Very-High Frequency): the TV band in the electronic spectrum from 30 to 300 megahertz, encompassing channels 1 through 13 in the United States and Canada.

Videotape: tape in the TV camera enabling recording, playback, and editing of film.

Voice-over: a recorded voice (also called a "tell") that describes or interprets the video portion; an off-camera announcer.

Recommended Reading

Agee, Warren K., Phillip H. Ault, and Edwin Emery. *Introduction to Mass Communications* (5th ed.). New York: Harper & Row, 1976.

Arbitron Cable Dictionary. New York: Arbitron Co., Inc., 1981.

Barnouw, Erik. *The Image Empire: A History of Broadcasting in the United States from 1953*, vol 3. New York: Oxford University Press, 1970.

Berlyn, David W. *Your Future in Television Careers.* New York: Richards Rosen Press, 1978.

Blanchard, Nina. *How to Break into Motion Pictures, Television Commercials, and Modeling.* Garden City, N.Y.: Doubleday & Co., 1978.

Brenner, Alfred. *The TV Scriptwriter's Handbook.* Cincinnati, Ohio: Writer's Digest Books, 1980.

Brooks, Tim, and Earle Marsh. *The Complete Directory to Prime Time Network TV Shows: 1946–Present* (rev.) New York: Ballantine Books, 1981.

Brown, Les. *The New York Times Encyclopedia of Television.* New York: Times Books, 1982.

Castleman, Harry, and Walter J. Podrazik. *Watching TV: Four Decades of American Television.* New York: McGraw-Hill, 1982.

Craft, Christine. *Christine Craft: An Anchorwoman's Story.* Santa Barbara, Cal.: Capra Press, 1986.

Fenten, D. X. *TV and Radio Careers.* New York: Franklin Watts, Inc., 1976.

Gelfman, Judith S. *Women in Television News.* New York: Columbia University Press, 1976.

Gradus, Ben. *Directing the Television Commercial.* New York: Hastings House, 1981.

Greenfield, Jeff. *Television: The First Fifty Years.* New York: Harry N. Abrams, 1977.

Grenade, Charles, Jr., and Margaret G. Butt. *The American Film Institute Guide to College Courses in Film and Television* (7th ed.). Princeton, N.J.: Peterson's Guides, 1980.

Hilliard, Robert L. *Writing for Television and Radio* (3rd ed.). New York: Hastings House, 1976.

Hyde, Stuart W. *Television and Radio Announcing* (3rd ed.). Boston: Houghton Mifflin Company, 1979.

Jessup, Cordland, and S. Lee Alpert. *The Actor's Guide to Breaking into TV Commercials.* New York: Pilot Books, 1980.

Levinson, Richard, and William Link. *Off Camera: Conversations with the Makers of Prime-Time Television.* New York: Plume, 1986.

Lichter, S. Robert, Stanley Rothman, and Linda S. Lichter. *The Media Elite: America's New Powerbrokers.* New York: Adler and Adler (Harper & Row, dist.), 1986.

McCabe, Peter. *Bad News at Black Rock: The Sellout of CBS News.* New York: Arbor House, 1987.

McNeil, Alex. *Total Television: A Comprehensive Guide to Programming from 1948 to the Present* (2nd ed.). New York: Penguin Books, 1984.

Matusow, Barbara. *The Evening Stars: The Making of the Network News Anchor.* Boston: Houghton Mifflin Company, 1983.

Millerson, Gerald. *TV Camera Operation.* New York: Hastings House, 1973.

Ravage, John W. *Television: The Director's Viewpoint.* Boulder, Colo: Westview Press, 1978.

Reed, Maxine K., and Robert M. Reed. *Career Opportunities in TV, Cable and Video* (rev. ed.). New York: Facts on File, 1986.

Root, Wells. *Writing the Script: A Practical Guide for Films and Television.* New York: Holt, Rinehart and Winston, 1980.

Shanks, Bob. *The Cool Fire: How to Make It in Television.* New York: Random House, 1976.

Shook, Frederick, and Dan Lattimore. *The Broadcast News Process.* Denver, Colo: Morton Publishing Co., 1979.

Terrace, Vincent. *The Complete Encyclopedia of Television Programs, 1947–1979* (2nd ed., rev.). San Diego, Calif: A. S. Barnes, 1979.

Wurtzel, Alan. *Television Production.* New York: McGraw-Hill, 1979.

In addition to the books listed, the reader will find the following pamphlets informative.

Careers in Broadcast News. A single free copy (with stamped self-addressed 6″ × 9″ envelope) is available from Radio Television News Directors Association, 1735 DeSales Street, N.W., Washington, DC 20036.

Careers in Cable. $3.50 per copy. Write to the National Cable Television Association, 1724 Massachusetts Avenue, N.W., Washington, DC 20036.

Careers in Radio. $1.00 per copy pre-paid. Write to the Publications Department, National Association of Broadcasters, 1771 N Street, N.W., Washington, DC 20036.

Careers in Television. $1.00 per copy pre-paid. Write to the Publications Department, National Association of Broadcasters, 1771 N Street, N.W., Washington, DC 20036.

Women on the Job: Careers in the Electronic Media. A single free copy is available from American Women in Radio and Television, Inc., 1321 Connecticut Avenue, N.W., Washington, DC 20036, or from the Women's Bureau, U.S. Department of Labor, 200 Constitution Avenue, N.W., Washington, DC 20010.

RADIO

When I was six, radio was fifteen years old, but we didn't have one. But I had a little friend whose family lived in the basement of their candy store. It was during the Depression and I don't know how they could afford it, but the family owned a wondrous invention in a brown oval-shaped box. When you turned a knob, a voice came out to talk to you. This marvelous contraption was a Fada radio. We would listen to it for hours, enchanted by its magical sounds. A few years later, my parents bought a Stromberg-Carlson. To me it was much better than a Fada, and besides, I didn't really like that kid and never would have been his best friend if it hadn't been for the radio.

I remember as high spots of my early radio years such gems as the songs of Rudy Vallee, Russ Colombo, and a guy with a mellow voice named Bing Crosby. And how can I forget such memorable commercial pitchmen as The Happiness Boys—Billy Jones and Ernie Hare—for Interwoven Socks?

When I was an eight-year-old, "The Uncle Don Radio Show" was my favorite program. Parents would write to Uncle Don, telling him their kid's birthday and where the present was hidden. Then, if the kid were lucky, he'd be listening when, miraculously, Uncle Don would mention his name and the little secret that a pair of skates was hidden in the top drawer of his parent's dresser.

When I was a bit older and crazy about baseball, I listened to the sportscaster Stan Lomax as he re-created the Brooklyn Dodgers' games on radio. It was almost as exciting as being there. We were such sports nuts, we "listened" to the fights on radio: "Left to the jaw, right to the chin." Whether the play-by-play announcer made it up or not, we still loved it.

Everyone of my generation will never forget that fateful day—December 7, 1941. We were listening to a football game. Suddenly, a voice interrupted with the announcement that the Japanese had bombed Pearl Harbor. After the initial shock, we joked about "getting out the uniforms" but then promptly resumed our concentration on the game.

Radio has been part of my life for a long time. These days I look forward to getting to the office early so that I can read the paper while wearing my Walkman tuned to my favorite classical station until the first phone call breaks my peaceful idyll.

A Short History of Radio

It all started with a Scot, James Maxwell, who in 1865 discovered that electrical impulses travel through space at the speed of light. Then, in 1888, the German physicist Heinrich Hertz demonstrated the wave theory and established a relationship between electrical waves and light waves.

In 1895, putting all this together, Guglielmo Marconi developed the first wireless telegraph, and by 1901, he received the first transatlantic radio message, from England to Newfoundland.

In 1904, the English electrical engineer John Ambrose Fleming invented a vacuum tube that could detect radio signals. An American, Lee De-Forest, developed the triode, or three-element vacuum tube, in 1907.

In 1918, President Woodrow Wilson became the first president to use radio when he broadcast from a ship to World War I troops aboard other vessels.

After World War I, manufacturers such as Westinghouse, General Electric, and American Marconi (a U.S. branch of a British company) began their push to develop the new medium. Because American Marconi held the patents, the other two companies and American Telephone & Telegraph (AT&T) bought it out and formed the Radio Corporation of America, the initials of which, you might notice, are RCA.

The career of radio pioneer David Sarnoff parallels the rise of radio. Sarnoff, an immigrant, taught himself Morse code and became a wireless operator with the American Marconi Company. He was at his post when the fateful message came through about the sinking of the *Titanic* on April 14, 1912. He was also there on May 7, 1915, when the *Lusitania* was sunk by German U-boats. This is considered the first scoop ever of electronic media.

RCA formed the National Broadcasting Company, which was to become the first network, in 1926. It was joined in 1927 by the fledgling Columbia Broadcasting System, founded by William S. Paley. These early commercial radio pioneers later became television pioneers and were the moving force in broadcasting for fifty years.

The earliest radio station was KDKA in Pittsburgh in 1920. It aroused public interest by broadcasting presidential election returns and, subsequently, musical programs.

The first use of wire telephone lines for interconnecting a station in New York with a station in Chicago was accomplished in 1922 when the stations broadcast a football game simultaneously.

The phenomenal expansion of radio in the early 1920s caused over-extension by many businesses in this field. Radio company stocks worth $160 million in 1924 fell to $65 million in 1926.

Radio in the 1930s

With radio stations being set up all across the country in the late 1920s and early '30s, programming proliferated, and radio advertising became big business. Of course, radio commercials on small-town stations were cheap. Old-timers refer to these commercials as "a dollar a holler."

The names of radio personalities became household words. The first well-known radio reporter was Graham McNamee. The announcer would introduce him with "Come in, Graham." It became ubiquitous. I worked with someone named Graham, and we always called him "Come in Graham."

Advertisers went into radio in a big way, beginning in the early '30s. Listeners associated a program with its sponsor much more so than viewers do now with television. It was a kind of shared intimacy. So, even fifty years later, some of us still remember the "A&P Gypsies," that "Amos 'n' Andy" was sponsored by Pepsodent, and that Jack Benny came on the air with "Jell-o, again, it's Jack Benny."

The late '30s and early '40s was the era of the Big Bands. We became accustomed to listening to live music on a radio network. On a Saturday night, a group of us might get together and dance to the music of Glen Gray and his Casa Loma orchestra from the famous Aragon ballroom, high atop the Belvedere Hotel in downtown "Anywhere." The Big Bands died at about the same time television took radio's place as the nation's favorite broadcast medium.

In 1938, in what some call the most famous of all radio programs, Orson Welles panicked millions of Americans listening to his production of H. G. Wells's "War of the Worlds" with a late news bulletin announcing that Martian spaceships had landed in New Jersey. Thousands of listeners called newspapers and radio stations for news of the invasion. The military was alerted, and people actually reported sighting the Martians. The program repeated warnings that the broadcast was fictional, but the damage had been done. The Federal Communications Commission (FCC) con-

Early radio drama, complete with round microphones. The actress to the right of the mike is Agnes Moorehead.

ducted an investigation and concluded that there would be no more fictional scare news bulletins.

Radio reigned in the period before World War II. Most families had only one radio, but as an entertainment medium it offered something for everyone. For the boys, it was "Jack Armstrong, the All-American Boy"; for the girls, "Little Orphan Annie." "Just Plain Bill" appealed to Mom, and Jack Benny, Fred Allen, and George Burns and Gracie Allen to the whole family— studio audiences, laugh machines, and all. (Laugh

tracks were introduced later on to provide more consistent laughter.)

World War II

The largest audience in radio history, estimated at 90 million listeners, heard President Franklin D. Roosevelt address the U.S. Congress two days after the Japanese attack on Pearl Harbor. Roosevelt, throughout his presidency, brought government to the people through his "fireside chats."

In Europe, the dictators Adolf Hitler and Benito Mussolini used radio to militarize Germany and Italy and later to soften up neighboring countries for conquest.

During the war, radio brought us reports from the fronts and news and commentary from the well-recognized voices of Gabriel Heatter, H. V. Kaltenborn, and Edward R. Murrow. Murrow was one of the few of this group to make the successful transition to television.

The End of "The Golden Era"

The "Golden Era" of radio ran from 1926 to 1940. By 1950, there were about 40 million radios in U.S. homes. By 1957, almost that many radios were installed in automobiles. Yet, when television came along in the early '50s, radio seemed doomed. It would become the networks' forgotten child. Successful radio station owners became successful television station owners, with emphasis on the latter.

But radio didn't take the ten count. It bounced back up and took advantage of unchartered opportunities. Radio went from being a medium of programs (e.g., "The Lone Ranger," "The Shadow") to a medium of formats finely tuned to a very specific audience (e.g., news, top forty, Big Band, talk). It experimented with new formats—all news, all music, interview shows. The term "deejay" became an integral part of radio language. Stations reached the vast car-radio audience with special "drive time" programming. If one format didn't work, the station changed to another.

In the early '80s, another phenomenon boosted radio listening—small, highly portable radios with lightweight headphones for personal listening anywhere, anytime. At this writing, there are more than 18 million people using these sets. Sony sells approximately 2 to 2.5 million of its Walkman sets a year. It has sold more than 10 million sets since the product first arrived on the market in 1982.

Today, well more than half a century after its commercial start, radio is far from dead. You'll learn all about it in this chapter.

The Scope of Radio

Radio is more than sixty-five years old, and it's doing very well, thank you. By 1987, it had adver-

tising revenues of more than $7 billion annually, or about a third of television's revenues. Television's production costs and capital expenditures, however, are many times those of radio. Conclusion: Radio is less glamorous but more profitable than television.

Acquisition fever in radio is unbridled. Consider Gene Autry, America's original singing cowboy and an early investor in radio: He owns a half-dozen radio stations, and they all make money. KMPC in Los Angeles, purchased by Autry and a partner in 1952 for $800,000, is worth about $40 million today. Profits from the station paid for Autry's purchase of a Los Angeles TV station in 1964 for $12 million. He sold it in 1982 for $245 million—not bad for a movie cowboy.

In what is believed to be the largest sale ever of a radio station group, in March 1986 Metromedia sold nine of its eleven stations to an investor group and Morgan Stanley and Company for $285 million. The nine stations are in six of the nation's largest markets and have a collective audience of about 44 million.

Prices for radio stations have zoomed in recent years because of the relatively small number of licenses available from the FCC. Furthermore, FCC regulations prohibit any company, regardless of size, from owning more than twelve AM and twelve FM stations. (AM, or amplitude-modulated, refers to this broadcasting system's frequency of signals, which bounce off the atmosphere in a zigzag pattern. FM, or frequency-modulated, refers to a higher frequency of signals, which travel in a straight line and are therefore less susceptible to atmospheric distortion.)

Of the nation's approximately 8,500 AM and FM stations, about 6,000 are owned by companies that operate in only one city or own only one station. As for the large companies, some of their mega-million acquisitions may be at risk in the late '80s as a result of the FCC's licensing of 700 new FM stations in March 1985, primarily to individual owners. Industry experts predict that there will be more than 10,000 stations by the close of the century.

CBS, NBC, and Capital Cities/ABC, Inc. are integrally involved in radio, although other media giants such as Gannett, RKO, and Westinghouse each own a dozen or more stations as well.

The networks in turn spawn other networks. (See the "Syndication and Networks" section later in this chapter.) So, for example, Capital Cities/ABC, while owning nine AM and eight FM stations outright, also provides programming for seven radio networks, with more than 1,900 affiliated radio stations. Its radio operations generated larger 1985 earnings than those of any other radio group in the United States.

These seven ABC radio networks air a variety of news, music, sports, and talk-show programs. It should be stressed here, however, that ABC does not own these networks. Rather, it has a contract with each of them to carry the particular body of programming it furnishes. One network, for example, carries Paul Harvey, who has been on the air for more than forty years and is carried on some 1,100 stations. During an average week, these combined networks reach 89 million people twelve years of age and older.

CBS is no radio slouch, either. In July 1985, it acquired five stations from Taft Broadcasting, giving it eighteen stations, seven AM and eleven FM. In addition, CBS News packages a news service that is heard over 400 affiliated stations thanks to an arrangement similar to that between ABC and its affiliates. Anchor Charles Osgood is a mainstay of this CBS network.

CBS and the other broadcasting majors own stations primarily in the major markets. CBS's lineup is in New York, Los Angeles, Chicago, San Francisco, Philadelphia, Boston, St. Louis, Houston, Dallas/Fort Worth, Tampa/St. Petersburg, and Washington, D.C.

Trends

Radio news was once the backbone of electronic journalism. It was often the first source of reporting. Now all of that is changing, with television taking over the live-news-reporting function. The reason: cost cutting on the part of the radio stations concomitant with their listeners' demand for more entertainment and less news.

Washington, D.C., had three all-news stations in the 1970s; now it has but one. Stations in New York, Chicago, and San Francisco that formerly devoted a great deal of air time to news have reduced this programming drastically.

Also a factor in the lessening of news-broadcast time is the decreasing audience of AM stations, traditionally the source for much news broadcasting. Today, FM stations claim 60 percent of the total radio audience.

If you're thinking of breaking into news reporting, we suggest concentrating on newspapers and television.

First there was pay television—now comes pay radio. Would you pay $9.95 a month for twenty-four hours a day of rock, jazz, classical, or country-and-western music without commercial interruption? It's now available to cable customers through Satellite Syndicated Systems Inc. The company believes that 10 percent of the 56 million homes with access to cable will buy this service. Subscribers will merely flip a switch to get commercial-free radio programming around the clock.

The Radio Advertising Bureau (RAB) reported recently that the average daily time spent by high school students listening to radio is 3½ hours; to TV it's 2¾ hours. The average daily time spent by college students listening to radio is 2¾ hours; to TV it's 2 hours. The RAB, by the way, is the industry's promotional organization; it has the responsibility to sell sponsors on the merits of radio as an advertising medium.

According to a recent Rand Youth Poll, teenagers picked radio as the most effective advertising medium for reaching people their own age. The research also shows that this group is persuasive in urging parents to buy such products and services as videocassette recorders, home computers, and cable television.

FM radio has overtaken AM in listener popularity, but both have prospered in the '80s.

In terms of audience, TV dominates in prime time, but during commuting hours (6:00 A.M. to 10:00 A.M. and 3:00 P.M. to 7:00 P.M.), radio has the upper hand. Ninety-five percent of all cars in the United States have radios. That's up from 55 percent in 1952. In the mid-1980s there were 127 million car radios in use.

The best format for drive time depends on the market and the station's execution. In the New York City area, the all-news format is very popular, and so is adult contemporary. In Kansas City, country is preferred.

With its 9,000 stations, radio offers enormous opportunity for the beginner. One can get started at a small local station and move up the ladder there or go to work for a big-city station.

In the early '70s, I met someone who had been the general manager of a major radio station in San Francisco. He left the station and bought a tiny one in a resort area in Massachusetts. He gave the station a soft rock and folk music format with editorial emphasis on ecology and social issues. The station was immediately successful. He was also progressive in his hiring policies, employing local college students for almost every job at the station, including sales. What a great start for people interested in broadcasting! It is certain that similar opportunities exist all over the country, especially if a high salary is not a primary consideration.

Facts on Radio

The Radio Advertising Bureau estimated that in 1986 there were 507 million radio sets in the United

States and 5.4 radios per household. Of these, 150 million are battery-operated radios, whose owners are called "walk-along" users—what else?

Of this group, 48.3 percent are adults between the ages of eighteen and thirty-four. Among "upscale" Americans, better than 95 percent listen to radio 3 or more hours a day. Between 10:00 A.M. and 3:00 P.M. radio reaches 163 million consumers each week, more than the TV audience at that time.

The largest audience group for midday is women, ages eighteen to thirty-four, but men in the same age group are not far behind. The lowest midday radio customer group is young men of eighteen.

Who Does What in Radio

For all those radios out there—in your car, bedroom, living room and kitchen, and on your wrist and ears—you need radio stations. There are 9,000 radio stations across the country and 75,000 full-time employees. You could be one of them.

Radio needs good people who are flexible, creative, dynamic, and hard working. It needs people to create and implement the variety of program formats. It needs people to interpret and deliver the news. It needs announcers, technicians, and administrators, and it needs salespeople to sell the advertising.

Because there is such a disparity in salary for each job described in this section, depending on the sales volume of the individual station, we list average salaries for both high- and low-volume stations. Jobs at stations in between will have proportionate average salaries. For certain support staff jobs, many of which are entry level, we will list the average starting compensation.

Salary levels are not given for every job described in this section because of the unavailability of data. The source for all data given is a recent study by the National Association of Broadcasters.

A word about unions in the radio field: Union people generally make more money than nonunion employees. The American Federation of Television and Radio Artists (AFTRA) is the only union representing on-air employees. In New York City, this union has contracts with twenty-seven out of twenty-eight major stations, which means these stations must hire union employees for all jobs covered by AFTRA.

Technical people belong to either the International Brotherhood of Electrical Workers (IBEW) or the National Association of Broadcast Employees and Technicians (NABET). However, there are now substantially fewer technical jobs in radio than there once were. These jobs are being phased out because of advances in technology.

Most stations' table of organization is broken down into four divisions. Following is a list of the divisions and their key job functions.

One should bear in mind that at a small radio station one person may perform a number of functions. That means more work—probably without more money—but it's a wonderful way to learn.

Programming
Program Director
News Director
Assistant News Director/Assignment
 Editor
Production Manager

General Administration
General Manager
Business Manager
Producer/Director
Announcer/Deejay
News Reporter
Sportscaster
Consumer Affairs Reporter
Business Editor
Various Freelancers
Music Director/Librarian
Continuity Writer
Traffic Manager
Promotion/Community Relations Director
Desk/News Assistant
Production/Traffic Assistant

Engineering
Chief Engineer
Studio Engineer
Production Engineer
Transmitter Engineer
Maintenance Engineer
Contract Engineer

Sales
General Sales Manager
Local Sales Manager
National Sales Manager
Account Executives
Sales Assistant
Research Director

Now we will specifically discuss each job.

General Administration

General Manager: If you're going into radio, this is the job to aspire to. The general manager—or station manager, as he's often called—is the boss. He has overall authority over operations, programming, advertising sales, personnel—the whole show. He's usually a corporate officer reporting directly to the station's owner or board of directors. At a station with a sales volume of $250,000 to $500,000, the salary is $35,000. At a station with a sales volume exceeding $2 million, the salary is $85,000. (These same sales-volume figures apply to all the salaries listed in this section.)

Business Manager: This professional handles all financial transactions, develops business plans and goals, prepares statements and budgets, and supervises the activities of accountants, bookkeepers, and billing clerks. Business-administration courses in college are a plus, as is an accounting or management degree. The average low-volume salary is $18,000; the average high-volume salary, $31,000.

Programming

Program Director: The program director is responsible for everything that is broadcast from the station. He works closely with the general manager, who runs the whole show, and the sales manager. The station's owners, of course, will have a major say regarding the station's programming. He plans the program schedule with considerations of the audience, the competition, the advertisers, and the budget. If shows are to be produced, the program director decides who will produce them.

Many program directors start out as announcers, some as deejays. (The word "deejay" stems, of course, from "D.J."—"disc jockey"—even though this term is seldom used today.) At some stations, program directors also host shows and do special events broadcasts. They are attuned to all the various radio formats and are prepared to make format changes when necessary. Program directors need long experience in radio. A liberal arts education, with courses in English, speech, and drama, is a plus. The average low-volume salary is $17,000; the average high-volume salary, $46,000.

News Director: This person sets the news policy of the station. Obviously, at an all-news station this function assumes greater importance than at a station with 5-minute hourly news breaks. The news director supervises reporters, monitors news printers (or computer screens), and takes telephoned news tips.

We learn later in this chapter that there are only about fifty all-news stations in the country. Some stations take their national news off the wire services' reports, avoiding the news network services. A communications major or college-level courses are helpful. A person usually moves into the news director's job after years of reporting experience. The average low-volume salary is $14,000; the average high-volume salary, $31,000.

Assistant News Director/Assignment Editor: This individual assists the news director with reporters' assignments. These positions exist only at larger stations with heavy news or all-news coverage.

Production Manager: The production manager is involved in assigning announcers, newscasters, and producers. He also arranges schedules and recording sessions. The job requires broadcast experience, especially an understanding of the physical limitations of the medium. The ability to supervise and organize is a *sine qua non* for this function. This position exists only at larger stations where original programs are produced.

Producer/Director: The producer/director plans, rehearses, and/or produces live or recorded programs. This person works with music, voices, and sound effects to achieve effective presentation. At talk show stations, of which there are about 250 at this writing, producers choose and schedule interviews. A producer/director must have experience in announcing, writing, and production. A liberal arts degree with a major in broadcasting or communications is preferred.

Announcer/Deejay: Earlier in this chapter, I wrote of my friend who ran a small, innovative radio station in Massachusetts in the early '70s. His deejays were paid $3.00 an hour. I dare say that most of those young people would have done it for nothing.

There are at present about 30,000 announcers in U.S. radio; and because supply far exceeds demand, beginning announcers work for low salaries. I wouldn't be surprised if some small FM stations paid their young talent with records.

Recently, the National Association of Broadcasters issued a report on radio on-air talent's gross annual salaries. "Talent," as used here, is an industry term for on-air people. It does not necessarily connote charisma, creativity, or artistic abilities. The term is used in this way in the entertainment industry, too.

Not surprisingly, news announcers, news reporters, and sports reporters receive lower salaries than the announcer/deejay. For example, a news reporter at the highest-revenue station earns an average of $22,000, and a sports reporter at the lowest-revenue station earns only an average of $10,000. These obviously are not high-paying professions. Also, as a rule, educational (nonprofit) stations pay less than commercial stations.

Here are some highlights of the NAB report:

Station Revenues	Average Annual Compensation	Average Starting Compensation
More than $2 million	$31,000	$19,000
$1 to $2 million	18,000	13,000
$500,000 to $1 million	15,000	11,000
$250,000 to $500,000	14,000	11,000

An announcer or deejay who attracts a large following will either move into a prime-time slot at the station with a big salary raise or be wooed by another large station. There are even consulting and talent agencies that recruit for the networks and major stations.

A candidate for an announcing job should use any means possible to get the interview that may lead to a job. Tapes sent to the program director may work, but unsolicited ones may never be heard. Want ads in trade publications are another source. (Information on *Broadcasting* and *Television/Radio Age* appears in the television chapter.) Making contact through a friend of a friend may work, too.

Announcers, or deejays, or other on-air personalities introduce programs and recordings, read commercial copy, give station identifications and recordings, and read promotional and public service announcements.

Announcers are often personalities with strong personal styles. They may host talk programs and deliver comments or information, often giving the show a distinctive tone. Some select the music to be played (at larger stations the program director selects the music) and operate some or all of the studio controls and equipment.

On 24-hour stations, announcers must be prepared to work odd hourly schedules. A prime requisite for the job is a good, clear, well-modulated voice conveying warmth and integrity, although at some hard-rock stations, a frantic personality seems to be the requirement.

An announcer at a talk or call-in show must be an informed generalist with an excellent educational background in the arts, history, and sociology. We've mentioned the low salary factor for this broadcast specialty. In contrast, we should also consider that big-city announcers on major stations may command six-figure salaries. It's worth a try.

News Reporter: The news reporter's function is similar to that of the announcer. The difference is that reporters gather the news. They may also edit

Deejay Al Bernstein looks like he's having a good time performing his chores for WLTW-FM in New York. (Photograph courtesy Charles West; reproduced with permission of Al Bernstein, WLTW Radio New York, and Viacom International, Inc.)

and produce taped segments to "illustrate" the news reports. The job requires a good vocal delivery, together with journalistic experience. A degree in broadcast journalism would be a distinct advantage for this job. The average low-volume salary is $13,000; the average high-volume salary, $22,000.

Sportscaster: In the introduction to this chapter, I told of the old-timer Stan Lomax who, in the '30s, had the ability to make a re-created baseball game sound like a live one. Today, with the increased interest in sports and the intense TV coverage, the job of radio sportscaster is quite complex.

The sportscaster gathers and reports the local and national sports news, often gives the play-by-play, and conducts interviews with athletes, managers, and coaches. Former athletes often do well at this job. The average low-volume salary is $10,000; the average high-volume salary, $28,000.

Consumer Affairs Reporter: This reporter helps listeners with shopping, health, and environmental news. In recent years, with growing consumer awareness, the job has become important in radio and TV.

The jobs of sportscaster and consumer affairs reporter are specialized versions of the news reporter function. Educational and occupational requirements are thus similar to those of the news reporter and announcer. Obviously, college courses in marketing would be good preparation for a consumer affairs reporter. Business-administration college courses are a must for a business reporter or editor.

Business Editor: Stock market reports and financial news stories and forecasts are the province of this reporting job. Often a freelancer handles this function.

Various Freelancers: Freelancers include traffic reporters, arts reviewers, and medical doctors. My nephew received a free pass from a large ski area just for reporting the conditions back to his local radio station.

Music Director/Librarian: If the station's format is music, a librarian is necessary to catalogue and store the records and tapes. Some librarians select the music for air play and may survey local stores to determine current popularity. This individual needs good organizational ability.

Continuity Writer: The continuity writer writes commercials for advertisers without agencies. Advertising agency experience is a plus.

Traffic Manager: The traffic manager handles data from the sales, programming, and engineering departments. He works with the sales department on commercial time availability. Computer training is a good asset for this job.

Promotion/Community Relations Director: At a large station, this position may be expanded to two separate jobs. The promotion director is concerned with image building, sales presentations, and relations with the local community. Public relations and advertising courses in college are good preparation for this job.

Desk/News Assistant and Production/Traffic Assistant: These are the entry-level jobs at a radio station. Some are merely "gofers." Yet, one can obtain excellent experience from a year or so in either of these positions. To differentiate between the two, the desk/news assistant works for the news department. The production/traffic assistant works for the production manager and, where the title exists, the traffic manager. If you're good, there's no place to go but up.

Engineering

Readers interested in the engineering function of radio should realize that, although broadcasting is technically complex, the technology is constantly changing and improving. The net effect is a reduction in the size of engineering staffs, with doubling up of many job categories.

Chief Engineer: Called, in some cases, director of engineering, this individual heads this department and supervises the technicians. At small stations, it may be a one-person department. A chief engineer needs at least five years' experience as a broadcast technician.

The chief engineer and the technical staff install and maintain studio and portable equipment and the station's transmitter. He generally has an engineering degree and a thorough understanding of the principles of electronics—and an FCC license.

The FCC no longer conducts examinations for broadcast engineers, and a license is needed only for transmitter operation and maintenance. Technical certification replaces the license examination and is conducted by several membership organizations such as the Society of Broadcast Engineers. For these engineering jobs, however, many employers do prefer to hire technicians with an FCC license and technical certification. The average low-volume salary is $15,000; the average high-volume salary, $35,000.

Studio Engineer: This job exists only at larger stations. The studio engineer is in charge of analyzing the technical requirements of programs produced in studios. He operates the control room during a broadcast to feed the program to the transmitter. During the broadcast, he controls the microphones, plays the records and tapes, incorporates the remote feeds (broadcasts originating outside the studio but channeled through it for broadcasting to the public), monitors the sound levels, and communicates with the producers and performers via headphones while the show is on the air. This position requires at least a high school diploma. Since competition for this job is so keen, however, we recommend a college degree plus courses in electronics as educational preparation.

Transmitter Engineer: The transmitter engineer cares for and monitors the transmitter. This includes testing the performance of and making technical adjustments and necessary repairs to both transmitter and tower. He also maintains records and logs of his tests and repairs.

Maintenance Engineer: The duties of the maintenance engineer include actual installation of and preventive maintenance on control consoles, boards, recording equipment, microphones, intercoms, two-way radios, remote facilities, and a variety of other station equipment and electronic systems. When systems fail to operate, the maintenance engineer performs the actual repair work.

Contract Engineer: The contract engineer performs inspection and maintenance duties on a regular basis for a number of small stations in an area. Large stations have on-staff contract engineers. This engineer is on call for emergencies.

Sales

As with television, airtime sales pay for a radio station's costs and ultimately account for its profits. This advertising revenue comes from two sources—local and national sales. The local sale is made by the station's own sales force. The national sale is usually handled by large rep firms that work on a commission basis.

If a local station is a network affiliate, the network may sometimes compensate the affiliate from advertising revenues earned by the networks.

General Sales Manager: The general sales manager directs the station's sales force and also sells air-time. He works closely with the program director and the general manager to evaluate the total amount of available air-time and to pinpoint those programs able to attract the highest-paying advertisers.

In directing the sales force, the sales manager must set sales goals, supervise sales presentations, and totally understand the local business market. Often the sales manager will go on sales calls with his salespeople.

Sales managers usually rank just below the general manager in a station's pecking order. They often succeed to the top spot at their own station. Training for this job comes from working at radio sales. A successful salesperson in any field, however, can make the jump to radio sales. An undergraduate degree in advertising or marketing is a good prerequisite. The average low-volume salary is $29,000; the average high-volume salary, $75,000.

Local Sales Manager: The local sales manager supervises the local salespeople, assigns accounts, and goes along on sales calls.

National Sales Manager: The national sales manager works with the station's national sales rep firm to solicit national advertising. The rep firm may have regional sales offices in key cities across the country.

Account Executives: The soldiers out on the line selling those 10-, 30-, and 60-second commercials are the account executives. These people must know the audience and match them with a particular program daypart (as in television, a particular segment of a broadcast day). Often salespeople assist an advertiser in the preparation of commercials. Account executives earn reasonably high salaries, especially as commission is a factor. A degree in marketing and advertising is a good prerequisite.

Sales Assistant: This employee monitors the activities of the sales staff, writes orders, maintains a schedule of available airtime, and often acts as the department's "gofer." This is an entry-level job that requires at least a high school diploma. Successful assistants often move into advertising sales jobs. The average salary for this job is low—about $10,000 to $12,000, but it's a foot in the door.

Research Director: The research director works for both the sales and programming departments, collecting information on the effectiveness and popularity of a station's programming and commercials and the relative strength of its competition. The job requires a college degree in business administration, advertising, accounting, or mass communications, in addition to computer and statistical skills. Average salaries range from $15,000 at a small station to about $28,000 at a larger station.

Syndication and the Networks

The terms *syndication* and *network* do not have the same meaning in radio that they have in television. Syndication in radio involves the packaging of a particular entertainment or information program (or segment thereof) and either selling or bartering it to radio stations. The station doesn't necessarily use this syndicated programming for its entire broadcasting day but rather for periods anywhere from 30 seconds to a few hours in length. The National Lampoon True Facts, for example, is a 2½-minute segment produced and packaged by a syndicator who also sells advertising sponsorship on the show. Syndication in radio, while offering limited job opportunities, can still be a stepping stone to the bigger time in television.

Here are some examples of this kind of syndication:

A Bit About Computers (90 seconds; ten per week)

Soap Opera News (six 60-second segments per day)

Car Care Tips (30-second format, sixty-five shows per quarter)

Off the Record with Mary Turner (1 hour per week)

Casey Kasem American Top 40 (4 hours)
National Lampoon True Facts (2½ minutes)
Great Sounds
King Biscuit Flour Hour
Pure Country (for men age forty-plus and
    women age thirty-six plus)
Detective Theater
Sacred Sounds of Praise
The Great American Woman
Health Care Tips
Investor's Guide
American Time Capsule
Swing! Era II
Music . . . Just for the Two of Us

As in television, the three networks—ABC, CBS, and NBC—each own a number of radio stations and have a large number of affiliated stations, interconnected by satellite. Whereas a television affiliate usually carries at least 70 percent of its network's programming, however, a radio affiliate has greater autonomy. ABC has seven separate networks, each with its own affiliated stations; NBC has three.

The following list identifies these ten networks along with their competition:

ABC Contemporary Radio Network
ABC Direction Radio Network
ABC Entertainment Radio Network
ABC FM Radio Network
ABC Information Radio Network
ABC Rock Radio Network
ABC Talkradio Network
Caballero Spanish Radio
CBS Radio
Concert Music Network
Mutual Broadcasting System
NBC Radio Network
NBC Talknet
NBC—The Source
Premiere Radio Network
Satellite Music Network
The Wall Street Journal Radio Network
Agri-News Network
Progressive Farmer Network
United Stations Radio Networks
Westwood One Radio Network

This form of networking is obviously profitable to the networks and the stations. Most of the networks listed have fifty or more affiliated stations. Again, as we pointed out in the section on format, there are many opportunities for innovation in radio, particularly in the area of selective programming.

Let's look at two of these networks.

Mutual Broadcasting System

Mutual has been in radio for more than 50 years. Today, it has the largest group of news affiliates in network radio. It feeds this network by the use of Westar IV and Satcom 1–R communications satellites. Mutual fills the gap in talk radio with other personalities such as Rona Barrett and Dr. Toni Grant, a psychologist. Mutual was acquired by Westwood in 1985 for $30 million.

Westwood One

Here's a success story in the true American tradition. Started in 1975 in a one-room office in Westwood, California, Westwood One is now the nation's largest producer and distributor of national radio programming with more than thirty regularly scheduled programs broadcast by more than 3,000 stations across the country.

Its gallery of programs ranges from 90-second featurettes such as "Earth News Radio," "Star Trak," and "Shooting the Breeze" to regularly scheduled long-form programs such as "Dr. Demento," "Live from the Apollo," and "Scott Shannon's Rockin' America Top Thirty Countdown."

In 1987 Westwood One paid $50 million to acquire General Electric's NBC radio networks. NBC had contracts with more than 700 stations.

Arbitron: The Research and Ratings Source

Advertisers and agencies committed to buying radio time must have the answers to many questions before they can make the proper media evaluation. The number of listeners, share of market, audience demography, listener loyalty—even attitudinal factors—add to a station's profile. The group that dominates radio research is Arbitron Ratings Company, a division of the Control Data Company.

Using this research, the radio stations can make programming decisions to increase the number of listeners as well as the length of time they listen. Also, a station's advertising and promotion people can use Arbitron estimates to plan on-air and off-air campaigns to garner a larger audience.

Here are some examples of Arbitron's research reports.

- Radio Market Reports: This comprehensive report, in the form of a small booklet, gives the audience estimates for all stations in a market for a specific survey period. These are sophisticated documents that present a wide variety of demographics and dayparts; for example, all the single males ages eighteen to twenty-four who listen to Monday-to-Friday radio from 7:00 P.M. to midnight.
- AID (Arbitron Information on Demand): The AID database gives advertisers such information as the hours teenagers or women with jobs listen to radio, the scheduling of specific programs or events, and the hours a particular group listens to radio away from home.
- Target AID: This research report describes where listeners live, what they buy, and how advertisers can reach them. It gives audience estimates by lifestyle in addition to standard age/sex demographics and also profiles the purchaser of specific products and brands.
- Arbitron Library: The library consists of a number of publications to assist stations in learning more about their markets, audience listening patterns, and the broadcast industry in general. Some examples of the publications include *Radio Today/In Your Market, Working Women: in Time with Radio,* and *Radio Today/The Black Listener.*

How Does Arbitron Get Its Information?

On a leisurely Sunday morning, someone in your neighborhood pours a cup of coffee, tunes in a favorite radio station, glances at the clock, and makes a notation of time and station in a booklet conveniently placed next to the radio. This booklet is a diary from Arbitron, and the information provided may determine how your local radio station serves its audience.

Before Arbitron came on the scene, radio research was very different. In the 1930s, a telephone survey asked listeners to recount their previous 24 hours of radio listening time. In the '40s, with the proliferation of multiple sets per household, plus in-car and out-of-home listening, phone calls didn't reach people at their source—so a mechanical device, the audimeter, was attached to car radio receivers. However, it couldn't withstand the bumps and jolts of driving and was soon dropped. The 1950s brought the birth of rock 'n' roll and changes in radio design. Smaller, less expensive radios helped

move the focus of research from metering the set to monitoring the behavior of individual listeners.

In 1964, a television research company called ARB (American Research Bureau) began measuring radio-listening habits, using a written, mailed survey technique that had worked well for television. Each listener got his or her own booklet, called a diary, to record listening habits.

From ARB eventually evolved the name Arbitron, and the company now measures 260 cities and towns, called "metro markets," every twelve weeks.

CAREER TIP: Note that station managers and their advertising departments carefully study Arbitron data. Advertisers and agencies use this information as a guide for their radio-buying decisions. For readers with a degree in computer science and an interest in radio, this phase of the business would make a good career choice. It pays well, and there are substantial employment opportunities in the media departments of advertising agencies.

As for Arbitron, it maintains executive and marketing headquarters in New York City and operations, production, and research facilities in Laurel and Beltsville, Maryland. It also has offices in Chicago, Atlanta, Dallas, Los Angeles, and San Francisco. Write for information on job opportunities to: Arbitron Ratings Company, 1350 Avenue of the Americas, New York, NY 10019.

Preparation for a survey begins four months before the actual survey period. Families of potential diary keepers are sent letters asking them to participate, followed by a phone call asking family members to track their radio listening for one week. One diary is mailed to each person in the house twelve years or older. A cash premium of about $1.00 is enclosed to encourage people to complete their diary and mail it back.

The diary records the hour of listening, the station, the location of the listener, and any personal comments. The household supplies demographic information including the age, sex, and geographic location of listeners, while keeping their actual identities confidential.

Once the diaries are sent back, the booklets are carefully reviewed. Editors check for accuracy and completeness. The data is then fed into a computer and then into a written report. This local market report lists all the stations and their share of the audience. More than 100,000 pieces of information are in each local market report. Each spring, Arbitron generates forty tons of market reports from 400 tons of data with more than 175 *billion* numbers. About 2,000 radio stations and 3,500 advertisers and ad agencies receive a local report; one hundred of the stations have electronic access to it.

The future of radio listening will tap into the most sophisticated high technology available, including electronic diaries, personal computers, and data transmitted over satellites.

Arbitron's range of information has grown to include lifestyle and product purchase data; it will continue to offer research as it is needed by its customers.

In the course of researching this section, I came upon a surprising radio fact. Those much-maligned teenage boys spend the fewest hours listening to radio each week, an average of 18 hours. Women over sixty-five spend the most time, 30 hours.

Fun with Formats

Arbitron monitors the size of radio audiences in the top 200 measured markets of the country. The Arbitron people measure the total week from 6:00 A.M. to midnight, Monday to Sunday. For what the industry calls the "fall sweeps," they recently ranked the stations for the fall period—roughly mid-September to mid-December of each year. (See "Arbitron: The Research and Ratings Source" later in this chapter for further details of its services.)

Included in this ranking is the format information for the top stations within each market. Because this section deals with formats, let's first list those designated by Simmons Market Research Bureau. Simmons does field studies for the magazine and broadcast industries (see chapter on magazines). In the course of its interviews, Simmons determines statistically the radio-listening habits of its subjects.

a:	album, easy listening, beautiful music
ac:	adult contemporary
ao:	album-oriented rock
bl:	black
cl:	classical
c:	country
e:	ethnic
g:	golden oldies
n:	all news
r:	rock
re:	religious
s:	Spanish
sc:	soft contemporary
st:	standard, nostalgia Big Band
nt:	talk, news/talk
v:	variety
uc:	urban contemporary
j:	jazz

Although there are only eighteen basic formats, within each format there are as many as ten subcategories. For example, within the category *bl* (black), there are the subcategories black contemporary, black oldies, black rock, and so forth.

An examination of the top ten in all one hundred markets shows no clear-cut domination of one particular format, although music of one kind or another remains the most popular.

Further, in major markets with ten or more stations, the share for the tenth-highest-rated station may be half of, or less than, the highest-rated station. Shares are what make the difference in advertising rates. Simply stated, WPLJ in New York, with 161,000 listeners and a 6.0 share, will be able to charge much more for its commercials than the tenth station, WPAT, with 91,700 listeners and a 3.4 share.

We have seen in this section the diversity of radio-station formats. This variety should encourage those with a particular interest in radio programming, because it proves there's a format for every aspiring radio professional. For further information, we suggest reading the trade publications discussed later in this chapter and in greater detail in the television chapter.

New York Leads the Way

The nation's largest radio market, New York City, boasts fifty AM and sixty-seven FM radio stations (see listing, page 180). In this mix there's a bit of everything, including two all-news stations, two all-classical-music stations (one owned by the *New York Times*), a municipal station that also carries public-radio programming, a college station (WNYU), and stations for call-ins to psychotherapists, psycholo-

New York AM stations				New York FM stations			
WABC	WHTG	WMTR	WQXR	WADB	WFDU	WMGO	WRCN
WADO	WHWH	WNBC	WRAN	WALK	WFME	WMJY	WRHU
WALK	WICC	WNEW	WRCN	WAWZ	WFMU	WNCN	WRKS
WBRW	WINS	WNJR	WRKL	WBAB	WFUV	WNEW	WRTN
WCBS	WJDM	WNNJ	WSKQ	WBAI	WHPC	WNSR	WRVH
WCTC	WJIT	WNYC	WTHE	WBAU	WHTG	WNWK	WSBH
WFAN	WJLK	WNYG	WVIP	WBGO	WHTZ	WNYC	WSIA
WFAS	WKDM	WNYM	WVOX	WBJB	WHUD	WNYE	WSOU
WGBB	WKMB	WOBM	WWDJ	WBLI	WJLK	WNYU	WSUS
WGLI	WLIB	WOR	WWRL	WBLS	WKCR	WOBM	WUSB
WGRC	WLIM	WPAT	WXMC	WCBS	WKJY	WPAT	WVIP
WGSM	WLIX	WPOW		WCTO	WKRB	WPIX	WVRM
WHLI	WMCA	WPUT		WCWP	WKWZ	WPLJ	WXRK
				WDHA	WKXW	WPRB	WYNY
				WEVD	WLIR	WPST	WYRS
				WEZN	WLTW	WQHT	WZFM
				WFAS	WMCX	WQXR	

gists, financial advisers, real estate experts, and sports editors. There are also foreign language stations, featuring Spanish, Greek, Russian, Yiddish, Polish, and Italian, and stations with every possible format of popular music.

New York is the most important radio-station city in the world. It is also the headquarters for the three giant radio and television networks. If radio is your career choice, what better place than New York to make your mark?

Format Trends

McGavren Guild Radio, a major radio rep firm, recently tracked format fluctuations. Its analysis covered thirty radio markets. Here are some facts about these formats and some of McGavren Guild's conclusions.

Contemporary Hit Radio: This format has many other names—top forty, parade, hot hits, boss hits—and continues to figure in many major markets. CHR fans want an unpredictable, trendy-sounding station that will keep them informed about all the latest hits. Basically the top forty, thirty, or twenty-five hits are played over and over again, while all the other music is ignored. One of the giants in this format is Casey Kasem, who has the syndicated show "American Top Forty." He gets his playing list from *Billboard* magazine, is the number-one authority in the business, and airs little-known facts about artists and their music.

Soft Rock: This format evolved from album-oriented rock in the mid-'70s. Soft-rock or mellow-rock stations feature music from the softer, less frantic and excited, side of the rock spectrum, mainly by artists like the Beatles, James Taylor,

Carly Simon, Elton John, and the like. Its audience is older than CHR's.

Album-Oriented Rock: The album-oriented rock format got its start in the 1960s, when it became evident that a lot of rock enthusiasts were tired of the constraints posed by contemporary-hit-radio (top forty) format. Deejays contended that progressive rock music was not getting on the air because songs were often too long or too controversial to fit into the tight top-forty format. This format now consists of a continuous flow of new album releases with comments pertaining to the artists, music, and writers from informed on-air, low-key personalities. The music consists of rock, rhythm and blues, country, folk, and jazz. Practically an exclusive FM format, it is targeted to an audience of people aged twelve to thirty-four. News and information segments are structured for a young audience.

Adult Contemporary: This format features the music of today, minus the most raucous tunes and abrasive talk (usually heard on rock stations), plus a mix of some old tunes, all presented in a pattern of 70 percent music, 10 percent news, 5 percent sports and special events, and 15 percent features. This format is directed mainly at a targeted audience of adults aged twenty-five to forty-nine and makes use of bright, on-air personalities and well-produced news, sports, weather, and feature segments.

Beautiful Music: This format consists of soothing, pleasant music drawn from movie sound tracks, Broadway shows, standard ballads, and rock and classical music arrangements, performed usually by string orchestras with occasional vocals. Its target is an adult audience of age thirty-five plus, and the format is usually found on FM.

Morning Zoo: A new format in morning radio that incorporates fast-talking deejays, sound effects, stunts, gags, and phone calls. Almost every market in the top 50 has a station with a "zoo" morning show. At this writing, ratings are high, but in radio no format really has long legs.

Conclusions

Contemporary hit radio and soft rock are rising formats on the FM band, while album-oriented rock on FM and the Big Band sound on AM are showing some declines. At this writing, the top-five formats are adult contemporary, contemporary hit radio, country, album-oriented rock, and beautiful music. Those wishing to pursue careers in radio should be knowledgeable of these ever-changing trends.

The Radio Information Center, an industry-supported non-profit organization in New York City, recently issued a report in which it ranked the top eighteen full-time formats as to number of stations.

Format	Number of stations
Country	2,233
Adult contemporary	1,933
Top 40	809
Nostalgia/MOR (middle of the road)	687
Beautiful music	524
Religious	510
AOR (album-oriented rock)	294
Black R&B	207
Oldies	173
Diversified	155
News/talk	135
Spanish	126
Soft rock	83
Classical	58
All news	48
Ethnic	43
Urban contemporary	37
Jazz	19

Changing Formats

The listening audience for radio has become older and more affluent. As the Baby Boom group approaches middle age, their tastes change, and this presents new opportunities for radio programmers. Also influencing radio stations is the interest of advertisers in this upscale age group.

What has developed is experimentation with innovative formats. One such format is EOR (eclectic-oriented rock), also known as "New Age" music. Although there are only a half-dozen FM stations testing this approach, more should follow. In EOR, listeners hear '70s stars such as James Taylor and Joni Mitchell, plus avant-gardists Kitaro and Hiroshima, and instrumentalists on the Windham Hill and Meadowlark labels.

If you don't like EOR, how about comedy radio stations? The *National Lampoon* laid the groundwork in the early 1970s. The "National Lampoon Radio Hour" was syndicated to more than 275 stations, but that was only for an hour at a time. Now there are all-comedy *stations*. KMDY-AM in Thousand Oaks, California, broadcasts cuts from albums by comedians daily from 5:30 A.M. to 1:00 A.M.—that's a lot of yocks. Cosby, Newhart, Dangerfield, and Murphy are the diet for KMDY's listeners, and it seems to be working.

As we noted earlier, there are only nineteen jazz stations in the United States. WNOP-AM in Newport, Kentucky, has tried a mix of comedy and jazz to appeal to listeners from twenty-five to fifty-four years old.

The growth of the all-news format has been slow. By the mid-1980s, there were only about fifty of these stations across the country. The basic appeal seems to be for the thirty-five-or-older audience in big cities. CBS owns all-news stations in New York, Los Angeles, San Francisco, and Chicago. There are also Group W (Westinghouse Broadcasting) stations in New York and Los Angeles as well as in Philadelphia. Other all-news stations are in Washington, Denver, and Hartford.

Although we have seen a great deal of cost cutting on some television news staffs, radio news offers increasing opportunities for those who aspire to be hard-core journalists rather than on-air personalities.

Ages and References

Arbitron reports that 96 percent of all persons aged twelve and older tune in a radio station at least once a week. But what are they listening to?

Young men under twenty-five are most likely to listen to AOR (album-oriented rock). Here you're sure to hear the Rolling Stones many times a day.

Teenagers and women under thirty choose the contemporary-hit format, usually on FM stations. The fare here is of the Prince, Madonna, Phil Collins, and Michael Jackson variety. When this music was on AM, it was called "top forty."

Many young people probably think that their elders listen exclusively to beautiful music—stations that play Streisand, Montovani, Dave Brubeck, and semiclassical selections. Not so. Most men and women fifty-five and older are fans of news and talk stations.

Men age forty-five and older often select the Big Band/nostalgia stations. Recently I switched to one of these stations and was rather pleased to hear such stalwarts as Patti Page, Billy Eckstine, Helen O'Connell, and Rosemary Clooney still going strong.

Geography plays an important role in radio formats. Country music works best in the South and West—the very best, Fargo, North Dakota, and Waco, Texas. Los Angeles is among the worst markets for country. Who knows why?

You and Formats

The wide variation in radio formats should prove to the reader that opportunities exist for talented programmers (program directors). A new idea that works at a small station can become an instant sensation, adopted by hundreds of other stations. Radio is less constricting than TV; there are more stations and more job shifting. So, be it deejay, programmer, or salesperson, why not give it a whirl?

Broadcast Sales: How to Sell Advertisers and Agencies on Why They Should Buy Radio Time Instead of TV, Newspaper, and Magazine Advertising

---

Radio stations live and profit on the sale of commercials. Selling them effectively is the formidable task of a corps of local, regional, and national salespeople. Here are some of the problems they face:

- There are many competitive forces at play. Advertisers in a local market can buy TV time, newspaper and magazine ads, and space in

shoppers (advertising circulars) and on billboards.

- Effectiveness of advertising is often difficult to prove.
- Radio is not always the most efficient medium on a "cost-per-thousand basis," the standard used in broadcast and print to evaluate the efficiency of advertising dollars. This standard always determines the cost necessary to reach a thousand people, never a hundred. For example, if a commercial costs $100 and the show has an audience of 10,000, the cost per thousand is $10.00. If, however, a newspaper ad in the same market can reach these 10,000 people for $80.00 (cost per thousand: $8.00), it is considered more "efficient" on a cost-per-thousand basis.
- Agencies are inclined to recommend television because it represents a bigger profit potential than radio.

The Radio Advertising Bureau

To overcome these problems and increase and expand the radio industry's share of advertising revenues by designing, developing, and implementing appropriate programs, research tools, and activities, the industry founded the Radio Advertising Bureau (RAB).

As mentioned previously, the RAB, formed in 1951, serves as the sales and marketing arm of America's commercial radio broadcast industry. The titles of its promotional literature provide an understanding of RAB's approach. We don't know how effective they are, but they certainly do present a cogent selling premise.

The following are some examples:

- "Two-thirds of Adult Americans Are Listening to Radio During TV's Prime Time." This piece goes on to add that 133 million people listen to their favorite radio stations each week from 7:00 P.M. to midnight and that an advertiser's radio message can reach 66 percent of all adults in the evening for moderate costs with high impact, recall, and awareness.
- "Daytime Radio Means Business." Quotes are given from a survey stating that the best customers and prospects tune in and rely on radio during midday for music, weather, information, and news.
- "Overnight Radio: Who's Listening." Here, the attempt is to convince advertisers that overnight radio listeners are not poorly educated people with low incomes.

• "Improving Advertising Impact and Effectiveness . . . by Combining Radio with Newspaper Ads." This booklet deals with local radio's main competitor, newspapers. In it are convincing arguments aiming to deter clients from advertising heavily in newspapers.

Another impressive piece, titled "Total Radio . . . Why It's First for Advertisers Now," contains a dozen definitive subheads, such as Radio Is First in People Reach, Radio Is First on Weekends, Radio Is First as a News Source, Radio Is First with the Auto Audience, and Radio Is First Indoors and Out.

In case there is any doubt about the commitment of America's top advertisers to radio, here is a recent list of the annual expenditures of some top national-spot radio advertisers:

Advertiser	Yearly Expenditure (in millions)
Anheuser-Busch	$40.0
Van Munching (Heineken and Amstel beer)	31.7
Pepsi Cola	29.9
General Motors	27.9
Chrysler	23.5
Southland (7-11 stores)	19.9
Delta Air Lines	19.9
Miller Brewing	19.7

Local businesses rely on radio advertising to sell their wares, too. Those types of firms spending the most are:

Category	Percentage Share of Expenditures
Auto dealers	10.7%
Department stores	8.4
Banks	8.0
Clothing stores	7.7
Restaurants	7.0
Supermarkets	6.7
Furniture stores	6.4
Bottlers	5.9

After digesting this diet of radio hard sell, one can picture the counterattack literature, prepared by the newspaper and TV ad salespeople. Oh, well—it makes for spirited competition, and that's what sales is all about.

Humor in Radio Commercials

Many radio commercials try to be funny. Few succeed. One noteworthy series is that of the advertising trade publication *ADWEEK*. Here's a 60-second bit that's hilarious when performed by talented actors. The commercial was written and produced by Dick Orkin's Radio Ranch in Los Angeles. It's called "Coming and Going" and is about the constant change in accounts and personnel at ad agencies. We're told by *ADWEEK*'s publisher that this entire series was extremely effective in drawing attention to the publication and how it keeps ad executives informed. This particular spot is soft sell at its best.

DICK: Hi, Bob. Hi, Jane.
M&W: Hi, Phil.
DICK: Can I buy you guys a drink?
MAN: Hey, do squirrels eat nuts?
DICK: Scotch over here, barkeep!!
MAN: So, how's the old ad game going?
DICK: Pretty good. We just won the "Beaver Bowling Ball Bag" at Kamper, Bowzer, Bingham, Bipper and Bowe.
MAN: I read in *ADWEEK* they pitched the Cooper-Kazoo business.
DICK: Yea, but they lost to Lifty, Libitz, Lumber and Lowe.
WOM.: That's not what I read in *ADWEEK*.
DICK: Really?
WOM.: *ADWEEK* said Cooper-Kazoo went with Kibell, Kop, Kibetz and Kabobo.
MAN: I thought Kabobo left Kibell, Kop and Kibetz.
DICK: He did. He joined Duper, Dink and Diddle.
WOM.: Well, according to *ADWEEK*, they just lost Dufus Drugs.
MAN: To who?
WOM.: Mirelli, Mooseman and Mum.
DICK: Mum just got the Royal Shaft.
WOM.: What a shame!
DICK: No, no. It's an ad club award . . . the story is in . . .
ALL: *ADWEEK*.
DICK: Last year, Wifflub, Walla, Wifley, Winky won that award.
MAN: I read that Winky went with Kabobo over to Duper, Dink and Diddle.
WOM.: Boy, that's gonna make Kabobo, Duper, Diddle, Winky and Dink a name to reckon with.
DICK: I thought Diddle would get top billing.
WOM.: Over Winky and Dink's dead body.

ANNCR: Sometimes it's hard to keep up with who's coming and who's going. That's why so many top ad executives stay informed with *ADWEEK*. When you want to have a little fun and gain a lot of perspective, better read *ADWEEK*.

MAN: I heard P. Peck, Peck and Olapepper joined Tearpiper, Abo, Pick and Smythe.

WOM.:   Now they're called . . .

ALL: Peter Piper Picked a Peck of Pickled Peppers . . . and Smythe.

Women in Broadcast Sales

The RAB publishes the fine monthly magazine *Sound Management* for its members, who are mostly radio-station executives and advertisers with radio accounts. A piece in its April 1986 issue reported that women hold 45.5 percent of all broadcast sales jobs, up from 37.5 percent in 1981. Along with minorities, women are making slight gains overall in the four highest job-classification categories (officials/managers, professionals, technicians, and salespeople). Women account for 28.6 percent of all these jobs; minority representation is 13.5 percent. The fact remains, however, that women and minorities are better represented at the bottom of the broadcast employment scale. Women account for 87.9 percent of all office/clerical jobs at the stations while minorities account for 26.3 percent.

One can conclude that there is progress in this area, but as in other areas of mass communications, the pace is still slow.

The Role of Regional Reps

Local stations cannot possibly afford to employ salespeople in the large metropolitan centers such as New York and Chicago where the major ad agencies that control the spending of national advertisers are concentrated.

Let's consider an example: Procter & Gamble, test-marketing a new soap product, wants to use radio in Columbus, Ohio. Rather than contacting the stations in that market directly, the agency calls the national reps for this area and then makes its buy on the basis of efficiency, reach, and other criteria. These data are provided by the rep firms for the Columbus stations.

Three national rep firms dominate the radio industry—John Blair Radio, McGavren Guild, and Katz Radio. McGavren, for example, has been selling radio for almost forty years and is the product of a consolidation of four firms. Interep is the holding company of these consolidated entities. They employ more than one hundred salespeople in forty-five offices across the country.

> CAREER TIP: Radio is a profitable, growing industry. Successful salespeople make as much money as their TV counterparts. Local sales jobs are not difficult to find and afford a good training ground for big-city sales situations.

Public Radio

Early History

One of the first broadcast stations in the United States, 9XM, was built in a University of Wisconsin physics laboratory. Renamed WHA-AM, it remains a major station in the public radio system.

By 1925, colleges and universities had 171 AM licenses. However, with the increased competition from commercial broadcasting, most of these stations were off the air by 1934 when the FCC was started.

In 1941, when regular FM broadcasting was initiated, five channels were authorized for noncommercial educational use as a substitution for AM allocations no longer in place.

In 1948, the FCC authorized 10-watt operation on educational FM channels. This enabled schools and colleges to broadcast to a limited area of two to five miles for an outlay of a few thousand dollars. By 1978, there were a total of 973 educational FM stations on the air.

Public broadcasting in its present form emerged with the passage of the Public Broadcasting Act of 1967. That act authorized the establishment of the Corporation for Public Broadcasting (CPB), whose primary function is to funnel federal funds to qualified noncommercial licensees.

The Scope of Public Radio Today

The Corporation for Public Broadcasting uses the designation "CPB-qualified stations" for those stations eligible for CPB financial support. The criteria cover facilities, funds, staff, quality of programming, and so forth. In 1970, there were ninety-six CPB-qualified stations; in 1985, 275 stations.

Subscriber support for public radio has grown as well. In 1973, there were only 64,000 subscribers; by 1983, there were 850,000. In the same period, listenership increased from a 2.6 million weekly cumulative audience to one of 8.7 million.

In the late '70s, when the Carnegie Commission made its report on public broadcasting, the largest station in the public-radio system had a budget of approximately $1.2 million, and the smallest had $100,000.

Programming

Public radio is by no means dull radio. The programming mix is eclectic and informed. Here is the breakdown from a recent CPB report:

Music	68.6%
News and Public Affairs	19.3%
Information	7.7%
Spoken Word/Performance	3.8%
Instructional	0.6%

Of this programming, 56.3 percent is locally originated; 24.7 percent comes from National Public Radio; the rest comes from other public broadcasters and other sources.

National Public Radio

National Public Radio (NPR) was established in 1970 to provide interconnection and programming service for public radio stations.

NPR is a network of about 325 noncommercial, nonprofit stations. The individual stations do their own programming in addition to those provided by NPR.

Their most significant programs are "Morning Edition" and "All Things Considered," both with a news and information format. With a reduction of federal funding in the early '80s, NPR sought revenues through commercial ventures. These efforts almost forced the network into bankruptcy. Fortunately, a $9 million loan from CPB bailed them out.

NPR member stations are independent, autonomous broadcast entities. Each station determines its own programming format based on the needs of the audience it serves. The network distributes its pro-

gramming through the public radio satellite system. According to Arbitron data, in spring '85 more than 9 million people listened each week to NPR member stations.

> CAREER TIP: Gain your experience as a volunteer in public radio, particularly when you're in college. You probably won't get paid, but at least you'll accumulate on-air or technical experience that may help you land a commercial radio job.

Important Addresses

If you are considering a career in radio, you'll want to contact these networks, unions, and trade organizations. You will probably have to apply through the human resources or personnel departments for interviews.

California

American Federation of Television and Radio Artists (AFTRA)
1717 North Highland Avenue
Hollywood, CA 90028

Capital Cities/ABC
2040 Avenue of the Stars
Los Angeles, CA 90067

CBS
7800 Beverly Boulevard
Los Angeles, CA 90036

National Broadcasting Co.
3000 West Alameda Avenue
Burbank, CA 91523

New York

American Federation of Television and Radio Artists
  (AFTRA)
1350 Avenue of the Americas
New York, NY 10019

Capital Cities/ABC
1330 Avenue of the Americas
New York, NY 10019

CBS, Inc.
51 West 52nd Street
New York, NY 10019

National Broadcasting Co.
30 Rockefeller Plaza
New York, NY 10020

Radio Advertising Bureau
485 Lexington Avenue
New York, NY 10017

Broadcasting and *Television/Radio Age*

The two leading publications in the broadcast industry are *Broadcasting* and *Television/Radio Age*. In addition to excellent articles on radio, they both contain employment/help-wanted ads relating to the broadcasting industry. See the chapter on television for details about these magazines.

Colleges and Universities Offering Degree Programs in Radio and/or TV

Those wishing to major in broadcasting at the college level or seeking a two-year program at a junior college should consult the organization set up by broadcasters and individual schools as a clearinghouse for this information. Write to: the president of the Broadcast Education Association, National Association of Broadcasters, 1771 N Street, N.W., Washington, DC 20036.

The following is a partial list of schools offering two-year, four-year, and graduate programs in broadcasting. For a complete list and information on scholarships, we recommend *Broadcast Programs in American Colleges and Universities*, available from the National Association of Broadcasters in Washington, D.C. The price is $5.00.

University of Alabama
University, AL 35486

American University
Washington, DC 20016

University of Arizona
Tucson, AZ 85721

Ball State University
Muncie, IN 47306

Boston University
Commonwealth Avenue
Boston, MA 02215

Brigham Young University
Provo, UT 84601

Brooklyn College of the City University of New
  York
Bedford Avenue and Avenue H
Brooklyn, NY 11210

University of California at Los Angeles
Los Angeles, CA 90024

Carnegie-Mellon University
Pittsburgh, PA 15213

University of Colorado
Boulder, CO 80302

Colorado State University
Fort Collins, CO 80521

Cornell University
Ithaca, NY 14850

University of Delaware
Newark, DE 19711

University of Denver
Denver, CO 80210

Emerson College
Boston, MA 02116

Florida State University
Tallahassee, FL 32306

University of Georgia
Athens, GA 30601

Hofstra University
Hempstead, NY 11550

Hunter College of the City University of New York
695 Park Avenue
New York, NY 10021

University of Illinois
Urbana, IL 61801

Indiana State University
Terre Haute, IN 47809

Indiana University
Bloomington, IN 47401

University of Iowa
Iowa City, IA 52240

University of Kansas
Lawrence, KS 66044

Marquette University
Milwaukee, WI 53233

University of Maryland
College Park, MD 20742

University of Massachusetts
Amherst, MA 01002

Miami University
Oxford, OH 45056

Michigan State University
East Lansing, MI 48823

University of Michigan
Ann Arbor, MI 48104

University of Mississippi
University, MS 38677

University of Missouri
Columbia, MO 65201

New York University
New York, NY 10003

University of North Carolina
Chapel Hill, NC 27514

Ohio State University
Columbus, OH 43210

Ohio University
Athens, OH 45701

Purdue University
Lafayette, IN 47907

University of Southern California
Los Angeles, CA 90007

Southern Methodist University
Dallas, TX 75222

University of Southern Mississippi
Hattiesburg, MS 39401

Stanford University
Stanford, CA 94305

Syracuse University
Syracuse, NY 13210

Temple University
Philadelphia, PA 19122

University of Texas
Austin, TX 78712

University of Utah
Salt Lake City, UT 84112

Wayne State University
Detroit, MI 48202

Radio Internships

The following is a partial list of radio stations offering four or more internship programs. Some pay minimum wage; some offer only college credit. Participation in any of these programs is excellent experience in the field of radio broadcasting. Many of the programs offer the possibility of future employment or will provide references for qualified people. Consult *Internships,* available from Writer's Digest books, for a complete updated listing. Some colleges with communication majors maintain internship information services.

KDBS/KRRV
1515 Jackson Street
Alexandria, LA 71301

KFDI Radio
Box 1402
Wichita, KS 67021

KFRC Radio AM
415 Bush Street
San Francisco, CA 94108

KKUA and/or 93FMQ (KQMQ)
765 Amana Street
Honolulu, Oahu, HI 96814

KNBR/NBC Radio
1700 Montgomery Street
San Francisco, CA 94111

KOFO/KKKX-FM Radio
Box 16
Ottawa, KS 66067

KOGO Radio
8665 Gibbs Drive
San Diego, CA 92123

KOLO Radio
4850 Ampere Drive
Reno, NV 89510

KQV Radio
411 Seventh Avenue
Pittsburgh, PA 15219

KYUU/FM Radio
530 Bush Street
San Francisco, CA 94108

RKO General, Inc., WRKO-AM, WROR-FM
3 Fenway Plaza
Boston, MA 02215

WBCN-FM
1265 Boylston Street
Boston, MA 02215

WBLI Radio
3090 Route 112
Medford, NY 11763

WCAU-AM Radio
City Line Avenue and Monument Road
Philadelphia, PA 19131

WEBR Newsradio 970
23 North Street
Buffalo, NY 14202

WGPR-FM/TV 62
3140-6 East Jefferson Avenue
Detroit, MI 48207

WHN Radio
400 Park Avenue
New York, NY 10019

WIND Radio, Westinghouse Broadcasting
625 North Michigan Avenue
Chicago, IL 60611

WKOX Radio
Fairbanks Broadcasting Company of Massachusetts, Inc.
100 Mount Wayte Avenue
Framingham, MA 01701

WMAL-AM and Q-107 (WRQX) Radio
4400 Jenifer Street, N.W.
Washington, DC 20015

WNCW Radio
Box 11788
Lexington, KY 40578

WNJR Radio
1700 Union Avenue
Union, NJ 07083

WPLW Radio
201 Ewing Road
Pittsburgh, PA 15205

WYSP Radio
1 Bala Cynwyd Place
Bala Cynwyd, PA 19004

WYXY Radio
1505 Dundee Road
Winter Haven, FL 33880

CAREER TIP: Those interested in a radio- or television-journalism job may apply directly to: General Broadcast Editor, Associated Press Broadcast Services, 1825 K Street, N.W., Washington, DC 20006-1253.

Two Interviews

We chose two individuals in very different phases of radio as our interviewees. John Scagliotti of WBAI—a provocative, controversial public-supported radio station in New York—has gone the commercial-radio route but now chooses public radio. Ellen Hulleberg of the major rep firm McGavren Guild has risen to the top in a traditionally male field—sales—after only ten years.

John Scagliotti is the program director of radio station WBAI in New York City. Before coming to WBAI, Scagliotti ran a small TV station in Vermont. He was graduated from New York University film school and has co-produced several films, including *Before Stonewall,* which documents the history of homosexuals in America. This film was selected as Best American Independent Feature Film at Filmex (Los Angeles Film Festival, 1985).

During the 1970s, Scagliotti was news and public affairs director for WBCN-FM, the Boston station that developed from a small late-night rock-and-roll den to one of the most successful radio stations in New England. While he was there, Scagliotti's radio documentaries won numerous awards, including a Major Armstrong award for "Down and Out in Boston," one of the first journalistic accounts of the plight of the homeless in contemporary American society.

WBAI is financed by listener subscriptions, the Pacifica Foundation, and various fund-raising activities. Approximately what percentage comes from each of these sources?

Well, the Pacifica Foundation owns the license and sets policy for WBAI. One policy is that we receive no corporate funding for any of our programs. Pacifica has a news bureau in Washington and provides a news service. Twenty-two percent of the money raised by WBAI goes to Pacifica. We raise 82 percent of our funds. We are a listener-sponsored station, more so than any other station in America. Unfortunately, we have to ask for money all the time. We are starting to organize more events—concerts and things—instead of asking for money hour after hour on the air. We'll say, go to the event, have a good time, learn something. It will cost you $5.00—$1.00 will go to pay for the event, and the rest will go to the station.

You're organizing a forum on nuclear power. Is that the kind of event you're talking about?

We really consider this one a service. The ticket will cost $4.00, all of which will go to pay for the hall. We're not going to make any money on that. We're also planning to do more entertaining things for our listeners, like concerts.

New York is the major radio market in the United States, and there are about one hundred stations in the city, of all possible formats. How does a station like WBAI find its audience? By having a particular kind of format? By catering to a lot of community concerns?

Well, these are questions we've been dealing with quite a bit in the past year or two. That's why I'm here. We try to find our audience by a combination of programming, defining our philosophy and ideals, and defining our audience. Obviously we're a public radio station and want everybody to listen to us. But Pacifica has its own philosophy, and

because of that, if we think that something is important, we'll talk about it, even if we know that not everyone will agree that it's important. We don't need to have thousands of people listening to us, because that's not our source of money. As far as knowing our audience, we listen to them. When they write to say that they think a topic should be covered, we listen. So subscribers help define what our programming should be. Now we're trying to grow a bit and bring in new people.

How large is your audience now, and how large was it at its peak?

It's hard to say. We get numbers from Arbitron Ratings Company, and they say we have a weekly accumulation of 100,000 listeners, but we might have the same people listening ten or fourteen times a week. We send out about 15,000 copies of *Folio,* our monthly programming and news sheet. Ten percent of them go to people who have pledged $5.00 or $10.00. We send these people the *Folio* for three months, hoping that they will become full-time subscribers. About 2,000 are sent to potential subscribers, especially after a marathon. I think we can say that we have a subscriber base of about 15,000 people. In 1974, we had a much larger number of subscribers—29,000 to 30,000—and we need to get up there once more.

New York City has its own station, WNYC. Are you two the only public radio stations in the market, and what are your essential differences?

Public radio is an interesting sort of thing. The CPB and Congress consider a public radio station any station that does not take advertising and commercials and is open to the public. I think the major difference between us is that WNYC is paid for by city government and by corporate foundations and by only a very small percent of listeners. We, on the other hand, are a listener-sponsored radio station.

Public radio needs volunteers. How can our readers gain experience in this area of broadcasting? What is the best outlet for their time and talents?

Over the next few months, we'll begin organizing volunteer coordinators. We are very interested in volunteers; however, we have a very small staff, and we don't have the wherewithal to organize their assignments in a structured way. We are starting a training program that will teach editing and the basics of producing a segment, interviewing and organizing a script, making a narration, and turning it into a radio program. Right now we have about 180 volunteers. They are different from the volunteers on public TV who man phones during a marathon. The people here are on the air and are considered part of BAI—part of the staff.

What is the annual budget of WBAI? Can you count on 82 percent of the budget coming in every year? And how many paid employees do you have?

Well, for years and years, people have supported WBAI. We base our budget on that, even though we have to get loans. To keep the station going, we need to raise about $1.2 million a year. We don't. We raise $800,000, which means that somebody doesn't get paid for what he or she is doing, and a lot of people get tired and work hard, putting in a lot of extra hours. Somehow the station survives, and I go to bed at night feeling kind of good about what I've done during the day. People here are beginning to realize that money is important, but that doesn't mean that we have to compromise principles. We need to look at how we manage ourselves, how we organize, and what our priorities are.

Regarding paid employees, the paid staff is maybe eight or ten out of 200; the bookkeeper, myself and other people in programming, some of the news people, and the person in charge of membership. That's it; all the rest are volunteers.

Is WBAI programmed by committee or coalition, or do you do all of it yourself? How does it work?

I am the program director, but I work with a number of people in the programming department such as the executive producer for the arts and the executive producer for information services. I am responsible, but I try to delegate responsibilities. We are very open here, and I try to encourage people who have interesting things to say—to provide time for them and set up an organization that allows that to happen. There are lots of fascinating ways to communicate through radio, other ways of expressing your feelings towards something, such as drama or sound collage, which will help people listen and feel and maybe learn something.

In 1986, **Ellen Hulleberg** was named president of McGavren Guild Radio, the nation's number-one radio rep firm. In the previous seven years, she was executive vice-president of marketing communications, and from 1975 to 1979 she was vice-president of research and client services.

In 1969, before coming to McGavren Guild, Hulleberg was an account and research executive at Brand Rating Index. Her first job, after completing her degree at Vermont College, was as a research assistant at ABC-owned radio stations.

Her credentials include CRMC-RAB (Certified

Radio Marketing Consultant, Radio Advertising Bureau), attendance at the Management Development Seminar at the Harvard School of Business Administration, and McGavren Guild Radio Management and Sales Training Program, including Xerox professional sales-training courses.

Tell us how you came to be at the top of what is traditionally a man's business. What kind of career path did you follow? What kind of training did you have?

I have an Associate Degree from a two-year college where I took secretarial courses. I wanted to work at a network and took a job at ABC because they had a training program in different areas of broadcasting. While serving my apprenticeship in the radio area, a job became available. I stayed for three years, becoming assistant to the research director. We worked with Brand Rating Index surveying audiences in terms of heavy product users. I left ABC and joined Brand Rating Index in sales and marketing. Shortly thereafter, I took a job at McGavren Guild, and within a month I was appointed research director.

In 1975, an executive committee was formed at McGavren Guild, and I was appointed to represent research and marketing. The executive committee was the governing body and set direction for the company. I had been working with these people for some time and was brought in because they respected my work, not as a token female.

At that time, we began a client survey with the help of a research company, and we were surprised at the results, which were rather disappointing. Task groups were set up to improve our image; as of the last survey, we are number one, especially in innovation and marketing. We are the only reps who deal only with radio, and we are the biggest company of that kind.

So the new organization really worked?

Yes, and it was truly a group effort with everyone involved. The president of the company, Ralph Guild, was very innovative and gave lots of autonomy. As research director, I always made my own decisions. If they were good, fine; if repeatedly bad, I would have been fired.

You mentioned that you also were in charge of the marketing function.

Yes, that was my last role before becoming president. As a marketing person, one really understands the entire company. Also, each member of the executive committee had the opportunity to act as president for about a month. We started this policy six years ago.

This reminds me of something that I read in Media and Marketing Decisions, *in which you said that you wanted McGavren to have the best salespeople in the business and you thought that it would be very useful if they spent time both in radio and in the ad agencies. Are you going to start some training program that would involve these two sides for people coming in and wanting to be sales reps?*

We have been sending people out to radio stations for some time. Now we are offering internships. Besides our summer program, we are starting a program where interns work in several offices, including research. This will help fill jobs when women must go on maternity leave. Internships bring in young people, which is healthy for an organization. We spend a lot of time working with schools; we give out scholarships so that we will always have a good force of people out there.

Do you work with schools only in the major cities or all around the country?

We have offices in sixteen cities, and each of those offices is in touch with the local schools and universities.

How many people in the United States do you think are selling radio and TV airtime?

Well, if you figure that there are 9,000 radio stations, and twelve salespeople in the large ones and maybe three in the small ones, that's an average of eight. Eight times 9,000, that's 72,000—and that's just selling at radio stations. Then there are the reps. We have about 300 people in our company, and there are probably a total of 1,500 people in the industry. That's just for radio. For television, the number is probably triple or quadruple.

In your experience, is selling for a rep firm more remunerative than selling for a network or a local station? Is there a real difference?

Not really. I know that the representative people are paid very well, but salespeople basically are paid well, especially those who rise to the top and are very effective.

Now that the FCC has eased its regulations, do you see that in the coming five to ten years there will be a proliferation of new radio stations? Is there going to be a spurt of growth in the industry?

Yes, we're expecting that there will be 900 to 1,100 new stations in the next few years. People are applying for licenses. Radio is a lucrative field. Of course, some will make it, and some won't.

Can you describe a day in the life of a McGavren salesperson?

We start at 8:30 A.M. with a sales meeting. Salespeople discuss techniques and opportunities, or a station person discusses qualitative data on a particular station. Then our people make calls at agencies. Another typical day would be to fly out to visit a station for a day or two. Or the salespeople make several agency calls during the day.

Do they have a certain number of calls that they have to complete during the week? Or is it really up to their own initiative?

It's really up to them. Of course, their compensation is based on sales, and a large part of their income is discretionary. In New York, each salesperson is a specialist for some of the stations, so he or she will spend a lot of time there. They must have up-to-date data on the stations when they visit the ad agencies, or the agencies will lose confidence. Our research system is called MRI—it's our memory system. New data goes into our computer. We regularly send a mail questionnaire, visit, or call to make sure we have the latest station information. And, of course, the sales people receive mail every day with all the changes in the marketplace.

Which medium do you primarily sell against in radio sales, TV or print?

Unfortunately, most of our time is spent going after existing radio dollars. We don't go after TV or newspaper. About six years ago, we started a business development department, and we now have six people who call on advertisers to interest them in radio. Radio is an expensive medium with a lot of paper work. We try to take care of the paper work for the customer. Another problem is that creative directors at agencies are interested in getting recognition by winning awards for television ads. We are starting to develop awards in radio, but TV really has that area locked in.

Would you say that there are still barriers against women in media sales?

In media sales, definitely not. I believe that almost three quarters of our sales force is female. Women have the edge in this business because they have been able to come in as secretaries and move up. Our sales assistants are constantly striving to get into sales or research or other areas. Lately, we have brought in some men at the assistant level. But it's unusual. There's a glut of people right now, so you really have to be willing to start at the bottom and eventually move up. This is something we are trying to accomplish with our intern program—get people to understand the company and its culture and move up a lot faster.

Is there right now an area of radio that you think might offer readers who are looking for a job the greatest opportunities?

Network radio is growing tremendously, and representation is doing very well, but local radio sales is probably the best area overall, because it is growing even more rapidly than national, and more emphasis is being placed on local business. The nice thing about local radio sales is that the local advertiser knows that the station was the reason for the success of the campaign, while on a national basis it is difficult to judge the success of a radio campaign.

For those people eager to get a job in radio sales, what do you think the best approach would be?

They should try to get their school to contact a company like ours or try to set up an internship program in other companies. Also, they should try to get their schools to give credit for internship work. More and more schools are doing this.

Glossary of Radio Terms

Affiliate: a station associated with a network that agrees to carry a portion of that network's programming in exchange for a fee or for carrying the network's commercials.

AM broadcast: amplitude modulation system of program transmission using power of 25 watts to 50 kilowatts, the maximum power permitted by the FCC.

Arbitron: the major radio research and ratings organization.

Continuity writer: a job at a radio station that may involve writing commercials for advertisers without agencies.

Cume: the estimated total number of different persons listening to radio for 5 minutes or more within a specified time period. The "cume rating" is the number of "cume persons" divided by all the population.

Daypart: a particular segment of a broadcasting day, such as drive time.

Drive time: the most popular radio-listening period: from 6:00 A.M. to 10:00 A.M. and from 3:00 P.M. to 7:00 P.M.

FM broadcast: frequency modulation method used to impress aural intelligence on the carrier wave.

Frequency: radio waves of different cycles per second that are "tuned"; hence, signals from many sources can be received on a radio set without interfering with one another.

Metro survey area: a region generally corresponding to the definitions of a metropolitan area set by the U.S. Government's Office of Management and Budget (OMB).

NPR: National Public Radio—a network of about 325 noncommercial, nonprofit stations.

RAB: Radio Advertising Bureau—the sales and marketing arm of America's commercial radio-broadcast industry.

Rating: the percentage of all people within a demographic group in a survey area who listen to a specific station: $\frac{\text{Listeners}}{\text{Population}} = \text{Rating (\%)}$

Share: the percentage of the radio audience in a particular market area listening to a specific program at a particular time.

Sweeps: a seasonal period when the audiences of radio stations are measured.

Transmitter: a tall tower that sends out a radio station's signal to its listening area.

TSA: Total Survey Area—an area including all counties in which there is a significant listening to radio stations located in the metro survey area.

Recommended Reading

Agee, Warren K., Phillip H. Ault, and Edwin Emery. *Introduction to Mass Communications* (5th ed.). New York: Harper & Row, 1976.

Barnouk, Erik. *A History of Broadcasting in the United States*. New York: Oxford University Press, 1970.

Beville, Hugh Malcolm, Jr. *Audience Ratings: Radio, Television, and Cable*. Hillsdale, N.J.: Lawrence Erlbaum Associates, 1985.

Book, Albert C., and Norman D. Cary. *The Radio and Television Commercial*. Chicago: Crain Books, 1978.

Broadcasting Yearbook. Washington, D.C.: Broadcasting Publications, Inc., 1982.

Coleman, Howard W. *Case Studies in Broadcast*

Management. New York: Hastings House, 1980.

Ellis, Elmo. *Opportunities in Broadcasting.* Skokie, Ill.: VGM Career Horizons, 1981.

Fenton, D. X. *TV and Radio Careers.* New York: Franklin Watts, Inc., 1976.

First 50 Years of Broadcasting, The. Washington, DC: Broadcasting Publications, Inc., 1982.

Fornatale, Peter, and Joshua Mills. *Radio in the Television Age.* New York: The Overlook Press, 1980.

Head, Sydney W. *Broadcasting in America: A Survey of Television, Radio and New Technologies* (4th ed.). Burlington, Mass.: Houghton Mifflin Co., 1982.

Heighton, Elizabeth J., and Don R. Cunningham. *Advertising in the Broadcast Media.* Belmont, Calif.: Wadsworth Publishing Co., 1976.

Hilliard, Robert L. *Writing for Television and Radio* (3rd ed.). New York: Hastings House, 1976.

Hyde, Stuart W. *Television and Radio Announcing* (3rd ed.). Burlington, Mass.: Houghton Mifflin Co., 1979.

Ouaal, Ward L., and James A. Brown. *Broadcast Management: Radio, Television* (2nd ed.). New York: Hastings House, 1976.

Shook, Frederick, and Dan Lattimore. *The Broadcast News Process.* Denver, Colo.: Morton Publishing Co., 1979.

Smith, F. Leslie. *Perspective on Radio and Television: Telecommunications in the United States.* New York: Harper & Row, 1985.

Sterling, Christopher H., and John M. Kittross. *Stay Tuned: A Concise History of American Broadcasting.* Belmont, Cal.: Wadsworth Publishing Co., 1978.

Zeigler, Sherilyn K., and Herbert H. Howard. *Broadcast Advertising: A Comprehensive Working Textbook.* Columbus, Ohio: GRID, 1978.

MOVIES

When I was a kid, the Saturday-afternoon movies cost 15¢, 10¢ if you got there before one o'clock. My friends and I would each "find" five milk bottles (3¢ deposit per bottle) and use the proceeds to go to our local movie palace. The extra nickel would go for candy or, if we made the trek to the Loew's Coney Island, for a sizzling, juicy hot dog from Nathan's Famous.

At each theater the presentation was similar: a double feature, the Fox Movietone News, a cartoon, two shorts, and an action-filled serial. Total time elapsed: four hours. We staggered out into the sunshine dazed and with a headache, but it was great fun.

The theater owner didn't want kids filling the seats all day, so he came up with the idea of "time tickets" stamped with the time you bought your ticket. Periodically, through the late afternoon, a matron inspected the "children's section" to check the time tickets. The trick was to say that we lost it. Sometimes this approach worked, but at other times we were unceremoniously kicked out of the theater.

I certainly never thought in those days that I would one day become a movie producer. I would have settled for just being a ticket taker so that I could get into the movies for free.

A Mini-History of the Movies

In 1889, Thomas Alva Edison bought a 50-foot strip of Eastman film for $2.50 and made a successful demonstration of his kinetoscope. The French Lumière brothers, in 1895, developed the cinematrographe, which was a camera, a film-printing machine, and a projector all in one—and the *flic* business was on its way.

The American director D. W. Griffith, in 1907, revolutionized film techniques introducing such significant developments as the "fade-out," "close-up," "cutback," and "dissolve." Soon the film pioneers Adolph Zukor, Jesse Lasky, and Cecil B. De Mille popularized the medium by bringing established stage actors to the screen in famous plays.

We've read of the early epic features *Quo Vadis?* and *The Birth of a Nation,* but how many know that the first feature-length comedy was produced by Mack Sennett in 1916? The title: *Tillie's Punctured Romance.*

Although America dominated the field in the early 1900s, film studios sprang up all over Western Europe.

In 1926, Warner Bros. broke the musical ice by presenting *Don Juan,* which had a score synchronized on disks. *The Jazz Singer,* starring Al Jolson, was released by the same company in 1929. It was the first picture with spoken dialogue.

With the introduction of "talkies," movies became the major entertainment medium. Only eight years later, in 1937, there were 89,000 motion picture theaters around the world. In that same year, the average movie theater ticket in the United States cost 22¢. The industry employed more than 40,000 people in production and distribution alone. The average picture cost $350,000 to produce. Today, the average Hollywood picture costs about $13 million. We'll not comment on whether or not they're better.

The Scope of the Movie Industry Today

Ron Howard was thirty-two years old in 1986 when the picture *Gung Ho,* which he directed, was released. Howard, the son of actors, made his acting debut in 1956 at the age of eighteen months. Many years later, in 1978, after two years of film school, Howard began his career as a director, when he was only twenty-four. He then went on to direct the hits *Night Shift, Splash*, and *Cocoon.*

The number-one and number-two people at Warner Bros. production, Mark Canton and Lucy Fisher; the president of Walt Disney Pictures, Jeff Katzenberg; the president of Universal Pictures production, Sean Daniel; and the most successful director of all time, Steven Spielberg—all achieved great success in their thirties.

If readers draw the instant conclusion that this is a young people's business, they're right. Stay with us. The quick road to success of these directors, studio executives, and actors is not the rule. We know of screenwriters who have sold dozens of scripts and treatments but have never had a picture produced and thus are lacking that all-important first screen credit.

In this chapter, we'll tell you all about what these people do in feature films. We'll also discuss documentaries, business and industrial films, videos, short subjects, and the rest. They may be less glamorous, but they're no less important. Bear in mind that the feature film business, from Sylvester Stallone to the kid who takes tickets at your neighborhood multiplex, employs only 200,000 people, a tiny fraction of those employed in banking and finance. But is selling tax-free bonds as much fun as the land of make-believe?

Those of us in the movie business read the ominous reports almost daily in the trade and consumer press. In a recent study commissioned by Columbia Pictures, these startling facts were developed:

- Motion picture attendance is declining in virtually all age groups.
- More films are watched on VCRs than in theaters.
- As the century draws to a close, 60 percent of all U.S. households will have a VCR.
- Three out of four Americans don't patronize movie theaters.

When one puts these facts together with the statistic that 80 percent of moviegoers are teenagers, we soon realize why most movies are geared for this young group. Director William Friedkin, who won an Academy Award for *The French Connection*, states it firmly: "Studios and producers have abandoned adult audiences while pandering to kids." Will this trend continue? The answer: probably yes, especially because studios can't gamble on making quality films that won't make money.

The Big Get Bigger

Antitrust legislation in the early '50s forced many of the larger Hollywood studios to divest their holdings of movie theaters. The government regarded this ownership as conflict of interest. Columbia and Universal were smaller studios at the time and therefore were not part of the decree.

In early 1986, Universal purchased a one-third share of a company that owned 1,117 theaters in the United States and Canada. Columbia, in 1985, bought controlling interest in Walter Reade, which owns eleven theaters in New York City.

Rupert Murdoch, who owns all of 20th Century–Fox, joined with Marvin Davis, the former owner of Fox, in a $1.5 billion purchase of six Metromedia TV stations including those in New York, Chicago, and Los Angeles.

Warner Bros.' parent company, Warner Communications, bought control of Warner Amex Cable, with its 101 cable systems, in twenty-four states, for $450 million.

The major studios are making these huge investments both for their profit-making potential and also as their means of controlling the outlets for their movie and TV products.

How a Movie Is Made

Having gone through the agonies and ecstacies of producing two pictures, I think it will be interesting and informational for the reader to learn about the stages in getting a hypothetical picture made. In doing this, I will be discussing the activities of various players in the movie game. Later on in this chapter, I will highlight in some detail the functions of people and departments mentioned in this narrative.

Development

When our fictitious producer launched this project, he was determined to do a quality science-fiction picture, although he knew that it would require many costly special effects. Realizing that his financing would be limited to $10 million, he opted for a picture with lesser production values than those of a *Star Wars*. (Production values refer to set design, special effects, background detail, costumes, sound, and so on.)

After scanning hundreds of science-fiction novels and short stories, he came upon a book that he thought was perfect. Bringing it to the screen would still run him over budget, but by shooting the picture in England or Canada, he thought, he could keep additional expenses to a minimum.

At this point, the producer engaged a specialist movie lawyer to purchase the option from the book's publisher. A price of $20,000 for a one-year option was agreed upon, with a 10 percent down payment and the balance upon exercise. (In this way, the producer is not gambling much up-front money, and he gives himself a year to get financing for the film project. If a book reaches bestseller status, the publisher (or the author, if he retains these rights) may insist on all the money at the signing of the agreement. Also, the author may receive "points"—a share of the picture's net profits.)

Now that the producer had located the literary property, he began the process of finding a screenwriter to develop the screenplay. His preference was for a writer with experience in the science-fiction genre and one with a "screen credit," that is, having written a picture that was actually made.

The plot of the book concerned a future society set in a multilevel environment like floors in a building. After much searching, the producer found a young English writer who had done one previous picture that had been produced. The writer had also written two sci-fi novels—another plus.

The fee arranged with the screenwriter's agent was $150,000, payable at various stages of his work. In addition, the writer was to receive 5 percent of the net profits of the picture.

Now the producer had to make a major decision: Should he finance the writing of the screenplay with his own money, or should he raise the money privately or through a major Hollywood studio? There are advantages and disadvantages to each approach. Did he want to risk his own money? If he raised the money privately, he would be giving up some equity ownership in the project. If he went to a major studio, that would involve an entirely different set of rules.

(There are eight "majors": Universal, Columbia, Paramount, 20th Century–Fox, MGM, United Artists, Walt Disney Pictures, and Warner Bros. All wield tremendous influence in the United States and in the worldwide film market. They are designated majors by the industry by virtue of their sizes and the number of films they each produce and distribute each year—usually twenty to twenty-five.)

The producer decided to go the major-studio route and thereby signed a development contract with his new rich and powerful partner. The major studio then owned the majority interest in the project and agreed to fund the development of the script and, if it elected, the further production of the film.

The producer then signed a contract with the screenwriter for $150,000 (the studio's money); it guaranteed the screenwriter an initial payment of $25,000 for a twenty-five-to-thirty-page treatment. (A treatment is an essay-style description of the story and characters.) The contract also gave the producer and the studio an option (the right to buy the work at a future date at a specified price) to allow the screenwriter to write the screenplay itself for the additional payment of $125,000; thus his $150,000 was not guaranteed. A studio is always in the position of having many ways out of a deal.

The writing of the treatment took four weeks. It took another six weeks for the producer and the studio to decide to go ahead with the writing of the screenplay.

For the $125,000 that the screenwriter would receive in various stages, he would be required to deliver a first draft, a revision, and a "polish" (the writing of changes in dialogue, narration, or action).

The screenwriter completed the screenplay in the required six-month period. The producer was pleased, but the studio wasn't—studios seldom are. Instead of a revision, the studio requested a second draft and agreed to pay another $20,000 for this work.

Four months later, the studio received the second draft and then decided to "pass" on the whole project, which meant it did not want to go ahead with production. The production went into "turnaround," which meant that the chagrined producer now had to interest another studio or group in the project, and repaying the original studio's investment. This bit of manipulation took another five months before he was able to place the project at another studio.

The second studio loved the material and promptly commissioned the producer to find an acceptable director and to provide an approved budget and a shooting schedule, at which point this new team would be ready to go into preproduction.

The budget was not too much of a problem for the producer. He decided to do his studio work in London, where costs are much less, and his location work in Mexico. The shooting schedule—or "prin-

cipal photography," as it's called in the movie business—was to be ten weeks, of which four weeks would be spent on location.

But finding a director acceptable to the studio proved to be a task akin to Hercules' cleaning the Augean stables. Directors are the rarest commodity in feature films. Good ones are booked years in advance; the others wouldn't pass the studio's muster. Promising "first-timers" (just what the name connotes) are considered risky.

This selection process took six weeks, complicated by the studio's insistence that it wouldn't budget more than $250,000 for a director. Both sides finally agreed to the employment of a thirty-two-year-old director who had done music videos and directed some action TV shows but had never directed a feature film. His fee: $125,000.

With this tedious development stage completed, the project now moved into the second stage.

Pre-Production

Many important decisions had to be made in the four months between the start of pre-production and the beginning of principal photography—the real thing. They included the following:

- Hiring the key production staff and department heads, including unit production manager, first assistant director, production designer, art director, costume designer, construction coordinator, and director of photography, plus all their assistants and crew
- Hiring the casting director and beginning casting
- Arranging for rental equipment
- Arranging for studio rental, processing facilities, catering, and so on
- Receiving estimates and contracting for set construction
- Scouting locations in Mexico; arranging for permits, crews, and the like
- Designing and renting or purchasing costumes

During the pre-production period, important decisions had to be made by the producer and his chief aide, the unit production manager, on how many people would be taken to Mexico for the location shooting and how many would be employed locally.

To accomplish this, the producer, the director, the unit production manager, and the production designer made a ten-day trip to Mexico to scout locations, arrange for equipment rental, and engage a crew for the actual shooting. The trip was successful except that our team learned from local authorities that there might be more rain during the shooting than had been originally predicted.

At the very outset of pre-production, a casting director was engaged. Because there were twenty-two speaking roles including four principal actors, the casting director estimated six weeks for the assignment.

She then prepared a cast breakdown, which is a brief synopsis of each role. The breakdowns were then sent to dozens of agents and personal managers across the country. The casting director then began the screening process. It was also her job to make the financial arrangements with the actors' agents—this, of course, after discussions with the producer and a careful study of the budget.

For the four principal players, she was given a total budget of $800,000. This may seem to be a large amount of money, but it isn't when one considers that Robert Redford earns $7 million per picture plus a percentage of the gross. Much-lesser-known actors who have achieved instant success on one picture often ask $750,000 to $1 million for their next picture.

Ultimately, the producer and director chose two unknowns and two established actors and came in at $675,000 for the four.

At this point, let us introduce another character in the production—the studio's executive in charge of production, in this case a vice-president. This is standard practice on all major studio productions. The executive in charge of production is placed on the set to watch the budget, offer creative opinions, and generally serve as liaison between the production and the studio back in Hollywood.

During the casting, there was much controversy over the starring role, with the studio demanding a name actor for marquee value and the producer and director bidding for a talented newcomer. Surprisingly, the producer and director won out.

After four frantic months of pre-production, it's off to Mexico.

Principal Photography

The location shooting in Mexico was turbulent. Crowd control was poor and often disrupted the day's schedule. The producer realized that more time should have been spent on selecting locations. One location had to be changed on a day's notice. Many of the local crew were not up to standard. The demands for graft were rife. The director and the DP (director of photography) clashed openly and often. This first-time director seemed to be in over his head.

On the positive side, the weather was beautiful,

not too many people developed "Montezuma's Revenge," and the "dailies" (processed film of the previous day's shooting) looked wonderful. Somehow there was cohesion over all the disparate elements; people in the production and our producer and his team flew back to London four weeks and four days later convinced that they had something good "in the can."

The studio shooting in London was at Twickenham studio just outside the city. The set construction had progressed well, but the production accountants notified the producer that it was over budget by 15 percent. When the shooting started, the director's inexperience and the complexity of the science-fiction plot resulted in many retakes. The studio grudgingly approved an extra week of shooting time. The total over-budget for the picture at the end of principal photography was $825,000. Not too bad if a studio is behind the production, but what happens to the independent production?

When the shooting was finally over, no one could say for sure, but everyone felt confident. For most of the staff and crew, it was goodbye. For the editor, director, and the sound and music people, there was still a long haul.

(Note: For an account of what happens when everything goes wrong, I recommend Steven Bach's excellent book on the Heaven's Gate fiasco, Final Cut, published by William Morrow.)

Post-Production

The producer had allocated six months for this last stage of production. It took seven.

Now a different group of specialists took over, under the close supervision of the director. The editor was the big star of this show. He worked for nine weeks of principal photography and twenty-seven weeks of post-production. His fee was $102,000, not an excessive amount considering his responsibility, for it was his skillful handling of the film that gave the picture its excellent pace. He had two assistants and one apprentice editor. In addition, there were two looping editors, a music editor and assistant, and three sound effects editors and assistants.

Music was a major factor in this production. A name composer scored the picture for a fee of $60,000 plus a share in the revenues from the sound track album. (Involved with the composer in the music process were musicians and an arranger/ orchestrator.) As we have seen more and more lately, a successful sound track album can boost a movie's "box office" and vice versa. Also, a music video from this album was used as a promotional tool.

Post-production sound and film-lab work are important aspects of this final stage of a production, which culminates in an "answer print" (the final master from which other prints are made and distributed to theaters across the country and overseas).

In our case, the studio's decision was to distribute the picture "wide." This meant the distribution of 1,100 prints at a cost of about $2 million.

During this six-month post-production period, our friend the producer has not exactly been sitting on the beach in Hawaii. He had extensive meetings with the studio brass on advertising, promotion, and marketing. He realized in these meetings that although he's the producer, the final decision on the advertising campaign for the movie belongs to the studio. It's the studio's money.

The studio decided to commit $5 million for advertising, not an insubstantial figure for a picture of this kind. The money was to be spent primarily on TV, radio, and newspaper advertising. Of course, if the movie had opened poorly the first weekend, the studio might have cut back on its commitment. However, the prevailing theory on a wide release of this kind is to pour out the advertising in the first weekend—to "take the money and run," in case the movie does not have "legs" (staying power).

(*Note:* Reviews, either positive or negative, do not seem to have an effect on youth-oriented pictures. As we'll see a little later in this chapter, young people just go to movies. For them, word of mouth is what counts—and you can't manipulate it.)

In addition to working with the advertising and marketing staff, the producer met regularly with the studio's domestic and foreign distribution people. These executives are consummate professionals who know all the nuances of how to distribute a picture, down to the selection of appropriate theaters for this particular picture. Again, the producer voiced opinion but deferred to the distribution people for decisions.

The producer also sat in on meetings regarding ancillary marketing; that is, records, TV, cable, merchandising, plus the new giant, videocassettes.

Another activity that took much of his time before the release date was attending screenings of the picture. This procedure has become quite scientific. By holding statistical screenings in various test cities for specialized audiences—with cards given out for qualitative analysis—the producer, director, and studio executives are still able to alter the film before it is released.

The producer was also involved in the public relations campaign. While the studio's people go

through this exercise fifteen or more times a year, each producer has his own thoughts about how PR should be handled, which is usually contradictory to the studio's PR program.

Finally, on a Friday in early August, the picture was released. For our hero the producer, it was more than two years of immense effort. He had seen the picture so often he'd lost all his perspective. He didn't know if it was good or not and in his weariness seemed not to care—he just wanted it to be over.

At a final private screening for studio execs, cast, and their families, the director and producer embraced warmly and said things like, "Let's do another picture together." They didn't.

The producer, who lives in New York, spent the whole first weekend of the picture's release tramping from theater to theater to catch the audiences' reactions. The Times Square area seemed to have the longest lines, but that didn't mean much. The picture had to do well all over the country.

Epilogue: After speaking to the studio's head of distribution a week after the opening, the producer was told the picture opened well. It had box-office gross receipts of $3 million, but would it have "legs"?

With this in mind, the producer went to the beach for a short vacation, his first in two and a half years. The picture ran through the end of September. By the time school started, it fizzed. Its domestic take totaled $28 million. It did fair business in the foreign market. It wasn't until two years after its U.S. release that the producer, director, and screenwriter began receiving checks for their share of the picture's profits—and not big ones at that.

By then, the producer was in development on another picture, this one about robots. The director had already completed a successful comedy, and the screenwriter had sold two more scripts, neither of which were in production.

A Typical Movie Budget

We have just traced the steps required in making a movie. Now we will document a budget for a movie with a total cost of just over $9 million, similar to the one we have just discussed. We will also analyze each of the budget items.

"Above the Line" refers to all nonproduction

items, "Below the Line" to people and services involved in the actual production phase. The account numbers refer to standards for each category and are used for compiling U.S. budgets.

Budgets for U.S. productions have a standard format. They vary a great deal from those in England. An understanding of a real budget will give the reader an insight into the makeup of the production.

First, see the the "Top Sheet" of a Production Budget. Now for an explanation of each budget line item:

- *Story, rights and continuity:* The screenwriter's fees plus the cost of the original story.
- *Producers unit:* The fees for the producer, executive producer, and their secretaries.
- *Direction:* The fees for the director and dance director and assistants. The director was paid $400,000.
- *Cast:* This picture was shot primarily on location. The line item includes the two stars and two other leads, the supporting cast, day players, stunt men, overtime, and the casting director. One star was paid $1.5 million.
- *Travel and living costs:* This included the cost from the United States to the location, plus the living allowance while there.
- *Fringe benefits and payroll taxes:* As the wording implies.
- *Production staff:* The fees for the unit production manager, assistants, first assistant director, second assistant director, script supervisors, dialogue coach, production secretaries, and miscellaneous costs.
- *Extra talent:* Extras, stand-ins, and piano player.
- *Set design:* Production designer, art director, draftsmen, model makers, sketch artists, buyers, and purchases.
- *Set construction:* Construction coordinator, purchases, and rentals.
- *Set striking:* Labor, materials, and the like.
- *Set operations:* Grips (individuals who move equipment and dollies and do carpentry) were paid $900/week on location; greensmen, painters, laborers, and outside rentals.
- *Special effects:* Labor, manufacturing, rigging, and rentals.
- *Property:* Property master, props, set-dressers, laborers, animals, picture vehicles, and studio charges.
- *Men's wardrobe:* Labor and purchases.
- *Makeup and hairdressing:* Makeup artist (came from the United States and was paid $2,000/week for eleven weeks), hairdressers, wigs, and purchases.
- *Lighting:* Rigging crew, gaffer (chief electrician),

Account	Description	$ Budget
1100	Story, rights, and conti-nuity	480,000
1200	Producers unit	590,000
1300	Direction	457,000
1400	Cast	2,042,000
1500	Travel and living costs	259,000
1700	Fringe benefits and payroll taxes	122,000
	Above the Line	**$3,950,000**
2000	Production staff	290,000
2100	Extra talent	188,000
2200	Set design	105,000
2300	Set construction	375,000
2400	Set striking	41,000
2500	Set operations	182,000
2600	Special effects	102,000
2800	Property	165,000
2900	Men's wardrobe	115,000
3100	Makeup & hairdressing	65,000
3200	Lighting	152,000
3300	Camera	127,000
3400	Production sound	37,000
3500	Transportation	428,000
3600	Location	1,047,000
3700	Production film and laboratory	106,000
4000	Second unit	302,000
4200	Miscellaneous production expense	81,000
4300	Production period fringe benefit	397,000
	Production Budget	**$4,305,000**
4500	Film editing	195,000
4600	Music	142,000
4700	Post-production sound	92,000
4800	Post-production film and laboratory	73,000
4900	Main and end titles	13,000
5000	First domestic trailer	20,000
5200	Post-production fringe benefits	62,000
	Post-Production Budget	**$597,000**
6500	Publicity	13,000
6700	Insurance	176,000
6800	General expense	78,000
	Other Costs	267,000
	Below the Line	**$5,169,000**
	Grand Total	**$9,119,000**

best boy (assistant electrician), laborers, purchases, and rentals.

- *Camera:* First cameraman (director of photography) was paid $3,000/week; camera operators, loaders, machinists, purchases, and rentals.
- *Production sound:* Recording crew, boom operator, purchases, and rentals.
- *Transportation:* Studio drivers.
- *Location:* Fares, site rentals, fees, permits, lodging, meals, shipping and forwarding costs, first aid, telephone and telegraph, accountants, security, and special equipment.
- *Production film and laboratory:* Negative film and developing, and printing dailies and stills.
- *Second unit:* Director, rentals, production staff, set operations, special effects, property, wardrobe, makeup and hairdressing, camera, transportation, lodging, catering, and overtime.
- *Miscellaneous production expense:* Outside stage rentals, rehearsal rooms, and staff.
- *Production period fringe benefit:* As the wording implies.
- *Film editing:* Editors ($2,500/week), production editors, assistant editors, music effects editors and assistants, sound effects editors, coding, projection, equipment rentals, shipping, projection rooms, and studio charges.
- *Music:* Musicians, composer ($40,000), arrangers, copyists, singers, music rights, and instrument rentals.
- *Post-production sound:* Dubbing crew, scoring crew, looping crew, film stock, rentals, and studio charges.
- *Post-production film and laboratory:* Stock footage, editorial reprints, sound negative, matte shots, answer print, optical manufacture, and negative cutting.
- *Main and end titles:* As the wording implies.
- *First domestic trailer:* What we used to call "coming attractions."
- *Post-production fringe benefits:* As the wording implies.
- *Publicity:* Production publicity person plus secretary/interpreter.
- *Insurance:* Cast insurance.
- *General expense:* Telephone and telegraph, photocopying, postage, executive entertainment, traveling and living expense, preview expense, and studio charges.

Now you know why making movies is so expensive. It takes many people, equipment, vehicles, and a certain amount of waste. This particular picture was budgeted at $9.3 million, so it actually came in under budget.

Who Does What in Making a Film

Here is a list of the key players involved in making a movie.

Producer

Screenwriter

Story Editor

Director

Cinematographer

Production Designer

Art Director

Casting Director

Actors

Editor

Special-Effects Director

Now let's outline their functions.

The Producer

What does a producer do, anyway? Our narrative of a production provided some insight into the role of the producer. Here is a simplified definition: If the director is responsible for all the creative and technical aspects of the film, the producer is responsible for the rest. If a picture goes over budget, it is the producer's responsibility even though it may be the director's fault.

The producer generally originates the project by optioning the literary property and engaging the screenwriter. Then, it is his job to find the money, hire a director, organize the production, and see it through to its completion.

When you see the credit "Executive Producer" on the screen, that generally relates to an individual who either found the property, found the money, or even in some cases delivered the star. The executive producer usually does not have day-to-day duties on the set.

In addition to the producer and executive producer, a production will sometimes have a line producer. This job is performed by a specialist in every phase of production. He will usually come on at the start of pre-production and stay until after principal photography. He must be skilled in budgeting and hiring. Often a line producer is engaged when the producer lacks expertise in the nuts and bolts of making films.

The Screenwriter

We don't think any authoritative poll has been taken on the preference of people wanting to get into the movie business. Clearly the three most popular careers are acting, directing, and screenwriting. From my publishing experience, I know how many would-be writers there are, but lately it seems that almost every writer wants to be a screenwriter.

No need to bemoan the sad state of the writing profession today. A handful of novelists and non-fiction writers can make a living just from writing books and articles. Most writers have teaching or other jobs to sustain themselves. Read any issue of *Writer's Digest* to confirm the reality of this situation.

The Writers Guild of America (WGA): The WGA is the writer's union. The screenwriter is very well paid—when he gets paid. The WGA doesn't provide statistics, but I'm certain that the plight of its average member is as sad as that of his counterpart, the actor in SAG (Screen Actors Guild).

First let's explain all about the WGA. The Writers Guild of America represents writers for film and television. There are approximately 2,900 members in its eastern branch, with headquarters in New York City, and about 6,000 in its western branch, with headquarters in Los Angeles.

Most major studios and medium- and large-size production companies are signatories of the guild, which means that they employ guild members at certain rate minimums and conditions. The employer also agrees to make contributions to the guild's pension, health, and welfare fund on behalf of the writer.

A writer does not have to become a member of the WGA to register a script with it. The guild's registration service assists members and nonmembers in establishing the completion date and the identity of their property. Registration does not confer any statutory protection; it merely provides evidence of the author's prior claim to authorship of the literary material involved and of the date of its completion.

A registration is valid for ten years and may be renewed. The fee is $15,000 for nonmembers. An example of the minimum compensation a WGA member receives for a screenplay is as follows:

Low Budget	(less than $2.5 million)
Screenplay (including treatment)	$24,169
Rewrite of screenplay	9,062
Polish of screenplay	4,533

High Budget	(more than $2.5 million)
Screenplay (including treatment)	$44,944
Rewrite of screenplay	13,814
Polish of screenplay	6,907

As to the meanings of the key terms in the table: a "Treatment" means an adaptation of a story, book, play, or other literary dramatic material for motion picture purposes in a form suitable for use as the basis of a screenplay. "Rewrite" means the writing of significant changes in plot, story line, or interrelationship of characters in a screenplay. "Polish" means the writing of changes in dialogue, narration, or action, but not including a rewrite.

For further information about joining the WGA, write to Writers Guild of America, 8955 Beverly Boulevard, Los Angeles, CA 90048 or to Writers Guild of America, 555 West 57th Street, New York, NY 10019.

From Short Story to Screenplay: Adapting a screenplay from a book or short story is perhaps easier than creating a completely original concept, but it is still extremely difficult. Here is a case in point.

A co-producer and I produced a movie called *Burning Chrome*, to be released in 1988. The short story, by science-fiction writer William Gibson, appeared in *Omni* magazine in July 1982. We optioned the piece and then assigned the screenplay to Scott Roberts, a young English writer who had done one other screenplay prior to this assignment.

The short story is only ten pages in length. It has an interesting futuristic premise about computers but not much more. Roberts delivered a first draft in three months. He had developed the concept far beyond that of the original piece, but it called for a film treatment that was too expensive. Other drafts were written by Roberts, each an improvement on the previous one. By the sixth draft, we had a script that was ready to go.

Many movies are made from original screenplays, but others come from a variety of sources. *National Lampoon's Animal House* came from a short story in *National Lampoon* magazine. *Urban Cowboy* and

Saturday Night Fever also were adapted from magazine stories. *Superman* was originally a comic book. *Ode to Billy Joe* originated as a song. The highly successful *Star Trek* movies are based on a defunct 1960s television series.

Writing and Surviving: In West Hollywood, an area heavily populated with screenwriters, the traffic is in VWs, not in Jags. I recently visited a reasonably successful screenwriter who lives in a $400,000 house in Santa Monica that he had purchased with money from his last screenplay. When I asked him why there were no trees on his property, he replied, "They cost $4,000 each, and I'm waiting until I sell another script."

Most movie writers who had not been discovered take any nine-to-five job to sustain themselves and then write at night and on weekends. This routine can work, but my advice is to save enough money to be able to just write, write, write all day long—this, of course, while seeing hundreds of movies to learn from other people's style.

An important ingredient for a screenwriter's success is a good agent, but getting one is not easy. The big agencies—William Morris, International Creative Management (ICM), and Creative Artists Agency (CAA)—are reluctant to take on young screenwriters without screen credits. There are, however, smaller agencies in Los Angeles and New York that totally understand the writing process and are better able to sell a client's talent to producers and studios than the writer himself.

Sending a treatment or a screenplay "cold" to an agent is unproductive. A better approach is to call the agent for an interview. In this call, the writer is able to display his personality and intellect. At the interview, the writer submits the manuscript and hopes that the agent will find the time to read it. At some agencies, if one agent likes a property, he will pass it on to other agents for their opinions. An alternative method for getting an agent is by recommendation from other writers.

As for unagented manuscripts (those not solicited, assigned, or requested by a studio), they get almost no consideration, because studios are reluctant to read them for fear of legal consequences. Agented or not, however, all manuscripts are read by all studios and production companies in the same way, by using the "reader" system—that is, an in-house or freelance person reads the script, writes a brief synopsis, and passes it along to the story editor for further evaluation.

If a script passes first muster and gets a favorable reaction at a major studio, it may then go to three or four other readers for their evaluation. Then, even if all the readers are positive about it, it still needs salable elements—a name director, stars, an impor-

tant producer—to be made into a motion picture. Sound like an oppressive system? It is.

Many writers in Hollywood write for TV with the dream of greater glory in feature films. Television pays less, but there's much more of it. When the producer of a successful TV series gets a good script, he will be inclined to use that writer often.

The Story Editor

Whether it's a Hollywood major studio, a mini-major, an independent producer, or even a record company such as Geffen or A&M that makes movies, they all have story editors. Depending on the size of the operation, the story editor and his staff of readers read and evaluate all types of submissions; outlines, treatments, or manuscripts for screenplays.

The individual holding this important job must be able to recognize and appreciate good dramatic writing. The story editor must also be thoroughly familiar with the styles and credits of hundreds of writers working in film and TV. This knowledge can be used to best advantage when a studio options a book or magazine piece and seeks a certain kind of writer to adapt the work into screenplay form.

Here is some advice for would-be screenwriters:

- Write screenplays on "spec," that is, without a paid assignment. If you have writing ability and handle dialogue well, your work will be noticed, and you may receive assignments for future projects.
- Next, you can try to send your manuscript directly to a studio executive *if* he first approves your sending it. Remember, though, that he will pass it straight to the story department. Better to send it through an agent, who may get the executive to read it, too.
- If you send an unsolicited manuscript to a studio or production company, it must be accompanied by a legal release. This protects the company from a lawsuit in case it rejects the proposal but later produces a movie using the same theme.
- Summer writing programs can also be helpful because they offer professional evaluation. A partial listing of these programs can be found in this book in the chapter on magazines. Film schools (discussed later in this chapter) involve a major commitment to the medium and should be given careful consideration.

One must use caution in recommending anyone to a career as precarious as screenwriting. Few succeed. The rewards for those few may be great, but what about all those who don't?

For an account of the woes and travails of a Hollywood screenwriter, I recommend William Goldman's excellent book *Adventures in the Screen Trade* (Warner Books).

The Director

Long before the *auteur* theory crept into our movie language, there were directors, and they were important. They seemed less important in the past because movie audiences were star-oriented, and critics did not articulate the nuances of directing.

Today, there are very few stars in the classic sense, even though many actors have achieved this status by virtue of their monumental fees. Meryl Streep, for example, is a very talented performer who has had judicious counsel in choosing her roles and has worked with excellent directors. These directors have been an important factor in her success. The charismatic rock star Sting has had a number of acting stints without much success. It was only when he played himself in the documentary *Bring on the Night*, and worked with the fine director Michael Apted that he came into his own as an actor. Or again, in the same genre, consider how Jonathan Demme elevated the level of concert films in David Byrne's *Stop Making Sense*.

One thinks of the accomplishments of the giant directors Fellini, Bergman, Antonioni, David Lean, and John Huston. Yet look at the film *Flashdance:* Adrian Lyne took a small story, cast it with unknowns, and directed a very successful picture that was brilliantly slick and visually exciting.

We are in an era of the director as king. We have hundreds of interchangeable actors. Only a handful are "box office." There are few innovative screenplays. It is the skilled director who can wade through the sea of mediocrity and come out on top of the wave.

The director is the creative leader. He directs not only the actors but also the camera, lighting, and sound people. He is responsible for the look of the picture and therefore supervises the activity of the designers as well.

How does a director learn his craft? Many, but certainly not all, go to film school. Others start out as editors and cameramen. Many have progressed from crew members to assistant directors and then finally won the support of producers who gave them their chance. Then, too, a number of directors started out as actors—like Ron Howard, Anthony Perkins, and Dennis Hopper.

The director of a $13 million or a $1.3 million picture must be in total charge. He can't wing it. He must make split-second decisions all day, every day,

for ten weeks or more during the shooting period, and keep his huge team together in one cohesive unit.

The Directors Guild of America (DGA): The DGA is the director's union. The DGA also has jurisdiction over unit production managers, first assistant directors, and second assistant directors. It covers TV as well as films.

There are 8,000 members of the DGA, of which 55 percent are directors; the rest are in other specialties. Of the 4,400 directors, many are employed as such for TV commercials and TV sports and entertainment programs. According to a recent listing, about 350 of these DGA directors are women.

The requirement for DGA membership is employment on a job with a signatory company and a $5,000 fee. (A signatory company is a production company that agrees to abide by all DGA contract terms.) In addition, the requirements for employment for each of the specialties in the DGA include a qualification test and a fixed minimum number of days of employment in similar work.

The DGA also has a trainee program for a very limited number of talented people. An information sheet on this coveted program is available on request. Write to DGA (East), 110 West 57th Street, New York, NY 10019 or to DGA (West) Training Program, 14144 Ventura Boulevard, Sherman Oaks, CA 91423.

Examples of DGA directors' weekly salaries as of this writing are as follows:

- Low Budget (less than $500,000): $4,136
- Medium Budget ($500,000 to $1,500,000): $4,700
- High Budget (more than $1,500,000): $6,580

These are minimum fees. A contemporary woman director who did two films, one a critical success, was paid $500,000 for her third picture. Journeymen directors on $5 to $10 million features are seldom paid less than $250,000. At least ten top directors are paid $1 million or more per picture.

Here are some examples of other DGA weekly salaries.

	Studio	Location
Unit production manager	$1,879	$2,631
First assistant director	1,785	2,479
Key second assistant director	1,196	1,671
Second assistant	1,129	1,579
Additional second assistant	689	965

The DGA conducts workshops and seminars. Here are some that were given by the New York branch recently.

- Master class in directing: an advanced workshop exploring such elements of the director's cinematic craft as interpretation, characterization, movement, and style
- Introduction to videotape production: a workshop focusing on multiple-camera talk shows
- *Star Trek III:* a writer-producer's perspective on the making of a major motion picture
- The assistant director and single camera production: includes an introduction to script breakdown and scheduling, location surveys, location planning, and script revisions

The Cinematographer

Some call him the cinematographer, others the DP (director of photography), still others simply the cameraman. He works under the director and with him is responsible for the look and lighting of each scene.

He selects the camera and lighting equipment for the production. On a feature film, although he does not operate the camera, he engages and supervises the camera crew—a camera operator, a first assistant, and a second assistant, or loader—and the lighting crew.

Cameramen need training, particularly to handle today's sophisticated equipment. Film schools offer excellent professional training. Apprentice work on documentaries and industrial films, where the union requirements are not as stringent as those on features, are good steps on the upward ladder.

Those planning a career in film camera work should consider as essential training the study of the work of such cameramen greats as James Wong Howe (*Funny Lady*), Haskell Wexler in documentaries (*Medium Cool*), and in feature films today, Caleb Deschanel (*The Black Stallion*) and David Watkin (*Catch-22*). A DP on a $10 million budget feature will earn about $60,000, a camera operator about $27,000.

The Set Designer and Art Director

I have been around magazine art directors all my professional life, but I really didn't know or appreciate what art directors do in films until I became involved in the animated feature *Heavy Metal*, which was produced in Canada.

We had dozens of characters that had to be visualized. The picture had a $9 million budget, so we were seeking highly developed production values. Mike Gross, an art director who worked for us on the *National Lampoon* magazine, was our production designer. He decided that because the closest thing to an animated movie is a comic strip, it would be smart to get the best people from that medium and have them do all the character visualizations.

We brought a talented Spanish artist, Juan Gimenez, to Ottawa to work with one of our units there. He was supposed to stay for three weeks—we kept him for three months. Gross also recruited two well-known New York–based comic-strip artists, Howard Chaykin and Neal Adams, to do other visualizations.

The result of their efforts was a long series of heavily detailed drawings in full color that served as a guide for the animators. We also created hundreds of beautifully executed background drawings. When we needed a spaceship, we drew an authentic one. When we needed a futuristic night club, we simply drew it.

Live-action film uses drawings to a certain extent, but most backgrounds must be built. (See section on special effects later in this chapter.) In the '30s and '40s, when we saw a western, the producer simply used the "Last Chance Bar & Grill" set on the studio's back lot, dressed it up a bit, changed the "Frank Jones, Prop." sign, and audiences thought it was all very authentic.

These days, pictures are either shot on locations where the whole environment has to be created, or a set has to be built, designed, and decorated on a sound stage.

On feature films, the budget for this phase of the production can run into the millions. On industrial films and documentaries, where budgets may be a fraction of what they are on features, the designer's ingenuity is challenged to come up with the same degree of realism.

The production designer and art director (often the same individual) are entrusted with the function of carrying out the producer and director's concept of the "look" of the film. This function includes designing the sets and working with the set construction people and set decorator. These are multi-talented people with a great deal of training. They are paid well, but, as with other phases of film, only when they're working.

There is seldom a situation where a brilliant designer comes out of art school and immediately gets a job as art director on a $10 million movie. There is always the need for on-the-job training. One can, however, gain valuable experience in scenic design by working in college theater or in summer stock and regional theater.

To better appreciate the "look" of a film, consider what it took to create the eighteenth-century environment in *Amadeus,* or colonial India in *Passage to India,* or the Russia of *Reds* (not shot in Russia). The accomplishments of these designers are sheer genius.

The Casting Directors

Those of us who pay attention to the credits on a feature film have noticed the line "Casting by . . ." Casting directors are very talented people who perform a distinct and integral function for the producer and director of a feature film. They operate in the following fashion.

A producer engages a casting director for a given number of weeks at either a flat rate or on a weekly basis. The usual range is $5,000 to $6,000 per week, but the figure depends on the number of roles the director has to cast.

The casting director reads the script carefully and meets with the director and producer to get their perspective on how the picture should be cast. The casting director then prepares a cast breakdown, which contains about fifty to sixty words describing each role. After this is approved by the producer and director, the casting director begins her (more women than men in this field) search.

The casting director and her staff rely on an encyclopedic photographic memory of actors. Looking at a cast breakdown, their minds immediately focus in on many actors, including those they might have seen as much as a year prior in a bit part. Of course, the producer, director, and studio all play an active role in the casting procedure. Often they give the casting director a "wish list," which contains a number of stars or name actors desired for each role.

In addition, they scan all the casting guides and submit the cast breakdown to talent agents and personal managers all over the country. They then call in likely prospects, screen them down to a limited number of actors per role, and ultimately hold auditions, readings, and, at times, screen tests for the director and producer.

Once the selections are made, it is the casting director's function to consummate financial arrangements with the actors and their agents— within the guidelines of the budget. The arrangements with stars are generally made by the producer and/or the studio.

Casting directors also work for TV productions and commercials, although some specialize in one medium only. Most maintain offices in Los Angeles or New York City; some have offices in both cities and travel between the two locations. There is no particular educational training for the job. To be qualified one should love movies and have a great eye and ear for talent. Casting directors are paid from $3,000 to $5,500 per week for their efforts, which may run six to eight weeks on a major feature.

Although casting is a very creative activity integral to the film-production process, it does not employ a large number of people. We therefore do not give it a high career priority in films.

The Actor

At any one time, 80 percent of the 55,000 members of SAG, the Screen Actors Guild, are out of work. Want more? Fifteen percent of SAG's members earn 90 percent of all acting revenues in any one year. We don't have statistics on how many SAG members are waiters and receptionists.

Earlier in this chapter, we referred to a statistic saying that only 200,000 people were employed in the whole feature film industry, including ticket takers. Then what percentage are working actors? Not a very high one, we will answer. So is it worth the try? No, we will swiftly reply. You're not convinced.

Movie stars have always been our most glamorous people. Athletes and rock stars get heavy press coverage and make lots of money, but they can't rival movie actors for the public's adulation.

Then there's money. According to a recent piece in *People* magazine, here's what some of our movie stars have made per picture:

Sylvester Stallone	$12,000,000
Robert Redford	6,000,000
Dustin Hoffman	6,000,000
Warren Beatty	6,000,000
Barbra Streisand	5,000,000
Dolly Parton	4,000,000
Meryl Streep	3,000,000
Debra Winger	2,000,000
Jessica Lange	2,000,000
Sean Penn	1,250,000
Madonna	1,000,000

The last-named, Madonna, was paid the million for *Shanghai Surprise,* which was not successful. Before she made this picture, she had played a small role in *Desperately Seeking Susan.* Eddie Murphy was still in his mid-twenties when he commanded an $8 million fee for *Beverly Hills Cop II.* Redford was paid the $6 million for his role in *Out of Africa.*

When you see it on screen you'll never guess it's not real. Here Michael Pangrazio, matte artist, puts the finishing touches on a painting of the Nepalese village seen in *Raiders of the Lost Ark*. (Courtesy of Lucasfilm Ltd. © Lucasfilm Ltd. [LFL] 1981. All rights reserved.)

Could these enormous fees be the motivating factor? Perhaps, yes. The publicity, certainly. Reduced to the simplest level, acting is a lot more fun than working in an office or pumping gas.

A well-known actor once said that there are few jobs in the movie industry—so few that, for every 150 people, there is maybe one job. In my opinion, that's a conservative estimate.

So there. If, however, we have not deterred a single would-be actor from the lawful pursuit of his career, we might as well be constructive and offer this advice:

- Act in school plays at college, where the direction is sometimes on a professional level.
- After graduation, consider a good acting school like New York City's Neighborhood Playhouse. The Neighborhood Playhouse was the training ground for such important film actors as Tony Randall, Gregory Peck, James Caan, Joanne Woodward, Diane Keaton, and Jeff Goldblum. It offers a two-year, full-time program in acting, with training in dance, speech, and voice. Only those students whose work is approved unanimously by the faculty are admitted for the second year. The Playhouse also offers a six-week summer program. If interested, write to the school at 340 East 54th Street, New York, NY 10022.
- Get a professional set of photographs.
- Act in summer stock; some of these companies are excellent training grounds.
- Use any contact you can to get a good agent.
- Act in little-theater groups or in off-off-Broadway productions. There is always the chance of being spotted by producers and casting directors.
- Go on all casting calls even if they seem hopeless and demeaning.

The Screen Actors Guild (SAG): One must get an acting job on a production that is under SAG's jurisdiction in order to join SAG. If a producer wishes to hire SAG actors, he must sign a guild agreement, thus giving SAG jurisdiction over the entire production. Employers of SAG

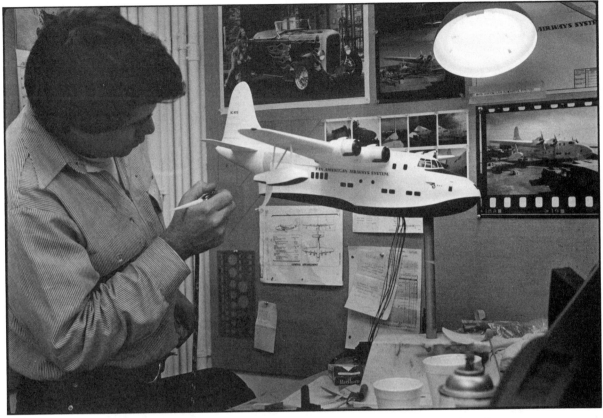

Modelmaking is a major aspect of special effects. Here Mike Fulmer works on a model of a Pan Am clipper for *Raiders of the Lost Ark*. It's a lot cheaper than locating and shooting the real thing. (Courtesy of Lucasfilm Ltd. © Lucasfilm Ltd. [LFL] 1981. All rights reserved.)

members are obligated to make a percentage contribution to SAG's health, dental, and retirement program.

SAG's membership dues vary according to the income of the member. New members currently pay an initiation fee of $63.50, which includes the $37.50-minimum semiannual dues. The fortunate SAG member who earns more than $100,000 a year pays semiannual dues of $575.00. SAG's two mailing addresses are: 7065 Hollywood Boulevard, Hollywood, CA 90028 and 1700 Broadway, 18th floor, New York, NY 10019.

Members of SAG regularly visit the guild offices for postings of registered productions. The posting will give the name of the production, director, and production manager; the names of the casting directors for principals and extras; the start date; and the length of the picture's shooting schedule.

SAG has a very fine program called "Conservatory" as support for its member actors. A member pays $25.00 a year for this valuable service. Conservatory is the most active and popular organiza-

tion within the SAG–New York framework. Here are some recent programs:

- A seminar on the contract between actor and agent
- A workshop discussion of the Alexander technique for body balance and alignment
- A joint SAG/AFTRA (American Federation of Television and Radio Artists) seminar entitled "Focus on Film," with directors and casting directors on hand to answer questions
- "From Film to Soap," an in-depth examination dealing with the transitions necessary for a performer adapting techniques for television

The Editor

After each day's shooting of a movie, the film is processed, and the "dailies" are viewed. Dailies are the positive prints of the director's choice of the numerous "takes" of each scene. Takes are the actual filming of scenes with actors. A director will usually do a number of takes of each scene written in the script. This is part of the "principal photography" phase.

Although the editor has been screening the dailies during principal photography, his work really begins during post-production. It is his job to cut and splice all these fragments into a finely woven story. To a lesser extent, then, the job is a technical one, and most feature-film editors possess these technical skills in abundance. The timing, pace, and creative demands of the editing process, however, are what separate the mere technician from the artist.

Feature films are not the only market for this talent. Editing is used in documentaries, industrial films, shorts, music videos, TV commercials, and TV news. Consequently, this work is available all over the country.

Since editing videotape is much less complex than editing film, one can gain valuable experience by editing tape and thus preparing for work on film. Experience can be gained as well by becoming an editorial-room assistant, then branching out after an apprentice period.

Editors work long hours under stressful and sometimes lonely conditions, but the job pays well. We certainly characterize film editing as a rewarding profession.

The Special Effects Director

In films, when we see a city destroyed in an earthquake or a spaceship flying over the Pentagon, those are special effects. When we see actors on sound stages in Hollywood performing in locales thousands of miles distant, those are special effects.

Audiences today have come to expect brilliance in this area of film-making—small wonder, with such "monsters" as *2001: A Space Odyssey*, *Alien* (and its sequel, *Aliens*), *Star Wars*, *Close Encounters of the Third Kind*, *Raiders of the Lost Ark*, and dozens of others in the science-fiction and fantasy genre.

Special effects in films are not a recent phenomenon. A Frenchman, Georges Melies, used glass shots as early as 1905. Norman Dawn used them in 1907. A glass shot employs a technique where replacement details are painted on a sheet of glass that is positioned between the camera and the live-action scene.

Today, special effects can be photographic (sometimes called visual or optical), mechanical, or computer generated. (A good example of this last

category can be seen in the film *Tron*.) The magicians of special effects ("FX" in the business) employ a broad variety of techniques from simple matte drawings (usually used to simulate backgrounds for live-action scenes) to split-screen photography, to miniaturization, to computer transformations. One need only study the work on film of special effects giant Doug Trumbull in Stanley Kubrick's *2001* to become aware of this creative process.

Special effects are used in feature films, TV commercials, animated films, and TV productions. The film industry employs a diverse group of technicians in this specialty, including matte painters, computer specialists, cameramen, and even sculptors.

Effects directors on high-budget action or sci-fi pictures are paid as much as cinematographers. Other special effects technicians are paid about $1,300 or $1,400 per week.

Most film schools, undergraduate or graduate, offer courses in special effects. (See the section on film schools later in this chapter.) With new advances, especially in the computer effects area, this specialty is a challenging one.

The Mighty Majors

Earlier in this chapter, in our narrative rendition of a feature production experience, we referred to the eight major studios. The majors are most filmmakers' favorite villains. We've all read hundreds of magazine and newspaper pieces about how the studios are run by lawyers and accountants with no taste. One may conclude that if they were run by high-minded independent filmmakers, we would see 200 *Out of Africa*s and no schlock horror pictures or slob comedies. That, however, is not the reality.

Those of us who understand the economic realities know that if an average picture costs $12 or $13 million, we're going to need the majors, with their financing capabilities and their marketing and distribution networks; and because most studios are owned by conglomerates, we're going to have M.B.A. types in charge.

As many of our readers who go into feature films will either work for, or be involved with, the majors in some way, we think an understanding of who they are and how they function is productive. These are the eight major studios: Columbia Pictures, MGM, Paramount Pictures, 20th Century–Fox, United Artists, Universal Pictures, Walt Disney Pictures, and Warner Bros.

Columbia is owned by the Coca-Cola Company. Paramount is owned by the Gulf & Western conglomerate, Universal by MCA, and Warner Bros. by Warner Communications. Fox is owned by Rupert Murdoch.

On a slightly lower level than the majors are these mini-majors: Orion, Lorimar/Telepictures, Tri-star, and the De Laurentiis Entertainment Group.

How the Majors Function

Although the majors are referred to as studios, only MGM, Paramount, Fox, and Universal have their own studios with sound stages and full production facilities. Columbia and Warner Bros. share studio facilities in Burbank, California.

However, this does not mean that all their pictures are shot on their own lots. In fact, very few are. The picture we detailed earlier in this chapter was shot on location and in an independent studio in London. Post-production was done in the studio's facilities in Hollywood.

Unlike the olden days when the studios' back lots were humming with feature film activity, these days TV production is the primary activity. Almost all the majors are knee-deep in TV activity, producing sitcoms, dramatic shows, and made-for-TV movies.

In addition to producing TV shows, the majors are active in the burgeoning field of videocassettes, known in the industry as "home video." Universal and Warner Bros. are also involved in the record business.

The majors each produce twelve to fourteen pictures a year. They distribute an additional ten or twelve pictures for independent producers. In most of the latter situations, the major gives the independent producer a cash advance upon delivery of the print. The major studio will usually commit an agreed amount of money for prints and advertising. All these monies, plus the studio's distribution fee, must be recouped by the studio before the independent producer begins to see new money.

On a picture actually produced by a major studio, the financial arrangement is quite another thing. In this case, an outside producer, often with offices on the studio's premises, will enter into a partnership with the studio whereby each entity owns half the picture. The studio provides the financing and exercises fiscal and creative authority for the picture.

There is an argument to be made for each approach. The producer should have excellent guidance before entering into a distribution or a production arrangement.

The Table of Organization of a Typical Major Studio

So, after all we've said, do you still want to get a job at a studio? And later, when you're about thirty-two, perhaps become an independent producer and make "quality" films? The accompanying illustration (page 212) shows how a major studio's organizational chart might look.

Corporate Division. In most situations, the chairman and chief executive officer and the president of the parent company are housed here. Although this division has authority over the others, we have shown them as equals. Within the corporate division are such housekeeping functions as finance, administration, and legal.

Theatrical Production. As we have discussed, when a studio actually produces a picture, whether it is on its lot or not, the production falls into this division. It is generally headed by a president, with a number of VPs. The business affairs department has the responsibility of making all the agreements that are a part of production.

Theatrical Distribution. These people maintain relationships and sell the exhibitors (theater owners) their various feature film product. Again, this division is run by a president.

Theatrical Marketing. The areas of advertising, promotion, and public relations are managed by this department, which is headed by a president.

Network TV Production and Video Distribution. This important division develops and produces TV programming. In some companies, it is as important as theatrical production. The division is also responsible for producing made-for-TV movies and distribution of videocassettes for the home video market.

International Distribution. These people sell pictures and TV shows that the company produces to the foreign market. As we have mentioned, they also sell products produced elsewhere.

Studio Division. The people in this division are charged with operations of the studio and its post-production facilities.

Although movie studios do not employ contract actors, directors, and producers—the custom in the '30s and '40s—they still employ hundreds of people in the activities described here.

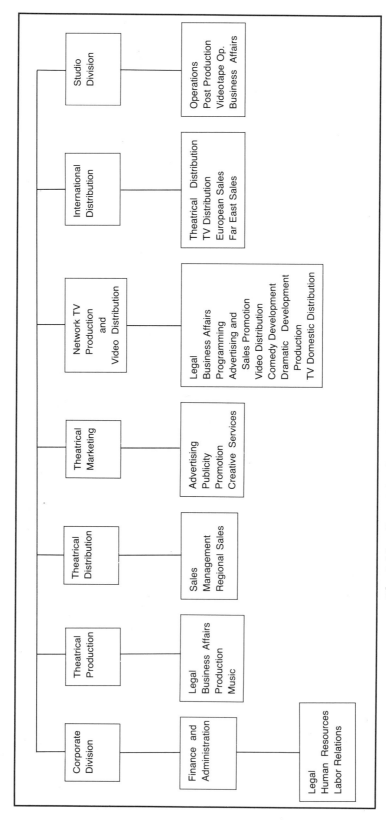

The table of organization of a typical Hollywood major studio.

Distribution, Marketing, and Public Relations

Distribution

Let's first discuss the distribution process. When a picture is completed, it must somehow find its way to the nation's theaters and, ultimately, to distributors and theaters all over the world. If a picture is produced by one of the eight major studios, the studio is responsible for its worldwide distribution. The producer has relatively little input in this process. For a fixed commission fee, studios will also distribute films they did not produce. When one of the mighty majors does not distribute a picture, there is a second level of domestic distributors that can handle the distribution as efficiently as the majors. These include Orion, Samuel Goldwyn, and New World. Many of these operate in the foreign market as well. In addition, there are organizations that sell only to foreign markets.

The key to effective domestic distribution is first to have a good distribution strategy and second to have "muscle." There are large chains of exhibitors (theater owners), some controlling a thousand screens. Obviously, the exhibitors will favor a big picture from a major distributor because they know it will be backed by a multimillion-dollar advertising campaign. They also know that the majors will be distributing twenty-five to thirty pictures a year and that they need this output to fill their theaters.

The exhibitors employ film buyers. The distributors have field salespeople and managers who call on the buyers. The field people also get involved with promotions and advertising campaigns.

In the foreign sales area, there are three major convocations bringing producers and distributors from all over the world: the well-publicized Cannes Film Festival, Mifed in Milan, and the American Film Market in Los Angeles. Hundreds of screenings are put on at these festivals for the benefit of buyers. A promising picture can sell all its world rights at one festival.

There is a rapid turnover in distribution field people, offering a good entry-level opportunity for those desiring employment in this area. Top distribution executives have gone on to run film studios.

Marketing

People in the film biz call it "ad-pub." They're referring to those individuals who plan advertising and publicity campaigns for pictures. Their function is extremely vital to a movie's distribution.

A campaign first involves the "trailer" (we used to call them "coming attractions"), which appears prior to a picture's screening. Trailers will sometimes run for a few months before a picture's release. They are often seductive and, in many instances, better than the picture itself. Trailers are sometimes cut by the picture's director. These days there are production companies that specialize in producing trailers.

After the trailer portion of the campaign, the ad-pub people concentrate on the test screenings. Here the picture gets its first critical audience reaction. The producer and director often attend these screenings along with studio brass. Changes, such as cutting a whole scene, using voice-overs as a narrative device, or partially altering the sound track, can still be made as a result of audience reaction. When new scenes have to be shot, it gets very expensive. In addition, the ad-pub people can get a final fix on the direction of their ad campaign.

If you plan to work in ad-pub, college courses in marketing and business will be helpful. A stint at an ad agency working on entertainment-industry clients is also good training. Salaries in ad-pub at the studio or production-company level are about the same as they are at the agencies. Beginners will start at about $15,000 to $17,000 a year, going to $22,000 to $25,000 in two to three years.

Ad-pub works with major advertising agencies and also with smaller boutique agencies that specialize in movie advertising. Television, radio, billboards, magazines, and newspapers are all used to advertise a picture. Specialized buys are made— "Saturday Night Live" for a comedy or MTV for a music-oriented picture like *Flashdance* or *Footloose*.

Every element of the campaign is significant. Much attention is given to the key art on the movie's poster. Artists have received as much as $25,000 for movie art. This art is used in print ads as well.

Public Relations

Months before a picture's release, the public relations staff is busy arranging trade publicity and magazine or newspaper stories that will break on the movie's release. For a picture I produced, Columbia Pictures arranged a large press breakfast the day before the picture's release. The media were given press kits and the opportunity to interview key people on the production.

On a big picture with stars, the PR staff arranges interviews on major talk shows. If handled effec-

Sometimes the job of the studio's promotional people is all fun. Universal Pictures promoted *National Lampoon's Animal House* in 1978 with a special screening at the book industry's ABA convention in Atlanta. This helped spread the word about the picture a full two months before its release. The ladies pictured here handed out invitations at the convention hall. The very successful movie also helped sales of a tie-in book published by *National Lampoon* and Universal Pictures' book division. (Courtesy National Lampoon, Inc.)

tively, this form of promotion can be more productive than advertising and is a lot cheaper.

College marketing majors, M.B.A.s, or people in entry-level jobs at advertising agencies would be wise to investigate jobs in ad-pub. The field pays well and has excellent upward mobility within the industry.

Business Affairs

When a studio commissions a screenwriter to write a treatment for a screenplay, the studio's business affairs department negotiates the deal, draws the contract, and then consummates it with the screenwriter's agent, manager, or lawyer.

When a small movie distributor agrees to distribute a picture for a small independent producer, the distributor's business affairs department (sometimes only one person) finalizes the deal with the independent producer.

Business affairs departments are staffed and run by shrewd negotiators, usually lawyers. For the independent producer, or anyone else for that matter, negotiating with a major studio's business affairs people can be a most frustrating experience because they usually hold all the cards.

Here, too, as in other phases of filmmaking, business affairs employs a limited number of people. Lawyers interested in the field can also seek opportunities in the general area of entertainment law.

214

Paramount Pictures Corporation

NEWS RELEASE

FOR IMMEDIATE RELEASE

JOHN HUGHES' "FERRIS BUELLER'S DAY OFF" OPENS TO $8,528,068 IN 5 DAYS

Paramount's second release of the summer, "Ferris Bueller's Day Off," has grossed $6,275,647 in its initial weekend of national release, it was announced today by Barry London, President, Distribution and Marketing for the Motion Picture Group of Paramount Pictures Corporation.

Playing on 1,330 screens in the United States and Canada, "Ferris Bueller's Day Off" opened on Wednesday (11), bringing the first five days boxoffice gross to an accumulative figure of $8,528,068.

The second John Hughes film under his pact with Paramount, "Ferris Bueller's Day Off" is also the second consecutive boxoffice success--the first being "Pretty in Pink," released earlier this year by Paramount, with a $39 million gross to date. "Ferris Bueller's Day Off" marks the biggest debut for a John Hughes film.

Starring Matthew Broderick in the title role, "Ferris Bueller's Day Off" is the story of one man's struggle to take it easy. Written and directed by John Hughes, with Michael Chinich as executive producer and John Hughes and Tom Jacobson as producers, the film also stars Alan Ruck, Mia Sara and Jeffrey Jones.

"Ferris Bueller's Day Off" is distributed in the United States and Canada by the Motion Picture Group of Paramount Pictures Corporation, a member of The Entertainment Group of Gulf+Western Inc.

061686   -0-   Printed in USA

1 Gulf+Western Plaza, New York, New York 10023 (212)-333-4600

A typical press release sent out to various industry sources. On a hit picture such as this one, Paramount is boasting about the strong opening. Follow-up releases are sent out by the studio's public relations department if the high grosses continue. (Courtesy Paramount Pictures.)

Who Goes to the Movies?

Many of the readers of this book are young people, college age and above, with an interest in mass communications. In the beginning of this chapter, we talked about how young people are running the motion picture industry. There is very good reason for this. Young people are the movie audience, and who can relate to them better than their peers?

The following striking statistics have been developed by the Motion Picture Association of America.

As you can see from Table 1, the bulk of motion picture admissions continues to be generated by those moviegoers under age forty, accounting for 85 percent of total yearly admissions.

Age groups showing the greatest discrepancy between proportions of yearly admissions and proportion in the population are as shown in Table 2. The total number of moviegoers age twelve and over moderately increased by 4 percent from 115 million in 1984 to 119.2 million in 1985.

The frequency of attendance statistics are as shown in Table 3. Here, frequent moviegoers constitute only 23 percent of the public age twelve and over but continue to account for 82 percent of admissions.

These data make the preponderance of youth-oriented films understandable. Videocassettes have chipped away at movie attendance, but not substantially at those moviegoers under age thirty.

Why There Are So Many Bad Movies

A few years ago I had the opportunity to arrange the financing for a wonderful script by talented writer/director John Sayles (*Return of the Secaucus Seven, Lianna, Baby It's You*) on a significant piece of Americana, the Chicago Black Sox baseball scandal of 1919. John was to direct, and the relatively low-budget picture was to be produced by the talented producers of *Desperately Seeking Susan*, Midge Sanford and Sarah Pillsbury (see interview at end of this chapter).

Studio after studio and dozens of financial sources acclaimed the screenplay only to turn down the project with statements like "It's a great story, but you know baseball is a no-no." When we mentioned *The Natural*, they explained that the only reason it was made was that Robert Redford wanted to do it. We worked very hard to overcome this attitude but could not prove that this quality script would have a chance for success. At this writing, the picture is finally being made.

Saul Zaentz is the courageous producer who spent ten years getting *One Flew Over the Cuckoo's Nest* made. Fortunately, he was able to buck the system. He provided his own financing to make *Amadeus* and proved that a good picture can attract large audiences.

Yet the much-maligned accountants and lawyers who are supposed to be running the major studios are not cultureless and tasteless fools. They are dealing with a reality. It takes a great deal of money to make a picture these days. The code of operations is this: If a formula works—do it again. Young people, the primary movie audience, do not want to be uplifted intellectually. They want to escape, as movie audiences always have. So producers give them what they want—and most of it is of low quality. Can anything be done about it? Not when the average picture's costs exceed $13 million.

Women in Film

The next time you read the end titles of a movie and get past the acting credits, you'll become aware of how few women participate in the making of films.

In the feature-film industry, there are very few female producers, directors, screenwriters, directors of photography, and technicians. And the gates of opportunity for women in the industry are opening very slowly.

By the mid-1980s, at the executive level of the eight major studios, for the rank of vice-president and above, there were only forty-six women out of a total of 292 executives, or 15 percent. One studio, Universal Pictures, had ten women VPs out of thirty-six, higher than the average, but this was balanced by another studio that had only one out of thirty-six.

To increase employment and promote equal opportunities for women in film, in 1973 Tichi Wilkerson, editor of the *Hollywood Reporter*, joined with

Table 1

Age Group (years)	Percent of Total Yearly Admissions			Percent of Population
	1985	1984	1983	1985
12 to 15	14%	13%	13%	8%
16 to 20	21	23	25	10
21 to 24	18	18	15	9
25 to 29	14	13	15	11
30 to 39	18	18	17	19
40 to 49	7	8	7	13
50 to 59	4	4	4	11
60 and over	4	3	4	20
	100%	**100%**	**100%**	**100%**
12 to 17	20%	21%	25%	11%
18 and over	80	79	75	89

Table 2

Age Group (years)	Yearly Admissions			Percent of Population
	1985	1984	1983	1984
12 to 29	67%	67%	68%	37%
12 to 39	85	85	86	56
16 to 39	72	72	73	48
40 and over	15	15	13	44

Table 3

	Total Public Age 12 and Over			Adult Public Age 18 and Over			Teenager Public Age 12 to 17		
	1985	1984	1983	1985	1984	1983	1985	1984	1983
Frequent[1]	22%	23%	23%	21%	21%	20%	48%	51%	54%
Occasional[2]	29	28	32	28	28	32	38	34	30
Infrequent[3]	9	8	9	9	9	10	3	6	4
Never	39	39	36	41	41	38	9	5	12
Not reported	1	2	—[4]	1	1	—[4]	2	4	0

[1] At least once a month.
[2] Once in 2 to 6 months.
[3] Less than once in 6 months.
[4] Less than ½ percent.

twelve women to found Women in Film. By the mid-1980s, the group had 1,100 members in the Los Angeles chapter alone, with other chapters in seven U.S. cities and with affiliated groups in Europe, Australia, and the Far East.

Women in Film, whose members are in television as well, represents virtually every occupation from network and studio executives to producers, performers, directors, designers, writers, editors—more than seventy-five professional categories.

This progressive organization has become a vital force in the film and entertainment industry. Some of its diverse activities are as follows:

- Job Referral Service: Provides professional assistance in hiring.
- Workshops: Industry leaders share expertise with members.
- Programs: Screenings of films by and for women; guest speakers on provocative and controversial subjects.
- Membership Directory: A reference guide listing members alphabetically and by job category.
- Speakers Bureau: Women in Film members address outside organizations.
- Women in Film Foundation: Offers grants and scholarships to students and others to inspire, create, and fund activities in motion pictures and television.

Through the efforts of Women in Film and non-sexist industry leaders, the role of women in the film business is increasing, perhaps at too slow a pace. However, most barriers to women should come down soon. I encourage women to enter this dynamic profession. Readers may receive information about this organization by writing to Women in Film, 8489 West Third Street, Los Angeles, CA 90048.

where, primarily for economic reasons but also for authenticity and realism.

Twickenham is one of three major studio facilities in London. We shot the studio phase of *National Lampoon's European Vacation* there and also on location in France and Italy. Even though we brought many people over from the States, it still cost far less to do the picture in England than it would have in the United States.

New York City, always a popular place for location shooting, now has available to producers a number of new first-rate studio facilities. In one recent year, there were ninety-four features and ninety-eight TV specials, made-for-TV movies, and series shot in New York. Seven soaps are resident in New York as of this writing.

Many states and cities have set up film commissions and actively pursue film production. Working with these commissions can be economically beneficial. They also provide the producer with favorable locations and other advantages. For example, Dino de Laurentiis expects to produce a substantial number of pictures in North Carolina. Run Run Shaw, the prolific Hong Kong filmmaker, has for years produced hundreds of pictures in that cosmopolitan city. Now western producers, attracted by lower costs and unusual locales, are packing their scripts and going east. *Shanghai Surprise*, with Sean Penn and Madonna, was shot in Hong Kong in 1986.

Canada emerged in the late '80s as Hollywood North. Dozens of feature films, made-for-TV movies, and other TV shows are now being made in Canada, attracted by the favorable money exchange and lower wage scales for qualified technical personnel.

What all that means for the would-be film person who doesn't necessarily want to fight the fierce competition in Hollywood is that there are films of all kinds being made all over this country and all over the world, even though the deals are still cut in Hollywood, New York, and London. This translates into new opportunities that have merely to be grasped.

From Hollywood to Twickenham to North Carolina

Two Good Magazines About Film

Time was when almost every movie was made in Hollywood. With the development of TV and its need for so much production space, the feature film went on the road. Today, pictures are made every-

For those interested in film as an art form and for those planning to make it their life's work, there are two excellent magazines: *Film Comment* and *American Film.*

Film Comment

Published by the Film Society of Lincoln Center, sponsor of the New York Film Festival, *Film Comment* is a bimonthly that offers crisp, literate writing about film viewing. Some articles indicative of their spirited editorial coverage include the following:

- "Fellinissimo!": a hard-hitting animated conversation with the master fabulist Federico Fellini
- "Ms. Treatment": a hard-hitting analysis of why the film business remains a bastion of puritanical, exploitative treatment of women
- "Mavericks": a review of those filmmakers working outside the mainstream, including profiles of Robert Altman, John Sayles, Martin Scorsese, and Alan Rudolph
- "Westerns: Dead or Alive": a fascinating new look at the genre that's refused to die, including interviews with Kevin Kline and Linda Hunt

A year's subscription is only $12.00. The address is 140 West 65th Street, New York, NY 10023.

American Film

The official publication of the American Film Institute is *American Film*. "It takes you inside the film industry—filling you in on the films of today and the stars of tomorrow, the latest in film technology, and the behind-the-scenes decision making that shapes the movies."

One issue had this provocative mix:

- "Wilder Times": Billy Wilder (*The Front Page, The Private Life of Sherlock Holmes, Some Like It Hot*) tells a young screenwriter how it was, is, and should be.
- "The Fascist Guns in the West": Are movies like *Red Dawn* and *Rambo* just good, clean American fun, or is Hollywood developing its own brand of fascism?
- "The Man Who Would Be Different": Alan Rudolph (*Choose Me, Trouble in Mind*) makes quirky personal movies that have earned him a cult following. Will his idiosyncratic vision survive his new respectability?
- "Dialogue of Film: Peter Weir": From the aborigine to the Amish, the Australian director (*Year of Living Dangerously, Witness, The Last Wave*) uses film to cross boundaries between people and cultures.

For a year's subscription, which is $20.00, write to *American Film*, 130 West 42nd Street, New York, NY 10036. (Also see the following section on the American Film Institute.) The magazine lists no employment opportunities or want ads.

The American Film Institute (AFI)

A membership in the American Film Institute, which costs $20.00, entitles the member to ten issues of *American Film* magazine, together with discounts on selected movies, seminars, lectures, books, and merchandise; invitations to film weekends and festivals; use of the Louis B. Mayer Library; and participation in a wide range of AFI programs conducted all over the country.

The work of the American Film Institute is supported by government, private enterprise, and philanthropy. Its board of trustees is composed of TV and movie industry leaders as well as a number of academics.

Here are some examples of typical AFI seminars and workshops:

- "Introduction to Screenwriting": designed for students with no training in screenwriting: covers original story ideas, plot points, biographies of major characters
- "Acting for the Camera": a demanding three-day seminar for the beginning and the professional actor whose goal is to work in film and/or TV
- "The Art of Film Direction": for those with no training, a workshop covering all phases of film production from the special point of view of the director
- "Motion Picture Marketing": a seminar presenting an in-depth analysis of motion picture marketing practices, financial considerations, and the like

For information on membership and on the locations and dates of these and a dozen other AFI programs, write to Public Service Programs, The American Film Institute, P.O. Box 27999, 2021 North Western Avenue, Los Angeles, CA 90027.

The "Trades": *Variety* and *The Hollywood Reporter*

This chapter would not be complete if it didn't cover those bibles of show business, *Variety* and *The Hollywood Reporter*. *Variety* has been published since 1905. It comes out daily and weekly. *The Hollywood Reporter* is a daily and dates back to 1930. Both offer indefatigable coverage of every phase of show business. They are read by show-biz buffs and professionals alike. One need only have breakfast at the coffee shop of cinemaland's Beverly Wilshire hotel and watch a typical show-business customer buy both trades, peruse them carefully, and only then have that first sip of coffee. How can one not be interested in a publication that has coined the words *feevee* for pay TV and *kidvid* for videocassettes for children?

Variety

Variety covers the film biz with dedication and understanding. Let's examine a typical page of the weekly, shown here. A translation is needed, as *Variety*'s language is explicit "show businessese."

- "Multimedia Buyers Blitz Boffo Mifed": Mifed is a giant convocation of film, TV, and video executives held each year in Milan in October. What they're saying is that business was terrific ("boffo"), with sales being made in many media and in many countries.
- "Munich Contingent Exits Fat & Happy": West Germany's film and video distributors came to Mifed with a lot of money and left with a lot of foreign product.
- "Listless Biz for Far East Sellers at Mifed Market": The Asian group didn't fare too well. For this important market, there were too many sellers and not enough buyers.

These three articles were just a small portion of this issue of weekly *Variety*. The issue had thirty-five pages of coverage of the motion picture industry including the following:

- Film grosses for all current films in all major cities

- New film starts: a lineup of the pictures that went into production in recent months
- Film reviews: reviews of ten pictures opening in the United States and abroad
- Top-fifty film chart: a tracking of the grosses of the fifty top pictures still in distribution

In addition to these regular features, there are dozens of movie industry articles about people and companies. *Variety* offers much more than colorful language. The reader planning to enter the business can learn much from reading it regularly. Also, weekly *Variety*'s readers receive excellent coverage of home video, TV-radio, cable, music-records, and legitimate theater. *Variety* is also published as a daily. A one-year subscription to the weekly costs $85.00. Write to *Variety*, 154 West 46th Street, New York, NY 10036.

The Hollywood Reporter

Although *The Hollywood Reporter*'s editorial approach is less flashy than *Variety*'s, it is no less effective.

A recent issue included the following columns and coverage:

- "Rambling Reporter": just what it sounds like— breezy items about show-business folk
- "Review": one review of a movie and another of a TV mini-series—both reviews incisive and knowledgeable
- "Legal Notes": who's getting sued by whom
- "People on the Move": keeping track of job shifts in movies, broadcasting, and music
- "Hollywood Report": an inside look at the business side of Hollywood
- "The Great Life": all about parties, pictures, and people who make them
- News items about everything that's happening in the business

The Hollywood Reporter publishes many special editions throughout the year. In late February, for example, it publishes its annual *American Film Market Special Report*, a volume of more than 400 pages devoted to the happenings of this important industry convocation.

A one-year subscription to *The Hollywood Reporter* is $89.00. Studying this publication for a year is akin to receiving a liberal arts degree in show business. For subscription information, write to *The Hollywood Reporter*, 6715 Sunset Boulevard, Hollywood, CA 90028.

MOVIES

Wednesday, November 5, 1986 VARIETY PICTURES 5

MULTIMEDIA BUYERS BLITZ BOFFO MIFED

Mifed Mutterings

Milan — Alan Kean, former U.K. theatrical distrib who became a consultant to Guild Home Video, noted here: "Theatrical circuits are getting more wary of being used just to provide a window for video. Most are doing more in-depth analysis on whether properties are worth theatrical release" ... The mini-boom in the sale of kid pics to video proved a plus for the Swedish Film Institute, which shifted its moppet inventory to Latin America vid companies. Biggest mover, it seems, is the animated feature "Americat" ... U.S. boxoffice exposure of Kaerne Film's "Twist & Shout" proved a powerful sales aid for the Danish company and it cleaned up some remaining territories with the pic, notably Germany, where it was licensed to **Erwin Dietrich**'s Ascot Film.

Rank Film Distributors was excited to close Shochiku for Japan release of "The Fourth Protocol." It's a rare thing for Rank to interest the Nipponese ... Despite a disappointing year in U.S. theatrical distribution, Cannon intends to stay in that side of the trade, per chairman **Menahem Golan.** "We will continue to seek outside investment for prints and advertising," he noted. The Cannon chief also said he had taken $5,000,000 out of the "Superman IV" budget, bringing its negative cost down to $30,000,000 ... Dutch banker **Franz Afman** (Credit Lyonnais Nederland) was in checking the time of day with his growing roster of clients — Cannon, Carolco, Empire Intl., Alex Salkind, Scotti Bros., Hemdale, Gladden Entertainment and others.

Having sold his Frankfurt-based Janus Film to the Beta Taurus

(Continued on page 22)

British Companies, Big And Small, Make Whoopee At Milan Market

By ROGER WATKINS

Milan — Like most other sellers at this year's Mifed film sales market, the British made whoopee, especially since Mifed was claimed to be "good for the little guy" in terms of sales action.

Typifying the notion, upstart British exporter The Sales Co., helmed by Carole Myer for partners British Screen, Palace Pictures and Zenith Prods., kicked off here with a hit, the Island-Zenith coproduction "Slam Dance," an American production nearing completion for which Myer garnered top dollar.

It has been sold to all European territories except France, plus Australia, Latin America and the Far East.

Myer claims a substantial deal with Virgin, a British-based multinational video distributor with output deals with theatrical distribs in a dozen territories allowing it to acquire all rights to available product. Virgin took "Slam Dance" for Spain, Germany and Scandinavia.

The Sales Co.'s other good mover was "High Season," which picked up some lucrative coin from key territories on the basis of a promo reel.

In its first Mifed, Myer's outfit

(Continued on page 28)

Norstar Pacts For Trio Of Film Four Features

Milan — Britain's Film Four Intl. and Canada's Norstar Releasing pacted an all-media licensing agreement at Mifed covering three Film Four feature films.

The deal worked out by Joy Pereths, international v.p. for New York-based Intl. Film Exchange and sales agent for Film Four, and Norstar Releasing prez Dan Weinzweig, gives Norstar rights to Film Four's "Fatherland," pic screened at this year's Toronto and Venice film fests, "The Good Father," toplining Anthony Hopkins and helmed by Mike Newell, and "Eat The Peach," which unspooled recently at the Edinburgh and Montreal festivals.

Norstar previously released Film Four's "Letter To Brezhnev" in Canada.

MUNICH CONTINGENT EXITS FAT & HAPPY; SEZ BIZ 'BEST EVER'

Milan — Munich's film exporters are rolling back over the Alps, happy to a man with the film trading concluded in Milan.

Mifed veterans such as Lilli Tyc Holm's Cine Intl. and Dieter Menz' Atlas Intl. unhesitatingly report "best-ever" business as theatrical and video buyers showed up in droves carrying money. Depending on product, Mifed divided the Germans into more or less clear sectors.

"Mifed is no longer a cinema market," says a beaming Eginhart Hillenbrand, "it is a video and television market." Among other activities, Hillenbrand is agent for

(Continued on page 31)

REVISED MARKET PLANNED FOR '87

By HANK WERBA

Milan — The unconditional success of the Mifed Indian Summer Market has many ramifications for the world entertainment community as well as for the fall Mifed markets under new manager Alfredo Bini.

Particularly significant was the multimedia spread among the 4,000 registered participants from 1,702 companies in action from Oct. 20-Nov. 1.

It was taken for granted that Indian Summer harbored film and homevideo in almost equal numbers for traders and trading. Not foreseen, except perhaps by Bini, was the strong participation by the television sector in acquisitions, program packaging, film co-ventures and software exponents of the high-definition process from Japan and elsewhere.

Not Just Suppliers

Completing the horizontal media attendance was the participation of almost all the second line of attack in production — the support services. As active as the film suppliers, who, according to one veteran distrib, "sold by the kilo and sold out," were reps from law firms, talent agencies, film studios, labs, postproduction facilities, raw stock companies, equipment-makers and furnishers, plus all the services. Tying it all together was the presence of many trade associations and national promo agencies in one big, cohesive event attended by reps from 75-80 countries.

Yank Record

The U.S. alone registered 277 companies, which has to be a new record for Americans on the wing to what was billed only as a film and homevid market.

Twenty-four hours before the curtain came down on Mifed, administration figures made available by Bini accented an equally record-breaking attendance from Latin America. Argentina was in with 92 reps from 59 film and homevid ban-

(Continued on page 28)

Many Yank Sellers Post Record Biz At Indian Summer Market

By DAN GILROY

Milan — The weakened dollar, sudden strengthening of homevideo and tv syndication in a number of territories and the product void left by the collapse of sales giant Producers Sales Organization all added up to record business for many American film sales companies by the Nov. 1 close of this year's Mifed Indian Summer Market.

Buyers from Argentina were out in force, and they brought money with them. U.S. sales personnel seemed surprised by the high level of activity registered by all Latin America, particularly in homevid.

Opinions on the state of the overseas theatrical market varied. Stateside sellers who also produce their own films saw a general upturn in theatrical sales, again aided by the PSO foldo. Sales agents with lower-quality pickups saw less theatrical action, the bulk of their biz registered in homevid.

U.S. film buyers at Mifed were less excited by what they found this year than their selling counterparts. No one foreign film leapt from the pack.

The currency situation, however, was the hot topic at the Mifed offices of U.S. companies. "The weakened dollar is helping tremendously," said Walter Manley, head of Manley Prods. and v.p. of the

(Continued on page 31)

'86 Showmanship Awards Presented By Orion Intl.

Milan — Orion Pictures Intl. chairman Ernst Goldschmidt handed out the 1986 Orion Showmanship Awards at a dinner for the company's overseas distribs.

Goldschmidt passed on Orion's highest award to Seven Stars Film Distributors of Israel for its promo campaign of "Remo Williams." Top award carries an all-expense-paid one-week vacation in New York.

Second prize went to Harry Anastassiadi, managing director of 20th Fox in Brazil. Other winners were Werner Kaspers, 20th Fox, West Germany; Robert Balk, 20th Fox, France; Steen Gregers of Denmark's Nordisk Films Distribution; Bob Howey, Ster-Kinekor Limited, South Africa, and Paul Takaki and Shoji Sato, Warner Bros. Japan.

Cannon Institutes New 3-Year Output Deal With Distribs

Milan — The only thing muted about Cannon this Mifed was its voice. The L.A.-based company, which has emerged as the outright leader of the indie sector, clearly was delighted by its week's trading on the Mifed floor, but the company policy now is to withhold the numbers.

In what in some ways was the company's roughest week since it became a significant force in independent film supply, Cannon figures to have emerged with its best sales performance ever. But the trade will have to wait for the company's official financial reports for verification.

What is known about Cannon's current international trading, however, is its family of offshore distri-

(Continued on page 29)

Fazer Musik Buys Stake In Finnkino

Milan — Fazer Musik, the dominant Finnish music and video company, has become one of three major shareholders in Finnkino, the nation's new, near-monopolistic film organization.

Erik Stenros, boss of Fazer, which has annual sales worth $50,000,000 and handles Warner Home Video among other labels in Finland, said that his company chipped into Finnkino as an investment and not as a means of securing the inside track on a product line for video releasing.

"We believe in the film business," he said, "and we will not be putting up any barriers. Finnkino will sell its video rights to the highest bidders."

Finnkino, which will be fully

(Continued on page 27)

Coproducer-Hunting Still A Major Part Of Mifed

Milan — Mifed Indian Summer market primarily was a supplier's picnic, with buyers around from all parts of the world. But within the hustle and bustle of over-the-counter trading in film features, specialized members of many delegations were prowling the corridors on a hunt for coventures.

In recent years, this specific mission has reached the kind of dimension justifying some special market arrangements, such as a Mifed club for coproducers; but through last week's event, the coventure aspect of Indian Summer still was merged chaotically with film feature supply and acquisitions.

Setting for top-draw packages is still the bar and salons of the Principe and Savoia Hotel or the Palace directly across the wide boulevard. But initial approach outside Mifed halls also could take place in one of the many other four-star restaurants generally overbooked with Mifed participants during Indian Summer.

Cannon toppers Menahem Golan and Yoram Globus, the swiftest coventure deal-makers in past years, this time concentrated on big game projects with Milan-based private tv kingpin Silvio Berlusconi. According to Golan, the film and tv moguls agreed in principle to coproduce four miniseries, two submitted by Cannon, the other two by Berlusconi's Reteitalia production and acquisition arm.

During negotiations, Cannon unloaded a package of 70 features (including Cannon's 16 pic fables) for programming on the three Berlusconi networks.

A much bigger product acquisition package was the subject of further negotiations. At stake are films from both Cannon and Cannon EMI. Berlusconi and Golan & Globus confirmed they were off to a good start for a longrange relationship.

Bob Rehme, head of New World, said he received scripts and joint venture proposals from France, Spain and Italy. He sees a U.S.-Spain coproduction taking shape, but insisted it would be an international film feature with an American cast and director, filmed in Spain with a Spanish crew with postproduction phase completed in England or Hollywood. Spanish partner would come in for half or one-third the negative cost.

On the supply side, Rehme said his New World team at Mifed "sold every major territory, including Japan and France, after the initial screening of 'Soul Man.' The market as a whole is very healthy."

Jerry Pickman was on hand for the Scotti Bros. banner. He said discussions for production packages were taking place with several companies. "We talked to Cinecittà. They are now open for joint production activity and hopefully we will be doing one with a German

(Continued on page 24)

LISTLESS BIZ FOR FAR EAST SELLERS AT MIFED MARKET

By HAROLD MYERS

Milan — With one or two notable exceptions, it hardly was a distinguished market for the Far East contingent at Mifed this year. Possibly one Hong Kong producer best summed it up by observing "Yes, there are a lot of buyers; but far too many sellers."

On the basis of a last-minute roundup, it would appear the most successful of the Japanese exporters was Toho Intl., thanks very largely to one pic, "The Adventures Of Chatran," that already has more than proved itself in its domestic market. It's a story of a cat that

(Continued on page 27)

A page from *Variety,* the entertainment industry's reliable and authoritative voice. (Reprinted with permission.)

Music Videos

In the late 1970s, some young filmmakers in England and the United States began making three- or four-minute films to promote bands and their record albums. Their budgets were small, but with the bands pitching in, they were able to do high-quality, innovative short films (later called music videos) that were then shown in clubs and on TV in England.

In 1981, MTV was launched, programming music videos twenty-four hours a day. The formula was an instant success, and soon videos were a mini-industry. Video directors became as celebrated as the bands they were filming. (See the chapter on television for more about MTV.)

Record companies supported music videos because they were convinced that after a young viewer saw a video on MTV, he would then rush down to the local record store to buy the single or the album. These companies poured money into videos and, in the process, forced production prices for a single video into six figures.

For established acts, the expense was justified, and, in many cases, the video's cost was even supplemented by a contribution from the performers. Nevertheless, the record people began to see a marketing problem. It seemed that for new performers, music videos didn't work or at least weren't worth all that money.

There had to be a shakeout, and, by 1985, fewer videos were commissioned. Recently, the average price of a video has fallen to $60,000. Superstars like Barbra Streisand still make lavish music videos with directors like William Friedkin. The Rolling Stones did the same with animation director Ralph Bakshi. For the lesser performer, however, video quality is down because of the smaller budgets.

As a training ground for young filmmakers, music videos remain a great place to be. You may be asked to move lights and cameras and "gofer" coffee—without getting paid. It's good experience. But if you think of music videos as a career opportunity, we'd say do it for six months, then enroll in film school.

A number of directors went from music videos to the big time—feature films. They include Julien Temple (*Absolute Beginners*), Russell Mulcahy (*Highlander*), and Steve Barron (*Electric Dreams*). None have had a box office success yet, but critically they've done some exciting work.

The Home-Video Revolution

When a movie producer projects a picture's revenues from all sources, he lists videocassettes for 50 percent. This substantial percentage becomes more meaningful when one considers that in 1984 it was about 20 percent, and in 1980 it didn't even exist.

We are seeing a videocassette revolution that the industry forecasts will not end until near the close of the century. By then, they are estimating, there will be 55.6 million VCR households—that's almost one for every home in America. The home-video software industry's volume is expected to reach $20 billion at retail. Videocassettes will become the nation's leading entertainment medium, with 85 percent of all U.S. homes expected to have at least one VCR by then.

In 1985, home-video software volume was already $3.5 billion. VCR penetration by late '87 was 42 percent, with 10 percent owning two or more units.

In its early days, the predominance of cassette sales were X-rated films. By the mid-1980s, this material accounted for only 13 percent of the market in stores that carry it. Feature films are now the major market in home video, followed by children's products and music video.

As of this writing, *Indiana Jones and the Temple of Doom* is the all-time number-one feature film on cassette, with 1.7 million units sold. "Jane Fonda's Workout" was the leading nontheatrical cassette, with 850,00 units sold worldwide, followed by "Making Michael Jackson's *Thriller*."

By the mid-1980s there were 35 million videocassette units sold in 20,000 video stores in the United States—for a dollar volume larger than that of the book industry although the bulk of the stores' business was still in rentals. Music videos were sold at $14.95 and $19.95 to attract purchasers as well, and the high prices of theatrical film cassettes were coming down from their $69.95-and-up price tags to more affordable levels.

Such is the impact of home video that even though the 1986 movie *Iron Eagle* with Lou Gossett, Jr., did not reach blockbuster proportions in its theatrical release, it generated $11 million in videocassette sales—and this resulted in a decision to make a sequel, *Iron Eagle II.*

Video clubs have been introducd by such formidable direct-mail marketers as Columbia House, Book-of-the-Month Club, and *Reader's Digest.*

222

We are already seeing a shakeout in this fast-paced new industry. Some retail chains have already gone bankrupt. Smaller distributors have failed, primarily because of a lack of viable product and an inability to compete with the movie-owned video distributors that distribute their own films.

One cannot predict even the near-term future growth for home video. Right now, it's still a novelty and very convenient to go down to the corner store and pay $2.00 or less for the rental of a movie that was released only three months earlier.

The movie industry, however, is looking forward to the time in the near future when technology will permit the following scenario:

A big picture opens—not in 1,200 theaters, but instead in 20 or 30 million homes for a set fee of $4.00 to $5.00. These homes will be hooked up to cable systems and be ''addressable,'' that is, they will have little boxes installed on their sets making them interactive with the cable company's computer.

The viewer presses a button on the box and receives the movie. He is automatically billed by his cable company for the right to see the movie. The picture may gross $80 to $100 million in just one night. Pay-per-view is definitely the future. For now, however, home video has the lead.

As a career choice, home video is challenging, particularly in the area of programming, but it still does not employ many people. Opening a neighborhood video store is quite risky. It requires a large amount of capital because the distributors do not consign the product but work on a straight purchase basis. We would recommend consideration of other phases of the film business as growth opportunities rather than the hot newcomer—home video.

Animation

An archivist of popular culture, Carl Macek, categorized animation as ''the purest form of cinema. It is the only form of filmmaking with the potential for unlimited growth and experimentation. Every element in an animated film is controllable; the characters, the backgrounds, the lighting, the movement, the camera angle, the color, the sounds, the relationship of volume to space—everything. The only limitation is the imagination of the animator.''

When one reflects on the imagination of the animator, one is drawn naturally to the work of the Walt Disney studios in the '30s and '40s. Feature after feature entranced generations of children with their vivid imagery. Disney was the first to create quality full-length animated films.

A feature-length animated film has to sustain interest over a long time, and it is a much more condensed and compelling form of film than live action.

Although not attracting a worldwide audience as did Disney, films such as George Orwell's *Animal Farm* (1954) broke new ground. Directed by the legendary animator John Halas, *Animal Farm* did not sentimentalize and cutely humanize animals (the usual treatment in most cartoon films). Rather, in this biting satire, the animals were seriously portrayed as characters in a live-action, human story.

And in Al Brodax and George Dunning's 1967 triumph, *Yellow Submarine,* set to the Beatles' music, the audience was exposed to wonderfully inventive and audacious visuals.

In the '70s, Ralph Bakshi innovated animation with his X-rated *Fritz the Cat.* Bakshi went on to the brilliant realism of films like *Lord of the Rings.* Animation enthusiasts add to their ''hall of fame'' the talents of such as John Hubley, Saul Bass, Norman McLaren, and Bruno Bozzetto.

In 1981, I was fortunate in being involved as executive producer of the animated feature *Heavy Metal,* which was called by one critic ''the most unusual animation movie since *Fantasia.*'' *Heavy Metal* had seven diverse segments—animated by as many animation studios in Canada, the United States, and England—and showcased many innovative animation techniques. Blended with this mix was the ''heavy metal'' music of thirteen world-class bands. The picture grossed $40 million worldwide, an enormous figure for an animated film.

Unfortunately, these days there are few animated feature releases. The expense and the time factor are two key reasons for this dearth of output. *Yellow Submarine*'s Al Brodax created *Strawberry Fields,* to be released in 1988, a film that introduces the latest developments in computer animation techniques.

Animation, and particularly computer-generated images, are used extensively in TV commercials. Saturday-morning children's animated programming is low budget with concomitant low quality. This is unfortunate, because children would clearly benefit from good animation combined with good scripts.

The field of computer-generated images and computer animation as exemplified by the feature films *Tron, Star Trek II,* and *Brainstorm* offers many new opportunities for the talented newcomer skilled in computer science and with an aptitude for graphic design. One has merely to see the magical effects of a computer graphic in its instant transformation of a woman's head to a cat's head and then back to a woman's head to appreciate how far this specialty has come.

Computer graphics and animation have wider applications than in feature films—title treatments and TV commercials, for example. Employment here requires computer training, ideally blended with a graphic arts background.

I find it difficult to recommend animation as a career opportunity. Although it is a people-intensive craft, there is just not enough available work to justify the training. Talented artists and graphic designers would best pursue careers in publishing or live-action film.

The Bright Future for Documentaries

The nine-and-a-half hour Holocaust documentary *Shoah* favorably impressed critics and audiences alike. The Oscar-winning *The Times of Harvey Milk* was a big favorite on college campuses and with film societies. *The Atomic Cafe* was adopted by antinuclear groups all over the world.

Good documentaries are like oases in the desert, yet we are not seeing a sudden surge of interest in documentaries as feature-film fare. One would have great difficulty in selling a documentary project to a major Hollywood studio. What makes documentaries more economically feasible today are their ancillary possibilities—videocassettes, plus the aforementioned college and film-society markets.

There is still, of course, a limited audience in TV and in theaters for films with intellectual values. One need only compare the competitive share of the TV audience of a PBS "Civilization" and a Judith Krantz "Princess Daisy" mini-series.

The crop of theatrically viable documentaries that emerged in the mid-1980s, such as the ones previously mentioned as well as *Huey Long, Streetwise,* and *Sixteen Days of Glory,* have opened the door to other quality films of this genre.

Young filmmakers attracted to the medium by its opportunity for honest filmmaking, without the commerciality of the Hollywood product, would be wise to consider the obstacles in financing even a very low-budget documentary.

A talented young filmmaker I know was determined to produce a documentary about the social evils of the reform-school system in Massachusetts. His funding was to come from foundations. He later told me that just doing the paperwork necessary to apply for the grants took many months. Finally, he raised less than he needed but somehow produced the film anyway.

Young filmmakers are lured to documentaries, too, because they usually require no script—more often just a plan-of-attack approach. Also, today's light camera equipment makes shooting in difficult locations easier than ever before. The documentary can be the simplest of film formats. As such, it is a popular activity for film students. Some documentaries have a crew of one—serving as director, cameraman, and producer.

Beginners in this challenging film specialty would be wise to study the work of documentary greats like Frederick Wiseman (*Titicut Follies, Basic Training*), Haskell Wexler (*The Bus, Report on Torture in Brazil*), and Barbara Kopple (*Harlan County U.S.A.*).

Business Films

Who can forget the soporific films we were shown in our elementary-school biology and geography classes on such stimulating subjects as "How peanuts are grown" or "How rope is manufactured"? These films, which all seemed to have been produced by the same company, were provided free to the schools by trade associations and similar organizations, with the implied purpose of augmenting the educational process. They neither implemented nor impeded the process; they just put us to sleep.

These films—once called "industrial" and now called "business" films—have developed in sophistication and quality. Recently, I became aware of the diverse activities of a leading company in this field, Jack Morton Productions, with offices in New York and four other cities. Although JMP's sphere encompasses the broad area of corporate communication, business films are a key aspect of their operation.

Here are some of JMP's film projects:

- For Bally shoes, four 18-minute filmstrip cassettes to train sales associates in the many aspects of selling Bally products

- A videotape for Ryder System, Inc., basically known for its rental trucks, showing the multifaceted nature of this company
- An animated audio-visual simulation of a sales call for American Express, used to guide sales representatives in convincing retail establishments to accept the American Express card as a form of payment
- For the Tailored Clothing Technology Corporation, a consortium of government, union, and business leaders in the garment industry, a videotape showing high-technology machinery making America more competitive to foreign apparel imports
- Calma, a subsidiary of General Electric, develops and produces computer software. JMP's videotapes illustrate how state-of-the-art computers can produce at rapid-fire speed what was accomplished slowly by engineers with drawing boards.

Industrial films are decidedly a growth area. Companies like JMP service businesses, trade associations, and tourist commissions. In the preparation of these productions, there is a need for producers, directors, writers, designers, photographers, and other creative personnel. Further, employment in this division of the film industry is much less transitory than that in feature films.

The Independent Production

In our narrative about an actual film earlier in this chapter, the producer chose to go the "production" route with a major studio; that is, the studio financed the whole production from the earliest stage of development, had creative input, distributed the picture, and received half the profits.

Had the producer opted instead for a "negative pick-up" deal, he would have had to finance the picture independently and then work out a distribution arrangement with the studio. The latter, in turn, might then have made a commitment up front with the producer calling for a fixed payment upon receipt of the negative or just prior to the release of the picture.

This latter arrangement would qualify the picture as an independent production. A major studio

distributes about ten or twelve pictures a year that it doesn't produce. If you multiply the nine majors by these figures, you get only about one hundred independent productions that the studios distribute. There are hundreds more that are produced independently. How are they distributed?

Of 141 independent releases (costing $362 million to produce) produced by U.S. companies during 1985, 104 received more than a test release and earned back approximately $162 million in domestic film rentals. Rentals are the amount the distributor receives after the exhibitors (theater owners) take their cut.

One doesn't have to be a financial genius to realize that $200 million had to be recovered by these independent producers from foreign sales, cable, home video, and so on. We can be certain this did not occur—and losses piled up.

Mini-Majors and Mini-Distributors

Companies like Orion, Cinecom, Lorimar, and Goldwyn distribute independent productions. They handle fewer pictures than the majors and often do an excellent job in marketing and distribution. We should realize, however, that there is huge competition for the nation's theaters, especially during the peak summer and Christmas periods. Exhibitors know that if a major is behind a picture, it will usually have a "major" advertising campaign. Also, they know that each major will distribute twenty or twenty-five pictures a year, thus putting the major in a favorable situation with the exhibitors.

When an independent producer strikes out with the majors and the mini-majors, he then pursues the smaller distributors—New World, Empire, Atlantic, Carolco, and others. For lower-budget pictures, these distributors are generally the only game in town, but in dealing with them, the independent producer can count only on small advances and little or no guarantees for prints and advertising.

In the mid-1980s, realizing the need for effective distribution of their product, about a dozen independent producers entered the fold. These included a major company in the record business, Scotti Bros. Pictures, and the number-two videocassette distributor, Vestron.

If any of our readers are would-be independent

producers and seem depressed and confused at this stage, I'd like to tell them the wonderful story of John Sayles and his *Return of the Secaucus Seven.* John made the picture for $60,000 of his own money. His original distributor was the very small Libra Films. The movie's worldwide gross was $2.5 million, most of that from the United States. Today, the rights to *Secaucus* are owned by Cinecom.

A neophyte producer should take heed of film business savants who say that a producer should not spend his own or his investors' money unless he knows who will distribute his picture.

IATSE

Known in the entertainment industry as "IA," the International Alliance of Theatrical Stage Employees and Moving Picture Machine Operators of the United States and Canada, originally a union of stage employees and movie projectionists, now encompasses a great variety of craftspersons in the theater, movies, and TV.

IA began in 1893 and in the next twenty years organized the carpenters, propertymen, and electricians working in theaters. In 1908, soon after the birth of the film industry, the union won recognition for projectionists throughout the country. When commercial TV got its start, right after World War II, IATSE was there to represent its craftspeople.

Today, there are more than 800 local unions of the IA in the United States and Canada. In the film business, these are some of the craftspersons represented:

art directors
story analysts
set designers
set decorators
scenic artists
grips
electricians
property persons
costumers
makeup artists
hair stylists
motion picture cameramen
still cameramen
sound technicians

editors
script supervisors
projectionists

Most major studios and production companies have contracts with IA. It is very difficult getting a job if one is not a union member, and it is difficult getting into the union. If an employer hires a young nonunion person in a lesser job function, it may then be possible for that person to get into the union. Once in the union, it is possible to move up the ladder to the more technical and highly paid specialties.

Most locals of the IA have qualification tests that include a written examination as well as an experience requirement. Union membership gives one the best job security possible in an industry with limited employment opportunities.

As there are so many individual locals in IA, covering so many crafts, we suggest writing to its New York City and Los Angeles headquarters for further information about training programs, membership requirements, and so on. The addresses are as follows: IATSE, 1515 Broadway, New York, NY 10036 and IATSE, 7715 Sunset Boulevard, Los Angeles, CA 90046.

The Case for Film School

Francis Ford Coppola (*The Godfather*) was graduated from the University of California at Los Angeles' film school in 1967. George Lucas's senior thesis at the University of Southern California in 1966, a science-fiction short called *Electronic Labyrinth: THX 1138:4EB,* was later developed as his first commercially released picture, *THX 1138.* Lucas achieved fame with *American Graffiti* and ultimately *Star Wars.* Both Coppola and Lucas are strong advocates of the film-school route to success in movies.

Steven Spielberg, the most successful director in Hollywood history, was turned down by USC and never went to film school. Nonetheless, he contributed $500,000 to USC's $15 million cinema-television center. Lucas donated $5.7 million.

The University of Southern California and the University of California at Los Angeles, along with New York University's film school, are the most prestigious in the country. Their graduates alone make up a "who's who in American films." But interest in filmmaking is so intense that more than one hundred other colleges offer undergraduate film study programs.

As we pointed out earlier in this chapter, the film business is, unfortunately, a small one and can't absorb the vast majority of film-school graduates; fewer than 10 percent actually enter the industry. We think, however, that the unique educational experience of film school justifies bucking the long odds.

What You Really Learn in Film School

Each school differs in its approach to filmmaking. Both USC and UCLA encourage students to make their own movies. Some are as elaborate as low-budget commercial features. Students at USC, the oldest and largest film school in the country, produce films within a strict budget. At UCLA, students can spend as much money as they can raise. Because all three of these major film schools offer distinctive programs, the following are highlights of each school's curriculum:

UCLA (undergraduate): The two-year major in Motion Picture/Television offers extensive training in all aspects of production, history, and criticism, rather than specialized technical training in one specific field. Students are exposed to scriptwriting, producing, directing, cinematography, design editing, sound recording, and mixing. Animated, experimental, ethnographic, documentary, and fictional films are studied.

These are some representative courses: History of the European Motion Picture, Producers and Their Films, Advanced Motion Picture/Television Writing, Color Cinematography, Motion Picture Editing, Technical Motion Picture/Television Laboratory, Motion Picture Internship, and Overview of the Motion Picture Industry.

UCLA (graduate): The master of arts degree is granted with specializations in animation, filmmaking, scriptwriting, or a subdiscipline in ethnographic film. Approximately one hundred films are produced and screened by students each quarter.

These are some representative courses: Seminar in American Motion Picture History, Seminar in Fictional Film, Seminar in Film Genres, Seminar in Film Criticism, Writing Scenes for Production, Advanced Design for Motion Pictures, Manuscript Evaluation, and Advanced Motion Picture/Television Directing and Photography.

NYU (undergraduate): In their own words, the goal of the Undergraduate Division of NYU's Department of Film and Television is: "to provide the student with 1) a variety of creative experiences in both the conceptual and production phases of film, television, and radio; 2) the opportunity to develop the technical skills for bringing these concepts to the audience; 3) an extensive critical and historical frame of reference; 4) an understanding of the relationship between society and the visual and sound media; 5) a personal philosophy that embraces the potential of these media as a means of expressing a wide range of human experience."

Here are some typical courses: Future Technologies: Image and Sound, Editing I: Techniques of the Film Cutting Room, Senior Production/Workshop and Seminar, Producing I: The Fundamentals of the Producing Craft for Film and Television, Animation Action Analysis, Writing the Short Screenplay, and Comedy Workshop.

Internships in film and television are arranged for those juniors and seniors who are qualified and wish to devote more hours than the regular classroom and/or laboratory hours provide.

NYU (graduate): A master of fine arts degree is provided for those talented men and women whose commitment toward work in film is solid. It is a three-year program.

Here are some representative courses: Film Editing I and II, Motion Picture Camera Technique I and II, Directing Actors I and II, Production Crews, and Writing for Film I and II.

NYU also offers an undergraduate and graduate program called Cinema Studies. Its general purpose is to ground the student in the principles, methods, and objectives of film study.

University of Southern California: One of the three great films schools in America, USC offers a B.A., M.A., M.F.A. and a Ph.D. in Film. Also, an M.S. in Film Education. There are 200 undergraduate film majors and 250 graduate students.

Following are some highlights from the USC catalogue's summary: "We hope to educate the film artist who will fulfill the traditional role of the artist in society, using his art not only to reflect but to improve, for social change. Our approach is professional in the best sense. We equally offer emphasis in history/criticism or production in film."

USC's part-time faculty is dotted with film giants including Blake Edwards, Jerry Lewis, John Milius, Bill Melendez, and King Vidor.

There are about 140 course titles available. Here are some typical courses for undergraduates: History of the American Film, Art and Industry of the Theatrical Film, Graphics-Animation, Practicum in Pre-Production, Film Directors, Music in Motion Pictures, Filmwriting, and Production Workshop. The following are some typical graduate courses: Advanced Motion Picture Script Analysis, Practicum in Screenwriting, Seminar in Film Analysis, Animation Camera Workshop, Censorship in Cinema, and History of the Sound Film in America. For more information on these film schools, write to the following:

New York University
Undergraduate Institute of Film and Television
51 West Fourth Street
New York, NY 10003
(212) 598–3703

New York University
Graduate Institute of Film and Television
40 East Seventh Street
New York, NY 10003
(212) 598–2416

University of Southern California (USC)
Division of Cinema (Film)
School of Journalism (TV)
University Park, CA 90007
(213) 746–2235 (Cinema)
(213) 746–2166 (TV/Journalism)

University of California, Los Angeles (UCLA)
Department of Theatre, Film, and Television
45 Hilgard
Los Angeles, CA 90024
(213) 825–5761

For those interested in film courses elsewhere, look for a book in your library published by the American Film Institute titled *American Film Institute Guide to College Courses in Film and Television*. If it is not available locally, write to the American Film Institute, Princeton, NJ 08540. The price is $12.75.

Two Interviews

As has been discussed in the section of this chapter on women in film, it has been difficult for women to establish themselves in the production and executive levels of the film business. Our interviewees, however, have achieved success in two different areas: Midge Sanford and Sarah Pillsbury as independent producers of feature films, and Ruth Vitale as an acquisition executive in the high-visibility field of home video.

Midge Sanford and **Sarah Pillsbury** made their team debut in 1985 with the popular hit *Desperately Seeking Susan*, which starred Rosanna Arquette and Madonna. The following year they produced their second feature film, *River's Edge*.

Pillsbury began her career working in independent films, acting as associate producer for *The California Reich* (1976; nominated for an Academy Award for Best Documentary Feature), followed by *With Babies and Banners* (1978; also Oscar-nominated), for which she was West Coast production coordinator. She also produced Ron Ellis's *Board and Care*, a love story about two people with Down's syndrome, which won the 1979 Academy Award for Best Live Action Short Subject.

Sanford got her training working with producer/film editor Bob Estrin for three years. There she received an extensive background in development and the Hollywood style of movie production.

Sanford and Pillsbury met through mutual friends and, in 1980, decided to form a partnership. After Pillsbury spent some time raising capital from private investors, they officially inaugurated Sanford/Pillsbury Productions in August 1982. They are currently developing a number of projects with such notable directors as John Sayles (*Baby It's You, The Brother from Another Planet*), and King Hu (*Touch of Zen*).

How long did it take you to make Desperately Seeking Susan *from idea to release?*

Midge: Four years. We optioned the original screenplay in February 1981. All the studios said to come back with a director, so in August 1982, after having seen Susan Seidelman's independent feature *Smithereens*, we sent her the script, and she agreed to direct. We made a development deal at Warner Bros. in April 1983. A rewrite was done, and the project was put into turnaround in December 1983. In February 1984, Orion decided to give *Desperately Seeking Susan* the go-ahead, and we began principal photography in September 1984. It was released in March 1985. From idea to release—four years.

What formal training in films did each of you have before producing your first picture?

Midge: My training began rather informally—typing synopses for my husband when he started out in the film business as a reader in 1963. He became a literary agent, and I often read scripts and galleys at home while raising children and later teaching school. I quit teaching and began reading screenplays and books for independent producers. Through a mutual friend, I met a film editor, Bob Estrin, who had started a production company and needed a reader/story editor. I worked for him for three years, gradually meeting writers, agents, and studio executives and learning how the development process worked. Then Sarah and I met and began talking about forming a company. I'd say that before *Desperately Seeking Susan,* I'd been on a movie set as a visitor about three times!

Sarah: I took some filmmaking and film-criticism courses at Yale and did a couple of videos for a public access network in Aspen, Colorado, one summer. I came to L.A. in 1974 to work on a documentary—*The California Reich*—about the American Nazi party in California. I was associate producer, but really I was part financier, part production assistant, part researcher, part assistant editor, and part sound recordist. I started UCLA film school in the fall of 1975 but never finished because I was doing production work on a couple of documentaries. Nonetheless, I feel the classes I took have helped a lot and, most important, I recommend film school because you meet your peers; and in a business where it's who you know that counts, your peers are really important. I did production assistant work on a couple of AFI [American Film Institute] projects and met two of the people I still see today. At UCLA, I met a guy who got an AFI grant for a short that I co-produced with him and that won an Academy Award. In the meantime, I worked as a production assistant on a feature, as a secretary to two young producers, and as a reader and researcher. In conclusion, being a producer means learning on the job, but I recommend film school and working for other producers before hanging out your own shingle.

Our readers already know that there is a paucity of women in the film business. In what areas do you think this gap is most prominent?

Midge: What comes to mind first is direction, although in the last couple of years women are being offered more opportunities in that area. Still, women directors must constantly prove themselves. The gap is greater below the line [in production positions]. There are very few women DPs (directors of photography), electricians, first ADs (assistant directors), grips, drivers. There are lots of middle-level studio executives, but none who really have the power to green-light a project, though a woman executive, Barbara Boyle, was instrumental in getting *Desperately Seeking Susan* made at Orion.

Sarah: There is still an old boy's network. What exists of a woman's network is still pretty poor and powerless.

Do you advocate film school for those who desire to enter the field, or do you suggest on-the-job training?

Midge: Film school definitely has its advantages, especially if one wants to learn a craft. On-the-job training can be just as valuable, though. It depends a lot on how one learns best. I always learned more doing the job than studying about it, especially when I went to graduate school to get a teaching credential. It frustrated me tremendously because I just wanted to get into the classroom and teach. I think I would have felt the same way in film school.

Do the major studios really trust women producers?

Midge: Women producers—alone, partnered with a man, or with another woman—*are* being given opportunities by studios to produce, but there are still very few of them. As more successful movies are produced by women, studios have to take them more seriously. This doesn't preclude the fact that there is a "boys' club" that has existed for a long time, and it's pretty hard for a woman to become a member. If an inexperienced woman has the rights to a book or script and a financier badly wants the project, the woman will be accepted as the producer. She may be bumped to another title, but the same is also true for a man.

Sarah: I think that there is unconscious sexism at work here. In other words, male executives don't *think* that they don't trust women, but I think many of the older men are still uncomfortable with women commanding that kind of power.

What areas of filmmaking seem to have the greatest opportunity?

Secretary/assistants, readers, story editors, development executives, studio production vice-presidents. The last is the closest a studio executive gets to physical production because overseeing the film projects from inception to conclusion is often a function of the job.

Also writers, agents, editors, production managers, art directors, casting directors, script supervisors, production coordinators, auditors, costume designers, and hair and makeup supervisors.

A tough final question: What one special tip can you offer college people and recent graduates who are eager to pursue film careers?

Midge: Believe in yourself and want it desperately. Contact your alumni office and find out who graduated from your college who is in the film business. Write to them and try to meet them. Use any other contact you have to get your foot in the door. Relationships are everything.

Sarah: Never take no for an answer, but don't bug

people. Either call back with new information about your project, or when someone says he can't talk to you now or he doesn't have a job now, ask when you might call back. Also ask who else he could call for you. Try to have an informal meeting if possible: "I know you don't have a lot of time, but could I just come in to meet with you for 15 minutes?" Usually if someone likes you in person, he'll try to come up with recommendations.

Ruth Vitale was until mid-1987 senior vice-president of feature-film programming at Vestron Video International. This interview was conducted while she was still at Vestron. Prior to joining Vestron, Vitale was director of film acquisition at Warner Amex Satellite Entertainment Company's The Movie Channel, a pay-TV service, for two years. Prior to that, she was part of the start-up operation for Hearst/ABC's basic cable service, Daytime, as manager of sales operations. For the previous two years, Vitale was vice-president of media account services for McCann-Erickson, an advertising agency. And for three years prior, she was a broadcast rep for the Post-Newsweek TV stations and RKO's then-owned Boston TV station, WNAC-TV, the CBS affiliate.

Vitale has an M.S. in journalism from Boston University and a B.A. in literature from Tufts University.

Home video is the new entertainment tiger. How long do you think it will roar?

Today, the domestic home-video retail revenues are almost equal to the domestic motion-picture box office and could be substantially larger very soon. With significant growth expected in the number of Americans using videocassette recorders, home video is becoming the dominant medium for the consumption of motion picture entertainment. From my perspective, the future of home video has never looked more promising. Like any young industry, there will be growing pains, but the industry as a whole will prosper.

You run the movie acquisitions group at Vestron. Just what does this work entail?

As senior vice-president of feature film programming for Vestron, my areas of responsibility include video acquisition, feature film story department, low-budget production, and Vestron Pictures production.

The department of video acquisitions is responsible for the purchase of 190 films released each year. This team concentrates solely on the acquisition of movie product for release in video, either domestically, foreign, or worldwide. It not only includes the

purchase of finished features, but also the pre-buying of features in script form. These people deal with theatrical distributors, producers, sales reps, and, in some cases, directors to negotiate for some variation on these rights.

The feature film story department is responsible for the evaluation and recommendation to purchase all feature films submitted to the company, either for video or for production and co-production.

The low-budget feature division is responsible for the production of feature films made for under $1 million. They are high-concept, clearly targeted genre pictures, which have a value not only in video but also in all markets. The talent here is to pick selectively and to choose the filmmakers that have demonstrated a continuing ability to bring films in for that price range.

In 1990, where will home video be in terms of coverage, product, and competition?

At present, videocassette recorders and players are used in 35 million, or 41 percent, of all American homes with TV sets. This represents a dramatic rate of expansion from 1982, when VCRs were present in 4.8 million, or 5.9 percent, of American homes. Market research studies indicate that VCR (and VCP) penetration will have grown to 45 million homes, or 50 percent, by the end of 1987. It is generally agreed that penetration will continue to grow well into the 1990s, but it is not yet clear what penetration level will constitute saturation of the market.

Certainly the growing pains of a young industry will weed out the weaker companies. Certainly the business will also mature to the point that taste levels will become more sophisticated. Beyond that, my crystal ball goes blank.

At this writing, the home-video industry, with its rapid growth pattern, still employs relatively few people. What areas of the business would you especially recommend for people wanting to get into it?

There is room for good people in every aspect of the business, both in the marketing and sales end and in the acquisition and business affairs end.

Finally, what are your thoughts about film or business school as a means of entering the movie and home video business?

I think that a combined master's degree in film and business is a very helpful tool for stepping into the business. The home-video business—specifically at Vestron—has become an area where a sound understanding of both film and business practices will be extremely helpful. Again, as it is a young business, you find yourself "hitting the ground running," as it were.

Glossary of Movie Terms

Ancillary markets: the areas of a production's revenues other than theatrical (movie theater admissions); includes home video, television, cable, merchandising, and records.

Answer print: the first trial print after all editing and mixing.

Cast breakdown: a brief description of each major role provided by the casting director to agents, managers, and the like.

Cinematographer: also known as director of photography and cameraman; responsible to director for all camera work and lighting.

Exhibitor: the theater owner; can be an individual or a chain; deals with distributors and subdistributors.

Film rentals: the revenues available to distributor after exhibitors take their share.

Industrial films: now called business films. These are films whose production is funded by industries, companies, trade associations, and others to tell their particular story.

Legs: staying power. A theatrical motion picture has "legs" if it survives the first two weeks, the period when it receives heavy support by advertising, publicity, and promotion.

Majors: the eight Hollywood production and distribution giants.

Mixing: the end of the post-production period, when voice, music, and sound effects are blended.

Negative pick-up: a distribution deal made by a major or mini-major agreeing to distribute a picture and, on receipt of the negative from the producer, to pay an agreed-upon advance.

Pay-per-view: a system whereby programmers of movies or other events are able to feed a program to specific addressable cable TV households for a fixed fee.

Polish: a revision of a particular draft of a screenplay, usually revisions of specific scenes only.

Post-production: a phase beginning when the principal photography, or shooting, ends. Editing, special effects, sound mixing, lab work, optical effects, and final dub are done in this period.

Pre-production: a preliminary stage of production consisting of script development, location choice, crew recruitment, cast selection, and set design and construction.

Principal photography: the actual shooting time of the picture; can be done in a studio or on location.

Sound track: in general, the music and voice tracks of the picture.

Storyboard: a comic book reenactment of the script, often with a separate panel for each camera setup.

Trailer: a short film using segments of the feature; used for promotion before the picture opens.

Treatment: a synopsis or outline—often thirty pages or less—of a story without dialogue.

Turnaround: when a major studio or production company has developed a project up to production and decides to drop it, it goes into "turnaround" and can be purchased by another group.

Work print: the protection material—pulled from the original film—used by the editor for cutting.

Recommended Reading

Bach, Steven. *Final Cut.* New York: William Morrow, 1985.

Beal, J. David. *Cine Craft.* Stoneham, Mass.: Focal Press, 1974.

Brady, John. *The Craft of the Screenwriter.* New York: Simon & Schuster, Touchstone, 1982.

Bronfeld, Stewart. *How to Produce a Film.* Englewood Cliffs, N.J.: Prentice-Hall, Spectrum Books, 1984.

———. *Writing for Film and Television.* Englewood Cliffs, N.J.: Prentice-Hall, Spectrum Books, 1981.

Daley, Ken. *Basic Film Technique.* Stoneham, Mass.: Focal Press, 1980.

Dmytryk, Edward. *On Filmmaking.* Stoneham, Mass.: Focal Press, 1986.

Geller, Stephen. *Screenwriting.* New York: Bantam Books, Inc., 1985.

Goldman, William. *Adventures in the Screen Trade.* New York: Warner Books, 1983.

Goodell, Gregory. *Independent Feature Film Production.* New York: St. Martin's Press, 1982.

Granade, Charles, Jr., ed. *American Film Institute Guide to College Courses in Film and Television.* Princeton, N.J.: American Film Institute, 1981.

Hyland, Wende, and Roberta Haynes. *How to Make it in Hollywood*. Chicago: Nelson Hall, 1975.

Lasky, Betty. *RKO: The Biggest Little Major of Them All*. Englewood Cliffs, N.J.: Prentice-Hall, 1984.

London, Mel. *Getting Into Film*. New York: Ballantine Books, 1982.

———. *Making it in Film*. New York: Fireside Books, 1985.

Pincus, Edward, and Steven Ascher. *The Filmmaker's Handbook*. New York: Plume Books, 1985.

Pollock, Dale. *Skywalking: The Life and Films of George Lucas*. New York: Harmony Books, 1983.

Rosenblum, Ralph, and Robert Karen. *When the Shooting Stops . . . the Cutting Begins*. New York: Da Capo Press, 1986.

Rubin, Susan. *Animation: The Art and the Industry*. Englewood Cliffs, N.J.: Prentice-Hall, Spectrum Books, 1984.

Squire, Jason. *The Movie Business*. New York: Simon & Schuster, Touchstone, 1983.

Wilkie, Bernard. *Creating Special Effects for TV and Films*. Stoneham, Mass.: Focal Press, 1977.

Withers, Robert S. *Introduction to Film*. New York: Barnes & Noble Outline Series/Division of Harper & Row, 1983.

ADVERTISING

My love affair with advertising agencies goes back forty-six years. In 1941, I was eighteen and no longer attending college full time. World War II was imminent and I knew I was going to be in it, so I took a daytime job delivering printing orders while going to City College in New York at night. Although we were edging out of the Depression, good jobs were not plentiful. I was paid $12.00 a week for forty hours, and time and a half if I worked four hours on Saturday. This would bring my salary up to $13.80 a week—not bad for those days, especially since I was picking up nine credits a semester at the same time.

Each day I arrived at the printing plant at 8:30 A.M., after an hour's ride on the subway. My first duty was to sweep up the small plant, a job made more difficult because of all the paper scraps strewn about, as well as the metal shavings near the Linotype machine.

My immediate boss was the shipping clerk, a stocky, cigar-chewing rather obnoxious type with a bellowing voice who, at 9:30 each morning, had me load my three-wheeled pushcart with about 150 pounds of deliveries destined for offices at various locations in the midtown business district.

I quickly learned all the tricks of the trade. During the summer, I would park my cart outside a Horn and Hardart automat, go through the revolving door, and make myself a free lemonade using the ice and lemons provided for purchasers of iced tea.

The delivery I enjoyed most was to an advertising agency with the imposing name of Monarch Advertising Associates. When I opened the etched glass doors, I was instantly transported into a world of glamour. The indirect lighting of the reception room was a perfect setting for its ebony and chrome modernistic furniture. Enthroned in the middle of the room was an elegant blonde about my age whose conversation with me was limited to a curt, "They go in the back."

Ten years later, older and wiser, I began to visit ad agencies regularly in the course of my work in magazine publishing. I was no longer intimidated by impressive reception rooms—maybe by receptionists occasionally—yet I never lost my fascination for the vibrant atmosphere of an ad agency. Had I not spent my life in publishing, perhaps I might have become a Madison Avenue huckster.

A History of Advertising

When I was a kid growing up in Brooklyn, a man would walk the streets with a sack on his back, singing to the housewives, "I cash clothes, I cash clothes." The ladies knew that was the time to bring old suits, dresses, and shoes to the street to sell for a few cents. The "I cash clothes" man illustrates the oldest form of advertising.

Personal selling, or word-of-mouth advertising, probably goes back to prehistoric times, whenever anyone had something he no longer needed and wanted to exchange it for something else.

When manufacturing began to develop, the people who made things would take to the streets carrying their merchandise and shouting their wares. As they expanded their operations, they hired "criers" with good loud voices to sell for them.

Outdoor advertising predates Burma-Shave signs, having been used by the Babylonians 5,000 years earlier. Because few persons could read in those days, a sign was placed outside an establishment with a crude illustration of the vendor's product. Today, in the small towns of Italy, this tradition continues! Local winemakers sometimes nail a small section of a vine to the door indicating that local wine is for sale.

The ancient Egyptians were more progressive. They carved advertising messages on stone slabs and placed them along the main roads for people to see. The same message was repeated on many tablets for emphasis—the earliest form of saturation advertising.

The first want ads go back 3,000 years to the Babylonians, who posted signs on walls to advertise for the return of runaway slaves.

Johann Gutenberg's invention of movable type around 1450 greatly increased the use of printed messages to sell merchandise and services. In 1480, William Caxton, England's first printer, posted a handbill on church doors advertising a book. Printed handbills, posters, and even newspaper advertising became common in the 1600s.

The first newspaper advertising in the United States was carried by the *Boston News-Letter* in 1704, but this was on a small scale, as the paper didn't reach a circulation of 300 until forty years later. Ben Franklin's *Journal Magazine*, founded in 1743, carried paid advertising. Although England had the jump on the United States in advertising, by the early 1800s we had the lead and never relinquished it. The use of advertising, however, was very limited in publications until the 1850s, when printing developed rapidly and literacy increased among the general population.

The Origin of Advertising Agencies

Newspapers proliferated from 1750 to 1850. Further, as is the case today, advertising revenue supported the operations of these newspapers. In those days, sellers purchased space directly from the newspaper publishers. When this practice became unwieldy, the publishers hired salesmen to implement their advertising sales programs.

The salesmen acted as "brokers" for the space, purchasing it in blocks from the publishers at a discount and then selling it to the customers at full price. The discount was usually 15 percent. The same commission structure and discount prevail today.

Soon advertisers depended on the brokers to prepare their advertising, and the brokers began hiring specialists to write the ads. And that's how advertising agencies started.

The first known U.S. agency was founded by Volney B. Palmer in Philadelphia in 1840. Ads of that period were full of boastful claims for strange elixirs with amazing curative powers for a dozen diseases.

A wonderful book on the history of advertising, *Advertising: Reflections of a Century,* by Bryan Holme, makes use of the author's graphics collection, which spans four family generations, supplemented by the collections of museums and libraries. Particularly enjoyable is the 1880–1890 section, which features the posters of Toulouse-Lautrec, Maxfield Parrish, and Aubrey Beardsley.

In the 1900–1920 period of the book, we see a new trend emerging in advertising—celebrity testimonials, with Ethel Barrymore for petticoats, the great dancer Anna Pavlova pitching O'Sullivan's rubber heels, and the noted actress Ina Claire pushing hats. Once we were exposed to celebrity testimonials, we had them with us forever.

In the early 1900s, Cyrus H.K. Curtis founded the first big national magazines (among them the *Saturday Evening Post*) that became important advertising media. Radio advertising got started in the early 1920s, and television advertising in the immediate post–World War II period. We've been exposed to modern advertising for a hundred years. Where would we be without it?

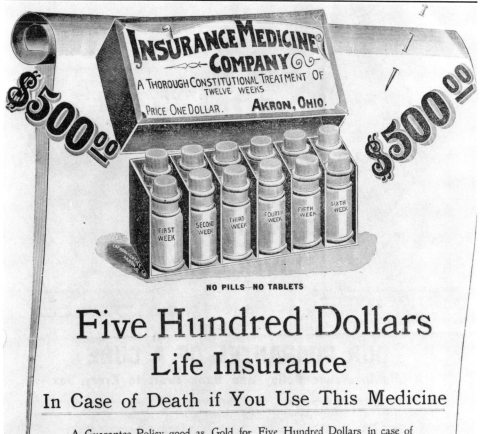

Five Hundred Dollars
Life Insurance
In Case of Death if You Use This Medicine

A Guarantee Policy good as Gold for Five Hundred Dollars in case of death, in every box of our medicine, which contains Twelve Weeks' Treatment and costs only One Dollar.

Issued as an evidence of good faith showing our confidence in the curative power of our medicine for certain diseases.

We simply defy disease if given a few weeks' trial and do not hesitate in issuing the above Guarantee when we know the power this medicine and treatment has over DISEASE, WEAKNESS and DECAY.

AND YET WE USE NOTHING BUT VEGETABLE AGENTS

"In his able work entitled 'Longevity' published a few years ago, Dr. John Gardner, of England, predicts that a vegetable agent will yet be found that shall so retard those changes that bring about old age as to prolong human life much beyond its present limit."

THE WORLD HAS WAITED A THOUSAND YEARS FOR THIS.

See other side for Medicine and Diseases.

We often see extravagant claims in our advertising today. However, as a result of government and industry standards, present-day advertising is tamer than that of earlier vintage. This circa-1890 ad requires a careful reading for one to fathom its unbelievable claims. Note the insidious quote about Dr. Gardner. They're not saying that this $1 vegetable agent treatment will prolong life, but that it *may* do so. In any case, if one happened to die from this treatment, the aptly named Insurance Medicine Company would have enriched his heirs with the munificent sum of Five Hundred Dollars. (Reprinted with permission of the Bettman Archive.)

That Extra 20 lbs.

Watch It Disappear

This is to men and women who weigh an extra twenty pounds or m o r e. It mars your beauty, quells your vivacity, threatens your health. You owe to yourself the removal of that excess, as people all around you now are doing.

Not by abnormal exercise or diet. That is too hard and too long, and sometimes too risky. You have probably tried those methods. Now try the modern way.

Twenty years ago scientific men discovered, by long research, a cause of excess fat. And they found a way to remedy that cause. They proved it first by thousands of experiments on animals, then on human beings.

When efforts were proved, the factors were embodied in Marmola Prescription Tablets, now used for two decades. Many people used them and watched the results, then told those results to others. Thus the use has grown until Marmola has attained an enormous sale.

Wherever y o u look today you can see how excess fat has disappeared in late years. Slenderness prevails. You must realize that people are employing a more efficient help.

The use of Marmola requires no starvation, no over-exercise. But moderation helps. Simply take four tablets daily until the weight comes down to normal. Then stop, unless a later gain suggests some further use.

The complete formula of Marmola comes in every box. Also an explanation of all good results that come. This is done to banish for you any fear of harm.

Go start Marmola now. Order a box before you forget it. Watch the results, not only in reduction but in new health and vitality. Weigh yourself every week. You will be amazed and delighted, we believe. Your whole life may be changed.

Marmola prescription tablets are sold by all druggists at $1 per box. Any druggist who is out will get them from his jobber for you.

MARMOLA Prescription Tablets
The Pleasant Way to Reduce

In the "nothing new under the sun" department, here is a weight-reduction ad that appeared in the prominent fashion magazine *Fashionable Dress* in February 1928. A similar ad today might have better layout and slicker copy, but the claims would probably remain the same. This ad says to forget about "abnormal exercises and diets" and just take the pills. Sound familiar?

Advertising Agencies: What They Are, What They Do, and How They Do It

Suppose you are in the business of selling four-wheeled trucks, shaving cream, or scotch whiskey. Before your product ever reaches the dealer, he must be willing to give it shelf space and, if possible, prominent display. Sales clerks must be encouraged to suggest and promote it, and, finally, customers in sufficient numbers must be moved to recognize it and persuaded to buy it.

How do you achieve all this? Most likely you will advertise, for advertising is an efficient sales force, reaching many potential customers at one time, quickly, and at a relatively low cost. Advertising expenditures are only 3 percent of the U.S. gross national product, but they act as a stimulus and lubricant to help our complex economy to function.

The Modern Way to Sell

Advertising now embraces television, radio, and films—sight and sound, as well as print. Advertising familiarizes people with brand names, spreads news about product improvements, cooperates with a dealer's own promotions, helps close the sale, and reassures customers after they have bought the product.

There are more than 20,000 national and regional advertisers in the United States today, and many more local ones, all competing for the buyer's attention. Unless advertising can attract, convince, and persuade, it is a complete waste.

We are barraged with advertising in every medium, from chalked messages on sidewalks to writing in the sky. Much of it reaches us subliminally; much we block from our minds. Recently, I heard a 60-second radio commercial for an Italian restaurant on my favorite music station. An authentic Italian-accented voice recited in rhyme some of the restaurant's specialties, intermittently interrupted with the restaurant's name and address. I was so taken with the charm and effectiveness of this commercial that I made sure to tune in and listen at 8:55 each morning so that I could hear it. I made sure my wife heard it as

well. We even patronized the restaurant. That's advertising at its best.

The Advertising Agency Business

Before the emergence of the modern advertising agency, advertising was a do-it-yourself affair. But that doesn't happen often these days. There are just too many talents and skills that must be combined to make advertising succeed. You could farm out the various elements individually, but that is a difficult approach. What you should do is take your problem to an advertising agency, for virtually all advertising is prepared in agencies.

An advertising agency is an organization of business and creative people dedicated to making advertising succeed. Agencies often become involved with other aspects of marketing and selling, but their fundamental concern is the development of successful advertising.

There are about 6,000 advertising agencies in the United States. Most are small. About a third are one-person operations; still another third have an average of only five employees, but these exist primarily in smaller cities to handle local accounts, or as branches of larger agencies; the last third includes large companies, some employing more than 1,000 people each.

To maintain standards of conduct and competency, "the four A's," or American Association of Advertising Agencies (AAAA) was formed in 1917. Membership is by application: An applicant's references and balance sheet are reviewed with respect to the 4A qualifications; the applicant is then investigated and voted on by the 4A board. Member agencies handle some 70 to 75 percent of all the agency business in the United States.

There are more than 400 4A member agencies, operating more than 1,000 offices in some 165 cities in nearly every state (and in some one hundred cities in other countries). They're big and small. The *Standard Directory of Advertising Agencies* (the Agency Red Book) lists all the agencies alphabetically and geographically and states their 4A affiliation, if any. A sample listing from this directory appears later in this chapter in the section on Saatchi & Saatchi Compton, Inc. This directory may be found in major public libraries and some college libraries.

What Advertising Agencies Do and How They Do It

When an agency takes on a client, or even when it's "pitching" the account, it performs the following basic functions.

The agency studies the product, compares it with the competition, and checks its uses and its pricing, its packaging, and what consumers say about it and the competitors' products. The agency also analyzes the competitive advertising. These facts are determined from interviews, field studies, trade associations, and so forth.

The agency makes a careful study of the present and potential market for the product or service. The study involves the kinds of people who can use the product, their demographics (social and economic characteristics such as sex, age, size of family, education, and economic levels), where they are located, other potential uses, seasonal and geographical factors, and how the business is affected by trade and economic conditions. The need for research is clear. It may be obtained from many sources, but much will depend on the agency's experience and ingenuity.

The agency puts into use its knowledge of how to get the product profitably to the point of sale and who are the best wholesalers, jobbers, retail stores, and chains. Agency people constantly visit and study these establishments, as well as interview consumers in their homes.

An advertiser can spend his money in thousands of different places—consumer and trade magazines; daily and weekly newspapers; national and local TV and radio; outdoor posters; subways, buses, trains, taxis; window and store displays; and direct mail. The agency must understand all these media and their configurations. It must identify the best potential customers and then propose the media that will get the message to the buyer at the lowest effective cost. Media selection and evaluation are the most intricate arts of the agency business.

We now reach a key stage known as formulating the plan. The first half consists of making the plan, the second of putting it into operation. In formulating the plan, the agency makes its recommendations on the following:

- market or markets to be reached
- distribution changes to be made
- pricing and discounts
- the media channels to be employed to carry the message to the consumer and the trade
- what appeals to employ
- what to say in each channel
- what merchandising factors are to be contacted and brought into the effort
- how much the advertising appropriation should be

We then go into the execution of the plan. The client may decide to cut the overall budget or test-market the campaign.

Now the agency's creative people take over, putting the advertising message into words and pictures.

Copywriters must be skilled in the use of words and the motivations that cause consumers to act. Art directors and their staff, working with copywriters, visually implement the writers' efforts.

For print ads, layouts are made. These are designed by art directors who also specify typefaces. Assistants then make the mechanical paste-ups of these pages. The final rendering of the art is usually done by freelancers outside the agency.

For TV commercials, frame-by-frame "storyboards" (cartoonlike representations of the action) are produced by writers, art directors, and producers.

At this point, the agency issues orders to the various media to be used. For many purposes, a standard 4A form is used as an insertion order. These forms are accepted by most media, as they facilitate transactions.

Before the agency can send print advertisements to publications, the ads must be converted by the agency into the proper mechanical materials. The agency's production department, dealing with outside suppliers, controls this flow of materials.

For TV and radio, the agency buys commercial announcements, not usually a sole sponsorship of a program. An example of this is Procter & Gamble's mini-series "A.D.," discussed later in this chapter. The agency people are involved in every stage of the production of the commercials, although the actual filming and taping is done by production companies. The agency also "traffics" these materials from place to place.

After an ad or commercial is run, the agency verifies its appearance and performance. If an ad is printed poorly in a magazine, it is the agency's job to request a rerun. If a commercial doesn't run as planned, the agency must be aware of it and request new showings.

Finally, the agency receives bills from its suppliers, media, and services, and then bills the client. The agency will adopt some formula for services—that is, cost plus a percentage. In the case of media, the client pays the full charge, but the media allow a discount to the agency, usually 15 percent. This is how the agency pays its salaries and overhead and earns a profit. So that the agency's and media's cash flows are in sync, the client generally pays the agency at or before the time payments are due the media.

Billing Range	Number of Agencies
More than $25 million	339
Between $10 million and $25 million	481
Between $5 million and $10 million	495
Between $1 million and $5 million	1,127
Less than $1 million	504

Agency/Client Contact

On a day-to-day basis, the agency provides an account executive or, for very large accounts, an account supervisor as well, to act as the client's proponent within the agency. In a small agency, one account executive may handle more than one account. AEs may also specialize in such areas as packaged goods, cosmetics, heavy industrial, and so forth.

A larger agency may be organized into groups so that one group of people handles the contact, planning, and creative work for one or more clients.

People are an agency's main cost, accounting for about two thirds of its gross-income dollar. The remaining third goes for rent, taxes, and other expenses. An agency's average net profit is only about 4 percent of its income.

We can now begin to understand the function of an advertising agency and its specialists. The nation's 6,000 agencies employ about 70,000 people, with a lesser number employed by their clients in advertising and marketing functions. Including those who write an occasional ad for a restaurant or an auto-supply store, there are only about 200,000 people employed in advertising. If you want to be one of them, be prepared for an extremely competitive, pressure-laden, and challenging career.

The Scope of Advertising Today

In advertising and publishing, the *Standard Directory of Advertising Agencies* ("The Agency Red Book") is the industry's most important reference book. A recent edition lists key information about 3,531 agencies in this country and many abroad. It is published three times a year by the National Register Publishing Company, Wilmette, IL 60091.

The Size of Agency Billings

Of the 2,946 agencies that list their annual billings—defined as the gross amount the agency bills its client for space, time, and so on—here is the range:

Although the highest category is stated as more than $25 million, there are actually thirty-eight giant agencies that bill more than $300 million—fifteen of them more than $1 billion. Conclusion: *This is a very big business.*

Geographically Speaking

There is one lone agency with headquarters in Alaska, none in Wyoming, three in North Dakota, and only four in Delaware. Recent figures show that New York State has 774 headquarters of agencies and 295 branch offices of agencies with headquarters elsewhere, of which about 75 percent are in New York City. California is in second place with 401 headquarters and 221 branch offices, of which about 185 are in Los Angeles and one hundred in San Francisco. The others, generally smaller in size, are spread throughout the state. Illinois is in third place with 331 headquarters and ninety-two branch offices, of which about 50 percent are in Chicago.

Specialization

Many agencies are generalists, yet there are some that either specialize in advertising to a specific group or have departments that specialize in communication with particular markets or product lines. Here are some examples of these areas:

Area	Number of Agencies
Black Market	18
Direct Response	124
Financial	27
Health and Medicine	80
Recruitment	87
Resort and Travel	45
Hispanic	37

Media Spending by Leading National Advertisers

The reason there are so many advertising agencies with huge billings is that there are so many giant-size advertisers with huge expenditures in various media. A recent issue of the trade publication *Advertising Age* listed the ten largest advertisers and a breakdown of where they spent their money in a given year. Here are the ten, listed in order of total advertising expenditures: Procter & Gamble, General Motors, Sears, Roebuck & Co., Beatrice Companies, R. J. Reynolds Industries, Philip Morris, Inc., A.T.&T., Ford Motor Company, K mart Corporation, and McDonald's Corporation.

Here are some interesting facts about their spending:

- Procter & Gamble spent almost $1 billion on advertising, with about 75 percent of it for television.
- R. J. Reynolds Industries owns Heublein (wines and liquors) and Del Monte (foods), as well as its own tobacco brands. The parent company purchased almost $700 million in advertising and was the largest user of magazine space—$200 million worth.
- McDonald's needed to spend about $500 million in advertising to sell all those Big Macs and other fast-food goodies.

Who Does What at an Advertising Agency

There are about forty different job classifications at an advertising agency. Following are the basic divisions, followed in turn by their description and salary range. At the top, there is usually a president and chairperson of the board, who report to a board of directors unless the agency is personally held.

The Business Side

Management Supervisor

Account Supervisor	Media Director
Account Executive	Senior Media Buyer
Assistant Account Executive	Research Director
Account Trainee	
Account Assistant	

The Creative Side

Creative Director

Art Director	Copy Chief
Assistant Art Director	Copywriter
Art Assistant	Production Manager
Illustrator	(Print and Broadcast)
Paste-up Artist	Producer
	Assistant Producer
	Production Assistant

The figures in the following job profiles were obtained from a recent *ADWEEK* survey. Salaries at a New York City agency will be at the top of this range; at a Southwest agency, at the bottom. Salaries also vary with advertising experience. For example, an account executive with zero to five years' experience will earn a median salary of $27,900; an executive with six to ten years' experience, $36,000.

Salaries will vary further still according to an agency's total annual billings. For example, these are the median salaries for account executives at agencies with these billings:

- Less than $1 million: $22,000
- $1 million to $4.9 million: $26,800
- $5 million to $19.9 million: $30,700
- $20 million to $99.9 million: $31,200
- More than $100 million: $35,400

Soon after our discussion of job categories, we will offer suggestions on educational preparation and occupational training for many of these jobs.

The Business Side

Management Supervisor: This is a top-managment executive, responsible for the administration of one or more major accounts at an agency. He must be experienced in marketing techniques, campaign planning, and making successful contacts with clients. He must be a good business administrator. Occasionally, he will be involved in new-business activity, that is, selling the agency's services to prospective clients. Usually, he comes up from the ranks of account executives and account supervisors. Management supervisors often succeed to the presidency of their own or other agencies. Salary range is from $60,000 to $100,000.

Account Supervisor: On very large accounts, the account supervisor acts as the principal liaison between the agency and the client and often has corporate-vice-president status. He must be a strong, knowledgeable, and diplomatic leader. The account supervisor is charged with seeing that accounts under his responsibility generate a profit at the agency. In some agencies, he is in charge of three or four account executives. Salary range is $44,800 to $59,000.

Account Executive: The account executive maintains day-to-day liaison with the client. He must be a skillful organizer and analyzer and work well with the creative staff, the media department, and the traffic/production staff. He makes regular calls on the client to discuss strategy and media, review creative work, develop plans, and monitor the budget. Salary range is $25,700 to $33,900.

Assistant Account Executive: This is usually an entry-level job. A year or two in the advertising department of a manufacturer or retailer will help you get that first agency job. Also, a first job in traffic or media research is often a practical stepping stone to the account management staff. The assistant account executive doesn't get a fancy office or have much prestige, but in assisting the AE, he can learn in a year what is necessary to become an AE. Salary range is $17,300 to $22,800.

Account Trainee and Account Assistant: These are entry-level jobs below that of the assistant account executive, whom they assist. Often secretarial skills are required in these job classifications. Salary range is from $12,500 to $17,000.

Media Director: This individual directs the formulation of the advertiser's media plan. He analyzes, recommends, and estimates costs of various media to fit the client's budget. The media director must be a good businessperson and a sharp negotiator, and he must be precise on details. He is responsible for the spending of large sums of money. The media director consults with media reps on rates, position, special packages, and so on. Total familiarity with research data is required. Salary range is from $34,000 to $45,500.

Senior Media Buyer: The senior media buyer and assistants spend the client's money according to an agreed media plan. They will buy printed space and broadcast time and, consequently, must have the ability to weigh competitive claims and negotiate the best deals. Salary range for senior media buyer is from $31,000 to $41,000. Media buyers' salaries range from $20,500 to $27,000. Media trainees are entry-level jobs. Their salaries range from $12,000 to $17,000.

Research Director: This individual and the specialists who work for him are charged with providing the vital intelligence that helps solve sales problems. Frequently he provides creative people with the central idea for an advertising approach. The research function involves interpretation of market research, product research, and copy research. Salaries range from $37,800 to $55,000.

The Creative Side

Creative Director: This individual is entrusted with creating the selling idea and often presenting concepts to clients. He is responsible for a client's total advertising program, including TV and radio commercials, print ads, and outdoor billboards. He directs the creative activity of the art directors, copywriters, producers, and so on. In most agencies, the creative director has corporate-vice-president status. He usually starts out as a copywriter or as an art director. Salary range is from $45,000 to $60,000.

Art Director: The art director creates visual images that are translated into TV commercials and print ads. He must have a fertile imagination. In many agencies, the art director is part of a two-person creative team—the art director and the copywriter. The art director selects layout, type, art, and photos for print ads. He often does storyboards for TV commercials and works closely with the TV producer. He may have started out by doing paste-ups of art mechanicals. Art-school training and a portfolio of sample work help in getting such a start. Salary range is from $25,000 to $34,000.

Assistant Art Director: This person performs many of the same functions as the art director. He usually has more contact with staff people than his superior. The salary range is from $20,000 to $30,000.

Art Assistant: Under the guidance of the art director, the assistant prepares layouts and rough sketches for ads in print and broadcast. Salary range is from $13,000 to $18,000.

Illustrator: Most agencies use freelance illustrators. In New York and other large cities, there are hundreds of talented people in this specialty. Large agencies, however, may have illustrators on staff for the convenience of rush presentations. Salary range for staff is from $18,000 to $27,000.

Paste-up Artist: This individual assembles all the elements of an ad—type, art, and photos—and mechanically places them on a board ready for the printing or reproduction process. Salary range is from $12,000 to $18,000.

Copy Chief: Words are the essence of this function. Prerequisite is long experience as a copywriter who can evaluate good copy writing and motivate a staff to produce it. He must be able to translate product- and consumer-research data into copy that will trigger a response. Salary range is from $27,000 to $39,000.

Copywriter: The copywriter generates scripts for TV and radio commercials and copy for print ads. The focus for all advertising often starts with the copywriter, who evolves the campaign theme—

although the advent of the art director/writer team has given equal status to the art side of creative development. The job requires strong writing and verbal skills. The copywriter must have the ability to create attention-getting themes and headlines and to write strong copy for both print ads and TV and radio commercials. It is difficult to get entry-level jobs; persistence and patience are essential. Salary range is from $24,000 to $36,000.

> CAREER TIP: If you're applying for a job either as an artist or a copywriter, a portfolio is very important. You can develop one by working for an advertiser, such as a department store or a manufacturer. Schools like New York's School of Visual Arts (see section later in this chapter) stress preparation of a portfolio. Concentrate on print advertising in your portfolio. Try to include a whole campaign rather than single ads. Communicate your ability to create campaign themes. Make sure the portfolio is neat and well organized, and keep the copy within readable limits.

Production Manager: The nuts-and-bolts people in an agency are the production managers. The *print* production manager supervises the production, printing, scheduling, and budgeting of all advertising, outdoor print, and all print "collateral" (brochures, folders, letters, fliers, and the like). He must know all graphic-arts and printing processes. The *broadcast* production manager supervises the production of all TV and radio commercials. He works with outside production houses and "the talent" (actors, singers, musicians, etc.). Salary range is from $25,000 to $34,000.
Producer: The producer coordinates the many production details common to the TV commercial. He prepares the budget and works closely with the copywriter and art director. He selects the director and cameraman best suited for the job. The producer consults with the set designer and works with the casting director and the sound and music specialists. Salary range is from $28,000 to $39,000.
Assistant Producer: The assistant performs many

of the same jobs as his boss but is more involved with details, such as the complex technical, legal, and cost factors of making TV and radio commercials. Salary range is from $22,000 to $31,000.
Production Assistant: This entry-level position is highly coveted for the training it offers in every facet of the commercial-making process. Promotion can be rapid for the talented individual. Salary range is from $12,000 to $18,500.

Note: In a medium-to-large-size agency, the mix of personnel in the key areas is as follows:

Account Management	25%
Creative	25%
Media	15%
Production	10%
Other	25%

What the Big Boys Make

As we have seen in the previous section, the troops at an ad agency do not receive munificent salaries. Their generals, on the other hand, do very well indeed. However, these are the people who bring the $50 to $100 million accounts to the agency and are ultimately responsible to their boards and stockholders for the agencies' profit. When they cease doing this, they're fired. Here are the 1985 estimated salaries for some agency heads:

- Tom Clark, *President,* BBD&O International: $573,600
- Don Johnston, *Chairman,* JWT Group: $742,318
- Leo-Arthur Kelmenson, *Chairman,* Bozell, Jacobs, Kenyon & Eckhardt: $432,750
- Bruce Crawford, *Chairman,* BBD&O International: $666,500
- Philip H. Geier, Jr., *Chairman/President,* Interpublic Group: $1,300,000
- Charles Goldschmidt, *Chairman,* Laurence, Charles, Free & Lawson: $711,830

Getting an Agency Job

SSC&B:Lintas Worldwide is a large international agency with its headquarters in New York and a staff of 3,765. It has published a fine booklet called *The DETERMINED Person's Guide to Getting a Job in Advertising.* To obtain a copy of the booklet, send $2.50, or for more information on career opportunities at the agency, write to the personnel department at One Dag Hammarskjöld Plaza, New York, NY 10017.

Here's a staggering statistic: Each year SSC&B:Lintas Worldwide receives *more than 10,000* inquiries for entry-level jobs. The firm hires only forty new people. But please don't turn to another chapter; there's still hope.

Shortage in the Talent Pool

Seemingly incongruous with what we've written about an agency's hiring only forty out of 10,000 applicants is the talent gap existing in the creative departments of ad agencies. The problem is not the number of bodies but the availability of creative stars.

As one senior creative director put it, "We've never had a shortage of candidates. Plenty of young people have come to us over the years wanting to be copywriters or art directors, but the problem traditionally has been finding the really terrific ones who can make a difference."

One thirty-year-old copywriter, with eight years' experience, makes close to $90,000 at a large New York packaged-goods agency. He has already been at four jobs and claims to get five offers a week to jump to another agency, with each agency offering an exciting compensation package.

Rather than raiding, agencies are now actively developing their own creative talent. Says the president of one prestigious agency, "The kids now being trained in the creative area are coming on so strong and so fast that people in our business are going to wonder why they ever stopped hiring entry-level talent in the first place." That's good news for college graduates wanting to become involved in the advertising process now.

Advertising Agency Training Programs

The top ten agencies have instituted active training programs for their new media employees. Here are some highlights:

- One agency has a forty-week program of lunch-hour seminars that cover media basics, presentation skills, research tools, and media buying.
- Another agency holds lecture series and participation sessions for twenty-eight weeks at lunchtime. The series covers TV and print production, media research, and the creative side of the industry.
- A large Chicago agency has six- to eight-month formal programs of media classes held twice a

week in the morning. Programs delve into the identification of the various media sources—newspapers, magazines, TV, radio—plus training in purchasing these media. Trainees also attend yearlong agency overview seminars taught by supervisors.

In an excellent book listed under "Recommended Reading" at the end of the chapter, *How to Get the Right Job in Advertising* by Frank Kirkpatrick, the author takes a look at the top twenty agencies, with special emphasis on their training programs. He also discusses promotion opportunities.

Educational Requirements for Various Agency and Client Jobs

Account Management: If you want to make it as an account executive, agency hiring practices lean toward a minimum of a bachelor's degree with some background in advertising, psychology, communications and/or business. Some agencies require an M.B.A. in marketing but face competition with advertising clients and Wall Street for these candidates.

Agencies also favor applicants with one or two years of full-time work experience, preferably in sales or an advertising-related field such as the advertising or marketing departments of a manufacturer or retailer.

Research: A bachelor's degree in math and statistics is required. Some agencies like to hire people who have had three or four years of full-time experience with an independent research firm or with an advertising research department.

Media: Educational preparation includes a bachelor's degree in areas such as marketing, economics, math, and statistics. General advertising experience helps as well.

Creative (includes art direction and copywriting): The first requirement is a bachelor's degree in English, psychology, sociology, or language. If you want to be an ad agency copywriter, try to get some experience writing for a local retail or department store or the sales or advertising department of a corporation, usually an entry-level situation.

Client Jobs: While the agency is responsible for the creation and placement of advertising, the client administers and approves. Client advertisers often operate on the product, or brand manager, system. This individual is the key liaison between a particular brand and the agency. Clients are more involved with marketing than with advertising. To be precise, marketing involves the whole sales process, whereas advertising gets the message to the public via the media. Generally, the same education requirements listed previously for account management apply to client advertising jobs.

CAREER TIP: New York's School of Visual Arts is an excellent place to develop a portfolio—or "book," as it's called in the business. There's a one-semester general advertising creative course taught by active professionals from New York's ad agencies. You learn by doing. At the conclusion of the course, you have created your own book of ads, which may become a big plus at job interviews. The School of Visual Arts also has follow-up courses in copywriting and art direction. For more information, see the "School of Visual Arts" section further on in this chapter. See section at the end of this chapter ("Internships and Employment Agencies") for information on similar educational training at other schools.

A Day in the Life of an Advertising Agency

You majored in communications at college. After graduation, you moved from your home town in Ohio to the Big Apple, where you found a share in an apartment in Greenwich Village with two other recent graduates, and then got a job at $15,000 in a large ad agency as an assistant account executive on an airlines account.

It wasn't much of a job—mainly typing reports and making phone calls for your boss, a female account executive—but it afforded you the opportunity to find out how an ad agency functioned.

You were determined to succeed and even had a timetable of how long it would take to become a full-fledged AE and outrank your boss. Here's what a typical day looked like in your early agency career.

This day is important because it is now a month since the client, a major airline, approved the media plan, and in the coming weeks, the plan must be implemented. The plan calls for a large TV and radio budget, a major newspaper push, and some outdoor advertising. Since deregulation, most airline campaigns emphasize price cutting, and your client is no exception.

Your immediate boss (the AE) and her superior (the account supervisor) have given you the day-to-day responsibility of monitoring the flow of work for the account from each department and reporting back to them on its progress, so on this day you begin your rounds.

Your first stop is to see the associate creative director on this airline account, who informs you that everything is proceeding apace. He suggests that you drop in on the copywriter, who is just then meeting with an art director to plan a series of full-page newspaper ads. The thrust: Other airlines *talk* about low fares but really have many restrictions; your airline *delivers* low fares. You look at sample layouts and are impressed.

Then you hurry down the hall to the radio department where another copywriter is working on a group of 30- and 60-second spots that will be used in all the major cities along this airline's route. The same approach as that of print is taken— legitimate low fares. The radio people are also working with a freelance music outfit on doing a new jingle for the radio commercials.

The in-house TV producer is a heavyweight. Her staff is working on a series of 30-second spots. This entails the biggest part of the budget. It means coordinating with an art director who is doing the storyboards, a copywriter doing the scripts, a director, and an outside production house to actually shoot the commercials, and the agent for the star who will appear on camera. Of course, the client is brought up to date on every phase of this key operation.

Down another floor to the media department. The media buyer is meeting with a newspaper rep who is proposing a twenty-city buy with a twice-a-week frequency for a month. The buyer knows it will be too costly and must cut the budget back. The associate media director is, at that moment, lunching at the Four Seasons with a rep from John Blair, who is putting together a package involving 10- and 30-second TV commercials, as well as 30-second radio spots to be broadcast during commuting hours (drive time). You have a ham-and-cheese sandwich at your desk.

In the afternoon, you pay a visit to the research department. The research people seem to work at a slower pace. They are consulting their data reports to locate the best target audience for budget vacation travel. They use statistics the client has provided, plus material they have received from outside market research specialists.

When you report back to your boss, the AE, you get a verbal pat on the back and are told to continue the good work.

All is well until a week later when you and your boss visit the client. The client is unhappy about the creative layouts of the print ads and is not sure of the thrust of the TV commercials. Oh well, nobody said advertising was going to be easy.

The World's Largest Advertising Agency

Take two creative brothers named Maurice and Charles. Add six large-size ad agencies in the United States and the United Kingdom. Put them all together and you get the world's largest advertising conglomerate—Saatchi & Saatchi. Its worldwide billings in 1986 were an astounding $7.6 billion.

It all started in London in 1970 when Maurice was twenty-four and Charles was twenty-seven. The two formed a partnership and in just a few short years dominated British advertising by turning out excellent creative work for such prestigious clients as British Leyland, Bristol-Meyers, and Dunlop, whose products included autos, toiletries, and tires.

In just four years, Saatchi & Saatchi had billings of $10 million and had risen to thirteenth position among U.K. ad agencies. In 1975, it pulled off a major coup by merging with a much larger agency, Garland Compton, which was partly owned by the U.S. agency Compton Advertising. With it came three high-billing accounts—two British companies and the U.K. division of Procter & Gamble. Acquisition fever was off and running.

Even before the Compton buy, Saatchi & Saatchi had been making smaller acquisitions—three regional agencies in the United Kingdom and agencies in France, Belgium, and Holland. Also, the Compton deal gave them access to a New York office.

Very early on, Saatchi & Saatchi was determined to ride the global advertising bandwagon. With the rapid rise of multinational companies, it became apparent that marketing economy could be effected if the same advertising campaign could be used in many different countries, with only cultural and regional changes. As Saatchi & Saatchi reckoned, get the multinational advertising account first; then set up branch agencies all over the world, or purchase agencies in those countries.

Its U.S. barrage began in earnest in 1983 when it picked up the major agency McCaffrey and McCall for $10 million. Dancer Fitzgerald Sample was acquired in '85 for $75 million, and Backer & Spielvogel in '86. It became number one worldwide the same year that it bought the tenth ranking U.S. agency, Ted Bates, for the extraordinary sum of $450 million.

At this point, Saatchi & Saatchi can boast of these achievements:

- Its U.K. agency works with six of Britain's top ten advertisers.
- The U.S. agency handles more number-one brands than any other agency in America.
- The international network does business with more than fifty of the world's top one hundred advertisers.

The combined Saatchi & Saatchi operation represents these prestigious clients in three or more countries:

American Motors	Gillette
Avis	IBM
Bacardi	Johnson & Johnson
British Airways	Mattel
Campbell's Soups	Nabisco Brands
Chesebrough-Ponds	Nestlé
Citicorp	Nissan
DuPont	Philips
Eastman Kodak	Procter & Gamble

With the acquisition of competitive agencies came client conflicts. How does Chesebrough-Ponds feel about being in the same agency "family" as its competitor Gillette? Saatchi & Saatchi's answer is that the agency units are operationally independent and, while they probably won't pitch each other's accounts, they will zealously protect their creative and marketing strategy.

Other Acquisitions

Not content with a global ad agency network of about 12,000 people in 150 offices in fifty-four countries, Saatchi & Saatchi has been extending its sway into allied fields. These include public relations companies, management consultants, sales promotion agencies, and market research and corporate communications companies. In 1984, for example, it acquired the Hay Group, a major U.S. management consulting company, for $80 million and a prominent market researcher, Yankelovich, Skelly and White, for $13.5 million.

The *Standard Directory of Advertising Agencies* lists all advertising agencies with the names of officers, lists of accounts, and a breakdown of how they spend their clients' money. This directory may be found at most large public libraries and at some college libraries. See page 247 for a recent listing of S&S (Saatchi & Saatchi) Compton, Inc.

This agency is a subsidiary of S&S Compton Worldwide, which is the parent organization for its group of agencies. Other agencies in the group have separate listings.

The Compton agency was founded in 1908. It is a member of the four A's (American Association of Advertising Agencies) and by itself has billings of $500 million. Its largest media spending by far, $350 million, goes for television, with a significant amount for magazines. There are agencies such as Young & Rubicam that spend more than *$1 billion* a year on TV.

There are four executive VPs who are management directors. These are the top people in liaison with the clients. Working with them are senior VPs (account management), account supervisors, and account executives—all with direct client contact.

There are two executive VPs who are group creative directors and six senior VPs (creative). These people head creative groups composed of copywriters, art directors, and producers. The senior VP (business development) is the team captain of the group seeking out new clients—this is an ongoing operation.

The four Senior VPs (media) are in charge of all the agency's media buying and evaluation. Under them is a corps of media directors, buyers, and planners. They are the people who primarily maintain day-to-day contact with the various media representatives.

The listing shows forty-six top executives out of the entire agency's complement of 686 people. Although we don't have access to salary levels, we can guess that these forty-six heavyweights are all in the six-figure salary range. We can also guess that *all* S&S Compton personnel are well paid.

Now let's look at the list of their clients, certainly a prestigious lot. Headed by IBM, the list includes American Motors, Johnson & Johnson, and Procter & Gamble. A company the size of Procter & Gamble

will have a number of agencies representing its various products. In fact, soon after this list appeared, P&G pulled $120 million in billings from S&S. Unquestionably, P&G did not want client conflicts between the various S&S agencies, which nevertheless still represent a dozen P&G products.

What can we learn from this saga of an emerging communications Goliath? Clearly, it is a textbook story of aggressive acquisitions and growth. But before S&S began swallowing agencies, it had made its reputation producing trend-setting advertising. S&S simply out-performed all competitors—and it paid off.

S&S has always rewarded its star performers. In Britain, where salaries tend to be lower than ours, a hotshot twenty-three-year-old TV buyer can earn more than $50,000 a year, with a BMW as a perk. Going to work for S&S at one of its agencies is a

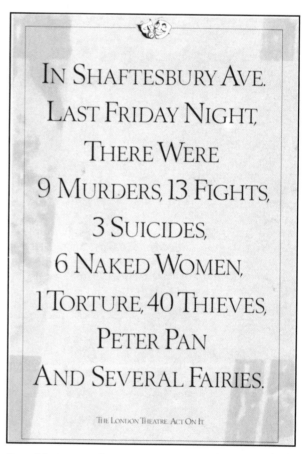

Saatchi & Saatchi Compton Ltd. established its reputation for creative excellence in England before making a foray into the U.S. market. Shaftesbury Avenue is London's theater section; the ad is a great piece of copywriting. (Reprinted with permission of Saatchi & Saatchi Compton Ltd. and The Society of West End Theatres.)

SAATCHI & SAATCHI COMPTON INC.

625 MADISON AVENUE, NEW YORK, NY 10022

TELEPHONE (212) 754-1100

(Subsidiary of Saatchi & Saatchi Compton Worldwide)

Employees: 686   Year Founded: 1908
National Agency Associations: AAAA—AAF—ABC—APA—BPA—DMA—MCA—TAAN
Approx. Annual Billing: $590,000,000
Breakdown of Gross Billings by Media:
 Newsp. $38,940,000; Bus. Publs. $6,490,000; Mags.
 $112,100,000; TV $413,000,000; Radio $19,470,000

Robert O. Jordan .... CHM. BD.
Edward L. Wax .... PRES. & CHIEF EXEC. OFFICER
Robert H. Levenson .... VICE CHM., CHIEF CREATIVE OFFICER
Philip Voss .... VICE CHM.
Gerald A. Kessler .... EXEC. V.P., CHIEF FIN. OFFICER
David Basch .... EXEC. V.P., MNGMT. DIR.
Ernst De Flines .... EXEC. V.P., MNGMT. DIR.
Thomas Lom .... EXEC. V.P., MNGMT. DIR.
Christopher A. Mill .... EXEC. V.P., MNGMT. DIR.
Edward Rosenstein .... EXEC. V.P., EXEC. RESEARCH & PING DIR.
Richard Earle .... EXEC. V.P., GRP. CREATIVE DIR.
Nadeen Peterson .... EXEC. V.P., GRP. CREATIVE DIR.
Charles Abrams .... SR. V.P., GRP. CREATIVE DIR.
Don Blauweiss .... SR. V.P., GRP. CREATIVE DIR.
Marcia Grace .... SR. V.P., GRP. CREATIVE DIR.
David J. Herzbrun .... SR. V.P., GRP. CREATIVE DIR.
William Harris .... SR. V.P., EXEC. ART DIR.
Robert Minicus .... SR. V.P., CREATIVE DIR.
Norm Weill .... SR. V.P., CREATIVE DIR.
Carole Cohan .... SR. V.P., DIR. BRDCST. PRODUCTION
Peter McGuggart .... SR. V.P., HEAD COLLATERAL SERVICE
Nancy J. Serlin .... V.P., MGR. CREATIVE SERVICES
John Ammon .... SR. V.P., ACCT. MNGMT.
Paula Forman .... SR. V.P., ACCT. MNGMT.
John Hayes .... SR. V.P., ACCT. MNGMT.
Ella Kelley .... SR. V.P., ACCT. MNGMT.
James Lomonosoff .... SR. V.P., ACCT. MNGMT.
Ericka Witnauer .... SR. V.P., ACCT. MNGMT.
Jeffrey Zeiller .... SR. V.P., ACCT. MNGMT.
John Dunmar .... SR. V.P., BUS. DEVEL.
John LaCroix .... SR. V.P., BUS. DEVEL.
Richard Mumma .... SR. V.P., ADMIN.
Stephen Fajen .... SR. V.P., EXEC. MEDIA DIR.
Joseph Burbeck .... SR. V.P., DIR. MEDIA SERVICE
Carol Karasick .... SR. V.P., N.Y. MEDIA DIR.
Donald Mohr .... SR. V.P., DIR. NETWORK BRDCST.
Robert Pape .... SR. V.P., DIR. P&G PING.
Abbott Wool .... SR. V.P., DIR. MEDIA RES.
Joseph Sansaverino .... SR. V.P., PERSONNEL DIR.
Bruce Cox .... SR. V.P., PROGRAMMING
Janine Linden .... SR. V.P., PUB. RELS.
Myrna Omang .... SR. V.P., FIN. ADMIN.
Richard Tompkins .... SR. V.P., DIR. EXEC. RECRUITMENT
Danielle Korn .... V.P. & DIR. TV & PRINT SERVICE
Sheldon A. Tankel .... V.P. & DIR. PRINT & BRDCST. TRAFFIC
Joseph Pedone .... V.P., DIR. PRINT PRODUCTION

Saatchi & Saatchi Compton Inc.
 8383 Wilshire Blvd., Beverly Hills, CA 90021
 Tel.: 213-852-1415

Shel Stuart .... V.P. & MGR.
Saatchi & Saatchi Compton Inc.
 American Center Bldg., 27777 Franklin Rd., Southfield,
MI 48034
 Tel.: 313-354-5400

David Welch .... PRES., MICHIGAN OFFICE
Richard Johnson .... SR. V.P., CREATIVE DIR.

Saatchi & Saatchi Compton Publicity
625 Madison Ave., New York, NY 10022
Tel.: 212-350-1815
 Janine Linden .... SR. V.P.

General Advertising

American Home Products
 Ayerst Laboratories Posture Calcium Supplement, Riopan, New Prods.
American Motors Corp. Detroit, MI Renault-Alliance, Encore, Jeep-CJ, Cherokee, Pickup, Scrambler, Comanche, Grand Wagoneer, Wagoneer Ltd., Jeep & Renault Fleet
AMC Intl. Opers.
Boehringer Ingelheim Ltd., Stamford, CT New Prods.
British Airways, New York, NY U.S. Adv.
Christian Broadcasting Network, Virginia Beach, VA The 700 Club
Cunard Line Ltd., New York, NY Consumer & Trade Adv.
IBM Corp., Armonk, NY
 National Marketing Div. (Sales Promo. & Related Literature)
 National Accounts Div.
 National Distribution Div.
 Customer Service Division
 Entry Systems Div.
 A/FE (America/Far East)
Jeffrey Martin Inc., Union, NJ Topol Toothpolish, Lavoris
Johnson & Johnson, New Brunswick, NJ
 McNeil Consumer Products Co., Ft. Washington, PA Tylenol Analgesic, Extra-Strength Tylenol, Co-Tylenol Cold Formula, Children's Tylenol, Children's Co-Tylenol, Max-Strength Tylenol Sinus Medication, Sine-Aid Sinus Medicine, Delsym Cough Medicine, New Prods.
 Personal Products Co., Milltown, NJ Take-Off Make Up Remover Cloths, Espree
 UroAbsorbent Pads, Stayfree Silhouettes
Krystal Co., Chattanooga, TN
Luden's Inc., Reading, PA Luden's Cough Drops & Confections
Mellon Bank Corporation, Pittsburgh, PA
New York Life Insurance Co., New York, NY Life, Group & Health Ins. Annuities, Pension Plans
Paine Webber, Inc. New York, NY
Phelps Dodge Industries, Inc. Corporate & Product Adv.
Portuguese Tourist Office, New York, NY
Procter & Gamble of Canada Ltd., The, Toronto, ON
Procter & Gamble Co., The Cincinnati, OH
 Packaged Soap & Detergent Div., Cincinnati, OH Cascade, Lemon Scented Cascade, Ivory Liquid, Tide, Liquid Tide
 Bar Soap & Household Cleaning Products Div., Cincinnati, OH
  Ivory Soap, Comet, Top Job, Comet Liquid, Liquid Ivory Soap
 Food Products Div., Cincinnati, OH Crisco Shortening, Crisco Oil, Duncan Hines Muffins, Duncan Hines Cake Mixes & Frostings, Duncan Hines Cookie Mix, Duncan Hines Brownies, Butter Flavored Crisco
 Folger Coffee Co., Cincinnati, OH High Point Decaffeinated Ground Coffee, High Point Decaffeinated Instant Coffee
 Industrial Chemicals Div., Cincinnati, OH Indus. Chemical, Grocery Trade, Drug Trade & Military Trade Adv.
Rums of Puerto Rico
Thompson Medical Co., Inc. New York, NY Dexatrim, Control, Slim Fast, Cortizone-5, Diar-Aid, Sleepinal, NP27, FiberFull, Slim Mints, New Prods.
Tyndale House Publishers. Publrs. of Religious Books
U.S. Health Care Systems Inc., PA HMO PA/NJ, U.S. Health Care, HealthWin, Medicare
Union Underwear, BVD Div., Bowing Green, KY
United States Steel Corp., Pittsburgh, PA Corporate & Product Adv.
WASA Intl., Copenhagen, Denmark. Crispbreads

Public Service Campaigns

American Economic System
Eye Bank for Sight Restoration
Productivity Campaign. Council of Independent Colleges
Religion in American Life

Updating information has been received directly from agency

good bet. Talent is its chief product, and you could be the superstar it is looking for.

A Look at a Small Agency

S&S Compton is a giant, and there are few in its class. However, there are many small ad agencies spread out across the country. Here is a listing of a typical small agency, Harper & Co., in Miami, Florida.

HARPER & CO.
75 S.W. 8TH ST., SUITE 306, MIAMI, FL 33130
TEL.: 305-358-6100

Employees: 15   Year Founded: 1977

Approx. Annual Billing: $4,220,000

Breakdown of Gross Billings by Media:
Newsp. $500,000; Bus. Publs. $100,000; Mags. $250,000; POP $50,000; Pub. Rels. $50,000; DM $400,000; Outdoor $50,000; Sls. Promo. $275,000; Production $80,000; Fees $100,000; Collateral $200,000; A/V $50,000; Radio & TV $2,000,000; Consumer Publs. $75,000; Cable TV $20,000; Trade Shows $20,000

David Harper .... Pres.
Alicia Martinez-Fonts .... V.P., Acct. Services
Judy Kaplan .... Media Dir.
Maria Madruga .... Art Dir.
Aleida M. Chao .... Office Mgr.

AeroPeru, Miami, Fla. Airline
Florida National Bank of Miami-Hispanic
Land Industries
Ontej/Orinoco Travel
Pizza Hut of Titusville, Inc.

There are only fifteen employees and billings are $4.22 million. If the agency works on a 15-percent-commission structure, its revenues are about $600,000. Many small agencies that perform special services such as designing brochures and display material on behalf of a client usually bill them on a fee basis for these services; sometimes, they operate on a part-commission, part-fee basis.

Radio and television get $2 million, or almost half the agency's billing. The agency keeps busy no doubt with the other spending categories listed. "POP" means point-of-purchase displays—for example, a counter card for drugstores. "DM" stands for direct mail. "Outdoor" refers to billboards and signs. "Collateral" usually means brochures, booklets, and the like, prepared for clients. "Trade Shows" refers to setting up exhibits for clients at conventions and trade shows.

There are only five key executives listed. In all probability, the account services VP maintains all the client control, and the media director is responsible for all the media buying. There are only five accounts listed, making the agency vulnerable to difficulty in the event of client loss.

For would-be advertising agency people among our readers, there is a case to be made for both the large and the small agency. In a large agency, one is in danger of being pigeonholed. In a small agency, one gets to do a number of jobs. The art director may also write copy, and the account services people also become involved with media selection.

CAREER TIP: If you are willing to work in a big city such as New York or Chicago, it is probably best to go the big-agency route because the salaries are better and the chances to switch jobs more opportune. By virtue of the numbers, it's easier to get a job in a big agency. In a small city, at a small agency, you will have the opportunity to gain a broader range of experience; then, if that is your desire, the move can be made to the glamorous big time.

The Ten Hottest Advertising Agencies

Periodically, the advertising trade publication *AD-WEEK* makes its choices of the ten hottest agencies.

WE MAKE THE SECOND BEST ROLLS IN THE WORLD.

MURRAY'S BAKERY & DELI
Skyway level · 701 Fourth Avenue South · 371-9429

Here's one reason why Fallon McElligott was chosen the hottest agency of 1985 by *ADWEEK*. The firm didn't need a shot of a warm, delectable roll to sell the bakery's quality—just a Rolls. (Reprinted with permission of Fallon McElligott.)

It is significant to note that four of the names on its recent list are located outside New York. These rankings are based on a performance index that includes both percentage and dollar growth in agency billings:

1. Fallon McElligott
2. Young & Rubicam
3. Ammurati & Puris
4. Allen & Dorward
5. Meldrum and Fewsmith
6. Saatchi & Saatchi Compton
7. BBD&O
8. The Richards Group
9. Kobs and Brady
10. Richard & Edward's

Fallon McElligott is in Minneapolis. Its billings skyrocketed as a result of successful campaigns for the *Wall Street Journal, US, Rolling Stone,* Prince Spaghetti and Armour Frozen Food. Young & Rubicam is a giant with worldwide billings of more than $3.25 billion. Meldrum and Fewsmith is in Cleveland and bills about $75 million. The Richards Group is in Dallas and ranks eighty-seventh among the top hundred agencies. Kobs and Brady is in Chicago and is in eighty-ninth place.

While New York predominates as home base for the top thirty hottest agencies, about one-third are west of Madison Avenue.

The preceding list is, of course, of the ten *hottest.* When we look at the top thirty agencies in terms of recent billings, we see only two of the top ten outside New York, three out of the top twenty, and seven out of the top thirty. Virtually all these New York–based agencies, however, have branch offices across the country and many worldwide (see section on Saatchi & Saatchi).

The Top Thirty

1. JWT Group, New York City
2. Young and Rubicam, New York City
3. The Ogilvy Group, New York City
4. Saatchi & Saatchi Compton, New York City
5. Ted Bates, New York City
6. BBD&O International, New York City
7. McCann-Erickson, New York City
8. Foote, Cone & Belding, Chicago
9. Doyle Dane Bernbach, New York City
10. Grey Advertising, New York City

11. Leo Burnett, Chicago
12. Benton & Bowles, New York City
13. Marschalk Campbell-Ewald, New York City
14. Dancer Fitzgerald Sample, New York City
15. Needham Harper, New York City
16. N. W. Ayer, New York City
17. Bozell & Jacobs, New York City
18. D'Arcy MacManus & Masius, New York City
19. Wells, Rich, Greene, New York City
20. SSC&B:Lintas Worldwide, London and New York City
21. William Esty, New York City
22. HCM, New York City
23. Campbell-Ewald, Warren, Michigan
24. Backer & Spielvogel, New York City
25. Ketchum Communications, Pittsburgh, Pennsylvania
26. Scali, McCabe, Sloves, New York City
27. K&E Holdings, New York City
28. C&W Group, New York City
29. Campbell-Mithun, Minneapolis and Chicago
30. TBWA, New York City

A Risky Business

In an industry with such frequent account changes, total billings are not the whole story. Small agencies turn out advertising as good as the biggies'. Accounts are lost for many reasons: The client is acquired and its advertising is handled by the parent company's agency; sales fall off, and the agency is fired; or the client hires a new management team who wants a new agency.

This points up the precariousness of the agency business. You get a job as an account executive at a hot agency, develop a strong relationship with the product manager on your account, and both the client and your agency group head think you're doing a good job. One day the president of the client company plays golf with the top executive of another agency, who tells him what great creative work they're turning out. You guessed it. The account switches agencies, and you're either out of a job or out of that account.

This does happen in advertising, but consider: You may be the hot account executive at the agency that *picks up* the new business. You then become account supervisor on the account and get to play golf with the client.

How an Advertising Agency Spends Its Money

Bozell, Jacobs, Kenyon & Eckhardt, Inc., is a giant advertising agency owned by the major entertainment company Lorimar–Telepictures. The agency had approximate annual billings of $1.1 billion in a recent year. It has branch offices in more than a dozen U.S. cities and in many foreign countries, in addition to its headquarters in New York. The agency employs about 4,000 people.

BJK&E is the agency for such prestigious accounts as American Airlines, Chrysler, Holiday Inns, Merrill Lynch, Revlon, Thomas J. Lipton, Fabergé, and Minolta copiers.

Here is a breakdown of the agency's gross billings as just cited. We will examine each medium for an understanding of where the money goes.

Breakdown of Gross Billings by Media

Newspapers	$ 91,000,000
Magazines	$152,300,000
Direct Mail	$ 800,000
Outdoor	$ 11,900,000
Television	$283,000,000
Radio	$102,000,000
Yellow Pages	$ 20,500,000
Production	$160,500,000
Fees	$167,900,000
Cable Television	$ 10,000,000
Other	$100,000,000

Source: *Standard Directory of Advertising Agencies.*

Newspapers: Most newspaper advertising is placed on a local basis. However, national advertisers, such as those BJK&E represents, place a great deal of space in Sunday magazine supplements of newspapers. Also, food advertisers do a great deal of co-op newspaper advertising with supermarkets in local papers. In co-op advertising, the advertiser pays for a portion of the advertising, and the supermarket or retailer pays the rest.

Magazines: BJK&E places $152.3 million in magazines. This includes business, or trade, publications, where advertisers reach their dealers, wholesalers, jobbers, and so forth. It's the agency's job to find the best publications to reach this audience. The category also includes farm publications and consumer magazines. At this agency, at least thirty accounts place major schedules in magazines.

Direct Mail: This category is referred to as "direct response." It relates to direct-response campaigns and coupon advertising.

Outdoor: Every time you see an outdoor sign, an ad agency had to prepare its creative aspects, in all probability became involved in the production of the sign poster, and placed the business with the sign's owner or representative.

Television: Here's the big bucks. BJK&E commits more than 25 percent of its annual billings to this potent medium. Some of it is in network buys, some in spot buys. We can be sure of one thing—this agency's media buyers and directors are highly skilled in the nuances of television buying. They have to be, especially when a 30-second spot during a highly rated show like the Super Bowl costs $550,000.

Radio: Radio is alive and well at BJK&E. It is one of the largest buyers of radio in adland, with an annual expenditure in the medium of $100 million. Because there is not much network radio, most of this money is spent at the local level. To facilitate these buys, the agency maintains eleven regional buying offices.

Yellow Pages: BJK&E has the Minolta account. When your fingers do the walking through your Yellow Pages directory under "Photocopiers," you'll see a small Minolta trademark listing and then a list of all their retailers in your city. This pattern is repeated all across the country. The agency gets it there—in this case, $20.5 million of it for Minolta and its other clients.

Production: When the agency does the production on a TV commercial, or tapes the radio commercial, or sets the type and makes the color separations for a magazine—that's a production charge that the agency bills to the client. It's usually handled with an agreed-upon markup for the agency.

Fees: This refers to the fees charged by the agency for services not included in the traditional practice of commissions deducted from media billing, usually 15 percent. When this practice is not feasible, the agency will agree with the client on a schedule of fees for services.

Cable Television: The growing field of cable TV is now achieving major advertising revenues, although it has been a slow starter because of its relatively small share of the viewing audiences. The figure of $10.1 million is a rather large one for this medium.

The spending of such huge sums of money re-

quires careful planning on the part of the account management people and, particularly, the media planners and buyers. The clients, of course, must approve the allocations of this spending and are integrally involved in the choice of media categories. Representatives of the media constantly visit the agency to ply their wares.

Other: In this category are included sales-promotional material for trade shows and conventions, point-of-sale (in-store displays), and printed material for sales meetings, industrial films, and so on.

Advertising and Marketing at a Major Bank

We have concentrated in this chapter on the role of agencies in the advertising and marketing process. Now we direct our focus to the client side—in this case, one of the nation's ten largest banks, with headquarters in New York City.

When we think of a bank's advertising, we think of radio commercials for IRAs or newspaper ads for mortgage loans or savings accounts. This bank has a $15 million ad budget, which it spends in TV, radio, newspapers, magazines, and point of sale. Its ad agency is one of the top five in the United States.

Organization

Advertising and marketing are under the aegis of a senior vice-president who heads a division that includes the branch sales network, human resources, product management, market research, facilities planning, and other functions.

A vice-president who reports to the senior vice-president controls marketing, advertising, direct mail, and promotional materials that go into the branches.

The advertising unit, under the vice-president, consists of three people. Their primary function is to act as a liaison between the ad agency and the various product managers in the bank, each of whom is responsible for a different production area. Products to a bank are IRAs, CDs, savings accounts, improvement loans, and the like. Most of this bank's collateral material is prepared out of house. A design firm works up different designs to be approved by the advertising unit and then given out to printers for execution. The agency creates advertising for each of these products.

How the Liaison Between the Bank and the Agency Works

The relationship between the bank and the ad agency is very close, with the agency at times practically living at the bank. Two account people at the agency work full time on the bank's account. There are another five to seven people at the agency who work on the account when the demand arises.

Although the bank looks to one account supervisor at the agency for overall responsibility, a whole team of people are involved, ranging from the president of the agency, occasionally, to the creative director, to the art directors, to the copywriters, and to the account executives.

The people in the bank's advertising group are on the phone with the agency about ten to fifteen times a day. It's the kind of close relationship where almost every decision—be it changing a word, a headline, or a sentence—is discussed between the agency and the bank before it's finally put to rest.

Although the advertising group at the bank consists only of three people, when a television shoot is done, someone from the bank is present at all phases, whether it's the pre-production meeting, the selection of locations, or the actual shooting and editing of the film.

Art and Copy Functions

The bank has an art director on staff who works with the commercial art studios that sell the department design work. Eighty percent of the bank's copywriting is written by outside sources. In-house writers will handle lesser chores, such as a simple form letter to a branch's customers.

The advertising/promotion group is responsible for direct-mail catalogues and brochures, "take one" (giveaway) material in banks, and trade shows. Requests for these specific materials come from the product management group. For example, the product manager for checking accounts needs brochures and take-ones. He requests these from the advertising/promotion group, which implements this by working with outside suppliers.

The advertising/promotion group, about eight people, differs in function from the advertising unit. In advertising/promotion, there are specialists in direct mail, copywriting, design, and printing production.

Radio and TV Commercials

When a radio commercial is made, there are about four or five in-house people involved—two on a full-time basis and the others, the product managers, at various points in the production.

A TV commercial may involve six or seven people—the three people in the advertising unit, plus some of the product managers and the senior managers who are shown the material at various stages of production to make decisions or recommendations.

Research

Advertising and marketing research for a large bank such as this one is a major activity. None of it, however, is done in house. The research department of the bank assists the agency in concept-testing research before an ad is produced. This is done through the use of focus groups, who are shown different ad solutions on boards and offer their comments on them.

Once the advertising has gone into production, a portfolio test is occasionally done in which people are shown a mock newspaper and asked to react to different advertisements in it. Surveys are also done in which test groups are asked to comment on commercials they have seen on TV or heard on radio. All of the bank's advertising is evaluated similarly.

Sales Promotion and Training Films

Promotions are generated by the in-house staff or by specialist sales promotion companies. Once a particular promotion is decided upon, the ad agency is brought in to execute it through various advertising media.

The bank has been doing some experimentation using videos for internal training and communications; however, the agency customarily does not get involved in this kind of production, so the bank uses a small video specialist company instead.

Opportunities in Bank Marketing and Advertising

Salaries paid to advertising people in house at banks are somewhat lower than salaries paid to their counterparts at an ad agency.

As the whole financial services and banking industry becomes deregulated, more and more emphasis is placed on the marketing and advertising functions; thus, this field becomes a good career opportunity for recent college graduates with advertising or marketing majors. Also, because banks are located all over the country, working for a bank does not necessarily require relocating to the three or four largest cities.

Note: Although we have pinpointed a bank to show agency/advertiser liaison, a similar process prevails with other kinds of accounts as well, such as those of packaged-goods companies, automobile makers and their dealer associations, fast-food franchises, and mutual funds.

How a Major Advertiser Handles a Television Event

Most of us have seen the "Hallmark Hall of Fame" on television. This advertiser carefully selects its programs, usually quality dramatic presentations, and becomes the single sponsor of a network broadcast.

In this situation, the network contracts with a production company that conceives the show—Paramount, Lorimar, Warners—and produces it. The network pays for the right to air it, and the client pays for the commercial time, which covers the network's cost and profit. (See Richard Low interview at the end of this chapter.)

An example of such a single sponsorship is Procter & Gamble's production of the mini-series "A.D." in 1985. Procter & Gamble paid for the production and worked with International Film Productions—the line producer, in a sense—on script, casting, director, and so forth. Ownership of the mini-series was held by P&G, with perhaps some participation by International Film Productions. P&G and its agencies then decided which of their brands would share the commercial time. The agencies contracted with NBC for the desired days and time slots. From a creative point of view, there was no significant difference in production values between this show and others that are merely "sponsored" by advertisers.

Huge amounts of money were at stake, first in the cost of production, then in the 12 hours of network prime time. Important sitcoms and dramatic series had to be pre-empted to make room for "A.D." Therefore, NBC, which didn't pay for the show, nonetheless had to be paid for the time.

To ensure a large audience for "A.D.," P&G incurred the additional expense of $600,000 for inserting a four-color booklet in *Reader's Digest* in the issue coincidental to the airing of the mini-series. The booklet told the story of "A.D." The magazine's audience of 55 million readers thus was exposed to an editorial approach to the mini-series with the hope of attracting them as viewers. P&G spent a great deal of money on this presentation. It represents top-drawer marketing.

How a TV Commercial Is Created

You may think you're mentally blocking out those pesky TV commercials. Some people actually zap them with their remote controls the way an electronic zapper demolishes mosquitoes on the back porch. The people who make commercials are aware of this and are redesigning commercials to be more like music videos, so that if you zap the sound with your remote control or fast-forward through a taped commercial, you'll still see the product name and a more or less comprehensible ad. Subliminally or otherwise, they're getting through. You're in their viselike grip. The only way to avoid them is to not watch commercial television. Commercials are big business: They cost hundreds of thousands of dollars to make and hundred thousands more to air. Here's how they are created.

The agency's copywriter and art director design commercials in very much the same way comic strips are drawn and written. First, they create a storyboard—a sequence of sketches of scenes approximating the action in the commercial with the spoken message written below each scene. This helps set up the shots and presents at a glance a visual outline of the commercial's structure.

The storyboard must then be approved by the client before actual production can start. Once it is approved, the copywriter and art director work closely with the agency's TV producer, who coordinates the production elements before filming or videotaping the spot.

The TV producer is a skilled specialist in many fields. He prepares a budget and tries to stick to it. He chooses the outside director and cameraman best suited to the job. He supervises the casting procedure, consults with the set designer, and works right at the director's side when the commercial is shot. Through it all, he adheres to a high standard of production values. After the shooting, he must follow through with the film editor, sound recording, and music sessions.

The TV producer is involved with the technical, legal, and cost factors in making commercials. He must also deal with contracts, unions, film studios, actors, musicians, and the toughest nut—the client. The job requires taste, skill, solid creative judgment, and talent.

Broadcast Operations

The broadcast operations department in an agency follows through on the whole process of a commercial from the early creative stage until it is delivered to the stations to be aired. In large agencies, broadcast operations have a big staff. The progress is monitored most closely by a broadcast coordinator. The coordinator works with the copywriter, art director, producer, legal department, account executives, and the production house that directs and actually shoots the commercial.

Business Affairs

When a commercial has been written and a storyboard prepared, the business affairs people are consulted on negotiations with talent and the production house. They send out bids, review them, and write contracts. The commercial must also be approved by network- or station-continuity acceptance people to make sure it meets with broadcast standards. This work demands knowledge and experience of every phase of TV commercial production.

Casting

Agencies employ specialists who handle the casting of actors, musicians, voice-over people, and singers—generically referred to as "the talent." Casting calls are conducted just as they would be for a feature film. Some agencies screen people in studio facilities that rival broadcasting station studios. Here, radio and TV commercials can be heard and viewed in all stages of completion by agency people and clients.

The equipment in these studios includes film projectors and screens, videotape players and monitors, audio-tape players, and slide projectors. These machines are handled and repaired by operators who have been hired for their skill or trained on the job, so one could conceivably be involved in TV commercials production with only "technical" training and expertise.

Talent is paid for the first performance in a commercial at the studio where it is recorded or filmed. If the commercial is used over and over again, the actors are paid residuals by the agency's talent reuse payment department. Residuals may be very lucrative, earning tens of thousands of dollars for the actors—more if the commercial receives heavy usage. That's why the competition among actors for work in commercials is so keen.

Traffic

When a spot is produced and given its final okay by the agency and the client sponsor, copies are turned over to one of the many broadcast traffic operators for shipment to the networks or stations in time to make air dates.

> CAREER TIP: As we have seen, many agency specialists are involved in the production of TV commercials. That means many agency jobs for qualified people. Education helps, but practical experience at a film studio, tape studio, TV station or production house is also essential. (See the chapter on television for information about technical training for these jobs.)

The Production Company

The agency people are specialists, but the TV production companies are the *auteurs*. Their special talents can make the commercial an award-winner and, at the same time, sell lots of soap or beer. Speaking of beer, some of the most outstanding beer commercials on television were created for Miller Lite by the renowned New York production company, Giraldi/Suarez. We talked with Phil Suarez, a partner. Here are some of his comments.

Basically, the production company executes the concept. The agency sends in the concept, and the production company handles all the producing. It does the casting, location scouting, costume designing, and takes care of the sets and the music. It sends the budget and the price to the agency for discussion. Often, the discussions entail some change in sets or costumes or locations to reduce the cost. Once the cost issue is settled, the creative work begins, and our director interacts closely with the agency's art director and creative people. However, the commercial director has most of the creative input while shooting the commercial. He is the one who takes the concept and develops it into the 60-second film, so he not only takes care of directing the actors, the lighting, and so on, but also creates the atmosphere of the whole film.

In our Miller Lite campaign, our problem in terms of actors was that the athletes used were not professional actors. They were, on the whole, very cooperative and delighted to be in the commercial, but they caused a lot more work for the director; consequently, the commercials took much longer to shoot. For instance, in the one with Steve Miserack, the pool player, there is a trick shot that took 180 takes to come out right. That was exhausting. However, such things happen only when you want the extraordinary to take place. Another instance of this was the commercial with John Madden [former NFL coach and current sports commentator], who had to crash through a wall. The crash had to be just right, and each time it didn't work, the wall had to be built all over again. Special effects are always time-consuming and expensive.

The price for a 30-second Miller Lite commercial is around $65,000. We have been working with Miller for fifteen years and have always tried to keep our prices reasonable. It's really in our own best interest. The average price for our 60-second commercial is only slightly higher—$75,000 to $80,000. We do so many during the year that we can afford to keep our prices reasonable. The only time our costs go up is when there are problems caused by bad weather. We try to absorb those costs, however, rather than pass them on to our client.

From the standpoint of where the action is, New York is a creative hotbed; all the major creative people are there. Commercials are produced mostly in New York, Chicago, and in Los Angeles, at times, because of the weather. Sometimes we shoot in Florida. The rest of the country really doesn't do much, although some cities like San Francisco have talented people doing this job. But New York is the place to be.

This is a huge industry, making and billing billions of dollars for TV commercials. There are hundreds of production companies in New York alone and, basically, if you own a camera and print up a card with your name on it and "Production Company" underneath, you're in business. Among all these companies, there are two or three dozen who are very, very good.

Regarding directors of commercials, the reason they have not really made the transition into feature films is that the film world—Hollywood—is not open to them. The film community doesn't really want to let people in from this side of the business. It is much easier to go in the other direction; that is, for a feature film director to start making commercials. If Sidney Lumet decided to do so, people in the commercial community would be very interested. Exceptions to the rule are directors of commercials in England, many of whom have made the transition from commercials to features—Ridley Scott [*Alien, Blade Runner*] and his brother Tony Scott [*Top Gun*] to name just two. Of course, even here we have people like Michael Cimino making the transition, but it's an exception.

The Two Most Important Advertising/Marketing Publications

Want a quick education in advertising and marketing without ever taking a college course? Just subscribe to *Advertising Age* and *ADWEEK*. You'll sound like an industry pro in a year and be able to "send it up the flagpole" with the best of them. Both *Ad Age* and *ADWEEK* have good want ads sections for jobs in advertising. Let's take a brief look at each publication.

Advertising Age

Ad Age, as we in the business refer to it, has been around since 1930. It comes out weekly on Mondays and has Special Reports that appear as separate Thursday editions. The Special Reports are on a diverse group of subjects including travel and tour

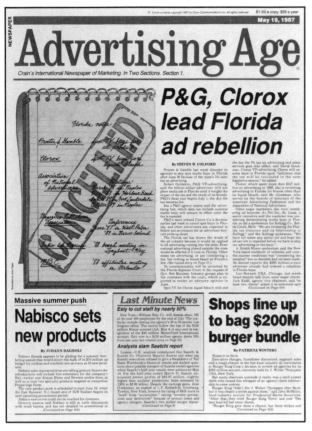

Ad Age is a powerhouse publication. Its coverage of the ad business is must Monday-morning reading. (Reprinted with permission.)

ism, liquor marketing, marketing to blacks, sports marketing, California, cable, and healthcare marketing. The publishers claim that each Special Report has more than 300,000 readers.

Ad Age's editorial package encompasses the media industry in great depth, both in the extent of its news stories and in its provocative columns. Magazines and newspapers receive the largest editorial coverage, but television and radio, direct response, and research also get heavy emphasis.

One is impressed with *Ad Age*'s editorial integrity. In its pages, unlike those of many trade publications, a press release is not reprinted with just the shifting of a few commas. If the story is worthy of coverage, an *Ad Age* reporter will call the subject of the release and do either a phone or a live interview.

Ad Age's "Special Reports" offer comprehensive coverage of a single subject. For example, the Wine and Beer report will deal with marketing trends, wholesaler and distributor attitudes, and valuable statistical and research information.

Advertisers in *Ad Age* are able to schedule advertising in any or all of the publication's regional

editions, which boast an overall paid circulation of about 90,000. Circulation is a significant factor in *Ad Age*'s tooth-and-nail battle with its archcompetitor, *ADWEEK.* The latter publication's recent circulation was about 75,000, but 20 percent of that was controlled, or free.

When it comes to ad dollars, *Ad Age* has the edge, selling about $24 million to *ADWEEK*'s $15 million. The two publications also engage in statistical research wars. The prospective advertiser is fed reams of figures and is expected to disseminate such arcane data as the fact that 20 percent of *Ad Age*'s readers read only *Ad Age,* but that *Ad Age* duplicates 88 percent of *ADWEEK*'s readers. Pity another industry magazine, *Madison Avenue,* which is read by only 8 percent of advertisers.

A subscription to *Ad Age* is $57.00 a year. Write to *Advertising Age,* Circulation Department, 965 East Jefferson, Detroit, MI 98207.

ADWEEK

Before *ADWEEK* was so named by new owners in 1981, the publication was composed of three regional advertising magazines with the funky titles *Anny* (Advertising News of New York), *Sam* (Serving Advertisers in the Midwest), and *Mac* (Media Advertisers and Clients).

ADWEEK is a network of seven regional advertising and marketing publications. It is edited by a staff of seventy-five, located in the nine major advertising centers of the country. What distinguishes *ADWEEK* from the competition is the liberal use of editorial color. But what really sets *ADWEEK* apart is a breezy, gossipy, hip style.

On a weekly basis, *ADWEEK* is a trade news magazine. In addition to this coverage, readers receive twenty-five bonus special issues with in-depth examination of specific subjects in advertising, marketing, and media.

Page one of a recent issue included the following articles: "First Amendment at Crossroads," "AMA: No Alcohol Ad Ban—For Now," and "Rehnquist: No Friend of the Ad Industry."

In the same issue, *ADWEEK*'s commercials' critic reviewed a new TV commercial for Burger King. She praised the music and visual presentation while rapping Burger King's joining "the already crowded patriotic jamboree." I'm sure this column draws much controversy, but it enjoys a high readership. The same thing can be said of this publication as a whole, because it is gutsy enough to criticize its own industry.

A subscription to *ADWEEK* is $50.00 a year. Write to *ADWEEK,* Subscription Department, 49 East 21st Street, New York, NY 10010.

256

ADWEEK

Vol. XXXVII No. 12   WESTERN ADVERTISING NEWS   March 9, 1987 ● $1.50

Merle Makes Up Its Mind: Grey Grabs a Beauty Prize

By Doreen Lee

LOS ANGELES—The courtship is over. After months of interviews and deliberation, Merle Norman Cosmetics has picked Grey as its new color for spring, handing the L.A. agency its $3-5-million account. The decision was made after Grey and fellow L.A. shops Ogilvy & Mather; Ramey Communications; and Asher/Gould and incumbent Della Femina, Travisano & Partners/N.Y. went through an unanticipated extra round of *(Continued on page 8)*

Merle Norman makes the difference.

Merle Norman will get a Grey make-over.

Oscar Winner: Revlon Starts A 'Star Watch'

By Betsy Sharkey

HOLLYWOOD—For the first time in its 59-year history, the Academy Awards will allow a sponsor to run a promotion prior to the March 30 ABC broadcast. And the winner is . . . Revlon.

The Academy Awards show has historically been extremely hard for advertisers to break into—long waiting lists, little turnover and additional *(Continued on page 8)*

(Continued on page 8)

Will Max mouth the "P" word?

Making Headway in the Cola Wars

Coke and Pepsi are squaring off in a new round of TV advertising. "Critique" columnist Barbara Lippert takes a look at two of the spots and finds a refreshing change in tactics.   *(See page 20)*

(INDEX CONTINUED ON PAGE 2)

Jacuzzi Sinks JWT/S.F. Again

By Jon Berry

WALNUT CREEK—For the second time in three years, Jacuzzi Whirlpool Bath has fired J. Walter Thompson/West, S.F., and splashed into review waters. Billings are $3 million, says Jacuzzi president Roy Jacuzzi.

Jacuzzi, which hopes to have a new shop by midsummer, says the move is the result of changes at JWT. The agency recently overhauled its senior management team and replaced general manager John Florida with cd Bill Lane.

"The first time we left, it was the same reason," says Jacuzzi, citing the parade of "five or six" gms at JWT in the account's 9½ years there. "We were promised *(Continued on page 63)*

THE EURO

Jacuzzi gives review a whirl without JWT.

ADWEEK can be counted on to report the news of the advertising world brilliantly. (Reprinted with permission of *ADWEEK*.)

The Advertiser's Side of Advertising

The large company that markets products to the public relies on its advertising agency for the research, creation, and placement of advertising. In addition, the company also maintains an in-house advertising department staffed with individuals with functions not dissimilar to those found in an advertising agency. The direction of a department such as this one is usually under a senior corporate officer, while its various divisions (food products, personal-care products, etc.) are each under a vice-president.

Take a look at the listing in the *Standard Directory* for Procter & Gamble, the nation's top advertiser, with expenditures of almost $900 million and total sales of approximately $13.55 billion.

Now let's identify the structure of this giant among marketers. The company is broken down into five subdivisions, each with its own roster of brands. "Soaps, Detergents & Household Cleaners" has thirty-three individual products, which are the responsibility of product managers within the subdivision. Seven different ad agencies divide the assignments for these brands. One of the agencies listed, Saatchi & Saatchi Compton, has fourteen brands from various subdivisions of P&G.

The mind-boggling reality is the size of P&G's advertising appropriations; TV accounts for about $650 million, while magazines receive a paltry $50 million. With numbers like these to spend, we can understand P&G's clout with the media.

Procter & Gamble has always been known as a master marketer. Business and marketing majors or M.B.A.s can launch profitable careers working for P&G while gaining incomparable experience with this talented giant.

This company hires approximately 1,000 college graduates each year. Not all of these are in advertising and marketing; some are in product management and development. Talk to P&G recruiters when they visit your campus.

How Much You Will Make

Salaries on the advertiser, or client, side of advertising/marketing for a company such as Procter & Gamble are comparable to those at the agency level. In order to attract top talent, a giant diversified company such as R. J. Reynolds, in Winston-Salem, North Carolina, will pay its people salaries as high as those at New York ad agencies. This is the case with any national advertiser with a budget of $100 million or more annually.

This factor should be considered by readers who want to get into the field but don't want to live in New York or Chicago. Recent figures for various advertiser jobs are as follows:

Job Classification	Median Salary (in thousands)
Top Advertising and Sales Promotion Executive	$52.3
Advertising Manager	34.7
Sales Promotion Manager	33.6
Brand or Product Manager	48.5
Media Manager	35.3
Media Planner/Buyer	24.0

Men earn substantially more money than women for similar jobs. The median salary for eight client, or advertiser, positions is $48,300 for men and only $32,000 for women. Women seem to be as underpaid in this glamorous activity as they are in other management situations.

Another chart of interest to would-be ad people is the one *ADWEEK* recently tabulated (below) on the salary increases that business and industry marketing executives (not agency) can expect for experience on the job.

Conclusion: Get promoted fast and stay on the job—or stay in school and get an M.B.A.

Job Classification	0–5 years	6–10 years	20+ years
Top Advertising and Sales Promotion Executive	$36.0	$44.7	$74.0
Advertising Manager	27.4	35.2	—
Sales Promotion Manager	28.7	35.2	—
Brand or Product Manager	42.0	51.0	—

The Procter & Gamble Co.

ONE PROCTER & GAMBLE PLAZA
CINCINNATI, OH 45202

MAILING ADDRESS: P.O. BOX 599
CINCINNATI, OH 45201
TEL.: 513-983-1100

Approx. Sales: $13,552,000,000
Approx. Number Employees: 62,000

Soaps, Detergents & Household Cleaners

Bold-3, Camay, Coast, Dawn, Downy, Dreft, Cascade, Cheer, Comet, Dash, Ivory Soap, Ivory Snow, Ivory Liquid, Joy, Lava, Mr. Clean, Oxydol, Safeguard, Spic and Span, Tide, Top Job, Zest, Biz, Gain, Era, Bounce, Comet Liquid, Kirk's, Solo, Liquid IvorySoap, Monchel, Pine Liquid, Liquid Tide

Food Products

Crisco, Crisco Oil, Duncan Hines Prepared Baking Mixes, Jif Peanut Butter, Pringle's Potato Chips, Puritan Oil, Crush, Hires, Sundrop, Fluffo, Citrus Hill Orange Juice and Citrus Prods., Duncan Hines Cookies

Personal Care Products

Crest, Gleem, Head & Shoulders, Norwich Asprin, Encaprin, Head & Chest, Chloroseptic, Pepto-Bismol, Prescription Drugs, Always Feminine Protection Prods., Ivory Hair Conditioner, Lilt, Wondra, Scope Mouthwash, Secret & Sure Deodorants, Ivory Shampoo, Pert Shampoo, Prell Shampoo

Household Paper Products

Charmin Bathroom Tissue, White Cloud Bathroom Tissue, Puffs Facial Tissues, Bounty Paper Towels, Pampers Diapers, Luvs Disposable Diapers, Attends, Banner Bathroom Tissue

Coffee Products

Folger's Vacuum Packed, Folger's Decaffeinated, Instant Folger's Coffee Crystals, High Point Decaffeinated Coffee

Advertising Agencies:

Saatchi & Saatchi Compton Inc.
625 Madison Ave
New York, NY 10022
Tel.: 212-754-1100
(Cascade, Comet, Crisco, Crisco Oil, Ivory Soap, Duncan Hines Quick Bread Mixes, Duncan Hines Brownie & Muffin Mixes, Duncan Hines Cookie Mix, Duncan Hines Layer & Creamy Ready-to-Spread Frosting, & Angel Food Cake Mixes, Duncan Hines Bakery Style Muffins & Flavored Brownies, Ivory Liquid, Tide & Liquid Tide, Top Job, High Point Decaffeinated Coffee)

D'Arcy Masius Benton & Bowles, Inc.
909 Third Ave.
New York, NY 10022
Tel.: 212-758-6200
(Always, Attends, Bounce, Charmin, Crest, Dash, Dawn, Ivory Shampoo & Conditioner, Ivory Snow, Norwich Asprin, Pampers, Pepto-Bismol, Scope, Vibrant, Wondra)

Leo Burnett Company, Inc.
Prudential Plaza
Chicago, IL 60601
Tel.: 312-565-5959
(Camay, Lava, Secret, Chloraseptic Throat Spray & Lozenges, Head & Chest Cold Medicines, Lilt Home Permanent, Cheer, Era, Gleem Toothpaste, Pert Shampoo, White Cloud Tissue)

Grey Advertising Inc.
777 Third Avenue
New York, NY 10017
Tel.: 718-546-2000
(Downy, Jif Peanut Butter, Monchel Soap, Duncan Hines Ready-to-Eat Chocolate Chip Cookies, Joy, Bold, Puritan Oil)

Tatham-Laird & Kudner
980 N. Michigan Ave.
Chicago, IL 60611
Tel.: 312-337-4400
(Mr. Clean, Head & Shoulders Shampoo & Conditioner, Biz, Coast Soap)

Northlich, Stolley, Inc
200 W. Fourth St.
Cincinnati, OH 45202
Tel.: 513-421-8840
(Industrial Prods., Folgers, Bar Soaps, Cleaning Products, Laundry Prods., High Point Coffee, Foodservice)

Burrell Advertising Inc.
625 N. Michigan Ave.
Chicago, IL 60611
Tel.: 312-266-4600
(Crest Toothpaste) (Appro.: $872,000,000; Daily News $6,547,000; Consumer Magazines Div. $49,735,000; Outdoor $380,000; Network Radio $3,900,000 Spot Radio $3,517,000, Network T.V. $412,747,000; Spot T.V. $239,331,000; Cable T.V. $24,182,000; Misc. $131,584,000)

Dancer Fitzgerald Sample, Inc.
405 Lexington Ave.
New York, NY 10174
Tel.: 212-661-0800
(Oxydol, Dreft, Luvs, Encaprin, Tenderleaf Tea, Bounty, Solo Detergent with Fabric Softener)

Cunningham & Walsh Inc.
260 Madison Ave.
New York, NY 10016
Tel.: 212-683-4900
(Folger's Instant & Red Brick Ground Coffee, Vacuum, Flaked, Certain, Hires, Sundrop, Puffs, Crush, Citrus Hill Orange Juice)

Wells, Rich, Greene, Inc.
9 West 57th St.
New York, NY 10019
Tel.: 212-303-5000
(Prell, Pringle's Potato Chips, Spic 'n Span No Rinse Cleaner, Safeguard & Sure, Banner Toilet Tissue)

Klemtner Advertising Inc.
625 Madison Ave.
New York, NY 10022
Tel.: 212-350-0400
(Didronel, Professional High Point Coffee)

Mandabach & Simms, Inc.
111 N. Canal St.
Chicago, IL 60606
Tel.: 312-902-1300
(Industrial Prods., Frymax, Prep & Sterling Oils)

The School of Visual Arts

New York City has many fine academic institutions for undergraduate and continuing education studies. None, however, can match the School of Visual Arts in the depth of its concentration in fine arts and media arts. Founded in 1947, SVA is the largest independent art school in the United States. It currently offers bachelor of fine arts degree programs in six areas: art teacher education, film, fine arts, media arts, photography, and journalism.

The school also offers master of fine arts degree programs in fine arts, illustration, and computer graphics. In addition to SVA's undergraduate and graduate programs, 4,000 students attend the continuing education program.

The 2,200 full-time undergraduate students are taught by a staff of 647 faculty members who are all working professionals. The SVA library houses 47,000 volumes, 75,000 art slides, and a picture collection of 225,000 pieces.

For the exhibit and sale of advanced student works, SVA maintains a professional gallery in New York's Soho district. There, approximately fourteen group shows are presented annually.

The school also has an in-house design studio that produces award-winning books, booklets, magazines, ads, and films. The Public Advertising System of SVA is a media arts department course, which functions like an advertising agency. Students develop ad campaigns, brochures, posters, and TV commercials for public service clients such as the President's Committee on Employment of the Handicapped, the New York City Department of Health, Planned Parenthood, and the Sickle Cell Disease Foundation.

Specialization

There are ten areas of specialization within SVA's curriculum. Each discipline has its first- through fourth-year requirements, with a liberal sprinkling of electives to widen the scope of the specialization. We list all ten disciplines.

- Film and Video: New York attracts the best writers, producers, directors, and editors. Professionals who work in commercial filmmaking, video and broadcasting and in advertising pro-

duction serve as faculty and inspiration for students in this specialty. Here are some representative courses: Introduction to Video Tape, Writing as Communication, Film Production, Advanced Editing, Advanced Cinematography, and Documentary Video.
- Fine Arts
- Art Education
- Art Therapy
- Media Arts
- Computer Graphics: Clearly, computers dominate our new technologies. Here, SVA offers a variety of computer graphics courses designed for artists wanting to learn the use of computers as a visual and creative tool.
- Communication Arts: In the glamorous world of print, broadcast journalism, and public relations, New York is the international hub. Students in this specialty benefit from the instruction of local professionals in radio, TV, and the newsroom. There is an eight-semester humanities core program intermixed with specialist courses in film, photography, and journalism.
- Photography: SVA's catalogue states the focus of this department: "Developing the artist behind the camera." This is a four-year program of technical information and experience offering about forty courses exploring this creative discipline.
- Humanities and Science
- Art History

SVA and Continuing Education

The school's motto, "When the job you have is not enough, but the job you want is out of reach," is the thrust of SVA's Visual Arts continuing education program. Go there, they say, when you're between jobs, and go there at night and on Saturdays while you're working and want to prepare for a new career.

This is just a sprinkling of the recent evening and weekend courses in media arts available at SVA:

Basic Graphic Design: For Advertising
Magazine Design Portfolio
Creating Television and Movie Posters
Magazine Design
Advanced Graphic Design
Principles of Pharmaceutical Advertising
Account Management
Advertising Media Planning
Producing a Commercial Spot
Basic Copywriting
Designing Collateral Graphics

Bernard Bragg has won critical acclaim as an actor.
He has never heard applause.

BERNARD BRAGG/CO-FOUNDER OF THE NATIONAL THEATRE OF THE DEAF.

Believe in them.
Break the barriers.

PRESIDENT'S COMMITTEE ON EMPLOYMENT OF THE HANDICAPPED, WASHINGTON D.C. 20210

PRODUCED BY THE SCHOOL OF VISUAL ARTS PRESS, LTD.

"Deafness is something you put beside you not in front of you."

LINDA BOVE/ACTRESS.

LINDA BOVE PERFORMED WITH THE NATIONAL THEATRE OF THE DEAF FOR NINE YEARS. SHE HAS ALSO STARRED IN THE TONY AWARD WINNING SHOW, CHILDREN OF A LESSER GOD.

Believe in them.
Break the barriers.

PRESIDENT'S COMMITTEE ON EMPLOYMENT OF THE HANDICAPPED, WASHINGTON D.C. 20210

PRODUCED BY THE SCHOOL OF VISUAL ARTS PRESS, LTD.

Victoria Ann-Lewis moves so gracefully on stage the audience doesn't even know she has polio.

VICTORIA ANN-LEWIS/ARTIST IN RESIDENCE AT THE MARK TAPER FORUM IN LOS ANGELES.

Believe in them.
Break the barriers.

PRESIDENT'S COMMITTEE ON EMPLOYMENT OF THE HANDICAPPED, WASHINGTON D.C. 20210

PRODUCED BY THE SCHOOL OF VISUAL ARTS PRESS, LTD.

Creating public-service ads such as these give students at New York's School of Visual Arts excellent on-the-job training. The students can also use the ads for their "book," or sample portfolio. (Reprinted with permission.)

The Concept Within a Concept Approach to Writing Body Copy

Advertising for People Who Are Already in Advertising

The Team Approach

How to Think Like a Creative Person

The Best Writers Are Good Art Directors—The Best Art Directors Are Good Writers

The cost of courses in continuing education at SVA averages $220 per semester. For further information about this exceptional school, write to School of Visual Arts, 209 East 23rd Street, New York, NY 10010.

The New Consumer Age

Affecting global advertising and marketing of the future is the growth of developing countries, their populations, and their mega-cities. These mega-cities, called greater metropolitan areas in most research, are termed "conurbations" by the United Nations in its studies. Here is an interesting listing of the world's ten largest conurbations in 1970 and a projected listing for the year 2000, both listed in descending order.

1970	2000
New York/Northeast New Jersey	Mexico City
Tokyo/Yokohama	São Paulo
Shanghai	Tokyo/Yokohama
London	Calcutta
Rhine/Ruhr	Bombay
Mexico City	New York/Northeast New Jersey
Greater Buenos Aires	Seoul
Los Angeles/Long Beach	Shanghai
Paris	Rio de Janeiro
Beijing	Delhi
Total Population: 105.2 million	Total Population: 169.1 million

From the same source, the United Nations, come figures of great significance to consumer marketing and advertising in the future—in this case, projected increases in median age from 1980 to 2000.

	1980	2000
United States	30.0	35.7
United Kingdom	34.3	37.4
France	32.5	37.6
Germany	36.6	41.1
Japan	32.7	39.2

One therefore realizes that unless these mega-cities are huge pockets of poverty, opportunities exist for mass marketing to groups previously not considered prime consumers.

Twenty Tips on Breaking into Advertising

Here are specific tips to help you in your pursuit of fame and fortune in the advertising world.

- If recruiters from ad agencies visit your campus, be sure to attend. Ask questions and try to learn their hiring practices, interview systems, attitudes about requirements for graduate work, and so forth.
- Advertising is a young people's business. You may be over the hill by the time you're forty-five; nevertheless, I know a copywriter at a top-three agency who spent almost forty years with the company, never made it to top management, earned an excellent salary, and feels that he has had a very fulfilling career.
- Use friends or any contact you can make to get an agency interview, preferably with an executive in the department that interests you. If a family member has a contact at a major advertiser, use it to get an interview with the agency.
- If you want to be a copywriter, you must have a sample book made up of hypothetical ads for real brands and services. One good way to get this book is to take a copywriting course at a school like New York's School of Visual Arts. (Unfortunately, similar courses on the continuing-education level do not exist in most other cities.) Then compile your book as part of your course work. Another way is to get a job at a large retailer or manufacturer that does its own advertising. The job won't pay much, but it will help build your portfolio.
- Consider any agency entry-level job, even sec-

retarial. There you can learn by just being around advertising.

- If you live in a large city, take an evening course in advertising and marketing taught by professionals at one of the city's colleges.
- Sell yourself in your résumé, but keep it to one page. Consider it your "unique selling proposition," which is the basic premise of all advertising. Don't waste space on clubs you belonged to in high school. Punctuation, spelling, and reproduction of the résumé must be perfect.
- Read every book you can find about advertising. Subscribe to *Ad Age, ADWEEK,* and *Media & Marketing Decisions.* (A year's subscription to this last publication is $45.00. Write to the magazine at 1140 Avenue of the Americas, New York, NY 10036.)
- The top hundred agencies have about 50,000 employees. If you choose to work for a small agency, note that salaries can be 20 to 50 percent less.
- New York agencies are not keen on transfers from agencies in smaller cities because of different work style and pace. But if you come from a *client*, say Procter & Gamble in Cincinnati, that's another story.
- Before you go to work for an agency, find out about its training program. Many don't have this important feature.
- If you're interested in advertising and marketing but don't want to work in New York or in an ad agency, consider employment at a major advertiser like Procter & Gamble. They spend $1 *billion* a year on advertising. If you become a product or brand manager, you will be responsible for all phases of a product's marketing including test marketing, product development, advertising campaign, packaging, and so on. It's a challenging, well-paid job.
- If you want to go into account management at an ad agency, you should think seriously about getting an M.B.A. You'll have a better chance to get that important first job and you'll earn much more money to start. Also, product managers who work most closely with account executives are often M.B.A.s. They prefer working with other M.B.A.s so they can talk "M.B.A.speak."
- When you get an agency job—be it account management, media, or creative—learn all you can about a client's business. Read the annual report and marketing literature. Study the competition and the trade practices in the industry.
- Persevere through the "assistant" stage. An assistant art director doesn't do many layouts. An assistant copywriter doesn't write very much. An assistant TV producer may just "gofer" coffee. But you'll be in the right place when the right time comes. Stick with it; everyone starts that way.
- Market research and media are good fields for people well versed in statistics and computer science. Salaries are on a par with those of other specialties.
- Packaged goods accounts are coveted at agencies, as are jobs working on them. People are paid more for these assignments, but the account fatality rate at agencies is high.
- Don't depend on too much job hopping. Build up your experience. It will eventually pay off.
- Going the big-agency route? In New York, Young & Rubicam and The Ogilvy Group, and in Chicago, Leo Burnett, seem to be actively interested in entry-level people. Y&R employs almost 4,000 people at its various offices. You might concentrate your efforts on these three.
- Don't overstress the glamour aspect of agency work. There are tremendous client pressures. When your account moves to another agency, you may be dropped as well. Also, you'll be competing against many bright, aggressive people. Becoming rich and famous in ten easy years is not the rule in advertising.

Internships and Employment Agencies

Internships

Unfortunately, there are not many internships available in the advertising business, although some colleges arrange for internships for their students. There is one important one, the American Association of Advertising Agencies, 666 Third Avenue, New York, NY 10017. This trade association offers twenty-five salaried, ten-week summer jobs in New York and Chicago for minority college students. Write for full information.

College Advertising Courses

There are more than one hundred U.S. colleges and universities offering courses in marketing and advertising. These programs take many forms: majors, sequences, specializations, emphases, and concentration. An excellent booklet detailing these programs may be obtained by sending $1.00 to Advertising Education Publications, 3429 55th Street, Lubbock, TX 79413. The title of the booklet is *Where Shall I Go to College to Study Advertising?* by Billy I. Ross, Ph.D.

For information about college courses and internships on a local level, contact the American Advertising Federation, Director of Educational Services, 1400 K Street, N.W., Washington, DC 20005.

Employment Agencies

Two agencies specializing in advertising agency jobs in the New York area are Jerry Fields Associates, Inc., 555 Madison Avenue, New York, NY 10022; and Judy Wald Agency, Inc., 110 East 59th Street, New York, NY 10022.

Career Booklets

Three valuable advertising career booklets are available:

Advertising: A Guide to Careers in Advertising. Single copy $1.00 postpaid. Available from the American Association of Advertising Agencies, Inc., 666 Third Avenue, New York, NY 10017.

Business-to-Business Communications. Single copy free. Available from Business/Professional Advertising Association, 205 East 42nd Street, New York, NY 10017.

Jobs in Advertising. Send 75¢ per copy and a self-addressed stamped envelope. Available from the Bureau of Education and Research, American Advertising Federation, 400 K Street, N.W., Washington, DC 20005.

Two Interviews

Our two guests in this section combine almost sixty years of experience in advertising. Bill Pitts' background is in the creative area of advertising with a strong emphasis on marketing. Dick Low retired from Young & Rubicam, one of the world's largest ad agencies, in the early 1980s. There, as executive vice-president, his responsibilities included the annual purchase of almost a billion dollars worth of television commercial time.

Bill Pitts, vice chairman and marketing director, Lois Pitts Gershon Pon GGK, is an accomplished marketing professional with unmatched experience in promotion, merchandising, and market research.

After three years in the U.S. Army during World War II, during which he served as French interpreter for the Thirteenth Airborne Division in France, he went off to Harvard College, where he studied liberal arts and was graduated *cum laude.* He began his advertising career in the early 1950s and has spent more than thirty-five years in this field.

Over the last decade, he has been marketing strategist on major ad campaigns for Olivetti, Honda, Sheraton, Qwip, Arby's Fast Food, Dictaphone, and the Dreyfus Corporation. He created and edits the prestigious Dreyfus newsletter "Letter from the Lion."

Many young people, seduced by the supposed glamour of Madison Avenue, are drawn to agencies right after college. What path would you chart for a bright, young liberal arts graduate determined to make it to the top in ten years?

The advertising business offers several sectors for career advancement: creative, account management, media. If the bright young liberal arts graduate is determined to make it to the top in ten years, he should first become professionally trained in media and/or account management. The best way to obtain this experience is through the training that certain large agencies like The Ogilvy Group offer to a limited number of applicants.

If the new graduate is interested in creative work, a good sample book of hypothetical ads for well-known advertising brands is absolutely essential. Astute creative directors study these books and can spot high potential talent. My partner, George Lois, our agency's chairman and creative director, can spot a spunky headline, flip through three more pages, and come away with an exact fix on that person's creative possibilities.

But whether the path is through media, account management, marketing or creative, anyone who wants to make it to the top in ten years has to risk himself in the classic entrepreneurial style: Get some basic experience, try like hell to be at the heart of at least one famous campaign, and start your own agency with a kindred, restive talent.

The earlier you start, the greater the risk because you bring limited background to your new agency— but if you don't compromise your basic philosophy of advertising and work like mad to turn out great work, you'll be noticed and publicized, and you'll have a good chance to go all the way.

I'd also be sure I could type.

You've been both a participant and a close observer of the creative side of the ad agency business for a long time. Where have you seen the greatest degree of change in this area in the past twenty-five years?

Artist/writer teams are now *de rigueur* in virtually all agencies that make any claim to doing original work—even if the work may ultimately not be that original. In addition, the concept of graphic and/or verbal imagery is now a given in the creative equation among an increasing number of advertising people, both creative and noncreative.

The most recent offshoot of this trend has been the evolution of that hybrid creative individual—the "creative planner," part creative personality, part marketer. All of this is intended to "direct" the agency's creative personnel toward the right marketing goals while discouraging, presumably, creativity that is not derived from the rich soil of marketing essence.

Large agencies have been accused of becoming ad factories. Yet we see award-winning print and broadcast advertising coming out of these same shops. How is it possible within a giant agency structure?

Large agencies are beset by the same continuing crises as those of small- and medium-sized agencies, except that the dimensions of their crises are more formidable and require the talents of their genuinely creative minorities during these times of stress.

Remember that large agencies have large accounts. A decline of market share or any of a number of circumstances summons forth a decree from management to dragoon all or most of its creative teams to come up with new approaches. In such a crisis, the "factory hands" quickly reveal the limits of their creative potential, while the mavericks swing for homers and often save the ball game. At the same time, those talented creative teams are probably disproportionately responsible for the award-winning advertising that often emerges from these giant shops.

One final word on the award issue: Our agency does not submit our work to award competitions. The application process is time-consuming and costly. By avoiding these frenetic exercises (unless requested to submit our work at the request of a proud client), we have more time to create advertising that brings results rather than awards. It is no fiction that too many award-winning campaigns deliver inconsequential results.

We know that there are pros and cons to each, but do you recommend a small or a large agency as the best training ground?

It's hard to give an unequivocal answer. Large agencies do offer newcomers professional training, and that's an invaluable way to start. But after the training, many—(not all)—big-agency people can end up feeling pigeonholed or stymied or unrecognized. They face, in effect, the underlying problem of bigness and hierarchy.

By contrast, the smaller agency is usually personnel-shy and calls on its people to go beyond their nonexistent job descriptions. The learning process here can be accelerated, but the disciplines that should accompany the learning are lacking. I began my career with a classic small shop in the 1950s, personally run by its charismatic founder, Ben Sackheim. I wrote copy, managed accounts, initiated TV buys, started the agency's broadcast production department, and so on. I now consider myself an astute generalist, but I always learn a lot from any smart alumnus of a big marketing shop on market share interpretation, research analysis, and the basic building blocks of marketing.

Ultimately, it comes down to personality. If you're spontaneous, resourceful, loose, and very smart, you can probably cut the mustard in a large or small shop. If you require more structure, if you're uncomfortable in working without moorings—and you'll have to be entirely honest with yourself in answering this question—you'll be miserable in a small shop but not necessarily a whiz in a big agency. It may be that you should not be in advertising at all—it's a profession that places intense demands on every aspect of your mind and heart. Therefore, if you *know* you're terrific, plunge in, work hard, speak up, and do your damnedest every day.

Although there are ad agencies in all fifty states, they predominate in New York, Chicago, and Los Angeles. Is there exceptional advertising produced in smaller cities, and are the salary levels substantially lower outside major metropolitan areas?

Well, of course there are many superb campaigns created in smaller cities. Boston, Washington, Dallas, Detroit, Pittsburgh, and San Francisco would probably fit the definition, however patronizing, of "smaller markets."

The most serious limitations of these markets is the limited number of large-size clients. It's not surprising, therefore, to see Steve Cosmopoulis's agency in Boston competing for New York–based clients.

My guess is that it's probably a lot of fun and potentially very profitable to *own* an agency in a smaller city, and because of the disproportionately high percentage of smaller clients—retailers, local franchise groups, hotels, restaurants, radio stations—it is far easier for a younger person to start up an agency in a smaller city than in the top three. If you start out working in a small-city shop, if you love the work and commute to your office in less than a half-hour, you may have everything that so many urban-shocked people are lusting for. If you can move up to an equity position, that's even closer to nirvana. On the other hand, despite the outward advantages of working in a smaller city, such as the lower cost of living, you probably earn less than in a major town and your chances for a job switch are probably quite limited.

Go through the *Standard Directory of Advertising Agencies* and count the agencies in the cities I've mentioned. Then go through the shops located in New York, and you'll get the picture.

Are copywriters born or made, and if the latter, how does one go about training to become a skillful copywriter?

Creative people are born with a rage to communicate. Ask me not the origins of this passion, but it's there. You have to start by being blessed—or cursed—by a touch of the poet. I speak seriously. You cannot possibly train to be a terrific copywriter, as you cannot train to write a sensitive novel unless you bring a formidable talent to the table. Writers are possessed people. If you *do* have this obsession, you can expand and even enrich this talent by linking up with a gifted art director. Create several original campaigns together, and you'll quickly understand that the melding of visual and verbal images can produce breathtaking work.

On another level, I would urge all copywriters to read everything in sight. In addition to newsweeklies and literary magazines, read John Updike, Norman Mailer, V. S. Naipaul, and all the works of Elmore Leonard. Copywriters should bathe their souls in the written word every day of their lives.

Who are the real elite in an ad agency—the creative, account, or media people?

The agency's elite are its creative people. Ultimately, after all the marketing analyses and research findings, copywriters and art directors must create the advertising that does the job. Simultaneously, account people, who have a strong, trusting relationship with the agency's clients and can communicate effectively with the agency's creative group, are surely the agency's elite as well.

Are there some areas of the ad agency business that seem to hold more opportunity than others?

The key word is *opportunity*. The field is being inundated by a growing generation of college-trained, would-be advertising people.

I came into the business, as everyone did of my generation, with no formal training because there were no courses in communications or in any of the disciplines of advertising. Nonetheless, I wanted to be a writer—either a journalist or a copywriter—and my years as a student of literature proved to be of inestimable pertinence.

I also pride myself in being a swift, accurate, two-finger typist. I am not being facetious in making the following suggestion: If you're starting out, you may want to look for a job as a *secretary* in an ad agency. The turnover is high, and the quality is generally lackluster. A smart, nimble secretary, male or female, is noticed quickly and appreciated. When this happens, it is remarkably easy to move into account work or media buying. Creative is another story—poets don't usually get discovered as secretaries, and they are probably lousy typists. In that famous putdown by Truman Capote, he described another author, whom he obviously hated, as a typist, not a writer.

Are there as many opportunities on the client side of marketing and advertising as there are on the agency side?

I don't have statistics to support my answer, but I have the impression that these days the client side offers a wider range of opportunities. American industry, in increasing numbers of categories, is becoming highly advertising-dependent, while more and more companies are being managed by marketing professionals. By contrast, the ad agency world is steadily trimming its payroll fat so that the ratio of employees to billings is shrinking. This retrenchment has been further abetted by the mega-merger trend among America's largest agencies, which account for a high percentage of total jobs.

I've seen too many young people sending out earnestly constructed résumés, determined beyond rational discourse to crack an impenetrable ad agency wall for an entry-level job, while they may hit earlier pay dirt by hunting for work in publishing, service industries, retailing, entertainment, and those many business categories that reflect the U.S.A. of the '80s and '90s: advertising-dependent, marketing-based—and always in need of intelligent, resourceful young people.

In going after a job in advertising, either in an ad agency or on the client side, what advice can you give in preparing a résumé?

Keep it short and make it a model of visual clarity: wide margins, neat typing, few bullets, minimum underlining and an appropriately modest roster of "achievements." Résumés are usually hard to read: short, to-the-point résumés *may* have a chance of being noticed.

Of perhaps greater importance: If you're sending a cover letter—and you should—keep it short and human. A one-paragraph letter should do the trick. If you can pack a modicum of charm and wit into this brief message, it will wash far better than those long, tedious tomes that are prepared for young people, at considerable cost, by résumé factories.

Advertising is the art of commercial communication; if you prepare a crowded résumé and send it out with a dense letter, you've begun by making two fundamental mistakes. You can, however, get off on the right foot by making your résumé and cover letter as crisp and inviting as a good ad.

Richard Low has been a part of network television since its inception as an advertising medium. His career in television began in 1952 at CBS, where he worked first in the news division and then for the television network. He joined Young & Rubicam in 1962 and in 1973 became head of its broadcast department, where he remained until his retirement in 1985.

Low's activity on behalf of clients covered the gamut from specials with Henry Kissinger and Steve Martin to special events such as coverage of the *Apollo* mission, the Tonys, and the Kennedy Center Honors. He was a member of the board of governors of the National Academy of Television Arts and Sciences, the National Council on the Arts Media Task Force, a judge of the International Emmys, and an adviser to the League of Women Voters' presidential TV debates. Currently, he is an independent film producer.

How do you decide which programs you would buy time in for a particular client?

That, as the saying goes, is the "$64,000 question." First, the whole process is not so arcane or mysterious as some might think. Yes, making judgments about which new programs will be successful requires all of the analysis and all of the experience and instincts that one can bring to bear; and still the failure rate for new programs in prime time is often higher than 60 percent. Certainly, a great many high-priced people at the networks with responsibility for spending millions of dollars felt that almost every one of their selections had a good chance of being a hit or at least of being watched by more than 26 percent of the available audience—a "share" that is considered acceptable today.

To begin with, you gather as much information as possible. The first step is to make an assessment of the number of households that use television in the time period the program is scheduled in and how that usage varies by time of the year. These usage levels are available from rating services such as A. C. Nielsen, and you make an estimate based on past performance. You then factor in the rating—percentage of the television universe—of the preceding program, the competition, and to some extent, even the program that follows. Obviously, the more that any of these elements involve programming with a track record, the easier it is to estimate the range of the audience that is possible for the new entry. The same process is then used, hopefully, by your research department, to give you a demographic breakdown for each program, again using as much of past history as is applicable.

Now you have to decide where the new program will fit inside the potential range for its audience and whether it is so appealing that it will bring new people into the time period and exceed the range or, on the other hand, be so bad that it will fall below the theoretical bottom of the range. All of this can happen and has happened.

At last, the $64,000 question: How do you decide that? You look at a pilot that a network screens for you. It is hoped that it will be a complete show, but sometimes you will only be able to see a "demo." Sometimes the pilot will be in the form of a made-for-television movie, which will be much longer than any episode in the series. In every case, more time and money has been spent on a complete pilot program than will be spent on any episodes in the series. More often than not, it is directed by a premier director who may not work on any series episode.

Did you like it? Not necessarily relevant. Was it well produced? Helpful, but not necessarily decisive. The key question is whether it will appeal to the large-scale audience of television today. Now we can refine the question even further. What types of programming seem to be declining in appeal, and what kinds of programming seem to be increasing in appeal? Does the appealing pilot have the ingredients for a successful series? Is there a pilot that is less than successful but has the ingredients for a successful series? Who is the producer, and what else has he done? Who are the stars? What kind of commitment has the head writer, assuming you liked the script? And, finally, does your "gut" tell you that this program will be successful?

And so you decide. Now you can begin to understand the enormous difficulty and failure rate, which is not unlike that in movies or theater and wherever creativity and assessing the marketplace are principal elements.

All right. I think I understand how you go about evaluating a program, but how do you determine which programs should be bought?

Here we begin with the client. What is the marketing strategy or plan for each of the client's brands? Based on the answer, a media plan is put together, which covers, among other things, the principal and secondary targets, that is, the prospective buyers broken down by sex and age—and sometimes by additional factors ranging from income and educational level to psychological/social values—what the budget is, when the advertising is to run, and how many of the potential prospects you want to reach and with what frequency.

The next element is to look at each of the programs and, in fact, at each of the different dayparts of television to see the breakdown of the components within the audience. For example, women are dominant in daytime, sports programming is viewed largely by men, and prime time is a dual audience vehicle, with a skew towards women.

To carry this one step further, assume that your principal target is women aged eighteen to thirty-four and you want the broader reach offered by prime time. You have your own estimates of how well each program will do and how the audience for each one will break down demographically. And the networks have their own estimates. You tell them how much money there is or how much of the budget they can try to obtain, and when the advertising has to run; then the negotiations begin. Usually, you want the added reach that is obtainable by having commercial units in a number of programs on at least two of the three networks; and while some advertisers will pay a premium for programs that have high ratings or some element of quality, ultimately the buy is made on the basis of negotiating and buying at the lowest cost-per-thousand against one's principal prospects.

What is the best career path for someone who aspires to your former agency position?

There is no one way, but if I had to chart an ideal path, it might be the following: First, obtain a job with an agency that offers a media training program; then buy network television for two to four years; then move to a supervisory position either at your first agency or at another one, or—probably best of all—get a job selling at one of the networks. From there, you can move to sales management, perhaps

to programming, or back to an agency where you might be running the buying operation.

To what extent does the client become involved in purchasing?

There are as many answers to this as there are clients, but essentially there are two kinds of involvement, depending on the type of buying that is being done. An overwhelming number of clients are interested in efficiency, with the right mix of quality and some reach and frequency requirements; they are not interested in sponsorships.

The client's dollars are largely spent in 30-second announcements, and now, increasingly, in 15-second announcements in a good number of programs on two or three of the networks. If it's a large advertiser, the buy is generally made for the fifty-two-week period, beginning with the "new season," which starts in mid-September because that's when vacations are over and people are less likely to be outdoors in the early evening.

Here, if you're doing your job properly, before you begin buying, you let the client know what you think the market will be like in pricing and efficiencies and what your estimates are of the audience and efficiencies for all the new and renewing programs. You also discuss your proposed buying strategies: how much you think should be put into the fifty-two-week "up-front" marketplace, how much you may wish to hold back for "opportunistic" buying in future quarters, and how you plan to approach the networks. As just one example, if you plan to make a buy on only two of the networks, you might wish to ask all three of them to come up with plans—a list of their programs and the number of announcements in them that they are offering, along with how they are scheduled—for half of the budget, 65 percent of the budget, and 35 percent of the budget. Then you can begin to negotiate and decide ultimately what you want to recommend to the client. Obviously, you are more likely to obtain that approval if you fill the client in as the negotiations proceed.

As for the relatively few instances where an advertiser will be a "sponsor" so that he will have some identification with a program, in addition to knowing the cost and the estimated audience, he will want to know as much as possible about the program. He will want to see it or a script and know who the stars, the director, and the writer are and, if possible, how the program can be merchandised and/or will be promoted for his benefit. If he is to be the sole sponsor, or a very large sponsor, he could have a voice in what the vehicle will be, what direction it will take, and who the performers will be, although this type of buying is available for less than a handful of advertisers because of the costs and risks involved today.

Are there any departments in an agency that seem to have more opportunities than others?

I think almost every department could lay claim to having many opportunities. One of the pleasures of a career in an advertising agency is that you get exposure to and must learn something about so many different businesses, apart from being at the forefront of helping clients to expand their business in an increasingly competitive marketplace. Ulcers maybe, excitement for sure.

If you're asking which departments are more likely to be the proving grounds for becoming the president of the agency, the answers are account management and creative, but there are exceptions including, not too long ago, a graduate of Y&R's broadcast department who went on to become the president of another very large agency.

All of which does not diminish the rewards of working in broadcast buying. You not only get to know something about your clients' businesses but also how the mass public of this democracy thinks and feels and, along the way, maybe you learn something about entertainment, news, sports, and, it is hoped, how to function in an ever-changing environment.

Glossary of Advertising Terms

AAAA: the American Association of Advertising Agencies, a group composed of 400 member agencies that have 1,000 offices in 165 cities.

Book: a portfolio of a creative person's own work or collaborative work—a must for job interviews.

Collateral: brochures, booklets, or any printed or visual materials, not including ads or commercials, used in the sales and marketing process; often prepared by agencies for clients.

Creative director: the head of a creative group at an advertising agency in charge of copywriters, art directors, and TV commercial producers; a senior management position, highly paid.

Demographics: a term used to categorize the various social and economic characteristics of a group of households or individuals. It refers to such statistics as sex, age, size of family, education, and economic levels.

Direct response: a type of advertising that covers mail order and allied fields; includes coupon advertising, direct mailings, and anything that brings a "direct response" from prospect to advertiser.

Focus group: a group of random or typical consumers used to test-market ads, ideas, or commercials.

Market share: the percentage of sales a particular product or service has in relation to its competitive brands.

Marketing plan: a comprehensive plan, prepared by the advertising agency for its clients, that defines such factors as the size of the market to be reached, the dollars per household needed to reach it, the media to be used, and the dollars needed for each medium.

Media plan: an adjunct to the marketing plan; covers the principal and secondary targets, that is, the prospective buyers broken down by sex and age and other demographics.

Point of purchase (POP): refers to both displays (in store windows, on store counters, etc.) and literature prepared by advertiser and agency to increase sales at the store or "point of sale."

Print: magazines (consumer and business) and newspapers where advertising is placed, as distinguished from broadcast media.

Product Manager: sometimes called brand manager; individual at advertiser who deals with a particular product's marketing, promotion, and advertising.

Reach: a determination of how many potential prospects for a particular product exist in an area or territory.

Residuals: an amount of money received by actors in a TV commercial for reuse.

Saturation: a large amount of advertising placed in one or many media enabling total coverage of all prospective consumers for a brand or service.

Sole sponsor: an advertiser who takes all commercial announcements on a network basis of a dramatic show or other entertainment on TV.

Storyboard: sketches of the sequence action in a TV commercial in comic-strip format; used as a guide by the producers and directors and also used for theatrical feature films and TV presentations.

Unique selling proposition: the basic premise of all advertising; tells the reader or viewer of the ad why a particular product or service should be purchased and is superior to its competitors.

Voice-over: a voice used off camera in a TV commercial.

Recommended Reading

Betancourt Hal. *Advertising Basics.* New York. Condor Publishing, 1978.

Bikke, James A., and Eugene Door, ed. *Careers in Marketing* (2nd ed.). New York: McGraw-Hill, 1978.

Bouvee, Courtland L., and William F. Arens. *Contemporary Advertising.* Homewood, Ill.: Richard D. Irwin, Inc., 1981.

Crompton, Alastair. *The Craft of Copywriting.* Englewood Cliffs, N.J.: Prentice-Hall, Spectrum Books, 1979.

Fletcher, Winston. *Teach Yourself Advertising.* New York: D. McKay, 1978.

Fujita, Neil S. *Aim for a Job in Graphic Design and Art.* Little Rock, Ark.: Rose Publishing Company, 1979.

Garfunkel, Stanley. *Developing the Advertising Plan: A Practical Guide.* New York: Random House, 1980.

Groome, Harry C., Jr. *Opportunities in Advertising Careers.* Louisville, Ky.: Vocational Guidance Manuals, 1976

Heighton, Elizabeth, and Don R. Cunningham. *Advertising in the Broadcast Media.* Belmont, Calif.: Wadsworth, 1976.

Holme, Bryan. *Advertising: Reflections of a Century.* New York: Viking, 1982.

Kirkpatrick, Frank. *How to Get the Right Job in Advertising.* Chicago: Contemporary Books, Inc., 1982.

National Advertising Company. *America's Advertisers: Who They Are, Where They Are, How They Developed, and What They Are Doing at the Present Time.* New York: The New York Times Book Company, 1976.

Ogilvy, David. *Ogilvy on Advertising.* New York: Random House, 1985.

Paetro, Maxine. *How to Put Your Book Together and Get a Job in Advertising.* New York: Dutton, 1980.

Pattis, William S. *Opportunities in Advertising Careers.* Lincolnwood, Ill.: VGM Career Horizons, 1984.

Wasserman, Dick. *How to Get Your First Copywriting Job.* New York: Center for Advancement of Advertising, 1986.

Watkins, Julina L. *The One Hundred Greatest Advertisements, Who Wrote Them and What They Did.* (2nd ed.). Mineola, N.Y.: Dover, 1959.

White, Roderick. *Advertising: What It Is and How To Do It.* New York: McGraw-Hill, 1981.

An Expert Talks About
Interviews and Résumés

We have been discussing the structure and opportunities in the seven major fields of mass communications. As a final note, we posed a few questions on job seeking to Roger Bumstead, a veteran media specialist.

Roger Bumstead has more than thirty years of broad-scope background in media and marketing and, most recently, in executive recruiting for the advertising and communications industries. Currently, he heads the media services/sales division of Jerry Fields Associates, the oldest and largest executive recruitment firm serving the advertising business.

Earlier, Bumstead served as advertising sales director for the Cableshop, the Consumer's Channel. For more than fifteen years he was a senior vice president and director of media services for Interpublic's Tinker Campbell-Ewald and the Marschalk Company. He held similar media management positions with Kelly-Nason, Inc., Campbell-Mithun, and MacManus, John & Adams, Inc.

Bumstead has served widely on industry committees for the American Association of Advertising Agencies, the International Radio and TV Executives Society, the Traffic Audit Bureau, and the Audit Bureau of Circulation.

How do you go about getting a job after graduation from college? Do you go to an employment agency, or a recruiting search firm like JFA, or do you do it yourself?

Your future depends on you and no one else. The competition for entry level jobs in the glamour industries—and, particularly, good ad agencies—is fierce.

Some employment agencies claim to be able to help get you a "starter" job in the ad business. Don't be fooled. They may be able to get you a job as a secretary if you type or can use a word processor or a job in the accounting department, *but not in any vital function offering a career path.*

Despite what college placement people may tell you or the mass media may depict, you are not living in the "Age of Entitlement"—that's a phrase coined by Ira Carlin, the executive vice-president and media director of the McCann-Erickson ad agency. No one owes you a job because you have a degree—even a masters.

Okay—enough philosophy. How do I get a good job?

First, you start thinking early about what you want to do. Use your college's guidance department as a resource to learn more about the types of careers you want to explore. Decide on *a few* types of jobs or career paths that you'd like—ones that best fit your skills and education and, most importantly, your personality. When I say "early," you should have been thinking this over back in high school. By your junior year in college, you should be on a career goal track to get what you want. Try to get summer jobs and internships that relate to

CHRISTINA M. SHEROVER

330 New Park Avenue
Anytown, NJ 07771
(201) 555-7531

OBJECTIVE: To obtain employment with an advertising/marketing agency or consumer
              products corporation, allowing me to utilize my marketing and communication
              skills and background.

EDUCATION: B.A. Management and Communications; Regis College, Weston, Mass.
              Related courses in Marketing Principles, Human Resource Management,
              Computer Programming, Graphic Arts, Writing for the Media,
              Administrative Theory, and Public Relations.

EXPERIENCE: American Tourister, Marketing and Communications Department: Warren, R.I.
              Internship, January through May 1985
              Expanded theory into practical application in both sales forecasting
              and demographics. Aided the Marketing Communications Manager in
              writing press releases, feature sheets, and new product information.
              Wrote reviews and recommendations in advertising scheduling in print
              media placement.

              WJAR-TV: Providence, R.I.
              Internship, May through December 1984
              Assistant in the news department. Duties encompassed research,
              monitored competitive network stations, assisted reporters on field
              assignments, and participated in promotional commercials.
              From May through August, averaged at least 20 hours weekly.
              While attending college, averaged 8 hours weekly.

              Merchandising and Marketing Corporation: Dobbs Ferry, N.Y.
              Marketing assistant, August 25 through September 13, 1984
              Aided at an international marketing conference in Paris, France; with
              representatives from 18 different countries. Planned and organized
              material for presentations, assisted in same, and processed requests
              for samples.

              December 1983 through January 1984
              Researched promotional material, organized same, and then assisted in
              the sales presentations to several clients. This New York-based
              marketing company's clients include major consumer products companies
              in food, beverage, drug, liquor, soft goods, and other industries.

              Merchandising and Marketing Corporation: Dobbs Ferry, N.Y.
              Internship, December 1982 through January 1983
              Participated in the implementation of new promotions, improved office
              promotional premium file system, and assisted in sales presentations.

              May through September 1982
              Developed promotional ideas with a new client, served as production
              assistant, organized office system, assisted in sales presentations
              and general clerical work.

              Professional References available.

that goal. The real world is goal-oriented, and a summer spent "bumming around Europe" or "surfing in Hawaii" doesn't look good on your résumé.

Be more specific.

You'll get your first job by cold calling, letter writing, and networking.

When you know what you want to do, make a long list of companies that might have those types of jobs. Try to get interviews on your vacation time. Most colleges have long Christmas or mid-winter breaks: No one will want to see you pre-Christmas, but early January is a great time to get in the door, with a prior appointment, of course.

I mentioned "networking." That's talking to people who are already working in the fields you have chosen for a career. They may be alumni. The alumni office usually has a readily available list of who does what and where, and someone in the class of '77 or '37 usually is more than willing to help someone from, say, "the good ol' Orange." I went to Syracuse, and any "Orange-person" sure gets preferential/deferential treatment from me.

Younger alums—in a class a few years ahead of you and in the field you're interested in—should be searched out. They've done it, and they'll sometimes share knowledge of who hires whom, along with the hows and whys. They also may have roommates or friends who work in other "shops."

What should my résumé be like?

It should sell you. It should clearly state what you bring "to the party." The best entry-level résumé I've ever seen is Christina Sherover's [see exhibit]. It's career specific right down to the exact dates she held any interim employment. It exudes energy and leadership.

A couple of other points: If you have a good grade point average—better than a 3.0—show it. If you've won any awards for educational excellence or leadership, detail them.

Last, if you know how to use a personal computer, mention it. We're already well into the computer age, and I'm amazed at how often recent graduates neglect to put that know-how on their résumés.

Covering letters should be short. Say just what you want—*an interview.*

How do I get experience interviewing?

If you're lucky, your school has a good placement department, and it should help by setting up some role-playing situations and giving advice. If it

doesn't, practice with a parent or a "stern-minded" older friend or sister or brother.

What should I say in an interview?

First, do your homework on the company you are interviewing at—its products or services or clients and its field. Learn to use the library. The *Readers' Guide* will lead you to relevant references in *Forbes, Fortune, Business Week,* or the trade press.

Next, talk about yourself—what you've learned, what you offer, and what you can do for Company X. Above all, be interested, enthusiastic, and alert. You'll probably be asked a "curve-ball" question or two. When this happens, the best gambit is to restate the question, verbally, yourself—this gives you time to think about a careful answer.

What turns you off in an interview?

Candidates without a career focus. Candidates who want me to do the talking. Candidates who "laze" in the chair across from me. Candidates who are either boring or arrogant. Candidates who don't dress properly because they think it doesn't matter when they're seeing a recruiter. Wow, are they wrong!

Your appearance is all-important. Your clothing may have been bought at Sears or Penney's, but it can and should look like it came from Brooks Brothers or Alcott & Andrews. We call it "The Corporate Look."

Do any of the "glamour fields" covered in this book offer greater opportunities—among themselves—than another?

Not really. One has to be aware of change and how it may impact your career goals. TV didn't kill radio, but it sure changed it. Cable TV has fractionated the viewing levels for the major networks and their affiliates, but it has literally created thousands of new job opportunities, as has videotape, minicams, and VCRs.

Right now, the specialist ad agencies—many are subsidiaries of the giants—are doing well, particularly in health care, direct marketing, and sales promotion. Look at the company, or at its clients if it's an ad agency, rather than the industry, per se.

What about job shifting in these fields?

I'm not encouraging it. Get a spot and stay there at least a year, maybe two. Don't sample one job and then try something else for another six months. You'll never get hired if your résumé shows "job-hopping." And, too, you can't really learn what a job is all about or what opportunities there are in six months.

After a year or so you'll move on, and a recruiter such as JFA can help you. *But don't change jobs just for the money.* Make sure your next job relates to your long-range career goal, *which may have changed by then.*

Should I try to work for a big firm or a small one?

I'd recommend a big, established company for several reasons. A big company is more likely to have in-house training programs. A big company may offer educational benefits if you want to go for a masters. A big company has disciplines—for example, there is a right way and a wrong way to write a report for Procter & Gamble. You'll gain a measure of what's good and what's bad about American big business. Most important, a big company—the higher in the top one hundred the better—will be very impressive on your résumé when you go for your next spot.

Working for smaller firms, or entrepreneurial firms, offers you the opportunity to learn more, do more, and have more fun doing it; however, later on, you may be turned down for jobs because your background is too eclectic.

While I "made it," so to speak, as a media director in the ad agency business, my own career growth and income potential was stunted because I had never worked on a major, high-spending, TV-oriented package-goods brand.

Should I try to get a job in one of the "power centers"— as New York is for magazine and book publishing and as Los Angeles is for movies and TV production—or should I try to get a job in one of the other top twenty-three "media markets"?

There isn't any yes or no answer to that one. What's happening today and what will happen in the years ahead is quite different from how things were twenty or thirty years ago.

If it's film or video or book publishing or magazine work you're after, you may get some experience in the hinterlands, but you should aim for large metropolitan meccas early on.

You can do many of the same things working for a TV station, a radio station, or a newspaper in Columbus, Ohio as you can working for the CBS radio networks or NBC-TV in New York or *USA Today* in Washington and New York.

You might not make as much money, but it will go farther. Your lifestyle will be more pleasant and you'll have quite a bit less stress. Finding a job, too, may be easier simply because there is less competi-

tion, even though there are fewer openings. If you stick it out in the hinterlands, and you're successful, you'll be a "power" in that pond before you are forty.

As to the advertising business, it is not nearly as concentrated as it once was in New York. One source tells me that around 90 percent of all national advertising was created and placed by New York ad agencies twenty-five years ago; now, it is reported to be between 50 and 60 percent.

To put it in perspective, there is an ad agency in Cedar Rapids, Iowa, a free-standing subsidiary of Y&R, that spent more than $70 million for its clients in 1985.

Or look at it another way: There are more than 190 ad agencies of substance in the state of Ohio, and they all aren't in Cleveland, Cincinnati, or Columbus.

Lever Brothers uses one agency in Detroit for a well-known brand. Campbell-Mithun, in Minneapolis, has been a major shop with very big clients for years, and then there's Fallon-McElligott in the same city.

In short, if you're good, *you can make it almost anywhere.*

There is one catch, however. If your lust or your ego dictates that you want to make it in New York—or Chicago, Detroit, or L.A.—adland, don't wait until your price is out of line with your experience!

Should I pursue a graduate degree?

You are better off with it than without it. It's almost a must for a career in marketing—the client side, or market research—and it's worth a few bucks more if you're headed in the direction of ad agency account work. It will be worth more in media services in the future than it is now.

Two practical thoughts, however: First, take a break from schooling. Get a job. Learn what the real world is all about. You'll get more out of getting that M.B.A. And not every M.B.A. means the same thing to potential employers—the perceived reputation of the school and its teaching staff is all-important. And, as I said before, find a beneficent first employer who will contribute to the cost, even if you have to be an indentured servant to that company for a few years.

Anything else?

It's there: the gold. Go for it—but it's only you who can make it happen!

INDEX